Europe's Birds: A guide to

see *pages 12–13* for m

Conservation status
(globally and in Europe)

Easy reference to
similar species

Status summary and date
range for migrants

Moult 'type'
indicated (for
passerines)

Detailed text
highlights key
ID features

Flight described
and strictly
nocturnal migrants
indicated

Distinctive features
highlighted

Comparison
species shown
to scale

Map showing
seasonal
and passage
distributions

Habitat
summary

Covers all
subspecies
for regular
breeders

Months when
each plumage
may be seen

At-a-glance
comparison
plates or
tables where
appropriate

Photos give a feel
for typical habitat

Unrivalled selection of
high-quality photos

SHRIKES

SHRIKES IN FLIGHT *p. 467*

LC **Woodchat Shrike** *Lanius senator*

LC ④ | **L** 24–25 cm | **W** 25–27 cm

Smallish, stocky, relatively short-tailed shrike; often perches on wire, bush top. **Ad** | back dark with **white oval patch each side**; broad white wing patch (except on ssp. *badius*). Underparts white. ♂ | **black 'mask'**; cap and nape **rufous**; back blackish, rump paler. ♀ | back 'mask' interrupted by whitish marks, cap pale rufous; back and rump brownish-grey. **Juv / 1W** | upperparts 'cold' **greyish**, **rump whitish** with grey barring. Line of **whitish feathers**, each with black crescent, along shoulder. Underparts whitish with grey barring ('scaly' effect). **1S** | like **Ad** but with some browner wing coverts and flight feathers.

V | Quick, harsh, chattering calls. Song fast, rambling, chattering and grating notes.

FL ● | Fast, direct, undulating. Sometimes hovers. White patches beside dark back; white band on outerwing (absent in ssp. *badius*).

Juv - Masked Shrike [Juv] *p. 467*
Juv - Red-backed Shrike [Juv] *p. 466*

Scarce and fairly local summer migrant MAR–OCT

Bushy arable land, heathland, orchards

Four sspp. occur: *senator* (widespread) broad white primary patch, little white on central tail feathers; *rutilans* (Iberia) white in primaries reduced; *badius* (W Mediterranean islands) thicker bill, less black on forehead, white primary patch absent; *niloticus* (Cyprus, S Turkey eastwards) extensive white across base of central tail feathers.

♂**1S**
ALL YEAR

well defined
black 'mask'

blacker back
than ♀

no white
primary
patch

ssp. *badius*

brownish
back

ssp. *senator*

♀ **1S**
MAR–AUG

♂ **Ad**
ALL YEAR

ssp. *rutilans*

Juv
JUN–AUG

ssp. *rutilans*

greyer back
than ♂

ssp. *senator*

♀ **Ad**
ALL YEAR

470

EUROPE'S BIRDS

An identification guide

Rob Hume, Robert Still, Andy Swash and Hugh Harrop

Consultant: Chris Batty
Photographic associate: Agami Photo Agency

WILDGuides

PRINCETON
press.princeton.edu

Published by Princeton University Press,
41 William Street, Princeton, New Jersey 08540
6 Oxford Street, Woodstock, Oxfordshire OX20 1TR
press.princeton.edu

Requests for permission to reproduce material from this work should be sent to
permissions@press.princeton.edu

First published 2021

British Library Cataloging-in-Publication Data is available

Library of Congress Control Number 2021935098
ISBN 978-0-691-17765-6
ISBN (ebook) 978-0-691-22279-0

Production and design by **WILD**Guides Ltd., Old Basing, Hampshire UK.
Printed in Italy

10 9 8 7 6 5 4 3 2 1

Contents

Introduction

This complete photographic identification guide to the wild birds of Europe can be used and enjoyed by anyone who is enthusiastic about birds. It has been created for anyone who is keen to learn more about them and wishes to identify all the fascinating species that Europe has to offer. It also offers an insight into the variety of Europe's birds, their status and movements, their habitats and their behaviour: birdwatching, after all, goes far beyond simple identification. With thousands of informative pictures, it is also a joy to browse its pages.

An identification handbook, rather than a pocket-sized field guide, it describes and illustrates 928 species. Following the best-selling Princeton **WILD**Guides title Britain's Birds, this book continues that book's hugely successful format and rationale. It has been put together by the same team of authors, editors, designer and photographers, who are all also experienced and well-travelled birdwatchers, who understand what is required.

In this book, 'Europe' is bounded to the south by the Mediterranean Sea (but encompasses its islands) and to the east by the Caspian Sea and the Ural Mountains. The isolated Atlantic island groups of the Azores, Madeira and the Canary Islands are also included.

The book covers all birds native to Europe and every species known to have wandered 'accidentally' from other parts of the world up to the end of March 2021. It also deals more briefly with those that have established self-sustaining populations following escapes from captivity or human introduction. Two species recorded historically (the globally extinct Canarian Oystercatcher *Haematopus meadewaldoi* and Eskimo Curlew *Numenius borealis*, probably now extinct) are not covered (Great Auk *Pinguinus impennis* became extinct much earlier). Sadly, Slender-billed Curlew, which is included in the book, may also now be globally extinct, and Common Buttonquail has probably now been lost as a European species.

Many people made invaluable contributions to the production of the book and in helping to ensure its accuracy (these are all gratefully acknowledged on *page 624*). However, special mention should be made here of **Chris Batty**, who checked many thousands of photographs to verify the identification, age and sex of the birds shown, and helped immeasurably in many other ways. The photographs and the way they have been presented undoubtedly distinguish this book. Although many were taken by the authors, no fewer than 349 bird photographers worldwide generously and enthusiastically contributed to filling the inevitable gaps. There is, however, no doubt that the production of the book would not have been possible without an especially close association with the **Agami Photo Agency** in the Netherlands (www.agami.nl), facilitating access to an unsurpassed array of high-quality images taken by many of Europe's top bird photographers. Viewing their images and selecting which to use became an informative, rewarding and hugely enjoyable task. This also enabled the vast majority of the images featured, including those of extreme rarities, to show individual birds that were actually photographed in Europe. All the contributing photographers are credited in the acknowledgements section on *pages 624–627*.

Each species found regularly in Europe has a map, adapted from distribution maps kindly supplied by **BirdLife International**, the global authority on the conservation status of wild birds (see *page 622*).

The treatment of species and subspecies in this book, and the scientific names used follows BirdLife International, as does the classification of the species' conservation status.

Recent environmental changes and pressures, finally reaching the public consciousness after decades of research and campaigning, reinforce the need to act to conserve birds and habitats worldwide. This book will help people identify what they see, but if that is just a first step towards more people appreciating birds to the full, and to understand the need to ensure their survival in a fast-changing world, it will have been worth the effort.

Map of the area covered by the book showing countries, key regions and key features.

In the table **BOLD CAPITALS** are used for regions (countries within those regions are colour coded); **bold text** is used for countries; light text is used for other locations, with areas in capitals.

AL	**Albania**	CRI	Crimea	IE	Ireland	NO	**Norway**
AD	**Andorra**	CY	**Cyprus**	IS	Iceland	PL	**Poland**
AM	**Armenia**	CZ	**Czech Republic**	IT	Italy	PT	**Portugal**
ASM	**ASIA MINOR**	DE	**Germany**	JMA	Jan Mayen (NO)	RO	**Romania**
AT	**Austria**	DK	**Denmark**	LV	Latvia	RS	**Serbia**
AZ	**Azerbaijan**	EE	Estonia	LI	**Liechtenstein**	RU	**Russia (European)**
AZO	AZORES (PT)	EL	Greece	LT	**Lithuania**	SAR	Sardinia (IT)
BA	**Bosnia & Herzegovina**	ES	**Spain**	LU	Luxembourg	SCA	**SCANDINAVIA**
BAI	BALEARIC ISLANDS	FAR	**Faroe Islands**	MAC	**MACARONESIA**	SE	**Sweden**
BAL	**BALKANS**	FI	**Finland**	MAD	Madeira	SI	**Slovenia**
BE	**Belgium**	FR	**France**	MC	Monaco	SK	**Slovakia**
BG	**Bulgaria**	GE	**Georgia**	MD	Moldova	SM	San Marino
BY	**Belarus**	GRL	**Greenland**	MK	**North Macedonia**	TR	**Turkey**
CAN	CANARY ISLANDS (ES)	HR	Croatia	MT	Malta	UA	**Ukraine**
CH	**Switzerland**	HU	**Hungary**	ME	**Montenegro**	UK	**United Kingdom**
COR	Corsica (FR)	IBE	**IBERIA**	NL	**Netherlands**	XK	**Kosovo**

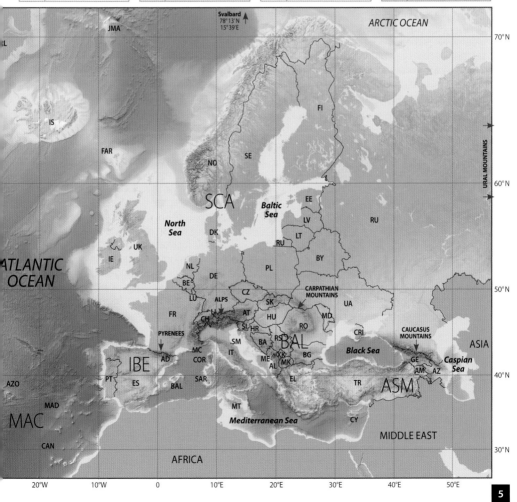

How to use this book

This book adopts a simple step-by-step approach combined with detailed descriptions, comparisons and an unparalleled set of photographs to help you identify any bird you see. This does, however, require adequate views and careful observation and depends on the species. Some remain extremely difficult. Identification requires care and objectivity, coupled with a degree of realism.

The identification process

1 If you see an unfamiliar bird, look carefully and try to note all points that may prove to be relevant to an identification: including shapes and structures, colours, patterns, behavioural features and voice.

2 Search the gallery of thumbnail images (*pages 14–19*) to find the kind of bird you are looking at – perhaps a duck, a gull, a woodpecker, a thrush or a finch. The birds in the book are arranged in logical groupings, reflecting their classification (taxonomic order) but deviating where necessary for better comparison (*e.g.* putting swifts close to swallows and falcons with birds of prey, rather than separating them according to strict evolutionary relationships).

3 Turn to the relevant section, where a short introduction will help to narrow down the possibilities. In some cases there may still be many options and where helpful these are further divided into sub-groups. This will help you to focus on the right kind of bird and highlight any others that might need to be considered, reducing the options to a handful of possibilities. The details given in the individual species accounts should then enable you to put a name to the bird.

4 ***If something is not right***, then look at the introductory section's information on commonly confused groups/species, or consider the possibility of an exotic 'escape' or a rare migrant or vagrant.

5 With increasing experience, you will be able to flick through the book to the most likely group, or the best fit, but leaping to conclusions often leads to mistakes.

Similar species to check are highlighted in a purple 'lookalike' box (with a page reference, unless on the same or facing page). Remember that rare birds are exactly that: they are rare! In the vast majority of cases, what you see will be a commoner alternative.

The photographs show birds in similar poses and lighting for ease of comparison – but it is all too easy to go wrong. In reality, colours are affected by factors such as bright or dull conditions and reflections from water or foliage. Close-up pictures show all the plumage details, but it is important to bear in mind that a more distant view might show a simpler, broader tonal 'pattern' and much less detail or colour. Becoming 'expert' is often about being able to identify birds at a greater distance, or with a poorer view. A Siskin on a garden feeder, or a Song Thrush on the lawn, will be easy: but identifying either seen as a distant 'dot' in the sky or on a treetop will need more experience.

Many characteristics of particular species become clear with experience and are difficult to illustrate in a book – but remain vitally important for identification. Each species has its own character (sometimes referred to as 'jizz'), and some even have a particular 'expression'. Behaviour often helps: a large flock of black birds flying closely together may be Starlings, but will not be Blackbirds. Over an estuary, a flock might be of Dunlins or Knots, but not Common Sandpipers; a flock of 100 larger waders could be Redshanks or godwits, but not Greenshanks. A large diving bird that settles on a post or buoy could be a Cormorant, but will not be a diver. A warbler that repeatedly dips its tail might be a Chiffchaff rather than a Willow Warbler. Happily, a keen observer never stops learning such important nuances of identification.

The parts of a bird

These annotated images show the basic, essential terms used throughout this book (other terms specific to a particular group are covered in the relevant introductory section).

Wingbars: The term 'wingbar' is used to describe any obvious 'bar' along the spread wing. This is typically formed of contrasting tips to the wing coverts and/or pale bases to the flight feathers. On some species such as **Blue Tit** (*right*) this bar is obvious on the closed wing, in others, such as **Sanderling** (*below*), it is barely discernible or not visible – particularly any pale bases to the flight feathers. Note that the term 'bar' usually refers to a 'crosswise' pattern or line, whereas 'streak' means a 'lengthwise' mark along the wing.

SANDERLING

covert tips

covert tips barely discernible

pale bases to flight feathers

covert tips (visible on closed wing)

stripe over eye (supercilium)

eyestripe

cap

wingbar

BLUE TIT

UPPERWING

rump

back

midwing
greater coverts

uppertail coverts

forewing
lesser and median coverts

innerwing
wing coverts and secondaries

SECONDARIES

PRIMARIES

hindwing
secondaries and inner primaries

primary coverts

outerwing
primary coverts and primaries

wingtip
outer primaries

UNDERWING

flight feathers

PRIMARIES

SECONDARIES

'wingpit' (axillaries)

undertail coverts

trailing edge

FIELDFARE

back

wing coverts

'shoulder' neck

nape

crown

greater median lesser

eyering

wingtip (closed)

forehead

lore

upper mandible

bill

rump

throat chin

uppertail coverts

'moustache' cheek

tail

alula

flank belly

breast

thigh

Ageing, sexing and moult

Individuals of any one species may differ according to age, sex and season, the effects of wear and bleaching (fading) on feather colours and patterns, and the state of moult (replacement of old feathers with new ones). In some, separate geographical populations with consistent differences may be classed as 'subspecies'. It is not possible to show every 'plumage', but all significant ones are described or illustrated.

With species such as Wren and Tawny Owl, male (♂) and female (♀) look alike all year round and juveniles are very similar. At the other extreme, male and female look very different, some have distinct breeding and non-breeding (or summer and winter) plumages, and juveniles can be told from other immature birds. Larger species may mature over several years, progressing towards adulthood at differing rates.

Throughout this book the pictures are labelled to indicate the months in which the plumage shown is likely to be seen, but it is important to be aware that *changes from one plumage to another proceed gradually* over a period of weeks, even months.

A photographic guide forces a different approach from most field guides. All must be accurate, but close-up, high-resolution photographs (which birdwatchers increasingly take for themselves) reveal details that might previously only have been properly appreciated when a bird was captured for ringing purposes, or on a museum specimen. A photograph cannot be labelled 'Adult' if, for example, some pale wing covert tips reveal that the bird is one year old. This adds a degree of complexity, but also enables a more detailed discussion on ageing.

In general, adult males in breeding or courtship plumage are the most brightly coloured, non-breeding and immature males more like females, and juveniles the least distinctive. With a very few species (phalaropes and Dotterel), male and female roles and plumages are reversed, with females being the brightest. The males of most species are generally larger than females, but in birds of prey the reverse is the case and the size difference can be particularly marked.

Plumage categories

In this book, simple terms are used to describe plumage categories; these are coded as follows:

Juvenile (Juv)	1st-winter (1W)	1st-summer (1S)	2nd-winter (2W)	2nd-summer (2W)	Adult (Ad)
the first plumage of a young bird able to fly	usually following a partial moult of head/body feathers only in the autumn	following further change through moult and/or bleaching, by the following spring	usually an entirely new set of feathers after a complete moult in late-summer/autumn	and so on until maturity when the bird becomes…	which may have breeding (Br) and non-breeding (Nb) plumages

Juv → 1W → 1S → 2W → AdBr → AdNb

This sequence of images shows the variation in plumages of Little Gull as a result of five moults over a period of two years, from juvenile to adult.

Birds in juvenile, 1st-winter and 1st-summer plumage – *i.e.* up to one year old – may be termed **'1st-year' (1Y)**. Some species become adult at one year old, with no discernible '1st-summer' plumage. Birds not old enough to breed are collectively **'immature' (Imm)**. 'Breeding plumage' is usually brightest in spring and summer (*i.e.* 'summer plumage'). Exceptions include most male ducks, brightest in winter ('breeding' or 'courtship plumage'): in summer, they moult into a duller 'eclipse' plumage – see *page 21*. Large gulls with a white head in breeding plumage acquire a streaked 'winter' head from midsummer but may become white-headed again by January.

Examples of plumage sequences are included in the relevant introductory sections throughout the book: see Mallard (*page 21*), Great Crested Grebe, Red-throated Diver and Cormorant (*page 72*), Black-headed Gull (*pages 106 and 109*), Herring Gull (*pages 108–109*), Pomarine Skua (*page 146*), Sanderling (*page 154*), Siskin (*page 480*) and Reed Bunting (*page 508*), and as well as in some of the individual species accounts, such as Common Gull (*page 116*), Red-footed Falcon (*page 313*) and Blackbird (*page 385*).

A brief explanation of moult

Feathers are tough but require replacement, can become very worn and can change colour with exposure to sun and saltwater. They are replaced in a process called 'moult'. This has a strict sequence in most species but the timing may vary and a complete moult involving replacement of all the feathers may take weeks or months, so the change from one plumage to another is a gradual one. On large or strongly patterned species moult can be seen quite easily with good views, but on most birds it is less easy to judge (except perhaps on photographs or in the hand).

Colours are remarkably consistent within species, but fade when exposed to sunlight (bleaching) or affected by wear (abrasion). Certain feathers (such as the pale grey of gulls and terns, or the grey of a Woodpigeon) become darker with wear as the surface 'bloom' is rubbed away. Black, grey or green can become browner over time. Even a relatively 'plain' or uniform bird may vary in appearance with these processes and observed patterns may not match basic descriptions. Pigments such as melanin produce dark markings that are stronger than unpigmented light-coloured fringes, which easily wear off. As a consequence, feathers can become surprisingly ragged, and patterns may change.

On a Curlew, for example, pale spots on the feather edge literally wear off, changing a 'spotted' pattern to a plainer one, without any replacement of feathers. Many gulls lose white spots from black wingtips, which fade browner. Some species, such as certain finches, buntings and chats, have a rapid loss of pale fringes in spring, revealing brighter colours beneath and producing a breeding plumage without any replacement of feathers. An adult Golden Eagle will have blackish body feathers (new) mixed almost randomly with browner ones (older) and pale buff, bleached ones (about a year old).

Moult itself can have a huge effect on shape and pattern, as feathers are shed or part-grown, creating obvious gaps. Consider the wings of gulls with distinctive grey, black and white patterns, which can be disrupted as some feathers are bright and new, others missing entirely or still part-grown, and others old and faded. During moult, shed or growing feathers will create gaps in wings and tail, or apparent breaks in patterns such as wingbars, until all new feathers are grown and normal patterns are restored. Also be aware that feathers, such as tail streamers, may break off.

Moult is either **'complete'** (replacing all the feathers on the head, body, wings and tail) or **'partial'** (usually involving the head and body and some wing coverts, but not the larger wing or tail feathers). A complete moult usually begins with the innermost primary, the other feathers being renewed during the time it takes to shed and regrow all the primaries. Most species complete their moult in a single unbroken sequence. A complete moult takes several weeks even for small species: Goldfinch, for example, takes an average of 77 days. Others have a 'suspended moult' (paused midway, usually during migration, to be completed later).

These adult **Black Terns** show how a bird's appearance may change according to wear (which may darken feathers by wearing off the paler surface), bleaching (which makes them paler) and the gradual progression of moult (which takes several weeks), so complex intermediate stages are commonly seen. Moult must always be considered if a bird does not look quite as expected. **MAY:** black head/underparts; immaculate tail; dark (worn) inner secondaries and outer primaries (grown during previous JUL–AUG); newer, paler outer secondaries/inner primaries (grown JAN–FEB). **JUL:** black head/underparts replaced by white from MAY/EARLY JUN, from face rearwards. Old tail feathers (grown OCT) worn to a point, new ones (grown MAR/APR) rounded. Dark inner secondaries, outer primaries and their coverts, but paler feathers also now wearing darker. **AUG:** body mostly white; wing feathers of different ages, blackish, brown and pale grey.

Most **non-passerines** have two moults per year when adult: **complete** in autumn/winter (August–December) and **partial** in spring (March–May). Northern waders may suspend moult during migration and complete it in their winter quarters. Large birds of prey moult almost continuously, but small birds of prey have a more defined, single annual moult (such as buzzards, May–September). In many wildfowl and a few other species (*e.g.* cranes) all flight feathers are shed together, rendering the bird flightless for 20 to 40 days.

Adult Black Tern (*above*) has a **complete moult**, starting with the head in late May/June, tail and wings from July/August, but paused during migration and completed by January/February. Before the return migration in spring a **partial moult** includes head, body, tail, inner primaries and some wing coverts, but the inner primaries are moulted again from as early as November, more usually February, but stopped during spring migration.

Passerines (or songbirds: in this book, from swallows/martins and larks to finches and buntings) mostly have a post-juvenile moult to first-winter, soon after fledging. Adults have a post-breeding moult in late summer. In late winter or spring, both age groups have a pre-breeding moult. Within this pattern are **four main moult strategies**, but with variations in detail. Typical date ranges given may differ between species. Age may be determined by features such as a difference between old (juvenile) and newly moulted (adult type) wing coverts on 1st-year birds. The contrast where the two types meet is referred to as a 'moult limit' (see Citril Finch, *right*).

These female **Citril Finches** illustrate the difference between the greater coverts of a 1st-summer bird (some juvenile feathers, others newly-moulted adult type) compared with an adult (coverts uniform age).

Actively moulting birds may, for a short time, show features (such as mixed old and new wing coverts) associated with other age groups. The four strategies are summarized below and a symbol (❶, ❷, ❸ or ❹) is included for each of the regularly occurring species to indicate which strategy it adopts.

❶ **Type 1** involves just **one complete moult per year** [June–September] for both adults and juveniles. Juveniles are easily distinguished but ageing is not possible after the moult (*i.e.* 1st-winter is identical to adult).

❷ **Type 2** involves a **partial moult** [July–September] for juveniles, and a **complete moult** [June–September] for adults. Juveniles may moult primaries but not their primary coverts, unlike adults: new primaries with old (juvenile) coverts after the moult will distinguish 1st-winter from adult birds. Adults have one generation of feathers, while 1st-year birds have two until the following summer.

❸ **Type 3** involves a **partial moult** [July–September] and a second **partial moult** [January–April] for juveniles, and a **complete moult** [June–October] and a **partial moult** [January–April] for adults. If their partial moult does not include any wing feathers, adults' wing feathers are all of one age, while 1st-year birds' wing coverts are of two different ages. The contrast (or 'moult limit') enables age to be determined in some circumstances. If the adults' winter moult includes some wing coverts, both one-year-old and adult birds show a difference in age within their coverts; ageing may or may not be possible. Some individuals can have three different ages of wing coverts. The winter moult may include some flight feathers, because of a suspended moult, and ageing is unreliable.

❹ **Type 4** involves a **partial moult** [July–September] and a **complete moult** [December–March] for both juveniles and adults.

Pied Flycatcher is an example of a passerine with a 'Type 3' (❸) moult strategy: the progression from juvenile to adult is illustrated by these photos.

1 Juvenile
(sexes indistinguishable)
JUN–JUL

Head and upperparts spotted.

PARTIAL MOULT in **JUL–AUG** becoming

2 1st-winter
(sexes often indistinguishable)
SEP–MAR

Juvenile wing/tail but new, unspotted head and body feathers.

PARTIAL MOULT in **MAR–APR** becoming

3 1st-summer [♂]
MAR–AUG

Black-and-white, with original brown (juvenile) wing and tail (breeds in this plumage).

COMPLETE MOULT in **JUN–AUG** becoming

4 Non-breeding [♂]
AUG–MAR

Resembles 1st-winter (or female) but has black wings and tail.

PARTIAL MOULT in **MAR–APR** becoming

5 Adult breeding [♂]
MAR–AUG

Black-and-white with blackish wing and tail feathers (can be faded).

COMPLETE MOULT in **JUN–AUG** becoming

4 Non-breeding [♂]
AUG–MAR

All the photographs in the book are labelled according to the **plumage type** shown (and, where transitional, with the actual date it was taken in square brackets). Where the sex or age is known, this is given, together with the **date range** during which this plumage might be seen (in some cases, the species concerned might not normally be present in Europe for part of this period). For some species, individuals may not be identifiable to a particular plumage type, so the captions indicate either/or categories – such as ♀/**Juv**, **1W/Ad** or **1Y/Ad** where the adult female and juvenile look alike, or individuals in their 1st-winter or 1st-year of life are inseparable from adults, or where the photograph does not clearly show crucial differences. Although some differences between plumages are slight, such as 1st-summer birds differing from adults by the presence of pale tips to a few wing coverts, recognizing such subtleties is informative and can be helpful in the identification of certain species.

The species accounts

The species accounts in this book are grouped into 38 sections. An introduction to each summarizes the number of species and their common features, and subdivides them where appropriate.

It is important to use all the information provided: a combination of factors is always more likely to give an accurate identification than one or two features. Study the photographs and note the captions, read the descriptions and annotations, but also check the status, distribution map and habitat preferences. Any bird *might* occur almost anywhere, but almost always the bird you see will be in the right place, in its proper habitat, at the right time of year.

As far as possible the species accounts follow a consistent approach in the order of information presented and the terminology used. The book is exhaustively cross-referenced to enable comparisons of similar species to be made as quickly as possible. Where relevant, potential confusion species are highlighted with a 👁 symbol in a purple box: species' names shown in *italics* indicate rare migrants or vagrants to the region as a whole; those with an asterisk (*) signify an 'escape' or introduction (*i.e.* not native to Europe). Where appropriate, references at the top of the page lead to comparison plates on which similar or related species are shown together (such as 'Geese in flight'). It is important to look at all the available information to minimize the risk of mistakes.

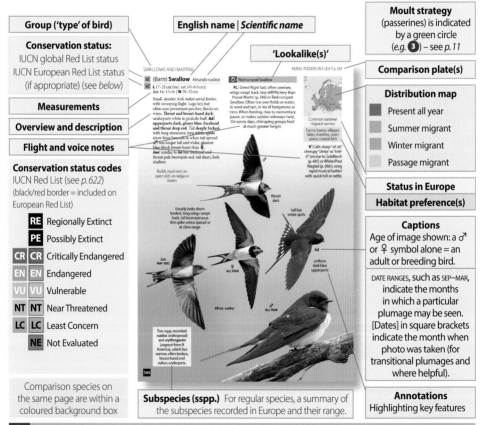

Moult strategy (passerines) is indicated by a green circle (*e.g.* ❸) – see *p. 11*

Group ('type' of bird)

English name | *Scientific name*

Conservation status:
IUCN global Red List status
IUCN European Red List status (if appropriate) (see *below*)

'Lookalike(s)'

Comparison plate(s)

Measurements

Distribution map

Overview and description

Present all year

Summer migrant

Flight and voice notes

Winter migrant

Conservation status codes
IUCN Red List (see *p. 622*)
(black/red border = included on European Red List)

Passage migrant

Status in Europe

Habitat preference(s)

RE	Regionally Extinct
PE	Possibly Extinct
CR CR	Critically Endangered
EN EN	Endangered
VU VU	Vulnerable
NT NT	Near Threatened
LC LC	Least Concern
NE	Not Evaluated

Captions
Age of image shown: a ♂ or ♀ symbol alone = an adult or breeding bird.

DATE RANGES, such as SEP–MAR, indicate the months in which a particular plumage may be seen. [Dates] in square brackets indicate the month when photo was taken (for transitional plumages and where helpful).

Comparison species on the same page are within a coloured background box

Subspecies (sspp.) For regular species, a summary of the subspecies recorded in Europe and their range.

Annotations
Highlighting key features

👁 **'Lookalikes'**

The 'lookalike' box indicates other species that are very similar or may be mistaken in some circumstances, and, in *italics*, similar rare species or established escapes (shown with an asterisk (*)) that should be checked.

Names, species and subspecies
Each species has a common **English name** and *scientific name* (in *italics*). Different text sizes distinguish between regular and rare migrants, vagrants and escaped/introduced species. The *scientific name* has two words: the first, the *Genus*, groups closely related species; the second creates a unique combination for every *species*. Variations in appearance and voice across a species' range may be sufficient to separate *subspecies*, identified by a third word. **The treatment of species and subspecies, and the scientific names used in this book follows BirdLife International. Common names are those most frequently used by English-speaking birdwatchers** (with commonly used qualifiers added in brackets).

Average differences between **subspecies** are best appreciated in a sample of museum specimens; it may not be possible to assign individual birds to a subspecies except by location. With the exception of a few species that have a large number of subspecies which are similar and/or intergrade, those occurring in Europe are named. As far as possible, the geographical range of each is summarized and a brief description provided for those that differ sufficiently to be *visibly* different. **In a few cases, birds treated as subspecies in this book are recognized as full species by other taxonomic authorities.** Nevertheless, the means of identifying them remain the same.

Measurements
Length (**L**) (bill-tip to tail-tip) and wingspan (**W**) are given as a range (male and female separately if appropriate). Interpretation is important, though: a very long bill or elongated tail feathers can give a misleading indication of size and a slim bird that is the same length as a rounded one may look much 'smaller' in reality. More subjective impressions of size may be given for species *within* groups, but these do not apply *between* groups (*e.g.* Blackbird is a 'large' thrush; Teal, much bigger, a 'small' duck).

Conservation status
The conservation status for each species is indicated with an icon next to the English name. This is based on the 2020 global Red List, which is coordinated by BirdLife International, the international authority on the status of wild birds. Information on the categories used is provided on *page 622* (and summarized on the front flap). For those species that occur naturally and regularly in Europe, a second icon is included that shows the European Red List status.

Overview and description
Descriptions begin with a summary of the general appearance and behaviour of the species, with an overview of features common to both sexes and all ages. This is followed by a description of 'adult' plumages, beginning, where relevant, with the male and where appropriate qualified with breeding (summer) or non-breeding, then female and in turn juvenile and other immature plumages. The term 'adult' on its own may be taken to mean that the sexes look alike; similarly, breeding/non-breeding plumages will be the same unless specified. Words in **bold** describe particularly important characters for identifying the species.

The codes used are: **Ad** = adult (qualified as necessary with **Br** = breeding or **Nb** = non-breeding); ♂ = male; ♀ = female; **Juv** = juvenile; **1W** = 1st-winter; **1S** = 1st-summer; **2W** = 2nd-winter (and so on); **1Y** = 1st year (and so on); **Imm** = immature. Combinations such as ♀/**1W** (female or 1st-winter) indicate that sex or age look much alike.

A ③ symbol shows the age at which a bird becomes fully mature. It may be difficult to determine the age of immatures (as in many gulls) which progress at differing rates.

V| introduces 'voice', the songs and/or calls of the species. Vocalizations can be essential clues to identification and although expressing them in words is often difficult, an attempt has been made to do so in order to serve as a useful *aide mémoire* if you have heard the bird already, or to give an indication of what to expect.

FL ●| (black dot indicates strictly a nocturnal migrant) describes flight actions and often plumage patterns (or shapes, such as a forked tail) that are visible in flight but may not be obvious on a perched or swimming bird. Typical flock size/behaviour is mentioned where appropriate.

Distribution map, status and habitat
A **map** is included for each regularly occurring species, showing breeding, wintering and passage distributions based on the latest information held by BirdLife international.

The **status** box indicates how common (or otherwise) the species is in Europe and shows the time of year it is generally seen. Birds referred to as 'migrants' travel to and from Europe on an annual cycle; those referred to as 'migratory' undertake movements at least partially within Europe. The term 'vagrant' is used to describe a species that is off its usual migration route; for such species their likely area of origin is given.

The **habitats** box indicates the type(s) of habitat(s) in which the species is most likely to be found. For rare migrants and vagrants this information is included in their status box.

Area modifiers are used throughout the text are: C = Central, E = East, N = North, S = South, W = West, or combinations (*e.g.* SW = South-west).

The types of bird

This gallery of thumbnail images of typical birds from each group should allow you to go quickly to the relevant **INTRODUCTION** or main sub-section/specific page(s) when trying to identify a bird.

WILDFOWL (*page 20*)

Swans *pages 26–27*

Geese *pages 28–37*

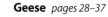

Shelducks
pages 36–37

Ducks (dabbling)
pages 38–47

Ducks (diving)
pages 48–66

'SEA DUCK'   'SAWBILL'

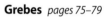

GREBES, DIVERS and **CORMORANTS** (*page 72*)

Cormorants *pages 84–86*

Divers *pages 80–83*

Grebes *pages 75–79*

SEABIRDS (*pages 87–89*)

Gannets
page 90

Shearwaters/Petrels
pages 91–97

Storm-petrels
pages 97–99

Auks *pages 101–105*

👁 RARE SEABIRDS

See *pages 539–544* for other (rare) seabirds that are different in form from those shown here.

LARGE WATERSIDE BIRDS (*page 198*)

Herons, Bitterns
pages 212–215

Egrets
pages 209–211

Spoonbills
page 208

Ibises
pages 203

BITTERN

HERON

Storks *pages 206–207*

Cranes *pages 204–205*

Flamingos *pages 202*

Pelicans
pages 200–201

GULLS and TERNS (*pages 106–107*)

Gulls *pages 114–131*

Terns *pages 136–145*

SKUAS (*page 146*)

Skuas *pages 150–153*

CRAKES and RAILS (*page 216*)

Moorhens / Coots / Swamphens	Rails	Crakes	Corncrake
pages 218–220	*page 221*	*page 216–217*	*page 221*

WADERS (*page 154*)

Snipe / Woodcocks
pages 193–195

Plovers (smaller)
pages 170–171

Plovers (larger)
pages 166–169

Lapwings
pages 163–165

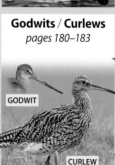

Sandpipers
pages 174–176, 184–192

'Shanks'
pages 177–179

Godwits / Curlews
pages 180–183

Stone-curlews
page 160

GODWIT

CURLEW

Avocets, Stilts
pages 158–159

Oystercatchers, Turnstones
pages 158, 161

Phalaropes
pages 196–197

Pratincoles, Coursers
pages 156–157, 160

STILT

AVOCET

TURNSTONE

OYSTERCATCHER

PRATINCOLE

COURSER

GALLIFORMS (also buttonquail and francolins) (*page 222*)

Grouse
pages 228–233

Partridges
pages 224–226

Pheasants
pages 227

BUSTARDS (*p. 236*)

Bustards
pages 236–238

ALL AT LEAST AS LARGE
AS PHEASANT

Vultures
page 268–269

BIRDS OF PREY (*page 265*)

Eagles
*pages 279–281,
292–298*

Kites
pages 278, 282

Harriers
pages 283–287

Osprey
page 278

'Buzzards'
pages 272–275

Hawks
pages 302–305

Falcons
pages 310–319

OWLS (*page 250*)

Owls *pages 251–264*

NIGHTJARS (*p. 248*)

Nightjars
page 249

AERIAL FEEDERS (*page 339*)

Swifts
pages 340–343

Swallows / Martins
pages 344–347

'HIGHER LANDBIRDS' (*page 320*)

Kingfishers
pages 324–325

Parrots
pages 618–619

PASSERINES 1/2 (page references in *bold* indicate introductory sections)

👁 AMERICAN PASSERINES

Vagrant passerines from America (*pages 609–615*) are either from, or bear a fairly close resemblance to, groups shown here. Using this initial guide and subsequent pointers should enable you to find these species.

Rollers *page 327*

Bee-eaters *page 326*

Orioles *page 376*

Shrikes
pages 466–470

Hoopoes *page 328*

Cuckoos
pages 321–323

Crows
pages 471, 474–477

Magpies
pages 471, 479

PIGEONS/DOVES, SANDGROUSE (*p. 239*)

Sandgrouse
pages 246–247

Pigeons & doves
pages 241–245

Jays, Nutcrackers
pages 471, 473, 478

NUTCRACKER

JAY

Dippers
page 381

WOODPECKERS (*page 329*)

Woodpeckers
pages 331–338

Wrynecks
page 337

Starlings
pages 378–380

Waxwings
pages 376, 377

PASSERINES 2/2 (page references in *bold* indicate introductory sections)

Larks
*pages **348**–357*

Pipits
*pages **348**, 360–365*

Wagtails
*pages **348**, 366–371*

Thrushes
*pages **383**, 384–387*

Wrens
*page **372***

Accentors
pages 373–375

Babblers
*page **382***

Bulbuls
*page **382***

Nuthatches
*pages **452**–455*

Treecreepers
*pages **452**, 456–457*

Wallcreeper
*pages **452**, 456*

Chats/Wheatears
*pages **383**, 390–411*

Crests
*pages **413**, 414*

Warblers, Cisticolas, Prinias
*pages **412–413**, 415–447*

'REED'

'LEAF'

'SYLVIA'

Flycatchers
*pages **448**–451*

Tits
*pages **452**, 458–465*

Finches
*pages **480**, 484–503*

Sparrows
*pages **480**, 504–507*

Buntings
*pages **508**–522*

19

Wildfowl

are water or waterside birds. Some use both water and drier habitats nearby, often feeding on land and resting or roosting on water, safe from predators. **3 swans**; **12 geese** [**3 vagrants**] **with several distinct subspecies** (sometimes treated as species) + **1 introduced resident** + **some 'escapes'**; **2 shelducks** and **45 ducks** [**some vagrants or rare**] + **several introductions and occasional 'escapes'**.

SWANS (pp. 22, 26–27, 69)

Very large, white (one 'escape' black); swim, upend, walk and feed on open ground, but lack agility. **Flight** Straight, powerful. **Sexing, Ageing and Moult** No seasonal changes, sexes alike. See *Ageing and moult, opposite*.

MUTE SWAN

Identify by size, bill colour and pattern, voice, wing noise in flight.

SHELDUCKS (pp. 23, 36–37, 71)

Large, heavy ducks; walk freely on mud or dry land near water. **Flight** Heavy, direct. **Sexing, Ageing and Moult** Seasonal changes slight; sexes look similar; juveniles duller than adults in first year.

SHELDUCK

Identify by bill, leg and body colour and wing pattern.

GEESE (pp. 23, 28–37, 68–69)

Large, sociable, water/waterside birds – obvious goose shape. Some introduced or re-established breeders, others largely winter visitors in most of Europe. **Flight** May form big flocks (mostly at traditional sites); dramatic and vocal in flight. **Sexing, Ageing and Moult** No seasonal change except fading of old feathers; sexes look alike. See also *Ageing and moult, opposite*.

GREYLAG GOOSE

Identify by overall colour and contrasts, specific patterns, bill and leg colour, voice.
'GREY GEESE' are grey-brown: check bill and leg colours, wing patterns, subtleties of shape, head/body contrasts. **Ageing** Juveniles less neatly barred with round-tipped feathers (not square) on the upperparts. **OTHER GEESE** are black and white on head, neck and chest and have black bills and legs: check patterns. **Ageing** Juveniles duller, less neat.

DUCKS (pp. 24–25, 38–71, 532–537)

Smaller, shorter-necked and shorter-legged than geese. Include 'dabbling ducks', 'diving ducks' and 'seaducks'. **Flight** Fast, direct; see *page 38*. **Sexing, Ageing and Moult** Seasonal plumages and sexes differ; juveniles are like females but distinguishable in some species; immature males retain juvenile wings – see also *Ageing and moult, opposite*.

MALLARD

♀

♂

Identify by bill, leg and overall body colour; head and wing patterns.
'DABBLING DUCKS' feed on water, mud, marsh or drier land, most walk quite well on land; males colourful for most of the year, females browner. 'DIVING DUCKS' (including 'SAWBILLS', 'STIFFTAILS' and 'SEADUCKS') dive from the surface; sometimes stand at the water's edge but cannot walk far.

Ageing and moult

SWANS (pp. 22, 26–27, 69)

MUTE SWAN

Juveniles dull; become white, with adult bill colours showing, during first winter (1W); retain some grey/brown feathers in following summer (1S).

Juv

1W

1S

GEESE (pp. 23, 28–37, 68–69)

GREYLAG GOOSE

Adults have square-tipped feathers above; juveniles have round-tipped feathers, are duller overall or lack adult patterns.

less neat

neat bars

Juv/1W

Ad

DUCKS (pp. 24–25, 38–71, 532–537)

Males brightest in winter/early spring ('breeding' or courtship plumage) but moult into dull ('eclipse') plumage by summer.

Juv
AUG-JAN

Juvenile moults head/body AUG-SEP and head/body again OCT-JAN.

♂ Br
OCT-MAY

MALLARD

♂ Nb ('eclipse')
JUN-SEP

♀
ALL YEAR

Females look the same all-year-round; juveniles appear similar but males increasingly obvious as adult patterns appear by early winter.

Adult moults head/body to breeding plumage SEP-NOV; undertakes a complete moult after breeding JUN-AUG (when briefly flightless), males starting earlier than females.

POSSIBLE CONFUSION GROUPS Coots, grebes, divers, auks and cormorants all swim and may be taken for ducks. **Coots** are often mixed with ducks on open water; round-backed, short-tailed (other 'crakes and rails' usually on land or water's edge, have longer legs and toes, walk/run with uptilted tails, but may swim); **grebes** round-bodied, sharp-billed, almost tailless; **divers** long-bodied, short-tailed, dagger-billed; **auks** squat, dumpy, small-winged; **cormorants** bigger, longer-tailed, hook-billed.

COOT
(p. 219)

AUK
(p. 100)

DIVER
(p. 73)

CORMORANT
(pp. 85–86)

MERGANSER (DUCK)
(p. 55)

GREBE
(p. 73)

Swans in flight

Immature Whooper Swan and Bewick's Swan upperwings relatively uniform.

Immature Mute Swan has strongest contrast: dark coverts/pale hindwing.

BEWICK'S SWAN

Imm

WHOOPER SWAN

Imm

Imm

MUTE SWAN

Ad

Adult swans have all-white upperwings.

MUTE SWAN
(p. 26)

Ad

huge; head/bill best visual features but loud humming throb of wingbeats distinctive

BEWICK'S SWAN
(p. 27)

Ad

smaller and with shorter neck than Whooper Swan (but hard to judge)

WHOOPER SWAN
(p. 27)

Ad

huge, angular, with fine-pointed head

Flight powerful and direct with long head/neck outstretched. Generally in shapeless groups (Whooper Swans often in 'V' or wavy line), descending with wings stiffly arched, body angled and legs lowered before splashing down on water or landing on the ground with a short run.

Geese and shelducks in flight

WHITE-FRONTED GOOSE
(p. 30)
Quick, agile, in lines/'V's. Adult **belly distinctively marked** (beware, juvenile is unmarked). Sharp, bright, laughing calls with yodelling 'catch.'

PINK-FOOTED GOOSE
(p. 28)
In long lines, 'V's or masses. Head and neck short and dark. Nasal, bubbly, deep chorus interspersed with high "wink-wink."

BEAN GOOSE (p. 29)
Long-winged; 'Taiga' (ssp. *fabalis*) long-necked. Nasal, deep double- or triple-note calls.

GREYLAG GOOSE (p. 31)
In lines, 'V's or a shapeless mass. Head large, chunky and pale. Coarse, clattering, cackling chorus.

darkest underwing

palest underwing

GREYLAG GOOSE

underwing paler than on Bean Goose

BEAN GOOSE

Juv

PINK-FOOTED GOOSE

WHITE-FRONTED GOOSE

upperwing pale bluish-grey contrasting with dark trailing edge

upperwing mid-grey on outer part

upperwing largely mid- or pale blue-grey

upperwing dark, mid-grey towards tip

'GREY' GEESE

OTHER GEESE

RED-BREASTED GOOSE
(p. 35)

BRENT GOOSE
(p. 34)

BARNACLE GOOSE
(p. 33)

CANADA GOOSE
(p. 32)

grey-brown

white 'collar'

white forehead

unmistakable

grey, plain

grey, patterned

white chin

red bill

pale grey, black wingtips

BLUE FORM

WHITE FORM

SNOW GOOSE
(p. 68)

EGYPTIAN GOOSE
(p. 37)

RUDDY SHELDUCK
(p. 37)

SHELDUCK (p. 36) for size comparison (also see p. 24)

23

Regularly occurring ducks in flight

SHELDUCK
(*p. 36*)

RED-BREASTED MERGANSER
(*p. 55*)

♀

GOOSANDER
(*p. 54*)

♀

♂

♂

MALLARD (*p. 40*)

♀

♂

♀

GADWALL (*p. 42*)

SHOVELER (*p. 41*)

♀

♂

♂

PINTAIL (*p. 43*)

♀

MARBLED TEAL
(*p. 38*)

♂

WHITE-HEADED DUCK
(*p. 57*)

♂

♀

♀

♀

♀

♀

♂

RED-CRESTED POCHARD
(*p. 47*)

♂

♂

TEAL
(*p. 44*)

♂

GARGANEY
(*p. 45*)

WIGEON (*p. 39*)

♂

POCHARD (*p. 51*)

♀

SMEW (p. 56)

♂

GOLDENEYE
(p. 52)

♀

♂

♀

HARLEQUIN DUCK
(p. 66)

♀

♂

BARROW'S
GOLDENEYE
(p. 53)

♀

LONG-TAILED
DUCK
(p. 64)

♂

STELLER'S
EIDER
(p. 61)

♂

COMMON
SCOTER
(p. 62)

♂

♀

♀

VELVET
SCOTER
(p. 63)

♂

♀

KING EIDER
(p. 60)

♂

♀

♀

SCAUP
(p. 49)

♀

EIDER
(p. 58)

♂

♂

TUFTED
DUCK
(p. 48)

♀

♂ 1W

KING EIDER
(p. 60)

♂ 1W

EIDER
(p. 58)

♂

FERRUGINOUS
DUCK
(p. 50)

25

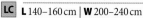
LC **Mute Swan** *Cygnus olor*

LC **L** 140–160 cm | **W** 200–240 cm

Very large; **approachable** in most of range. Neck 'S'-shaped or straight with head typically **down-tilted**. Wings often slightly **arched** (dramatically in threat). **Tail pointed, usually raised.** **Ad**| all-white; **orange bill** has **black knob, base and tip. Juv**| brown, wings whiter (increasingly white overall with age); bill grey with black tip/lower edge and lacks knob. **Black between eye and bill.**

V| Frequent quiet grunts, hisses, squeaky trumpeting.

FL| Wings create unique, rhythmic, **loud, humming** sound.

Sexes look alike but in breeding pair, bird with largest knob on bill is male.

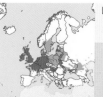

Locally common resident/local migrant

Saltwater and freshwater edges, lakes, rivers, marshes, pastures

♀

♂

pointed tail raised

Ad
ALL YEAR

JUVENILE SWANS are like adults in form, but have drab grey-brown plumage (which becomes whiter as winter progresses). The bill is duller than an adult's but shows the pattern that distinguishes the species.

'Polish' **Mute Swan** – locally frequent genetic variant: juveniles all-white; adults' legs pinkish-grey.

raspberry-red type

BEWICK'S SWAN

pink/black type

WHOOPER SWAN

diagnostic pale 'wedge'

rounded pale base

black between eye and bill

MUTE SWAN

.C Bewick's Swan *Cygnus columbianus*

.EN **L** 115–130 cm | **W** 170–195 cm

Smallest swan (size often difficult to judge); generally wary. Neck relatively short and thick but can appear quite thin and 'looped' when feeding. Long bill typically **held horizontally**. Tail short, square, **held low**. **Ad**| all-white; bill black with **rounded yellow patch** at base. **Juv**| **plainer, greyer** than Mute Swan, becoming whiter with age; **bill pattern like adult** but pinkish or raspberry-red, with pale cream/grey at base that becomes yellower through the winter.

FL| Wings 'creak' but lack the loud hum made by Mute Swan.

> Two sspp. occur: *bewickii* (widespread); *columbianus* (vagrant from N America) has minute yellow spot near base of bill; occasional intermediates difficult.

V| Yapping, **honking, whooping notes**, less bugling than Whooper Swan; usually **one or two** notes.

Ad

ssp. *columbianus*

Scarce, localized winter migrant SEP–MAY

Breeds freshwater lakes, tundra; winters saltwater and freshwater edges, lakes, pastures, farmland

Ad
ALL YEAR

ssp. *bewickii*

BEWICK'S SWAN

yellow patch rounded, usually beneath black stripe; yellow across top of bill on some

.C Whooper Swan *Cygnus cygnus*

.C **L** 140–160 cm | **W** 205–235 cm

As large as Mute Swan but more like Bewick's Swan; usually wary. Long neck upright when alert but curved when relaxed. Long bill typically **held horizontally**. Tail short, square, **held low**. **Ad**| all-white; bill black with **long, yellow, triangular 'wedge'** from base to beneath nostril. **Juv**| as Bewick's Swan. Bill pattern like adult: dark but with a **pointed whitish 'wedge'** that turns pale yellow through the winter.

FL| Wingbeats lack the loud hum made by Mute Swan.

> Although territorial when breeding, all three swans form flocks (sometimes 100s, often mixed) in winter and frequently feed on grassland (Bewick's Swan also commonly on ploughed fields).

V| Deep, nasal **bugling or clanging**, often **three/four notes** in a series. Flock chorus noisy, confused and varied.

yellow patch wedge-shaped, extends beyond nostril; top of bill usually yellow

WHOOPER SWAN

Ad
ALL YEAR

square tail held low

Scarce, localized migrant

Breeds Arctic tundra; winters, salt and fresh water edges, lakes, pastures, farmland

27

Pink-footed Goose *Anser brachyrhynchus*

LC

L 64–76 cm | **W** 137–161 cm

Medium-sized, rounded, dark goose with small head/bill and barred grey back. In winter, often in large, crowded flocks of 100s-1,000s. **Ad** | **round, dark head contrasts with pale buff-grey breast; flank darker than back**; pale feather edges give barred appearance to dusky blue-grey upperparts. **Short, dark bill** with a **pink** patch. Legs **pink** to darker purple-pink. **Juv** | drabber, with 'scaly' effect on upperparts; dark bill rules out juvenile White-fronted Goose.

V | Deep, nasal, gabbling chorus from flock, with frequent distinctive, high, sharp "wink-wink" interspersed.

 Bean Goose | White-fronted Goose *p. 30*

Migratory; locally numerous

Breeds freshwater lakes, marshes, islands; winters saltwater and freshwater edges, lakes, pastures, farmland

FL | Paler back/upperwing, greyer back, darker flank than Bean Goose. **Grey** on forewing narrower and **darker** than on Greylag Goose (*p. 31*); broad white tail tip. Skeins can be lines, 'V's or shapeless; usually 'clumped' and changing in form.

Ad

underwing paler than on Bean Goose

Shape and amount of colour on bill varies between individuals in both Bean and Pink-footed Geese.

Back dusky blue-grey, square white bars, less brown than Bean Goose.

Ad
ALL YEAR

Juv
JUN–MAR

Bean Goose *Anser fabalis*

L 69–88 cm | **W** 140–174 cm

Pink-footed Goose | Greylag Goose *p. 31*

Migratory; locally numerous

Breeds on tundra and taiga lakes and marshes; winters saltwater and freshwater edges, lakes, pastures, farmland

Large, dark goose: longer head/bill than that of Pink-footed Goose (but often difficult to pick out in mixed flocks); slimmer than Greylag Goose. **Ad** | rich brown overall; rather long **dark head contrasts with paler breast**; back dark brown, **neatly barred white**; **flank same tone as back**. **Legs orange or yellow-orange**, although colour can be hard to judge in poor light. **Juv** | irregular 'scaly' appearance on upperparts.

V | Calls "*ung-ung*" or "*yak-ak-ak*," lower than White-fronted (*p. 30*) and Pink-footed Geese; less 'clattering' than Greylag Goose.

FL | Dark, long-necked; no obvious grey on upperwing, underwing distinctively dark; narrow pale 'U' above dark tail.

BEAN GOOSE SUBSPECIES

Two: '**Taiga**' (*fabalis*) and '**Tundra**' (*rossicus*), sometimes regarded as separate species. Intermediate birds difficult to assign.

PINK-FOOTED GOOSE
BILL: small, with pink patch (extent varies between individuals).

'**Tundra**' **BEAN GOOSE**
SSP. *rossicus*
BILL: usually has **narrow orange band** and bulging black base; shorter and thicker than *fabalis*, longer than Pink-footed Goose. NECK: dark, contrasting with pale breast as on Pink-footed Goose; shorter than *fabalis*.

bulging

'**Taiga**' **BEAN GOOSE**
SSP. *fabalis*
BILL: long, **largely orange**. NECK: longer than that of Pink-footed Goose.

straight

Ad

underwing darker than on Pink-footed Goose

Ad
ALL YEAR

'**TAIGA**' **BEAN GOOSE**

'**TUNDRA**' **BEAN GOOSE**

Ad
ALL YEAR

Juv
JUN–FEB

LC (Greater) **White-fronted Goose** *Anser albifrons*

LC | **L** 64–78 cm | **W** 130–160 cm

Medium-sized, boldly marked, lively, agile goose (readily leaps into flight); two distinct subspecies. **Ad**| mid-brown with **white stripe** along flank. **White forehead** has vertical edge in side view. Belly **barred black**, all black in some individuals. Legs vivid **orange**. European ssp. *albifrons* bill pale **pink**; Greenland ssp. *flavirostris* darker, 'oily' brown, black belly bars often more extensive, bill larger, **orange** (colour often difficult to see in poor light). **Juv/1W**| no white on face until NOV or later; no black belly bars: combination of orange legs and pale pinkish or orange bill help separate from other juvenile geese.

V| High, laughing, yodelling with a catch in the middle: "*kyu-yu*" or "*lyo-lyok*." Flock chorus high, yapping/yodelling.

Lesser White-fronted Goose | Greylag Goose | Pink-footed Goose *p. 28*

Locally numerous winter visitor, usually in flocks

Breeds freshwater lakes, tundra; winters salt- and freshwater edges, lakes, pastures, farmland

FL| **Ad** plain greyish underwings, distinct black barring on belly. **Juv** plain beneath except white vent. Upperwing dark; grey forewing less obvious than on Pink-footed Goose. Flies in long lines or 'V's.

Juv

Ad

WHITE-FRONTED GOOSE IDENTIFICATION

white blaze on forehead

white curves back above eye

adults

no eyering

yellow eyering

juveniles

dark nail

pale nail

WHITE-FRONTED

LESSER WHITE-FRONTED

'Greenland' **WHITE-FRONTED GOOSE**

Ad **ALL YEAR**

'European' **WHITE-FRONTED GOOSE**

Ad **ALL YEAR**

Juv **JUN–JAN**

c Greylag Goose *Anser anser*

L 74–84 cm | **W** 149–168 cm

Large, heavy, **big-headed** goose (generic 'farmyard' goose shape). Widespread introduced flocks confiding and approachable; wilder in much of range. **Ad** | pale brown with **large, deep-based, orange bill** with pale tip (not always obvious). **Legs pale pink** (some pale to bright orange, at least in introduced flocks). May have some white near bill and small black spots on belly (recalling White-fronted Goose, which is smaller, darker and has a thinner bill). **Juv** | has irregular bars on back.

V | Noisy; clattering, **clanging or cackling chorus** from flock; calls "*kya-gaa-gaa*" or "*ang-ang-ank*."

Greylag Geese are obviously larger and heavier than other 'grey' geese.

Two sspp. occur:
anser (widespread);
rubirostris (E Europe) larger, paler.

FL | Very pale forewing; underwing strongly contrasted. Skeins in lines or 'V's, generally not 'clumped' or changing shape.

Ad

Low light creates strong contrasts; **breast pale**; prominent **white rear end**.

SSP. *anser*

Ad
ALL YEAR

Locally common resident/migrant

Breeds freshwater lakes, marshes, islands; winters salt- and freshwater edges, lakes, pastures, farmland

👁 White-fronted Goose [Juv]

U N Lesser White-fronted Goose *Anser erythropus*

L 56–66 cm | **W** 115–135 cm

Like small, compact White-fronted Goose but less barred above, less black beneath and with a chunkier head, shorter neck and **smaller bill**. Distinctly **quicker feeding action**. **Ad** | white forehead curves back above eye. **Bill bright pink**. Obvious **yellow eyering** even at distance (weak on White-fronted Goose). **Juv** | no white forehead but has **yellow eyering**; **pale nail** on bill (see *opposite*).

V | Similar to White-fronted Goose, but higher-pitched.

FL | Much like White-fronted Goose unless size can be assessed in direct comparison.

Hard to find among other species: search flocks for long white forehead flash first, then eyering/bill; fast feeding rate is a useful clue.

Ad

Ad
ALL YEAR

Migratory: rare, local; occasional escapes

Breeds freshwater marshes, bogs; winters salt- and freshwater edges, lakes, farmland

👁 White-fronted Goose

31

LC **Canada Goose** *Branta canadensis*

LC **L** 80–110 cm | **W** 155–180 cm

Large, **long-necked**, striking goose, usually approachable; dramatic in large flocks. **Ad** | brown with paler bars and **pale breast**. Black 'stocking' on neck and **bright white 'chinstrap'**. **Black bill and legs**, striking white rear end. **Juv** | similar to **Ad** but duller, with narrower, rounder feather tips on upperparts.

V | Loud, deep, full, **trumpeting honks**, including double "*arr-onk.*"

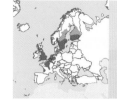

Locally common resident, introduced; vagrant from N America

Freshwater lakes, rivers, marshes, pastures, parks, farmland

FL | Lanky, long-necked; dark with white chest and obvious white rear end; long, dark wings.

Ad

Flocks of Canada Geese are less likely to contain individuals of other species (or vagrant Canada Geese) than other 'carrier' species such as White-fronted and Pink-footed Geese.

Ad

Heavy body, but the tallest, longest-necked goose if standing upright.

Retains some worn, rounded juvenile feathers on back for first year.

Ad
ALL YEAR

CANADA/CACKLING GOOSE IDENTIFICATION

CANADA GEESE
Gently sloping forehead, long bill, long-necked

large-bodied

CACKLING GEESE
Steep forehead, stubby bill, short-necked

small-bodied

LC **Cackling Goose** *Branta hutchinsii*

L 55–75 cm | **W** 120 cm

Very like **small** Canada Goose, but with **steep forehead, stubby bill** and shorter neck. Three subspecies recorded, *hutchinsii* the most likely vagrant (see *opposite*).

V | Quite high, rhythmic "*ah-ya*" or "*oo-yoo,*" calls from flock resembling Pink-footed Goose (*p. 28*) more than Canada Goose.

Ad
ALL YEAR

Vagrant from N America and occasional escape

Marshes, pastures

Canada Goose and Cackling Goose each have several subspecies which may occur in Europe as natural vagrants, but which also wander from collections.

CANADA GOOSE SUBSPECIES

Europe's resident, naturalized population is **'Atlantic' Canada Goose** (ssp. *canadensis*)
Large, averages palest, black neck separated from brown back with clear white.

Vagrants from N America rare, generally smaller forms that differ in head and bill characters: note extent of pale/white on base of neck and upper breast, as well as size and structure – beware overlap between subspecies and sexes (males average 5% larger than females).

'Todd's Canada Goose' (ssp. *interior*)
Similar in size to 'Atlantic' but generally has a darker, browner back that meets the shorter black neck; breast averages darker. *Only safely identified when accompanying migrant Greylag Geese from the north, 'Greenland' White-fronted Geese, Pink-footed Geese or Barnacle Geese.*

(NOTE: So-called **'Lesser Canada Goose'** (ssp. *parvipes*) is not well-defined and may not be sufficiently distinct to be a subspecies.)

CACKLING GOOSE SUBSPECIES

'Richardson's Cackling Goose' (ssp. *hutchinsii*) Dumpy body, short legs, pale breast; 5–10% have dark stripe under chin.

'Ridgway's Cackling Goose' (ssp. *minima*) Smallest, with small bill, short neck and relatively long legs. Dark brown with purplish breast; wing coverts each have dark band before pale tip; chin all-white.

'Taverner's Cackling Goose' (ssp. *taverneri*) As 'Richardson's' but averages larger and darker, with a more rounded head (similar to paler-breasted Canada Goose ssp. *interior*, with which it may intergrade); 40–75% have dark stripe under chin.

Barnacle Goose
Branta leucopsis

L 58–70 cm | **W** 120–142 cm

Small, strikingly patterned goose (no brown). Bright pale grey with sharp vertical divide against black front. Black bill short and stubby; legs black. **Black neck** widens into black 'breastplate', above **white belly**. Large white/yellowish-white face patch with black eyeline. **Ad** | back neatly **barred black, white and grey**. **Juv** | duller than **Ad** with irregular bars on upperparts. **1W** | becomes bolder black-and-white but still has browner, irregular barring on upperparts until **2W**.

V | Barking "*kaw*" calls, varying in pitch; yapping chorus from flock.

FL | Pale underwing; steel-grey upperwing with blacker tip; black breast/white belly. Flocks often in irregular, elongated packs or wavy lines.

Ad

👁 *Emperor Goose p. 69*

Locally common resident/local migrant

Saline and freshwater edges, lakes, rivers, marshes, pastures

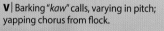

Ad
ALL YEAR

Looks black-and-white at long range.

Retains some worn, less regular juvenile feathers on back until second year.

2W (probably)
AUG–MAY

LC Brent Goose
LC *Branta bernicla*

L 55–62 cm | **W** 105–117 cm

Small goose (length of Mallard
(*p. 40*) but looks bigger); swims
and upends in saltmarsh creeks
and around seaweed-covered rocks;
grazes on fields, parks. **Dark with
striking white rear end** and **black
head, neck and breast**. Three/four
subspecies (or species) occur (see
opposite). **Ad** | white on upper neck.
Juv | neat pale bars on wings, no
neck patch until midwinter.
1W | gradually gains small white
neck patch during the winter.

V | Deep, rolling croaks, "*krr-r-ongk*,"
conversational character; quick,
higher/ringing chorus from big flock.

Feeds in tight groups, raising neck and walking away if mildly alarmed prior to taking flight. All the birds in this group are adults.

FL | Long-winged, heavy, thickset, dark goose with extended black head, neck and breast; bold white rear end. Flies in irregular flocks, but small groups form lines and 'V's.

Locally numerous
winter visitor (small
groups to 1,000s)
SEP–MAY

Breeds Arctic tundra;
winters on estuaries,
mudflats, coastal fields,
grassland

Ad

Ad
ALL YEAR

1W
NOV–MAR

'Dark-bellied'
BRENT GOOSE

Juv
JUN–NOV

BRENT GOOSE SUBSPECIES

'Pale-bellied' (ssp. hrota)

Brownest on back; sharp contrast between **black breast and pale belly**; flank whitish with greyer bars, darker at rear. Pale belly, **no dark between legs**. Narrow, spidery white neck marks.

'Dark-bellied' (ssp. bernicla)

Dark. Black breast sharp against browner belly (depends on angle and light). Small **white patch** high on side of neck may just meet in front. **Plain grey** back. Flank barred pale; **dark belly extends between legs**.

'Black Brant' (ssp. nigricans)

Darkest, dark brown above, **shining white flank patch**, two/three dark bars at rear. Little contrast between breast and belly; **dark extends between legs. Broad white neck patches meet in front**; head domed.

Rare **'Grey-bellied'** (taxonomic status uncertain) NOT SHOWN, individually variable, between subspecies *hrota* and *nigricans* (perhaps 'hybrid'); like *hrota* with darker, brownish-grey belly, dark **barely extending** between legs, diffuse paler flank and darker back; wider white neck bands may just meet in front.

Red-breasted Goose
Branta ruficollis

L 54–60 cm | **W** 110–125 cm

Striking small goose which 'disappears' surprisingly easily in large flocks of other geese, especially Brent Geese. **Ad** | black-and-white with **deep rust-red panels** on head and neck; black breast, white belly; **broad white flank stripe**. **Juv** | has browner bars on upperwing and duller head/neck than **Ad**. **1W** | like **Ad** but often extra thin white bar on wing coverts, and slightly duller head and neck.

V | High, sharp *"kik-wik."*

FL | Small, long-winged goose; looks black-and-white with narrow white bars along upperwing.

Ad

Rare, localized winter migrant SEP–MAY; occasional vagrant and escape

Breeds Arctic tundra; winters farmland, lakes

1W
AUG–MAR

Adult

LC LC (Common) **Shelduck**

Tadorna tadorna

L 55–65 cm | **W** 100–120 cm

Large, heavy, long-legged duck, found on dry ground, mud or water. Adults striking and unmistakable; juveniles less well marked but unlike anything else. **Ad** | **bright white** with blackish-green head, **black bands** along back and **broad orange-brown breast-band**. Legs pink. **Bill vivid red**, that of ♂ | with large basal knob (OCT–APR). ♀ | often has whitish marks on face/cheek. **Juv** | size and shape as adult but looks slim-necked. Head and neck dark brownish, face and throat white; back brown; no breast-band. **Legs greyish, bill pinkish**. Resembles juvenile Egyptian Goose but has a whiter body.

V | Wings whistle in flight; calls variable, whistling notes and deep, nasal "*ah-ahnk*" and "*grrah-grrah*."

♂ Br

Highly distinctive upcurved, spoon-like, vivid red bill; black bands along white body; and orange-brown breast-band

Locally numerous resident/migrant

Breeds estuaries, saline lagoons, freshwater lakes; winters saltwater and freshwater habitats, farmland

FL | Large, elongated but heavy with long wings. Mostly white; wings largely white with black flight feathers.

♀

smudgy brown-and-white head

orange-brown breast-band

♂

Juv
JUN–OCT

no breast-band

Some ♀ s have whitish face marks

♀
ALL YEAR

♀
ALL YEAR

duller feather edges in summer

♂
ALL YEAR
(bill knob enlarged Oct-Apr)

C
C

Ruddy Shelduck
Tadorna ferruginea

L 58–70 cm | **W** 110–135 cm

Large, heavy duck; obvious shelduck shape/size with long-legged gait. Rich **orange-brown with pale head**; black bill and legs. ♂ **Br** | black neck ring; ♂ **Nb** / ♀ | whiter face; **Juv** | greyer on head.

V | Quick, bubbling or cackling notes.

FL | Bold white forewing and black-and-white underwing.

Beware similar escaped species: *South African Shelduck p. 71; *Australian Shelduck Tadorna tadornoides* (not illustrated), ♂ very dark overall but ♀ greyish orange-buff with wholly white head and neck.

♂ **Br**
OCT–APR

♀
ALL YEAR

Local resident/ migrant breeder

Lakes and low-lying lagoons, rivers, drier hillsides

Egyptian Goose
Alopochen aegyptiaca

L 63–73 cm | **W** 110–120 cm

Medium-sized, upright goose; tall and long-legged but relatively short-necked. **Ad** | pale; olive-brown on back, greyer or rufous towards rear; **pale breast and head**, small black spot on lower breast. Pale crown; dark mask and neck ring. Bill small, pink-and-black; legs pink. Striking white forewing often shows at rest. **Juv** | head brown, forehead and throat white.

V | Monotonous, repetitive, rhythmic bark or babble in alarm, various hissing and gagging notes.

FL | Fast, direct; **bold white forewing** (mottled until MAY on **1S**).

Ad

Juvenile drabber than adult and has darker head.

Grey form has pale head and weak mask.

Rufous form has strong mask

Juv
JUN–FEB

Ad
ALL YEAR

Ad
ALL YEAR

Ad
ALL YEAR

Scarce, local resident, increasing; introduced

Lakes, parkland, pastures

37

The types of duck

DABBLING DUCKS are surface-feeders that swim with slightly raised tail on open water or among flooded vegetation, or paddle in muddy shallows; some feed on land, often at night. Flight fast, agile, with quick take-off from water or land.

tail held clear of water

Some graze

Some feed by upending

DIVING DUCKS are round-backed, hold their tail low and dive from the surface while swimming. Some drift in flocks by day or when asleep; others disperse when feeding. Some stand at the water's edge, but can barely walk. Flight low, straight and fast but less agile than dabbling ducks, with pattering run at take-off; settle onto water, not dry ground. **'SAWBILLS'** (except Smew) have an elongated shape, with long, serrated bills. **'STIFFTAILS'** often hold their tail high. **SEA DUCKS** are diving ducks (such as eiders and scoters) that are essentially marine except when nesting; occasional on inland waters, often ones and twos among commoner species.

'SAWBILL'

DIVING DUCK

'STIFFTAIL'

Most dive by leaping forwards

tail low

Marbled Teal
VU VU

Marmaronetta angustirostris

L 39–42 cm | **W** 55–60 cm

Small, pale, mottled, teal-like duck; sexes similar. **Ad**| dull sandy-brown with darker back and more or less obvious **dark mask; dark bill**. Flank **spotted with pale buff**, not streaked. Eye-catching pale forehead and lower face surrounding blackish smudge through eye; **short, drooped crest** (shorter on ♀). Bill slim, blackish-grey, recalling Pintail. **Juv**| similar to **Ad** but pale flank spots indistinct.

V| Silent except sharp whistle in display.

Pintail [♀] *p. 43*

Ad

Ad

Juv
JUN–DEC

♂
ALL YEAR

Rare, local migrant/ resident

Lowland, shallow lakes

FL| Pale without strong pattern: whitish hindwing, dark beyond angle of wing; white underwing.

(Eurasian) **Wigeon**

Mareca penelope

L 43–50 cm | **W** 72–85 cm

Medium-sized (smaller than Mallard
(*p. 40*), larger than Teal (*p. 44*)),
short-legged, **short-billed**, round-bodied
grazing/dabbling duck with a **white
belly**. **Grey legs and bill** useful clue.
Noisy flocks **graze on land** or swim.
♂ **Br** | blue-grey; **black-and-white
rear end**. Head **red-brown with pale
forehead**; body paler (darker on Teal).
White forewing may show at rest.
♂ **1W** | lacks white on wing; ♂ **Nb** | like
♀ but **redder**, with **white wing patch**.
Colourful/patchy intermediates often
seen in autumn. ♀ | barred/spotted, not
streaked like Mallard/Gadwall (*p. 42*)/
Pintail (*p. 43*), grey-brown to **tawny**
with greyer head and smudge (varies
between individuals) behind eye; often
looks dark at distance. **White belly**, **plain
flank**.

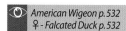

American Wigeon p. 532
♀ - Falcated Duck p. 532

V | Distinctive: ♂ an explosive whistle,
"*whe-ooo*" or "*whew!*;" ♀ a low growl, "*ra-
kraa*." Chatty flock chorus.

FL | Fast; tapered, swept-back wings and
short, pointed tail. ♂ white forewing;
dark hindwing; ♂ **1W** as adult but with
dull forewing. ♀ dull forewing; brownish
hindwing narrowly outlined with white.
Flocks tend to rise as one if disturbed.

Locally numerous;
migratory

Breeds tundra pools,
lakes, marshes; winters
low-lying coasts,
grassland, lakes, rivers

♀

♂ 1W

♂ Br

some grey
feathers on back

♂ Nb
MAY–OCT
[OCT]

Short,
triangular bill,
steep forehead
and domed
crown make
distinctive
shape.

♀
ALL YEAR

distinctive
head
pattern

♂ Br
NOV–APR

black-and-white
rear end

pink breast (striking
on sleeping birds)

LC Mallard *Anas platyrhynchos*

LC | **L** 50–60 cm | **W** 81–95 cm

Familiar large dabbling duck. Less often in tight flocks than Wigeon (*p. 39*) or Shoveler. Surface-feeding, upends; often feeds away from water. ♂ **Br** | broad brown bands along pale body; dark breast; black-and-white rear end. Head **green** (with blue/purple gloss) above white ring. **Bill yellow; legs bright orange**. ♂ **Nb** | like a rufous ♀ but **bill yellow**; cap and eyestripe green-black. ♀ | dull **brown**, flank marked with dark 'V'-shapes and creamy feather edges; belly brown. Creamy-white streak on tail. Dark eyestripe; bill brown with orange/yellowish markings. **Legs bright orange**. **Juv** | like ♀ but crown blacker, breast streaked (less spotted) and tail browner (see *p. 21*).

V | ♀ loud, short quack and long, coarse, descending series of longer quacks. ♂ | quiet quack, nasal whistles.

Shoveler | ♀ - *Am. Black Duck p. 532*
Many free-flying Mallards show influence of domestic varieties, often patched white; some males are pale brown with dark brown head, others blackish-brown with a white breast and yellow bill.

FL | Large, long-necked, long-winged; wingbeats mostly below body level. **Purple-blue hindwing between parallel white stripes**; underwing white.

Common resident/ migrant

Freshwater lakes, rivers, marshes, islands; winters salt and fresh water, pastures, farmland, parks

SSP. *platyrhynchos* occurs in Europe.

♀

♂ **Br**

In summer, Nb ('eclipse') ♂ loses strong colours and pattern, may look greyish or rusty; head greyer than on ♀; bill remains yellow.

Long bill sweeps into long, low forehead.

♂ **Nb**
JUN–NOV
[NOV]

♀
ALL YEAR

♂ **Br**
OCT–MAY

Shoveler *Spatula clypeata*

L 44–52 cm | **W** 73–82 cm

Medium-sized, large-headed dabbling duck with **long, heavy, broad bill**. Long-bodied, with shoulders low in water and head held low and well forward. Surface-feeding, sometimes in dense flock, often upends showing markedly long wing points. Feeds/rests in water or shallows at water's edge, not wandering far over drier land. ♂ **Br** | head greenish-black (looks blacker than Mallard's) with **yellow eye** and black bill; **breast white**, flank red-brown and **rear end black-and-white**. ♂ **Nb** | like ♀ but body often redder, head darker and with an **upright whitish crescent** (individually variable in extent and brightness) on the face in autumn. Eye yellow. ♀ | (best told by shape and big bill) dull pale brown, with darker blotches on flank; head paler greyish-brown; **brown belly**, **orange legs** (like Mallard). **Juv** | like ♀ but more finely marked.

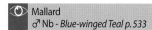
Mallard
♂ Nb - *Blue-winged Teal p. 533*

V | Calls weak, ♂ a nasal "*too-took*," ♀ a quiet, hoarse quack. Taking flight, wings make loud whoosh.

FL | ♂ **forewing pale blue**; hindwing dark green, **no white line at rear**. ♀ forewing grey-blue; broad white midwing bar. ♂ **1W** duller blue forewing; thin midwing bar. ♀ **1W** forewing brownish.

Locally common
resident/migrant

Shallow lakes, wet
marshes, estuaries

♀ 1W

♀

♂ Br

Nb ('eclipse') ♂ gradually develops a white crescent on the face, which becomes most distinct in autumn.

♂ Nb
APR–OCT
[OCT]

bill blackish

♀
ALL YEAR

bill orange

Combination of white foreparts and reddish flank is unique.

♂ Br
SEP–APR

41

LC # Gadwall *Mareca strepera*

LC **L** 46–56 cm | **W** 78–90 cm

Large, long-bodied dabbling duck, much like Mallard but squarer head with steep forehead and slim bill. Square **white patch** on inner hindwing (usually shows as triangle or diamond on swimming bird). ♂ **Br** | **grey body** with paler head and **black rear end (no white).**
♂ **Nb** | like ♀ but greyer head; barred grey on back and body, and black rump.
♀ | pale brown with darker brown blotches; head paler greyish-brown or buff, weakly marked; tail dull, less white than on ♀ Mallard; belly has clearly defined **white patch**. Orange side to bill; **legs orange-yellow. Juv/1W** | like ♀ but belly mottled and breast more streaked; small white wing patch (more like ♀ Wigeon).

V | Quiet quacks and frequent nasal "*nhek-nhek*" from ♂; very vocal in displays from late summer onwards.

Mallard *p. 40* | Wigeon *p. 39*

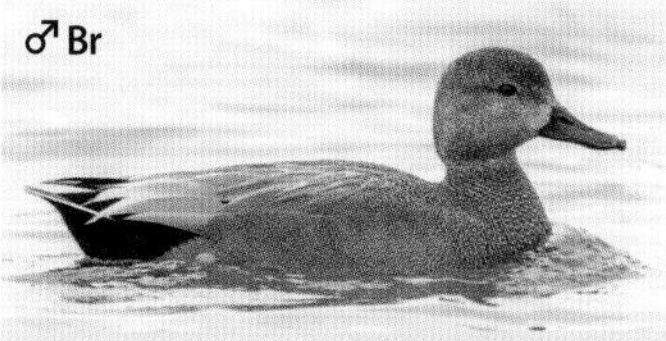

♂ **Br**

The diagnostic white wing patch is not always visible.

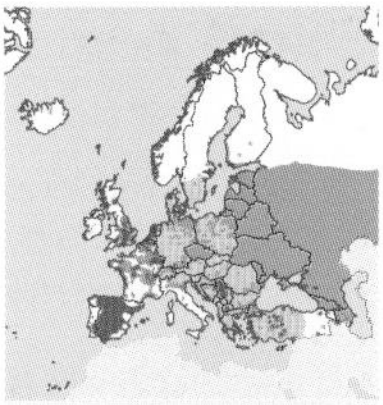

FL | Slim, narrow-winged; faster action than Mallard. Upperwing dark with chestnut and black, and obvious white square on hindwing close to body; ♀ has white belly.

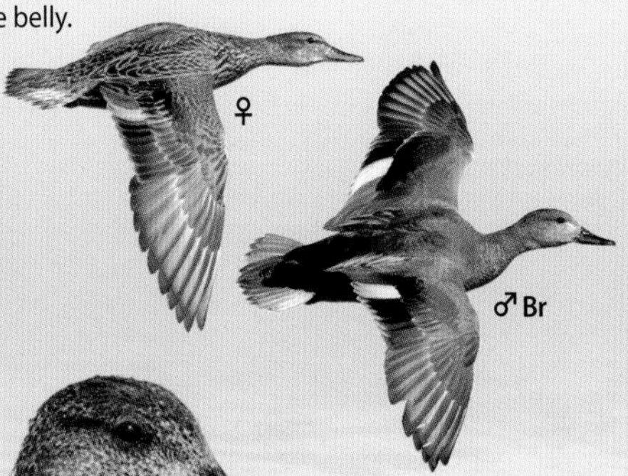

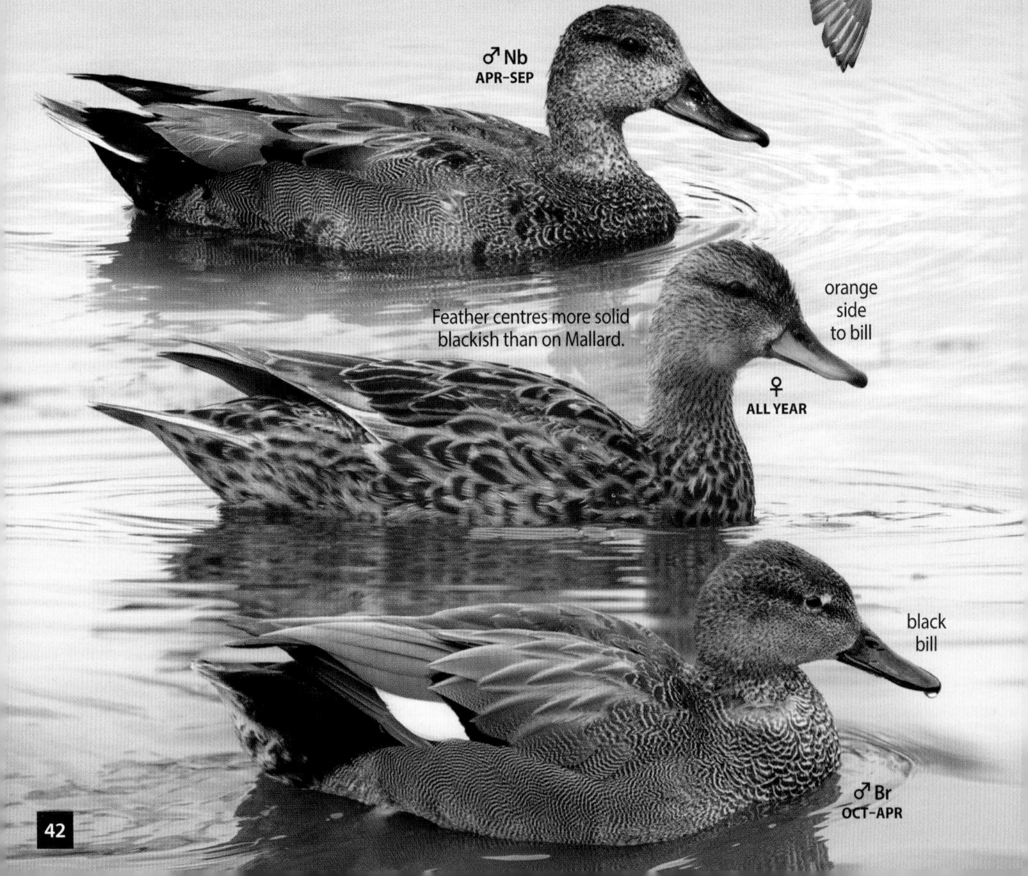

Locally common resident/migrant

Lakes, open marshes, saline lagoons

♀

♂ **Br**

♂ **Nb**
APR–SEP

Feather centres more solid blackish than on Mallard.

orange side to bill

♀
ALL YEAR

black bill

♂ **Br**
OCT–APR

Pintail *Anas acuta*

L 51–62 cm | **W** 79–87 cm

Large, heavy-bodied surface-feeding/grazing duck with slimmer bill and longer neck and tail than on Mallard. **♂ Br** | lead-grey body with **white breast** (often stained) extending as narrow **white stripe** towards back of dark head. Rear end black with yellow-buff patch and **long tail spike** (easy to see even at long range). **Legs grey**; bill bluish with black stripe. **♂ Nb** | can be puzzling: pale, blurry buffish with soft bars and streaks, dark chequering on upperparts, increasingly patched with grey; gingery head against long, **blue-sided, black bill**. **♀/Juv/♀ 1W** | brown with dark brown blotches and pale buff feather edges; head plain buffy-brown, less striped than on ♀ Mallard. **Bill grey; legs grey**.

V | **♂ Br** whistles; ♀ gives short, low quacks.

👁 ♀ - Mallard *p. 40*

♀

Blue-grey legs and bill rule out Mallard, Shoveler and Gadwall, but not Wigeon.

FL | Long, slim; narrow wings. ♂ has long tail, greenish-black hindwing; ♀ shows long white trailing edge.

Locally common; migratory

Breeds on tundra, moorland pools, saltmarsh; winters estuaries, lakes, marshes, floods

♀

♂ Br

1W ♂ similar but gradually develops breeding plumage as winter progresses.

blue-sided black bill

♂ Nb
JUL–OCT
[OCT]

no stripes on head

slim grey bill

♀
ALL YEAR

white neck stripe

♂ Br
NOV–JUN

distinctive long tail

DUCKS IN FLIGHT *pp. 24–25*

LC (Common) **Teal** *Anas crecca*

LC | **L** 34–38 cm | **W** 53–59 cm

Small, agile dabbling duck with a bright green wing patch (often hidden at rest). **♂ Br** | dark grey with **white stripe** along body and black-edged **mustard-yellow triangle** at rear; head dark brown with **buff-edged** glossy **green panel** behind eye. **Bill and legs black. ♀ / ♂ Nb** | coarsely mottled dark brown and grey-buff; **white streak beside tail** most useful mark. **Juv** | like ♀ but more finely streaked.

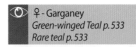

♀ - Garganey
Green-winged Teal p. 533
Rare teal p. 533

Dabbles in shallow water/wet mud.

V | Often heard from hidden or distant birds on marsh or reservoir: ♂ high, sharp, ringing whistle, *"crree"* or *"krik"* (may not bring 'duck' to mind); ♀ has low, gruff, nasal quack.

Locally common resident/migrant

Breeds freshwater edges, peat bogs, marshes; winters salt- and freshwater edges

FL | Fast with quick wingbeats; flocks twist/turn like waders; near-vertical take-off. **White border to hindwing patch broader in front than rear; flashy grass-green** between white lines rules out Garganey. ♀ has dark outerwing (unlike Garganey).

♂ Nb
MAY–OCT
[OCT]

Brownish edge to forewing

narrow grey bars

♀

Brilliant green and black patch between two white lines along wing.

♂ Br

'Eclipse' ♂ like ♀ ; often shows dark cap and pale cheek; any narrow grey bars indicate bird is a ♂ . Rapidly gains full breeding plumage from SEP–OCT onwards.

♂ Nb
MAY–OCT
[OCT]

Green on head/wing of male may flash vivid violet from certain angles against low sun.

♀
ALL YEAR

Breeding ♂ compact, looks dark (but bright when lit by e.g. low winter sun).

White streak near tail shows at long range.

♂ Br
OCT–APR

pale triangle

Garganey *Spatula querquedula*

C
C

L 37–41 cm | **W** 59–67 cm

Small dabbling duck; like Teal but slightly larger; male distinctive in spring. ♂ **Br** | **white crescent over eye**; head and breast warm brown; pale, drooping feathers over wing. ♂ **Nb** | like dark ♀ with bolder whitish stripes above and below eye, and white chin. ♀ /**Juv** | like Teal but flank spots bolder and with a dark brown cap; a dark brown stripe through the eye and a dark band across the cheek; **long whitish stripe over eye** (thin in middle) and whitish upper cheek line. Conspicuous **pale spot by bill**.

👁 ♀ - Teal | *Rare teal p. 533*

Spring birds often favour tall, flooded vegetation and are often very elusive.

V | Infrequent: ♂ gives curious dry rattle in spring; ♀ has nasal "*ga ga ga*" and weak quack.

Scarce
summer migrant
MAR–OCT

Shallow lakes, marshes

FL | ♂ forewing pale blue. ♀ milky-grey midwing stripe continues onto outerwing. **White borders to hindwing patch equal front and rear** (like Mallard (*p. 40*) (unequal on Teal)). Contrasted blackish edge to forewing beneath.

♂ **Juv**
JUN–OCT
[AUG]

'Eclipse' ♂ (MAY–SEP) similar to juvenile but underparts unstreaked white: like ♀ but darker; head usually more boldly patterned; forewing bluer, greater coverts more broadly tipped white; hindwing band greener.

Blackish edge to forewing

♀

Dull dark band between two white lines along wing.

♂ **Br**

Autumn migrants often located by head pattern; dark olive hindwing patch and greyish forewing help confirm identification.

Pale streak near tail weak or absent.

Pale stripe above and below dark eyestripe; pale spot near bill.

♀
ALL YEAR

♂ **Br**
SEP–MAY

Identifying speckled female/juvenile dabbling ducks

These surface-feeding ducks can look very similar. On birds flying overhead, take note of underwing patterns and any underwing/body contrast. On standing birds check the overall shape, bill size and colour, head shape, belly colour and leg length.

TEAL (*p. 40*): shown here for size comparison; averages 30% smaller than the other ducks shown below.

Identification of speckled female/juvenile dabbling ducks				
	Shoveler (*p. 41*)	**Mallard** (*p. 40*)	**Gadwall** (*p. 42*)	**Pintail** (*p. 43*)
Bill	orange; spatulate	diffuse orange and brown	well-defined orange side	grey
Legs	orange		orange (pale)	grey
Belly	brown		sharp white	blended white

TEAL (comparison)

dark underwing

SHOVELER

PINTAIL

GADWALL white

WIGEON (comparison)

MALLARD brown

TEAL

Shoveler stands with back level, belly tapering to high tail.

PINTAIL grey

SHOVELER spatulate

grey

MALLARD

blue wing patch

GADWALL

white wing patch

brown

white

bright orange

pale orange

Red-crested Pochard
Netta rufina

L 53–57 cm | **W** 85–90 cm

Big, bulky, large-headed duck; sits high in the water; generally a surface-feeder but also dives. ♂ **Br** | **brown head with high orange crown**, sharply contrasting with black neck and breast; body pale brown and white with black rear end; bill and eye **red**. ♂ **Nb** | brownish overall with a dark cap that extends to just below the eye; cheek pale buff-white; **bill and eye red**. ♀ / **Juv** | pale brown body; top half of head brown with darker eye patch, **lower half pale buff-white**; bill dark grey with pink patch near tip. (♀ Common Scoter similar but darker overall, with all-dark wings in flight.)

V | Quiet and insignificant, but squeaky 'sneeze' in display.

👁 ♀ - Common Scoter [♀] *p.62*

FL | Dark body, pale flank and **broad white band** along whole of wing; ♂ also has white leading edge.

Scarce, local resident/migrant; some introduced populations

Large marshy lakes, saline lagoons; winters mainly freshwater lakes

♀

♂ Br

♂ Juv
JUN–OCT
[OCT]

Nb ('eclipse') ♂ (MAY–SEP) looks similar to juvenile ♂ but eye bright and bill all-red.

♀
ALL YEAR

♂ Br
NOV–MAY

47

Tufted Duck *Aythya fuligula*

LC

LC **L** 40–47 cm | **W** 65–72 cm

Medium-sized, buoyant, round-headed diving duck with **tuft on back of head**. Bill slim and grey with a wide **black tip**. **♂ Br** | **black-and-white** (bright purple gloss on cheek). **Head, breast and back black; flank panel bright white**. Drooping tuft; yellow eyes. **♀** | dark, rich, plain chocolate brown; **'bump' or slight tuft on back of head** (rules out Scaup). **♀/♂ Nb/Juv** | may have white facial marks, often sharply defined but rarely as extensive as on Scaup. Often whitish under tail (less prominent than on Ferruginous Duck). **♂ 1W** | gradually becomes blacker on upperparts and white on flank.

V | Loud, rough growling notes; bubbling whistles from displaying ♂.

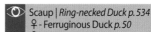

Scaup | *Ring-necked Duck p. 534*
♀ - Ferruginous Duck p. 50
♀ - *Lesser Scaup p. 534*

FL | Fast, direct; long white wing stripe along whole wing (grey on Pochard (*p. 51*)).

Locally common resident/migrant

Freshwater lakes, saline lagoons, rivers, sheltered coasts

♀

white under tail absent or dull (compare with Ferruginous Duck)

♀ darker brown and more streamlined than Scaup

♂ back and head same colour

♀

♂ Br

May be very like ♀ but back blacker, eye brighter yellow.

♂ Nb
MAY–SEP

♂ 1W
OCT–MAR

Some have larger Scaup-like face patches.

♀
MAR–OCT

♀
SEP–APR

♂ Br
SEP–MAY

(Greater) **Scaup** *Aythya marila*

L 42–51 cm | **W** 71–80 cm

Medium-sized diving duck, similar shape to Tufted Duck and Pochard but bulkier. Broader body than Tufted Duck and wider bill with **smaller black tip**; **rounded head** with steep forehead has **no trace of tuft**. ♂ **Br** | pale in middle, black at both ends, **white flank** excludes Pochard, **grey back** rules out Tufted Duck. ♂ **Nb** | flank browner. ♀ | grey-brown to ginger-brown, back with fine whitish bars. **White blaze on face** extends above bill; pale **ear patch** (variable in extent and brightness over time). **Juv/♀ 1W** | more like Tufted Duck but **larger** with **rounded head** and broader bill (dark tip wider and less well-defined than on adult). White face patch small or diffuse; may show pale ear patch.

Tufted Duck | *Lesser Scaup p.534*
Scaup is typically a marine duck – flocks at sea highly unlikely to be Tufted Duck or Pochard *p.51*.

V | Mostly silent; nasal bubbling note from displaying ♂, short growl from ♀; flight call a short "*ahng*."

FL | Fast, direct; white wing stripe along whole wing (grey on Pochard).

Scarce migrant breeder, locally numerous in winter

Breeds tundra and northern lakes, sea coasts, islands; winters mainly on sea

SSP. *marila* occurs in Europe.

♀ greyer and more robust than Tufted Duck but can look similar at distance.

♀

Grey back contrasts with darker head.

♂ **Br**

♂ **1W**
OCT–MAR

1W has smaller face patches than adult.

White cheek patches and larger white face patch in summer.

♀ **1W**
OCT–MAR

1W and 'eclipse' ♂ look similar and less like ♀ than Tufted Duck, gaining grey back, blacker head and white flank as moult progresses, so various intermediate stages may be seen.

♀
MAR–SEP

♀
SEP–MAR

♂ **Br**
SEP–JUN

NT LC Ferruginous Duck

Aythya nyroca

L 38–42 cm | **W** 60–67 cm

Small diving duck, like sleek, bright ♀ Tufted Duck with a slender bill.
♂ Br | glossy mahogany-brown with dark back and collar; **white under tail** edged black. **Eye white.** Bill grey with soft pale band. **♂ Nb** | duller but retains white eye. **♀** | dark brown, blacker on back; dark eye. Smooth, peaked head shape. **Upperparts always unmarked** (grey bars indicate hybrid (see *p. 67*)) (♀ Tufted Duck may show white under tail but rarely so prominent or bright.)
Juv | as ♀ but dark cap/paler cheek and white under tail duller or faintly spotted dark.

👁 Tufted Duck [♀] *p. 48*

V | Mostly silent; purring *"prr-prrr."*

Scarce, local resident/ migrant

Reedy freshwater lakes and tree-lined pools

FL | Long, wide white band on upperwing; underwing white.

white under tail (compare with Tufted Duck)

♀

♀ richer brown than Tufted Duck

♀

♂ Br

♀ (LEFT) and ♂ with raised head, showing flattened crown and revealing dark collar.

♀
ALL YEAR

Crown feathers can be flattened into less domed shape but high peak usually distinctive.

Smoothly curved, pale flank like Tufted Duck, but much richer red-brown.

♂ Br
SEP–MAY

(Common) **Pochard**
Aythya ferina

L 42–49 cm | **W** 7–75 cm

Medium-sized, round-backed diving duck; tends to swim with tail down; often rests by day with slightly smaller, more active, Tufted Ducks (*p. 48*). Round-headed with long bill running into sloping forehead. ♂ **Br** | pale grey, dark at both ends; head red-brown, bright in good light; eye red; pale band across dark bill. ♀ /♂ **Nb** | individually variable; greyish, darker front and rear. ♀ | brown on breast and at rear, diffusely mottled brownish on grey body; head pale brown with whitish eyering and around bill and throat, pale stripe curls over cheek; long, grey bill. **Juv**/ ♀ **1W** | dull brown with darker brown cap, pale patches on cheek, beside bill and on chin.

♀ / Juv - Scaup *p. 49*
Redhead *p. 535* | Canvasback *p. 535*
♀ / Juv - Ring-necked Duck *p. 534*

V | Infrequent: ♂ gives nasal "*wha-oo*" in display; ♀ a purring growl.

Scarce resident and migrant breeder; locally common winter visitor

Breeds reedy lakes, marshes; winters mainly freshwater lakes

FL | Fast, direct; short take-off run. Pale grey band along wing, palest on ♀ (white on Tufted Duck and Scaup).

♀

♂ **Br**

♂ **Nb**
MAY–SEP
[AUG]

'Eclipse' ♂ similar to ♀ but eye remains red and face lacks pale markings.

Adult females individually variable and ageing often difficult: **Juv/1W** look like dull adult ♀ but told by old, faded tertials/wing coverts.

♀
ALL YEAR

♀
ALL YEAR

♂ **Br**
SEP–MAY

LC (Common) **Goldeneye**
LC *Bucephalus clangula*

L 40–48 cm | **W** 62–77 cm

Medium-sized, rounded diving duck with large, domed or peaked head; dives frequently when feeding but rests in groups with head back and long tail raised. ♂ **Br** | strikingly **black-and-white** at distance; head green-black with **round white face patch**. Eyes yellow, legs orange. ♂ **Nb** | like ♀ but bigger white wing patch and often a hint of white face patch. ♀ | **dark: grey body** and dark brown head often sunk into shoulders; white collar; **triangular bill** with orange band. White wing markings (often hidden). Eyes yellow or white. **Juv / 1W** | like ♀ but neck darker; male develops white body and face patch during winter.

SSP. *clangula* occurs in Europe.

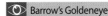

👁 Barrow's Goldeneye

V | ♂ makes creaky "*nhair-nhairr*" sounds in display; ♀ deep growls. Wings (especially adult males') whistle loudly in fast flight, often heard before birds seen.

♀

white patch on forewing

♂ **Br**

no black bar across white in wing

Locally common; migratory

Breeds forest lakes; winters on coast and freshwater lakes

FL | ♂ innerwing white, outerwing black; **underwing black**. ♀ innerwing mostly white, crossed by two dark bars; belly white. **Juv** like ♀ but forewing dark, one dark bar across white hindwing patch (like ♀ Barrow's Goldeneye).

♂Nb ('eclipse') (MAY–SEP) and ♂1W have a white face patch; this can be curved but never extends above the eye as on Barrow's Goldeneye.

♂ **1W**
NOV–MAR
[FEB]

Displaying ♂ jerks head back towards tail, then forward with kick of orange feet and gives grating call.

grey body (looks dark at distance)

peaked head, triangular bill

May show triangle or patches of white on wing, or no white at all.

♀
ALL YEAR

round white face patch

black streaks on white

♂ **Br**
OCT–JUN

Barrow's Goldeneye
Bucephala islandica

L 44–54 cm | **W** 77–83 cm

Medium-sized, rounded diving duck with large head, steep forehead and bulky nape; deep, triangular bill slightly **upcurved** with a bulging tip, tapering to a narrow point when seen head-on (Goldeneye has broader tip). ♂ **Br** | mostly white with **row of white spots** on black back and **long white face patch** extending up above front of eye. Black point beside breast. ♂ **Nb** | like ♀ but bigger white wing patch. ♀ | dull grey with dark brown head, white collar and underparts; rounder crown, longer head profile than on Goldeneye; bill dark, with patch of bright yellow or narrow dull orange-yellow band. (NOTE: North American birds (possible vagrants) have all-yellow bill from NOV–MAY.) **Juv / 1W** | like ♀ but no white on forewing; male develops white face patch during winter.

Goldeneye

V | Short, low, grunting notes; in display, ♂ makes hard, rasping or creaking double-note. Wings create whistle in flight.

Scarce, very local resident; occasional vagrant

Tundra pools and larger lakes

FL | ♂ has white forewing crossed by black bar. ♀ forewing mostly grey.

♀ forewing mostly grey (as juvenile Goldeneye)

black bar across white in wing

♂ **Br**

♂ **1W**
OCT–MAY
[FEB]

Bill size is not a reliable feature for distinguishing Goldeneye and Barrow's Goldeneye because of overlap, but extreme examples of Barrow's Goldeneye look heavy and deep-based.

bushy nape

steep forehead, triangular bill

♀ **ALL YEAR**

long white face patch extends above eye

row of white spots

♂ **Br** OCT–MAY

LC **Goosander**
LC *Mergus merganser*

L 58–68 cm | **W** 78–94 cm

Large, long-bodied, long-billed diving duck, only likely to be confused with Red-breasted Merganser (but see Great Crested Grebe (*p. 78*)). Frequently stands on shore, revealing **bright red legs**. ♂ **Br** | white/pale salmon-pink (yellowish in evening light) with black back. Large **green-black head**; dark eye. Bill thick, strongly hooked; deep **plum-red**. ♂ **Nb** | like ♀, with brown head, but with large white wing patch. ♀ | **pale grey body** with whitish breast and lower neck; **sharp divide against red-brown head** and upper neck. Well-defined **white chin patch**. Long red bill. Belly white, often stained orange. **Juv / 1W** | like ♀ but has stripes from bill to eye, a duller bill and less white on wing.

V | Croaking flight note.

ssp. ***merganser*** occurs in Europe.

Red-breasted Merganser

May show a flat crown, or raise feathers to make a rounder, bulging shape.

Locally common resident/migrant (ones/twos to 100+)

Breeds rivers, fresh-water lakes (nests in tree holes); winters lakes and coasts

FL | Long, heavy cross-shape with head outstretched; fast, direct.
♂ innerwing white (**no black cross-bars**); outerwing black.
♀ inner hindwing white (**usually no cross-bar**); forewing grey; outerwing black.

♂ **Br**

no bars across white in wing

usually no bars across white in wing

♀

♂ **Nb**
JUL–OCT
[OCT]

'Eclipse' and 1W ♂ moult into breeding plumage, with gradual change from grey/brown to black/white, so various intermediate stages may be seen.

Rounded, drooping crest (paler, more ragged in summer), raised in 'anvil' shape in courtship.

♀
ALL YEAR

distinct brown/white divide on neck

♂ **Br**
NOV–JUL

Red-breasted Merganser
Mergus serrator

L 52–58 cm | **W** 67–82 cm

Large, long-bodied, long-billed diving duck, males with striking patterns, and dramatic shapes in display. ♂ **Br** | dark head and back, with white band above **grey flank**, and **dark breast** (much less obviously pale than male Goosander). White collar beneath green-black head with **long, wispy crest**; **red eye**. Bill slender, **bright red**. ♂ **Nb** / ♀ / **Juv** / **1W** | brownish-grey (dark in dull light), less bright, darker grey than Goosander. Paler gingery head with thin, short crest fades into throat and dull, pale breast. Bill pale red; slim, slightly upswept and with a more curved gape line than on Goosander.

V | Insignificant, deep growl.

Goosander | *Hooded Merganser p. 535*

Goosander
nostril midway between eye and bill tip

Red-breasted Merganser
nostril closer to eye.

Locally common resident/migrant (ones/twos to 100+)

Breeds coasts, rivers (nests on the ground); winters at sea and in estuaries

FL | Long body, with head projecting, wings straight and narrow; rapid wing beats below body level. ♂ innerwing mainly white, crossed by two black bars; outerwing black. ♀ inner hindwing white crossed by black bar; forewing grey; outerwing black.

two black bars across white in wing

♂ **Br**

black bar across white in wing

♀

♂ **Nb**
MAY–OCT
[OCT]

'Eclipse' and 1W ♂ develop breeding plumage progressively, so intermediate stages are frequent. Sometimes stands at the water's edge, but less often than Goosander; shows vivid orange legs.

begins to gain black head by midwinter

Typically has a spiky, upright crest.

♂ **1W**
OCT–MAY
[JAN]

♀
ALL YEAR

blurred brown/white on neck

♂ **Br**
NOV–MAY

55

LC **Smew** *Mergellus albellus*

LC **L** 38–44 cm | **W** 56–69 cm

Small, lively, relatively small-headed, short-billed diving duck; often elusive (may hide under flooded waterside bushes or in reeds). ♂ **Br** | unmistakable: **mostly white** with pale grey flank and **black eye patch**. At close range, black nape beneath white crest, fine black chest lines, black back and grey rear end more noticeable. ♂ **Nb** | like ♀ with whiter breast. ♀ | lead grey body; relatively small head **red-brown** with **lower third white**, blacker around eye. **Juv** | like ♀ but redder head without dark eye patch. ♂ **1W** | develops white during winter.

V | Hoarse croak, otherwise mostly silent.

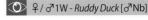
♀ / ♂ 1W - Ruddy Duck [♂ Nb]

Generally scarce, locally common; migratory

Forested lakes, larger rivers; winters on lakes, sheltered coasts

FL | Elongated but quite deep-bellied. ♂ and ♀ upperwing blackish with broad white forewing patch. Flight fast and direct, with quick, deep beats.

white on forewing

♂ Br

♀

Males court females throughout the winter, frequently throwing their head far back over their body – a typical diving duck display.

brown between eye and bill

Gradually develops white on body in late winter, increasingly patchy from January.

♂ 1W
OCT–MAY
[DEC]

bill dark grey

Non-breeding male Ruddy Duck has similar head pattern.

blackish between eye and bill

Crest can be flattened or held forwards.

lead-grey body

♀
ALL YEAR

white body with black markings

♂ Br
OCT–MAY

White-headed Duck

Oxyura leucocephala

L 43–48 cm | **W** 55–65 cm

Europe's native 'stifftail': a medium-sized, dumpy, round-backed and wide-bodied diving duck. **Long, stiff tail** raised (very obvious) or held flat (hardly visible). Bill noticeably **thick and swollen at base** in both sexes and at all ages (unlike similar Ruddy Duck). ♂ **Br** | ginger-brown body; **white head** with isolated black eye, small black cap, white hindneck, black collar. Bill pale blue. ♂ **Nb** | sandy-brown with more extensive black cap. ♂ **1S** | can have wholly black head, bright blue bill. ♀/**Juv** | finely barred overall, with black cap to below eye and bold blackish cheek stripe; bill swollen at base.

V | Usually silent.

Ruddy Duck

FL | Heavy, hump-backed, long-tailed, wings all-dark.

♂ Br

♀

Rare and local resident/migrant

Shallow freshwater lakes

♂ 1S
APR–SEP

♀
ALL YEAR

♂ Br
MAR–SEP

♂ Nb
SEP–FEB

Unlike most ducks, ♂ White-headed and Ruddy Ducks have a dull plumage through the winter and are most colourful in summer.

Ruddy Duck

Oxyura jamaicensis

L 35–43 cm | **W** 50–55 cm

Small, round-backed, large-headed diving duck with long, stiff tail (often held flat on water, inconspicuous until raised). ♂ **Br** | bright coppery-red with bold black cap, nape and neck **enclosing white face**; bill blue. ♂ **Nb** | dark, with black cap and **stark white face**; bill becomes grey in winter. ♀/**Juv** | dull, face dark with **pale cheek, crossed by dark band**.

V | Usually silent.

Rare resident, introduced (largely eradicated); vagrant from N America

Freshwater lakes

FL | Small, dumpy, fast and low; upperwing plain dark brown.

♀

♂ Nb

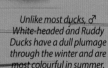
♂ Nb
SEP–FEB
(see ♀ Smew)

♀
ALL YEAR

♂ Br
APR–SEP

NT (Common) **Eider**
VU *Somateria mollissima*

L 60–70 cm | **W** 95–105 cm

Large, long, heavy sea duck with a **wedge-shaped head** and short tail often cocked. No similar common duck, but immature/summer males can confuse. **♂ Br** | black-and-white with salmon-pink breast (fades paler/yellower); **white back** and spot on rear flank; black body; green patch on nape. **Long white 'wedge'** beside bill. **♂ Nb** | piebald, brown-black face, breast and back. Pale greenish-grey bill blends into pale line over eye and cheek. **♂ 1W** | similar or very dark with whiter breast and mottled upperparts. **♀** | rich brown, **barred**; dark at distance; striking bars over flank, chequered/barred back. Pale **brown 'wedge' beside bill** (which has a pale 'blob'-tip). **Juv** | like ♀ but plainer, greyer brown.

V | Passionate cooing *"aa-ooh"* from ♂ and guttural *"gak-ak-ak-ak-ak"* from ♀.

 ♀ - King Eider [♀] *p. 60*
♀ - Steller's Eider [♀] *p. 61*
♀ - Spectacled Eider [♀] *p. 537*

FL | ♂ white in front/on top, black behind/beneath. **♀** hindwing dark, plain or edged by two parallel white lines.

Locally numerous resident/migrant

Breeds on coasts, islands; winters on open sea, estuaries

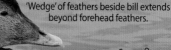

♂ **Br**

♀

♂ **1W**

'Wedge' of feathers beside bill extends beyond forehead feathers.

♀
ALL YEAR

Some ♀s are greyer, others more rufous, but always have chequered back and barred flank.

Steep, dark forehead curves forward into long bill profile.

♀
ALL YEAR

Northern ♀ (ssp. *faeroeensis*) is darker and more finely barred than southern (ssp. *mollissima*); all are darker in winter than in summer due to wear (pale edges reduced).

♀
ALL YEAR

EIDER SUBSPECIES

♂ **Nearctic**
ssp. *dresseri*
(from American N Atlantic)

small white 'sails' on back

pointed (shortest)

greenish-yellow

Northern European
ssp. *mollissima/faeroeensis*

slightly rounded

orange-yellow

Northern ssp. *borealis*

♂ **Northern**
ssp. *borealis*
(from Arctic N Atlantic)

small white 'sails' on back

rounded (longest)

orange

green line under eye

Nearctic ssp. *dresseri*

Slim tail often raised clear of water

♂ Nb
JUL–SEP

♂ 1W
AUG–MAY

♂ Br
OCT–JUN

59

King Eider *Somateria spectabilis*

LC

LC **L** 55–63 cm | **W** 87–100 cm

Large, heavy sea duck; rare associate of Eider flocks outside restricted regular range; beware unfamiliar plumages of moulting/immature Eider. ♂ immediately obvious but ♀ difficult. **♂ Br** | black body with white stripe and rear flank spot, and salmon-pink breast; **head pale blue-grey**, with **red bill** and bulging **orange/yellow frontal shield**. **♂ Nb** | dusky brownish on head and breast. **♂ 1W** | dark brown, but **bill reddish** and **frontal shield yellow**. ♀ | rusty, neatly marked with bars and **'V'-shapes on flank** (straighter bars on Eider). At close range may show tiny 'sails' on back and has a 'smiling' dark gape line with a short facial 'wedge' against **small bill with dark tip,** giving expression unlike Eider.

V | Usually silent.

Eider *p. 58*

All three regularly occurring species of eider can be seen together in parts of N Norway (NOV–APR); King Eider flocks tend to be shy if approached openly.

Rare and local; migratory

Breeds in tundra; winters usually with Eiders on coast

FL | **♂ Br** black-and-white with pink foreparts, 'colourful' head and bill. **♀** brown, underwing white (head shape only real difference from Eider - see opposite).

♂ Br

♀

♂ 1W

Usually shows subtle pale area around eye, no dark eyestripe.

♀
ALL YEAR

Rounded feathering beside bill falls short of forehead feathers.

♂ 1S
MAY–AUG

♂ 1W
AUG–MAY

♂ Br
OCT–JUN

Steller's Eider *Polysticta stelleri*

L 42–48 cm | **W** 68–77 cm

Medium-sized sea duck with a square head; not obviously an 'eider' but often associates with other eider species.
♂ Br | unmistakable: pale **yellow-buff** with black back and rear end; **white head** with black neck ring and **dark nape spot**.
♂ Nb / ♀ / Imm | dark brown, faintly barred; pale eyering; bill thick, plain grey and without the 'lobes' of other eiders (see inset illustrations); tail spike-like.

V | Usually silent.

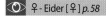

♀ - Eider [♀] *p.58*

Flocks of Steller's Eider occur in N Scandinavia and the Baltic (NOV–APR) but this is the rarest of the three eiders.

FL | ♂ Br strikingly black-and-white with buff body. **♀** dark with two white lines on hindwing, recalling Mallard (*p.40*), and white underwing flash.

Rare breeder; migratory; occasional vagrant

At sea

♂ Br

♀

♂ 2W → 2S
MAR–MAY
[MAR]

tertials curve down in all plumages

♂ 1W → 1S
MAR–MAY
[MAR]

Square head, pale eyering and deep-based bill give a distinct character.

♀ EIDER IDENTIFICATION

Concentrate on head shape, bill profile and shape of gape.

narrow 'lobe'

straight gape

EIDER

wide 'lobe'

'smiling' gape

KING EIDER

'bump'

no 'lobe'

STELLER'S EIDER

♀
ALL YEAR

Tuft on nape and dark 'collar'/pale breast contrast can be striking.

♂ Br
SEP–JUN

LC Common Scoter
LC *Melanitta nigra*

L 44–54 cm | **W** 70–84 cm

Medium-sized sea duck; heavy-bodied but elegant shape, with pointed tail and slender neck. On sea in long, ragged groups, showing on rising swell; often raises head and tail. Sits up from water with lowered head, to flap wings. Legs blackish. Usually dives with closed wings. ♂ **Br** | **entirely black**, except for yellow patch on top of bill beyond basal bulge. ♂ **Nb** / ♂ **1W** | brown, blotched black from NOV. ♀ / **Juv** | dark brown, obscurely barred, **blackish-brown cap**, **dusky-buff/whitish cheek**, darker face and throat. Summer birds fade and may have irregular pale patches on upperparts. (Resembles ♀ Red-crested Pochard but but darker, with plain wings in flight).

V | Whistled, piping notes and growling note from ♀.

Black Scoter p. 536
♀ - Red-crested Pochard p. 47

Scoter flocks trail across the waves, rising and falling in a 'roller coaster' effect. Flocks of non-breeding birds may be seen at sea all summer.

Generally scarce, locally numerous, resident/migrant

Breeds near lakes in moorland, northern forests, tundra; winters at sea

FL | Lacks white on hindwing; outerwing paler than innerwing.

round body and slim neck

♀

♂ **Br**

♂ **Br**

♀ in summer has pale feather edges above; pale cheek tends to form double patch; bill may show pink/red; cheek fades whiter by winter.

♀
MAY–OCT

♀
OCT–APR

Yellow/orange bill patch may extend as line over basal knob.

♂ **Br**
OCT–JUN

Slim tail often raised clear of water.

Velvet Scoter
Melanitta fusca

L 51–58 cm | **W** 79–97 cm

Large sea duck, outside breeding season often associates with similar Common Scoter, from which told by **white wing-patch** (although often hidden). Angular, wedge-shaped head recalls Eider (*p.58*) but bill slimmer and tail short. Usually dives with open wings.
♂ Br | black with **white 'tick'** under pale eye; bill yellow with black top; **legs red**.
♂ Nb / ♀ | very dark brown overall with white **cheek spot** and **pale patch near bill**. Bill deep-based, tapering (slightly upwards) to slender tip; legs reddish.
Juv / ♀ 1W | like **Ad ♀** with well-marked face, whiter belly. **♂ 1W / ♂ 1S** | like adult but with mixture of browner juvenile feathers above, whiter belly, until midsummer.

V | Hoarse double notes in summer.

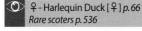
♀ - Harlequin Duck [♀] *p.66*
Rare scoters p.536

♂ Br

Velvet Scoters tend to hide their distinctive white wing panel when at rest (often showing a thin white line at best), so watch scoter flocks to catch frequent wing-flapping, when a bright white flash shows clearly.

Scarce and local; migratory

Breeds near northern coasts, tundra pools; winters at sea

FL | Shows prominent white hindwing panel.

♀

♂ Br

♂ Br

♀ 1W
belly white (unlike adult ♀)

♂ 1S
APR–OCT

bill tip slender, slightly uptilted

two pale patches on head

Short, raised tail and thick neck give an eider-like profile.

♀
ALL YEAR

curved yellow patch on bill

♂ Br
AUG–MAY

VU **Long-tailed Duck** *Clangula hyemalis*

VU **L** ♂ 49–62 cm (incl. 10–15 cm tail); ♀ 39–47 cm | **W** 65–82 cm

Medium-sized sea duck with complex plumages, but recognisable character: thickset, squat, or humped at rear; large, rounded head; and **short, deep, triangular bill.** ♂ | long, whippy tail feathers (see Pintail (*p. 43*) but Long-tailed Duck does not stand on mud or grass). ♂ **Br** | dark brown, streaked rusty-buff; head and breast black with **pale face patch**. ♂ **Nb** | white with **dark brown back** and drooped pale grey scapulars; black breast-band and grey flank; two-tone **dark head patch** below bright **white crown**; bill dark with pink ring. ♀ | in winter, dark upperparts, pale underparts; white head with dark cap and dark smudge on cheek; grey bill. In summer darker, more extensive dark cap and cheek marking, leaving fine whitish line behind eye, and white neck. **Juv** | (sometimes solitary, sometimes inland) like ♀ but greyer face, **whitish around eye** and **larger dark cheek patch**. ♂ **1W** | slowly develops adult pattern.

Complex moult patterns plus bleaching create striking changes in plumage: **Juv** moults body (to **1W**) SEP-DEC, or later; moults head/body again (to **1S**) APR-MAY, then wing/tail JUL-AUG. ♂**Ad** moults head/body APR-MAY, wing/tail JUN-OCT (flightless JUL-AUG); head/body again SEP-OCT, head/neck OCT-NOV. ♀**Ad** as ♂ but slightly later.

V | ♂ gives frequent, nasal, yodelling "*ar-ar-ardl-ow*;" quiet "*gag*" notes; ♀ makes short, nasal quacks and "*naah*" call.

Scarce, very locally numerous; migratory

Breeds on tundra, marshes, near coasts; winters at sea

FL | ♂ **Br** dark underwing, dark breast, white belly.

♂ **Br**

Juv
JUN-SEP

Dumpy, rather auk-like on water; triangular bill, round head; dives with wingtips slightly splayed.

♀ **Br**
MAY-JUN

♂ **Br**
MAY-JUN

Long-tailed Ducks form long, straggling flocks flying low over the sea, often with scoters (*pp. 62–63*).

FL | ♂ **Nb** extensively white with dark breast-band. ♀ wings very dark, rump **dark with white** sides, recalling Guillemot (*pp. 103*) or Razorbill (*pp. 102*).

♀

♂ **Nb**

♀ **Nb [dark]**
NOV–APR

♂ **1W**
DEC–MAY

♀ **Nb [light]**
NOV–APR

♂ **Nb**
OCT–APR

DUCKS IN FLIGHT pp. 24–25

LC Harlequin Duck

LC *Histrionicus histrionicus*

L 38–43 cm | **W** 65–68 cm

Small, round, small-billed sea duck. White face and cheek spots in all plumages. ♂ **Br** | dark slate-blue with rusty-red flank; **bold white patch on face** extending to rufous streak beside crown; white cheek spot, collar and **stripe on side of breast**. Complex moult: ♂ **Nb**/♂ **1W** | like ♀ but shows traces of breeding pattern. ♀/**Juv** | dark brown with **white cheek spot** and more diffuse white marks above and below eye (compare face pattern with larger Velvet Scoter).

V | Piping notes in display, otherwise silent.

♀/♂ Nb - Velvet Scoter [♀] *p. 63*

Both sexes are remarkably well camouflaged when standing on rocks.

Scarce, very local resident; occasional vagrant

Breeds on fast-flowing rivers; winters on coasts

FL | ♂ dark with white line along edge of back; all-dark wing. ♀ wings and body dark but belly slightly paler.

♂ Br

♂ Br

♀

♀

Nb ('eclipse') ♂ (MAY-SEP) looks very similar.

♂ 1W
SEP–MAY
[FEB]

white face and cheek spots in all plumages

Round head with steep forehead, often held low and pushed forwards.

♀
ALL YEAR

♂ Br
SEP–JUN

Hybrid ducks

Ducks interbreed more often than most birds, mainly in captivity. The resulting hybrids differ according to which species is the male parent, and female progeny are generally less recognizable than males. They usually show obviously mixed features, but may look remarkably like a third species. Many combinations occur: the males shown below include both subtle and distinctive examples. Hybrid possibilities must always be borne in mind when identifying wildfowl outside their normal range, especially Ferruginous Duck (*p. 50*), Redhead (*p. 535*) and Lesser Scaup (*p. 534*).

Mallard × Pintail
Male combines colours and shape of both parents, clearly differs from either.

Shoveler × Gadwall
Body largely like male Gadwall but peculiar head pattern incorporates Shoveler green.

Wigeon × American Wigeon
Intermediate, or closer to one parent; pale head with dark band, and grey body frequent.

Tufted Duck × Pochard
Like dark Scaup with a tuft, or Lesser Scaup with a uniform back; broader black bill tip.

Tufted Duck × Ferruginous Duck
Like Ferruginous Duck but with a duller eye and a 'tuft'; or Tufted Duck with dark flank.

Pochard × Ferruginous Duck
Like Ferruginous Duck but often reddish eye, greyer body, little white under tail.

Tufted Duck × Ring-necked Duck
Like Ring-necked Duck but with a tuft on the nape; grey flank may lack white peak at front.

Scaup × Tufted Duck
Both sexes like Scaup but with more black on the bill; male darker, with a tuft.

INTRODUCTIONS, ESCAPES and VAGRANTS

Several species of ducks, geese and swans may occasionally be seen as escapes (from ornamental collections) and introductions (released in the hope that they will breed and add interest to indigenous bird life). Shown here are some of the more frequently encountered escapes that look similar to naturally occurring (wild) species and which may cause confusion: note that Snow Goose and Ross's Goose also occur as wild vagrants.

 Ross's Goose | **Emperor Goose* | Beware: hybrids between Canada Goose (*p. 32*) and other geese often have a white head, but dark legs.

LC ## Snow Goose *Anser caerulescens*

L 65–75 cm | **W** 133–156 cm

Medium-sized, thickset goose; two subspecies: *caerulescens* (**Lesser**) and *atlanticus* (**Greater**), which differ in average size (although there is considerable overlap). **Ad** | both subspecies **pure white** (commonest form) with **black wingtips**; bill and feet red/pink. 'Lesser' also has dark form ('blue goose'): **white head, dark blue-grey body**, paler wings. **Juv / 1W** | pale brownish-grey upperparts, white neck, with dark eyeline, dark bill and grey legs.

V | Cackling notes and loud "*ang-ang-ank*."

FL | Black wingtips beyond small grey patch on leading edge.

Vagrant from N America; escapes/ introductions locally established

Farmland, marshes

Ad

Ad 'white form'
ALL YEAR

Beware 'farmyard goose' escapes (usually larger and less compact).

Same shape and proportions as adult, but drab.

1W
OCT–MAR

LESSER SNOW GOOSE
'blue goose'

Ad
ALL YEAR

'Open' patch along cutting edges of bill gives a 'grinning' effect.

LESSER SNOW GOOSE
'intermediate'

Ad
ALL YEAR

Ross's Goose *Anser rossii*

L 53–66 cm | **W** 115–130 cm

Small, short-necked white goose with black wingtips; very like Snow Goose but smaller, with rounder head; **short bill, grey at base**, without open 'grin' effect.
Juv / 1W duller, washed brownish-grey, with dark eyeline.

Escapes and vagrant from N America, typically with Pink-footed Geese (*p. 28*)

Marshes, pastures

SNOW GOOSE

red

Ad

ROSS'S GOOSE

grey

Ad
ALL YEAR

1W

1W
OCT–MAR

NT Emperor Goose *Anser canagicus*

L 68–89 cm | **W** 120 cm

Medium-sized, lead-grey goose (feather edges fade bronzy-brown) with dark bars, **white head and hindneck**, black foreneck and white tail. Bill pink and **legs bright orange** (Snow Goose has pink legs and lacks obvious bars on back).

Occasional escapes

Lakes/pastures

Ad
ALL YEAR

Bar-headed Goose *Anser indicus*

L 71–76 cm | **W** 140–160 cm

Medium-sized, pale grey goose; two black bands on white head, white neck stripe; very pale forewing. Legs orange.

Frequent escapes, usually with other geese

Lakes/rivers

Ad

Ad
ALL YEAR

LC Black Swan *Cygnus atratus*

L 110–140 cm | **W** 160–200 cm

Unmistakable large **black** swan with red bill and **white flight feathers** (obvious in flight).

Escaped birds frequent, sometimes breeds

Rivers, lakes, wet pasture

Ad

Often associates closely with Mute Swan (*p. 26*), sometimes joining family parties.

Ad
ALL YEAR

69

LC **Mandarin Duck** *Aix galericulata*

L 41–49 cm | **W** 65–75 cm

Medium-sized, unobtrusive, surface-feeding duck, often in or near trees.
♂ **Br** | unmistakable: **broad white band over eye** beneath long crest overlying back; lower face forms a broad orange-red fan. **Unique upright orange 'sails'** along back. ♂ **Nb** | like ♀ but has weaker 'spectacle', dull orange patch on cheek and dull orange-pink or red on bill. ♀ / **Juv** | small-headed; dark brown, breast finely streaked white, **flank boldly spotted**; blunt, thick crest above fine **white 'spectacle'**; white chin; small grey bill with **pale nail**.

👁 ♂ Nb/ ♀ Mandarin and Wood Ducks are similar.

V | High, squeaky whistle in flight.

FL | Small, dark, fast-flying; quite plain; dark upperwing with glossy hindwing patch, thin white trailing edge.

Scarce, local; introduced

Lakes, rivers in wooded areas, parks

Facial feathers against base of bill form straight line (curved on Wood Duck).

♂ **Br**
OCT–JUN

♂ **Nb**
APR–SEP

♀
ALL YEAR

LC **Wood Duck** *Aix sponsa*

L 47–54 cm | **W** 66–73 cm

Medium-sized surface-feeding duck.
♂ | unmistakable: black/white patterned head, drooping crest edged white; back dark, flank pale orange, bordered with black and white stripes. ♀ | like ♀ Mandarin Duck but broader white 'spectacle', no whitish flank stripe, **darker bill tip**.

Vagrant from N America/escape

Wooded lakes

♂ **Br**
OCT–MAY

♀ *Aix* IDENTIFICATION

MANDARIN DUCK	WOOD DUCK

NAIL
pale

NAIL
dark

WHITE 'SPECTACLE'	BILL BASE	WHITE 'SPECTACLE'	BILL BASE
narrow	**straight**	**broad**	**curved**

♀
ALL YEAR

Cinnamon Teal *Spatula cyanoptera*

L 41 cm | **W** 56–60 cm

Small dabbling duck. **♂ Br | bright mahogany** with blue forewing in flight; red eye; blackish bill long and heavy, wide at tip. **♀/♂ Nb/Juv** | like Blue-winged Teal but warmer brown and with less well-marked face (white spot near bill duller and dark eyestripe falls short of dark nape); eye brighter red-brown; bill wider, heavier, more spatulate.

Vagrant from
N America/escape

Lakes, marshes

♂ 1W
JUN–MAR

♀
ALL YEAR

♂ Br
OCT–MAY

👁 Blue-winged Teal p. 533

LC Fulvous Whistling-duck
Dendrocygna bicolor

L 45–53 cm | **W** 75–85 cm

Medium-sized, long-legged, long-billed duck. Bright tawny-brown with a plain head. Back barred black and rufous; flank pale brown with long, curved buff streaks towards rear. Bill and legs grey.

FL | Upperwing dark, rump white above black tail; underwing black.

Vagrant from
N America or
Africa/escape

Marshes, lakes

Upright neck, horizontal bill when swimming; flank plumes sweep upwards.

Ad

Ad
ALL YEAR

South African Shelduck *Tadorna cana*

L 71–76 cm | **W** 120–130 cm

Like a dark Ruddy Shelduck (*p. 37*). **♂** | has a grey head; **♀** | a grey head with white face.

♀
ALL YEAR

♂
ALL YEAR

Occasional
escape

Lakes

LC Muscovy Duck *Cairina moschata*

L 66–84 cm | **W** 120–140 cm

Large, bulky duck; widely domesticated, with very variable forms. **Mostly glossy blackish**; bill long and dark with pink band, and **red basal knob**. Domestic/escaped birds often have white head and underparts; large, wrinkled red face and bill.

Local; introduced

Rivers, ponds

white wing
patches

♀
ALL YEAR

♂
ALL YEAR

Grebes, divers and cormorants

Waterbirds, spending all or most of their time swimming and diving; legs are set far back along the body.

GREAT CRESTED GREBE

AdBr

Juv

AdNb

AdBr

GREBES 6 species [1 vagrant] *(pp. 73, 75–79, 538)*
Small to medium-sized; rounded; bill pointed; tail minute. Social. Strictly waterbirds (unless on floating nest); may stand but cannot walk. Swim high on water, neck erect or lowered, bill resting on breast; dive from the surface, smaller species 'disappear' in quick roll and bob up again like corks. **Flight** Fast, direct, large feet trailing; skitter across surface and splash down breast-first. **Sexing, Ageing and Moult** Sexes alike, obvious seasonal differences with head adornments in spring/summer; juveniles have a striped head at first, but are very like adults by winter. Juveniles moult head/body Jul-Dec and again Jan-May; adults moult head/body into breeding plumage Jan-Apr and complete moult to winter Jun-Nov.

Identify by SUMMER size | head and neck pattern and colour; WINTER bill shape and colour | head pattern

RED-THROATED DIVER

1W

1W

AdNb

AdBr → Nb

AdBr

DIVERS 5 species [1 vagrant] *(pp. 73, 74, 80–83, 538)*
Medium to large-sized; bill tapers to sharp point, tail short. Solitary or in loose groups; strictly waterbirds unless on nest at water's edge; cannot stand upright or walk. Swim low, neck erect, diving with smooth roll from surface. **Flight** Fast, direct; little agility on long, slender wings with head stretched forwards and feet trailing. All have white underparts and underwing, with dark band along top of flank. **Sexing, Ageing and Moult** Sexes alike but obvious seasonal changes: adults moult head/body into breeding plumage Feb-Apr, complete moult to winter plumage Sep-Dec. Juveniles differ slightly from winter adults in having more 'rounded' (less square) feather edges on upperparts; moult head/body Nov-Feb and again Apr-May.

Identify by SUMMER head/throat/back pattern and colour; WINTER bill shape | head/neck/flank pattern

CORMORANT

Juv

AdBr

Juv

CORMORANTS 4 species [1 vagrant] *(pp. 74, 84–86, 538)*Medium to large-sized; bill long with blunt hook at tip; feet large (webbed between all four toes). Social. Swim low in water with neck erect or curved, longish tail flat on surface; dive from surface with forward roll or small leap. Frequently stand on rocks, cliffs, islands and sandbars, on rafts/buoys *etc.* (unlike divers and grebes), upright or more horizontal, often with wings widely spread; some species perch freely (and may nest) in trees. **Flight** Often in lines/'V's, showing long tail; Cormorant may soar high up, can be seen anywhere over dry land. **Sexing, Ageing and Moult** Adults all-dark or marked with white in spring; sexes alike: have complete moult Jun-Dec and head/body Jan-Apr. Juveniles differ (browner) and older immatures intermediate; juveniles moult head/body Aug-Dec, then prolonged moult Feb-Dec and again Jun-Dec creating transitional stages.

Identify by head pattern | bill size | colour of underparts

POSSIBLE CONFUSION GROUPS Coots *(p. 219)*, diving ducks *(pp. 48–55)* and auks *(p. 100)* may be taken for divers and grebes.

Identifying grebes in winter

GREAT CRESTED GREBE (*p. 78*)
long, **pinkish bill**; black cap; **white stripe above black line from eye to bill**; slightly **'horned'** head; white cheek; slim neck; dark on nape narrow, foreneck white

RED-NECKED GREBE (*p. 79*)
dark bill with **yellow base**; dark in front of eye, rounded black cap and dull white cheek; thick neck; **dark on hindneck broad**, foreneck dull

SLAVONIAN GREBE (*p. 77*)
short, straight bill; **sloping forehead** and **flat crown**; flat back; dark cap usually very distinct from **white cheek**

BLACK-NECKED GREBE (*p. 76*)
short, slightly upturned bill; **steep forehead**; back round; dark cap merges into pale cheek

LITTLE GREBE (*p. 75*)
dull: buff and brown; darker, round cap

GREAT CRESTED GREBE

RED-NECKED GREBE

SLAVONIAN GREBE

BLACK-NECKED GREBE

LITTLE GREBE

Identifying divers in winter

WHITE-BILLED DIVER (*p. 83*)
side of head and neck pale brown, contrasting with **darker crown and hindneck**; bill pale, uptilted, angled

GREAT NORTHERN DIVER (*p. 82*)
dark cap broken by white around eye; cap/hindneck **darker than/same tone as** back; no white flank patch

RED-THROATED DIVER (*p. 80*)
pale, silvery at distance; **'button' eye** in pale face; **cap/neck much paler** and dark on hindneck **narrow**

BLACK-THROATED DIVER (*p. 81*)
dark cap to eye level; **cap/hindneck paler than back**; **white flank patch**
(see Pacific Diver *p. 538*)

WHITE-BILLED DIVER

GREAT NORTHERN DIVER

RED-THROATED DIVER

BLACK-THROATED DIVER

Cormorants and divers in flight

Imm

CORMORANT (*p. 84*)

Juv

PYGMY CORMORANT (*p. 86*)

Ad

SHAG (*p. 85*)

AdBr

AdBr

AdBr

WHITE-BILLED DIVER (*p. 83*)

AdBr

AdBr

GREAT NORTHERN DIVER (*p. 82*)

AdBr

RED-THROATED DIVER (*p. 80*)

BLACK-THROATED DIVER (*p. 81*)

PACIFIC DIVER (*p. 538*)

Juv

Nb [1W]

Nb [Juv]

Nb [Juv]

GREAT NORTHERN DIVER (*p. 82*)

Nb [1W → 1S]

WHITE-BILLED DIVER (*p. 83*)

Grebes in flight

white patch on forewing does not extend beside back (all plumages)

AdBr

RED-NECKED GREBE (p.79)

white spot on shoulder

short white band (all plumages)

AdNb

SLAVONIAN GREBE (p.77)

AdBr

white patch on forewing extends back (all plumages)

AdNb

GREAT CRESTED GREBE (p.78)

no white spot on shoulder

BLACK-NECKED GREBE (p.76)

AdNb

long white band (all plumages)

AdBr

Little Grebe
Tachybaptus ruficollis

L 23–29 cm | **W** 40–45 cm

Very small, brown, dumpy grebe; floats with cork-like buoyancy, occasionally sits at water's edge but rarely stands upright. Eye dark. **AdBr** | **very dark** with **chestnut-red face**, orange-buff flank and paler, 'fluffy', rear end; bill short with pale yellow spot at base. **AdNb/1W** | paler, browner than **AdBr**; back dark, flank paler buff and cap dark, contrasting with paler cheek, but less black-and-white than other small grebes; bill has a **whitish basal spot. Juv** | face and cap dark, cheek striped; bill short and stout.

V | Loud, sudden whinnying trill – characteristic waterside sound in summer. Various short, thin, puzzling whistles from juveniles. Frequent short pipes and trills in autumn/winter.

 Black-necked Grebe *p.76*
Pied-billed Grebe *p.538*

FL | Wings dull dark brown; appears longer-necked and has trailing dark feet when skittering across water.

Locally common resident/migrant

Freshwater lakes, rivers, marshes; often winters on sheltered estuaries

Two sspp. occur: *ruficollis* (widespread) has brown eye; *albescens* (Caucasus) has yellow eye.

Fledgling MAY–AUG

often shows strong contrast on head, but brown/ buff, not black-and-white

Juv JUL–OCT

All ssp. *ruficollis*

AdNb/1W SEP–MAR

AdBr APR–SEP

Black-necked Grebe

LC

LC *Podiceps nigricollis*

L 28–34 cm| **W** 45–50 cm

Small, round-backed grebe. Bill short, slim, **slightly upturned**, all-dark: **forehead steep**; crown high, peaked in the middle. Usually ones or twos, but occasionally forms large, tight flocks. **AdBr**| black with coppery-red flank and **drooping golden-yellow 'fan'** behind eye. **AdNb**| black-and-white. Black cap typically merges behind the eye into dusky cheek (unlike Slavonian Grebe), although some can show marked contrast; lower part of cheek paler and often shows a whitish 'hook' at the rear; broad dark stripe down hindneck; grey foreneck. Bright red eyes, often obvious even at long range. **Juv**| thin white stripes on head. **1W**| loses stripes; like **AdNb** but face and neck orange-buff, resembling Little Grebe.

👁 Slavonian Grebe | Little Grebe *p. 75*

Black-necked Grebes bunch together in lively and active flocks where they are common; note the variety of transitional plumages in this flock.

V| Weak trills and rising whistles; silent in winter.

Scarce, local; migratory

Breeds freshwater lakes; winters lakes, sea coasts

SSP. *nigricollis* occurs in Europe.

FL| White on hindwing extends to outerwing (no 'shoulder' spot as on Slavonian Grebe).

AdNb

no white spot

white reaches outerwing

AdBr

small pink patch on face, fine white lines over eye

high crown; dusky cheek with blurred border

Fledgling
JUN–AUG

often shows hint of brown on face and neck

dark bill slightly upturned

AdNb / 1W
SEP–APR

looks black-and-white in strong winter sun

AdBr
APR–OCT

black neck

Slavonian Grebe
Podiceps auritus

L 31–38 cm | **W** 46–55 cm

Fairly small relatively flat-backed grebe. Bill short, **straight**, dark with a **pale tip**; **forehead gently sloping**; crown low, peaked at rear. Less social than other small grebes: usually ones or twos, but may associate with Black-necked Grebes. **AdBr**| head black with **broad yellow 'wedge'** behind eye; **neck and flank deep rusty-red**. **AdNb**| black-and-white. Black cap **sharply defined** against white cheek; narrow black stripe down hindneck; silky-white foreneck. Typically has a whitish patch in front of bright red eye. **Juv**| broad black and white stripes on head. **1W**| loses stripes; like **AdNb** but dusky/buff marks on head and neck, more like Black-necked Grebe (or a small Red-necked Grebe).

👁 Black-necked Grebe
Red-necked Grebe *p. 79*

AdBr → Nb
[SEP]

In spring transition, white cheeks darken and yellow appears on head; in autumn, cheeks become white, and yellow is gradually lost, as shown here.

V| Rather insignificant whinnies in summer; silent in winter.

Rare, local; migratory
Breeds freshwater lakes; winters lakes, sea coasts

ssp. *auritus* occurs in Europe.

FL| White on hindwing on innerwing only; usually small white 'shoulder' spot.

white spot

white only on innerwing

AdNb

AdBr

large pink patch on face, broad white stripes on head

Fledgling
JUN–AUG

low, flat crown peaks at rear; white cheek with distinct border

head/neck more contrastingly black-and-white than Black-necked Grebe

AdNb
JUL–MAR

dark bill straight; pale tip

pink line from bill to eye

AdBr
MAR–JUL

rufous neck

77

LC Great Crested Grebe

LC *Podiceps cristatus*

L 46–51 cm | **W** 59–73 cm

Largest grebe, although size difficult to judge as slim neck can be held upright or withdrawn into shoulders: can look dumpy or sleek. Black cap **stops above eye; white patch above black stripe from eye to bill.** Bill **dagger-like, pinkish**; eye red. Makes frequent 'smooth' dives from surface. Solitary/ pairs or large groups. **AdBr** | **black crest**; broad **chestnut-orange ruff**; white face, foreneck and breast. **AdNb** | **neck bright white**; narrow dark line down hindneck. **Juv** | nondescript pale brown with whiter breast; black-and-white stripes on head but moults to look like **AdNb** by **1W.**

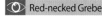
Red-necked Grebe

Breeding pairs frequently display together with spread ruffs and head-wagging ceremonies while facing each other.

V | Summer calls loud, croaking or nasal. Chicks' persistent loud, whistling "*pli-pli-pli*" common wetland sound in summer; occasional croaks in winter.

Locally common resident/migrant

Breeds freshwater lakes, rivers; winters lakes, rivers, sea coasts

SSP. *cristatus* occurs in Europe.

FL | Fast, direct; gangly neck; large, trailing feet drooped. White patches on narrow wings.

AdNb
white patch on forewing extends back (all plumages)

Juv
MAY–AUG

AdNb
AUG–MAR

some are less bright on cheek

dark cap stops above eye (unlike Red-necked Grebe)

bill pink

AdNb
AUG–MAR
[JAN]

cheek bright white

AdBr
MAR–JUL

black crest and chestnut-orange 'ruff'

Red-necked Grebe
Podiceps grisegena

L 40–46 cm | **W** 55–60 cm

Large grebe with heavy, **yellow-based dark bill**, thick neck and large head. **Dark cap extends below** dark or yellow (not red) eye; no white in front of eye. Solitary or in pairs, locally 50 or more, often with other grebes. **AdBr** cap black with short tuft; **cheek pale grey, edged white; neck and breast rusty-orange. AdNb** black, white and grey/brown (like a dull, thickset Great Crested Grebe or large Slavonian Grebe). Lower half of head smudgy grey or dull white, with slight white 'hook' at rear of cheek. **Broad dark band** down hindneck; **foreneck greyish-brown** to rusty buff. **Juv** bill and eye yellowish; face striped, neck rusty-red, but like AdNb by **1W**.

Great Crested Grebe
Slavonian Grebe *p. 77*

Dives with a slight 'leap', unlike the 'smooth' dive of Great Crested Grebe.

V Noisy, grating, wailing and chattering notes in the breeding season; silent in winter.

Scarce, local resident/migrant

Breeds on reedy freshwater lakes, rivers; winters lakes, rivers, sea coasts

Two sspp. occur: *grisegena* widespread; *holbollii* (vagrant from N America) has larger bill.

FL Fast, direct; large, trailing feet. Settles breast-first. White patches on narrow wings.

white patch on forewing only
(all plumages)

AdBr

Juvenile yellow iris reduced to thin ring on 1W; all-dark on AdNb.

Juv
MAY–AUG

Autumn adults and juveniles more or less rusty on neck; juveniles retain some black-and-white striping on head.

AdNb/1W
SEP–FEB

dark cap extends below eye
(unlike Great Crested Grebe)

bill yellow-and-black

cheek pale grey

AdBr
MAR–SEP

LC **Red-throated Diver**
LC *Gavia stellata*

L 55–67 cm | **W** 91–110 cm

Smallest diver. **Neck upright, straight,** with **head and bill uptilted**; bill tapered, **upper edge straight**. Most social of the diver species in winter. **AdBr** | back plain grey-brown. Head grey with fine lines on hindneck; **throat patch narrow** and **dark red. AdNb** | very pale; back grey with **white flecks**; flank whiter, mottled. Breast and foreneck white; cap and **narrow** band down hindneck dark grey-brown; **face white** with **dark, button-like eye. Juv** | like **AdNb** but foreneck and cheek browner; small white chevrons on back. **1W** | as **Juv** but small white flecks on back (adult more heavily spotted). **1S** | like **AdBr** but some feathers on back and flight feathers old and faded.

◉ Black-throated Diver

V | Silent in winter; in summer, varied calls include loud quacking "*kwuk kwuk kwuk*" in flight, rising wail "*eeaaooow.*" Pair make fast quacking and rhythmic, grating, notes in duet.

Scarce, local; migratory

Breeds on tundra and moorland pools, islands; winters at sea

FL | Elongated; long, **narrow wings** dark above, white beneath; narrow dark flank line; **head/bill slightly drooped**; trailing feet quite small, so looks longer in front and shorter behind wings than other divers. Wingbeats quicker and deeper than other divers; distinctive head bobbing in time with wingbeats.

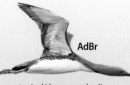

AdBr

typical 'droop-necked' flight profile

no white on back

AdBr
APR–NOV

Complete moult after breeding, partial in spring (reverse of sequence in other divers), with transitional stages in between (see *p. 72*)

AdNb
AUG–MAR

white speckling on back diagnostic

1W
AUG–FEB

Black-throated Diver
Gavia arctica

L 63–75 cm | **W** 100–122 cm

Medium-sized diver. Neck sinuous; bill **dagger-shaped** and **held horizontally**. From rear, body narrow, head **bulbous** on thin neck (Great Northern Diver is broad-bodied, with head and neck of equal width). Typically dives with slight backward jerk of the head. **AdBr** back black with oval patch of white spots. Head grey, face dark; neck striped, **throat patch wide** and **black**. **AdNb** upperparts blackish but **hindneck paler than back** (unlike Great Northern Diver). **White patch on rear flank** usually visible. Wing coverts spotted white. **Juv** like **AdNb** but browner with pale fringes to back feathers. **1W** like **AdNb** but scaly, pale-fringed juvenile feathers on back; wing coverts dark. **1S** like **AdNb** but few or no white spots on wing coverts. **2S** like **AdBr** but throat patch brown-black.

ssp. *arctica* occurs in Europe.

Great Northern Diver *p. 82*
Pacific Diver p. 538
Red-throated Diver

V | Calls growling, rolling "*rrow rrow*," goose-like, honking "*oo-uw*;" song in summer loud, high, rhythmic wail "*klow-owww-oh, lyo-lyow-oh.*"

Rare, local; migratory

Breeds on large lakes with islands; winters at sea

FL | Long, straight neck **thick, tube-like, hardly drooped**; trailing feet long, so wings appear more central than on Red-throated Diver. Direct, low flight with stiff, deep beats.

AdBr

typical straight-necked flight profile

In breeding season, large head and neck appear almost 'inflated'.

AdBr
FEB–OCT

bluish bill in winter

AdNb
OCT–MAR

even border between grey-brown and white on neck; small grey point below white cheek

white flank patch

Juv
JUN–DEC

moult continuous over following year to 2W

LC Great Northern Diver
VU *Gavia immer*

| White-billed Diver
| Black-throated Diver *p. 81*

Scarce, local; migratory

Breeds by large lakes,
on tundra; winters
manly on sea

L 73–88 cm | **W** 122–148 cm

Large, thick-necked diver, with variably shaped 'bump' on forehead. Bill **deep-based** and **dagger-shaped, held horizontally. AdBr** | head black; neck black with patch of white stripes on side; breast white; back black with rows of **square white spots. Bill dark. AdNb** | dark grey with scattered white spots on upperparts; white throat and foreneck (recalls immature Cormorant (*p. 84*) but tail very short). **Cap and rear half of neck darker than back** (slightly paler on Black-throated Diver), with **white indentation** above **dark half-collar.** Back faintly barred (less scaly than Black-throated Diver). **Flank all-dark** (no white patch as on Black-throated Diver). Bill grey/whitish with **dark upper edge and tip. Juv / 1W / 1S** | like **AdNb** but more scaled on upperparts and with browner head. **2W** | as **AdNb** but back plain.

V | Call fast, laughing or bubbling note, sometimes heard from birds on sea; breeding birds have loud, rising wail "*ooor-loooh*" leading into "*we a-wee-a, we a-weee-oh.*"

FL | Big, heavy head barely drooped; long, centrally set wings; feet large, protruding. Wingbeats more whippy than smaller divers, but large bill and bulk best clues. Dark band on flank.

Juv
AUG–APR
[DEC]

bill thicker, more greyish or yellowish, than Black-throated Diver

cap and hindneck darker than back

1W
AUG–APR

white indentation above dark half-collar low on neck

AdNb
OCT–MAR

back covered with white squares (oval patches of white spots on Black-throated Diver)

AdBr
APR–OCT

White-billed Diver

Gavia adamsii

Great Northern Diver

L 77–90 cm | **W** 135–150 cm

Large, bulky diver, with thick neck and bulbous head, typically held **uptilted**; variably shaped 'bump' on forehead. Bill deep-based, lower edge **angled up to sharp tip**. **AdBr** | **head black**; neck black with patch of white stripes on side; breast white; black back with rows of **large, square white spots. Bill pale yellow/ivory. AdNb** | dark grey with scattered white spots on upperparts; white throat and foreneck; dark brown rear half of neck and **narrow dark band down hindneck**; dark 'half-collar' patches often join to form brownish band above white breast. Top of bill **dark only at base; tip and cutting edges all-pale. Juv / 1W / 1S** | browner than **AdNb**, with broad, **buff-white crescentic bars** ('scaly' effect) on upperparts. Head largely pale; crown, rear of hindneck and collar brown; **dark cheek patch**; dark eye isolated in pale face; lower neck ginger-buff. **2W** | as **AdNb** but back plain.

V | Bubbling, laughing notes, low mournful "*ooo-o*" and loud, rhythmic, rising wail "*ooo oo-o, oo-oolu, oo-oour-lu*" during the breeding season. Silent in winter.

Rare and very local breeder/rare winter migrant

Coastal waters

FL | Heaviest diver, deep-bellied, wingbeats slow; large, pale head and upturned bill may be visible.

1W → 1S
MAR–MAY
[MAY]

moult continuous from Feb-Sep

Juv/1W has pale, crescentic bars on back and wing coverts.

1S
MAR–OCT

GREAT NORTHERN DIVER
The bill of a non-breeding Great Northern Diver looks pale, but **AdNb** always has a dark ridge and tip.

AdNb (SEP-APR) similar but retains scattered white spots on upperparts.

2W
OCT–MAR

Head and bill are typically uptilted, as if looking upwards.

larger white spots on back than Great Northern Diver

AdBr
APR–OCT

LC (Great) **Cormorant**
LC *Phalacrocorax carbo*

L 77–94 cm | **W** 121–149 cm

Large, dark waterbird. Feeds alone, in small groups, or in larger excitable flocks; roosts socially, often in trees. Dives with smooth roll. Stands upright, often with wings spread (see *p. 72*), or more horizontally, with neck 'S'-shaped and thick **bill uptilted; forehead low, sloping**. **AdBr** | blackish, with **white chin and thigh**. Whitish head plumes, or largely white head in spring. Eye green. **AdNb** | cheek/throat dull white; yellow skin on face. **Juv** | black-brown, whiter beneath by winter; head dark down to eye; chin whitish, face yellow. **Imm** | mottled black, whiter on underparts; orange-yellow facial patch, **whitish cheek**; eye dull until **2W**.

👁 Shag
Double-crested Cormorant p. 538

FL | Steady rhythm; neck extended; **long, broad, rounded tail**. Parties (5–100) synchronized, in 'V's or lines; glides and soars well on broad wings; tilts over to lose height.

neck uniform thickness

AdNb

Locally common resident/migrant

Breeds freshwater lakes, marshes, coastal cliffs; winters on salt and fresh waters

V | Calls low, deep, guttural or cooing notes.

AdNb
JUN–MAR

AdBr
SSP. *carbo*
[MAR]

AdBr
SSP. *sinensis*
[FEB]

AdBr
SSP. *carbo*
JAN–JUN
[MAR]

Imm
ALL YEAR

Matures over 3–4 years: 1S (1 year old) glossy patches on back; 2W upperparts mostly glossy, underparts white, mottled dark; 2S (2 years old) belly mottled blue-black; 3W like adult but has new (black), older (dull) and juvenile (pale brown) flight feathers.

Two sspp. occur: *sinensis* is glossed blue-green, *carbo* more purple; *sinensis* has whiter head earlier in spring; more parallel white band behind square yellow skin (see *below*).

Cormorant subspecies

Separating sspp. *carbo* and *sinensis* may be difficult. Bare yellow skin below eye pointed on *carbo*, squarer on most *sinensis*.

SSP. *carbo*

Angle 30°–72°

SSP. *sinensis*

Angle 66°–111°

Shag *Gulosus aristotelis*

L 68–78 cm | **W** 95–110 cm

Large, dark seabird; like small, delicate Cormorant. Social, may feed in **large flocks**; does not perch in trees. Dives from surface with a marked leap. Wings broad, tail long and rounded. Frequently stands with wings outstretched. **Bill slim** with small hook; rounded head with **steep forehead**. **Ad** | green-black; yellow gape and chin (**no white**). Eye emerald-green. **AdBr** | upright crest. **Juv** | dark brown; head dark to below eye; whitish chin spot and eyering. Legs pale, rarely yellowish. Often pale panel of worn feathers on wing by **1S**. **Imm** | upperparts dull green, underparts brown; eye yellow-green by **2Y**.

V | Grunts and cackling alarm from ♂ at nest.

Cormorant
Double-crested Cormorant p. 538

Often leaps into a dive (Cormorant rolls).

Locally common resident

Breeds coastal cliffs; winters on sea, estuaries

FL | Direct; quick action, no glides (Cormorant slower, heavier); usually low over sea, neither high nor over land. Neck slender; wings set well back; tail relatively short.

neck narrows in middle

AdBr

Moult continues irregularly until Dec of following year; matures over 4 years.

crest not always raised

AdBr
MAR–JUN

SSP. *aristotelis*

Juv
JUN–SEP

Imm
SSP. *desmarestii*
ALL YEAR

Two sspp. occur: *aristotelis* (widespread) and *desmarestii* (Mediterranean) – longer, paler bill; adult may retain crest longer in autumn than *aristotelis*; juvenile has stronger pale upperwing panel, whiter underparts (see Cormorant). Legs can be pale yellow.

Cormorant and Shag juveniles compared

dark cap extends onto cheek

thin bill

white chin spot

SHAG

thick bill

yellow skin

CORMORANT

85

LC Pygmy Cormorant

LC *Microcarbo pygmaeus*

L 45–55 cm | **W** 80–90 cm

Small, thick-necked, **short-billed** cormorant; typical cormorant shape and postures. Mostly in remote marshes/deltas but may roost in suburban riverside willows. Soars high in warm conditions. **Ad** black-brown with paler sheen on upperwing. **AdBr** in spring, head **glossy bronze** with fine white plumes, which wear away; facial skin black. Bill black, becoming pale by MAY/JUN. **AdNb** head **dull brown**; bill yellowish. **Juv** drab, with white chin and dull white belly. Matures over 3–4 years with prolonged, complex moults, giving a variety of intermediate stages.

AdBr
FEB–JUL
[APR]

The brownish head and neck have fine white plumes (filoplumes) for a short time early in the breeding season.

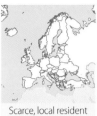

Scarce, local resident

Freshwater lakes, marshes, rivers

FL | Long tail slim or fanned; head extended, thick neck kinked near base; wingbeats quick, wings bowed in glides.

V | Silent except croaks and grunting calls at colony.

Juv

tail/rear body longer than head and neck

By May/June the bill becomes pale and the white head plumes are lost.

AdBr
FEB–JUL

Juv/1W
JUN–APR

tail feathers new, fresh

tail feathers old, badly worn

In water, typical cormorant profile with neck erect, bill uptilted and back often almost awash.

Juv/1W
AUG–APR

Seabirds are essentially marine birds, coming to land only to nest. Most are best seen by watching
from coast (headlands or bays into which seabirds may be driven by strong winds), or from ships/ferries; only
a few easily seen at breeding colonies by day. Occasionally 'storm-driven' into coastal or inland waters

'TUBENOSES' 35 species [17 vagrants] Include several subgroups, all with tubular nostrils on
top of bill for excreting excess salt, detecting pressure changes above waves, and smell.
Sexing, Ageing and Moult Sexes and ages (except albatrosses) alike; no seasonal changes.

Shearwaters 11 species [3 vagrants] (*pp. 91–95, 539*) and **Fulmar** (*p. 91*)
Small to large, long-winged. Sit on the sea (shearwaters in flocks); dive to feed.
Shearwaters visit nest burrows only after dark; Fulmar nests on cliffs. **Flight** Low over
the sea with few wingbeats between glides or higher, 'shearing' in strong wind.

Identify by size | colour of upperparts and underside | underwing detail |
bill colour and head pattern

Petrels 11 species [8 vagrants] (*pp. 96–97, 539–541*)
Like smaller shearwaters; round-faced, short-billed, some longer-tailed.
Flight Agile and bounding, flap-and-glide or almost constant glides in wind.

Identify by presence and pattern of white | head pattern | bill size and shape |
tail shape

Storm-petrels 8 species [2 vagrants] (*pp. 98–99, 541*)
Very small, dark; small head, wings angled or more curved; tail rounded or
inconspicuously forked. **Flight** Fly low over water, sometimes 'pattering' over waves
(even along beach in onshore gale).

Identify by presence/absence and extent of white rump | tail shape |
upperwing pattern | underwing pattern | colour of underside

Albatrosses 3 species [all vagrants] (*p. 543*) and **giant-petrels 1 species**
[vagrant] (*p. 541*)
Huge, very long-winged with thick, hooked bill and short tail. **Flight** Glide over
the sea, exploiting wind and updraughts above waves to travel with little effort.
Sexing, Ageing and Moult Sexes alike, no seasonal change, but several years of
immaturity: young birds darker/duller than adults, different bill colour.

Identify by size, bill colour | pattern of white, and especially underwing detail

GANNETS and BOOBIES 5 species [4 vagrants] (*pp. 90, 542*)
Very large, long-winged plunge-divers with thick neck, dagger-like bill and pointed
tail. **Flight** Fly well above water with steady flaps between glides, or low over the
waves, tilting into the wind; occasional shallow beats in wind, easily handling gales.
Sexing, Ageing and Moult Sexes alike, no seasonal change, but juveniles dark;
immatures progress through intermediate stages (piebald or chequered in 'white'
species) to adulthood.

Identify by shape, overall colour | precise distribution of black/white on wings and
tail or white on belly/underwing | precise observation of facial patterns/throat stripes

FRIGATEBIRDS 2 species [both vagrants] (*p. 544*)
Very long winged aerial birds with long, forked tail (spread or closed into a single point); slim, hooked bill; and tiny feet. **Flight** Flight includes high soaring; prolonged glides on pointed, angled wings; and acrobatic feeding (chasing other seabirds, dipping/plunging to surface, but not diving). **Sexing, Ageing and Moult** Male all-dark; female (larger than male) and juvenile have white on head and underparts.

Identify by precise patterns of white markings (females and Juveniles); males difficult without measurements and colour of plumage gloss

TROPICBIRDS 2 species [1 vagrant] (*pp. 97, 544*)
Like large terns with thick, pointed bill and long tail projections; cannot walk.
Flight Flight steady, direct, but acrobatic when feeding by plunge-diving. Large, projecting head/bill merge into sleek body; tail short and slim but has very long, 'whippy' central feathers. **Sexing, Ageing and Moult** Sexes look similar (male has longer streamers); juveniles lack streamers and have dark bars on the back, but otherwise wing patterns are the same as an adult.

Identify by upperwing pattern | underwing pattern

Seabirds compared

RESTING SHEARWATERS Shearwaters (and Fulmar) will rest on the sea, where they may be mistaken for gulls. At close range the 'tubenose' that is diagnostic of the group may be seen.

Gulls and skuas
fairly bowed wings, round tail, relaxed flight action

Imm

GULL
(*p. 106*)

GANNET
(*p. 90*)

SKUA
(*p. 146*)

Juv

GULL
(*p. 106*)

AUKS 11 species [5 vagrants] (*pp. 100–105, 545*)
Specialized, web-footed seabirds with a pointed, or stout, colourful bill.
They are mostly black-and-white or dark brown and white. Typical form
is distinctive: large head, thick neck; barrel-shaped body; short tail; and
small, quite slender wings. Short legs set well back give an upright stance
on flexed legs (Puffin can walk). On water, swim low, head upright; dive
from surface to feed, using wings for propulsion. At sea for most of the
year, but breed on sea cliffs and islands. Some (*e.g.* Razorbill) may be
inshore in winter, others (*e.g.* Puffin) are usually far out at sea, brought
inshore by severe weather. Breeding colonies may be large and dense
(*e.g.* Guillemot, on cliff ledges, and Puffin, in burrows on rocky or grassy
slopes) but Black Guillemots nest in single pairs, at foot of cliffs or on
small islands. Adults come to land in early spring, Puffins performing
wheeling flights over colonies. Young Puffins leave for the sea alone,
while others (*e.g.* Guillemot) leap off cliffs before reaching full size,
accompanied by a parent, and swim to sea with an adult. **Flight** Fast,
direct and low, with whirring wingbeats and no glides except when
rising towards breeding ledge, but Puffins may hang in updraughts
beside cliff tops on flexed wings. **Sexing, Ageing and Moult** Sexes are
alike. Adults have marked seasonal differences; juveniles hardly differ
from non-breeding adults.

Identify by size | bill shape, colour and pattern | details of head pattern
(in winter)

Guillemot breeding colony

POSSIBLE CONFUSION GROUPS In flight **gulls** (*p. 106*) (typically long, bowed wings, short square tail, but
flight varies according to size and weather conditions); **terns** (*p. 107*) (slim bill, angled wings, forked tail);
skuas (*p. 146*) (slim, long-winged, often dark). On the sea gulls and skuas (usually hunched, rear/wingtips
long and upswept). Other types of bird that are commonly seen at sea are wildfowl (*p. 20*), cormorants
divers and grebes (*p. 72*).

*Fulmar white head, grey tail;
stiff wings, flap-and-glide*

*Petrels long, slender wings,
buoyant/bounding flight*

*Storm petrels tiny,
dark; erratic flight*

PETREL
(*p. 96*)

*Shearwaters small
head, thin bill; stiff wings,
'shearing' or flap-and-glide*

STORM-PETREL
(*p. 98*)

*Auk heavy-bodied,
narrow-winged;
direct flight
with whirring
wingbeats*

FULMAR
(*p. 91*)

SHEARWATER
(*p. 92*)

AUK
(*p. 100*)

(Northern) **Gannet**
LC *Morus bassanus*

L 85–97 cm | **W** 170–192 cm

Large, elegant seabird with dagger-like
bill, slim pointed tail and long wings.
Ad| **gleaming white**, with **black wingtips**:
distinctive even at long range. Head
golden-buff. **Juv**| dark brown; small white
spots make head and neck appear greyish
(see also *p. 88*). **Imm**| **chequered black
and white**: striking two- to three-year-
old birds piebald with yellow head.

V| Calls at colony have repetitive,
mechanical effect in guttural chorus.

FL| Steady flight, singly or in lines,
well above the sea or shearing
close to waves; periodically
circles and **plunge-dives**. Flight
controlled even in a gale: head/
neck extended and slightly raised,
longer than **spiky tail**; wings taut,
straight, with shallow downbeats
of wingtips (unlike gulls, which fly
with bowed wings).

Rare gannets and boobies p. 542

Ad
ALL YEAR

Locally numerous
resident/migrant

Breeds sea cliffs and
islands; at sea

Ad
ALL YEAR

**Imm
3-year-old**
ALL YEAR

**Imm
(1)-2-year-old**
ALL YEAR

**TYPICAL
1-YEAR-OLD**
Some remain this dark well
into 2nd year.

**LATE 1ST-YEAR
or 2ND-YEAR**
Some 2nd-year birds
more boldly chequered
with white.

3RD-YEAR
Typically few dark
secondaries and tail feathers,
and small black marks on
back. Less advanced 3rd-
year birds have a 'piano key'
hindwing and black-and-
white patches on back; more
advanced individuals closer
to adult.

**Imm
1-(2)-year-old**
ALL YEAR

**Juv
AUG–DEC**

Wing moult continuous,
three generations of feathers
may be seen at once: may
be asymmetrical. Individuals
develop at different rates,
plumages variable and
ageing difficult.

Sits high on water when resting on the
surface or after a dive.

Often plunges near
vertically, entering
water with a splash.
Closer to the surface,
may slip in at an angle.

Fulmar *Fulmarus glacialis*

L 43–52 cm | **W** 101–117 cm

Fairly large, gull-like seabird but cannot stand or walk, shuffling at best; present around coastal cliffs much of the year. Sexes and ages alike; no seasonal changes. Pale grey and white. Grey upperwing with dusky wingtips (**no black**) and whitish patch beyond joint. **Plain grey rump and tail** (unlike any gull). Underwing white with dark rim.

V| Tuneless, loud, throaty, choking, cackling notes from ledge.

Two sspp. occur: *glacialis* (widespread); *auduboni* (sub-Arctic) larger overall, but bill smaller.

Petrels p. 96 | Rare petrels pp. 540–541

FL| Wings rather stiff, straight, or angled in glides around cliffs; quick, slightly whippy beats in calm air, but masterful glides over sea in strong winds. Grey with **bold white head**.

Worn or moulting birds show mottled effect on upperside.

Dark form ('Blue Fulmar') commoner in north: dusky brownish-grey head and body. Intermediates occur.

On sea, swims high on water, head and tail raised, leaning forward.

head white, with dark eye-patch; bill stubby

Locally common resident/ disperses at sea

Breeds sea cliffs and islands, some buildings, some a little inland; at sea

Sooty Shearwater
Ardenna grisea

L 40–50 cm | **W** 93–106 cm

Angular, large, dark shearwater. Quite heavy, long-bodied and pot-bellied; long, pointed, slender wings set centrally, often held angled at bend (like half-size juvenile Gannet). Sexes and ages alike; no seasonal changes. **Dark brown** ; slightly paler inner trailing edge and largely **pale underwing** both flash silvery-white in good light.

Beware dark **Balearic Shearwater** (which is smaller with shorter wings) and dark skuas.

V| Occasional high, nasal *"nair nair."*

Balearic Shearwater p. 92 | Skuas (dark form) pp. 148–149 | Bulwer's Petrel p. 97 Rare dark shearwaters and petrels p. 539

FL| In strong wind, few flaps close to the surface between long, high, curving glides. In calm winds, flies low; 3–7 quick, stiff-winged beats between glides of 3–5 seconds.

Typical shearwater flight: shearing, belly-to-wind, to gain speed in sweeping glides.

Scarce but regular migrant MAR–NOV, but particularly late summer-autumn

At sea

91

Small shearwaters
The four small shearwaters are similar in basic colour, shape and actions. Sexes and ages look alike; no seasonal changes. All are nocturnal at breeding colony (gathering offshore before dark) but best seen over the sea by day. **Flight** low, spread out or in lines, with quick, stiff flaps and short glides in calm conditions, increasingly using long glides and steep, belly-to-wind banking ('shearing') in stronger winds. They look like a small, dark cross-shape at a distance, alternating dark and light as upperside and underside show; Manx Shearwater is especially obvious black-and-white.

CR Balearic Shearwater
CR *Puffinus mauretanicus*

L 34–39 cm | **W** 78–90 cm

Small **dark, brown** W Mediterranean shearwater (scarce in the Atlantic). Smaller and paler than Sooty Shearwater, shorter-winged, less angular; dark cap with indistinct border, dull cheek fades into neck. **No white on rear flank.**

V | Harsh, throaty notes at colony, *e.g.* "*ah-ee-ah-eeh.*"

FL | Deep-bodied; flappy flight with quick beats.

Sooty Shearwater *p. 91*

VU Yelkouan Shearwater
VU *Puffinus yelkouan*

L 30–35 cm | **W** 70–84 cm

The common small shearwater of most of the Mediterranean, offshore and from ferries between islands. Upperparts **dark brown**, fading to paler brown than Balearic Shearwater, but individually variable; dark cap, with small white 'hook' from throat behind dark cheek. Darker forms in west Mediterranean often browner on belly and vent, and hard to tell from Balearic Shearwater.

V | Raucous cackling at colony.

FL | Fast flight low over waves with quick beats, short glides.

dark patch in wingpit

dark line

pale individuals white on underparts; darkest all-brown, but many intermediates

undertail coverts dark, even on palest birds

dark line

distinct dark bar on underwing

Feet extend well beyond tail (appears as central spike).

Feet extend beyond slim tail (appears as pointed tail).

BALEARIC SHEARWATER

no white on rear flank

YELKOUAN SHEARWATER

small white patch on rear flank

Manx Shearwater
Puffinus puffinus

L 30–35 cm | **W** 71–83 cm

Small, slim shearwater, common in the Atlantic. Upperparts **blackish** (fade browner), greyer in strong light; underparts white. Dark cap to below eye, distinct against white lower face and obvious white 'hook' behind cheek, neck side greyish; **white rear flank patch.**

V | Chorus of guttural croaks, laughing notes and deep cooing calls at colony.

FL | Wingbeats quick, flicked between glides – in wind, more elegant, almost all glides, tilting over from side to side.

LC NT Macaronesian Shearwater
Puffinus lherminieri

L 25–30 cm | **W** 58–67 cm

Very small, black-and-white shearwater, off E Atlantic islands; black cap small, above **white, disk-like face.** May show whitish bar across rear wing, or silvery hindwing.

V | From burrow in scree; higher than Manx Shearwater, penetrating, rhythmic *"pi-pi-pi-poo, pi-poo."*

FL | Fast wingbeats but progress slow; wings may be slightly bowed in short glides; settles with wings raised.

Three sspp. occur: *baroli* (Azores, Canary Is.); *boydi* (vagrant from Cape Verde), sometimes treated as a species, **'Boyd's Shearwater'** *Puffinus boydi*, slightly larger, upperwing plainer, face and undertail coverts darker; *lherminieri* (historical vagrant from W Atlantic/ Caribbean), also sometimes treated as a species, **'Audubon's Shearwater'** *Puffinus lherminieri*, like *boydi* but fractionally larger with larger bill – but identification at sea not feasible.

Balearic Shearwater

Rare, locally fairly common resident; ranges N to English Channel JUL–OCT

Breeds coastal cliffs; at sea

Yelkouan Shearwater

Locally common resident; vagrant

Breeds coastal cliffs; at sea

Manx Shearwater

Locally abundant resident/migrant

Breeds islands, cliffs, screes; at sea

Macaronesian Shearwater

Rare, local resident; vagrant elsewhere

Breeds in holes/ crevices; at sea

unmarked white flank

indistinct dark bar on underwing

dark eye in white cheek

unmarked white flank

MANX SHEARWATER

White rear flank patch (may extend onto side of rump).

MACARONESIAN SHEARWATER

Feet do not extend far beyond tail.

Pale hindwing may be obvious.

small white patch on rear flank

Large shearwaters

Four species, very similar in colour, shape and actions. Sexes and ages look alike; no seasonal changes. Two breed; nocturnal at breeding colony (gathering offshore at dusk). **Flight** low, slow and rather languid in calm conditions; long glides and steep 'shearing' in stronger winds.

LC Great Shearwater *Ardenna gravis*

L 43–51 cm | **W** 105–122 cm

Large shearwater: usually far out at sea. Upperparts dark brown, underparts white with smudgy dark marks on belly and underwing; sharply contrasted **dark brown cap** (blackish at distance) and white crescent at base of tail. (Manx Shearwater smaller, fades browner, and white flank patch can give illusion of white at base of tail.) **Bill blackish.**

V | Silent at sea.

FL | Wingbeats stiffer and quicker than Cory's Shearwater, like Fulmar; high, sweeping glides in gale.

LC Cory's Shearwater *Calonectris borealis*

LC **L** 50–56 cm | **W** 118–126 cm

Large, heavy-bodied shearwater. **Brown-and-white;** on water, dark with white breast and flank but greyer head. In flight, weak dark 'W' across upperside; white at base of tail (individually variable). **Greyish hood merges into white throat,** neck may shine greyish in low light; underside **gleams white. Bill pale yellow** against dark water.

V | Loud, nasal, mechanical notes, very like Scopoli's Shearwater, at colony and offshore at dusk.

FL | Lethargic in calm air, with 2–4 slow, even, shallow downbeats (often seemingly pivoting on lowered wingtip, sometimes dipped into water as banks) followed by glides on bowed wings. More active in wind; high, towering climbs in gale. Juvenile Gannet (*p. 90*) is larger, with longer, more pointed bill and tail.

white patch at base of tail (more obvious than almost all Cory's Shearwaters)

weak dark 'W' across upperside

GREAT SHEARWATER

Moulting birds in autumn show ragged whitish mid-upperwing.

Dark marks on belly and underwing may be visible.

CORY'S SHEARWATER

two dark spots on primary coverts

underparts and underwing plain white

wingtip all-dark

In low evening sunlight a swimming bird shows strong contrast, with gleaming white breast and flank.

Scopoli's Shearwater
Calonectris diomedea

L 44–49 cm | **W** 117–135 cm

Large, heavy, **brown-and-white** shearwater with **diffuse hood** and **yellow bill** (replaces Cory's Shearwater in Mediterranean). Distinct 'W' across upperwing; underwing white, dark tip with **white line along each primary** (all-dark on Cory's Shearwater); one dark spot on primary coverts under wing (two on Cory's Shearwater) very difficult to see except on photographs.

V | Loud, strangled, nasal and mechanical notes, mostly triple, "*aary-aary-aary, arrwa-arrwa-arrwa, prrrr-prrrr-prrrr*," around colony at dusk.

NT # Cape Verde Shearwater
Calonectris edwardsii

L 42–47 cm | **W** 100–112 cm

Like Cory's and Scopoli's Shearwaters, but slightly smaller. **Bill dark grey** with black band; dark 'W' across upperparts; dark cap clearly defined against white throat. Underwing as Cory's Shearwater.

Great Shearwater

Scarce but regular migrant MAY–NOV, most late summer-autumn

At sea

dark grey bill

dark 'W' across upperside

dark cap clearly defined

CAPE VERDE SHEARWATER

FL | Like Cory's Shearwater but occasional bursts of 5–7 flaps between glides.

SCOPOLI'S SHEARWATER

single dark spot on primary coverts

wingtip dark with white lines

underwing white with thin dark rim

Cory's Shearwater

Locally numerous resident/migrant

Breeds sea cliffs, islands; winters at sea

Scopoli's Shearwater

Locally numerous resident/migrant

Breeds sea cliffs, islands; winters at sea

Cape Verde Shearwater

Vagrant from Cape Verde

At sea

Fulmar p. 91 | *Rare petrels p. 540*

Pterodroma petrels

Three *Pterodroma* species breed on Macaronesian islands (Fea's Petrel only on Cape Verde, outside the area covered by this book, but recorded within it).

Medium-sized, long-winged seabirds (about the size of Manx Shearwater (*p. 93*)): dark grey-brown above with a **subtle dark 'W' across the upperwing**; **grey rump/tail**; **dark eye patch** and dusky lower neck; and bright **white underparts** with a **dark underwing**. Very difficult or near-impossible to tell apart with certainty except by measurements (particularly of the bill).

Primary feather moult can be helpful: **Zino's** moults Aug-Dec, **Fea's** Mar-Aug, **Desertas** Oct-Apr.

DESERTAS PETREL

ZINO'S PETREL

Desertas Petrel has a thick, heavy bill; Zino's Petrel has a slender bill.

DESERTAS PETREL

ZINO'S PETREL

FL | Fast with distinctive steeply banking glides on angled wings; pendulum-like side-to-side sweeps in strong wind.

VU **VU** ## Desertas Petrel
Pterodroma deserta

NT ## Fea's (Cape Verde) **Petrel**
Pterodroma feae [NOT ILLUSTRATED]

L 33–36 cm | **W** 86–94 cm

Inseparable except by measurements in the hand: **Desertas Petrel** has slightly larger bill than **Fea's Petrel** but differences < 3 mm. Extremely similar to Zino's Petrel but heavier build, with slower, more gull-like wing beats; wingtip fractionally longer and broader; more distinct dark 'W' across upperwing and no white stripe on underwing. Stouter, deeper bill.

V | Moaning or groaning notes, deeper than Zino's Petrel, often "*gon-gon.*"

EN **EN** ## Zino's Petrel
Pterodroma madeira

L 30–35 cm | **W** 80–90 cm

Slightly smaller and more lightly built and slimmer-billed than Desertas/Fea's Petrels; **grey rump/ tail**; long **white stripe** on dark underwing on many.

V | Loud, mournful wails "*hoo-o-oww*" at nest, a little higher than those of Desertas Petrel.

Resident; endemic to Desertas Is.; migrant/ vagrant elsewhere

Nests in burrows; at sea

Desertas Petrel

Resident; endemic to Madeira; migrant/ vagrant elsewhere

Nests in burrows; at sea

Zino's Petrel

 White-tailed Tropicbird p. 544

Red-billed Tropicbird
Phaethon aethereus

L 45–50 cm (plus streamers of 46–56 cm)
W 100–115 cm

Like a large, stocky tern (*p. 107*) with a **thick red bill. Ad**|very long, flexible, central tail streamer. White upperwings with dark bars; **black on wingtips. Juv**|lacks tail streamer; heavily barred upperparts.

V|Shrill whistle near colony.

ssp. **mesonauta** occurs in Europe.

FL|Fast, gliding or direct with shallow wingbeats; grey back/forewing with darker diagonal band, white hindwing and black wingtips give striking three-toned effect.

Ad

RED-BILLED TROPICBIRD

 Sooty Shearwater p. 91
Swinhoe's Storm-petrel p. 541

Bulwer's Petrel
Bulweria bulwerii

L 26–28 cm | **W** 67 cm

Small, **dark brown** shearwater-like petrel with **long, slightly angled, pointed wings** and rather long, **tapered** tail (**not forked**). Paler band across upperwing can be striking; hindwing and underwing may show paler reflections; bill relatively large, thick.

V|Deep, barking notes from nest.

FL|Buoyant, rolling, wavering flight low over waves, wings held well forward.

BULWER'S PETREL

White-faced Storm-petrel
Pelagrodoma marina

L 18–21 cm | **W** 38–45 cm

Small, dainty, long-legged, round-winged storm-petrel. Upperparts **pale brownish-grey** with **pale grey crescent** at base of black tail, black flight feathers; **face white with dark cap and cheek**; underparts white.

V|Moaning, mournful "*oo-aa-oo*" from nest.

ssp. **marina** occurs in Europe.

FL|Buoyant, skipping, bouncing; patters on surface.

WHITE-FACED STORM-PETREL

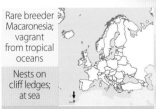

Rare breeder Macaronesia; vagrant from tropical oceans

Nests on cliff ledges; at sea

Red-billed Tropicbird

Scarce resident in Macaronesia; vagrant farther north

Nests in cliff cavities; at sea

Bulwer's Petrel

Breeds locally in Macaronesia, vagrant farther north

Nests in burrows near sea; at sea

White-faced Storm-petrel

Storm-petrels are all similar.

Wilson's Storm-petrel

Rare but regular migrant Aug-Oct

At sea

European Storm-petrel

Locally common resident/migrant

Breeds islands, cliffs, screes, coastal ruins, nests in crevices; at sea

Leach's Storm-petrel

Scarce, locally fairly common resident

Breeds islands, cliffs, screes, nesting in crevices; at sea

Madeiran Storm-petrel
Monteiro's Storm-petrel

Resident Macaronesian islands; Madeiran Storm-petrel vagrant elsewhere

Nests in rock crevices near coast; at sea

LC Wilson's Storm-petrel
Oceanites oceanicus

L 16–18·5 cm | **W** 38–42 cm

Dark, **white-rumped** storm-petrel with **round or square tail** (raised sides give concave effect), **wide grey upperwing band** not quite reaching leading edge (does so on Leach's Storm-petrel); **all-dark underwing** (white band on European Storm-petrel) and broad white rump extending to rear flank. Moulting birds may look patchy.

FL| Steady, swallow-like, with regular beats; low, bouncing, skipping with wings raised when feeding. Wings wider than those of European Storm-petrel, smoothly rounded on leading edge, tapering back to a point in direct flight; trailing edge straighter than on Leach's Storm-petrel. Long legs trail beyond tail (but can be held forward).

ssp. *oceanicus* occurs in Europe.

LC European Storm-petrel
LC *Hydrobates pelagicus*

L 15–16 cm | **W** 37–41 cm

Tiny, delicate seabird with white rump (resembles House Martin (*p. 346*)). Most likely in flight low over sea; often seen from ships, may follow in wake. Smoky brown-black, except **bold white rump** wrapping around each side and **broad white band along underwing**. **Juv**| weak, fine, pale wingbar on top.

V| Visits nesting burrow at night, giving prolonged, slightly squeaky, rolling purr, punctuated by short, deeper note.

FL| Light, smooth, rolling or swooping, twirling action, depending on circumstance. Wings curve back, with slightly rounded tips; tail wide and rounded; feet do not project past tail.

Two sspp.: *pelagicus* (widespread) and *melitensis* (Mediterranean), which averages longer wings and heavier bill.

Most likely from headlands near breeding areas in summer; otherwise usually well offshore.

Yellow webs between toes show best in photographs.

white band on underwing

EUROPEAN STORM-PETREL
Both ssp. *pelagicus*

pale band does not reach leading edge

WILSON'S STORM-PETREL

rump patch nearly rectangular

feet usually project

feet do not project

from side, broad white band may seem to surround tail.

Black-bellied Storm-petrel p. 541

Leach's Storm-petrel
Hydrobates leucorhous

L 18–21 cm | **W** 43–48 cm

Large, angular, dark brown storm-petrel with relatively small 'V'- or 'W'-shaped **white rump** (rarely absent). **Pale upperwing band** reaches front edge of wing. **Underwing all-dark. Juv** | pale upperwing band brighter, greyer. Breeding sites more remote than those of European Storm-petrel, but more likely inland or inshore after an autumn gale.

V | Visits nesting burrow at night, giving a long, high-pitched purring, punctuated by higher double note.

FL | Erratic, sudden turns or rising twists. **Wings long, pushed forward and angled**; tail forked or notched (hard to see); tail shape very variable.

ssp. *leucorhous* occurs in Europe.

LC Madeiran (Band-rumped)
LC Storm-petrel *Hydrobates castro*
VU Monteiro's Storm-petrel
VU *Hydrobates monteiroi*

L 20 cm | **W** 43–49 cm

Madeiran (Madeira) and Monteiro's Storm-petrels (Azores) are treated as separate species, based on breeding seasons, moult and detailed morphological differences; identification at sea is not yet possible. Large, angular storm-petrels with slightly notched tail; **white rump narrow, 'U'-shaped**; pale upperwing bands fall short of front edge of wing. Feet do not project beyond tail.

V | At nest, both have throaty purring interspersed with sporadic sharp notes or 'hiccup' at end, "*prr-rr-rr-rr-hu-chup.*"

FL | Zigzagging, with flicked or erratic wingbeats between glides.

When feeding, stalls or hangs into wind, foot-patters; in gales, may patter along beach.

LEACH'S STORM-PETREL

MADEIRAN STORM-PETREL

MONTEIRO'S STORM-PETREL

Curved white rump of even width, no dark central line; white extends down side more than on Leach's Storm-petrel.

rump patch usually elongated or 'V'-shaped, often with dark stripe up middle

pale band reaches leading edge

rump patch crescentic, extending slightly onto undertail coverts

pale band does not reach leading edge

Swinhoe's Storm-petrel p. 541

99

Auks in flight

PUFFIN
(p. 101)
AdBr

BLACK
GUILLEMOT
(p. 105)
1S

AdBr

LITTLE AUK
(p. 101)

AdBr

RAZORBILL
(p. 102)

AdNb/1W

BRÜNNICH'S
GUILLEMOT
(p. 104)
AdBr

AdBr

GUILLEMOT
(p. 103)

AdNb

AdNb

BLACK GUILLEMOT
(p. 105)

AdNb/1W

AdNb/1W

Auks in winter

AdNb/1W
('bridled')

AdNb/1W

1W

GUILLEMOT
(p. 103)

BRÜNNICH'S
GUILLEMOT
(p. 104)

RAZORBILL
(p. 102)

GUILLEMOT
(p. 103)

AdNb/1W

AdNb

BLACK
GUILLEMOT
(p. 105)

RAZORBILL
(p. 102)

Juv→1W

AdNb/1W

BRÜNNICH'S
GUILLEMOT
(p. 104)

PUFFIN
(p. 101)

AdNb/1W

LITTLE AUK
(p. 101)

AdNb

(Atlantic) **Puffin**
Fratercula arctica

L 28–34 cm | **W** 50–60 cm

Small, black-and-white; colourful, triangular bill; large, round head; short, rounded tail. Often on cliffs with Razorbills (*p. 102*) and Guillemots (*p. 103*), but nests in burrows. **AdBr** | upperparts plain black, face grey; underparts white. **Bill deep, triangular; red, yellow and grey** (has 1 groove in **2Y**, 1½ in **3Y**, 2 in **4Y**). Male's bill larger than female's in same colony, but colonies vary, so most impossible to sex. **Legs orange. AdNb** | like AdBr but face darker; bill smaller, duller and darker. **Juv** | bill small, dull; cheek dusky (Little Auk has darker cheek and white streaks on back). **1Y** | remains at sea; bill drab.

Scarce, locally numerous summer migrant; scarce winter

Breeds on islands, grassy screes on rocky coasts; winters at sea

V | Low, hard cooing and "*arrk arrk*" notes.

FL | Short, rounded body; small, whirring wings; upperwing and **underwing black** (no white trailing edge); face pale, outlined by black collar; rear flank black.

Face becomes dusky and bill smaller and duller after breeding.

LC **Little Auk** *Alle alle*

LC **L** 17–19 cm | **W** 40–48 cm

Very small, dumpy, black-and-white; **short, stubby black bill**; short, rounded tail. Swims with tail raised, wingtips drooped, flicked open as dives. **AdBr** | head, neck and upperparts black with white streaks on shoulder and thin white wingbar; underparts white. **AdNb / 1W** | **cap and cheek sharply defined black**; chin, throat and neck white. **White streaks** retained on shoulder. **Juv** | slightly browner than **Ad** (juvenile Puffin has dusky cheek and a plain back).

2 sspp.: *alle* (Iceland, Svalbard); *polaris* (Franz Josef Ld) larger.

Locally numerous summer migrant, regular winter migrant

At sea, cliff ledges; rare inland after autumn/ winter gales

V | Ringing chorus at breeding cliffs and in song flights, mixing short yelps, "*chyow-chyow-crrow-crrow-yo-yo*," and long trills. Silent away from breeding colony.

FL | Low, fast; groups sometimes twisting and turning like small waders; body bulky; head large; tail broad; wings small, black with **white trailing edge** on innerwing; **underwing blackish**.

AdNb / 1W

Tired birds driven close inshore by storms often have a sunken head and drooped wings.

AdBr

AdNb
JUL-MAR

Juv
JUN-OCT

AdBr

AdBr
FEB-OCT

AdBr

AdNb / 1W

AdNb / 1W
AUG-FEB

All ssp. *alle*

AdBr
JAN-JUL

NT **Razorbill** *Alca torda*

NT **L** 38–43 cm | **W** 60–69 cm

Small, black-and-white seabird with **blunt bill** and pointed tail. Nests in cavities, usually scattered among Guillemots; stands upright, resting on lower leg. On sea, thick neck held upright, tail often raised. **Ad** | head, neck and upperparts plain **black** with narrow white wingbar; underparts white, unmarked; bill **blade-shaped**, blunt, black with **white cross-band** and **line to eye**. **AdBr** | white on breast extends to a **point** up front of dark neck. **AdNb** | crown black; foreneck, throat and cheek white with dark line across cheek (less well defined than on Guillemot); bill like **AdBr** but no white line to eye. **Juv** | initially identifiable by small size and call. **1W** | like **AdNb** but bill all-dark.

V | Calls at nest guttural, growling *"goarrr;"* at sea, young bird calls are loud, a far-carrying, musical whistle, *"plee-u."*

Guillemot
Brünnich's Guillemot *p. 104*
Long-tailed Duck *p. 64*

Locally numerous migrant

Breeds on sea cliffs, coastal islands; winters at sea or in estuaries

Two sspp. occur: *torda* (Scandinavia, Baltic); *islandica* (Iceland, NW Europe), which averages fractionally smaller.

FL | Fast, whirring action over sea; body oval, wings slim. Difficult to tell from Guillemot unless bill shape seen, but blacker and a little shorter, dumpier, thicker-necked; dark rump has **wide white sides**; narrow white trailing edge to wing; **underwing and 'wingpit' white, unmarked.**

AdNb

A tired bird close inshore looks squat, with with head sunk low, tail raised.

All ssp. *islandica*

AdBr

1W
OCT–MAY

AdBr
FEB–AUG

AdNb
AUG–MAR

AdBr
FEB–AUG

(Common) **Guillemot** *Uria aalge*

L 38–46 cm | **W** 61–73 cm

Small, brown/black-and-white seabird with **pointed bill** (slimmer than on Brünnich's Guillemot) and short, square tail. Nests on open ledge, stands upright, resting on lower leg. On sea, long, low profile, with neck erect or held low. **Ad** | head, neck and upperparts plain **dark brown** to blackish with short white wingbar; underparts white with **dark streaking on flank**; bill pointed, black. **AdBr** | white on breast **rounded** along bottom of dark neck. A few (particularly in N) have white eyering and line behind eye ('bridled'). **AdNb / 1W** | crown/nape dark; cheek and throat white with **well-defined dark line bisecting cheek**; narrow, dark brown collar. **Juv** | initially identifiable by small size and call.

V | Calls on cliffs long, rather musical whirring notes; at sea, young bird calls loud, a far-carrying musical whistle, "*plee-u.*"

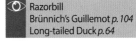

Razorbill
Brünnich's Guillemot *p. 104*
Long-tailed Duck *p. 64*

Locally numerous migrant

Breeds on sea cliffs, coastal islands; winters at sea

Two sspp.: southern *albionis* browner than blackish northern *aalge*, but much overlap.

FL | Fast, rather whirring action over sea (not high except when visiting cliff). Difficult to tell from Razorbill unless bill shape seen, but more tapered at both ends, fat in middle with narrow, mid-set wing; dark rump has **narrow white side**; narrow white trailing edge to wing; **dark 'wingpit'**.

AdNb

Storm-driven birds swim close inshore, and may sometimes be stranded on the tideline.

AdBr

AdBr

All ssp. *albionis*

AdBr
('bridled')
DEC–JUL

AdNb
AUG–MAR

AdBr
DEC–JUL

AdNb
AUG–MAR

AdBr
DEC–JUL

LC Brünnich's Guillemot
LC *Uria lomvia*

L 40–44 cm | **W** 64–75 cm

Small, brown/black-and-white seabird with **thick, pointed bill** (thicker than on Guillemot, more pointed than on Razorbill). **Ad**|upperparts **dark brown** to blackish, underparts white; head slightly peaked; **flank unmarked; white streak along cutting edge of bill; AdBr**|white on breast extends to a **point** up front of dark neck. **AdNb/1W**|dark cap to beneath eye (**no white behind eye**). May have thin dark chinstrap. **Juv**|identifiable by small size and food-begging call; full-grown by SEP.

V|Deep, guttural growling notes at colony.

👁 Guillemot *p. 103* | Razorbill *p. 102*

Breeding birds (TWO: TOP CENTRE) often in mixed auk colonies; here with Guillemots and Razorbill (TOP RIGHT).

FL|Fast, whirring action, like similar auks. Thickset oval shape with slim wing, deep body; less tapered than Guillemot. 'Wingpit' unmarked.

Locally numerous resident/migrant; occasional vagrant

Breeds on northern sea cliffs, coastal islands; winters at sea

SSP. *lomvia* occurs in Europe.

AdBr

AdNb/1W
AUG–MAR

AdBr

AdBr
DEC–JUL

AdNb
AUG–MAR

AdBr
DEC–JUL

Black Guillemot
Cepphus grylle

L 32–38 cm | **W** 49–58 cm

Small oval-shaped seabird; slim, dagger-like bill. Swims buoyantly, offshore or in harbours/inlets; sits on rocks, piers, breakwaters (not on high cliff ledges). **AdBr** smoky black; **oval white wing patch** striking even at long range. **Legs bright red. AdNb** head and body white, mottled grey; back barred grey-black; wing black with large white patch. **Juv** flank barred black and white; head brownish; wing patch barred grey. **1W** like **AdNb** but white wing patch has black spots/bars. **1S** as **AdBr** but dark parts brownish. **2Y/3Y** as **AdBr** but only in JUN-JUL.

V High, shrill whistle.

Winter grebes *p. 73*

1W→1S
[FEB]

Moulting birds are mottled grey and white, but the white wing patch remains distinct.

FL Low, whirring; big oval white patch on upperwing and white underwing obvious, especially on breeding adults.

Generally scarce, locally common resident

Breeds coastal islands, rocky shores; winters at sea, sheltered inlets

Five similar sspp.: *mandtii* (Arctic islands) has largest white wing patch and whitest head and body in winter.

AdBr
FEB-AUG

The bright red mouth is striking when an adult calls in the breeding season.

AdNb

AdBr

Juv→1W
JUN-MAY

Nests in isolated pairs or small groups around rocky islets, or at the foot of larger cliffs.

AdNb
AUG-MAR

AdBr
FEB-AUG

AdBr
FEB-AUG

Gulls
are stout-bodied, long-winged, web-footed birds with strong bills, pointed in the smaller species but stout and more or less hooked in the larger ones. Except for some immature plumages, they usually show a lot of white, with grey to black upperparts. They fly expertly on somewhat bowed or angled wings, swim buoyantly, and most walk easily, being quite at home on dry land.

31 species [15 breed; 3 regular, but scarce, migrants; 13 vagrants] with several distinct subspecies

Gulls are associated with water, on which they usually roost overnight, but most are opportunistic, exploiting habitats from sea level to high peaks, from open sea and freshwater to grasslands, and man-made situations from arable fields to urban sites. On coasts, their daily routine is largely dictated by the tides. Some are familiar in parts of Europe, such as Herring Gull in north-west Europe and Yellow-legged Gull in the Mediterranean, and Black-headed Gull, which is widespread inland. Others breed in remote places and simply pass by as scarce migrants. **Flight** Direct flight strong, with regular beats of bowed, angled wings between glides; flocks often in long lines and Vs; acrobatic, twisting flight when attracting others to roosting sites and feeding areas; most soar frequently; some hawk for flying insects. **Sexing, Ageing and Moult** (see also *pp. 108–109*) Sexes are alike except for size; seasonal differences are often marked. Adults are mostly either white-headed in summer but streaky-headed in winter, or dark-hooded in summer and pale-headed in winter. Juveniles are very different from adults, mostly browner, with duller head and wing patterns and bill and leg colours. Different species mature over two to four years, with a succession of intermediate stages. Immature gulls are usually harder to identify to species than adults, becoming easier as they mature. Breeding plumage may be attained very early in spring but lost by early summer, with intermediate stages obvious in 'hooded' species.

Given individual variation, seasonal differences, intermediate stages during moult, and the effects of wear, gulls can seem overwhelmingly difficult even for experienced observers. They can, however, simply be enjoyed for what they are, and adults, at least, are mostly relatively easy to identify!

> **Identify by** age/time of year | bill and leg colour | head pattern | wing pattern | details of wingtip and other feather areas
> See *page 14* for full details of gull feather areas.

KITTIWAKE

BLACK-HEADED GULLS

Juv

1W

1S

AdNb

AdBr

Black-headed Gull ageing sequence over two years (see *p. 109* for more detail)

A feeding flock of Herring Gulls and Kittiwakes, and a Great Black-backed Gull.

POSSIBLE CONFUSION GROUPS –
see comparison on *pages 88–89*
Terns are more slender, sharper-billed, shorter-legged and longer-tailed.
Skuas (*p. 146*) are more strictly sea and coastal, and are darker/browner and much less streaked or patterned than most immature gulls.
Shearwaters (*p. 92*) are also strictly marine birds, which fly low and frequently swim but never stand out on beaches, piers or posts, as gulls often do.

Terns are like slender, dark-capped gulls with pointed bill, short legs and forked tail.

19 species [9 vagrants]; 2 with distinct subspecies (sometimes treated as species)

All are long-distance migrants, most wintering at sea, off West Africa or farther south, returning to Europe in spring. The commoner species form two distinct groups: 'sea' terns and 'marsh' terns.

'SEA' TERNS (7 regular species) include Common and Little Terns that breed widely inland, and Arctic Tern that does so in northern Scandinavia and Iceland; although most migrate at sea, some also do so overland. However, they are mainly associated with coasts, breeding on lagoons, dunes, shingle and islands (although Gull-billed Tern normally feeds over land). All are basically pale grey and white, with a black cap during the breeding season. They are gull-like, but have a pointed bill, short legs and forked tail (some have long, slender outer tail feathers). **Flight** Gull-like, but generally faster, lighter and more elegant with slimmer, angled wings; larger species quite powerful. Most hover with head down and plunge-dive for food, but they sometimes dip and pick food from the surface.

'SEA' TERN
(ARCTIC TERN)

'MARSH' TERNS (3 species) breed inland but are more widespread on migration, inland and along coasts. They frequently perch on buoys, posts, rafts *etc*. All have a short, slightly notched tail and lack elongated outer tail feathers. Breeding plumages are darker than 'sea' terns, although non-breeding and immature plumages are similar, being pale with a dark cap. **Flight** Rather buoyant. Do not plunge-dive but instead fly into the wind, twisting and dipping to the surface to take food. Most gulls do this at times, but only Little Gull (*p. 122*) consistently behaves in this way.

'MARSH' TERN
(WHISKERED TERN)

Sexing, Ageing and Moult Sexes alike. Marked seasonal differences: all bar Little Tern have full black cap in breeding plumage but partly white cap in non-breeding plumage (from June in Sandwich Tern, not until reaching winter quarters in Arctic Tern). Complex moult varies between species: some start wing moult before autumn migration, others not until they reach their winter quarters. Some (*e.g.* Common Tern) moult wing twice a year and can have 3, even 4, ages of feathers in the wing (visible in the field). Others (*e.g.* Arctic Tern) moult wings just once per year so wing more uniform. Juveniles brown/barred but quickly moult body to look like winter adults, although retain flight feathers into following year.

COMMON TERN

Juv

1W

AdBr

A migrating flock of Common Terns, Sandwich Tern and Black-headed Gull in spring. Dark marks on outerwing of Common Terns rules out Arctic Tern.

Identify by size | shade of grey/black | bill colour | leg colour | wing pattern | feeding behaviour

POSSIBLE CONFUSION GROUPS -

Gulls are heavier-bodied, shorter-billed and mostly have a shorter, rounded or square-ended tail.

Moult sequence in gulls

Gulls, like other birds, renew their feathers in a regular sequence of moults, producing distinct plumages. Because gull feathers are big and strongly patterned, the process is easily appreciated; it is summarized here for a gull that takes two years to reach maturity (Black-headed Gull) and one that takes four or five years (Herring Gull). An understanding of this process is key to establishing the age of a gull, an important factor in the safe identification of some species.

Primary moult

Primaries are moulted in sequence, outwards from the innermost primary (P1) to the outermost primary (P10). Numbering the primaries helps to describe patterns with precision. This is especially important in the identification of some closely related species, as is the time of year the moult takes place.

inner primaries (P1-P4)

3rd-winter [JAN]

outer primaries (P5-P10) and their coverts

P1
P2
P3
P4
P5
P6
P7
P8
P9 P10

'mirror'

primary tip

Adult [OCT]

trailing edge

LESSER BLACK-BACKED GULL

White streaks on the midwing show where feathers (wing coverts) have been shed.

P1
P2
P3
P4
P5
[P6]
P7 P8 P9 P10

'mirror'

primary tip (worn away)

On the bird shown here, a 'notch' shows on the trailing edge where the primaries are regrowing after being shed: **P1** and **P2** are fully grown; **P3** is almost fully grown; **P4** is growing; **P5** is just appearing; [P6] is missing (shed); **P7–P10** are old, with white tips worn off (compare with full wing *inset above right*).

Herring Gull – 4 years to maturity ④

Juvenile
MAY-SEP
[AUG]

1st-winter
SEP-APR
[FEB]

1st-summer
MAR-OCT
[JUN]

2nd-winter
MAY-MAR
[FEB]

1st moult	**2nd moult**	**3rd moult**	**4th moult**
JUVENILE	1ST-WINTER	1ST-SUMMER	2ND-WINTER
↓	↓	↓	↓
1ST-WINTER	1ST-SUMMER	2ND-WINTER	2ND-SUMMER
Head and body feathers replaced	Partial moult of head and body feathers; wing and tail feathers now a year old.	Prolonged complete moult of head, body, tail and wing feathers. Bill colour progressively changes with age.	Partial moult of head and body feathers only.
	(Some larger species such as Herring Gull moult few feathers and just fade paler.)		

JUVENILE	1st moult	1ST-WINTER	2nd moult	1ST-SUMMER	3rd moult	2ND-WINTER	4th moult
Jun	Jul	Aug	Sep	Oct	Nov	Dec	Jan	Feb	Mar	Apr	May	Jun	Jul	Aug	Sep	Oct	Nov	Dec	Jan	Feb	M

1st calendar ← year

2nd calendar year →

3rd calendar year →

Black-headed Gull – 2 years to maturity ②

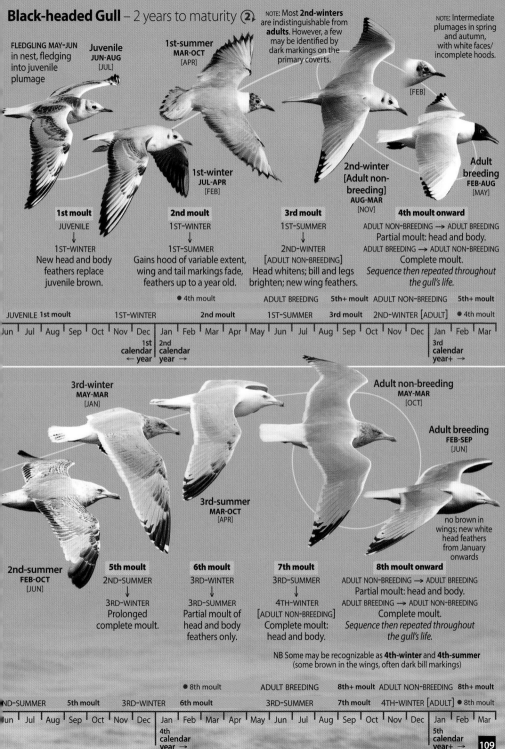

FLEDGLING MAY-JUN in nest, fledging into juvenile plumage

Juvenile JUN-AUG [JUL]

1st-summer MAR-OCT [APR]

NOTE: Most **2nd-winters** are indistinguishable from **adults**. However, a few may be identified by dark markings on the primary coverts.

NOTE: Intermediate plumages in spring and autumn, with white faces/ incomplete hoods.

[FEB]

1st-winter JUL-APR [FEB]

2nd-winter [Adult non-breeding] AUG-MAR [NOV]

Adult breeding FEB-AUG [MAY]

1st moult	2nd moult	3rd moult	4th moult onward
JUVENILE ↓ 1ST-WINTER	1ST-WINTER ↓ 1ST-SUMMER	1ST-SUMMER ↓ 2ND-WINTER [ADULT NON-BREEDING]	ADULT NON-BREEDING → ADULT BREEDING Partial moult: head and body. ADULT BREEDING → ADULT NON-BREEDING Complete moult. *Sequence then repeated throughout the gull's life.*
New head and body feathers replace juvenile brown.	Gains hood of variable extent, wing and tail markings fade, feathers up to a year old.	Head whitens; bill and legs brighten; new wing feathers.	

● 4th moult   ADULT BREEDING   5th+ moult   ADULT NON-BREEDING   5th+ moult

JUVENILE **1st moult**	1ST-WINTER	**2nd moult**	1ST-SUMMER	**3rd moult**	2ND-WINTER [ADULT]	● **4th moult**
Jun Jul Aug Sep Oct Nov Dec	Jan Feb Mar Apr May	Jun Jul Aug Sep Oct Nov Dec	Jan Feb Mar			

1st calendar ← year | 2nd calendar year → | 3rd calendar year+ →

3rd-winter MAY-MAR [JAN]

Adult non-breeding MAY-MAR [OCT]

3rd-summer MAR-OCT [APR]

Adult breeding FEB-SEP [JUN]

no brown in wings; new white head feathers from January onwards

2nd-summer FEB-OCT [JUN]

5th moult	6th moult	7th moult	8th moult onward
2ND-SUMMER ↓ 3RD-WINTER	3RD-WINTER ↓ 3RD-SUMMER	3RD-SUMMER ↓ 4TH-WINTER [ADULT NON-BREEDING]	ADULT NON-BREEDING → ADULT BREEDING Partial moult: head and body. ADULT BREEDING → ADULT NON-BREEDING Complete moult. *Sequence then repeated throughout the gull's life.*
Prolonged complete moult.	Partial moult of head and body feathers only.	Complete moult: head and body.	

NB Some may be recognizable as **4th-winter** and **4th-summer** (some brown in the wings, often dark bill markings)

● 8th moult   ADULT BREEDING   8th+ moult   ADULT NON-BREEDING   8th+ moult

...ND-SUMMER	**5th moult**	3RD-WINTER	**6th moult**	3RD-SUMMER	**7th moult**	4TH-WINTER [ADULT]	● **8th moult**
Jun Jul Aug Sep Oct Nov Dec	Jan Feb Mar Apr May	Jun Jul Aug Sep Oct Nov Dec	Jan Feb Mar				

4th calendar year → | 5th calendar year+ →

Regularly occurring gulls in flight (juveniles/1st-years)

AUDOUIN'S GULL
(p. 117)

Juv

ssp. *fuscus*

Juv

Juv

COMMON GULL
(p. 116)

1W

LESSER BLACK-BACKED GULL
(p. 124)

1W

MEDITERRANEAN GULL
(p. 120)

Juv

SLENDER-BILLED GULL
(p. 118)

1W

BLACK-HEADED GULL
(p. 119)

1W

GREAT BLACK-HEADED GULL
(p. 121)

Ross's Gull p. 134

Juv

SABINE'S GULL
(p. 115)

Juv

1W

LITTLE GULL
(p. 122)

KITTIWAKE
(p. 114)

AdNb

ARMENIAN GULL
(*p. 127*)

1W

Juv

GREAT BLACK-BACKED GULL
(*p. 123*)

1W

YELLOW-LEGGED GULL
(*p. 126*)

1W

NOTE: See annotation on *p. 127* regarding the identification of juvenile/1st-winter Armenian Gulls outside breeding range.

1W

CASPIAN GULL
(*p. 129*)

1W

Juv

HERRING GULL
(*p. 128*)

Juv/1S

Juv

ICELAND GULL
(*p. 131*)

Juv / 1W

SSP.
glaucoides

GLAUCOUS GULL
(*p. 130*)

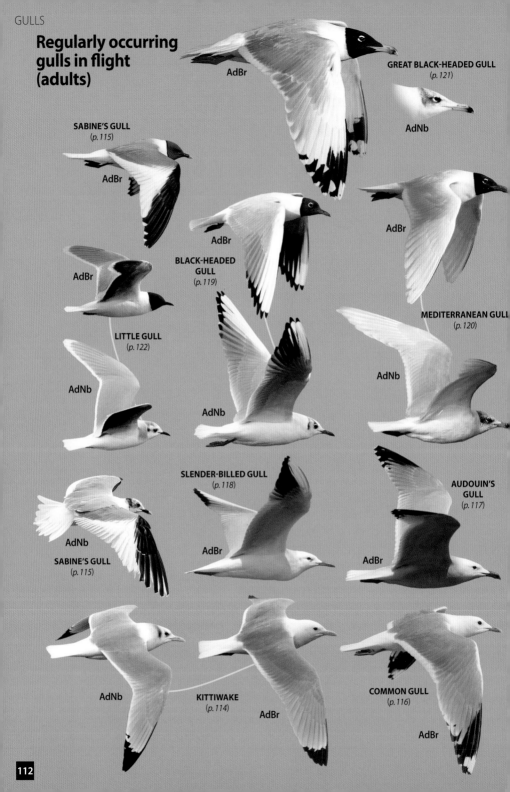

Regularly occurring gulls in flight (adults)

AdBr

GREAT BLACK-HEADED GULL
(*p. 121*)

AdNb

SABINE'S GULL
(*p. 115*)

AdBr

AdBr

AdBr

BLACK-HEADED GULL
(*p. 119*)

AdBr

MEDITERRANEAN GULL
(*p. 120*)

LITTLE GULL
(*p. 122*)

AdNb

AdNb

AdNb

AdNb

SLENDER-BILLED GULL
(*p. 118*)

AUDOUIN'S GULL
(*p. 117*)

AdNb

SABINE'S GULL
(*p. 115*)

AdBr

AdBr

AdNb

KITTIWAKE
(*p. 114*)

AdBr

COMMON GULL
(*p. 116*)

AdBr

GREAT BLACK-
BACKED GULL
(p. 123)

AdNb

LESSER BLACK-
BACKED GULL
(p. 124)

AdBr

HERRING GULL
(p. 128)

AdNb

AdNb

CASPIAN GULL
(p. 129)

3W

YELLOW-LEGGED GULL
(p. 126)

AdNb

AdNb

ARMENIAN GULL
(p. 127)

YELLOW-
LEGGED GULL
(p. 126)

CASPIAN GULL
(p. 129)

Ad

typically P10 has
a more extensive
white tip

AdNb

GREAT BLACK-
BACKED GULL
(p. 123)

AdBr

AdBr

LESSER BLACK-
BACKED GULL
(p. 124)

HERRING
GULL
(p. 128)

AdNb

GLAUCOUS
GULL
(p. 130)

ICELAND GULL
(p. 131)

AdNb

AdNb

SSP.
glaucoides

SSP.
kumlieni

113

Kittiwake   *Rissa tridactyla*

VU **VU**

③ **L** 37–42 cm | **W** 93–105 cm

Fairly small marine gull with a rounded head, slim wings and short tail. **Legs short, blackish** (some brown). Does not forage on the ground (but does land to collect nest material). **AdBr**| head white, bill yellow (no red spot); **eye black**. **AdNb**| grey nape, dark cheek spot. **Juv**| black bill; dark band along wing; black collar. Gradual change through **1W** (loses collar) to **1S** (when wing bands are faded and fragmented). **2W** / **2S** | looks like **Ad**, or has dusky 'winter' head in summer, often with black marks on bill.

V | Around colony, occasionally elsewhere, loud, wailing, piercing, rhythmic "*kitti-a-waike*;" long, high, whining notes.

SSP. *tridactyla* occurs in Europe.

AdBr - Common Gull *p. 116*
Juv - Little Gull *p. 122* | Sabine's Gull

AdBr
MAR–SEP

Stands quite upright on narrow ledges (in **crowded colonies**), on cliffs or buildings.

Generally uncommon although locally abundant; migratory

Breeds sea cliffs, islands, coastal buildings, rests on beaches; winters at sea

FL | Wings slender and tapered; steep, banking flight in strong wind. **Ad** wingtip black (no white spots); outerwing paler than innerwing; **underwing white**. **Juv** black collar; **black 'W' across wings** broken by grey back; underwing white (dusky underwing band on Sabine's Gull). **1W** / **1S** prolonged moult (OCT-JUN): loses collar and dark 'W' fades by spring; hindwing white. **2W** / **2S** like **Ad** but black streaks on primary coverts and outer primaries.

1W
OCT–APR

Juv
JUN–JAN

1S
FEB–SEP

2S
FEB–SEP

underwing white, primaries semi-translucent against the light

AdNb
OCT–FEB

Juv
JUN–JAN

AdBr
MAR–SEP

Sabine's Gull *Xema sabini*

② **L** 30–36 cm | **W** 80–87 cm

Small marine gull with **black, grey and white triangles** on spread wing. On water, dark and slim; closed tail forked. Head dove-like; bill fairly short and thick. Picks food from surface while swimming or dips down in flight. **AdBr** | hood lead-grey; bill black with yellow tip; outerwing black with **white primary tips** (which wear away). **AdNb** | head white, with black nape and ear spot. **Juv / 1W** | crown, breast side and back grey-brown with dark bars and buff feather tips. **1S / 2W** | develop grey back before grey wing coverts; area of smudgy grey on side of neck and breast.

V | Insignificant sharp *"kik."*

Two similar sspp. occur: *palaearctica* (Svalbard eastwards); *sabini* (Nearctic) adult/1st-summer slightly paler.

Moult sequence is reverse of most other gulls: complete in early spring before migrating north; partial in winter after returning south.

👁 Juv - Kittiwake | Little Gull *p. 122*
AdBr – Black-headed Gull *p. 119*

AdNb
OCT–MAR

The 'triple-triangle' pattern is always much clearer than on any immature Kittiwake; white streaks on the wingtip show only when it is fully spread. Non-breeding adults like this one are rare in Europe.

Rare passage migrant
Breeds Arctic tundra; migrates at sea

FL | Broad, angled wings give great agility. **Triple-triangle upperwing** diagnostic (immature Kittiwake's black innerwing band may be almost absent in 1S, but upperwing always lacks well-defined triangles). Dusky underwing band, especially on **Juv**.

In all plumages, clear white triangle across hindwing.

Juv

1S
FEB–DEC

AdBr

Juv
JUN–JAN
(NOTE: Moults in winter range.)

AdNb
OCT–MAR

AdBr
FEB–OCT

LC Common Gull *Larus canus*

LC ③ **L** 40–46 cm | **W** 100–115 cm

Most widespread medium-sized gull.
AdBr | head white, back mid-grey;
wingtip black-and-white; **eye dark**; bill
yellow, **no red spot**; **legs green**.
AdNb | head streaked (some birds have
a dusky hood); bill duller than **AdBr**,
often with dark band. **Juv** | upperparts
brown with neat pale fringes; flank and
undertail white with brown barring, the
extent of which is individually variable.
1W | back plain grey (some retain brown
juvenile feathers); wings brown with buff
feather edges. **1S** | grey back darker than
faded wing. **2Y** | like dull **Ad** with more
brown-black on wingtip.

AdBr - Kittiwake *p. 114*
1W - Mediterranean Gull *p. 120*
Ring-billed Gull *p. 547*
1W, AdNb - *Relict Gull p. 551*

Juv
JUN–OCT

Juveniles are elongated, with small head
and bill; back moulted to grey in autumn,
some retaining brown feathers into winter.

V | High-pitched, squealing "*keeea*,"
"*klee-u*" and long, laughing, wailing
"*ke-ke-ke-kleee-a kleee-a.*"

Locally common
migrant/resident

Breeds on peat bogs,
sea coasts; widespread
on coasts and inland
in winter

FL | **Ad** wingtip black
with **large white spots** on
two outermost primaries.
1W outerwing blackish,
innerwing browner; tail
white with **clear-cut black
tail-band**. **2W** as **Ad** but
smaller white spots in more
extensive brown-black
wingtip.

1W

grey back darker
than faded wing
(Mediterranean Gull
similar but paler on
back); dark parts
fade browner

1S
APR–JUL
(NOTE: Starting
moult to 2W)

2W
(NOTE: Outer
primaries still
growing)

AdBr

All SSP. *canus*

White in
wingtip
rules out
Kittiwake.

dark band on bill
varies between
individuals

1W
AUG–MAR

AdNb
AUG–MAR

2W
AUG–MAR

long black
wingtip without
white spots

AdBr
FEB–JUL

SSP. *canus* widespread; becomes darker
with more black on primaries in E,
merging into dark-backed, paler-eyed
SSP. *heinei*. SSP. *brachyrhynchus* (vagrant
from N America) has a shorter bill on
average and more white on wingtip.

Audouin's Gull *Larus audouinii*

(4) **L** 44–52 cm | **W** 117–128 cm

Medium-large, slim-winged, pale gull with long 'snout'; **legs grey**; **eye dark**. **Ad** | back pale grey; underparts paler grey; head white all year. Bill **red with black band**. White spots on black wingtip (wear off by AUG). **Juv** | brown overall, with neat buff fringes to upperparts; bill pink-grey with black tip. Dusky smudge around eye; **tertials have narrow pale edges**. **1W** | pale grey back; dark 'mask'. Bill grey to pinkish with black tip; base redder by **1S**. **2W / 2S** | pale grey with blackish wingtip and tail-band. **3W / 3S** | like **Ad** but smaller white spots on wingtip.

Herring Gull *p. 128*
Caspian Gull *p. 129*
Yellow-legged Gull *p. 126*

Juv
JUN–OCT

Juveniles are elongated, with long wingtip and long, heavy bill; combination of grey legs and pinkish-grey bill distinctive.

V | Typical large-gull staccato, nasal notes and squealing calls.

Scarce, locally common resident/migrant

Breeds on rocky islands; winters on sandy or rocky shores, lagoons

FL | **Ad** wingtip black with small white 'mirror'; underwing white with strongly contrasted black tip. **Juv** dark brown, with white rump and black hindwing band and tail-band; underwing dark with white band along middle. **1W** gains grey back. **2W / 2S** pale grey with blackish primary coverts, hindwing band and tail-band.

Juv
JUN–SEP

2S

AdBr

Juv has black hindwing band and tail-band, and white band along dark underwing; 1W is similar but has grey on back.

1W
SEP–APR

2S
MAR–SEP

AdBr
FEB–SEP

Large white spots on wingtip in autumn, wear off by AUG.

GULLS

LC **Slender-billed Gull**
LC *Larus genei*

(2) **L** 37–42 cm | **W** 90–102 cm

Small but long-necked gull; silvery-grey
and white with **pale head**. Forehead
extends to long, rather thick, pointed bill,
longest on ♂. Looks bigger than similar
Black-headed Gull: appears bulkier
on water, longer-legged on land.
AdBr| head and body white, flushed **pink**
(but degree individually variable); **bill
red to blackish; legs red**. Eye whitish
or buff (especially in E) to mid-brown
(mostly in W). **AdNb**| grey ear-spot; bill
orange: eye pale. **Juv**| pale grey and white
with brown on neck and back; dusky
ear-spot; slim bill; long legs. **1W**| head
white, back pale grey; **eye pale**; bill and
legs pale orange.

V| "*Kee-er*" and squabbling notes (like
Black-headed Gull).

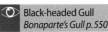

Black-headed Gull
Bonaparte's Gull p.550

AdBr
FEB–AUG

May stand with long neck erect; in
breeding season often intensely pink, bill
can look blackish.

Scarce and local;
migratory

Breeds on lakes, saline
lagoons; winters
mainly on coasts

FL| Long-winged, long-
headed shape; white
and pale grey with
broad **white outerwing
'blaze'**; black trailing
edge to outer primaries.
Underwing darkens
towards tip, contrasting
with **white outermost
primaries**. **1W** has
faint brown innerwing
band, brown hindwing
band and black-brown
tail-band.

1W

AdNb

bill markedly longer and
thicker than on Black-headed
Gull, especially on ♂

Bill colour varies
from pale to
very dark red;
often looks
almost black.

AdBr
MAR–JUL

1W
AUG–MAR

Long grey back and small black
wingtip when standing or swimming
(Black-headed Gull has shorter grey
back and longer wingtip).

AdNb
AUG–APR

Black-headed Gull
Larus ridibundus

②↓ **L** 35–39 cm | **W** 86–99 cm

Small, vocal gull; widespread in many habitats. **AdBr**│silver-grey and white with **dark brown hood** and thin white eye-crescents (hood fades but retains darker edge: **white face** during spring and summer moults). Bill dark red (does not contrast with hood). Wingtip black. **AdNb**│head white with **black ear-spot**; legs and bill **bright red**. **Juv**│neck, back and wings **dark tawny-brown** and silver-grey. **1W**│head and neck white with dark ear-spot; back grey, wings retain brown markings; eye dark. **1S**│patchy or full hood; brown wing markings fade paler.

V│Calls strident, shouted, screaming or grating - *"krree-arr," "karr,"* abrupt *"kek"* or *"kekek."*

👁 Mediterranean Gull *p. 120*
Little Gull *p. 122*
AdBr - Sabine's Gull *p. 115*
Slender-billed Gull
Rare 'hooded' gulls pp. 550–551

Juv
JUN–JUL

Juveniles are dark, mostly brown on the neck and upperside, and have a black ear-spot and dark band over the crown.

Locally abundant resident/migrant

Breeds freshwater pools, marshes, islands in lakes, saltmarshes; widespread in winter

FL│Light, buoyant, on sharp, angled wings; soars, dips to water, and hawks insects.
Ad broad white outerwing 'blaze'; black trailing edge to outer primaries; **underwing blackish** with white outermost primaries. **Juv/1W/1S** black streaks along white outerwing; underwing grey, contrasting with white outermost primaries.

1W

AdNb

AdBr

Black-brown trailing edge, fades browner; brown innerwing band also fades to pale brown by 1S; white forewing 'flash' marked with black.

Dark hood develops from rear to front during moult to AdBr or 1S, but is lost gradually from front to rear during moult to AdNb, giving a white-faced effect during transition.

1W
SEP–MAR

1S
MAR–SEP

AdBr→AdNb
JUN–SEP

AdNb
JUL–MAR

closed wingtip a thin black wedge with tiny white spots and white lower edge

AdBr
JAN–JUL

LC Mediterranean Gull
LC *Larus melanocephalus*

③ **L** 37–40 cm | **W** 94–102 cm

Small, very pale gull with a **thick, blunt bill** and rounded head. **AdBr** | wingtip white; **hood black** with bold **white eye-crescents**; **red bill contrasts** with hood. **AdNb** | **pale grey and white**; head white with blackish smudge through eye and grey nape; bill and legs red or blackish. **Juv** | upperparts brown with buff feather edges; breast pale brown-buff; bill black. **1W** | back pale grey, underparts white; dark smudge behind eye; white eye-crescents; bill thick, blackish (some orange/red at base); wingtip blackish. **2W** | like **Ad** but black marks on wingtip; often distinct broad 'mask'. **2S** | has full hood, bill and legs as **Ad** but black marks on wingtip.

V | Distinctive **loud, nasal** *"yaa-uh"* or *"ee-ow"* often reveals bird in mixed flock overhead in spring/summer.

Black-headed Gull *p. 119*
1W - Common Gull *p. 116*
Rare 'hooded' gulls *pp. 550–551*

Juv
JUN–SEP

Juvenile has buff feather edges on brown back, grey greater coverts (forming band) and grey-brown breast side and flank.

FL | **Ad** Wingtip and underwing white. **1W** dark forewing and hindwing band; midwing and back very pale grey; primaries blackish. **1S** dark areas fade browner. **2Y** upperwing pale grey, with black streaks; **white underwing**.

Generally scarce, locally common migrant/resident

Breeds freshwater pools, marshes, lakes, saltmarsh; winters mainly on coasts

Pale back (faded 1S Common Gull similar but has darker 'saddle').

1W

pale midwing panel

white streaks on blackish primaries

AdNb

2S
FEB–JUL

AdNb
JUL–MAR

1W
SEP–MAR

AdBr
JAN–JUL

Great Black-headed
(Pallas's) Gull *Larus ichthyaetus*

③↓ **L** 58–67 cm | **W** 146–162 cm

Large gull, bigger than Yellow-legged Gull, with **long head/bill profile** and white eye-crescents. **Ad** pale grey and white with black wingtip; **legs yellow**; bill long, yellow with black/red band. **AdBr** **black hood**. **AdNb** head white with **dusky 'mask'**. **Juv** back and wings buff-brown with whitish feather edges. **1W** back grey, patched brown; dark 'mask', mottled collar. **2W** like 1W but back plainer grey. **2S** has blackish hood.

V Deep, throaty calls at colony.

👁 Imm - Yellow-legged *p. 126*, Armenian *p. 127*, Caspian *p. 129* and Herring Gulls *p. 128*

Juv
JUN–SEP

The combination of long bill, white eye-crescents, dark 'mask' and large size helps to identify juveniles.

Rare, local; migratory, occasional vagrant
Breeds marshes, islands in lakes; winters on sea coasts

FL **Ad** white wingtip with black band. **Juv** blackish hindwing, grey midwing; white tail with black band. **1W** grey back, wing brown with darker flight feathers; black tail-band. **2W** tail-band reduced, black wingtip and primary coverts, small white 'mirror'. **3Y** like **Ad** but more black on wingtip.

1W

2W
AUG–APR

AdNb

1W
JUL–APR

2W
JUL–APR

AdNb
AUG–APR

long, flat profile when swimming; large head and bill

AdBr
FEB–AUG

long yellow legs

121

Little Gull *Hydrocoloeus minutus*

LC
NT ② **L** 24–28 cm | **W** 62–69 cm

Tiny, slim, lightweight gull; feeds buoyantly (like Black Tern), dipping head-to-wind over water. **AdBr** | pale grey and white with **black hood (no white eye-crescents)**; **wingtip white**; bill dark; legs red. **AdNb** | blackish cap and ear-spot; legs pink. **Juv** | upperparts densely barred black/brown; breast side dark brown. **1W** | back pale grey; head/neck like **AdNb**; dark innerwing band. **1S** | dark areas on wing fade browner; full or patchy hood. **2W** | like **AdNb** but black marks on wingtip (retained to **2S**).

V | Calls insignificant "kik," "kek."

1W - Kittiwake p. 114 | Sabine's Gull p. 115
Black-headed Gull p. 119 | Black Tern p. 136
1W, AdNb - Ross's Gull p. 546 | Bonaparte's Gull p. 550

1W

Generally scarce, locally common; migratory

Juv / 1W Little Gulls have white underwing, dull blackish feathers appearing only in 2W plumage after JUL/AUG.

Breeds freshwater marshes; winters lakes, sea coasts

FL | Buoyant, sometimes 'towering' in high, erratic flight. **Ad** upperwing pale grey with **white trailing edge and wingtip**; underwing **blackish with white rim**. **Juv** dusky hindneck and breast side (thin collar on similar Kittiwake); **blackish 'W' across wings** and lower back. **1W** back/rump grey; dark spots on secondaries and streaked inner primaries (Kittiwake's whiter); outer primaries striped black and white. **2W** as **Ad** but has black spots or streaks on outerwing; underwing mottled dull black.

Juv

1W

1S MAR–AUG

NOTE: 1W Kittiwake has whiter hindwing and unstreaked black wingtip.

2W SEP–MAR

AdNb

This 1st-summer bird has a nearly complete hood and new, all-white tail feathers, but still has juvenile wing feathers, now almost a year old.

AdBr

Juv JUN–SEP

1W SEP–MAR

Wingtip white, but black underside often shows.

AdNb SEP–MAR

All ages may have pink underparts during the breeding season.

AdBr FEB–JUL

Great Black-backed Gull   *Larus marinus*

④ ↓ L 61–74 cm | **W** 144–166 cm

Largest, most predatory gull. Adult black-backed and white-headed, only likely to be confused with smaller Lesser Black-backed Gull. Massive broad head; huge bill on male. **AdBr** | **black** above, darker than most Lesser Black-backed Gulls, with more white in wingtip. Legs long: **pale, pinkish** or whitish. **AdNb** | **head remains largely white** (streaked until FEB on Lesser Black-backed Gull). **Juv / 1W** | **heavy, black bill**; pale head and underparts (more obviously so than same-age Herring or Lesser Black-backed Gulls); **boldly chequered** black, brown and buff above. **2W** | increasingly black above. **3W** | similar to **Ad**, but wing patched with brown (extent varies between individuals).

FL | Long, bowed wings; strong, steady beats; soars well in wind. **Ad** back and wings black, with no contrast between black wingtip and rest of wing. **Juv / 1W** like pale juvenile Herring Gull but pale area on inner primaries less contrasted and upperside boldly chequered grey and brown. **2Y** and **3Y** increasingly marked with black above.

👁 Lesser Black-backed *p. 124* | Kelp Gull *p. 548* | Imm - Herring Gull *p. 128*

Locally common resident/migrant

Breeds on coastal cliffs, islands; winters on coasts, scarcer inland

V | Generally the deepest of all gulls – a loud, distinctive barking "*huh-huh-huh;*" long, deep, choking "*hou-oow-o, how-how-ow-ow-ow o o o.*"

AdNb

3W
JUL–MAR

2W
JUL–MAR

Juv
MAY–OCT

4W
JUL–MAR

AdNb
JUL–MAR

1W
JUL–MAR

NOTE: Some birds take six years to become fully mature.

AdBr
FEB–AUG

Intermediate plumages (2W and 3W) are shown on *p. 132*

123

LC **Lesser Black-backed Gull** *Larus fuscus*

LC ④ **L** 48–56 cm | **W** 117–134 cm

Common large gull of N and W Europe. Adult dark-backed, only likely to be confused with larger Great Black-backed Gull; immatures mottled brown, can be difficult to identify. Three subspecies occur (*see opposite*). **AdBr**| upperparts **dark grey**, otherwise white except black-and-white wingtip; **legs bright yellow. AdNb**| head/breast grey-brown; legs dull yellow. **Juv / 1W**| pale buff, heavily mottled grey/brown; tertials with **narrow pale fringes**; greater coverts wear to dark brown. **2W / 3W**| become grey on upperparts, more or less blotched dark brown (individuals mature at differing rates, so ageing unreliable): **2W** upperparts dark dull brown, but bright white head and underparts by **3S**.

FL| **Ad** grey upperwing with black wingtip (no contrast on ssp. *fuscus* or Great Black-backed Gull); small white 'mirrors'; dark grey beneath flight feathers. **Juv / 1W** primaries all-dark; dark hindwing band plus dark midwing band; thick black tail-band of even width. **2W dark grey 'saddle'** between brown wings.

Great Black-backed Gull *p. 123*
'Yellow-legged' gulls *pp. 126–127*
Imm - Herring Gull *p. 128*
Imm - Caspian Gull *p. 129*
Slaty-backed p. 549 | Kelp Gulls *p. 548*

Locally common resident/migrant

Breeds moors, coastal cliffs and islands, buildings; some on roofs far inland; winters on coasts and inland

V| Deep, throaty "*kyow*" and squealing notes; long, laughing calls deeper than Herring Gull (often heard from migrating flocks overhead inland).

3S
MAR–SEP

AdBr

2S
MAR–SEP

1S
MAR–SEP

Juv
JUN–AUG

dark midwing band (absent on Herring Gull)

dark hindwing band

Juv
JUN–OCT

AdNb
JUL–MAR

AdBr
FEB–AUG

Intermediate plumages (2W and 3W) are shown on *p. 133*

ssp. *graellsii*   ssp. *intermedius*   ssp. *fuscus*

Lesser Black-backed Gull subspecies

Three subspecies breed: *graellsii* (Great Britain and Ireland) palest; *intermedius* (NW Europe) darker, but intergrades; *fuscus* blackest, may be separate species, **'Baltic Gull'** (Baltic, migrates S and E; rare in W Europe) – has relatively long-wings, small head, slender bill and short legs; adult black above, no contrast with wingtip; almost white head in winter. Unlike the other subspecies., which after first year moult all flight feathers May-Nov (with only the outer 1–2 primaries still growing by Oct), ssp. *fuscus* replaces **only 1–4 innermost feathers, in Oct-Nov**, the rest after migrating. One/two vagrant subspecies: *heuglini* and perhaps *barabensis* vagrants from Siberia.

Identifying 'yellow-legged' gulls

Lesser Black-backed, Yellow-legged, Armenian, Caspian and Herring Gulls often present identification problems. The key differences in the pattern and colour of wing feathers are summarized below.

Wingtips of adults   **Wings and tertials of juveniles/1st-winters**   Tertial pattern can be useful, but there is considerable individual variation and feathers are often bleached.

Lesser Black-backed Gull

Black extensive, on outer 6 feathers, contrasts slightly against dark grey; two small white 'mirrors'.   Outerwing all-dark; innerwing has dark band across coverts, as well as dark hindwing.   Dark brown with narrow pale fringes.

Yellow-legged Gull
(*p. 126*)

P10
P5

Black extensive; white 'mirror' or rarely full white tip to P10; broad black band on P5.   Outerwing dark; inner primaries slightly paler.   Dark base in solid crescent; pale fringes only at tip.

Armenian Gull
(*p. 127*)

P10
P5

Black extensive, squared with no indentations, on outer 7 feathers; one or two white 'mirrors'.   Outerwing dark; inner primaries striped dark brown and silver-grey.   Dark brown with pale tips, fading whitish.

Caspian Gull
(*p. 129*)

'fingers'
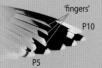
P10
P5

Pale grey 'fingers' extend into black of P7–P10; long white tip to P10; usually black band on P5. Beneath, long white 'tongue' on P10.   Outerwing dark; inner primaries streaked slightly paler towards base.   Dark base in solid crescent; pale fringes only at tip.

Herring Gull
(*p. 128*) ssp. *argenteus*

P10
P5

ssp. *argentatus* overlaps fully with Caspian Gull. ssp. *argenteus* has black bar between white 'mirror'. and tip of P10; black spot on outer web of P5.   Outerwing dark; inner primaries obviously pale; innerwing has pale coverts; dark hindwing band.   Brown with buff tips and fringes in 'oak-leaf' pattern.

LC Yellow-legged Gull
LC *Larus michahellis*

(4) **L** 52–58 cm | **W** 120–140 cm

Common large gull of S and E Europe. **Ad** | head white, upperparts grey (**darker** than Herring Gull, **paler** than Lesser Black-backed Gull); wingtip black-and-white. Bill large, rich yellow with red spot. **Legs yellow**; eye deep yellow with red ring. **AdNb** | head streaked behind eye in JUL-SEP, then striking **white** (Herring and Lesser Black-backed Gulls streaked dark until JAN/FEB). **Juv** | dull grey-brown; ginger-brown by **1W** | when head whiter with slight mask, greyish 'shawl'. **Tertials dark with thin pale tips** (plus pale fringes on some birds). Later ageing unreliable, but **2W** | gains grey on upperparts. **3W** | blotched brown on grey, underparts white; bill blackish to bright yellow with black band. Some **3Y/4Y** like **Ad** with black bill band, very like Armenian Gull.

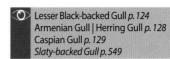

Lesser Black-backed Gull *p. 124*
Armenian Gull | Herring Gull *p. 128*
Caspian Gull *p. 129*
Slaty-backed Gull *p. 549*

3W
[OCT]

AdNb
[OCT]

Two sspp. occur: *atlantis* (Macaronesian Is.) ('Azorean' or 'Atlantic Gull') (ABOVE) **AdNb** has variably dark hood and even in 3rd-winter often has blackish bill base. Widespread ssp. is *michahellis*.

FL | **Ad** upperwing grey; more extensive black on wingtip than Herring Gull, with large white 'mirror' or tip on outer primary (see *p. 125*). **1W** innerwing brown, faint pale inner primary patch; thick black tail-band, broadest in centre. **2W** grey on back. **3W** like **Ad** but some brown on upperwing and dusky tail markings.

Locally common resident/migrant

Breeds on coastal cliffs, islands, buildings; in winter, often inland

V | Low-pitched barking notes. Long call **slow, separated** laughing notes.

1W

3W
SEP–MAR

AdNb
JUL–SEP

All SSP. *michahellis*

AdBr
OCT–JUL

2W
SEP–MAR

Minority have black on bill, like Armenian Gull.

NOTE: Adult Herring Gulls from the Baltic may have dull yellow legs, but the head and breast are streaked in winter.

1W
SEP–MAR

AdBr
OCT–JUL

Intermediate plumages (2W and 3W) are shown on *p. 133*

Armenian Gull   *Larus armenicus*

④ **L** 52–60 cm | **W** 120–140 cm

Large, elegant gull; very like Yellow-legged Gull but bill shorter and thicker; long-legged, upright stance. **AdBr** grey-and-white; bill **vivid yellow** with red spot and often a **black band**. Legs bright yellow; eye usually dark. **AdNb** hind-neck spotted dark; bill yellow with black band, with or without red (similar on some Yellow-legged Gulls): ♂ has longer bill, flatter head than round-headed ♀. **Juv / 1W** upperparts greyish, blotched brown. Head white, grey around eye. Underparts white; dark spots on hindneck and breast side; bill black; legs pinkish. **1S** pale brown, some fade almost to white. **2W** back grey, wing barred grey-brown and whitish, tertials largely pale; collar and breast spotted dark brown; bill dull with dusky band; legs pinkish. **3W** upperparts grey with brown wash across coverts; tertials spotted dark brown; wingtip black-brown; bill and legs as **Ad**; eye dark.

FL **Ad** extensive black wingtip (black on outer 7 primaries) square against grey; one white 'mirror', less often two (see *p. 125*). **1W / 2W** like Yellow-legged Gull but bill shorter, inner primaries striped, underwing paler; thick black tail-band of even width. **3W** like **Ad** but smudged brown on wing, smaller white 'mirror' on wingtip and a few dusky tail markings.

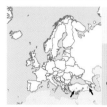

Yellow-legged Gull
Caspian Gull *p. 129*
Lesser Black-backed Gull *p. 124*
Herring Gull *p. 128*

Very local resident/ migrant

Breeds lakes, marshes; winters on coasts, shallow lagoons

V Nasal "*ow-ow-ow*," deep barking notes and yapping "*kyaa-ap-ap-ap-ap-ap….*"

2S
FEB–SEP

3S
MAR–SEP

AdNb

Juv
JUN–SEP

AdNb
MAY–MAR

NOTE: Outside breeding range (and particularly outside the area covered by this book) identification may not be possible due to similarity with other species. The image of a Juv above was taken in Israel, where virtually identical 'Steppe Gull' (species/ssp. *barabensis* of Lesser Black-backed Gull) occurs.

1W
AUG–MAR

Juv is darker brown, but soon bleaches paler by 1W

AdBr
JAN–JUN

Intermediate plumage (2S or 3S) shown on *p. 133*

Herring Gull *Larus argentatus*

LC
LC

④ L 54–60 cm | **W** 123–148 cm

Common large gull of N and W Europe.
Ad | upperparts **pale grey**; wingtip black
with white spots (smallest wear off by
MAY). **Eye pale** with yellow/orange ring;
bill yellow with red spot, **legs pink**.
Northern SSP. *argentatus* larger and
darker than W European SSP. *argenteus*
(which is paler than Common Gull
(*p. 116*)). **AdBr** | head and body white.
AdNb | head heavily streaked. **Juv / 1W** |
grey-brown, fading paler; tertials have
pale tips and notches. Bill and eye dark.
Plumage bleached paler by **1S**. **2W** | bill
has pale base and tip; eye pale. **3W** | **pale
grey** back; bill yellow with dark marks
and reddish spot. **2Y / 3Y** develop at
varying rates, so ageing unreliable.

Caspian Gull | 'Yellow-legged' gulls *pp. 126–127* | Imm - Great
Black-backed Gull *p. 123* | Imm - Great Black-headed Gull *p. 121*
American Herring Gull *p. 548* | 'Thayer's Gull' *p. 547*
Glaucous-winged Gull *p. 549*

AdBr

Extreme
examples of north
Scandinavian
SSP. *argentatus*
(migrates S) have
more white on
wingtip, often
with very little
black beneath.
In Iceland,
similar birds may
result from past
hybridization with
Glaucous Gull.

Locally abundant
resident/migrant

Breeds coastal cliffs,
islands, buildings (even
far inland); winters on
coasts and inland

V | **High-pitched**, strident yelps, whines and deep barks; soft "*gag-ag-
gag.*" Long call loud, higher-pitched than Yellow-legged Gull (*p. 126*).

FL | Powerful; soars and glides well.
Ad wingtip black, two white 'mirrors' (or full
white tip on outer feather) (see *p. 125*).
Pale grey beneath flight feathers.
Juv / 1W wingtip dark, **striking pale inner
primary patch**; dark hindwing band; thick
brown/black tail-band, broadest in centre.
2Y / 3Y become grey on back; pale inner
primaries remain distinctive.

SSP. *argenteus*

SSP. *argentatus*

3W
MAY–MAR

AdBr

SSP.
argentatus

SSP. *argenteus*

MAY–MAR

2W
MAY–MAR

Juv
MAY–SEP

Juv

dark hindwing
band, but no
dark midwing
band (unlike
Lesser Black-
backed Gull)

Adult head ranges
from lightly marked
to heavily blotched/
streaked, NOV–MAR.

Intermediate plumages (2W
and 3W) are shown on *p. 132*

Some Baltic breeders have
dull yellow legs (see Yellow-
legged Gull) but the head and
breast are streaked in winter.

AdBr
FEB–SEP

SSP. *argenteus*

Caspian Gull *Larus cachinnans*

(4) **L** 55–60 cm | **W** 138–147 cm

Large gull; often has upright stance, breast/shoulders high and broad, back sloping steeply down to long wingtip; head 'pear-shaped' with eye set well forward; legs long, slender. Others less distinctive, and identification problematic due to hybrids/intergrades. ♂ has long, parallel-edged bill; forehead slopes to high nape. ♀ has shorter bill and legs. **Ad** back pale grey; wingtip black-and-white; **head white all year**. Eye yellow or dark, with red ring. Bill greenish-yellow with dull red spot. Legs dull yellowish or pinkish-grey. **AdNb** bill often has dark band. **Juv / 1W** brownish; head and underparts whitish, hindneck darker; by SEP, new back/scapular feathers grey with dark spots; tertials blackish, with white tips, forming a dark crescent; wingtip blackish; bill and eye dark. **2Y** like 1W but back grey, plain or with fine dark streaks/'anchor' shapes; darker 'shawl'. **3Y** back and wing plain grey.

V Low-pitched barks and yelling notes, similar to Lesser Black-backed Gull; laughing note higher than Yellow-legged Gull.

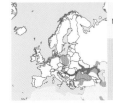

Herring Gull
'Yellow-legged' gulls *pp. 126–127*
Imm - Audouin's Gull *p. 117*
Imm - Great Black-headed Gull *p. 121*

Scarce, local resident/migrant

Breeds lakes in semi-arid regions; winters on coasts, lakes, rivers

FL | **Underwing pale** at all ages. **Ad** black on outer 6/7 primaries, **indented by pale grey 'fingers'** (see *p. 125*). **1W** thick black tail-band of even width; two dark innerwing bands plus black hindwing band; faint pale inner primary patch. **2W** pale innerwing with dark hindwing band; clear-cut black tail-band. **3W** like Ad with darker primary coverts, less white in wingtip and a few dark tail markings.

NOTE: Tail may be almost solidly blackish on some 1Y and 2Y birds.

2W
SEP–MAR

3W
SEP–MAR

Ad

NOTE: 2Y, 3Y, 4Y develop at varying rates, so ageing unreliable.

1W

head whiter than other large gulls of same age

Adult has white head all year.

1W
SEP–MAR

Ad
ALL YEAR

Intermediate plumages (2W and 3W) are shown on *p. 133*.

'WHITE-WINGED' GULLS **Glaucous Gull** and **Iceland Gull** are large, pale gulls that lack any black on their wings, unlike any other regularly occurring gulls of a similar size. The two species have similar plumages at comparable ages but can be distinguished as follows:

Glaucous Gull (rear): larger than Herring Gull; bulky body; large head; **forehead less steeply sloped to typically lower, smoothly rounded crown**; large head, bulky nape, staring eye and deep 'chin' and large, **long** bill give 'strong' expression; wingtip projects **slightly beyond** tail.

Iceland Gull (front): size **similar to or smaller** than Herring Gull; rounded breast; rounded head with **steep forehead** sloping to **high 'domed' crown**; rounded nape, short 'chin' and **short** bill give 'gentle' look; wingtip long, pointed, projects **well beyond** tail.

Juv / 1W

LC Glaucous Gull *Larus hyperboreus*

👁 Iceland Gull | Herring Gull *p. 128*
Glaucous-winged Gull p. 549

LC ④ **L** 63–68 cm | **W** 138–158 cm

Ad | pale grey and white; **wingtip white**; bill yellow with red spot; legs pink. **AdBr** | head white; eye yellow with yellow ring. **AdNb** | as **AdBr** but head/breast streaked brown. **Juv** | buff, mottled/barred coffee-brown; **wingtip pale buff**; tail buff-brown. Fades paler to **1W** | . Bill pink with **well-defined black tip**. Eye dark. **1S** | like 1W but blotched white. **2W** | like 1W but eye pale; back has a little grey; bill pink with dark band and pale tip. **3W** | upperparts largely pale grey; wingtip white.

V | Yelps and thin squealing notes; long, slightly strangled, ringing call in summer.

FL | Heavy, long-winged. **Ad** pale grey; **white wingtip** and trailing edge. **1W / 2W** striking sandy-buff, wings fading to long, pointed **pale tips**; tail barred but has no dark band.

Generally scarce, locally common migrant/resident

Breeds on coastal cliffs, islands; in winter, widespread but local on coasts, scarcer inland

Up to four sspp. recognized around Arctic; *hyperboreus* and *leuceretes* breed in Europe but are poorly differentiated.

2W
SEP–MAR

3W
SEP–MAR

AdNb

Juv / 1W

Juv / 1W
JUN–MAR

AdBr
APR–AUG

AdNb
SEP–APR

Juv / 1W very variable: some darker on underparts than upperparts, others pale overall (see image on *p. 132*).

Intermediate plumages (2W and 3W) shown on *p. 132*

Iceland Gull *Larus glaucoides*

④ **L** 52–60 cm | **W** 123–139 cm

Ad| pale grey and white; **wingtip white**; bill yellow with red spot; legs dusky pink. **AdBr**| head white; eye yellow with dark red ring. **AdNb**| as AdBr but head/breast streaked grey-brown. **Juv / 1W**| pale sandy-buff, mottled pale brown; wingtip and tail buff-brown. **Bill brownish, black tip extends back into point**. Eye dark. Some birds fade very white by **1S**. **2W**| some grey feathers on upperparts; bill dull greyish-pink with pale tip and dark band; eye gradually becomes paler. **3W**| upperparts pale grey; wingtip white.

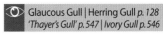

Glaucous Gull | Herring Gull *p. 128*
'Thayer's Gull' *p. 547* | Ivory Gull *p. 546*

Scarce winter visitor SEP–MAR, some all year

Local on coasts, especially harbours, scarcer inland

V| Short, yelping and laughing calls, slightly higher-pitched than Herring Gull.

FL| Wings broad-based, taper to narrower tip than Glaucous Gull; more pot-bellied, but size/ shape often difficult to assess. **Ad** has white wingtip. **1W / 2W** pale buff with pale wingtip, no dark hindwing or tail-band. ssp. *kumlieni* has dusky innerwing and hindwing bands and dusky tail.

Three subspecies occur: *glaucoides* (Iceland Gull) (from Greenland), and *kumlieni* ('Kumlien's Gull') (vagrant from NE Canada) intergrade and some birds are difficult to identify; *thayeri* ('Thayer's Gull') (vagrant from N America) is rather distinct (see *p. 547*).

ssp. *kumlieni* 'Kumlien's Gull'

1W| wingtip buff to brown with **dark streaks**, fine buff edges.

Ad| wingtip has **grey streaks** and white spots (extent and pattern individually rather variable).

NOTE: **Unless otherwise indicated, all the images on this page are ssp. *glaucoides*.**

AdNb

ssp. *kumlieni*

3W
SEP–MAR

SSP. *kumlieni*

Juv / 1W

2W
SEP–MAR

Juv / 1W
JUN–MAR

AdBr
APR–AUG

AdNb
SEP–MAR

Intermediate plumages (2W and 3W) shown on *p. 132*

Regularly occurring 'larger' gulls (immatures)

GREAT BLACK-BACKED GULL (p. 123)

1W

2W

3W

HERRING GULL (p. 128)

Juv

2W

3W

GLAUCOUS GULL (p. 130)

Juv / 1W

2W

3W

ICELAND GULL (p. 131)

For both these species, on water, long pale triangle of tertial tips/wingtip first clue.

Juv / 1W

2W

3W

CASPIAN GULL (*p. 129*)

1W

2W

3W

LESSER BLACK-BACKED GULL (*p. 124*)

Juv

2W

3W

YELLOW-LEGGED GULL (*p. 126*)

1W

2W

3W

ARMENIAN GULL (*p. 127*)

See note on *p. 127* regarding the inclusion in this book of images of Juv / 1W Armenian Gull taken outside Europe.

1W

2S

NOTE: Legs of 2Y and 3Y birds may be dull, pale yellow or vivid yellow, like Ad.

Regularly occurring terns in flight
(adults in breeding plumage)

SANDWICH TERN
(p. 141)

LITTLE TERN
(p. 139)

GULL-BILLED TERN
(p. 140)

ARCTIC TERN
(p. 143)

COMMON TERN
(p. 142)

WHISKERED TERN
(p. 138)

ROSEATE TERN
(p. 144)

WHITE-WINGED
BLACK TERN
(p. 137)

CASPIAN TERN
(p. 145)

BLACK TERN
(p. 136)

Regularly occurring terns in flight (juveniles)

SANDWICH TERN
(p. 141)

LITTLE TERN
(p. 139)

GULL-BILLED TERN
(p. 140)

COMMON TERN
(p. 142)

ARCTIC TERN
(p. 143)

ROSEATE TERN
(p. 144)

WHISKERED TERN
(p. 138)

WHITE-WINGED BLACK TERN
(p. 137)

BLACK TERN
(p. 136)

CASPIAN TERN
(p. 145)

LC Black Tern *Chlidonias niger*

LC **L** 22–26 cm | **W** 56–62 cm

Small 'marsh' tern with slender bill and short legs. **AdBr**| upperparts grey, **underparts black** (mottled white after breeding as black is gradually lost). Bill and legs black. **AdNb**| upperparts grey, underparts white. **Black cap**, extending onto nape and cheek; white around eye. **Dusky patch on side of breast**. Legs dull reddish. **Juv**| like **AdNb** but back barred brown.

V| Call insignificant, slightly squeaky, "*ki-ki-ki*" or "*kyeh;*" at colony, a chorus of longer, squealing notes.

White-winged Black Tern
Whiskered Tern *p. 138*
AdNb, Juv - Little Gull *p. 122*

FL| Flies into wind, dips to surface to feed. **AdBr** upperside dark grey, underside smoky-black, **white under tail**. **AdNb** back mid-grey, rump pale grey; underparts white with **dark patch on side of breast**. **Juv** no strong pattern on upperside: back grey-brown; innerwing greyish, darker along front and rear; some individuals have darker back, paler rump (White-winged Black Tern has darker back, paler wings, white rump).

Scarce, locally common summer migrant MAR–OCT

Breeds freshwater marshes; migrants lakes, coasts

Juv

Juv

Juv

dusky patch on side of breast

Vagrant N American SSP. *surinamensis* (ABOVE) **AdBr**| head/breast jet-black; **Juv**| **crown grey**, ear coverts black, large black patch on front of **grey flank**. SSP. *niger* is widespread in Europe.

AdNb
SEP–FEB

Juv
JUN–SEP

AdBr

AdBr
MAR–AUG

White-winged Black Tern
Chlidonias leucopterus

L 20–24 cm | **W** 50–56 cm

Small, stocky 'marsh' tern; similar to Black Tern but rather **dumpy, longer-legged** and **shorter-billed**. **AdBr** | glossy **black** (increasingly patched white after breeding), with **white tail** and **forewing**. Bill black; **legs red**. **AdNb** | upperparts grey, underparts white. **Black cap** extends onto nape and cheek; white around eye. Breast white, **unmarked (no dusky patch on side** as on Black Tern). **Juv** | head like **AdNb**; back **dark brown**; wing grey with brown bars.

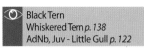

Black Tern
Whiskered Tern *p. 138*
AdNb, Juv - Little Gull *p. 122*

FL | Flies into wind, dips to surface to feed. Wings held relatively straight and flight action stiffer compared with other 'marsh' terns. **AdBr** black-and-white. **AdNb** back pale grey, **rump almost white**; white below (**side of breast unmarked**). Often has blackish line along middle of underwing. **Juv** back dark (forming distinct 'saddle'); wings pale; **rump white**.

V | Short, squeaky "*kik*" notes; louder, grating "*kerk*" or "*kow-erk*" alarm at colony.

Scarce, local summer migrant APR–OCT

Breeds freshwater marshes; migrants lakes, coasts

Juv

AdNb

AdBr

mottled black during moult but no dusky breast patch

dark back contrasts with white rump and pale wings; no trace of dark patch on side of breast

AdNb
SEP–MAR

Juv
JUN–SEP

AdBr
MAR–AUG

137

LC Whiskered Tern
LC *Chlidonias hybrida*
L 24–28 cm | **W** 57–63 cm

Small, robustly built 'marsh' tern with long, thick bill and long legs.
AdBr | upperparts grey, underparts dark grey; black cap contrasting with **white cheek and throat**. Bill and legs red.
AdNb | upperparts pale grey, underparts white; only a hint of a dark patch on side of breast; cap blackish, streaked white (lacks clearly defined head markings of other 'marsh' terns). Bill black, reddish at base; legs brown or blackish. **Juv** | head like **AdNb** but washed brown; back barred dark brown; wing pale brownish-grey.

V | Short, hoarse "*chrep;*" at colony abrupt, rasping "*djerp, djerp.*"

Black Tern *p. 136*
White-winged Black Tern *p. 137*
AdNb, Juv - Common Tern *p. 142*

FL | Direct, but dipping action when feeding. **AdBr** upperside mid-grey, **blackish below**, cheek and vent white. **AdNb** upperside pale grey (like Common Tern (*p. 142*), but rump greyer, tail shorter). **Juv** wings silvery-grey; back **barred** brown (more so than White-winged Black Tern) until AUG/SEP when grey; scapulars barred brown. Grey hindwing band (like juvenile Common Tern, but lacks obvious blackish forewing). Tail has dark tip and white sides (Common Tern has pale tip and blackish sides).

Scarce, local summer migrant MAR–OCT
Breeds lakes, freshwater marshes; migrants lakes, coasts

SSP. *hybrida* occurs in Europe.

Juv

AdBr

AdBr

AdNb

Juv
JUN–SEP

AdNb
SEP–FEB

AdBr
MAR–AUG

Little Tern *Sternula albifrons*

L 21–25 cm | **W** 41–47 cm

Very small, fast, very pale, long-winged tern. **Ad** | pale grey and white; black cap/eyestripe; **white forehead** all year. **Bill yellow** with black tip; legs yellow to orange. Closed wingtip shows black lower edge. **Juv** | barred, dusky on crown; legs yellowish.

V | Quick, rasping "*kreet*" and fast, rhythmic chatter "*kiereet kiereet kiereet.*"

FL | Fast, direct flight, quick, regular deep beats of swept wings. More erratic when feeding, frequent **fast hovers** and splashing headlong dives. **Outer primaries blackish.**

Least Tern *p. 553*
Juv - Sandwich Tern [Juv] *p. 141*
Juv - Roseate Tern [Juv] *p. 144*

The Little Tern has the quickest wingbeats of all terns when hovering.

Rare, local summer migrant APR–OCT; very local resident

Breeds sand/shingle beaches; migrants on coasts, rare inland

SSP. *albifrons* occurs in Europe.

Juv

AdBr

AdBr

Juv
JUN–OCT

AdBr→AdNb
AUG–SEP
[AUG]

AdBr
APR–SEP

LC Gull-billed Tern
LC *Gelochelidon nilotica*

L 35–42 cm | **W** 76–86 cm

Medium-large, pale grey and white tern; **head rounded** with no crest; tail short; bill **stout, all-black** (compare with juvenile Sandwich Tern); legs black. **AdBr** | back grey, underparts white; rounded black cap. **AdNb** | head white with small **dark mark behind eye**. **Juv** | cap streaked grey, cheek darker; back pale sandy-brown; bill pale at base but soon darkens. **1W** | very pale; crown white, small dark patch behind eye; nape greyish; bill black.

V | Call a low, harsh "*ker-wick.*"

Sandwich Tern

FL | Long wings swept back; head short; tail has shallow notch. Dips/hawks over land; does not normally plunge-dive. **Ad** rump and tail pale grey. Outerwing darkens with wear but may still be pale grey by AUG; fresh primaries have **dark trailing edge** on upper- and undersides (weaker on Sandwich Tern). **Juv** / **1W** back grey; pale brown on wing coverts; rump whitish; tail pale grey with white tip.

Scarce and local summer migrant
APR–OCT

Breeds freshwater and saline marshes, lakes; migrants on coasts

SSP. *nilotica* occurs in Europe.

AdBr

AdNb

Juv

AdNb
AUG–MAR

Juv
JUN–DEC

AdBr
MAR–SEP

Sandwich Tern
Thalasseus sandvicensis

L 37–43 cm | **W** 85–97 cm

Medium-large, very pale grey and white, angular tern with short crest; tail short; bill slim, **black with** pale tip (all-black on **Juv**); legs black. Larger, longer-billed and paler than Common Tern and Arctic Tern. **Ad** | back silvery-grey, underparts **pure white**; cap black with spiky crest (white forehead from JUN). **Juv** | cap dusky; back and wing coverts barred; tail pale grey with white sides, dark corners/tip; bill and legs blackish. **1W** | after JUL/AUG has blackish mask, white forehead, plain grey back; wing and tail as **Juv**.

V | Highly distinctive, loud, rhythmic, abrupt, short, tearing "*kierr-ik, ki-rink*" or "*ko-yok*." Young birds make high, whining "*srreee-i*."

Gull-billed Tern
Common *p. 142* | Arctic Tern *p. 143*
Roseate Tern *p. 144*
Juv - Little Tern *p. 139*
Lesser Crested & Elegant Terns p. 554

FL | Long-winged; flies high, direct, fast; dives from height with big splash. **Ad** underside white; very pale after autumn moult, outer 4/5 primaries streaked darker by spring, wearing to black by JUL. **Juv / 1W** upperwing grey, flecked brown; tail short, notched, tip blackish. Very young birds trail behind adult, calling to be fed.

Generally scarce, locally common summer migrant MAR–NOV; rare in winter

Breeds sandy beaches, dunes, lagoons, islands; migrants on coasts, rare inland

Juv

AdBr

AdNb

AdNb
JUN–FEB

Juv
JUN–DEC

AdBr
FEB–JUL

Two sspp. recorded: *sandvicensis* (widespread) and *acuflavidus* (**'Cabot's Tern'**, sometimes treated as a species) (vagrant from N America), **AdNb** (AUG-MAR) has a slightly shorter, thicker bill, thinner white fringes on inner webs of outer primaries and more sharply defined black nape/white crown.

141

LC **Common Tern** *Sterna hirundo*

LC **L** 34–37 cm | **W** 70–80 cm

Very like Arctic Tern but legs longer (and, in flight, outer primaries opaque). **AdBr**| upperparts grey, underparts paler grey. **Closed wingtip dark grey with contrasting pale feather tip at base**. Bill **scarlet** with black tip. **AdNb**| forehead white (from JUL), underparts white; dark grey shoulder; bill blackish. **Juv**| back gingery-brown; cap black, pale forehead tinged buff-brown; shoulder **blackish**; bill **orange**, tipped black. **1W**| some pale grey feathers on back, wings faded. **1S**| like **AdNb** but primaries more uniform or juvenile outer ones retained (most **1S** birds remain in winter range). **2S**| most are like **AdBr** but some are like **AdNb**.

Two sspp. occur: *hirundo* (widespread); *longipennis* ('Eastern' or 'Siberian Common Tern') (vagrant from Asia), **Ad** underparts darker, bill blackish.

Roseate Tern *p. 144* | AdNb/Imm - Whiskered Tern [AdNb] *p. 138* Sandwich Tern *p. 141* | Forster's Tern *p. 553* | Aleutian Tern *p. 552*

V| Calls sharp "*kit*," squabbling "*kit-it-it-it*" and long-drawn, nasal "*kierri-kierri*," with emphasis on first syllable.

FL| Hovers before direct plunge (may dip to surface like 'marsh' terns (*pp. 136–138*), especially inland). Compared with Arctic Tern, has longer innerwing, broader outerwing, longer bill/head/neck (**long** in front of wing); **AdBr** has shorter tail; inner primaries translucent, **outer ones opaque**. AdNb Whiskered Tern similar, but rump greyer, tail shorter. Darker than on Sandwich Tern.

Locally common summer migrant
MAR–OCT

Breeds on beaches and islands on coast, lakes and rivers inland; migrants widespread

AdBr UPPERWING **contrast** between pale inner and dark outer primaries, least obvious APR–MAY; by JUL/AUG clear **dark streaks** on outer 5–6 primaries, inner ones all-pale

RUMP grey

Juv/1W
UPPERWING blackish shoulder, pale midwing, **grey hindwing band**

Juv

UNDERWING pale/**translucent patch** on inner primaries, outer 5–6 **opaque** with blackish tips forming **broad dark trailing edge**

AdBr

relatively long-necked

RUMP grey

UPPERWING strong dark 'wedge' on outer 5–6 primaries and their coverts

1S/AdNb
[AUG]

1W
JUL–DEC

usually shows prominent black shoulder bar

Juv
JUN–OCT

PRIMARIES innermost contrasting pale

AdBr
MAR–SEP

LEGS relatively long

Arctic Tern *Sterna paradisaea*

L 33–39 cm | **W** 66–77 cm

Very like Common Tern but **legs very short** (and, in flight, all primaries translucent). **AdBr** | upperparts grey, underparts slightly paler grey with contrasting white cheek. **Closed wing uniform grey. Bill deep red. AdNb** | (very rare/absent in Europe) forehead white (from SEP/OCT), underparts white; dark grey shoulder; bill black. **Juv** | back brownish; cap black, forehead buff; shoulder dark grey; bill red at base. By autumn (JUL–SEP), back grey with black/brown scales, forehead white, **bill black. 1S** | indistinguishable from AdNb unless retains darker **Juv** inner forewing and darker grey marks on secondaries (most **1S** birds remain S of Europe).

Roseate Tern *p. 144*
Sandwich Tern *p. 141*
Forster's Tern *p. 553*
Aleutian Tern *p. 552*

V | Calls "*kit*" and sharp chatter; "*ki-eerr*," more ringing than Common Tern, with emphasis on last syllable.

FL | Light, buoyant, 'bouncy'; hover and dive hesitant. Compared with Common Tern, has shorter innerwing, longer, finely tapered outerwing, shorter bill/head/neck (**short** in front of wing); **AdBr** has longer tail; **all primaries translucent**; does not moult wing in autumn and forehead black until SEP/OCT.

Generally scarce, locally common summer migrant
MAR–OCT

Breeds on coastal beaches, rocky islands; migrants widespread on coasts, inland lakes

1S
APR–OCT

RUMP **white**

Juv
UPPERWING dusky shoulder, grey midwing, white trailing edge

Juv

AdBr
UPPERWING pale grey; primaries very pale, darker by AUG/SEP, but no contrast between inner and outer

TAIL forked; outer feathers very long

AdBr

dumpy, thick-necked

RUMP **white**

1S

UPPERWING plain grey

Juv (fresh)
JUN–OCT
[AUG]

BILL base red initially but soon darkens

Juv (faded)
JUN–OCT
[AUG]

PRIMARIES uniform

AdBr
MAR–NOV

LEGS relatively short

143

LC **Roseate Tern** *Sterna dougallii*

LC **L** 33–36 cm | **W** 67–76 cm

Small, very pale tern; upperparts grey, underparts white or pale pink. **AdBr** | body **white, flushed pink without grey** (pink fades, but may persist to OCT). Cap long, black, curves down hindneck. Blackish stripe along closed wingtip. Tail very long. Bill all-black in spring, **black** with dark **red at base** by JUN/JUL, bright red with black tip by AUG. **AdNb** | forehead white after OCT; shoulder dark grey; bill black. **Juv** | upperparts grey, scaled blackish; forehead dark (fades whiter); cap black; bill and legs blackish. **1S** | like **AdNb** but shoulder darker and greater contrast between new (pale grey) inner and worn (dark) outer primaries.

V | Calls include distinct hard "*chewk*," double "*chivik*." At colony, calls rather quick, low and harsh, "*chyow*," or "*kitter-i-tik*."

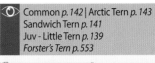

Common *p. 142* | Arctic Tern *p. 143*
Sandwich Tern *p. 141*
Juv - Little Tern *p. 139*
Forster's Tern *p. 553*

Rare and local summer migrant
APR–OCT

Breeds rocky islands; migrants around coasts, rare inland

FL | Quite stiff, quick, shallow beats; often 'flies down' into direct dive without hovering. Rounded head, long bill. **AdBr** noticeably pale; very long tail; blackish outer primaries (like Sandwich and Common, but unlike Arctic Tern). Underwing has dusky streaks but no dark trailing edge; inner primaries translucent. **Juv** dark 'scales' on back, dark streaks on tail; pale midwing/dark hindwing band like juvenile Common Tern but shoulder less black; underwing as **Ad**. By **1W** (SEP), back plainer grey, flight feathers darker and browner.

Juv

AdNb
[SEP]

AdBr

Juv
JUN–OCT
[SEP]

AdBr
[AUG]

AdBr
[JUL]

AdBr
[JUN]

A juvenile, with dark bill and legs and dark bars or crescents above, looks like a small, slim juvenile Sandwich Tern; the forehead is usually grey, unlike juvenile Common and Arctic Terns.

AdBr
MAR–OCT
[JUL]

AdNb
AUG–FEB
[AUG]

AdNb
AUG–FEB
[SEP]

SSP. *dougallii* occurs in Europe.

Caspian Tern

Hydroprogne caspia

L 48–55 cm | **W** 96–111 cm

Huge, pale grey tern (size of large gull); long head/neck/bill, short tail. Bill obviously large close-up. Heavy bodied and **gull-like** on ground; **legs black**. **AdBr**| **cap black**, slightly crested. Bill thick, **dagger-like; red with dark patch near tip. AdNb**| like **AdBr** but cap finely streaked white. **Juv**| brown-black 'V'-shapes on upperparts; cap grey-black, mottled white; bill orange-red with dark tip; back plain grey by **1W**. **1S**| like AdNb but crown streaks whiter.

V| Calls include deep, heron-like, shouted "*kree-ahk.*"

Royal Tern p.554

A juvenile is clearly a very large tern, with a dark-streaked cap above blacker cheek, and a short but heavy, orange-red bill.

Scarce, local summer migrant APR–NOV; very local resident

Breeds on offshore islands; migrants on coasts, rare inland

FL| Pale, with long, **pointed, angled wings** and short tail. **Ad** pale grey; outer primaries blacker by AUG/SEP. **Underwing white with extensive black tip. Juv** back pale grey, mottled brown, rump white, tail dark; innerwing pale with dark hindwing band. **1W** brown shoulder and hindwing band; blackish outer primaries; dark tip to tail. **1S** like **Ad** but darker tips to primary coverts, fresh pale inner primaries and darker old outer ones, and less black beneath wingtip.

AdBr

bill held more or less horizontal in direct flight

1W
AUG–APR

Juv

AdNb
AUG–APR

AdBr
MAR–SEP

Skuas are predatory, gull-like seabirds and frequently steal food from gulls and terns. Away from breeding areas, most likely in spring (Mar-May) and autumn (Aug-Nov), passing headlands or closer inshore in winds; occasional strays storm-blown inland.

5 species [1 vagrant]; four breed (Pomarine Skua only in extreme NE) and are regular migrants on coasts

Gull-like with a sleek but quite heavy body, a hook-tipped bill and short legs. Tail is broad and short; three species have extended central feathers (longest on adults). Adult Arctic and Pomarine Skuas have pale, intermediate and dark forms, which interbreed; most adult Long-tailed Skuas are pale, the dark form being very rare, while Great Skua is dark and more streaked. All are long-distance migrants. **Flight** Direct, effortless and graceful, over sea, coastal islands, moorland and tundra. Skuas chase other birds, forcing them to disgorge food, or kill birds and small mammals to eat; when chasing terns, gulls *etc.*, flight exceptionally aerobatic, with tight twists, easily recognizable at long range. Typically look very dark over the sea, more uniform than immature gulls, with a pale 'flash' of varying extent on the outer primaries. **Sexing, Ageing and Moult** Sexes look alike, but plumages differ seasonally; sub-adult plumages, and non-breeding Long-tailed Skua, are rare or not seen in Europe. Juveniles are different from adults and more difficult to identify. Moult is complex, often incomplete and prolonged, and moult of flight feathers may be 'suspended' for a period, so highly variable patterns of new dark feathers and old ones, bleached much paler, often result. It is usually difficult to assign any immature bird to specific plumage types, and 'Juv', '1W' and '1S' merge together during a long period of wear, bleaching and moult. In the three smaller skuas, adult body moult is partial or incomplete Aug-Nov, complete Feb-Apr; wing moult continues from Aug-Mar and tail feathers may be replaced twice in a year. From spring to autumn in Europe, all are in breeding plumage. Juveniles have a complete or partial body moult Feb-Apr (so may have many juvenile feathers in their first summer) and moult flight feathers from Sep-Mar (but beginning as early as Jul in some Pomarine Skuas, and as late as Feb in Long-tailed Skua). The first complete moult produces 2W plumage. Great Skua adult moults its body Jun-Nov, wings Aug-Mar. Juvenile moults Sep-May, with a restricted head and body moult again from May or Jun.

Identify by size and shape | wing pattern | tail shape

POSSIBLE CONFUSION GROUPS – see *pages 88-89*
Gulls (*pp. 106, 108-133*), although a skua's smooth or barred appearance and lack of a white rump rules out most immature gulls. **Terns** (*pp. 107, 134-145*) are mostly smaller and paler. **Shearwaters** (*pp. 91-95*) have a different flight action, longer, slimmer bill, narrow tail and no white 'flash' on outerwing.

Pomarine Skuas migrating north in spring are often in larger groups (10–20) than Arctic Skuas.

Juv
JUL-OCT
[OCT]

Years 2–(5) Immature moults are often not completed, hence the confusing array of plumages that may be encountered – most immature birds have shorter central tail feathers than adults.

1W–1S
NOV-JUN
[MAY]

2W–2S
JUL-APR
[AUG]

AdBr
APR-JUN
[MAY]

AdNb
JUL-APR
[OCT]

Pomarine Skua ageing sequence, maturing over 3–5 years

Skua forms
(in flight – see also *pp. 148–149*)

Arctic (shown) and Pomarine Skuas have recognizable forms: pale and dark. However, these interbreed freely and produce a more or less continuous gradation between the extremes (hence there are also intermediate birds). Almost all adult Long-tailed Skuas are pale, with dark birds very rare.

PALE FORM

INTERMEDIATE

DARK FORM

Identification of juvenile skuas

Adult skuas in fresh plumage have patterns, tail projections and size differences that easily distinguish them. Juveniles and 1st-winter birds are much harder: although size, shape and actions may make them seem distinctive at a distance, birds seen more closely often provoke controversy. It might seem unlikely that a Pomarine Skua could be confused with a Great Skua, for example, but a very dark bird sitting on a beach can be surprisingly difficult. That in itself might help rule out the smaller Arctic Skua: but flying Arctic/Pomarine Skua juveniles, especially in poor viewing conditions, may often be left unidentified even by experienced observers.

NOTE: Forms cannot be strictly applied to juveniles, as they are variable; 'dark' juveniles may mature to become 'pale form' adults and *vice versa*.

LONG-TAILED SKUA
(p. 151)   bill short, stubby
PALE   DARK

LONG-TAILED SKUA *(p. 151)*
Most are cold, greyish brown; barred under tail; rump pale-barred; belly often whitish; white on just two primary shafts may be visible. **1W** tail spike very short, blunt; pointed by **1S**.

ARCTIC SKUA
(p. 152)   **PALE**   bill slim   **INTERMEDIATE**

ARCTIC SKUA *(p. 152)*
Most are rufous-brown, yellowish or rusty on head/underparts. Head/neck streaked, neck often pale buff. Rump dark; **bars under tail wavy**.

POMARINE SKUA
(p. 153)   bill thick   **GREAT SKUA**
(p. 150)

ochre streaks on neck and wing coverts

POMARINE SKUA *(p. 153)*
Most are dark brown; often with all-brown head and barred underparts, unlike any Arctic Skua. Head/neck may be lightly barred, not streaked, and neck not contrastingly pale. Rump usually paler than nape; **bars above and below tail straight**. Tail rounded, spike absent or very short and blunt.

GREAT SKUA *(p. 150)*
Lacks barring on rump and vent; white primary 'flash' on upperside and larger crescent on underwing. Tail short, square or wedge-shaped or with small blunt central point. Largest, most streaked, but dark individuals much like dark Pomarine Skua.

Adult skuas in flight

LONG-TAILED SKUA
(*p. 151*)

grey

ARCTIC SKUA
(*p. 152*)

brown

POMARINE SKUA
(*p. 153*)

brown

PALE

PALE

PALE

PALE

TAIL SPIKE
very long, flexible

TAIL SPIKE
long, pointed

TAIL SPIKE
'blob-tipped'

pale breast merges
with dark belly

breast-band, plain flank

breast-band,
barred flank

DARK

INTERMEDIATE

DARK

tail short
and blunt

broad-based wings
with white band across
primaries on upperwing,
broader white triangle
or crescent beneath.
Tail short and blunt.

GREAT SKUA
(*p. 150*)

Immature skuas in flight

small primary 'flash'

generally greyer than Arctic Skua

pale-barred rump

white 'flash' on darkest birds

LONG-TAILED SKUA (p. 151)

INTERMEDIATE/DARK

barred

tail rather long and slender, with bunt central projection

PALE/INTERMEDIATE

central tail feathers typically rounded but can be pointed or thin

paler birds: blackish

PALE

ARCTIC SKUA (p. 152)

DARK

short tail point

white 'flash' on upperwing

most are rufous-brown with yellow/rusty-brown head and underparts; palest have paler neck, broad, pale bars under tail and dark rump

may show second crescent but not as strong as on Pomarine

INTERMEDIATE

short, blunt, or no tail point

pale crescent on wing coverts can be striking

whitish primary patch plus second crescent on underwing primary coverts

palest are barred buff across rump and under tail; barred underwing

PALE

PALE

POMARINE SKUA (p. 153)

INTERMEDIATE

resembles dark Pomarine Skua but lacks pale barring on rump and vent

tail short: square or wedge-shaped; central feathers barely protruding

GREAT SKUA (p. 150)

large white wing patches

LC Great Skua *Catharacta skua*

LC **L** 50–58 cm | **W** 125–140 cm

Large, dark, gull-like seabird: biggest and heaviest skua; short-tailed. **Ad** | brown, streaked buff with darker cap; wingtip blacker with prominent **white 'flash'** at base. **Juv / 1W** | like **Ad** but darker; underparts uniform rufous, upperparts more barred.

V | Short barking calls at colony; silent at sea.

FL | At sea flies low, direct with steady wingbeats, but may rise much higher, particularly when chasing prey and on migration. Dark brown; looks heavy-bodied and short-tailed, with broad-based wings. Prominent **white crescent** or triangle (smaller on **Juv**) across base of primaries on both upperwing and underwing, widest on outer edge. Fast, twisting pursuit of birds as large as Gannet (*p. 90*); may dive on prey and kill it with bill. Aggressive to people when breeding, approaching at chest height and swooping overhead.

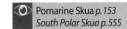

Pomarine Skua *p. 153*
South Polar Skua *p. 555*

Generally scarce, locally common; migratory

Breeds on northern islands; migrants around coasts, rare inland

Ad

A dramatic pose with raised wings is adopted by displaying birds, and often when defending floating food or a 'kill'.

NOTE: 1S moults inner primaries from MAY, much earlier than Ad (from AUG).

Ad

Ad

Juv
JUL–NOV

Ad
ALL YEAR

Long-tailed Skua
Stercorarius longicaudus

L 35–43 cm (plus up to 15 cm tail spike) **W** 102–117 cm

Slender seabird (about size of Kittiwake (*p. 114*)); deep-chested.
Ad PALE FORM pale grey-brown with **white breast**, greyish belly
and **dark grey under tail**. DARK FORM very rare: all black-brown,
except two white primary shafts. **Tail spike very long and slender**
(missing for short time between SEP–JAN). **Juv / 1Y** ranges from
greyish-brown with buff head and paler belly, to darker brown with
paler nape, and all-dark brown with blackish face; all have fine buff
edges to feathers on upperparts, giving 'scaly' effect, and black and
whitish bars under tail. **2Y** gains Ad plumage, but tail spike short.

V High-pitched squealing notes around colony.

FL Tern-like, but direct over sea. **Deep-chested** (Arctic Skua deeper
at belly). **Ad** tail spike very long, flexible. PALE FORM greyish with blacker
trailing edge on upperwing; two white shaft streaks on outerwing. No
breast-band. Underwing all-dark. Very rare DARK FORM all-brown with
white shafts to outermost two primaries. **Juv / 1Y** tail usually has short,
rounded central spike, easily broken or worn to a point.

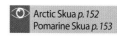

Arctic Skua *p. 152*
Pomarine Skua *p. 153*

Scarce, local
summer migrant
MAR–NOV; rare on
passage

Breeds on Arctic
tundra; migrants
around coasts,
rare inland

Juv
JUL–OCT

Juveniles may be pale or dark, typically
cold grey-brown and rarely rufous. Bill
short; looks dark with little contrast.

SSP. *longicaudus* occurs in Europe
(SSP. *pallescens* (possible vagrant from
N America, Greenland) paler.)

Juv

AdBr
(PALE)

AdBr
(DARK)

1S (1Y)
APR–SEP

AdBr
(PALE)

All SSP. *longicaudus*

very long, flexible tail
spike, longest in ♀ (short or
missing during SEP–JAN)

AdBr
MAR–OCT

LC Arctic Skua
LC *Stercorarius parasiticus*

L 38–41 cm (plus up to 7 cm tail spike)
W 107–125 cm

Elegant, tapered; slimmer than similar Pomarine Skua. Has pale, intermediate and dark forms in all plumages.
Ad | PALE FORM **plain brown** above; underparts white or yellowish with grey-brown breast-band or side to breast (less mottled than Pomarine Skua); flank unmarked. DARK FORM uniform brown. **Tail spike thin, pointed** (missing for short time between SEP–JAN). **Juv / 1Y** | typically yellowish- or rufous-brown, finely barred; primary tips **pale**. Some birds are uniformly black. **2Y** | gains **Ad** plumage but tail spike short.

Pomarine Skua
Long-tailed Skua p. 151
Sooty Shearwater p. 91

FL | Relaxed, direct; supple action. Slim, deepest at belly (Pomarine Skua heavy-bodied; Long-tailed Skua deep-chested). **Ad** tail narrow with long, pointed spike. PALE FORM upperparts brown, black cap; underparts white/yellowish, pale or dark greyish breast-band; flank unmarked; DARK FORM all-brown. Thin white outerwing 'flash', broader on underside. **Juv / 1Y** tail has short, pointed central spike.

Scarce, local summer/ passage migrant
MAR–NOV

Breeds on tundra, islands, remote moors; migrants around coasts, scarce inland

V | In diving display flights, calls loud, nasal, mewing "*waaa-ooh*" or "*mee-ah!*"

AdBr
(INTERMEDIATE)

Juv
(INTERMEDIATE)
JUL–NOV

thin, pointed tail spike (short or missing SEP–JAN)

Juv
(INTERMEDIATE)

AdBr
(PALE)

Juveniles may be dull brown or yellowish but most are tinged rufous. Bill slim; about two-thirds grey with a dull black tip.

AdBr (DARK)
MAR–OCT

AdBr (INTERMEDIATE)
MAR–OCT

Mixed pairs are frequent and, as a result, gradations between the forms may be seen at any age.

AdBr (PALE)
MAR–OCT

Pomarine Skua
Stercorarius pomarinus

L 38–57 cm (plus up to 10 cm tail spike)
W 110–138 cm

Heavy-bodied, bulkier than similar Arctic Skua. Has pale, intermediate and dark forms in all plumages. **Ad** | **PALE FORM** upperparts dark grey-brown, underparts yellowish, with patchy brownish breast-band and flank; **DARK FORM** uniform brown to blackish. **Tail spike broad**, blunt-tipped or twisted (may break off, and missing for short time between SEP–JAN). **Juv** / **1Y** | ranges from brown to black, but typically darker than Arctic Skua; primary tips **dark. 2Y** / **3Y** | gain **Ad** plumage, with pale, bleached old feathers and dark new ones in wing; tail spike short.

👁 Arctic Skua
Long-tailed Skua *p. 151*
Great Skua *p. 150*

FL | Large, heavy-bodied, broad-winged and 'muscular' (Arctic and Long-tailed Skuas more lightly built). **Ad** long, 'blob-tipped' tail spike (shorter in autumn/winter). **PALE FORM** upperparts brown, black cap; underparts yellowish, brown breast-band and flank; **DARK FORM** all-brown. Narrow white outerwing 'flash', broader crescent on underside. **Juv** / **1Y** tail square or with short, blunt central spike.

Scarce, local migrant
MAR–NOV, rare DEC–FEB

Breeds on exposed tundra; migrants around coasts, rare inland

V | Short, harsh notes near nest; may call *"wich-yew"* at sea.

Juv
(INTERMEDIATE)
JUL–NOV

Most juveniles are dark/mid-brown, less often pale-headed or very dark. Bill thick; mostly pale grey with a contrasted black tip. Heavy body, thick legs characteristic.

AdBr
(DARK)

Juv
(DARK)

AdBr
(PALE)

AdBr
(DARK)
MAR–OCT

broad tail spike (often bitten off or broken from JUN, and short or missing in moult SEP–JAN)

AdBr
(PALE)
MAR–OCT

Waders

Waders, with few exceptions, feed on or near the water's edge. Some are smaller than a sparrow (*p. 504*), the biggest larger than a crow (*p. 471*). They are long-legged, but their bills vary from short to very long, and can be straight, upswept or downcurved. Other species wade, but most birds walking in shallow water, on mud or at the water's edge, probing or picking food from the surface, will be waders.

89 species [39 rare migrants or vagrants + 2 possibly now extinct]:
1 avocet; **1 stilt**; **1 oystercatcher**; **1 stone-curlew**; **1 courser**;
3 pratincoles [1 vagrant]; **3 phalaropes** [1 vagrant];
23 plovers and lapwings [11 vagrants]; **3 godwits** [1 vagrant];
4 curlews [1 vagrant, 1 possibly extinct];
8 snipes and woodcocks [3 vagrants]; **39 sandpipers** [21 vagrants];
1 buttonquail [possibly extinct] (included with Galliforms (*p. 223*)).

Waders **walk** or run: they do not hop. Some breed on fields, moorland or northern tundra, but spend most of the year on estuaries, or on rocky, sandy or shingle beaches. A few use all of these habitats, and also feed beside fresh water inland. At the coast, waders spread out as the tide recedes and roost together at high tide. Most are sociable, others are not: a large flock of waders might include several species. Some defend breeding territories, but flock once the breeding season is over; a few defend feeding territories in winter but roost together at high tide. Most waders are long-distance migrants but some are resident in parts of Europe, joined by summer visitors, winter visitors and passage migrants of the same species, as different populations move through at various times. Arctic breeding areas are inhabitable only for a short time in summer, so winter visitors linger until May, when spring migrants, having wintered farther south, move quickly northwards. In autumn, adults move south in Jul/Aug, juveniles often later in Aug/Sep. Lapwings form 'autumn' flocks, after breeding, as early as June.

Ageing and moult

Adults usually have a complete moult after breeding (August–November) and moult head and body feathers again in late winter (January–April). Juveniles moult head and body feathers soon after fledging (September–November) and some do so again the following spring. The complete moult begins with the rapid replacement of five or six inner primaries; the coverts, secondaries, tail and body feathers follow as the outer primaries are replaced. Some northern breeders start their moult in the Arctic, suspend it when on migration, then complete it in their wintering grounds. Many species have distinctive breeding and non-breeding plumages (with patchy intermediate stages), plus a distinct juvenile plumage; only a few have obvious differences between male and female.

Wader ageing and moult
Some waders have a range of plumages; others look the same year-round.

SANDERLING
Juv
JUL–OCT

moult as adult from **MAY**

1W (AdNb similar)
OCT–FEB

AdBr
FEB–MAY

Pale feather edges wear off to reveal full colours.

AdBr
JUN–JUL

AdBr→AdNb
AUG–SEP

Waders vary in size from the sparrow-sized stints to the Curlew, which is as large as a medium-sized gull.

CURLEW

BAR-TAILED GODWIT

KNOT

SANDERLING

REDSHANK

DUNLIN

LITTLE STINT

Bill length and shape
Focus on the relative length and
overall shape of the bill

SHORT, STOUT, POINTED
**Plovers,
Turnstones**

GOLDEN PLOVER

LONG, SLIGHTLY DOWNCURVED
Sandpipers

CURLEW
SANDPIPER

LONG, SLIM, SLIGHTLY UPCURVED
**Godwits,
sandpipers**

GREENSHANK

LONG, STRAIGHT, TAPERED
**Godwits, larger
sandpipers, 'shanks',
phalaropes, snipes,
woodcocks**

REDSHANK

LONG, EVENLY DOWNCURVED
Curlews

CURLEW

Patterns in flight
e.g. wings plain or with white
wingbar; rump white/dark or dark
with white sides

rump and tail
pattern

presence or
absence of
wingbar

SANDERLING

The 'types' of wader

Waders include groups of closely similar, related species and some that are unlike any others in Europe. The family groups, or 'types', into which waders are divided in this book are shown below. Most waders can usually be assigned to a distinctive species, or at least to one of these groups, within which some are difficult to identify. Differences due to age and season must be appreciated for correct identifications.

AVOCETS (*p. 158*) Mostly white; feeds in shallow water.

STILTS (*p. 159*) Extremely long legs; feeds in shallow water.

OYSTERCATCHERS (*p. 158*) Bright orange bill; feed on mud, rocks or pastures.

STONE-CURLEWS (*p. 160*) Cryptic, brown; on dry ground.

COURSERS (*p. 160*) Small, upright, short-billed; on arid ground.

PRATINCOLES (*pp. 156–157*) Short-billed, long-winged; feed in the air.

PHALAROPES (*pp. 173, 196–197, 555*) Habitually swim; live at sea in winter.

LAPWINGS (*pp. 162–165, 556*) Short-billed; on dry ground; tilting feeding action.

PLOVERS (*pp. 162, 166–171, 556–559*) Short-billed; run-stop-tilt feeding action.

CURLEWS (*pp. 172, 182–183, 561*) Large; bill downcurved; from dry ground to coastal mud.

GODWITS (*pp. 172, 180–181, 564*) Medium-large; long-billed, long-legged.

SNIPE & **WOODCOCKS** (*pp. 173, 194–195, 568*) Cryptic, brown; in wet, boggy or wooded areas.

SANDPIPERS (*pp. 172–179, 184–192, 561–568*), most of which fall into sub-groups: **'shanks'**, medium-sized with long, distinctively coloured legs and a long bill; smaller, less social **larger sandpipers** that bob their head and longish tail as they walk; and a large and varied group of **small sandpipers**, including stints, which are relatively short-legged, mostly social and highly migratory, but which occupy a variety of inland and coastal habitats.

Pratincoles rest on open ground (looking rounded, or more elongated if alert) and feed in the air. All are short-billed, with brown upperparts and pale underparts with a white belly. **AdBr** throat buff, outlined in black. **AdNb** usually lose the black and buff. **Juv** have a complete autumn moult from AUG, so **1W** often inseparable from AdNb except by browner bill-base.

FL Buoyant and swooping or erratic action; sleek shape with flat head held up; wings long and tapered; tail forked; rump white.

  Black-winged, Collared, and Oriental Pratincoles are all similar

underwing black

underwing rusty-red

underwing rusty-red

no white trailing edge

white trailing edge

no white trailing edge

ORIENTAL PRATINCOLE

BLACK-WINGED PRATINCOLE

short tail

AdB
MAR-S

long tail

AdBr
MAR-SEP

long tail (unless moulting)

AdBr
MAR-SEP

upperwing little contrast

upperwing contrasted

upperwing little contrast

COLLARED PRATINCOLE

NT VU # Black-winged Pratincole   *Glareola nordmanni*

L 24–28 cm | **W** 60–70 cm

Relatively dark pratincole; tail **falls short** of closed wingtip; nostril a long oval. **Ad** bill has **small** red patch at base. **Juv** back shows dark spots and pale scaly fringes. **1W** like AdNb but bill base browner.

FL Upperwing dark, with little contrast and no white trailing edge. Underwing **all blackish**, contrasting with white body.

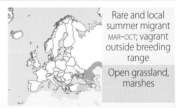

Rare and local summer migrant MAR–OCT; vagrant outside breeding range

Open grassland, marshes

V Dry, hard "*ketek*" or "*kit-i-kit*."

LONG OVAL

AdBr
MAR-AUG

1W
SEP-FEB

Collared Pratincole *Glareola pratincola*

L 24–28 cm | **W** 60–70 cm

Pale pratincole, tends to have horizontal stance; tail **extends beyond** closed wingtip (may be shorter in moult, like Oriental Pratincole); nostril a narrow slit. **Ad** | bill has **large** red patch at base. **Juv** | back heavily barred black and cream; breast spotted. **1W** | some moult early, with black-edged buff bib appearing from OCT.

FL | Upperwing brown with **blacker outer half; dark secondaries** (on Ad outermost few often **paler**) with **whitish trailing edge** (may wear away MAR-JUL). Underwing dark, with white trailing edge, but **rusty-red** inner half shows in good light. Outer tail feather clearly elongated, with extensive dark tip.

Scarce summer migrant MAR–OCT; vagrant outside breeding range

Open grassland, pastures, drier marshes

SSP. *pratincola* occurs in Europe.

V | Loud, tern-like "*kit-ik*" and longer chattering calls.

SLIT

inner primaries paler on inner webs

AdNb
AUG-MAR

AdBr
MAR-AUG

Juv
JUN-OCT

Oriental Pratincole
Glareola maldivarum

L 23–27 cm | **W** 55–65 cm

Much like Collared Pratincole, but tends to be more upright and rear part of body less elongated; tail **usually does not reach** closed wingtip; nostril oval. **AdBr** | bill has red patch at base (overlaps with Collared Pratincole). **AdNb** | bill **all-black** on some; may retain thick black surround to streaky bib; lower breast often **orange-buff**.

FL | Upperwing has **little contrast**; underwing red but **no white trailing edge** (worn Collared Pratincole (MAR-JUL) may have white reduced or absent). Outer tail feather not elongated, has restricted dark tip.

Vagrant from Asia
Open ground

OVAL

inner primaries uniform

wingtip tip of tail

AdBr
MAR-AUG

157

NT | VU | **Oystercatcher** *Haematopus ostralegus*

L 39–44 cm | **W** 72–83 cm

Large, bulky, **black-and-white** wader with strident calls. Classic sight and sound of estuaries, sandy or shingle beaches, upland fields; often in flocks (up to 1,000+) on coast. **AdBr** | **bill orange**; legs pale pink. **AdNb / 1W** | like AdBr but has a white frontal collar, browner back and darker tip to bill. **Juv** | feathers on 'dark' areas dull brownish; legs grey.

V | Shrill, piping, penetrating *"peep," "k-peep," "kip-kip-kip"* and fast, bubbling, ecstatic piping from small groups with open bills pointing down.

Two sspp. occur: ***ostralegus*** (widespread) and ***longipes*** (Russia), which has browner back and longer nasal groove.

FL | White 'V' rump and long, broad white wingbars create 'dazzle' effect in flock.

1Y / 2Y dull; hard to age as timing of moult varies with location; colour of bill / legs varies with quality of food.

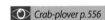
1W
SEP–MAR

AdNb has white collar (like 1W)
SEP–MAR

Locally common migrant/resident

Breeds coastal fields, dunes, beaches, islands, some on inland pastures; winters on coasts

AdBr
DEC–SEP

LC | LC | **Avocet** *Recurvirostra avosetta*

L 42–46 cm | **W** 67–77 cm

⊙ Crab-plover p. 556

Large, white-and-black wader; elegant but quite heavy-bodied. **Bill upcurved**, distinctive at close range, but 'white' bird can be overlooked at a distance among gulls. Feeds in shallow water with regular sideswipes of bill; swims with tail uptilted. Winter flocks up to 500. **Ad** | bright white; curved **black bands** on closed wing; cap and hindneck black. Legs long, grey; bill black. **Juv** | crown pale brown; upper back mottled brown; wingtip dark brown. **1W** | like **Ad** but crown dark brown. **1S** | like **Ad** but flight feathers dull and worn.

V | Calls ringing, piping *"klute"* or *"krup krup krup."*

FL | Quick, stiff, flickery wingbeats. Strikingly white with black wingtip and innerwing band.

Juv
JUN–SEP

Juveniles' black-and-white pattern is blurred by brown.

Ad
ALL YEAR

Chick

Generally scarce, locally common migrant/resident

Breeds on coastal saline lagoons, muddy lakes; winters, on estuaries, coastal pools

OYSTERCATCHER

AdBr

AVOCET

1S
APR–OCT

BLACK-WINGED STILT

Black-winged Stilt
Himantopus himantopus

L 33–36 cm | **W** 60 cm

Elegant shallow-water wader with long wing, slender body, needle-like bill and very long legs. ♂ | back black, glossed green; underparts white; head may be white, dusky black or grey. Legs pink-red. ♀ | as ♂ but back browner. **Juv** | dull; head and neck washed brownish; back brown; legs yellowish-ochre to pink.

V | Loud, frenetic, tern-like "*kyik kyik kyik*" near nest; migrants usually silent.

FL | Underwing black; long white 'wedge' up back. Legs trail far beyond tail (feet often crossed). **Juv** pale trailing edge to wing.

Generally scarce, locally common migrant/resident

Breeds on coastal saline lagoons, muddy lakes; winters, on estuaries, coastal pools

Juv → 1W
JUN–SEP
[AUG]

Juveniles have dull legs and less contrasting plumage than adults but still unlike any other wader.

♂ and ♀ head patterns vary: ♂ more extreme (blackest, whitest), ♀ duskier, but ♀ head darker than ♂ in many pairs.

♀
ALL YEAR

♂
ALL YEAR

SSP. *himantopus* occurs in Europe.

LC Stone-curlew
LC *Burhinus oedicnemus*

L 38–45 cm | **W** 76–88 cm

Large, long-tailed, dry-ground wader, with creeping, hesitant walk or run between long, upright pauses. Secretive, but noisy at dusk. Forms loose flocks before autumn migration. Often squats with lower part of leg flat on ground. **Ad** | streaked brown; wing has **dark-edged white band**. White forehead and yellow bill base create **pale face**, more striking than yellow eye at distance; legs yellow. **Juv** | as **Ad** but weaker dark edge to duller band across wing.

V | Calls at dusk: loud, Oystercatcher-like (*p. 158*) pipes and sharp "*ki-vi-vi*," and Curlew-like (*p. 183*) whistles.

Scarce summer migrant/resident	
Sandy/shingly open ground on farmland, heaths, coasts	

Four sspp. occur with minor differences in size and colour but much variability.

FL | Strong and direct on stiff, bowed wings. Upperwing mostly blackish with white bands and spots; underwing white.

♂Ad

ssp. *saharae* (Mediterranea islands)

Ad broad white band on wing edged black on ♂, lower edge browner on ♀; on **Juv**, broad buff/white band without black.

♂Ad
ALL YEAR

ssp. *insularum* (E Canary Islands)

LC Cream-coloured Courser
NT *Cursorius cursor*

L 24–27 cm | **W** 51–57 cm

Small, oval, upright bird with plover-like run-and-stop action on ground. **Plain sandy-buff**. Bill black, short, faintly downcurved; legs long, whitish. **Ad** | **black and white stripes** behind eye, dark patch at rear of grey crown. **Juv** | back faintly barred, head stripes dull.

V | Quiet, nasal "*whit*" or "*croo, whet whet*."

Rare resident (Canary Islands); rare and local summer migrant (Turkey)	
Semi-arid open ground	

Two similar sspp. occur: *cursor* (Canary Is.) reddish; *bogolubovi* (Turkey) yellowish.

FL | Back and innerwing pale, outerwing black; underwing black.

All ssp. *cursor*

Ad

Ad
ALL YEAR

Juv → 1W
AUG–MAR

Turnstone *Arenaria interpres*

L 21–24 cm | **W** 43–49 cm

Small, stocky wader; dark with **white belly**, **black breast-band**; short **orange legs**. Bill thick, tapers to a point. Busy but inconspicuous on weed/rocks/strandline, often with other waders, probing under stones and weed. Plumage pattern constant, but seasonal changes marked. **AdBr** | head black-and-white, back bright **rusty-orange and black**. **AdNb** | head dark; **back dark brown**. **Juv** | cheek pale; back dark with neat 'V'-shaped buff feather edges. **1W** | like **AdNb** but wing feathers edged paler.

V | Calls short, fast, low-pitched, or strung into quick chattering trills if flushed, "*kew*" or "*tuk-a-tuk*;" song a longer repetition of similar notes.

Locally common migrant/resident

Breeds tundra, northern islands; widespread on coasts in winter, scarce inland

SSP. *interpres* occurs in Europe.

FL | **White patches** on back and shoulder; white wingbar and tail base conspicuous against dark background.

AdNb

Juv
AUG–SEP

♂Br

♂**Br** head more black-and-white, chestnut on back less streaked, than ♀**Br**, but unreliable unless pair seen together.

♂Br
APR–SEP

♀Br
APR–SEP

AdNb
SEP–MAY

1W
JUL–MAY

Lapwings and regularly occurring plovers in flight

LAPWING
(p. 163)

AdNb

AdBr

WHITE-TAILED LAPWING
(p. 164)

AdBr

AdBr

SOCIABLE LAPWING
(p. 164)

AdBr

1W

COLLARED PRATINCOLE
(p. 157)

SPUR-WINGED LAPWING
(p. 165)

RED-WATTLED LAPWING
(p. 165)

Ad

KENTISH PLOVER
(p. 170)

LITTLE RINGED PLOVER
(p. 170)

♂Br

♂Br

Juv

RINGED PLOVER
(p. 170)

♂Br

GREY PLOVER
(p. 166)

Juv

Juv

AdBr

Juv

Juv

GOLDEN PLOVER
(p. 168)

DOTTEREL
(p. 167)

Juv

Juv

AdNb/1W

GREATER SANDPLOVER
(p. 558)

Juv

CASPIAN PLOVER
(p. 559)

Juv

DUNLIN
(p. 188)

(Northern) **Lapwing**
Vanellus vanellus

L 28–31 cm | **W** 82–87 cm

Large, eye-catching, social wader; feeds
mostly on drier ground; black-and-white
at distance, rich colours at close range.
Ad | back **rich green**; crown black with
long, **upswept, wispy crest**. Breast black,
underparts white. Closed wing **glossed
emerald, purple and bronze; undertail
orange**; legs pink-red. **♂ Br** | black
throat and extensive black marks, with
contrasting white face. **♀ Br** | less
extensive black marks and duller face
than ♂. **AdNb / 1W** | throat pale; back
has rusty-buff feather edges. **Juv** | crest
short; back has broad buff bars.

V | Calls creaky, nasal *"pee-wit," "wheet"*
and emphatic, shrill *"pwee-y-weet."* Song
wheezy, rasping in tumbling flight, with
ripping, throbbing wing noise.

Flocks in flight have a flickering black-
and-white effect.

Locally common
migrant/resident

Breeds moors,
marshes, lakesides,
pastures; winters on
drier fields, saltmarshes

FL | Flocks (JUN onwards) in lines, or
irregular masses, often 'thickest in the
middle', trailing behind. Slower flight
than other waders, gulls, pigeons.
Broadly rounded wing, **black outer half**,
black-and-white beneath.

♂ white band near tip of
outer three primaries broad,
well-defined; on ♀ white
narrower, blends into black

aerobatic
display flight

♂ Br

♂ Br

♀ Br
FEB–AUG

Crest lengths of
the sexes overlap,
but 2× head length
suggests ♂.

♂ Br
FEB–AUG

Juv
APR–SEP

AdNb / 1W
JUN–MAR

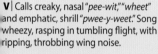

CR Sociable Lapwing *Vanellus gregarius*

CR L 27–30 cm | W 65–70 cm

Medium-sized lapwing with bold head and wing patterns; **long black legs**. **AdBr** | pale grey; cap and eyestripe black, long **white stripe over eye**; **belly black** and dark red; bill black. **AdNb** | dull brownish-grey, belly white; head pattern similar to **AdBr** but cap dark brown and eyestripe indistinct. **Juv / 1W** | sandy-brown with pale fringes; head pattern as **AdNb** but stripe over eye buff.

V | Chattering "*kretch-ech-ech.*"

 Dotterel *p. 167*

Rare and local passage migrant, formerly bred; vagrant elsewhere
Marshes, pastures

FL | Black outerwing; broad white hindwing; black band on white tail.

AdBr

AdBr
MAR–AUG

AdNb / 1W
JUN–MAR

Migrants often join flocks of Lapwings (*p. 163*).

LC White-tailed Lapwing *Vanellus leucurus*

LC L 26–29 cm | W 75–85 cm

Unmistakable: tall, upstanding, medium-sized lapwing. Body purplish-brown; **legs long, slender, yellow**; head **plain, rounded**; bill slim, black. **AdBr** | head pale buff; breast purplish-grey (often darkest on ♂); belly pink-buff. **AdNb** | head brown; breast pale greyish. **Juv** | back sandy-buff with black spots.

V | Short, nasal "*ki-ri-yah*" notes in rhythmic sequence.

 Grey-headed Lapwing *p. 556*

Rare and local summer migrant MAR–OCT; very rare and local resident
Watersides

FL | Black outerwing, **broad white midwing band; rump and tail pure white**. Long yellow legs trail.

AdBr

AdBr
FEB–SEP

AdNb
SEP–MAR

Juv
MAY–AUG

Newly fledged juveniles, like other waders, have a slightly untidy, clumsy appearance.

Spur-winged Lapwing *Vanellus spinosus*

L 25–28 cm | **W** 69–81 cm

Striking and unmistakable medium-sized lapwing, found on dry land or waterside habitats. **Ad** | back and wing uniform pale brown; **crown black**, **side of head and neck white**; throat and **underparts black**. Bill and legs black. **Juv** | resembles **Ad** but crown and back barred buff and brown.

V | Strident, piercing *"pik pik pik pik."*

FL | Innerwing brown, outerwing/hindwing black, separated by **broad white band**.

Ad

Ad
ALL YEAR

Juv
MAY–OCT

Narrow pale fringes quickly wear off juvenile's upperpart feathers.

Rare and local summer migrant MAR–OCT

Sandy riversides, lagoons

Red-wattled Lapwing *Vanellus indicus*

L 32–35 cm | **W** 80–85 cm

Large, slender, long-tailed lapwing; head black, white and red; breast black; underparts white; legs long, yellow. **Ad** | bill red with black tip; **facial stripe and eyering red**. **Juv** | similar pattern to **Ad** but throat white; crown and back feathers have pale fringes.

V | Strident *"cree"* and *"cree-crik-ki-ik-ik."*

SSP. *aigneri* occurs in Europe.

FL | Forewing brown, hindwing/wingtip black, narrow white midwing stripe.

Ad

Ad
ALL YEAR

Juv
MAY–AUG

Rare and local resident

Marshes and coasts

Juvenile is an easily recognizable, slightly duller version of the adult.

LC **Grey Plover** *Pluvialis squatarola*

LC **L** 26–29 cm | **W** 56–63 cm

Thickset, dumpy plover with a relatively **thick bill**. Easily overlooked on mudflats but rounded shape with short bill distinctive. Run-stop-tilt feeding action (slower than Golden Plover). Widely scattered when feeding, tight flocks at roost. **AdBr** | mottled black and grey on back and wing; **white patch on side of breast**; **face and belly solid black** (lacks white flank stripe of Golden Plover). During spring and autumn moult, patchy black-and-white. **AdNb** | dull, mottled grey, underparts whiter (looks dark in dull light, pale close-up). **Juv / 1W** | brownish-grey; back with yellow-buff spots.

V | Relaxed, plaintive, trisyllabic whistle with downslur in middle, "*tee-yoo-eee;*" a frequent estuary sound, also regularly at night. Song a low "*tsee-lu-ee.*"

Ssp. *squatarola* occurs in Europe.

👁 Golden plovers *pp. 168–169*

Note slightly smaller than accompanying Bar-tailed Godwit; the most boldly patterned birds are probably males.

Locally frequent (scarce and local breeder); migratory

Breeds Arctic tundra; winters on muddy estuaries, scarcer on open coasts, rare inland

FL | In all plumages, white wingbar and **white rump**; unique **black 'wingpit'**

black 'wingpit' diagnostic

Juv
JUN–OCT

AdBr
MAR–SEP

1W
SEP–APR

AdBr → AdNb
AUG–OCT
[OCT]

AdNb
SEP–MAR

Dotterel *Eudromias morinellus*

L 20·5–24 cm | **W** 57–64 cm

Small plover with bold colours in breeding plumage. Upright, long-legged, slender when alert, rounded when relaxed; often confiding. **AdBr** | sandy-greyish, pale at distance; ♀ darker than ♂. White band below black cap forms **striking white 'V'** from rear. Narrow white breast-band, rusty underparts and **black belly**, most prominent on ♀. Legs greenish-yellow, often 'lost' against background or in long grass/crops. **Juv** | pale grey-brown, with buff scales on back; **whitish stripe over eye**; pale breast-band weak but distinctive.

V | Purring *"pyurr"* and sharp *"pwit"* repeated as song.

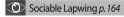

◑ Sociable Lapwing *p. 164*

Spring migrants (mixed males and females above) settle in lowland fields, as well as on high hills: their black bellies standing out against short crops or ploughed earth.

Scarce and local summer migrant APR–OCT, local in winter

Breeds on hills and high stony plateaux; spring migrants on hills and inland cereal fields, autumn migrants near coast

FL | Upperwing plain, no wingbar, underwing whiter.

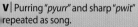

Juv

AdBr

Juv
JUN–NOV

♀ Br
APR–AUG

♂ Br
APR–AUG

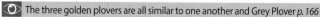 The three golden plovers are all similar to one another and Grey Plover *p. 166*

LC (Eurasian) **Golden Plover** *Pluvialis apricaria*
LC | **L** 25–28 cm | **W** 53–59 cm

Round-bodied, short-billed plover of dry ground. Often with Lapwings (*p. 163*) on pastures and cereal fields. Small head and relatively thin bill (compared with Grey Plover). **AdBr** | back spangled yellow, cream and black; **face and belly black**. N European breeders have **wide black band on neck, broadly edged white**. British/Irish breeders, black on foreneck narrow, mottled white. **AdNb** | yellowish; back spotted yellow on grey; breast softly streaked. **White belly** conspicuous in upright stance. **Juv** | back spotted yellow on black, breast softly barred grey. **1W** | like AdNb but pale spots bleached to off-white, yellow on new feathers.

V | Call loud, piping, mournful whistle, "*peeuw*." Rhythmic song given in flight over moors, repeated "*poo-peeee-oo*."

Locally common, migratory

Breeds tundra, moors, upland pastures; winters salt-marshes, scarce on open coasts, also pastures/arable fields inland

FL | **White underwing** and belly (show as bird settles or stretches wings); feet do not project beyond tail; **rump and tail dark**; upperwing has whitish wingbar. Large flocks form long, wavering, fast-moving lines.

Juv

AdBr

♀ Br
(SOUTHERN)
FEB–AUG

Can start to moult as early as MAY.

♀ Br
(NORTHERN)
or ♂ Br
(SOUTHERN)
FEB–AUG

♂ Br
(NORTHERN)
FEB–AUG

AdNb
MAY–MAR

Juv
JUN–DEC

Many are like **AdNb** by OCT.

Annual vagrant from N America

Pastures, lakesides

American Golden Plover *Pluvialis dominica*

L 24–27 cm | **W** 55–60 cm

Slim, long-legged 'golden' plover. **Wingtip projects well beyond tail** (approximately equal on Golden Plover); tertial tips short of tail tip. **AdBr** | upper-parts dark, **little yellow**; white around black face, but **little or no white on flank. AdNb / Juv / 1W** | greyish; dark cap; broad **whitish stripe over eye**; dark smudge between eye and bill.

V | Double "*clu-eet.*"

FL | Underwing dusky grey; feet project beyond tail.

Annual vagrant from Asia

Pastures, lakesides

LC Pacific Golden Plover *Pluvialis fulva*

L 21–25 cm | **W** 50–55 cm

Smallest, roundest of the three 'golden' plovers; long-legged. Wingtip projects slightly beyond tail; **tertial tips close to tail tip** (fall short on the other 'golden' plovers). **AdBr** | upperparts spangled yellow, cream and black; **mottled white line along flank. AdNb / Juv / 1W** | yellowish; dark cap, narrow yellowish stripe over eye.

V | Definite "*tchoo-it.*"

FL | Underwing dusky grey; feet project beyond tail.

ALL HAVE DARK RUMP AND TAIL

AMERICAN GOLDEN PLOVER

underwing dusky

feet project

1W

underwing white

feet do not project

GOLDEN PLOVER

Juv

PACIFIC GOLDEN PLOVER

underwing dusky

feet project

AdNb

AMERICAN GOLDEN PLOVER

AdBr FEB-AUG

GOLDEN PLOVER

♂Br (NORTHERN)

PACIFIC GOLDEN PLOVER

AdBr FEB-AUG

wingtip **well beyond** tail

tertial tips **short** of tail tip

wingtip slightly beyond tail

tertial tips **short** of tail tip

wingtip slightly beyond tail

tertial tips **close** to tail tip

AMERICAN GOLDEN PLOVER

1W OCT-MAY

1W / AdNb OCT-MAY

PACIFIC GOLDEN PLOVER

LC **Kentish Plover**
LC *Charadrius alexandrinus*

L 15–17 cm | **W** 31–32 cm

Small, pale 'ringed' plover. **Breast-band always incomplete; bill black; legs grey to black.** Usually small flocks, 1–5. ♂**Br** | **cap rufous** with **black frontal band**; forehead and stripe over eye white; **black patch on side of breast.** ♂**Nb** | loses rufous, black patches becoming brown with black flecks. ♀/**1W** | forehead and breast patches **brown**; cinnamon on crown, cheek and breast patch quickly wears off. **Juv** | back scaly, breast patches diffuse; legs greyish or dark ochre.

SSP. *alexandrinus* occurs in Europe.

Kittlitz's Plover p. 557

cinnamon fringes to feathers after autumn moult

♀
ALL YEAR

bill
blac

Breeding plumage may be attained by JAN, lost by JUN.

♂**Br**
JAN–SEP

LC **Little Ringed Plover**
LC *Charadrius dubius*

L 15·5–18 cm | **W** 32–35 cm

Small, freshwater 'ringed' plover with black breast-band. Bill small, dark; legs pinkish. **Yellow eyering.** Usually small flocks, 1–5. **AdBr** | cap brown with **white line** above black frontal band. Breast-band broad, black on ♂, narrower, smudged brown, on ♀. **AdNb/1W/Juv** | head brownish, buff over eye. Weak pale eyering. Breast-band brown, broken in front. Legs dull yellow-ochre.

SSP. *curonicus* occurs in Europe.

bill has sma
pale patch
at base

♂**Br**
FEB–OCT

♀**Br**
FEB–OCT

LC (Common) **Ringed Plover**
LC *Charadrius hiaticula*

L 17–19·5 cm | **W** 35–41 cm

Commonest 'ringed' plover with black breast-band, especially on coasts; typical run-stop-tilt action. **Bill orange** with black tip; **legs orange.** Usually larger flocks, up to 500. **AdBr** | cap brown with black frontal band but no white 'dividing' line. Breast-band black (widest on ♂). **AdNb/1W** | cheek and breast-band browner. **Juv** | white forehead joins **white band over eye**; breast-band brown. Bill dark; legs yellowish.

Three similar sspp. occur: *hiaticula* (widespread); *psammodromus* (Iceland); *tundrae* (Scandinavia) smaller and darker.

Semipalmated Plover p. 557

bill orange
with black ti

♂**Br**
MAR–SEP

♀**Br**
MAR–SEP

All SSP. *hiaticula*

170

V | Calls a short, hard "*pwit*," "*bip*" or metallic "*tip*" (distinctly different from other 'ringed' plovers). Song a sharp "*tjek-e tjek-e tjek-e*" and twanging "*dzwee-dwee-dwee*" in flight.

FL | White wingbar; tail short, square with **white sides**, central black patch.

steep forehead

Juv

♂Br

cinnamon fringes to feathers worn off

AdNB/1W
AUG–MAR

Scarce, locally common resident/ summer migrant FEB–SEP

Sandy/muddy shores; breeds beside lagoons, on sandy ground

dumpy, short-tailed, rounded shape

V | Abrupt, "*tew*" or "*te-u*" with **downward** inflection; song a hard, rolling "*crree-a crree-a*" in swerving, bat-like display flight.

FL | Wings plain brown (may show pale feather edges but **no white wingbar**); tail has dark bar near tip.

Juv

♀Br

Juv
MAY–OCT

Scarce summer migrant MAR–OCT; very local resident

Breeds on sand or shingle beside lakes and rivers; migrants scarce on sea coasts

Smaller and with longer, more tapered rear than bulky Ringed Plover.

V | Loud, musical, soft "*too-ee*" or "*ploo-eep*" with **upward** inflection; alarm a shorter pipe; song rhythmic "*too looee*," usually in low, waving, straight-winged flight.

FL | Long white wingbar; tail wedge-shaped, sides mostly brown and central black 'blob' in all plumages.

Juv

♂Br

Juv
MAY–SEP

Locally common resident/migrant

Breeds sand/shingle beaches, freshwater lakes, rivers; in winter widespread on coasts; migrants on inland lake shores

Heavier, longer bodied than Little Ringed Plover, with shorter rear-end.

171

Regularly occurring sandpipers, godwits, curlews, snipes and Woodcock in flight

WHIMBREL

CURLEW

WHIMBREL
(*p. 182*)

Ad

CURLEW
(*p. 183*)

♂

BLACK-TAILED
GODWIT

BAR-TAILED
GODWIT

Juv

**BLACK-TAILED
GODWIT**
(*p. 181*)

Juv

**BAR-TAILED
GODWIT**
(*p. 180*)

AdBr

REDSHANK
(*p. 178*)

AdBr

Juv → 1W

**SPOTTED
REDSHANK**
(*p. 179*)

AdNb

**MARSH
SANDPIPER**
(*p. 176*)

GREENSHANK
(*p. 177*)

TURNSTONE
(p. 161)

AdNb

**GREY
PHALAROPE**
(p. 197)

Juv → 1W

**RED-NECKED
PHALAROPE**
(p. 196)

Juv

**RINGED
PLOVER**
(p. 170)

Juv

**TEMMINCK'S
STINT**
(p. 185)

Ad

Juv

**LITTLE
STINT**
(p. 184)

Juv

**BROAD-BILLED
SANDPIPER**
(p. 187)

Juv

DUNLIN
(p. 188)

Juv

CURLEW SANDPIPER
(p. 189)

Juv

SANDERLING
(p. 190)

AdNb/
1W

PURPLE SANDPIPER
(p. 186)

Ad

RUFF
(p. 192)

AdNb/
1W

KNOT
(p. 191)

**WOOD
SANDPIPER**
(p. 176)

Ad

**GREAT
SNIPE**
(p. 195)

Ad

SNIPE
(p. 194)

Ad

**GREEN
SANDPIPER**
(p. 175)

JACK SNIPE
(p. 195)

Juv

**COMMON
SANDPIPER**
(p. 174)

AdBr

WOODCOCK
(p. 193)

**TEREK
SANDPIPER**
(p. 174)

LC Terek Sandpiper *Xenus cinereus*

LC | **L** 22–25 cm | **W** 32–35 cm

Small-medium-sized, greyish sandpiper with hunched or horizontal posture; **bill long, slightly upcurved**; legs short, **orange-yellow**. **AdBr**| back grey-brown with long dark stripes; underparts bright white. **AdNb/1W**| like **AdBr** but back plain, pale grey. **Juv**| back greyish with pale fringes to feathers and fine dark streaks.

👁 Redshank *p. 178*

V| Call a fluty "*dududududu*" and slower "*du-du*;" song a rich, varied "*per-rrrrrr-eeee*."

FL| Rump grey; wide **white trailing edge to wing** behind black stripe (see Redshank).

Scarce, local summer migrant MAR–NOV

Breeds forest bogs; migrants on coasts

Ad
ALL YEAR
[MAY]

Juv
JUL–OCT

LC Common Sandpiper

LC *Actitis hypoleucos*

L 18–20·5 cm | **W** 32–35 cm

Small, slim, rather elongated wader. Usually solitary or in groups of up to 5. Constantly bobs head and **'pumps' rear-end up and down**. Back plain sandy-olive-brown, **underparts gleaming white**; breast side dusky with **white 'hook' in front of shoulder**. Bill straight, pale at base; **legs dull greenish-ochre (inconspicuous)**. **AdBr**| upperparts flecked blackish. **AdNb**| (OCT–MAR) like **AdBr** but less flecked; wing coverts each with single dark bar. **Juv**| wing coverts have close double bars of blackish-brown and cream; pale 'notches' on tertials and tail side. **1W**| has some juvenile wing coverts, but hard to distinguish.

👁 Spotted Sandpiper *p. 564*

V| Often gives loud, **ringing calls** in flight, slight melancholy fall in pitch and volume – "*swee-wee-wee-wee*." Song runs calls together with fast rhythmic trills.

FL| **White wingbar**; white sides to tail, rounded, dark 'blob' tip. Flies low on flicked, or fluttering, beats of **stiff, arched wings**.

Locally common, scarce in winter; migratory

Rivers and lakes with stony shores; migrants on inland freshwater and sheltered coasts

AdBr
MAR–AUG

Tail extends well beyond wingtip (compare with Spotted Sandpiper).

Juv
JUN–SEP

TEREK SANDPIPER — Ad

AdNb — GREEN SANDPIPER — AdNb

AdBr

Juv — COMMON SANDPIPER

Juv

Green Sandpiper *Tringa ochropus*

L 20–24 cm | **W** 39–44 cm

Dark-backed sandpiper, bright white beneath but **no white 'hook'** in front of shoulder (obvious on smaller, paler Common Sandpiper). Usually solitary or in groups of up to 5. Bobs head and 'pumps' rear-end up and down. **White line from bill to top of eye** (extends behind eye on Wood Sandpiper); breast-band dark. Bill straight (longer, heavier than Common Sandpiper's). **AdBr**|back greenish-brown-black with small, dull white spots. **AdNb**|like AdBr but lacks pale spots on upperparts. **Juv**|back/wing coverts clearly spotted buffish (not so chequered as on Wood Sandpiper). **1W**|like AdNb but retains some Juv wing/tail feathers.

Wood Sandpiper p.176
Solitary Sandpiper p.564

V| Loud, rich, fluty, yodelling "*tluee-wee-wee*" call. Song a rapid, rhythmic repetition in display flight.

FL| Wings plain, rump white; few dark bands on tail: looks **'black-and-white'** as it flies up high and far away when disturbed. Belly white with contrasting **blackish underwings**, unlike any other common wader.

Scarce, locally fairly common; migratory

Breeds forest lakes, bogs; migrants/winters freshwater pools, streams, estuarine marshes

AdBr has small white spots on upperparts

AdBr
AUG–MAR

Juv
JUN–SEP

underparts gleaming white (brighter than Common or Wood Sandpiper)

LC Wood Sandpiper *Tringa glareola*

LC **L** 18·5–21 cm | **W** 35–39 cm

Rounded sandpiper with slender neck and tail/wingtip, and long, pale legs (paler, less robust than Green Sandpiper). Usually solitary or in groups of up to 5. **Long pale stripe extends behind eye** (only in front on Green Sandpiper). **AdBr**| back brown, strongly chequered white. **AdNb**| like **AdBr** but back greyer and plainer. **Juv**| back brown with **bold pale spots** (Green Sandpiper darker, spots smaller); breast streaked, without clear breast-band; bill slender; legs long, **yellowish**. **1W**| like AdNb but retains some juvenile wing coverts.

👁 Green Sandpiper *p. 175*
Marsh Sandpiper
Lesser Yellowlegs p. 562

V| Call thin, high, quick, "*chiff-if-if*" on even note. Song fast, yodelling sequence.

FL| Rises high, showing **square white rump** against brown wings and back (similar to Green Sandpiper but less contrasted); underwing **dusky grey-buff**. Tail narrowly barred; feet project beyond tail.

Scarce summer migrant APR–NOV; rare and local in winter

Breeds by forest lakes, bogs; migrants shallow freshwater/coastal pools

Juv
JUN–DEC

AdBr
MAR–AUG

LC Marsh Sandpiper

LC *Tringa stagnatilis*

L 22–25 cm | **W** 55–59 cm

Delicate brown-and-white sandpiper (like a small Greenshank or slim Wood Sandpiper); bill **thin**, straight, dark; **legs long, slender**. **AdBr**| back buff-brown with black spots. **AdNb / 1W**| back less spotted than **AdBr**; cap dark, pale stripe over eye. **Juv**| upperparts have broad buff feather edges.

👁 Greenshank
Wood Sandpiper
Lesser Yellowlegs p. 562

V| Call "*kyew*" or "*kyu-kyu-kyu*," higher, quicker, weaker than Greenshank; song a melodious "*tyu-ur-lyu*."

FL| Pattern like Greenshank, with plain dark wings, but white 'wedge' on back is longer and thinner; toes project more beyond tail.

Scarce, local summer migrant MAR–OCT; rare and local in winter

Breeds on marshes, forest pools; migrants on shallow lagoons, estuaries

AdBr
MAR–AUG

AdNb
AUG–MAR

Juv → 1W
JUL–MAR
[SEP]

GREENSHANK

Juv → 1W

MARSH SANDPIPER

Ad

WOOD SANDPIPER

AdBr

Greenshank *Tringa nebularia*

L 30–34 cm | **W** 55–62 cm

Large, elegant, **pale greyish** wader; **legs long, yellow-green** (grey-green in winter); bill long, **slightly upturned, pale grey**. **Larger, greyer** than Redshank; darker back than non-breeding Spotted Redshank; larger, heavier and thicker-billed than Marsh Sandpiper. Feeds sedately, sometimes wading deeply or with fast runs. Usually solitary or in groups of up to 10. **AdBr** | head and back streaked/spotted blackish and grey. **AdNb** | head and back greyish, whitish streaks merge on hindneck; **pale-faced** with dark eye; white fringes to wing coverts complete. **Juv** | like **AdNb** but pale wing covert fringes broken at tip and legs pale yellowish; some juvenile wing/back feathers retained into **1W**.

Marsh Sandpiper | Ruff *p. 192*
Spotted Redshank *p. 179*
Redshank *p. 178*
Greater Yellowlegs p. 562

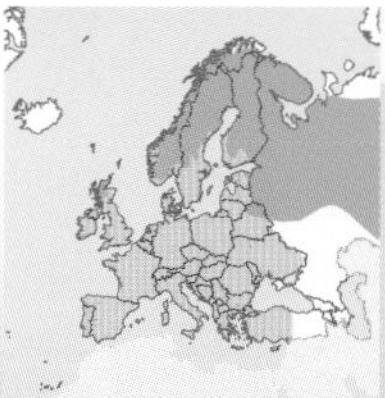

Scarce, migratory

Breeds northern moors, by forest lakes; migrants mostly on shallow coastal lagoons, edges of estuaries, inland watersides

V | Loud and **distinctive**, frequent estuary sound: ringing, powerful "*tyew-tyew-tyew*" of even strength/pitch (unlike 'fading' notes of similar Redshank); song when breeding repeated, rich, down-up double notes, "*tu-hoo tu-hoo*."

FL | Wings dark; white 'wedge' on lower back; toes project beyond tail.

leg colour often indistinct against muddy background, while Redshank's usually obviously red

Juv
JUN–NOV

AdBr
MAR–JUL

AdNb
AUG–MAR

LC (Common) **Redshank** *Tringa totanus*

LC **L** 24–27 cm | **W** 47–53 cm

Medium-small brown wader of estuary/marsh/pools. Noisy, active, bobs head; breeding birds often call anxiously from posts. Dumpier shape than Spotted Redshank or Greenshank, taller than Knot (*p. 191*). Usually in small groups but roosts in jostling flocks of up to 300. **Back brown**, underparts paler; **legs bright red** (rules out all but Spotted Redshank and Ruff). Bill straight, thick at base; red with dark tip. **AdBr** | back brown, chequered black; breast whitish, blotched black. **AdNb/1W** | back and breast plain, grey-brown. Whitish line over dark eyestripe (bolder than Ruff, weaker than Spotted Redshank). **Juv** | back has buff feather fringes; **legs yellow-orange**.

V | Rich, bright, musical "*teu*" or sad "*teu-hu*"; 'bouncy' "*teu-huhu*" or "*tyew-yewyew*" (quicker, less even than Greenshank). Frenetic "*pit-u-pit-u-pit-u*" when flushed, "*kyip*" in alarm; rhythmic, musical "*t'leeo-t'leeo-t'leeo*" song.

Spotted Redshank | Ruff [Nb] *p. 192*
Greenshank *p. 177* | Terek Sandpiper *p. 174*
| *Lesser Yellowlegs p. 562*
| *Willet p. 568* | *Grey-tailed Tattler p. 568*

Generally scarce, locally common resident/migrant

Breeds on wet grassland, freshwater marshes, saltmarsh; widespread inland and on most coast types

FL | White 'wedge' on back; **broad white hindwing** instantly obvious. Quick to take flight. Often settles with wings raised, flashing white underside.

AdBr
MAR–OCT

SSP. *robusta*

Two sspp. occur: *totanus* (widespread); *robusta* (Iceland, Faroe Islands) (ABOVE) larger on average and moult to breeding plumage is usually incomplete.

broad white hindwing

AdBr

Highly variable, with greyer, browner and more boldly marked 'types'.

AdNb (JUL–MAR) similar but wing coverts unspotted

1W
JUL–MAR

indistinct white line in front of eye

dark blotches

AdBr
MAR–OCT

whole bill base red

buff fringes

Juv
MAY–DEC

vivid red legs

legs may be yellowish

Some juvenile feathers are retained until spring, but edges wear or bleach.

Spotted Redshank *Tringa erythropus*

L 29–33 cm | **W** 61–67 cm

Medium-sized, deep-bodied, long-legged wading bird of shallow pools. Usually in small groups of up to 10. Wades deeply, runs/darts, upends, swims. **Bill long and fine-tipped, black with red base. AdBr** | body blackish, with wide white fringes that wear away, all-**black** by JUN; legs blackish (by JUL/AUG, plumage patchy black, grey and white; legs red). **AdNb/1W** | back **pale grey** (no hint of brown), underparts whiter; eyestripe black with **white line above** (unbroken over eye and widest towards bill, unlike Redshank); **legs red. Juv** | back grey-brown, spotted paler; **brownish bars** on flank.

V | **Distinctive call** invaluable clue: sharp, clearly enunciated *"tchew-it!"* Song when breeding mixes creaking/grating whistles with *"chip-chip"* notes like Blackbird's (*p. 385*) alarm.

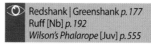
Redshank | Greenshank *p. 177*
Ruff [Nb] *p. 192*
Wilson's Phalarope [Juv] *p. 555*

Scarce and local; migratory

Breeds northern forest lakes, tundra; migrants mostly on shallow coastal lagoons, marshes; rare inland, mainly in autumn

FL | Wings plain; long **white oval on back** (see Greenshank). Wings quite short, arched; long body but pot-bellied appearance. Legs extend well beyond tail tip (can be withdrawn).

AdBr →AdNb
AUG–SEP
[AUG]

AdBr
MAR–MAY

Adults are black, barred with white feather fringes in early spring, blackest in summer, and black, increasingly patched with white, as autumn moult progresses.

no white on hindwing

Juv

distinct white line, widest in front of eye

AdNb
JUN–MAR

long, bright red legs

long, slightly droop-tipped bill; red on lower edge of bill only

AdBr
MAY–JUL

Juv
JUN–SEP

some juvenile feathers are retained into winter

179

NT **Bar-tailed Godwit**
LC *Limosa lapponica*

L 33–41 cm | **W** 62–72 cm

Large, **long-billed** wader; coastal, on estuaries in winter. Legs black, medium-long (shorter above 'knee' than on Black-tailed Godwit); bill slightly upcurved to fine tip. ♂**Br**| back brown; **head, breast and flank/belly/undertail plain bright coppery-red**, with little or no white; fades duller by JUL. Bill black. ♀**Br**| paler orange-red than ♂. **AdNb**| head, back and breast pale greyish-brown with **soft darker markings**. Bill dark pink with black tip. **Juv**| back brown with blackish streaks; pale 'notches' on tertials (pattern like Curlew); breast as **AdNb** but buffier. **1W**| like **AdNb** but retains some juvenile wing feathers.

SSP. *lapponica* occurs in Europe.

As with many other waders, flocks of birds in non-breeding plumage may include one or two individuals in full breeding colours.

👁 Black-tailed Godwit | Curlew *p. 183*

AdNb
SEP–MAY

Sleeping birds with bill hidden resemble Curlew, but are smaller, paler and less bulky.

FL| Upperwing has pale inner/dark outer half but no white; long **white triangle on rump/lower back**. Flocks going to roost make fast, aerobatic descents from high over estuary.

Locally common; migratory

Breeds on Arctic tundra; winters mostly on sandy or muddy coasts

V| Nasal, wickering "*ki-wee ki-wee*" or "*ik-ik-ik.*" Song when breeding variable in pitch and pace, a sweet or squeaky "*a-wik a-wik a-wik.*"

♂**Br**

Juv

♂**Br**
FEB–AUG

Juv
JUL–OCT

legs relatively short (compared with Black-tailed Godwit, much shorter above 'knee')

back and wing streaked

♀**Br**
FEB–AUG

AdNb
SEP–MAY

Feeds well-spaced out on open mud but roosts in tight flocks up to 1,000+.

Black-tailed Godwit
Limosa limosa

L 37–42 cm | **W** 63–74 cm

Large, **long-legged, long-billed** wader; on coast and inland. Legs black, **long above 'knee'**; bill long, straight, thick-based, **mostly orange or pink**. **♂Br** | back brown; head and breast coppery-red; flank and undertail white; belly and flank with **black bars**. **♀Br** | head and breast pale orange. **AdNb** | **head, back and breast plain grey-brown**. **Juv** | head and breast orange-buff; back mottled dark brown with **rusty fringes**. **1W** | like **AdNb** but retains some juvenile wing feathers.

Bar-tailed Godwit
Hudsonian Godwit p. 564

V | Many calls: quick, nasal notes like Lapwing (*p. 163*); mechanical/metallic bickering when feeding/quarrelling. Song a varied "*tur-ee-tur.*"

FL | Long, striking **white wingbar**; underwing **white with black edges**; rump square, white; tail black-banded, feet project well beyond tail. Flight fast, deep beats of bowed wings: can look rather small; flocks manoeuvre tightly.

Locally common; migratory

Breeds in wet grassland, moorland; winters/passage migrants on muddy estuaries, flooded grassland

Forms excitable groups outside breeding season.

Two sspp. occur: ssp. *islandica* (Iceland, widespread in W in winter) has shorter bill and darker chestnut breeding plumage than ssp. *limosa*. (Europe, Siberia)

♂Br
FEB–JUL

ssp. *islandica*

♂Br

ssp. *islandica*

AdNb

Juv
MAY–OCT

legs long (compared with Bar-tailed Godwit, much longer above 'knee')

♀Br
FEB–JUL

ssp. *limosa*

♂Br
FEB–JUL

back and wing plain

AdNb
JUN–MAR

Feeds in shallow water/ wet mud, often in narrow, hidden creeks; roosts in tight flocks up to 3,000+.

LC **Whimbrel** *Numenius phaeopus*
LC **L** 37–45 cm | **W** 78–88 cm

Large, streaked, brown wader with long, curved bill. Spring migrant flocks (up to 500), sometimes inland; scattered on coasts when not breeding. Like Curlew but smaller and darker with boldly striped head pattern. Bill **downcurved**, slightly more **angular bend** than Curlew. Legs greyish. **Ad** | back and breast darker or greyer brown than Curlew. Pale spots on upperparts, which wear off to create 'notches' by JUL. Crown dark with **pale central stripe**; dark eyestripe. Bill black in summer, but pink base after JUN/JUL. **Juv** | like Ad but has larger pale spots on tertials and scapulars.

V | Call diagnostic: short whistles in **rapid trill**: "*pipipipipipipip*." Song long whistles developing into even, sad trill.

Curlew | *Rare curlews p. 561*

Ad
ALL YEAR

Breeding birds are mostly on north-western isles and northern tundra (not more southerly moors, heaths and meadows where some Curlews breed).

Scarce, locally common summer migrant, rare and local in winter

moorland, forest bogs, tundra; migrants around coasts, scarcer inland

FL | Deep-chested; quicker action than Curlew; wings brown with outer half darker; long white triangle on rump/lower back.

Juv
JUN–SEP

Ad

Ad

Ad

ssp. *hudsonicus*

ssp. *hudsonicus*

pale band over eye

obvious pale crown stripe

dark line through eye

Ad
ALL YEAR
[JUN]

Three sspp. occur: *islandicus* and slightly smaller *phaeopus* (both widespread); *hudsonicus* ('Hudsonian Whimbrel', sometimes treated as a species (ABOVE)) (vagrant from N America) paler buffish-brown; head more contrasted brown and buff; **back/rump all-dark**.

bill shorter than Curlew's and distinctly angled towards tip

Ad
ALL YEAR
[AUG]

colder brown than Curlew

(Eurasian) **Curlew**
Numenius arquata

L 48–57 cm | **W** 89–106 cm

Large, heavy, streaked brown wader with long, curved bill. Feeds singly or spread out; roosts in tighter groups, sometimes flocks up to 1,000+. **Bill downcurved**: on ♀ very long; ♂ less curved, shorter. Legs greyish. **Ad** | mid-brown or buffy-brown, closely streaked, spotted and barred darker; belly and undertail white with dark arrows/bars. Pale spots on upperparts, which wear off to create wavy feather edges by JUL. **Head plain**, or paler over eye beneath darker cap, without marked central stripe or dark eyestripe. **Juv** | like **Ad** but tertials have bold pale 'notches' (less barred); white belly less marked, bill shorter.

V | Hoarse or barking notes; loud "*vi-vi-vi*" of alarm; clear, fluty "*cur-lee*" and "*cue-cue-cue.*" Song a loud, mournful, accelerating into mesmeric bubbling trill, often heard on estuaries but most ecstatic in breeding areas.

Whimbrel | Bar-tailed Godwit *p. 180*
Rare curlews p. 561

Ad [APR]

Looks very dark on mud in dull light; looks much paler against dark vegetation or in bright sun.

Scarce, locally common migrant/resident

Breeds marshes, bogs, damp grassland; winters mainly estuaries, but widespread on coasts, rough/wet pasture inland

FL | Steady, gull-like, shallow beats; head/bill protrude. Outerwing dark, innerwing mottled pale; long white or triangle on rump/lower back (pattern like Whimbrel and Bar-tailed Godwit); long bill usually obvious. Flocks form lines or 'V's, reminiscent of gulls.

plain crown (sometimes with faint stripe)

Ad

♂Ad

All ssp. *arquata*

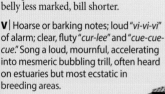

♂Ad
ALL YEAR

♂ has shorter bill than ♀

plain 'face' with 'isolated' dark eye

bill long and smoothly curved

♀ has longer bill than ♂

♀ Ad
ALL YEAR

Two sspp. occur, but intergrade: *arquata* (widespread); *orientalis* (Urals), which has streaked, not barred flank.

brighter and more buffy than Whimbrel

LC **Little Stint** *Calidris minuta*

LC | **L** 14–15·5 cm | **W** 28–31 cm

Tiny wader (smaller than a sparrow/wagtail) with **black legs** (compare with larger Dunlin and Sanderling). Dainty, quick-moving, legs often flexed. **Bill short**, straight, black. Usually small numbers (1–10). **Underparts white. AdBr** | back black-and-rufous; neck/ breast side pale rufous. **AdNb** | upperparts grey with darker mottles. **Juv** | upperparts rufous, black and cream (black spots isolated within paler buff as rufous fades). Cream stripes form **pale 'V'** as seen from rear. Cap streaked (dark in centre, rufous at side) above wide whitish line, subtly forked in front of eye. Breast side grey-buff, softly streaked; no dark smudges on flank. **1W** | like **AdNb** but browner, with hint of pale 'V' above.

V | Call distinctive, short, hard "*tip*," sometimes tripled. Song when breeding a quiet "*svee svee svee*."

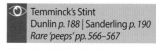

Temminck's Stint
Dunlin *p. 188* | Sanderling *p. 190*
Rare '*peeps*' *pp. 566–567*

Scarce and local; migratory

Breeds in Arctic; migrants on coasts, lagoons, scarcer by freshwater inland

FL | Wingbar and sides of rump white; tail grey (overall pattern very like Dunlin).

AdBr
APR–AUG

AdBr

sides of rump white but tail grey

Juv

Adults in breeding plumage have broad white fringes, which wear away to reveal brighter colours on upperparts.

♀ slightly longer-billed than ♂

AdBr
APR–AUG

legs black

Juv
JUN–DEC
(GREYISH INDIVIDUAL)

Juveniles are typically rufous, buff and white, with a clear pale 'V' above, but some are greyer overall.

Juv moults Oct–Jan, Ad in autumn Aug–Dec.

Juv
JUL–OCT

(RUFOUS INDIVIDUAL)

AdNb / 1W
SEP–MAR

underparts bright white, unmarked

Temminck's Stint *Calidris temminckii*

L 13.5-15 cm | **W** 30-35 cm

Little Stint | *Rare 'peeps' pp. 566–567*

Tiny, rather drab wader with **pale legs**. Creeps secretively along freshwater margins. Migrants usually solitary or in groups of up to 5. Elongated, **long-winged**; **upperparts/breast dull brown**; underparts white. Bill short, faintly downcurved, black. **AdBr** | back olive-brown, **blotched blackish** with rufous feather edges. Breast-band finely marked; throat whitish; belly white; legs pale ochre/greenish. **AdNb** | as **AdBr** but back plain brown. **Juv** | back brown with thin, dark-and-cream feather fringes forming wide, curved scales; breast-band dull grey-buff, paler in centre; throat white; legs pale yellowish. **1W** | like **AdNb** but retains some juvenile wing coverts.

V | Call a distinctive dry, rippled trill: "*si-si-si-si-si.*" Song when breeding, a continuous rising and falling trill up to several minutes long.

Scarce and local; migratory

Breeds northern bogs, by forest pools, tundra; migrants mostly on freshwater shallow lagoons

FL | Wingbar and **sides of rump white, extending onto outer tail feathers** (best seen as bird takes off). Tends to fly far away if flushed.

long wing

sides of tail white

AdBr

AdNb

AdBr
MAR-AUG

Variable moult and feather wear give blotchy effect above: new, blackish, feathers with rufous edges mixed with old grey ones.

legs pale ochre/greenish

AdBr
MAR-AUG

like tiny Common Sandpiper (p. 174)

AdNb
AUG-APR

distinctive black crescent and buff tip to scapulars and wing coverts

Juv
JUN-DEC

distinct breast-band

legs pale yellowish

185

Purple Sandpiper

Calidris maritima

L 19–22 cm | **W** 37–42 cm

Dark, thickset shoreline wader, with subtle pattern; bill thick-based, slightly downcurved, dark with **orange-yellow at base**; legs short, dull **orange-yellow**. **AdBr** | dark; head and back **chequered with black and rufous** (retains rufous and cream fringes, and blackish feather centres, until OCT); underparts finely streaked black. **AdNb** | **grey/mauve-brown**, with paler feather edges; eyering and chin white; underparts dull white; **breast soft grey**. **Juv / 1W** | like **AdNb** but most of upperparts have scaly white feather fringes.

V | Call a weak, sharp "*quit*" or "*quit-it*." Song when breeding recalls Tree Pipit (*p. 362*) with short trills repeated in long sequence.

Dunlin *p. 188* | Great Knot *p. 568*

Locally fairly common migrant/resident

Breeds high northern plateaux; winters mainly on rocky coasts, around groynes, piers; migrants rare inland

FL | Stocky but fast direct (leaps/flutters over breaking waves), dark with white wingbar; **broad black rump with white sides**

Purple Sandpipers on coastal rocks can be very approachable, but are likely to fly off if they are with more nervous Turnstones.

AdNb

AdNb

AdNb

1W
SEP–MAY

Juv
JUN–SEP

AdNb
OCT–APR

becomes brighter with wear

AdBr
MAR–OCT

Broad-billed Sandpiper
Calidris falcinellus

L 15–18 cm | W 34–37 cm

Small, short-legged wader, size between Dunlin and Little Stint (*p. 184*). Bill **thick-based**, with **downward tilt at tip**. Head strongly patterned, **white line forked above eye** in narrow 'V'. **AdBr** back has broad buff-white feather edges that wear off to reveal dark brown, rufous edges; hint of a pale 'V' on back. Breast streaked black, belly white. **AdNb / 1W** back plain grey-brown; underparts white; head pattern like **AdBr** but less distinct. **Juv** back bright brown, striped black and buff; underparts white; flank mottled buff.

V | Dry, upward buzz or trill, "*brrree-et*." Song when breeding comprises rhythmic, buzzing notes and faster, whirring trills.

◉ Dunlin *p. 188*

AdBr
MAR–AUG

Frosty white feather edges in spring have worn away by JUL, when adults look very dark; note characteristic bill shape.

SSP. ***falcinellus*** occurs in Europe.

Rare and local summer migrant MAR–OCT

Breeds in wet bogs; migrants on coasts, freshwater margins

FL | Dark with thin white wingbar, black rump with white sides (similar to Dunlin).

white fringes wear off, leaving rufous blotches on back

AdBr
MAR–AUG

Juv

AdNb
AUG–MAR

Juv
JUN–OCT

LC **Dunlin** *Calidris alpina*

LC | **L** 17–21 cm | **W** 32–36 cm

Usually commonest small wader on coast or inland; roosts in
packed groups with other species (up to 5,000+). Larger than
Little Stint; smaller than Knot. Forward-leaning, picks more
than probes when feeding; makes quick runs. Long bill
tapers to **downcurved tip** (giving long, front-heavy effect);
legs dark green-grey. **AdBr** | upperparts **rusty-brown**,
blackish and cream; **belly black**; breast-band finely streaked.
AdNb | **mouse-brown**, underparts white. On shiny mud shows
dark breast/white belly; in direct sun, paler brown and white.
Juv | back bright buffish with long, **cream lines**; head plain;
underparts pale, with **dusky streaks or blackish blotches on
flank**. Back mixed with new greyer winter feathers during
moult to **1W**.

Curlew Sandpiper | Knot *p. 191* | Little Stint
p. 184 | Sanderling *p. 565* | Broad-billed
Sandpiper *p. 187* | Purple Sandpiper *p. 186*
Rare 'peeps' pp. 566–567

Locally numerous
migrant/resident

Breeds on tundra,
moorland, bogs, wet
grassland; winters
mainly on sandy/muddy
coasts but widespread;
migrants frequent inland

V | Call thin, scratchy/'reedy', vibrant "*trreee*." Song
often from spring flocks, develops into vibran
'referee's whistle' which runs down - "*shrree-ruee
ruee-we-we-we-wee wee*"

FL | Rump dark with
white sides; wingba
white. Fast, direct; larg
flocks tight, swirling ir
synchronized twists and
turns

♀ **Br**
MAR–SEP
SSP. *alpina*

SSP. *alpina*

♂ **Br**

Juv

Juv → 1W

Juv → 1W
JUN–OCT

Five sspp. occur: two common – *alpina*
(N Scandinavia, winters W Europe/
Mediterranean), *schinzii* (N Europe, winters
S Europe); two scarce winter migrants –
arctica (coastal W Europe) and *centralis* (E
Mediterranean); *hudsonia* (vagrant from
N America). All similar, varying in size,
bill length/shape and colour/vibrancy
of breeding plumage (*alpina* averages
largest, and longest-billed; AdBr deeper
rusty-red on back than smaller *schinzii*).

♀ **Br**
MAR–SEP

♂ **Br has whitish
hindneck;
♀ Br has brown
hindneck and
less contrast with
crown and back**

SSP.
schinzii

Bill thick-based,
fine-tipped, slightl
downcurved; lengt
and curvature vary

AdNb
JUN–MAR

♂ **Br**
MAR–SEP

Curlew Sandpiper
Calidris ferruginea

L 19–22 cm | **W** 37–42 cm

Small, tall, long-necked sandpiper. Wades deeply, so long legs often hidden. **Bill long, smoothly downcurved**. Usually found as single birds or groups of up to 10 among other waders. **AdBr** | broad white feather tips on head, back and underparts wear off to reveal **coppery-red**; eyering and chin white; rump white, mottled rufous. Post-breeding migrants have **faded red patches** on dull white underparts. **AdNb** | head and back grey, underparts white; **rump clear white**. **Juv** | back has **neat cream fringes/spangles**. Underparts pale; **breast bright peachy-buff, flank unmarked**. **Juv** | back increasingly mixed with grey; like AdNb by NOV.

Dunlin | *Stilt Sandpiper p. 566*

[AUG]

A Curlew Sandpiper's wide white rump is conspicuous in a mixed wader flock (here with Dunlins).

Scarce winter visitor and passage migrant

Breeds in Arctic; migrants on coasts, lagoons, scarcer by freshwater inland

V | Call a rich trill *"chirrup"* (draws attention among thin Dunlin notes in a mixed flock).

FL | Broad **white rump**; thin white wingbar.

AdBr→AdNb
JUL-OCT
[OCT]

Juv

AdBr

Juv
JUN-OCT

AdBr
MAR-JUL
[JUL]

Breeding plumage initially has white feather edges (MAIN PLATE, BELOW) which wear off to reveal full red coloration (ABOVE, LOWER IMAGE); by OCT, most red has been replaced by white (ABOVE, UPPER IMAGE).

Autumn migrants mostly Ads. in JUL/AUG, Juvs. later, often with smaller Dunlin and Little Stint (p. 184).

AdBr
MAR-JUL
[JUN]

AdNb/1W
SEP-MAR

189

LC **Sanderling** *Calidris alba*

LC **L** 18–21 cm | **W** 35–39 cm

Small, fast-moving sandpiper, typically seen at water's edge on open sand or mud. Usually up to 300. **Chases receding waves**, picking invertebrates from the surface, occasionally probing. Bill short, straight (thicker than Dunlin's). **Legs black; no hind toe. AdBr** | back rufous, mottled dark; breast marbled black/rufous/white; white wears off to reveal brighter colours by MAY. Duller by JUL, but may retain rusty-red neck. **AdNb / 1W** | head and back **pale grey**; underparts white, **breast hardly marked** (conspicuously bright in mixed winter roosts). **Juv** | back grey with distinct three-lobed **black spots**; blackish 'shoulder'; side of breast streaked; neck warm buff; **underparts clean white**.

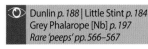

Dunlin *p. 188* | Little Stint *p. 184*
Grey Phalarope [Nb] *p. 197*
Rare 'peeps' pp. 566–567

AdNb / 1W
[FEB]

Typically feeds by picking from the surface between fast, long-striding runs.

V | Short, hard *"plit"* or *"twik"* call lacks any 'musical' quality.

Locally common winter migrant

Breeds in Arctic; winters mainly on sandy/muddy coasts; migrants occasionally inland in spring

SSP. ***alba*** occurs in Europe.

FL | Broad whit‣ wingbar on dar‣ wing

AdBr → AdNb
JUL–OCT
[AUG]

AdBr
MAR–AUG
[JUN]

Breeding plumage initially has fresh white feather edges (MAIN PLATE, BELOW), which wear off to reveal tawny-rufous (ABOVE, LOWER IMAGE); by AUG, little tawny-buff remains (ABOVE, UPPER IMAGE).

Juv

AdBr

AdNb / 1W

Juv
JUL–OCT

AdBr
MAR–AUG
[MAY]

AdNb
AUG–MAR

(Red) **Knot** *Calidris canutus*

L 23–26 cm | **W** 45–54 cm

Stocky, pigeon-shaped wader: **a little larger** than Dunlin; **smaller** and stands lower than Redshank (*p. 178*). Bill tapered, longer than a plover's (see Grey Plover (*p. 166*)), slightly downcurved. **Legs short, greenish**. Small groups among smaller, browner, less tightly grouped Dunlins stand out as bigger and greyer, moving more slowly, often closer together. **AdBr** | back blackish, mottled buff and grey; head and breast coppery-orange, faded orange by JUL/AUG. **AdNb / 1W** | dull **grey**, underparts paler. **Juv** | greyish; back feathers have lacy **grey and white crescents**; underparts pale peach-buff with fine, pale grey lines.

V | Obscure, soft "*whet*" or "*nut*," unmusical rapid chorus from jostling flocks at roost.

Two sspp. occur: **canutus** (Eurasia) and **islandica** (N America), often impossible to distinguish.

Dunlin *p. 188*
Great Knot *p. 568* | Willet *p. 568*
Grey-tailed Tattler *p. 568*

[APR]

Knot roosts at high tide on large estuaries are typically large and tightly packed.

Locally numerous winter migrant

Breeds in Arctic; winters mainly on sandy/muddy coasts but widespread; scarce inland

FL | White wingbar; pale grey rump. Synchronized tight, rolling flocks, which may number 10,000 or more, flashing white and smoky grey at distance.

Juv

AdBr

1W
AUG–MAR

AdBr
FEB–SEP

Juv
JUL–OCT

LC **Ruff** *Calidris pugnax*

LC | **L** ♂ 29–32 cm; ♀ 22–26 cm | **W** ♂ 54–60 cm; ♀ 46–49 cm

Medium-sized wader with **short, faintly downcurved bill** and small, rounded head. Legs **yellow-ochre or greenish** (orange or red on breeding birds and non-breeding ♂). ♀ smaller than similar Redshank, ♂ larger. Usually in flocks of up to 50. **♂Br** | from JAN much like ♀ **Br** but APR–JUN most are extravagantly patterned, with **coloured crest** and flamboyant **ruff** (highly individually variable, see *opposite*); some fail to develop a ruff. **♀Br** | buff- or grey-brown, chequered blackish; breast blotched black-brown on buff. **AdNb** | grey-brown, with white belly; ♂ often has **white face**. **Juv** | distinctive; back dark with prominent **cream scales; neck and breast clean olive-buff** (unlike Redshank). **1W** | like AdNb but feather edges more buff, less grey.

V | Usually silent, even in display; occasional low, quacking call.

Redshank *p. 178* | Greenshank *p. 177*
Spotted Redshank *p. 179*
Buff-breasted Sandpiper p. 561
Wilson's Phalarope [Juv] *p. 555*
Pectoral Sandpiper p. 565
Sharp-tailed Sandpiper p. 565

Generally scarce, locally fairly common; migratory

Breeds on wet grassland, marshes otherwise mostly by freshwater, on coastal lagoons

FL | Thin white wingbar, **white rump side** form broken or complete 'V'. Quite broad winged; flight rather slow, relaxed

♂ AdNb → AdBr

A male Ruff's boldly marked breeding plumage is briefly embellished by a crest and ruff, but transitional plumages are more often seen away from breeding areas.

♀ Br

♀ Br

When not in display plumage, ♂ looks similar to ♀, but is larger.

♂ Br
APR–JUN

♀ Br
MAR–JUL

♂ Nb
JUL–FEB

Juv
JUN–OCT

Ruff Males in full display plumage (APR–JUN) show a wide array of colour combinations (common types shown below, but others are more barred on the ruff); incomplete ruffs may be seen before and after this period.

Striking white-headed 'satellite' males on the fringes of the display ground attract females' attention.

Black-ruffed males may have black, white or rufous ear-tufts and equally varied upperpart colours.

Rufous-ruffed males look dark, but no two displaying Ruffs look exactly the same.

(Eurasian) **Woodcock**
Scolopax rusticola

L 33–38 cm | **W** 55–65 cm

Medium-sized, thickset, **camouflaged** woodland bird with **long, straight bill**; rather Snipe-like (*p. 194*) but bigger, more barrel-shaped; habitat and behaviour different. Usually flushed within woodland or seen **in flight at dusk**; feeds at night in damp fields and ditches. Back rusty-brown with 'dead-leaf' patterning; underparts closely barred. Forehead pale, peaked; **crosswise black bands over rear crown**. Sex, age and seasonal differences minor.

V | Alternate sharp, whistled "*tsiwik!*" and low, croaking grunt, "*rorrk-rorrk*" during display flight.

 Great Snipe *p. 195*
American Woodcock p. 568

FL | **Rufous on rump and tail**. Wings long, broad-based, evenly barred. Rises fast, twisting, with whoosh of wings. Flies over trees, calling, in twilight display (roding); pot-bellied with quick, flickering action seemingly superimposed on slower beats. Head up, thick bill angled down; feet often slightly lowered.

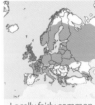

Locally fairly common migrant/resident

Woodland, fields; migrants also in dense cover on coasts

black bands across back of head

ALL YEAR

plumage patterned like leaf-litter

193

Snipe, Jack Snipe and Great Snipe are all similar. | *Rare snipes p. 560*

Snipe

Small/medium-sized waders of wet/muddy places; long-/very-long-billed; feed sedately but fast in flight.

Identify by size | head pattern | upperwing pattern | tail pattern | voice

Jack Snipe (LEFT) is much smaller than **Snipe** and has no pale stripe down the centre of the dark crown.

Snipe tail patterns compared

SNIPE	GREAT SNIPE

14 (12–18) feathers, **all with narrow white tips**

16 (14–18) feathers, **outer 4 white** (Ad) or **white with dark bars** (Juv)

LC **LC** (Common) **Snipe** *Gallinago gallinago*

L 23–28 cm | **W** 39–45 cm

Medium-sized snipe with **very long, straight bill** (points down, even in flight) and short, green legs. Often inconspicuous, in or near long vegetation on wet mud. Feeding flocks may number 100+. Typically flies off in quick **rolling zigzag**, with **noisy calls**. Overall bright brown, black and buff with white belly; cream stripes on back (can look very dark). Head has **pale central line** and buff stripe over eye. **Flank barred**, belly white. Age, sex and seasonal differences minor.

V | Loud harsh "*skaarch*;" calls (often from post or wire) rhythmically repeated "*chip-per chip-per*" spring/summer; harsh "*chip.*" Tail feathers vibrate during display flight, making a loud, buzzing "*h'h'hhhhhhh'h*" sound.

Scarce, locally common resident/migrant

Breeds moorland, marshes, bogs, wet pasture; winters marshes, saltmarsh, wet grassland

FL | Dark with whit[e] belly; **white trailin[g] edge** to dark win[g;] rufous on tail. Settle[s] with tail fanne[d,] revealing **white ti[ps]**

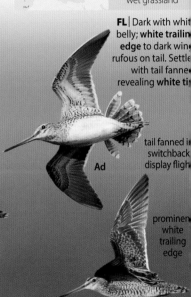

Ad

tail fanned i[n] switchback display fligh[t]

prominen[t] white trailing edge

Two sspp. occur: *gallinago* (LEFT) (widespread); *faeroeensis* (RIGHT) (Iceland, Faeroes), which is darker, more rufous and redder-faced, with thinner pale back stripes. (Birds from Shetland/Orkney are intermediate.)

bill very long

belly white

ALL YEAR

Jack Snipe *Lymnocryptes minimus*

L 18–20 cm | **W** 33–36 cm

Small snipe with dark, cryptic plumage; **bill not excessively long**. Hard to see unless almost trodden on, when flies up quickly, **quietly**, circling before dropping again close by. Usually small numbers (1–5). Feeds inconspicuously with bouncy action. Back dark, with two **long, golden-buff stripes** down each side; green gloss to dark feathers between. Head shows **dark crown** (no pale central line as on Snipe) and double pale band over eye. Age, sex and seasonal differences minor.

√ | Usually silent when flushed; sometimes a quiet croak. Hollow double note repeated in fast, undulating display flight.

FL | Wings quite long and rather straight, dark, with faint pale trailing edge; dark, pointed tail; **dark underwing** against white belly. Bill long but noticeably less so than Snipe's.

faint pale trailing edge

Scarce and local; migratory

Breeds northern bogs; winters wet grassland, marshes, saltmarshes

bill relatively short

ALL YEAR

Great Snipe *Gallinago media*

L 26–30 cm | **W** 43–50 cm

Large snipe, difficult to find, see and identify. Migrants often in drier areas than Snipe (but not invariably so). Brown overall; coarsely marked, 'marbled' effect make it an obvious snipe, but bill thicker, shorter than Snipe's. Pale central crown stripe. **Ad** | dark brown with pale streaks; **white tips to wing coverts**. Long, crescentic **bars across flank and under belly**. **Juv** | like **Ad** but paler and with narrower pale stripes on upperparts and narrower bars on underparts.

√ | Short, insignificant "*brad*" and rush of wings on rising. Strange whining, ticking and trilling notes from displaying ♂.

FL | Blackish midwing panel, edged white, extending to leading edge; faint white trailing edge. Head/neck held quite straight. Spread tail has triangular **white corners**.

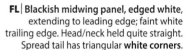

dark, pale-edged, midwing panel

Ad

◉ Woodcock *p. 193*

Scarce and local summer migrant
MAR–OCT

Wet meadows, lowland marshes

Ad
ALL YEAR

belly barred

white tips to wing coverts

WADERS IN FLIGHT pp. 172–1

Phalaropes swim buoyantly with high shoulders tapering to the tail, wingtip/tail raised clear of the water.

LC **Red-necked Phalarope** *Phalaropus lobatus*

LC **L** 17–19 cm | **W** 30–34 cm

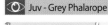

Juv - Grey Phalarope

Small water/waterside bird, usually seen swimming. Smaller than Grey Phalarope but size hard to judge. Bill all-black, **needle-like**. **AdBr**| dark with **long buff lines on back**; white throat more or less surrounded by **rufous band** (brightest on ♀) above **dark grey breast. AdNb**| back grey, striped white; dark eye-patch tends to **turn down at rear. Juv**| (AUG/SEP) body dark, **back striped** with long lines of buff. Neck pale pinkish (quickly fades to white). **1W**| striped grey/white/blackish (Grey Phalarope shows broader clear grey bands). Bill all-black; legs blackish.

Local summer migrant APR–NOV scarce on passag

Breeds near marshy pools, northern lakes; migrants mostly on coast; at sea

V| Calls short, sharp "*kwit*," "*chek-chek-chek*," "*plip*" and squeaky twittering; ♂ gives 'warbling' notes and ♀ a repeated "*wewewewewe*" when breeding.

FL| White stripe on very dark win **AdNb / 1W** not safely separable fro Grey Phalarope unless bill/head deta visible at close rang

Juv

♀ Br

1W
OCT–APR

Juv
JUN–OCT

♂ Br
APR–AUG

♂ cares for eggs/ chicks: begins moult during incubation.

♀ Br
APR–AUG

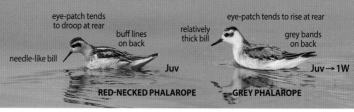

juvenile phalaropes compared

eye-patch tends to droop at rear

buff lines on back

needle-like bill

Juv

RED-NECKED PHALAROPE

eye-patch tends to rise at rear

relatively thick bill

grey bands on back

Juv → 1W

GREY PHALAROPE

Grey Phalarope *Phalaropus fulicarius*

20–22 cm | **W** 36–41 cm

mall wader, usually on water; generally commonest phalarope in W urope in autumn/early winter, especially after gales. Inshore, swims nd leaps over breaking waves; sometimes wades at water's edge. ill slim, but **thicker, broader** than on Red-necked Phalarope (not asy to judge). **AdBr** | brick-red (brightest on ♀); face white, back riped black and buff. **AdNb** | **pale grey and white**, dark eye-patch nds to **rise at rear**. **Juv** | back streaked buff at first (like Red-necked halarope), soon gaining broad **grey bands**; foreneck buff/apricot. **W** | back grey, wing blackish; **small pale patch at base of bill**; legs nged ochre.

| Calls short "*pit*" or "*cruit-cruit;*" when breeding, ♀ calls buzzing *hee*" in flight and "*kwee kwee kwee.*"

Juv, 1W - Red-necked Phalarope
AdNb, 1W - Sanderling p. 190

Rare and local summer migrant APR–DEC; scarce on passage

Breeds Arctic tundra pools; migrants on coasts, at sea

FL | White stripe on dark wing, like long-winged, pot-bellied Sanderling.

Juv → 1W

Juv → 1W

SANDERLING

Juv → 1W

AdNb / 1W

1W
OCT–APR

Juv → 1W
SEP–NOV

♂**Br**
APR–AUG

♀**Br**
APR–AUG

Large waterside birds

are a mixed group of birds that feed in shallow water, at the water's edge, or in marshes and reedbeds. The sexes look alike and there are slight seasonal differences (*e.g.* the growth of long plumes used in display) in some species, and a short period when bill, leg and facial skin colours change in the breeding season. Juveniles are separable (less so in egrets).

IBISES 3 species [1 'escape', becoming established] (*pp. 203, 571*)
Round-bodied, with long neck, round head and downcurved bill; probe in mud. **Flight** Head and feet outstretched. **Sexing, Ageing and Moult** Sexes alike. Adult has full moult to duller plumage Jun-Nov, partial moult Dec-May; duller juvenile moults to 1W Aug-Mar.

Identify by overall colour

STORKS 2 species [2 vagrants] (*pp. 206–207, 569*)
Tall, long-legged birds, with dagger-like bill. **Flight** Long, broad wings; head and feet extended. Migrating flocks soar to gain height, then glide long distances. **Sexing, Ageing and Moult** Sexes look alike. No seasonal changes, single prolonged moult; juvenile drab, with dull bill/legs, complete moult Dec-May; becomes adult over 1–2 years.

Identify by colour of head, neck and back | bill and leg colour | pattern on wing

HERONS 25 species [16 vagrants] (*pp. 209–215, 571–575*)
Long-necked birds with dagger-like bill. **Bitterns** are reedbed birds, larger herons typically waterside species, **egrets** use wet and dry habitats. **Night-herons** are active around dusk/dawn. **Flight** Wings bowed, neck withdrawn, legs extended. **Sexing, Ageing and Moult** Sexes look alike. Adult has seasonal differences in bare part colours, moult complete, prolonged and variable, Jun-Nov; juvenile duller, partial moult Sep-Feb, then like adult.

Identify by overall colour | colour of head and neck, bill, legs and feet | pattern on wing

FLAMINGOS 4 species [1 vagrant and 2 regular 'escapes'] (*pp. 202, 569*)
Very large, slender, very long-legged birds with short, uniquely angled bill. Sweep bill upside down through water; often swim. **Flight** Strong, direct; head and legs outstretched. **Sexing, Ageing and Moult** Sexes look alike. Juvenile drab for first year. Moult variable, almost continuous.

Identify by colour of bill and legs

SPOONBILLS 2 species [1 vagrant] (*pp. 208, 569*)
Heron/egret-like; bill has spatulate tip. **Flight** Neck and legs extended. **Sexing, Ageing and Moult** Sexes look alike. Minor seasonal changes; full moult Aug-Mar, head/body moulted again Jan-Mar; juvenile drab, full moult Dec-May; different bill colours for two years.

Identify by bill and leg colour

CRANES 3 species [1 vagrant] (*pp. 204–205, 570*)
Very large, greyish, with thick-based, tapered neck, short bill, horizontal carriage and plumes over tail. **Flight** Long, straight wings, neck extended. **Sexing, Ageing and Moult** Sexes look alike. No seasonal changes; flightless during post-breeding moult every 2–4 years; juvenile duller than adult, lacking head patterns until at least a year old.

Identify by head and neck pattern | pattern on wing

Identify by colour of eye, facial skin and bill pouch | pattern on wing above and below

PELICANS 3 species [1 vagrant] (*pp. 200–201, 570*)
Huge, distinctive waterbirds with long, pouched bill and short legs and tail.

EGRET (Heron) SPOONBILL HERON CRANE STORK FLAMINGO IB

rge waterside
irds in flight

FLAMINGO

WHITE
STORK
(p.206)

CRANE

WHITE
PELICAN
(p.201)

Ad

CRANE
(p.204)

STORK

Ad

HERON

Ad

DEMOISELLE
CRANE
(p.205)

BLACK
STORK
(p.207)

Ad

Ad

Ad

GLOSSY
IBIS
(p.203)

Ad

Ad

PURPLE HERON
(p.213)

1S

Ad

BITTERN
(p.215)

Ad

GREY HERON
(p.212)

NIGHT
HERON
(p.214)

Ad

Juv

Ad

SPOONBILL
(p.208)

♂

♀

GREAT
WHITE
EGRET
(p.211)

Ad

LITTLE BITTERN
(p.215)

Ad

Ad

Ad

SQUACCO
HERON
(p.209)

LITTLE EGRET
(p.210)

CATTLE EGRET
(p.209)

PELICANS Massive waterbirds; mostly on water but stand on shore or in trees. Social. On water, high, bulky; neck upright or curved; long bill angled down. **Flight** Head/bill withdrawn, much longer than short tail/legs; wings long, wide, fingered at tip. Low, heavy until well aloft, then graceful; slow, deep or shallow beats, long glides; often in lines or 'V'-shapes; soars on flat wings, flocks in co-ordinated circling manoeuvres. **Sexing, Ageing and Moult** Sexes alike. Adult has seasonal differences in bill/face colours; complete moult starts Jul, crest grows by Mar. Juveniles browner, moult when 1 year old; become like adult over 2–3 years.

NT LC Dalmatian Pelican
Pelecanus crispus

L 160–180 cm | **W** 290–345 cm

Huge, grey-white pelican, often mixes with White Pelicans. **Ad** | **crest short, curly; legs grey**; eye pale in pink/yellow skin. **AdBr** | silvery-white; bill pouch deep orange or reddish. **AdNb** | grey-white; bill pouch pinkish-yellow. **Juv / 1Y** | grey-brown above, but paler, less contrasted than juvenile White Pelican; bill pouch pale pink/yellowish. **2Y** | like dull **Ad**; eye darker.

V | Mostly silent.

White Pelican
Pink-backed Pelican p. 570

FL | Upperwing dull black, grey and whitish (less black-and-white than White Pelican, hindwing darkens with wear). Underwing distinctive: **grey with whitish central band** and dusky tip at all ages.

Rare, local, partial migrant

Breeds on shallow lakes, coastal marshes

Ad

Juv/1W

Two adults with a 1st-winter bird (left): the adult on the right already has bright breeding-season face and bill coloration.

slight crest

drab brownish; bill pouch pale

forehead feathering **blunt or 'W'-shaped** above bill

eye pale

slow change to adult over 2–3 years

Juv / 1W
ALL YEAR

Ad
ALL YEAR

Breeding colours on face and bill soon fade.

dull white

White Pelican
Pelecanus onocrotalus

L 140–180 cm | **W** 225–360 cm

Huge pelican, mixes with other waterside species. **Ad** | white or **pink**, yellower on breast; wide, drooping crest. **Eye black in wide patch of pale skin**. Bill grey, pouch yellow. **Legs yellow or pink**. **Juv/1Y** | head and neck brown, face/bill pinkish, pouch yellow; like dull **Ad** by **2W/2S**.

V | Low grunts; mostly silent.

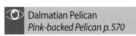

Dalmatian Pelican
Pink-backed Pelican p. 570

FL | **Ad** **black-and-white** above and below (pattern like White Stork (*p. 206*)). **Juv/1Y** broad **pale midwing band** on dark underwing; upperside dark with pale, 'V'-shaped rump. Groups soar on thermals/updraughts, then glide between lakes; bigger flocks synchronized, unlike storks, which tend to criss-cross within circling flocks.

Rare, local; migratory

Breeds on shallow lakes, coastal marshes

AdBr
MAR–AUG

In MAR-APR, facial skin becomes pinkish (male) or orange-yellow (female before egg-laying), and yellow bill pouch turns orange or yellow-ochre.

Ad

Juv/1W

slow change to adult over 2–3 years

Juv/1W
ALL YEAR

brown-and-white; bill pouch yellow

forehead feathering **pointed** above bill

eye dark

Ad
ALL YEAR

bright pinkish

201

LC **Greater Flamingo** *Phoenicopterus roseus*

LC **L** 110–180 cm | **W** 140–170 cm

Huge, pale, slender-necked and long-legged waterbird, unique in Europe (but beware escaped Chilean and American Flamingos). Feeds in flocks (10s to 1,000s), swims like swan, wades deeply or in shallows, **head reaching down to toes**, bill inverted. **Long, sinuous neck; long legs; angled bill. Ad** | pale pink, **bill pale pink with black tip**, eye yellow. Closed wing shows a little red. Legs pink. **Juv** | duller, slightly browner than **Ad**; bill greyish, legs dark. **1W / 1S** | dull white; bill yellowish; legs dull grey-pink.

V | Goose-like gargling and cackling notes.

FL | Flies in lines or 'V's. Neck and legs create long 'javelin'-shape crossed by narrow wings. **Ad** wings black with crimson coverts, striking **red-and-black** below. **Juv** upperwing has brown bands.

👁 *Rare and escaped flamingos p. 569*

Scarce, locally abundant resident

Saline lakes, shallow coastal lagoons, saltpans

First-year birds are whiter than juvenile, but moult and rate of development individually variable, so exact ageing not possible.

Juv
JUN–MAR

Ad

Ad
ALL YEAR

1S
FEB–OCT

legs grey-pink to yellowish

legs pink

Glossy Ibis *Plegadis falcinellus*

L 55–65 cm | **W** 88–105 cm

Very dark, long-legged bird of wet meadows, floods and swamps. Blackish overall; thick-legged; **bill thick, arched**, suggestive of Curlew (*p. 183*) in silhouette. **AdBr**| red-brown; green and copper gloss. **AdNb**/**Imm**| dark grey-brown, with whitish neck streaks.

♫| Usually silent except quiet grunts when breeding.

FL| Slender; outstretched head drooped, legs trailing, wings rounded.

AdBr

AdBr
APR–AUG

looks black at long range

AdNb
AUG–MAR

Scarce, locally common migrant/resident

Freshwater margins, lakes, floods, saltmarsh pools

Northern Bald Ibis
Geronticus eremita

L 70–80 cm | **W** 125–135 cm

Large, thickset, blackish ibis with slightly curved bill and shortish legs. **Ad**| glossed purplish, red-brown on shoulder; long, spiky black crest; bill red; face bare, pink; legs pink. **Juv**| duller, greyer than **Ad**, with no crest; bill and legs greyish-pink.

♫| Throaty croaks and hoarse "*hyo.*"

FL| Fast and elegant; head/bill extended but tail very short and wings taper towards long tip.

Ad

Ad
ALL YEAR

Extinct breeder, reintroduced birds free-flying only in summer; very rare vagrant elsewhere

Cliffs, grassland

LC **(Common) Crane**   *Grus grus*

LC **L** 96–119 cm | **W** 180–222 cm

Huge, stands tall; flies with **legs and head outstretched**, on **flat wings** (unlike herons). **Ad** | grey (back wears browner); **black-tipped tertials droop** over tail. Face black, **nape white**, crown red. **Juv / Imm** | like **Ad** but head grey-brown.

V | Loud, ringing or jarring "*krroo*."

Two sspp. occur: *grus* (widespread); and *archibaldi* (SE Europe), which lacks red on the crown.

Demoiselle Crane
Sandhill Crane p. 570

FL | Wingtip and trailing edge smoky black (like Grey Heron (*p. 212*)). Heavy-bellied; tapers into outstretched neck; wings broad, tips upcurved. Migrant flocks (10s to 100s strong) form long chevrons or 'V's.

Scarce, locally common summer migrant/resident

Extensive marshes, freshwater margins; on farmland, grassland

Ad

Breeding birds are very secretive once eggs hatch and their upperparts wear to a less conspicuous dull, dark brown.

AdBr

Every two to four years, has complete moult before autumn migration, when flightless for six weeks.

Ad
ALL YEAR

gradual change to adult over two years

Juv
JUN–MAY

Demoiselle Crane
Anthropoides virgo

L 85–100 cm | **W** 155–180

Tall, elongated crane (size of Grey Heron (*p. 212*)). **Ad** | grey, fades browner; like Crane but longer, more tapered; **all-grey plumes overhang tail in long, straight point**. Black face, white streak behind eye extends to tapered plume. Black foreneck and **black, pointed plumes on breast**. **Juv** | like **Ad** but greyer head.

V | Call rasping or creaking "*krik*," "*krri-er*," "*krraa*," higher and less musical than Crane.

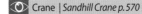
Crane | *Sandhill Crane p. 570*

FL | Flat wings, extended neck, trailed legs and grey colour indicate a crane; wings slightly more tapered, neck slightly shorter than Crane; best feature (not easy to see against sky) is **black breast**. Upperside of flight feathers **grey**, wear to dull black by summer, like Crane. (Grey Heron has pale spots on forewing, wings bowed, head withdrawn.)

Rare and local summer migrant MAR–SEP

Marshes, grassland

Ad

Unlike most cranes, does not become flightless during annual moult.

Juvenile/1w has a pale crown and face but already show the adult's distinctive character, which continues to develop gradually over two years.

1W
AUG–MAY

Ad
ALL YEAR

black breast

long breast plumes

205

LC White Stork *Ciconia ciconia*

LC **L** 95–110 cm | **W** 180–218 cm

Very large **white** or dirty white stork with **black wingtip**. Long-legged; long-necked, with long, dagger-like bill. Feeds with slow, striding walk. **Ad**│**bill and legs red**. **Juv**│like **Ad** but bill black at first; red with black tip in first year.

V│Silent, but loud bill-clapping at nest.

ssp. *ciconia* occurs in Europe.

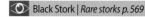
Black Stork | *Rare storks p. 569*

Nests in trees, on buildings, and often on specially provided high platforms; nests can be enormous, with pairs or large young very obvious.

Locally common summer migrant MAR–SEP; local resident

Marshes, farmland, open grassland; nests on trees, buildings, poles

FL│Black-and-white (pattern recalls White Pelican (*p. 201*) and Egyptian Vulture (*p. 269*)); head and long **neck all-white** outstretched; tail short, white; **legs long, red, straight out behind**. Wings **long, broad, deeply fingered**, in smooth bow with tips upturned. Low flight heavy, but soars perfectly. Flocks (10s to 100s strong) circle randomly (pelicans synchronized).

Ad

Flight feathers moult irregularly throughout the year: white edges on new feathers gradually wear off.

sexes look alike

Juv
JUN–JUL

Wades freely in shallow water or feeds on dry ground.

Ad
ALL YEAR

Black Stork *Ciconia nigra*

L 90–105 cm | **W** 173–205 cm

Very large, rather slender **black-and-white** stork. Long-legged; long-necked, with long, dagger-like bill. Feeds along forest streams as well as in open areas.
Ad | head, neck, upper breast and **upperparts blackish**, glossed purplish-green. Bill and face red; legs red.
Juv / 1W | duller, browner than **Ad**; bill and legs pinkish-brown or olive-green.

V | Almost mute; rattles bill like other storks.

White Stork | *Rare storks p. 569*

The black neck and underwing, with a prominent white triangle at the base, prevent confusion with White Stork.

Scarce summer migrant MAR–SEP; very local resident

Forests, cliffs, open grassland; nests on cliffs

FL | Black above (White Stork has white back, wing coverts and tail). **Black breast** obvious; **underwing all-dark** except for white triangle at base. Soars expertly; migrating flocks <100 strong.

Ad

sexes look alike

1W
JUN–MAY

Immature has mixture of new glossy and old brown feathers.

Ad
ALL YEAR

LC (Eurasian) **Spoonbill** *Platalea leucorodia*

LC **L** 80–93 cm | **W** 120–135 cm

Large, **thick-legged**, white wading bird; stance often **horizontal**; egrets typically more upright and elegant. Colonial breeder and also social outside breeding season. Stands in shallows or on tree, bill hidden, crest splayed, when sleeping. Long, slow strides when feeding, **open bill swept sideways** through water. **Ad** | **white**, yellow chin. Bill long, broad, black with **wide, rounded, flat yellow tip**. Legs black. **AdBr** | yellow-buff on neck. Bushy **crest on nape**, raised or blown aside in wind. **AdNb** | loses crest and yellow on neck. **Juv** / **1W** | drab; black wingtip spots. Bill pink, becoming blackish without yellow tip, pale beneath. **2W** | like **Ad** but bill mainly yellow.

V | Silent except bill-snapping at nest.

ssp. *leucorodia* occurs in Europe.

👁 African Spoonbill p. 569

Scarce, locally common migrant/resident

Reedy lakes, marshes; nests in trees; winters on estuaries, saline lagoons

FL | Head outstretched, legs trai vaguely swan-like (*p. 22*) but muc smaller; longer, slimmer, with quicke action than similar-sized Great Whit Egret (*p. 211*)

Juv

AdBr

Juv
JUN–MAY

AdBr
FEB–JUL

Squacco Heron *Ardeola ralloides*

L 40–49 cm | **W** 71–86 cm

Small, **white-winged, brown-bodied** heron; inconspicuous and secretive when feeding. **AdBr** | **peachy-pink or buff**; long plumes from nape; bill blue with black tip; legs pinkish. **AdNb / Juv / 1W** | drab sandy-brown, head/neck streaked grey-brown.

V | Quacking "*kaaahk.*"

Rare pond-herons p.574

FL | Striking **white wings and tail** (usually hidden at rest); dark back.

AdBr

AdNb

AdBr
FEB–JUL

1W / AdNb
JUL–APR

Scarce and local summer migrant
FEB–NOV

Freshwater margins, lakes, rivers, marshes

Cattle Egret *Bubulcus ibis*

L 45–52 cm | **W** 82–95 cm

Small white egret with **rounded head**, short neck and short, **yellow bill**. Feeds among cattle and horses (NOTE: Little Egrets do so, too). Throat feathers bulge under bill (smoothly tapered on Little Egret). **AdBr** | crown, breast and back **buff**. Bill and facial skin briefly turn red in spring, legs reddish, yellow or blackish. **AdNb / 1W** | all-white; legs dusky **greenish** or **greyish-brown**. **Juv** | white; legs black.

V | Short croaks.

Little Egret p.210
Rare egrets/herons pp.572–573

FL | Quick action; short neck/bill, short legs. Flocks fly fast to roost in trees.

May feed and fly in flocks up to 100 or so (Little Egret less social except at roost).

AdBr
FEB–JUL

AdBr
FEB–JUL

bill yellow

AdNb
JUL–MAR

bill often soiled

AdNb

Red colours last only about 10 days during egg-laying period.

Locally common resident/migrant

Farmland, wet grassland, floods, marshes; nests in trees

SSP. *ibis* occurs in Europe.

209

EGRETS are white, heron-like birds of watersides and meadows, nesting, roosting and often perching in trees. They use patient, heron-like feeding techniques, standing or wading slowly, but smaller species also tremble their feet in shallow water and sometimes dash about with raised wings, grabbing small fish with the bill. Cattle Egrets often perch on large grazing animals. Size is important for identification but can be difficult to judge, especially of lone birds or birds in flight.

CATTLE EGRET   GREAT WHITE EGRET   LITTLE EGRET

LC **Little Egret** *Egretta garzetta*

LC | **L** 55–65 cm | **W** 88–106 cm

Medium-sized, **white egret**, stands, wades, leaps or runs; often shuffles feet to disturb prey when feeding. **Ad** | two long plumes from nape; **bill grey-black**; facial skin grey or yellowish. Legs blackish, **bright yellow feet** (beware mud). **AdBr** | wispy, undivided plumes shroud tail and wingtip; facial colour varies from pink/blue to yellowish FEB-AUG. **AdNb** | head plumes reduced, back plumes untidy. **Juv** | bill greener than **Ad** or yellow base to lower mandible; legs greenish, yellowish on feet extending up to joint.

V | Call short, deep croak; croaks and growls at nest.

Cattle Egret *p. 209*
Rare egrets/herons pp. 572–573

Locally common resident/migrant

Salt- and freshwater margins, floods, wet pastures; nests in trees

FL | Angular neck withdrawn; wings arched, feet trailed (Great White Egret has more bowed wings and longer legs).

NOTE: Very rarely, birds occur that are mottled grey or dark grey overall.

Feeds/flies in groups up to 10–20, but roosts may be 100+

AdBr
FEB-AUG

AdBr

AdNb
JUL–MAR

Juv
JUN–NOV

SSP. *garzetta* occurs in Europe.

Great White Egret *Ardea alba*

L 85–105 cm | **W** 140–170 cm

Very large, **white**, heron-like egret with slender neck (**size of Grey Heron** (*p. 212*)). **AdBr** | bill black with yellow/green at base; legs black with yellow, pink or red above joint. No head plumes (unlike Little Egret); broad **cloak of fine, wispy plumes** on back, spread in display. **AdNb / Juv** | bill **bright yellow** (best clue by far); legs and feet dark, often **yellowish above joint**.

V | A dry croak.

Yellow-billed Egret *p. 572*

Scarce and fairly local migrant/ resident

Freshwater margins, floods, marshes, flooded thickets

FL | Direct, relatively slow, on bowed wings (action in between heavier Grey Heron and lighter Little Egret).

Less numerous than smaller egrets but may associate with them.

AdBr

AdBr
MAR–MAY

AdNb
MAY–APR

Two sspp. recorded in Europe: *alba* (widespread resident) and smaller *egretta* (vagrant from N America (to *e.g.* Azores)), safely identifiable only by measurements.

LC **Grey Heron** *Ardea cinerea*

LC **L** 84–102 cm | **W** 155–175 cm

Very large, long-legged, **long-necked**, pale **grey** waterside heron. Bill dagger-like; neck withdrawn or extended, forward-leaning or in 'S' bend allowing forward lunge. **Ad** | **head white** with **black band** extending into long plume from nape. **AdBr** | back grey, with pale plumes; neck whitish, flushed pinkish-grey, with black streaks down front; shoulder and flank black; bill orange or pink-red. **AdNb** | neck white or pale greyish; bill yellow. **Juv** | dull grey; side of crown and nape dark grey without long plume, and blackish streaks down front of neck; bluer-grey above by **1W**.

V | Loud, harsh or higher *"fraank!"* At nest, rhythmic bill clattering, croaks, grunts and challenging screams.

SSP. *cinerea* occurs in Europe.

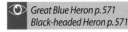
Great Blue Heron p. 571
Black-headed Heron p. 571

FL | Upperwing grey with dull black flight feathers and white patches on leading edge beyond bend of wing; underwing grey, leading edge white, hindwing slightly darker; flank black. Neck withdrawn (or briefly held straight out), legs trailing. Wings broad, **strongly arched**; wingbeats slow. Capable of high soaring and steep, twisting descents.

Locally common migrant/resident

Rivers, lakes, sea coasts; breeds in woods, marshes

wings uniformly broad, with a rounded tip, bowed; feet relatively small; coiled neck shallow (compare with Purple Heron)

Ad

Occasionally makes a low plunge into water from the air to catch fish.

AdBr
FEB–JUN

1W is grey overall, less contrasted than Ad.

1W
AUG–MAY

Purple Heron *Ardea purpurea*

L 70–90 cm | **W** 120–138 cm

Large, slender, secretive heron; more often in dense vegetation than Grey Heron; sinuous neck, slim bill.
AdBr | dark grey, back with long pale plumes; **bend of wing and flank purple-red; neck striped black, white and chestnut**; bill bright orange-yellow.
AdNb | short plumes on back; bill yellow.
Juv | pale rusty-brown; face striped grey and white; cap and hindneck rufous; foreneck buff streaked/spotted black (Bittern is superficially similar but much thicker-necked). **1W / 1S** | like **Juv** but has pointed scapulars and breast feathers.

V | Short, harsh croak.

ssp. *purpurea* occurs in Europe.

Feeds by watching or quiet stalking, often within reeds; may fly down from a perch to plunge into water after a fish.

Imm - Bittern *p. 215*

FL | Wings long, bowed, rather narrow, with 'S'-shaped trailing edge; **coiled neck deep** and narrow; very long toes.

Scarce summer migrant MAR–OCT

Reedbeds, marshes, lakes, riversides

wings narrow-based, tapered to tip; feet relatively large; coiled neck deep (compare with Grey Heron)

Ad

1S
FEB–AUG

Juv
JUN–SEP

AdBr
FEB–JUL

LC (Black-crowned) **Night**
LC **Heron** *Nycticorax nycticorax*

L 56–65 cm | **W** 105–112 cm

Medium-sized, dumpy heron. Hides in foliage by day, flies at dusk, dispersing to feed. **Ad** | cap and back black; forehead white; long white plume from nape. **Wings grey.** Breast pale buff-grey, belly white. Legs yellow-green. **AdBr** | legs red or orange. **Juv** | brown, with teardrop-shaped **white spots over back** and wing coverts. **1Y** | adult-like pattern but dingier, brownish-buff.

V | Coarse, frog-like or crow-like calls in flight.

SSP. *nycticorax* occurs in Europe.

Juv - *Yellow-crowned Night Heron* p.571

FL | Regular crow-like wingbeats, head withdrawn to give bulky oval body shape with deep, angular breast. Often flies at dusk.

Scarce, locally common summer migrant, rare resident

Lakes with water-logged trees, thickets; marshes, riversides

AdBr

Juv

AdBr
FEB–MAY

1S
FEB–OCT

Gains black on back and crown.

Juv
JUN–OCT

Little Bittern
Ixobrychus minutus

L 33–38 cm | **W** 49–58 cm

Small, secretive heron. Oval at rest, elongated when active, stretches down to water. Bill yellow; legs green. ♂| cap and back black; breast peachy-buff; **wing pale buff.** ♀| streaked brown, **wing buff. Juv**| streaked brown, wing mottled buff.

V| Short nasal notes; song single, low, muffled croak repeated every 2·5 seconds. Most vocal at night.

FL| ♂ oval wings black with immediately eye-catching **large, broad, rounded pale patch,** ♀ dark brown, deeper buff patch.

Schrenck's and *Least* Bitterns p. 575

Scarce and local summer migrant
MAR–OCT

Reeds/thickets beside lakes, marshes and riversides

NOTE: Bittern is more than twice the size.

♀
ALL YEAR

Juv
JUN–NOV

♂
ALL YEAR

Reddish face/bill brief, temporary coloration early in breeding season.

SSP. *minutus* occurs in Europe.

(Eurasian) **Bittern**
Botaurus stellaris

L 69–81 cm | **W** 100–130 cm

Large, cryptic heron. **Creeps through dense vegetation** in low crouch; stands still for long periods, bill often raised skywards. Sexes/ages similar. **Yellowish tawny-brown,** marked black/brown all over; **cap black, black streak from bill, long brown stripes on foreneck.** Bill stout, dagger-like; legs green, toes very long.

V| Song of male late JAN-JUN unmistakable 'boom' – loud, very deep "*ah-whump!*"

SSP. *stellaris* occurs in Europe.

FL| Yellowish/rusty-brown, pale forewing band. Wing broad, arched, barred. Head hunched back into a thick 'wedge'-shape or more extended.

American Bittern p. 574
Purple Heron [Imm] p. 213

ALL YEAR

Remarkably hard to see in brown, winter reeds, but may cross open ditch or emerge on edge of clear water.

Scarce/rare and local migrant/resident

Wet reedbeds; reeds, fens, lakes and rivers

Crakes and rails

are small to large birds with rounded head, short wings and long toes. Most are marsh or waterside species, living in dense vegetation. **16 species** [7 vagrants (*pp. 576–577*)]

Coots, gallinules and moorhens have bare facial shield from bill to forehead; **Water Rail** (long bill) and **crakes** (short bill) have no shield. All have long, slender toes, except coots, which have lobed toes and swim more like diving ducks; **Corncrake** is a dry-land bird of hay meadows. **Flight** All weak and laboured, with trailing feet, yet some are long-distance migrants and also perform display flights at night. **Sexing, Ageing and Moult** Sexes look alike in most, but not all, species. Adult has little or no seasonal variation; complete moult after breeding (some species become flightless), head/body moult in spring. Juveniles, and in some species first-year birds, are usually separable from adults, with different colours/patterns and duller bill and legs. Juvenile moults in autumn and again in spring, often into breeding plumage.

Identify by overall colour and shape | bill colour | detailed pattern on upperparts, flank and under tail

POSSIBLE CONFUSION GROUPS Wildfowl (**coots/moorhens** (particularly juveniles) may be mistaken for **diving ducks** (*pp. 48–52*)); grebes (*pp. 75–79*).

LC ## Little Crake *Zapornia parva*

LC **L** 17–19 cm | **W** 34–39 cm

Small, slender crake, with creeping, springy walk. **Wingtip projection beyond tertials rather long**; tail often **cocked**. Pale crescentic streak beside rump. ♂ | back brown with dark stripes and small white streaks; underparts blue-grey, barred only behind legs and under tail. Bill **short**, green with **red base** (may lose red in winter). **Legs yellow-green**. Eye dull red. ♀ | pale buff-brown, back and shoulder patch darker; bill/leg colours as ♂. **Juv** | flank weakly barred, brown with white spots above, bill has very little red (Baillon's Crake has shorter wingtips; Spotted Crake has greyer breast with white spots). Legs green.

👁 Baillon's Crake | *Rare crakes p. 577*

Scarce and local summer migrant
FEB–NOV

Reedbeds, fen, pools

V | Low yapping croak accelerating into a hard, stammering trill, heard at night.

FL ● | Short, fast burst to cover; wing coverts pale, wingtips dark.

Juv
JUN–OCT

red at base of bill

♂
ALL YEAR

♀
ALL YEAR

Spotted Crake *Porzana porzana*

L 19–22·5 cm | **W** 37–42 cm

Small, squat, dark grey-brown, **short-billed** crake; typically secretive but not shy, may walk onto open mud. **Legs green.** **Ad** | bill **red at base**; breast spotted white, rear flank barred; buff under tail. **Juv** | dull, breast brown; bill dark with yellow base. **1W** | like **Ad** but chin whitish, bill dark until FEB.

FL ● | White leading edge to wing (similar to Water Rail (*p. 221*)) shows in brief whirring rise from waterside cover before sudden 'collapse' back out of sight.

Rare crakes p. 577

Scarce and local summer migrant MAR–NOV

Flooded grassland, marshes, muddy pools

V | Sings at night: a sharp, upslurred whistle ending in a 'whiplash' or dripping effect, endlessly repeated.

Ad
ALL YEAR

Female and non-breeding male tend to be more heavily spotted white on breast than breeding male.

Juv
JUN–OCT

Baillon's Crake *Zapornia pusilla*

L 16–18 cm | **W** 33–37 cm

Very small, rounded crake; on mud or in waterside vegetation. **Wingtip projection beyond tertials short**; no pale crescent on tertials. Bill green (no red). **Ad** | sexes alike (but ♀ may have white zigzag bars on scapulars): back brown, with black streaks and narrow white lines and spots; underparts grey, **rear flank barred**. Eye bright red. Legs pinkish to dull greenish. **Juv** | brown, with pale spots/streaks; bill dull yellow-green; legs pinkish/ochre (like Spotted Crake with fewer breast spots, legs less green and sparrow-sized rather than thrush-sized).

Two sspp. occur: *intermedia* (widespread) and *pusilla* (E Europe), which is paler, ♀ often largely white below.

Little Crake | Rare crakes p. 577

Scarce and local summer migrant MAR–OCT

Reedbeds, fen, pools

V | Spring call nocturnal, a low, dry rattle, 1–2 seconds.

FL ● | Brief whirring flutter/run to cover.

no red on bill

Ad
ALL YEAR

Juv
JUN–DEC

CRAKES AND RAILS

MOORHENS AND COOTS are easily separated: **moorhens** have an uptilted, pointed tail; **coots** have a short, blunt tail and rounded back.

MOORHEN

Moorhens skitter across water surface on long, slender toes, dashing clumsily into cover. White under wing, on flank and under tail show well.

They feed on water, drier ground, even in bushes, with typical forward-leaning shape. Usually 1–2, or up to 10–20 in loose groups.

COOT

Coots often run across water on flat, broadly lobed toes, **rounded wings raised.**

They are more strictly water birds, but feed on adjacent grass; rounded, hump-backed, large-footed. Loose groups or larger flocks on open water.

LC (Common) **Moorhen**
LC *Gallinula chloropus*

L 30–38 cm | **W** 55–60 cm

Medium-sized, dark, often rounded rail. Rhythmic, creeping action on ground; dips head, flicks pointed tail both on water and on land. Swims, feeds on open grass, in overgrown ditches. **Ad** | dark glossy brown and grey; **white under tail** and **white stripe along flank; facial shield red, bill red-and-yellow;** eye red; legs green with red top. **Juv** | dull brown, throat whitish; white under tail and on flank. Bill olive-brown; eye dark. **1W** | like **Ad** with dark bill.

V | Varied, typically bubbling, explosive "*kurrt;*" abrupt "*ki-yek*" and "*krek-krek-krek.*"

👁 Lesser Moorhen, rare gallinules p.576

Juv
JUN–OCT

Juvenile plumage lasts until OCT; 1W becomes increasingly grey on underparts and has red eyes by JAN.

Common resident/ summer migrant

Freshwater margins, wet grassland, rivers; semi-saline pools

FL ● | Heavy, weak or sluggish over distance; fluttering, pattering in quick 'escape' across water

Ad
ALL YEAR

SSP. *chloropus* occurs in Europe.

(Common) **Coot** *Fulica atra*

L 36–39 cm | **W** 70–80 cm

Large, rounded, greyish-black, social rail. On ground, heavy, big-footed, not very agile. Usually on inland waters, rarely on sea, loose flocks 10–1,000 or among ducks; 'bobs up' back-first from dive. Swims with head up, **back rounded, tail low; dives frequently. Ad** | slaty-black; **bill pinkish-white; white facial shield** widens to rounded top. **Juv** | dull white lower face and breast.

V | Loud, sudden *"kowk!;"* various sharp, metallic notes. Young have feeble but far-carrying whistles.

Juv
JUN–DEC

Juvenile plumage persists until DEC; facial shield small until early summer.

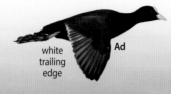

white trailing edge

Ad

pointed

Ad
ALL YEAR

Common, locally numerous resident/ migrant

Lakes, large rivers, sheltered estuaries/ coastal pools

FL ● | Heavy, cumbersome, with deep wingbeats but no agility; **white trailing edge.** Runs open-winged across water.

Ssp. *atra* occurs in Europe.

Red-knobbed Coot

Fulica cristata

L 38–40 cm | **W** 75–85 cm

Large, rounded, black rail; similar to Coot but back tapers more to rear when swimming. On ground, heavy, large footed. **AdBr** | bill bluish-white, **facial shield white; two red 'knobs' on forehead. AdNb** | bill greyish. Facial shield widens to square top (rounded on Coot); black facial feathers blunt against bill (pointed on Coot). **Juv** | greyish; face and breast darker than Coot; bill heavy, greenish.

V | Fast, shrill double notes and 'moaning' call.

Juv
JUN–DEC

Juvenile plumage lasts until AUG/SEP, but the white facial shield may not be fully developed for a year.

no white trailing edge

AdBr

AdBr
MAR–MAY

blunt

AdNb
MAY–MAR

Rare and local resident

Reed-fringed lakes

FL | As Coot but **wings uniform**, no white trailing edge.

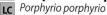

Purple Swamphen
Porphyrio porphyrio

LC
LC

L 38–50 cm | **W** 90–100 cm

Very large, heavy, dark, wetland rail that
strides slowly through vegetation, tail
raised; manipulates stems with feet and
bill. Body unmarked except for **white
patch beneath tail**; **big red bill and
facial shield**; legs and long toes red.
Ad | glossy blue, brighter turquoise on
face and foreneck. **Juv** | paler, greyer than
Ad, especially on breast, whitish belly;
bill and legs dark greyish. **1W** | like dull
Ad, bill dark greyish-red.

V | Sharp "*chock chock*," "*chuck*" and various
bleating and hooting calls.

Ad
ALL YEAR

African ssp. *madagascariensis* (treated as
a species, **'African Swamphen'**, by some)
has green back, blue throat; occasional
escape.

Rare and local
resident/summer
migrant; occasional
vagrant elsewhere

Dense vegetation
beside lakes, marshes

Ad

Juv
MAY–OCT

Ad
ALL YEAR

ssp. *caspius* (Turkey and Caspian region)
has blue-grey head, turquoise throat,
greener wing; sometimes treated
as a separate species, **'Grey-headed
Swamphen'** *P. poliocephalus*.

Ad
ALL YEAR

ssp. *porphyrio* (SW Europe) has dark head
with bright turquoise-blue face/throat.

Corncrake *Crex crex*

L 27–30 cm | **W** 42–53 cm

Large, secretive, dry land crake; usually heard from hay crop or patch of irises/nettles but sometimes calls from stone wall. Pale yellowish-brown, **spread wing rufous**. Face and breast greyish, flank barred rufous. ♂ / ♀ / **Imm** alike, except ♂ tends to be greyest on breast.

V | Unique, rhythmic, dry, rasping double "*craikr-craikr*," with open bill, head thrown upwards, sometimes from rock or wall, most frequent after dark; it is a loud, hard rattle at close range.

upright when calling, otherwise low and squat

FL ● | Low, quick on quite slender but rounded rufous wings; head outstretched; legs trailing.

Ad

Ad
ALL YEAR

Locally fairly common summer migrant
MAR–OCT

Grassland, hay, crops, iris/nettle beds

Water Rail *Rallus aquaticus*

L 23–26 cm | **W** 38–45 cm

Small, long-billed wetland rail; deep-bodied but slender, heard more often than seen. Secretive; walks, runs to cover. **Ad** | dark unless seen closely or in bright light. **Bill long, red at base**. Back streaked brown; **breast slate-grey**; flank barred; **short, raised tail** with white-tipped **buff patch beneath**. **Juv** | pale on breast and over eye; bill and legs dull grey-pink.

V | 'Piglet-like' squeals, moaning and repeated, loud "*kip*;" song an accelerating series of short notes, often at night.

👁 *African Crake p.577*

FL ● | Small wings; legs dangle; outstretched head/bill, white streak under leading edge of wing.

1W
SEP–MAR

Juv
MAY–OCT

Ad
ALL YEAR

Locally common resident/migrant

Dense vegetation beside lakes and rivers, marshes, flooded woodland, upper edge of saltmarsh

Two sspp. occur: *aquaticus* (widespread) and *hibernans* (Iceland [possibly extinct]).

Galliforms (quails, partridges, francolins, pheasants and grouse) have a rounded head,
strong, curved bill and short legs; grouse have fully feathered feet. **Flight** Wings broad, rounded or fingered;
fly with exhausting bursts of rapid wingbeats and long glides before 'collapsing' to the ground. Social; in
most species family groups remain together, flying up as small parties if disturbed. **Sexing, Ageing and Moult**
Males and females differ, slightly or very markedly. Seasonal differences in adults slight (complete moult after
breeding, males may have a brief summer 'eclipse' plumage; some have partial spring moult). Juveniles can
fly when 3–15 days old and start moult to more adult-like plumages when a month old.

Other 'familiar' species in this group that are widely introduced and may be encountered, but do not have
established breeding populations, are Helmeted Guineafowl, Indian Peafowl and Wild Turkey (all *p. 234*).

QUAILS 4 spp. [2 introduced; 1 occasional 'escape'] (*pp. 223, 234*)
Very small, rounded, short-legged, secretive birds. **Flight** Reluctant to fly
(although long-distance migrants), but quite fast; wings relatively long, tail
very short.

QUAIL

Identify by voice | head pattern

PARTRIDGES 6 spp. (*pp. 224–226*)
Rather small, secretive birds of open spaces; small-billed, round-bodied and rather
short-legged; like grouse but bare-legged, more distinctly barred on the flank; all have
a short, rounded tail. **Flight** Fast and low; whirring beats between long glides on stiff,
broad wings.

RED-LEGGED PARTRIDGE

Identify by head patterns | flank barring | leg/bill colour | voice

FRANCOLINS 2 spp. [1 introduced] (*pp. 232, 234*)
Chicken-like with longish neck, short tail. **Flight** Infrequent;
whirring wingbeats between glides.

BLACK FRANCOLIN

Identify by head and neck patterns | flank stripes

PHEASANTS 5 spp. [all introduced or 'escapes', one widespread]
(*pp. 227, 235*) Deep-bodied, short-necked, long-tailed birds of dense woodland
and more open spaces, sometimes in denser vegetation such as reedbeds. Males
(with the longest tails) and females differ markedly. **Flight** Rapid, low, with bursts of
wingbeats between long, flat glides.

PHEASANT

Identify by plumage | females by detailed patterns of barring, leg and bill colour

GROUSE 8 spp. [including 2 snowcocks] (*pp. 228–233*)
Inhabit woodland, heathland and moors, bushy slopes or stony ground (on
mountain tops or lower down in the north). They are chicken-like but squat, small
to very large. Some display together at regular sites (leks) in spring. **Flight** Low, fast,
with bursts of powerful wingbeats between glides.

BLACK GROUSE

Identify by size and shape | tail shape | wing/tail patterns

BUTTONQUAIL 1 sp. [possibly extinct] (*p. 223*)
Inhabit grassland and scrub. Although actually tiny waders (see *p. 154*),
buttonquails are included here as they most closely resemble quails and are almost
like small rails. **Flight** Short, fast, low flights before dropping to cover.

COMMON BUTTONQUAIL

Identify by breast pattern | upperwing pattern | voice

(Common) **Quail**

Coturnix coturnix

L 16–18 cm | **W** 32–35 cm

Very small crouching/creeping terrestrial bird; heard more often than seen. Pale brown; head striped brown and cream; back mottled black, with **buff streaks**; flank rufous with **cream stripes**. ♂ | black **'anchor-shaped' throat stripe** (rarely chestnut). ♀ / **Juv** | throat white, brown crescent on cheek; breast and flank spotted dark.

🔊 | Calls (close range) soft "*miaow*" or "*ma-nah.*" Song of male carries far: a liquid, rhythmic, low "*quik-wik-ik*" or "*wit-wi-wit,*" usually only clue to bird's presence.

L ● | Long, pointed wings. May take off with sudden burst from underfoot, but usually reluctant to fly.

Locally common summer migrant MAR–OCT; local resident

Grassland, cereal crops, scrub

Common Buttonquail | NOTE: *Japanese Quail C. japonica* (rare 'escape' from captivity) is indistinguishable from Quail in the field but has a distinctive voice: alarm call a thin "*tswieet;*" song a scratchy "*druit-dit*" or "*drit-it-dit.*"

Some males are pale-throated

♂

♀
ALL YEAR

♂
ALL YEAR

Two sspp. occur: *coturnix* (widespread) and *confisa* (Canary Is., Madeira, Azores) poorly defined.

Common Buttonquail

Turnix sylvaticus

L 13–16 cm | **W** 25–30 cm

Tiny, elusive and hard to see, behaves like small crake. Similar to Quail but bill longer and eye pale. **Ad** / **Juv** | rufous-brown, whiter below, with **rusty-orange breast-side/shoulder** and **black spots on upper flank**. ♂ | streaked blackish above.

🔊 | Female call a slow, resonant, hooting "*hooop hooop hooop;*" male a lighter "*kek-kek-kek.*"

L | Rarely seen in flight but **pale forewing patch** shows well if flushed.

Very rare local resident (possibly extinct) in Europe

Grassland, scrub

Quail | Small crakes *pp. 216–217*

NOTE: Asian SSP. *dussumier*

Ad
ALL YEAR

Iberian/NW African SSP. *sylvaticus*

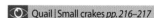

GALLIFORMS

Grey Partridge *p.226* | [Juv] See-see Partridge *p.226*

'Red-legged' partridges

are boldly patterned, large partridges with red/pinkish legs, red bill, plain grey-brown upperparts, grey rump, grey breast, orange belly and barred flank. Most have a white 'face' bordered black. They have a waddling walk and a fast, almost 'clockwork' run. The species are similar; adults differ in their head/neck, flank and tail patterns. Juveniles are pale, plain buff-brown and best identified by their accompanying adults. **Flight** infrequent: fast, low, on stiff wings with quick bursts of beats between glides.

NT Red-legged Partridge
NT *Alectoris rufa*

L 34–38 cm | **W** 47–50 cm

Western 'red-legged' partridge. **Ad** | grey and pale sandy-brown overall (*see table opposite*). **Juv** | plain weak, buff-brown head and neck pattern; bill dark.

V | Mix of croaks and rhythmic, grating, mechanical chuffing sounds, often "*chu chu chu chu ka-chekchek ca-chekchek cachekchek...*" sometimes from high perch.

Locally common resident, widely introduced

Grassland, heathland; dry bushy/rocky slopes; dry, sandy fields

Three sspp. occur but intergrade: *rufa* (widespread); *hispanica* (N & W Iberia) large, dark; *intercedens* (E & S Iberia) small.

FL | Rump grey; tail dark orange with darker central feathers

♀ has grey forecrown

Ad

Black border to 'face' breaks into streaks on neck

♂ ALL

Juv APR–SEP

LC Chukar *Alectoris chukar*
NT **L** 38–39 cm | **W** 47–52 cm

SE European 'red-legged' partridge widely introduced elsewhere; hybrids with Red-legged Partridge may persist in some areas. **Ad** | rather pale sandy-grey overall (*see table opposite*). **Juv** | head and neck buff; bill dark.

V | Loud, prolonged, rhythmic series of hollow, chuckling/coughing notes: "*chok-chok-chok ok chuk-a-ha chuk-a-ha chuk-arr-a*" etc.

Locally common resident and introduction

Open grassy places, dry sandy fields

Three similar sspp. occur but intergrade: *kleini* (SE Europe); *cypriotes* (Crete, Rhodes, Cyprus, SW & SC Turkey) and *kurdestanica* (SE Turkey) paler, browner.

FL | Rump and tail uniformly grey except outer tail feathers grey base, rufous at tip

Ad

diffuse white line above black eyestripe

Brown 'bloom' on fresh feathers wears off to give greyer back.

A ALL

Fledgling APR–SEP

224

Identification of 'red-legged' partridges

	Red-legged Partridge	Chukar	Rock Partridge
Face	white with black collar	creamy white with black collar	white or greyish with black collar
Neck	grey, **streaked black**	pale grey, **plain**	
Flank	barred black, rufous, grey and white; **white bars thinnest**	**barred evenly black and white** (minimal rufous and grey)	**barred evenly black and white** (variable amount of rufous and grey)
Tail	**dark centre, dark orange outer**	**grey base, rufous tip**	**all-rufous**

Rock Partridge *Alectoris graeca*

FL Rump/uppertail coverts grey, contrasting with all-rufous tail.

32–37 cm | **W** 46–53 cm

European 'red-legged' partridge.
Ad back bluish-grey to olive-brown (see table above). **Juv** head/neck greybrown; bill dark.

V Quick, rhythmic, scraping and clicking notes, "ribi-dip tik-i-tik."

Scarce and local resident

High altitude pastures, rocky slopes, alpine meadows

Four sspp. occur: *graeca* (S/E Balkans) greyest back, narrow collar; *saxatilis* (Alps, N Balkans) back dark greyish, tinged olive-brown, thickest collar; *orlandoi* (Italy) as *graeca* but back more bluish-grey, palest underparts; *whitakeri* (Sicily) smallest, with brownest back, darkest underparts, palest ear coverts, narrowest neck collar (often broken) and vermiculations on uppertail coverts and tail.

brightest red bill and legs of these four species

thin white line above black eyestripe (diffuse on Chukar, wider on Red-legged Partridge)

Ad
ALL YEAR

SSP. *saxatilis*

SSP. *whitakeri*

Ad
ALL YEAR

Barbary Partridge

Alectoris barbara

38 cm | **W** 46–49 cm

Ad pale brown; **narrow brown cap, long pale grey stripe** over eye; face pale grey with orange patch behind eye; hindneck and narrow necklace **dark red-brown, spotted white**; flank patch **broadly striped black/rufous/white. Bill red; legs pale pinkish. Juv** head and neck buff; bill dark.

V Rough 'hiccuping' notes and longer, coarse, rising "krrrr-ee;" flight note a sharp splutter.

FL Rump grey-brown; tail rufous with darker central feathers.

SSP. *koenigi* occurs in Europe.

Ad

Ad
ALL YEAR

Rare and local; presumed introduction to Sicily and Canary Islands; introduced Gibraltar

Rocky/grassy slopes

♀ - 'Red-legged' partridges [Juv] pp. 224–225

LC **See-see Partridge**
LC *Ammoperdix griseogularis*

L 22–25 cm | **W** 40–42 cm

Small, pale, orange-billed partridge that is usually found in small groups. Legs yellow. ♂ sandy-brown; crown pale; **forehead and stripe over eye black** above **white cheek streak; long, curved, dark streaks on flank.** ♀ / ♀ **Juv** buff; head almost plain. ♂ **Juv** like ♀ but has grey cap.

V Far-carrying, repetitive "*wheet-div.*"

FL Rarely flies, usually a brief burst, gliding to land with a run.

Very local resident

Sandy slopes

♀ ALL YEAR

♂ ALL YEAR

 'Red-legged' partridges pp. 224–225

LC **Grey Partridge** *Perdix perdix*
LC **L** 28–32 cm | **W** 45–48 cm

Medium-sized partridge with orange/ buff face, grey bill and pale brown legs. **Back brown, streaked buff;** neck, rump and underparts **grey; flank barred red-brown.** ♂ **face orange;** large **dark breast patch.** ♀ as ♂ but face buffish, breast patch small. **Juv** head and breast brown; no dark patch; flank bars short.

V Male calls during slow, upright walk, a creaky, wheezy "*ke-er-it*" or "*cheevit.*"

FL Pale brown; tail wide, rounded, da rusty-orange; wings **barred**, slight downcurved (plain and straighter o other partridge

♂

♂ ALL YEAR

♀ ALL YEAR

Scarce resident

Grassland, dunes, farmland

Five sspp. occur; overall colour, and size of belly patch variable and intergrade: *perdix* (N Europe to Greece); *armoricana* (W & S France); *hispaniensis* (N Iberia); *lucida* (Finland to Urals/N Caucasus); *canescens* (Turkey/Caucasus eastwards).

(Common) **Pheasant**

Phasianus colchicus

♂ 70–90 cm (incl. tail 35–45 cm);
♀ 55–70 cm (incl. tail 20–25 cm)
♦ 70–90 cm

Large, heavy-bodied, chicken-like,
terrestrial bird with **long, tapered tail**.
♂ individually variable: generally red-
brown overall; head green-black with
conspicuous **red facial wattle**; white
neck ring (may be weak or absent);
wing grey, flank copper (or golden) with
black spots; rump brown, bronze or pale
grey-green. ♀ pale sandy brown with
dark spots and 'V'-shaped markings; tail
barred black and buff. **Juv** like small ♀.

👁 *Escaped/introduced pheasants (especially females) p. 235*

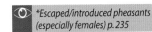

Males individually variable, especially
in rump colour, presence/absence of a
white collar, and wing colour (pale/dark).

Common introduced
resident

Woodland, adjacent
fields, heathland,
moorland, edges of
reedbeds

V Calls "*kutuk kutuk*"
and loud "*kork-kok*"
(with thrum of wings).

FL Fast, low and straight after initial
explosive burst with loud whirr of wings;
long tail obvious (but beware, half-
grown young can fly, but more pointed
tail than partridges (*pp. 224–226*)).

♂

♀

♂
ALL YEAR

♀
ALL YEAR

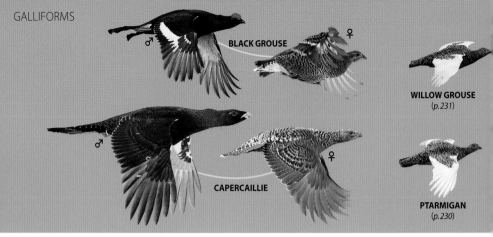

BLACK GROUSE ♂ ♀

WILLOW GROUSE
(p.231)

♂ **CAPERCAILLIE** ♀

PTARMIGAN
(p.230)

LC
LC

Capercaillie *Tetrao urogallus*

L ♂ 74–90 cm; ♀ 54–63 cm | **W** 87–125 cm

Very large, heavy, woodland grouse. ♂| dark blue-grey, wings brown; **white shoulder spot and flank stripe**. Bill large, pale, hooked. Tail rounded, blackish with thin white marks, raised in half-circular fan in display. ♀/**Imm**| large; pale brown; flank and belly white, heavily **spotted black**; **breast orange**, unmarked; tail broad, rounded.

V| Various croaking notes; display song unique series of clicks building into a 'popped cork' note.

FL| Low; noisy take-off from tree or ground fast and direct, with quick, deep wingbeats; often only a glimpse of a large, dark shape disappearing through the trees.
♂ underwing white.
♀ tail wide, rounded, rufous; rump greyer.

Scarce resident

Forest and adjacent moorland heathland

♂
ALL YEAR

Despite its size, often feeds and roosts in pine trees.

♂
ALL YEAR

♀
ALL YEAR

Nine sspp. occur but variable and intergrade.

Caucasian Grouse and Black Grouse are similar but ranges do not overlap.

GALLIFORMS

Caucasian Grouse
Tetrurus mlokosiewiczi

♂ 50–55 cm; ♀ 37–42 cm | **W** 60–70 cm

Local counterpart of Black Grouse.
♂ | **glossy blue-black**, with small white shoulder spot (but no white wingbar); **no white under tail**; red wattle over eye. Tail long, slender, **tip downcurved**.
♀ / **Imm** | long-tailed; olive-brown above, greyish-brown below, barred dark brown; pale stripe over eye above darkish cheek patch, and pale throat.

♪ | Mostly silent; low cackle from ♀.

FL | Fast, direct, with bursts of beats between glides; wings straight, fingered.
♂ upperwing all-dark; underwing white; tail long, notched. ♀ / **Imm** upperwing uniform; tail long (but shorter than ♂), notched or square.

Scarce and local resident

Bushy slopes, high meadows

♂
ALL YEAR

wing plain

♀
ALL YEAR

Black Grouse *Lyrurus tetrix*

♂ 49–58 cm; ♀ 40–45 cm | **W** 65–80 cm

Large grouse (but much smaller than superficially similar Capercaillie); obvious in open pasture, otherwise elusive.
♂ | **blue-black**, with white shoulder spot, **white wingbar** and **white under tail**. Large red wattle over eye; bill small. Tail wide, long outer feathers **curve outwards**.
♀ / **Imm** | head, neck and upperparts rufous/brown and underparts grey/rufous, all barred black; **breast finely barred black, rufous and white**.

♪ | Calls of male far-carrying: rolling, repeated crooning note and 'sneezing' "schuwee."

FL | Fast, with bursts of beats between long glides.
♂ broad white wingbar.
♀ / **Imm** tail notched, barred brown (less rufous than Capercaillie, uniform with rump; not contrastingly blackish as on Red Grouse (p. 231)); **weak white wingbar**.

In display, tail fanned above brilliant white 'cushion' (see p. 222). ♂ briefly loses long tail and is mottled brown on back, JUL–AUG.

Scarce resident

Bushy hillsides, moorland/ heathland/ woodland edge

Three sspp. occur; very slight differences in size and colour, and intergrade.

♂
ALL YEAR

white wingbar

♀
ALL YEAR

LC NT Ptarmigan *Lagopus muta*

L 31–35 cm | **W** 55–65 cm

Small, delicate grouse with distinct seasonal plumages. **Wings white, tail black** at all times (very similar to Willow Grouse, but **bill averages smaller**, although sizes overlap). ♂**Br**| grey, with fine black and white spots; wings, belly and feet white. ♂**Nb**| white except for black tail and **black between eye and bill**. ♀**Br**| grey-brown, tinged yellowish, barred/spotted black. ♀**Nb**| white except for black tail; head **all-white**. **Juv**| grey-black with fine pale fringes above; white with thick, blackish bars below.

FL| Low, short flights, but in display rises steeply before long, descending glide. **Wings white** in all plumages.

Willow/Red Grouse

Locally common resident

Stony plateau mountains and tundra; winter sometimes forest edge

V| Varied low, belching, croaking note typically "*arr-oo-a-karrrr*," "*aa-kaa-kaa kaka*" in song-flight

♀ Nb → Br [APR]

♂ Nb → Br [JUN]

♂ Br → Nb [JUN]

♂ Nb

♂ Br

Three plumages a year match changing snow cover and vegetation creating complex variations, often strikingly piebald during moult.

note difference in bill size: averages smaller on ♀ but much overlap

♀ Nb OCT–APR

♂ Nb OCT–APR

red wattle largest on ♂ but much individual variation

♂ Br JUN–NOV

♀ Br JUN–NOV

♂ Nb OCT–APR

Six sspp. occur, in geographically isolated groups: slight visible variation in breeding plumage (identify by range): *hyperborea* (Svalbard, Franz Josef Land); *islandorum* (Iceland); *muta* (N Scandinavia); *millaisi* (Scotland); *helvetica* (Alps); *pyrenaica* (Pyrenees).

Willow/Red Grouse *Lagopus lagopus*

33–38 cm | **W** 55–66 cm

nall grouse. **Willow Grouse** (sspp. *lagopus* (Scandinavia, N Russia), *riegata* (islets off W Norway) and *rossica* (Baltic eastwards)) has **hite wings all year**, and **white non-breeding plumage** (Ptarmigan as smaller bill, ♂ black on face). Patchy white, dark 'hood' during oult. ♂**Br** | (MAR–JUN) head, neck and breast plain red-brown, back rgely white but increasingly barred brown and black; underparts hite; red wattle over eye. From JUN–SEP, head, back, breast and flank arred tawny-brown and black, less rufous. ♀**Br** | like late-summer ♂ ut upperparts greyer; no red wattle. **AdNb** | white with black tail. **w** | brown mottling on white wings. **Red Grouse** (ssp. *scotica* (Great ritain/Ireland)) has **dark wings** and remains dark all year (see *inset*).

L | Fast; glides on arched wings. **Willow Grouse** has white wings; **ed Grouse** very dark except some **white on underwing**.

Ptarmigan

Scarce, locally common resident/ migrant

Willow Grouse tundra with trees; **Red Grouse** moors

V | Loud, abrupt stutter *"kaa-kaa-kaa - karr-rr-rr-rr-cok cok go-bak go bak bak bak..."*

AdNb

AdNb

♀ ALL YEAR

♂**Br**

♂ ALL YEAR

Red Grouse (SSP. *scoticus*) ♂ **dark red-brown** all year, with white-feathered feet; red wattle over eye. ♀/**Juv** yellowish-brown with broad buff feather edges.

WILLOW GROUSE

♂**Nb** [APR]

♀**Nb** AUG–MAR

♂**Br** MAR–JUN

♀**Br** FEB–SEP

LC Black Francolin
LC *Francolinus francolinus*

L 33–36 cm | **W** 50–55 cm

Chicken-like; longer-necked than partridges (*pp. 224–226*); terrestrial. ♂| head black, **white cheek spot**; rufous collar; underparts black with **white spots**. Back brown, with golden-buff feather edges; rump greyer, barred black and white. ♀| **dark cap, eyestripe and cheek stripe**; dark eye in pale face. **Hindneck rufous**; back brown with pale feather edges; underparts barred buff, brown and black. **Juv**| bright buff, upperparts closely barred dark; tail narrowly barred with black.

SSP. *francolinus* occurs in Europe.

FL| Short glides between bursts of wingbeats. **Tail black.**

♂

♀ - *Erckel's Francolin p. 234*

Scarce, local resident

Grassland

V| Harsh clicks and loud ringing ca "*chlik, cheea-cheea-cheeraki*

♂ **ALL YEAR**

♀ **ALL YEAR**

LC Hazel Grouse
LC *Bonasa bonasia*

L 35–39 cm | **W** 48–54 cm

Partridge-sized, shy grouse of dense forest and undergrowth. Angular head, peaked crown; tail quite long, often raised and spread. ♂| grey; **black throat with white border**. Breast white with dense black and rufous crescentic spots; **flank spotted rusty-red and black**. ♀| as ♂ but throat brown with paler speckling. **Juv**| as ♀ but throat white, tail short.

Up to eight sspp. occur: two colour forms (rufous and grey) and individual variation make separation difficult.

FL| Pale grey rump, **black tail-band**. Wing noise may draw attention as it crashes through branches.

♂

Scarce resident

Forests (mostly mixed or coniferous sometimes pure deciduous)

V| Remarkably high and thin, almo pipit-like. Alarm call a repeated singl sharp note; song a thin, whistled "*tsi-s ti, ti-ti-ti-*

♂ **ALL YEAR**

♀ **ALL YEAR**

Snowcocks

Snowcocks are grouse-like, large and wary; if disturbed will run or make a low, fast glide downhill on straight wings. Shape varies from heavy-bodied with head raised, to hump-backed with head lowered. Often ruffles then tightens dense plumage while walking; legs very short.

Caspian Snowcock

Tetraogallus caspius

L 56–63 cm | **W** 95–105 cm

Pale grey, back with pale spots; white under dark tail. **Tawny-buff around eye and bill**; cap and cheek grey; dark grey band down side of white neck; dark collar. **Hindneck pale grey**. Subtle pale crescent between breast and darker belly. Stripes along flank fine and indistinct, **buff streaks** usually more obvious than dark ones. **♂** breast finely spotted; **♀** breast barred (both look plain at distance). **Juv** like ♀ but dull greyish with plain head.

V Musical whistle with rising inflection, "*wor-lor-le-ee.*"

Caucasian Snowcock

Tetraogallus caucasicus

L 52–56 cm | **W** 80–95 cm

Grey; white under dark tail. Pale **yellowish-buff around eye**; cap and cheek grey; dark grey band down side of white neck; dark collar. **Breast scaled grey and white** (looks plain at distance). **♂** hindneck dark rufous; flank has 5–6 wide, **rusty-black stripes**. **♀** slightly duller and paler than ♂ with thinner, less regular, buff and rufous flank stripes. **Juv** as **Ad** but lacks flank stripes.

V Far-carrying, long, even-pitched musical whistle, "*wu-oo-lee-shluh*" and loud cackles.

FL White band along wing, wider towards tip; **tail sides blackish**; vent white. 'Wrist' patch **dark** grey.

Rare, local resident

High, rocky slopes, snow patches; lower, drier subalpine fringe than Caucasian Snowcock

Two sspp. occur: *tauricus* (S & E Turkey to W Armenia); *caspius* (W Azerbaijan).

♂ ALL YEAR

FL White band along wing, wider towards tip; **tail sides reddish**; vent white. 'Wrist' patch **pale** grey.

Scarce, local resident

High altitude rocky slopes and gorges, avoids deep snow

♂ ALL YEAR

INTRODUCTIONS and ESCAPES

Pheasants, partridges, quails and related species (Galliforms) have been brought to Europe for ornament, shooting, farming and conservation purposes; some were deliberately released ('introduced'), others accidentally 'escaped'. A few species are established (and have full treatment in this book), others remain erratic or temporary additions in very small areas. Those most likely to be seen apparently wild are covered briefly here (but other species might also be encountered from time to time).

LC Indian Peafowl *Pavo cristatus*

L ♂ 100–115 cm (plus 'train' 160 cm); ♀ 95 cm | **W** 130–160 cm

Larger, longer-legged than pheasant. ♂ | brilliant blue head and neck; **huge 'train'** with 'eyed' feathers. ♀ | brown-and-white; greenish neck.
V | Loud, nasal, braying "*ah-yaaah!*"

♀
ALL YEAR

♂
ALL YEAR

UK, Portugal (rare); woodland, parkland

LC Wild Turkey *Meleagris gallopavo*

L ♂ 100–125 cm; ♀ 75–95 cm | **W** 120–140 cm

Very large. ♂ | blackish; head small, pale, red wattle; **tail broad, rounded.** ♀ | brown, barred dark; head dull.
V | Soft, rising, bubbling purr; descending gobble.

♂
ALL YEAR

♀
ALL YEAR

Germany, Russia, Austria (rare and local); forests, orchards, farmland

LC Helmeted Guineafowl *Numida meleagris*

L 53–58 cm | **W** 95–100 cm

Ad | round body, small head, short legs; grey with small white spots; bony red casque on pale blue head. **Juv** | browner, with larger pale spots and bars.
V | Loud, harsh, chattering/gobbling notes.

Ad
ALL YEAR

Rare but widespread; grassland, bushy areas

Smaller galliforms North American quails are much larger and more partridge-like than Europe's native Quail (*p. 223*). Introduced francolins are more clearly related to Europe's Black Francolin (*p. 232*).

LC Erckel's Francolin
Pternistis erckelii

L 38–43 cm | **W** 55–60 cm

Italy; grassland (poss. extirpated)

♂
ALL YEAR

head buff-grey

crown brown

NT Northern Bobwhite
Colinus virginianus

L 25 cm | **W** 33–38 cm

Italy, France; farmland, grassland

face orange

white stripe over eye

♀
ALL YEAR

white throat

♂
ALL YEAR

LC California Quail
Callipepla californica

L 25 cm | **W** 32–34 cm

Corsica, Italy; grassland, scrub

rufous cap

striped black/w

♀
ALL YEAR

♂
ALL YEAR

👁 Green Pheasant [♂ & ♀] and ♀ introduced pheasants are similar to Pheasant *p. 227*

Pheasants Males distinctive but females difficult to identify, all being brownish, spotted and barred, and most having a long, slender tail.

Golden Pheasant
Chrysolophus pictus

L ♂ 90–105 cm; ♀ 60–80 cm
W 87–125 cm

♂ | crown yellow, body orange and dark red; yellow rump edged red. ♀/**Juv** | closely **barred grey**, olive and black; plain rump; long tail **barred black and buff**.

V | ♂ song a scraping "*che-chairk*."

NW Europe, UK; woodland — ♀ ALL YEAR — ♂ ALL YEAR

Green Pheasant
Phasianus versicolor

L ♂ 75–85 cm; ♀ 55–70 cm
W 70–90 cm

Like Pheasant, with which hybridizes. 'Pure' ♂ | dark green; pale bluish shoulders and rump; head glossed deep blue. ♀/**Juv** | streaked dark brown back and rump; barred flank.

Erratic (mostly hybrids); woodland — ♀ ALL YEAR — ♂ ALL YEAR

Silver Pheasant
Lophura nycthemera

L ♂ 120–125 cm; ♀ 70 cm
W 75–90 cm

'Pure' **Ad** | broad, arched tail; red legs. ♂ | white above, black below; large red wattle. ♀/**Juv** | dark olive-brown; red around eye; very short, dark crest; tail broad, rounded, plain, finely barred on side. NOTE: Grey legs may indicate hybrid (frequent) with Kalij Pheasant *Lophura tremarctos*.

V | Short crowing call.

Germany; woodland — ♂ ALL YEAR — ♀ ALL YEAR

Reeves's Pheasant
Syrmaticus reevesii

L ♂ 180–210 cm; ♀ 70–80 cm
W 85–130 cm

♂ | exceptionally long tail; golden-buff with black crescents; rufous, black and white below; black and white head. ♀/**Juv** | long tail; pale yellow around eye and on throat; rufous blotches below, with white arrowhead spots.

V | Song fast, staccato, squeaky, "*chok-chok-cho-cho*."

France, UK, Czech Republic; dense thickets — ♀ ALL YEAR — ♂ ALL YEAR

Bustards

Bustards are medium-large to huge terrestrial birds. Plumages cryptic, but spread wing reveals white. All are declining, rare and restricted in range, although very locally Great and Little Bustards may still be seen in flocks. **Flight** Powerful, direct; neck outstretched. **Sexing, Ageing and Moult** Male and female differ markedly or slightly. Adult seasonal differences small; full moult May-Mar, some have partial moult Dec-May (mostly Mar-Apr). Juvenile like female; moult starts soon after fledging, complete by spring.
4 species [**1 vagrant**, formerly bred but now possibly extinct in Europe]

GREAT BUSTARDS

NT **VU**

Little Bustard   *Tetrax tetrax*

L 40–45 cm | **W** 83–91 cm

Small, pale brown bustard, Pheasant-sized (*p. 227*) (size remarkably difficult to judge when isolated bird crouches in vegetation; often slowly raises rounded head on slender neck). Long legs; short bill. Social: 10s to 100+. **♂Br** | back buff-brown, belly white; **cheek grey, neck black-and-white**. **♂Nb / ♀ / Imm** | like ♂Br but head and neck pale brown, without black-and-white pattern; ♀ finely speckled black on upperparts.

V | Song abrupt rasp or dry croak, repeated; otherwise mostly silent.

👁 ♀ - Pheasant *p. 227*

FL | Rapid, with fast beats like a duck or pigeon, wings flashing **white**; glides on long, square-tipped, arched wings.

♀

♂Br

♂Br
FEB–AUG

Scarce, locally common resident/migrant

Open grassland, crops

Stands with slim neck and small, round head erect; crouched bird looks rather like a female Pheasant.

♀
ALL YEAR

black-and-white neck from two years old, expanded in display

Great Bustard *Otis tarda*

L ♂ 90–105 cm | ♀ 75–85 cm
W ♂ 210–240 cm | ♀ 170–190 cm

Huge, heavy bustard, typically on extensive plains; more or less horizontal stance with neck erect. Despite size, elusive; can hide in tall crops. Dull, grey at long range; brighter, richer colours close-up. Social. ♂**Br**| head grey; neck and breast dark rufous-orange; whitish plumes from base of bill. Back barred black and **bright ginger-brown**; underparts white. ♂**Nb**| loses facial plumes. ♀/♂**Imm**/**Juv**| similar to ♂**Nb** but smaller, duller, slimmer; head greyish without plumes; collar orange.

V| Short bark; mostly silent.

FL| Spread wing reveals extensive white. Large, dramatic; wings long, straight with fingered tips; crane- or stork-like but body heavy and **tail square with no leg projection**.

♀/♂ Imm

Rare and local resident/migrant

Open grassland, crops, steppe

SSP. *tarda* occurs in Europe.

♂Br
FEB–MAY

♀/♂ Imm
ALL YEAR

African Houbara

VU
NT

Chlamydotis undulata

L 45–65 cm | **W** 115–150 cm

Medium-sized bustard: sandy-brown above, **closely barred** with grey; white below. **Foreneck dusky grey; breast and belly white.** ♂| has black stripe down side of neck (wider patch in display; **crest white**. ♀| small, grey-brown; neck stripe thin. **Juv**| like ♀ but lacks neck stripe.

V| Short, mechanical notes in display, otherwise silent.

Rare and local resident (Fuerteventura); possibly vagrant

Scrubby semi-desert

FL| Neck outstretched; wings long, flat, largely black with broad white band near tip.

 Asian Houbara

ssp. ***fuertaventurae*** occurs in Europe.

Ad

wingtip pattern disrupted by moult

Ad
ALL YEAR

Asian Houbara

VU
PE

Chlamydotis macqueenii

L 55–75 cm | **W** 135–170 cm

Medium-large bustard: sandy-brown above, sparsely barred/spotted blackish; white below. **Foreneck and breast pale grey** above white belly. ♂| has black stripe down side of neck (long, broad black patch in display); **crest mixed black and white**. ♀| near-identical to ♂ but averages smaller (often indistinguishable from female African Houbara). **Juv**| like ♀ but lacks neck stripe.

V| Mechanical notes repeated in display, otherwise silent.

Very rare; migratory

Scrubby semi-desert

FL| Black outerwing with **broad white patch.**

African Houbara
NB: past vagrant African/Asian Houbaras in Europe probably involved Asian Houbaras, but most records not identifiable to species.

Ad

Ad
ALL YEAR

Pigeons and doves are medium-sized to large birds of woodland, gardens, farmland,
moorland, cliffs and urban areas. They have a round head and small bill with a fleshy patch (cere) at base; and short, heavily scaled legs. **Flight** Quick, clattering take-off, steady but powerful over long distance with deep, regular or more downward, flicked wingbeats and occasional glides. **Voice** Most have a cooing song but few other calls, although more varied at nest; wings can whistle loudly and make loud 'clap' or clatter.
Sexing, Ageing and Moult Sexes look alike. No seasonal differences; juveniles are duller than adults but differ only slightly in most species. Juveniles begin a complete moult soon after fledging; adult has a complete moult after breeding (any time from May–Dec). Ageing difficult on 'grey' pigeons, as retained browner juvenile feathers look much like faded older ones intermixed with fresh grey new feathers on adults.

23 species [3 vagrants; 3 endemic + 1 introduced on Macaronesian islands]

Identify by wing and, especially, tail patterns (distinctive on most species) | song (most do not have flight calls)

WOODPIGEON   MADEIRA LAUREL-PIGEON

Macaronesian 'laurel' pigeons
Three species of pigeon are restricted to the upland laurel and tree-heath forests of Madeira and the Canary Islands (see p.524)

Sandgrouse recall crouching partridges on the ground, or long-winged, streamlined pigeons
in flight. They are sociable and inconspicuous, shuffling and feeding on the ground in dry to semi-arid areas.
Flight Elongated, long-tailed; fast-flying with quick, deep wingbeats; noisy flocks fly each day to drink at pools, when calls aid identification. **Sexing, Ageing and Moult** Sexes look different. Adults of most species have no seasonal changes, and one complete moult in autumn. The exception is Pin-tailed Sandgrouse, which also has a partial pre-breeding moult and slight plumage differences in male. Juvenile much like female; moult to adult plumage within a few weeks.

5 species [2 vagrants] (pp.246–247, 579)

PIN-TAILED SANDGROUSE

Identify by wing pattern | belly colour | tail shape

PIN-TAILED SANDGROUSE

Regularly occurring pigeons and doves

LAUGHING DOVE
(p. 245)

TURTLE DOVE
(p. 244)

COLLARED DOVE
(p. 245)

ROCK DOVE

STOCK DOVE
(p. 242)

WOODPIGEON
(p. 243)

LAUGHING DOVE (p. 245)

TURTLE DOVE (p. 244)

COLLARED DOVE (p. 245)

Juv

ROCK DOVE

FERAL PIGEON

STOCK DOVE (p. 242)

WOODPIGEON (p. 243)

Rock Dove / Feral Pigeon *Columba livia*

L 30–35 cm | **W** 62–68 cm

Wild Rock Dove is a medium-sized pigeon of wilder places. Feral descendants (including those in towns) occur in a variety of forms. **Rock Dove Ad** is pale blue-grey; lower back/rump **white**, upperwing has two long black bars; **underwing white**. Compared with domestic/town birds, **small** white fleshy patch ('cere') above slim bill (large cere and thick bill on many domestic pigeons). **Juv** like **Ad** but dull and pale.

V Deep, rolling "*coo*" and long "*crrroo-rroo*" notes.

FL **White lower back**, dark tail, **white underwing** distinctive on wild birds. May sway from side to side, gliding on raised wings.

○ Stock Dove *p. 242*

Locally common resident; wild populations mostly mixed with feral birds

Rocky coasts, cliffs, adjacent moor and fields; feral birds widespread

Feral birds on cliffs often like Rock Dove but many are darker, more or less chequered above, some with white patches. Town birds include rusty, blue-grey, white and blackish types. Rock Dove-types have a larger cere than wild birds. Domestic birds circle in tight flocks above loft; racers fly across country in ragged groups, looking long-necked with slimmer, swept-back wings in streamlined evolution of basic shape.

FERAL PIGEON ('Rock Dove' type)

Ad

Ad

ROCK DOVE

'Blue barred'

'Brown'

'Chequered'

'Pied'

Key features of wild Rock Dove
- white rump
- small cere
- white underwing
- two bars across wing coverts

Both Rock Doves ssp. *livia*

FERAL PIGEON

ROCK DOVE

Ad
ALL YEAR

Two sspp. occur: *livia* (widespread) intergrades with *gaddi* (extreme E Europe), which is large/pale.

LC **Stock Dove** *Columba oenas*

LC **L** 28–32 cm | **W** 60–66 cm

Small pigeon, often feeding with Woodpigeon or flying in fast-moving groups. **Ad** | blue-grey overall, side of neck emerald with **no white** (unlike Woodpigeon); innerwing crossed by **two short dark bars**. Legs bright coral-red, bill pink with yellow tip. **Juv / 1W** | like **Ad** but duller; no bright neck patch.

V | Song a deep, rolling, rhythmic "oorr-oo."

SSP. *oenas* occurs in Europe.

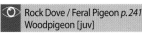

Rock Dove / Feral Pigeon *p. 241*
Woodpigeon [juv]

FL | Dull black around **pale grey midwing**; blue-grey rump, black tail-band; **grey underwing**. No white. Quick, deep beats of arched wings. Display flight has 'stall' and glide with innerwing raised, outer half flat (straighter on Woodpigeon). Stock Dove round-headed, broad wings curved back to slightly rounded tips; Feral Pigeons (and domestic homing pigeons) longer-necked, sharper-winged, with irregular plumage patterns.

Common resident/ migrant

Woods, parkland with old trees, farmland, moorland cliffs and quarries

Ad

Ad

cere inconspicuous (small and white on Rock Dove (p. 241); large and white on Feral Pigeon and Woodpigeon)

dull neck

Juv
MAR–NOV

glossy green on neck

Ad
ALL YEAR

Woodpigeon
Columba palumbus

L 38–43 cm | **W** 68–77 cm

Large, long-winged, blue-grey pigeon with **white band on wing**; sits motionless, feeds on ground and clumsily in trees, solitary to flocks of thousands. **Ad** | neck has **vivid white patch**; breast pink; bill red-and-yellow. **Juv** | duller than **Ad**, no white on neck. **1W** | like **Ad** but some dull juvenile feathers remain (timing variable due to long breeding season).

V | Song rhythmic "*coo, crroo-crroo, cu-coo, cuk crroo-crru, cuk.*" No flight call; strained cooing, moaning and grunting notes near nest. Wings may whistle loudly, also **clatter in alarm** and make **sudden 'slap'**.

Two sspp. occur: *azorica* (Azores) is duller, with smaller white neck patch, than widespread SSP. *palumbus*. [NOTE: SSP. *maderensis* (Madeira) is extinct.]

Juv - Stock Dove

FL | Direct, steady over longer distances after initial clattering climb; often rises to **momentary 'stall'**. Long, narrow head; long wings taper to blunt point; longish, wide-tipped tail; deep chest. Upperwing has unique **white band**; tail grey with paler central band above, black with **white band** beneath.

Common, locally abundant resident/ migrant

Woods, parks, gardens, farmland of all kinds

1W

Ad

no white on neck

Juv
ALL YEAR

white on neck

Ad
ALL YEAR

DOVES

Some larger 'pigeons' may be called 'doves' but smaller species are mostly more slender with a longer tail. Tail patterns, above and below, are useful features, especially obvious in display flights.

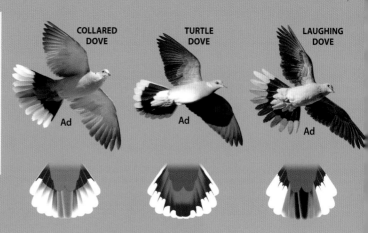

COLLARED DOVE

Ad

TURTLE DOVE

Ad

LAUGHING DOVE

Ad

 # (European) **Turtle Dove**
Streptopelia turtur

L 25–26 cm | **W** 45–50 cm

Small dove, absent in winter. Compared with Collared Dove, smaller, small-headed, more variegated. **Ad/1W**| upperparts **chequered orange-brown**; neck has small **streaked** patch. Breast pale pink, belly white. **Juv**| like **Ad** but paler, duller, greyish; back has blurred dark spots and broad, pale feather fringes; dull neck patch; **more rufous** than Collared Dove.

V| Prolonged, purring, soporific coo: "*currr-currurrr-curr.*"

SSP. **turtur** occurs in Europe.

 Oriental Turtle Dove p.578

FL| Light, agile, **narrow-tipped wings curled back**, tilting or rolling. Display flight high, long, soaring glide and descent with spread tail. Wings show small blue-grey cross-band and dark grey underside. Breast dark, belly **contrastingly white**. Tail grey with dark band and **wide, bright white tip**; underside black with striking white rim.

Scarce but increasingly uncommon summer migrant APR–OCT

Woodland/farmland/downland edge, thickets

Juv
JUN–SEP

Ad
ALL YEAR

Collared Dove
Streptopelia decaocto

L 29–33 cm | **W** 48–53 cm

Medium-sized, slim dove, typically near buildings, on wires, roofs. **Ad** upperparts pale sandy-grey; breast pinkish; narrow **black collar**. **Juv** like **Ad** but faint pale feather fringes, no black collar at first.

V | **Three-note** "*cu-coo-cuk*," middle note strongest but varied emphasis; strained or hoarse versions frequent. Flight call a nasal, slurred "*kwurrrr*." Wings clatter less than pigeons but can whistle loudly in flight.

👁 Juv - Laughing Dove (Juv)
Mourning Dove p. 578
*Barbary Dove p. 525

FL | Direct; display flight a steep climb and gliding descent. Nondescript but upperwing has **blue-grey band**; tail has pale tip, white with **black base** beneath.

Common resident, disperses widely

Farmland, gardens, docks/grain stores/ distilleries

Ad
ALL YEAR

Juv
ALL YEAR

Laughing Dove
Spilopelia senegalensis

L 25–28 cm | **W** 40–45 cm

Small, dark, rusty-brown dove. **Ad** | upperparts pale rufous, wing **blue-grey**; neck orange with **black spots**. **Juv** | rufous, bleaching to sandy-grey; lacks neck spots.

V | Soft, rhythmic, laughing coo, "*du-luooo-d'-d'-do*."

Probably introduced; ssp. uncertain.

👁 Juv - Collared Dove (Juv)
Juv - **Barbary Dove p. 525*

FL | Rump/uppertail dark grey with whitish corners; underside of tail has black band between white vent and broad white tip; underwing soft grey.

Local resident

Urban areas, parks, farmland

Juv
MAR-OCT

Ad
ALL YEAR

Sandgrouse in flight

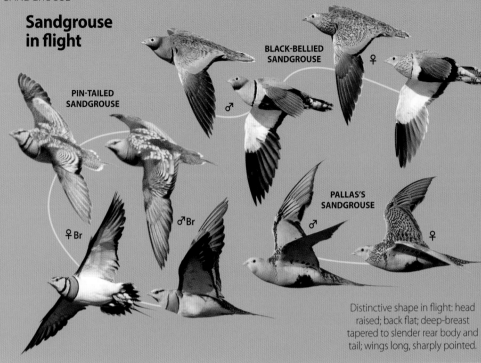

PIN-TAILED SANDGROUSE

BLACK-BELLIED SANDGROUSE ♀

♂

♀ Br

♂ Br

PALLAS'S SANDGROUSE

♂

♀

Distinctive shape in flight: head raised; back flat; deep-breast tapered to slender rear body and tail; wings long, sharply pointed.

LC **Pin-tailed Sandgrouse**

LC *Pterocles alchata*

L 31–39 cm | **W** 54–65 cm

Slim, lightly built sandgrouse with pointed central tail feathers. **Breast rufous or buff bordered by black lines:** ♂ | one line above and one below rufous panel; ♀ | two lines above, one below rufous panel. Underparts **bright white.** ♂**Br** | throat black; back greenish, from MAR with large yellow spots that fade to buff. ♀**Br** | throat white; back barred grey. **AdNb** | throat white; back barred buff, rufous, black. **Juv** | like ♀ but tail short.

Two sspp. occur: *alchata* (Iberia & SE France); *caudacutus* (SE Turkey) paler, shorter-winged.

V | Flies to drink in morning; chorus of nasal, descending *"catarr-catarr."*

Locally common resident

Open steppe grassland, dry riversides

FL | Fast, whirring action, in irregula packs, sometimes large flock Upperwing brown with grey tip an black trailing edge; underwing whit with black border; tail has long thi poin

♀ Br
MAR–SEP

♂Br
MAR–SEP

'Early-phase' breeding plumage, NOV–MAR, lacks yellow spots on back.

Black-bellied Sandgrouse
Pterocles orientalis

L 33–39 cm | **W** 70–73 cm

Large, rounded, pigeon-shaped sandgrouse with **short tail**; head small, round; bill and legs short. Breast **grey**, edged black, above broad cream breast-band; **belly black**. ♂| back pale sandy-buff with orange-buff and grey mottling. ♀/**Juv**| back finely barred black, breast spotted dark.

SSP. *orientalis* occurs in Europe.

V| Flies to drink in morning, with chorus of loud, rolling, gurgling or bubbling notes like "*churrr-rr-eka*."

Scarce and local resident/ migrant

Open steppe grassland, upland slopes

FL| Dumpy body with **black underside, short tail**, pigeon-like head. Wings long and pointed, two-tone above, sandy with black tips; underside has big white patch and black tips.

♀
ALL YEAR

♂
ALL YEAR

Pallas's Sandgrouse
Syrrhaptes paradoxus

L 30–41 cm | **W** 60–71 cm

Pale sandgrouse with long tail. Neck and face orange (head resembles Grey Partridge's (*p. 226*)); **belly has small black patch**; back barred black. ♂| breast-band grey-buff; shoulders/lower breast plain pink-buff. ♀/**Juv**| head pale orange, cheek grey; black spots on neck; back closely barred.

V| Simple nasal "*chup*," repeated, in flight.

FL| Upperwing pale, black trailing edge, narrow, tapered, grey tip; **underwing all-pale**.

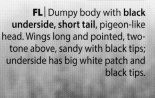

Rare and local resident; irruptive but most records historic

Open steppe grassland

♂
ALL YEAR

♀
ALL YEAR

Nightjars

Nightjars are active from dusk onwards and seen only by chance in daylight: identification rests largely on location and song. They have a broad, flat head, large mouth but tiny bill, and large eyes; their feet are small, suited only for sitting on the ground or bare perches, often lengthwise along a branch. They produce remarkable songs, quite unlike other birds, with a long, monotonous, mechanical effect, as well as calls and wing-clapping. **Flight** Effortless, wheeling, swerving and dipping hunting flight, with wings and long tail spread wide, while catching aerial insects; direct flight is low and relaxed, without the speed of other superficially similar long-winged birds such as cuckoos and falcons.

Sexing, Ageing and Moult Sexes differ slightly. Adults have no seasonal variation: complete moult after breeding; head and body moult in spring. Juvenile similar to adult female, like adult after 5–10 months.

4 species [2 vagrants].

Identify by location | wing/tail pattern | voice

♂ has white spots on wingtip and tail corners (eye-catching in moderate light); other detail hard to make out. ♂1S buff tail spots. ♀/Juv lack white spots.

♀

♂

♂

♀

NIGHTJAR

♂ has squared/diamond-shaped spots on wingtip; ♀ has smaller spots, narrow and rounded on their leading edge.

RED-NECKED NIGHTJAR

NIGHTJAR

Males sing in fading light, on open perches, where they are most easily seen against the paler sky. They can also be seen in silhouette, catching insects in the twilight.

(European) **Nightjar**
Caprimulgus europaeus

L 24–28 cm | **W** 52–59 cm

Small (Blackbird-sized (*p. 385*)); grey-brown and buff 'dead-branch' camouflage pattern, but usually seen as a silhouette **at dusk** in flight or perched on branch or log, near-horizontal. **Head flat, tapered**; bill minute; body slim; wings long; legs very short. **Ad** white streak below cheek, brown throat; **dark** forewing and broad pale band along closed wing. ♂ white on wing and tail. ♀ / **Juv** lacks white.

Two sspp. occur: *europaeus* (widespread); *meridionalis* (Iberia to SE Europe), which is paler and greyer, with larger white spots.

V Call and song **diagnostic**: abrupt, nasal, mechanical "*gooik!*" (beware Tawny Owl's (*p. 258*) "*ke-wick*"). Song vibrating **churr** for **minutes on end** – wooden, hollow, rattling, periodically abruptly changing pitch; 'runs down' before whiplash clap of wings as flies off. (Grasshopper Warbler (*p. 416*) has prolonged trill, high, metallic, ticking.)

FL ● Wings long, tapered; **tail almost as long**, narrow or widely spread, tilted sideways; light, floating swoops, glides and dives; may approach people. ♂ **Ad** three white spots near wingtip and white corners to tail.

Scarce, locally common summer migrant MAR–OCT

Heathland, moorland/woodland edge, woodland clearings

Ad
ALL YEAR

Red-necked **Nightjar**
Caprimulgus ruficollis

L 30–34 cm | **W** 60–65 cm

Large nightjar; nocturnal, best found by following up **characteristic song**. **Ad** shape and complex grey/brown/buff 'dead-wood' pattern very like Nightjar, but back more sandy-rufous. Rufous collar and larger white throat hard to detect. Closed wing shows **grey** forewing (dark brown on Nightjar) and **four rows of pale spots** (pale band on Nightjar). **Juv** greyer than **Ad**.

ssp. *ruficollis* occurs in Europe.

V Song prolonged sequence of hollow but slightly squeaked or nasal notes, "*k'tok k'tok k'tok k'tok….*"

FL ● Wings long, narrow; tail long, narrow or broadly spread in twists and turns of silent, agile flight against fading sky. Like Nightjar but all plumages have white wingtip spots and bold white corners to tail.

Scarce, locally common summer migrant MAR–OCT

Low-lying sandy heathland and bushy places with scattered trees

Ad
ALL YEAR

Owls

Owls are predators with a large, rounded or broadly flattened head, some with 'ear tufts' (not connected with hearing) that can be raised or flattened beside the crown. They have forward-facing eyes and a hooked bill more or less hidden in facial feathers; some have a distinct facial disk outlined with a rim of stiff feathers. Their feet are strong, with hooked claws. Most are woodland birds, hidden in foliage or cavities by day, hunting from perches by night. Others are birds of more open country, Short-eared Owl, for example, behaving more like a harrier in daylight. Little Owls are often easily seen on open perches by day although they hunt mainly at dusk. Calls and song are frequent and useful both in locating and identifying owls. **Flight** Some make short, heavy but silent flights from perch to perch, others have more bounding undulations and some more prolonged, buoyant hunting forays (*e.g.* Barn Owl) with periodic plunges into vegetation to catch prey. **Sexing, Ageing and Moult** Sexes alike in most species; adults show no seasonal differences. Moults are long and complex: Barn Owl replaces plumage with partial moults over several years; other species have almost-complete moult, but different sets of flight feathers are replaced each year. Juveniles are like adults once they lose their first downy covering. **17 species [1 vagrant]**

BROWN FISH-OWL (*p.264*)

EAGLE OWL (*p.261*)

Identify by size | shape | habitat | plumage | eye colour/facial pattern | wing pattern

SCOPS OWLS
(*pp.252–253*)

PYGMY OWL
(*p.255*)

TENGMALM'S OWL
(*p.255*)

LITTLE OWL
(*p.254*)

GREAT GREY OWL
(*p.260*)

URAL OWL
(*p.259*)

TAWNY OWL
(*p.258*)

LONG-EARED OWL (*p.256*)

SNOWY OWL
(*p.263*)

HAWK OWL
(*p.262*)

SHORT-EARED OWL (*p.257*)

BARN OWL

Barn Owl *Tyto alba*

L 33–39 cm | **W** 80–95 cm

Medium-large, narrow bodied, pale owl with broad head and **heart-shaped face** (round when relaxed); eyes black; narrow dark 'V' over bill. **Sandy or golden-buff** above, grey and white speckling evident close-up. Subspecies *alba* (see below for differences from other sspp.) ♂| underparts unspotted, white beside facial disk; ♀| underparts buffish with dark spots, buff beside facial disk, broader bars on flight feathers: variation makes many hard to sex.

V| Shrill, bubbly shriek; various hissing, squealing notes.

FL| Head very large; wings quite short, broad-based, with narrow, rounded tip. Wingbeats slightly jerky; **hovers briefly before headlong dive** onto prey. Outerwing pale with greyish bands; underwing white.

Scarce resident/ migrant

Farmland, woodland/ moorland edge, rough grassland, marshes

Six sspp. occur, which intergrade: *alba* (W and S) white below (Iberian birds speckled beneath); *guttata* (N, NE and E) orange-buff below, greyer above, dark flecking under wing and tail, larger dark patch around eye; *schmitzi* (Madeira) like *guttata* but paler buff below; *gracilirostris* (Canary Islands) underparts between *guttata* and *schmitzi*; *ernesti* (Corsica, Sardinia) pure unspotted white below; *erlangeri* (Crete, Aegean, Cyprus) like *ernesti* but yellower above.

ssp. *alba*

Ad

Ad
ALL YEAR

ssp. *alba*

ssp. *alba*

ssp. *guttata*

ssp. *gracilirostris*

All three scops owls are similar and best separated by voice.

LC (Eurasian) **Scops Owl** *Otus scops*

LC **L** 16–20 cm | **W** 53–64 cm

Common owl in S Europe; strictly nocturnal but may be seen near street lights: follow up song from roofs, wires, trees in villages, olive groves *etc*. Small, slender, **square-headed owl**. **'Ear tufts' short, flat or triangular**. Body greyish, rarely rufous, with 'tree-bark' pattern, streaked, barred and spotted with blackish and whitish marks; wing more rufous. Shoulder has row of **white-tipped pale spots**. Eyes yellow.

V | Rich, deep, musical, abrupt "*tioo*" or "*chew*," repeated every 2–3 seconds, often in prolonged sequence; familiar Mediterranean sound just after dusk. Sometimes main call is preceded by faint, shorter note.

FL ● | Short undulating swoops.

> Three sspp. occur: *scops* (widespread); *mallorcae* (Iberia/Balearic islands) darker, greyer, more streaked; *cycladum* (Greece/Turkey) coarsely marked, spots on upperparts pure white.

Locally common summer migrant/resident

Farmland/town parks/gardens/villages with trees

Ad
ALL YEAR

SSP. *scops*

Sleeping or alert birds stretch upright, eyes closed or reduced to slits, enhancing 'broken-branch' camouflage.

Ad

SSP. *mallorcae*

upright with 'ear' tufts raised

Ad
ALL YEAR

SSP. *scops*

alert or alarmed, ear tufts laid back flat

SSP. *mallorcae*

Ad
ALL YEAR

Pallid Scops Owl
Otus brucei

L 18–21 cm | **W** 54–64 cm

Small, pale greyish owl, much like Scops Owl but with **no rufous**. 'Ear tufts' short; facial disk grey, edged black each side, yellowish-buff near bill; shoulder has indistinct row of **yellow-buff** spots. Back has fine, contrasting dark streaks; belly has fine dark streaks and cross-bars. Eyes dull pale yellow, look dark when half-closed.

V | Soft, low "*huw huw huw huw…*," endlessly repeated, notes a little less than a second apart.

FL ● | Swooping undulations.

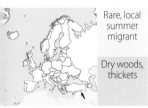

Rare, local summer migrant

Dry woods, thickets

Scops Owl

Cyprus Scops Owl
Otus cyprius

L 16–20 cm | **W** 53–64 cm

Very like Scops Owl but rather dark grey-brown; identified by restricted range and **song**. Facial disk dark. Underparts pale grey, with long streaks of black and bars of grey, whiter central stripe; white leading edge to underwing may show.

V | **Diagnostic song**, two notes alternate 2 seconds apart in long sequence, a low, short one followed by a soft, higher one like Scops Owl: "*dlu, dloo; dlu, dloo … .*"

FL | Short, undulating swoops.

Local resident

Dry woods, thickets

Ad
ALL YEAR

Ad
ALL YEAR

Fledgling **'small' owls** are all brown, round-headed, and yellow-eyed. **Little Owl** has broad head, eyes set well apart, and stands up on slim legs, in open habitat; **Tengmalm's Owl** is quite uniform and dark, with eyes close together; **Pygmy Owl** is tiny with a small, round head, longish tail, and short legs often hidden.

Little Owl (MAY–JUL)   Tengmalm's Owl (APR–JUL)   Pygmy Owl (MAY–JUL)

LC

LC # Little Owl *Athene noctua*

L 23–27·5 cm | **W** 50–57 cm

Small, thickset, thrush-sized owl. Body barrel-shaped; legs long; often in open on branch, stump or rock. Brown, paler below; back **mottled white**, belly streaked dark (becomes paler overall and less streaked on the underparts farther east). Head large, broad with rounded crown. **Eyes yellow** with black rings, beneath **long white, angled brows**; facial disk weak, greyish.

V | Loud, clear, nasal whistles, "*kleee-ow*" or "*chi-chi-chi.*" Song evenly repeated, rising "*keeeah.*"

Five sspp. occur: *noctua* (S/E Europe) rufous, 2 pale tail bands; *vidalii* (W Europe) dark, dull brown, 3 tail bands, long legs; *indigena* (E/SE Europe) pale, rufous, 1 tail band; *lilith* (Cyprus/SE Europe) pale olive-grey, tail spotted, shortest legs; *bactriana* (Azerbaijan) pale greyish. Intergrades occur.

👁 Tengmalm's Owl | Pygmy Owl

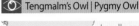

Locally common resident

Farmland/parks with old trees, farm buildings/ruins, rocky islands

FL | Quick, swooping/bounding woodpecker-like before **upward sweep to perch**

ssp. *vidalii*

Ad

Ad
ALL YEAR

ssp. *indigena/lilith* (E Turkey)

Ad
ALL YEAR

ssp. *vidalii*

Ad
ALL YEAR

Often sits on open perch by day but hunts at dusk.

ssp. *noctua*

Motionless, or bobs head; may run on ground after prey

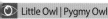

Little Owl | Pygmy Owl

Tengmalm's Owl
Aegolius funereus

21–25 cm | **W** 50–60 cm

Small, strictly nocturnal forest owl, hard to see in tree canopy. Plumage like Little Owl; back brown with sparse white spots, underparts pale with soft brown streaks. Head large with flat crown. Eyes yellow with black rings beneath high brows, giving 'quizzical' look; facial disk wide, rounded, white.

V | Rough, dry "*chiak*." Song a quick series of deep, soft whistles, slightly accelerating, "*pu-pu-po-po-popopopo*," sometimes drawn out into longer sequence.

L | Strong, direct.

Scarce resident

Dense forest with clearings

Ad
ALL YEAR

Flight direct (action like Tawny Owl (*p.258*)).

Ad

Ad

Both SSP. *funereus*

typically inside dense forest

Two similar sspp. occur: *funereus* (widespread) and slightly greyer *caucasicus* (Caucasus).

Little Owl | Tengmalm's Owl

Pygmy Owl
Glaucidium passerinum

15–19 cm | **W** 34–36 cm

Very small owl, smaller than Little or Tengmalm's Owls (size between sparrow and Starling). Oval shaped with smallish, round head, **long tail**. Underparts white with brown streaks, barred across flank. Eyes yellow below **white brows**; facial disk obscure.

V | Thin "*seeee*." Song a series of piping whistles, flatter than note of Scops Owl (*p.252*), a little more than a second apart, or quick, rising squeaks.

L | Bounding undulations.

Scarce, locally common resident

Upland/ northern coniferous or mixed forests

SSP. *passerinum* occurs in Europe.

Ad

'False face' pattern on the back of the head.

Flight undulating (action like a woodpecker).

Ad

White tail bars and lack of shoulder spots separate Pygmy Owl from Tengmalm's Owl.

Ad
ALL YEAR

Often on open treetop perch, waving and flicking tail upwards; hunts by day

LC Long-eared Owl
LC *Asio otus*

L 31–37 cm | **W** 86–98 cm

Medium-large, round-headed, upright owl of dense foliage; **nocturnal feeder**, but droppings/pellets concentrated under daytime roost. **Ad**| streaked brown (more olive than Tawny Owl); belly streaked; closed wing has orange-buff patch. **'Ear tufts' long,** wide, often laid flat. **Eyes deep orange,** surrounded by black; facial disk wide, with white **'V' above bill. Juv**| has dark face for first few weeks.

Short-eared Owl | Tawny Owl *p. 258*

V| Short, moaning hoot, "*oh*" or "*ooh*." Young bird calls like 'squeaky-gate', a plaintive "*pee-ee*" or "*pyeee*," louder, less hissing than young Tawny Owl.

FL| Slow, wavering action similar to Short-eared Owl but wings marginally broader. Beware – ear tufts usually not apparent in flight.

Scarce migrant/ resident

Forest, copses, marshy thickets, hedgerows

Juv
JUN–SEP

Relaxes into broad oval, like Tawny Owl but longer-tailed and more yellow-buff; eye colour obvious if fully awake.

Ad
ALL YEAR

When alert or alarmed, stretches tall, slender and upright, ears raised and face pattern tightened into a narrower shape.

orange eyes; pale shoulder spots

barred trailing edge

Ad

Ad

heavily streaked belly

All ssp. *otus*

finely barred and streaked upperparts

Ad
ALL YEAR

Ad
ALL YEAR

Two sspp. occur: *canariensis* (Canary Is.) is 10% smaller and slightly darker grey-brown than widespread ssp. *otus*.

Short-eared Owl

Asio flammeus

L 33–40 cm | **W** 95–105 cm

Medium-large, round-headed owl of open ground (nests on open moors and tundra, not in trees; winter roosts on ground or in low scrub). Often **flies by day. Ad** yellowish, some very pale, others dark, more rufous; belly white; closed wing has pale golden-yellow patch. Eyes **pale yellow**, broadly surrounded by black; facial disk rounded, edged white; broad whitish fan around bill. **Juv** like **Ad** but buff below and face blackish.

Asio owls in flight

Both Long-eared and Short-eared Owls have a similar wing pattern: upperwing has dark 'wrist' and wingtip separated by contrasting golden-buff patch; underwing is white with a small black mark and dark wingtip. They can be differentiated, even at distance, as follows:

Short-eared Owl	
WINGTIP:	black, solid
TRAILING EDGE:	white line
TAIL:	broad bars
BELLY:	sparsely streaked
Long-eared Owl	
WINGTIP:	barred
TRAILING EDGE:	barred grey
TAIL:	narrow bars
BELLY:	heavily streaked

Ad
ALL YEAR

Short 'ear' tufts are rarely visible, usually only on an alert or alarmed individual stretching upright on the ground.

Long-eared Owl | *Marsh Owl p. 584*

V Emphatic, tuneless, wheezy *"eeyah!;"* song in flight, deep, booming *"bu-bu-bu-bu"* combined with sharp wing-clap.

FL **Low over open ground**, wavering, harrier-like action, frequent glides.

Scarce migrant/ resident

Moorland, heathland; winters also wet pasture, marshes

yellow eyes; blotched pattern on back

white trailing edge

Ad

Ad

whiter belly than Long-eared Owl

marbled/spotted upperparts with bold pale spots

Ad
ALL YEAR

SSP. *flammeus* occurs in Europe.

LC **Tawny Owl** *Strix aluco*

LC **L** 37–43 cm | **W** 81–96 cm

👁 Long-eared Owl p. 256 | Ural Owl

The commonest large owl in most of Europe (size of Woodpigeon (*p. 243*)), but nocturnal, hard to see; voice and silhouette distinctive. Presence indicated by small birds noisily mobbing in tree/ivy, or white droppings under roost (pellets more widely dispersed than Long-eared Owl's). Large, round head, short tail. **Rufous** or **grey-brown**, with row of **white spots diagonally along 'shoulder'**; underparts pale with complex dark, cross-barred streaks. **Eyes dark**; facial disk wide, rounded, greyish, edged darker with pale 'X' between eyes/over bill.

V | Loud, emphatic nasal "*ke-wick!*," "*wik-wik-wik*" and variations. Pure or breathless **hoot** – "*hooo! hu - hu - huwooooo-oo*." Occasionally sings during the day. Young call hissing "*he-wik*" and "*shee-eep*."

FL | Large head, broad wingtips, quick beats.

Common and widespread resident

Woodland, parks, large gardens

Four sspp. occur, differ slightly in size but intergrade: *aluco* (N, C & SE Europe) and *siberiae* (Urals) largest; *sylvatica* (W Europe) and *willkonskii* (NE Turkey) smallest.

Ad
ALL YEAR

In W Europe most are rufous, but grey form (*above*) frequent. Pale grey form common in E, dark grey form in S.

Ad

All ssp. *aluco*

Ad
ALL YEAR

Fledgling
MAR–JUN

Fledgling Tawny Owl already has typically rounded, bulky character; eyes black

ural Owl *Strix uralensis*

50–62 cm | **W** 124–134 cm

arge, upright, greyish owl (but smaller than Great Grey Owl); Tawny wl shape but **tail longer, tapered**. Greyish, strongly streaked dark own; paler than Tawny Owl, but slightly browner than Great Grey wl. **Eyes small, black**; **facial disk wide**, plain greyish with no white 'X' s on Tawny Owl) nor concentric rings (as on Great Grey Owl).

Call harsh, deep, "*grr-ew*." Song deep, cooing, one/three notes "*hoo-oub-hooo*" or quicker, rhythmic series, "*hu pu-pu-pupupu-pu pu*."

Wings uniformly barred, primary patch obscure; long wings and give shape similar to Goshawk (*p. 302*) or Buzzard (*p. 272*).

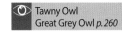

Tawny Owl
Great Grey Owl *p. 260*

Scarce and local resident

Old, damp lowland forest

Three sspp. occur: *liturata* (N Europe); *macroura* (C & SE Europe) larger and slightly darker; and *uralensis* (E European Russia) palest.

ssp. *liturata*

Ad

ssp. *macroura*

Ad
ALL YEAR

Chick
APR–JUN

he large, downy chick already shows the typical upright, round-headed shape; the large bill will quickly become almost hidden by feathers.

LC

Great Grey Owl *Strix nebulosa*

LC **L** 59–69 cm | **W** 160–180 cm

Huge, upright, greyish owl; size close to Eagle Owl but slimmer, more tapered towards tail; head **enormous**. **Ad**|mostly **greyish**; eyes small, **yellow**; facial disk very wide with narrow, concentric arcs of darker grey and striking **white 'X'-shape** between eyes; black bib under pale bill. **Juv**|like **Ad** but less strongly barred.

V|Nasal "*chi-ep chi-ep*" or "*wek-wiek.*" Deep "*grook-grook-grook.*" Song deep, rough, rhythmic hoot "*who-oo*" repeated every few seconds, fading away, not carrying far.

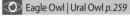

Eagle Owl | Ural Owl *p.259*

Rare and local reside

Lowland, damp fore

FL|Very broad wings show pale b patch towards

Ad
ALL YEAR

Ad

SSP. *lapponica* occur in Europe.

agle Owl *Bubo bubo*

58–71 cm | **W** 160–188 cm

assive owl, size of Buzzard (*p. 272*); head very large, broad, with
ng **'ear tufts'**. Rich, warm brown, buffier on front, streaked dark.
es **flame-orange**. Sex/age hard to judge.

Loud, repeated, staccato bark. Song deep, soft, seemingly 'quiet',
oming, rise-and-fall "*oo-hu*" or flatter "*ooh*," but actually carrying a
uple of kilometres or more, repeated about every 10 seconds.

Arched wings and broad head give front-heavy
ok, unlike large, diurnal birds of prey.

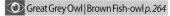

👁 Great Grey Owl | Brown Fish-owl *p. 264*

Scarce but
widespread
resident

Mountain cliffs,
gorges, quarries,
forest

edgling
MAR–JUL

Almost ready to fly, a young Eagle
Owl already looks large and fierce
with vivid orange eyes.

Ad

Ad
ALL YEAR

Four sspp. occur, but
difficult to separate
due to variation,
intergradation and
tendency for each
to be smaller in S of
their range.

LC

LC **Hawk Owl** *Surnia ulula*

L 39–41 cm | **W** 74–81 cm

Small, **long-tailed** owl of forest clearings. Upright or angled on perch, with tail held down; head broad, rounded or flat-topped. **Grey**, mottled, with large, whitish shoulder patches; head boldly marked. Eyes yellow; face white edged with **vertical black band**, and **white 'V'** over eyes. Pale stripes meet in **broad 'V' on nape** giving false 'face' effect from rear.

V | Shrill, hissy, rising *"srrrr-r-r-ik."* Song a long, rapid, hollow, bubbling trill.

FL | Wings broad, rounded; tail long; like Sparrowhawk (*p. 303*) with big, wide head and barrel chest.

Rare and loca resident/ winter migran occasional vagrant

Mixed, boggy mountain slop forest

Fledgling
MAR–JUL

Once it is able to fly, the juvenile is little different from the adult except for pointed, white-tipped tail feathers.

Ad

Ad

Ad

Ad
ALL YEAR

ssp. *ulula* occurs in Europe.

Snowy Owl *Bubo scandiacus*

L 53–65 cm | **W** 125–150 cm

Huge, rounded, 'white' owl; size of Buzzard (*p. 272*), with large, broad head. **Perches upright on ground.** ♂ | **white**; few or no dark marks. Bill shows tiny dark tip; **eyes yellow (can look dark from distance).** ♀ | back barred **grey-black** on white; narrower grey bars on underparts but underwing pure white; eyes yellow but deceptively dark. **Imm** | like ♀ but crown, body and upperwing more barred (♂**Imm** tends to have larger white nape patch and three or fewer tail bands; three to five on ♀**Imm**).

♫ | Short, deep "*huw huw*" and various screeches.

Rare migrant/ nomadic

Arctic tundra, islands, mountain plateaux

FL | Wingbeats steady, rhythmic with slowish downbeat, quicker upbeat.

♀
ALL YEAR

Nesting Snowy Owls may become soiled around the face when feeding a hungry brood several times daily.

♂
ALL YEAR

A fresh-plumaged adult male is pristine white: only the yellow eyes and dark bill tip stand out.

♂**Imm**
ALL YEAR

♂
ALL YEAR

♀
ALL YEAR

LC

Brown Fish-owl *Ketupa zeylonensis*

CR **L** 48–58 cm | **W** 125–140 cm

Large, heavy, 'eared' owl; perches and walks beside water to catch fish. 'Ear-tufts' usually flat or in **wide, shallow 'V'**, may be spiky or inconspicuous. Rich brown; breast and belly pale with fine, dark streaks all over (on Eagle Owl, broad streaks on breast, fine bars lower down). Eyes large, **yellow**; bill **long, prominent** with obvious nostrils; no facial disk: all give different expression from Eagle Owl.

V | Deep, muffled booming "*tu-hu, hoo-hoo, hu-hu;*" whistled, rising "*schrr-ip.*"

👁 Eagle Owl *p. 261*

Status uncertain; very local resident

Rocky or tree-lined streams

FL | Short flights between streamside perches, may skim water with feet lowere

Ad
ALL YEAR

SSP. *semenowi* occurs in Europe.

Birds of prey

Birds of prey are small to very large, with a hooked bill. Some species have distinct plumage forms. **Flight** Direct flight involves flaps and glides; many species 'sail' in long glides with wings flat, bowed or drooped and 'soar', circling to gain height, with wings raised or flat. Falcons, hawks and eagles 'stoop', diving with wings folded back. Harriers glide on raised wings. **Sexing, Ageing and Moult** In most species, sexes differ in size (females larger) and, in some, in plumage. If adult is barred beneath, juvenile is usually streaked and more closely barred on tail. Larger 'brown' eagles have distinct patterns on juveniles/immatures. Smaller species moult each year, the female often while incubating; juvenile looks like adult within one or two years. Larger species have almost constant moult in adults, but a definite sequence in immatures over several years. NOTE: Native, exotic, even hybrid birds of prey, used in falconry/displays, may fly free, creating identification problems.

43 species [13 vagrants] in several distinct groups, not all closely related.

POSSIBLE CONFUSION GROUPS (especially in flight)

LARGER SPECIES, with storks, cranes, herons and bitterns (p. 198); crows (p. 471).

SMALLER SPECIES, with crows, pigeons (p. 240), cuckoos (p. 320), nightjars (p. 248), diurnal owls (p. 250).

In some circumstances, soaring gulls (p. 106), cormorants (p. 74).

HAWKS 4 species
(pp. 299–305) Small to large; secretive, catch prey in short, fast chase or sudden foray; soar well. Plumages of sexes differ slightly; females much larger than males. Bulky nests in trees.

SPARROWHAWK [TOP] | GOSHAWK [BOTTOM]

Identify by wing and body shape | plumage details

FALCONS 13 species
[3 vagrants] (pp. 306–319, 583) Small to large; long-winged. Plumages of sexes differ slightly; females larger than males. Some social, most solitary. Do not build nest: use ledge or tree cavity, or old nest of another species.

KESTREL [TOP] | PEREGRINE [BOTTOM]

Identify by plumage and bare part details

OSPREY 1 species
(p. 278) Large, fish-eating; long-winged, short-tailed. Large nest in tree.

OSPREY

Identify by unique plumage | bowed wings

HARRIERS 5 species [1 vagrant]
(pp. 277, 283–287, 582) Slim; glides on raised wings. Sexes differ; females larger than males. Nest on the ground.

HEN HARRIER

Identify by plumage details | number of 'fingered' primaries

BUZZARDS AND HONEY-BUZZARDS 5 species
[1 vagrant] (pp. 270–275, 582) Large, broad-winged predators/scavengers; smaller than most eagles, weaker bill. Bulky nests in trees.

BUZZARD

Identify by shape and plumage

KITES 4 species [1 vagrant]
(pp. 277–278, 282, 582) Medium-sized to large predators and scavengers; long wings and notched, forked or square tail. Flight very 'buoyant'. Bulky nests in trees.

BLACK KITE

Identify by plumage details

EAGLES 14 species [4 vagrants]
(pp. 276–281, 288–298, 580, 582) Medium-sized to very large; big hooked bill, large feet. Female larger than male (known pairs). Mostly solitary. Large nests in trees/ledges.

LESSER SPOTTED EAGLE

Identify by plumage details | number of 'fingered' primaries

VULTURES 7 species
[3 vagrants] (pp. 267–269, 581) Large to very large scavengers; social; some colonial nesters on cliffs, others solitary in trees; use rising air to gain height, then long glides.

BLACK VULTURE

Identify by shape and plumage

Identifying birds of prey in flight

Remember that birds of prey use their wings and tail to gain or lose height, hover, dive or chase, or perform courtship and territorial display flights, so shape can vary greatly within short periods. All will tend to look 'dark' against a bright sky. Even so, groups have recognizable shapes, flight actions and patterns.

HONEY-BUZZARDS
(pp. 270, 275)
Head slender; tail long, slim or fanned; wings bowed/drooped

HONEY-BUZZARD

BUZZARDS
(pp. 271–274)
Head bulky; tail short; wings raised, flat, bowed/drooped

BUZZARD

EAGLES
(pp. 276–281, 288–298)
Head large; tail short or medium-length, broad; wings long, broad, flat, raised, bowed or drooped

GOLDEN EAGLE

OSPREY (p. 278)
Head small; tail short; wings long, typically kinked or bowed

OSPREY

KITES
(pp. 278, 282)
Head small; tail long, often twisted/tilted; wings long, angled or bowed

RED KITE

VULTURES
(pp. 267–269)
Head small; tail very short or long; wings very long, broad, raised, flat or bowed

GRIFFON VULTURE

HARRIERS
(pp. 277, 283–287)
Small head; long tail; long wings, raised in glide

HEN HARRIER

FALCONS
(pp. 306–319)
Head small; tail longish; wings long, tapered, often angled/swept back, pointed

HOBBY

SPARROWHAWK

HAWKS
(pp. 299–305)
Head small or protruding; tail longish; wings broad-based or long and tapered, typical flap-and-glide bursts in level flight

Rook
(for comparison

Vultures in flight

Vultures are broad-winged, largely reliant on warm, rising air to gain height, then glide over long distances. In cold conditions, prolonged heavy flapping or use of strong winds sweeping up over hillsides may be needed. Separated tips of outer primaries increase stability.

GRIFFON VULTURE
(p.268)

Ad

Ad

Imm

BLACK VULTURE
(p.268)

Ad

Ad

Ad

Ad

Imm

LAMMERGEIER
(p.269)

Ad

Juv

EGYPTIAN VULTURE
(p.269)

Imm

Ad

Ad

Imm

267

NT Black Vulture *Aegypius monachus*

LC | **L** 100–120 cm | **W** 250–295 cm

Huge, square-winged vulture. Nests **in trees**. Short, feathered neck. **Ad** | **dark brown**; 'mask' and throat blackish, crown pale; neck dark brown; bill large, pale bluish and black. **Juv** | head brownish; bill pink at base.

V | Usually silent.

Rare and local resident

Mountains, plateaux, forested plains

FL | **Wings flat or bowed when soaring**, tips drooped. Trailing edge straight. Great variations in apparent shape as bird circles, due to arched wings, upswept outer primaries. Tail short, wedge-tipped. **All-dark above**; dark below, **forewing black**. Pale feet obvious. **Ad** flight feathers often worn. Hindwing has distinct sawtooth, especially on neatly feathered **Juv**.

Juv

Ad

Juv
ALL YEAR

Ad
ALL YEAR

LC Griffon Vulture *Gyps fulvus*

LC | **L** 93–110 cm | **W** 234–270 cm

Huge vulture (larger than eagles). Cliff colonies/roosts revealed by 'whitewash'. Long neck; leaps with spread wings. **Ad** | **buff-brown**; head and downy ruff whitish; bill and eye pale; wing coverts rounded. **Juv** | ruff long, brown; bill black, eye dark; upperwing coverts pointed. **Imm** | intermediate until 6–9 years old.

V | Hissing, squabbling notes.

Scarce, locally common resident/ summer migrant

Gorges, peaks, open plains

FL | **Wings flat when gliding, rais when soaring**. Fast, synchronized gli around cliffs. Trailing edge 'S'-shap tips pointed or square as bird circles. short. **Ad** upperside **buff-brown**, fli feathers and band on coverts **bla** Beneath, forewing more or less bar with whitish lines. **Juv** / **Imm** wea covert band abo

Ad

Ad

Ad
ALL YEAR

Imm
ALL YEAR

SSP. *fulvus* occurs in Europe.

Egyptian Vulture *Neophron percnopterus*

L 54–70 cm | **W** 146–175 cm

Smallest vulture (larger than buzzards (*pp. 270–275*), smaller than Golden Eagle (*p. 292*)). Head and bill slim; tail wedge-shaped. **Ad** | **black-and-white**, soiled ochre; face yellow. **Juv** | dark brown or brown-and-cream. **Imm** | patchy intermediate stages until 5 years old (most remain in Africa).

V | Usually silent.

Rare, locally common summer migrant MAR–OCT; resident on E Canary Islands

Wooded slopes, cliffs, open plains, villages; scavenges at tips

Two sspp. occur: *percnopterus* (widespread, migratory); *majorensis* (Canary Is., resident), larger.

Booted Eagle *p. 280*
White Stork *p. 206*

FL | Agile; deep, kite-like beats. Wings arched or **flat** when soaring. **Ad** upper and underside whitish; **flight feathers black** (streaked pale above); tail white, wedge-shaped. **Juv** dark brown; slim head/bill and pointed tail rule out eagles and larger vultures.

Ad

Imm

Ad
ALL YEAR

Imm
ALL YEAR

NT Lammergeier *Gypaetus barbatus*
VU

L 94–125 cm | **W** 231–283 cm

Huge, long-tailed vulture: beside Griffon Vulture, looks slightly smaller. **Ad** | upperparts charcoal/brown; **head buff-white**; black eyestripe and 'beard'. Underparts stained **orange-buff**. **Juv** | grey, back and belly paler; **blackish hood**. **Imm** | patched dark and pale grey, mature at 6 years old.

V | Very occasionally gives a shrill whistle.

Rare and local resident

Cliffs, gorges, open plains and plateaux

FL | Wings flat or bowed when soaring or in long glides. Drops bones, following down in spiralling dive. Spread tail **wedge-tipped**. Direct flight on angled wings; tail **long and slim**. **Ad** white head; underwing coverts dark. **Juv** grey; dark hood; flight feathers and tail blackish; underwing has pale grey midwing band. **Imm** increasingly dark above, pale below.

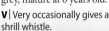

Ad

Ad

SSP. **barbatus** occurs in Europe.

Imm
ALL YEAR

Ad
ALL YEAR

269

'Buzzards' in flight

Buzzards and Honey-buzzard can be difficult to identify, but as a group are usually easy to tell from **harriers** (*pp. 277, 283–287*), which are slimmer-winged and longer-tailed; 'brown' **kites** (*pp. 278, 282*), which have a square-ended or forked tail; and **eagles** (*pp. 276–281, 290–298*), most of which are larger and longer-winged. Buzzard and Long-legged Buzzard can look remarkably eagle-like, but size, habitat, location and underwing pattern are all useful characters.

Identify by shape (including the 'set' of the wings: whether in a 'V', flat or drooped) | flight action | tail pattern | underside coloration

HONEY-BUZZARD (*p. 275*)

Much like Buzzard but slender head, **longer tail** (often held closed, when appears widest in middle). Action more relaxed, 'elastic' than Buzzard (more like Rough-legged Buzzard); soars on **flat wings**. Relatively narrow wings can look round-tipped, trailing edge straight, 'S'-shaped or angled. Often flies between distant feeding areas at considerable height. Highly variable in plumage at all ages; both pale and dark forms occur.

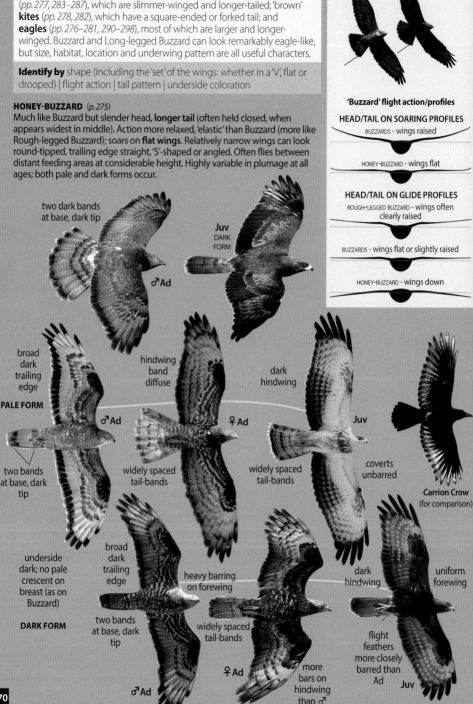

HONEY-BUZZARD   BUZZARD

'Buzzard' flight action/profiles

HEAD/TAIL ON SOARING PROFILES

BUZZARDS - wings raised

HONEY-BUZZARD - wings flat

HEAD/TAIL ON GLIDE PROFILES

ROUGH-LEGGED BUZZARD - wings often clearly raised

BUZZARDS - wings flat or slightly raised

HONEY-BUZZARD - wings down

two dark bands at base, dark tip

Juv
DARK FORM

♂Ad

broad dark trailing edge

PALE FORM

hindwing band diffuse

dark hindwing

♂Ad

♀Ad

Juv

two bands at base, dark tip

widely spaced tail-bands

widely spaced tail-bands

coverts unbarred

Carrion Crow
(for comparison)

underside dark; no pale crescent on breast (as on Buzzard)

DARK FORM

broad dark trailing edge

heavy barring on forewing

dark hindwing

uniform forewing

two bands at base, dark tip

widely spaced tail-bands

♀Ad

more bars on hindwing than ♂

dark hindwing

flight feathers more closely barred than Ad

Juv

♂Ad

ROUGH-LEGGED BUZZARD
(p.274)

black
band
white
tail

BUZZARD
(p.272)

dark
tail-band
on barred
tail

Ad

'STEPPE BUZZARD'
(p.273)

Ad

a wide
range of
plumages,
from very
pale to very
dark

Ad

LONG-LEGGED BUZZARD
(p.273)

♂2W

♂Ad

Ad
(TYPICAL)

Ad
(TYPICAL)

Ad
RUFOUS
FORM

Juv

Ad
DARK
FORM

1S
DARK
FORM

Ad
PALE
FORM

black belly,
in tail-band

**ROUGH-LEGGED
BUZZARD**
(p.274)

diffuse
tail-band

1S
PALE
FORM

complete
dark
trailing
edge and
tail-band;
barred
belly

1S
DARK
FORM

Ad
DARK
FORM

BUZZARD
(p.272)

OSPREY
(p.278)

white
body

**LONG-
LEGGED
BUZZARD**
(p.273)

Ad

dark
midwing
band

fine bars;
no tail-band

finely barred on
secondaries and tail;
streaked belly, pale
crescent on breast

Juv

'STEPPE BUZZARD'
(p.273)

Juv

'BUZZARDS' IN FLIGHT pp. 270–2.

LC LC (Common) **Buzzard**
Buteo buteo

L 48–56 cm | **W** 113–128 cm

Large, upright, creamy-white to dark brown buzzard; bare yellow legs. **Ad** | upperparts brown, underparts whitish with **pale 'U'** between brown streaks on breast and brown bars on belly. **Juv** | belly streaked; greater coverts tipped pale.

V | Loud, sharp "*pi-yaaa*," explosive close-up. Late summer, squealing wails from juveniles (perched or up high).

Eight sspp. occur: *buteo* (widespread); *menetriesi* (Caucasus, E Turkey); migratory *vulpinus* (N and E Europe) and resident sspp. on the Macaronesian Is. (3), Italy/Sicily, and Corsica/Sardinia. Only ssp. *vulpinus* ('**Steppe Buzzard**') distinctive (see *opposite*).

Other buzzards *pp. 273–274*
Honey-buzzard *p. 275*
Marsh Harrier *p. 283*
Booted Eagle *p. 280*
Short-toed Eagle *p. 281*

FL | Quite quick, stiff wingbeats, slower in display flights. Wings usually **raised when soaring** (juvenile flatter); slight upward kink in glide. Switchbacks and plunge-dives in display. Underwing **whitish beyond dark 'wrist'. Ad** broad, dark hindwing band and tail tip. **Juv** dark hindwing band weak, no tail-band.

Common resident/ migrant

Woodland, wooded mountain slopes, heaths and moors

Buzzards hover, but less often than Rough-legged Buzzard.

Juv
DARK FORM

Juv
PALE FORM

Wide plumage variation, but most sspp. have less well-defined colour forms than ssp. *vulpinus* and **Long-legged Buzzard** (*opposite*). Other plumage variations are shown on *p. 271*.

1S
PALE FORM
ALL YEAR

Ad

Ad

Juv

All ssp. *buteo*

Ad
ALL YEAR

Juv
JUL–OCT

'Steppe Buzzard' (SSP. *vulpinus*) (summer migrant to N and E Europe MAR–OCT), sometimes treated as a species (including SSP. *menetriesi*). **FL**| Compared with SSP. *buteo*, smaller, wings flatter, tail longer. Plumages like Long-legged Buzzard: grey-brown (N), rufous (NE) and blackish-grey (SE) forms. Primaries have a flash of white above (small/absent on SSP. *buteo*). **Ad**| underwing coverts dark, flight feathers white with black tips; tail whitish or rufous, tipped dark above; black tail-band on dark rufous birds. **Juv**| streaked below (Ad barred); narrow dark tail tip.

LC / LC Long-legged Buzzard
Buteo rufinus

L 43–62 cm | **W** 112–160 cm

Large buzzard; plumages like smaller 'Steppe Buzzard', but intergrade. **Ad**| PALE FORM rufous-brown, head buff, belly dark brown, tail white; RUFOUS FORM dark rufous-brown with white tail; DARK FORM blackish-brown with whitish tail. **Juv**| head buff/white, breast creamy-white, flank brown or blackish. Eye distinctively **pale**.

V| Infrequent mewing note.

'Steppe Buzzard'

Scarce resident/ summer migrant

Dry plains, rocky slopes

FL| Eagle-like (*pp. 276-281*) shape, head protruding. **Long wings raised in 'V' when soaring**; hovers frequently. **Ad** upperwing typically pale with darker flight feathers and **white patch on primaries**. Tail unmarked, **whitish** or **pale cinnamon**. Pale birds (commonest), head pale, **belly dark**. Below, innerwing pale or with dark forewing, streaked not barred, hindwing whitish with fine black barring and broad **blackish trailing edge**; dark 'wrist' patches; large area of white towards wingtip. **Juv** paler forms have all-dark hindwing, fine bars making tail darker; dark forms like Ad.

Ad

Ad

Ad
DARK
FORM

SSP. *rufinus*

Ad
(TYPICAL)

Juv
PALE
FORM

Juv
JUN–APR

2W
JUL–APR
SSP. *cirtensis*

Ad
ALL YEAR

Ad
ALL YEAR

1S
APR–JUL

Juv
JUN–APR

Two sspp.: *rufinus* (SE) and smaller *cirtensis* (from N Africa; has bred).

273

Rough-legged Buzzard

LC
LC

Buteo lagopus

L 49–59 cm | **W** 120–150 cm

Large buzzard, often on high perch, or hovering; lower leg feathered (hard to see). **Ad** mottled grey-brown and white; head and breast pale, **belly blackish**, thighs pale. **Juv / 1W** head and upperwing coverts whiter than **Ad** but **underparts solidly dark brown**. Eye pale.

Two sspp. recorded: *lagopus* (widespread); *sanctijohannis* (vagrant from N America), most indistinguishable but 25–40% in E Canada are of dark form (unknown in *lagopus*), with head, body and underwing coverts solidly dark brown and tail greyish.

Other buzzards *pp. 272–273*

FL Soars like Buzzard; glides on more upwardly 'bent' wings; active flight more 'elastic'; often hovers. Upperside shows **pale band across primaries**, diagonal pale innerwing band and **broad white base to tail**. Underwing has black patch on each 'wrist' and white towards wingtip; **belly black; tail white with blackish band**. ♂ 1–3 narrow bars above broad black tail-band; ♀ 1–2 fine bars above narrow tail-band; **Juv** broad greyish-black tip to white tail.

V Sharp wail, falling at end "*peee-ya;*" silent outside breeding season.

Rare, locally common; migratory

High, craggy tundra; winters on farmland, marshes

Hovers with deep flaps in calm air, shallow flickers in wind.

♂2W

Juv

Pale patch on upper primaries strongest on Juv/1W, usually more distinct than on Buzzard.

♂ Ad

♀ Ad

Juv

Looks longer-winged, and has more relaxed flight action, than 'stiffer' Buzzard.

Juv / 1W
JUL–MAR

♂ Ad
ALL YEAR

(European) **Honey-buzzard**
Pernis apivorus

L 52–59 cm | **W** 135–150 cm

Similar to Buzzard; much individual variation. Unobtrusive, much less likely to be seen perched in the open than other buzzards. **Ad** | **eyes yellow** (brown in buzzards); base of bill dark grey. ♂ | head grey, back greyish; underparts whitish (pale form) or brown (dark form). ♀ | browner overall. **Juv** | may be whitish with dark mask, more rufous, or very dark; eyes dark; base of bill yellow.

V | Melodious "*whee-ooo*" or "*whi-whee-oo.*"

Buzzards *pp. 272–274*
Oriental Honey-buzzard *p. 582*

FL | Like juvenile Buzzard, but head long, narrow; tail longer. Wings **smoothly drooped** in glide, flat or slightly raised when soaring. Male flutters wings over back between upward swoops in display. From above, ♂**Ad** has broad blackish trailing edge to grey-brown wing, tail has dark tip and two/three bands at base; ♀**Ad** browner above than ♂**Ad**, with pale primary patch and fainter bands on hindwing and tail. From below, dark trailing edge to wing; tail as above, or single band at base on ♂. Lacks Buzzard's pale breast-band. **Juv** many have more, thinner bars under tail and inner primaries.

Locally common summer migrant
APR–OCT

All kinds of mature forest, wooded plains, parkland; migrates over narrow sea crossings

Plumage highly variable, not all can be sexed (see also *p. 270*).

Ad

Juv
DARK FORM
ALL YEAR

Juv
DARK FORM

♂Ad

♂Ad

slim head held slightly raised in flight

♂ more grey-and-white than ♀

♀Ad
ALL YEAR

♂Ad
PALE FORM
ALL YEAR

♂Ad
DARK FORM
ALL YEAR

Smaller eagles, kites and Marsh Harrier in flight

Smaller/medium-sized eagles have their individual character and are neither related to each other nor to the larger, 'brown' eagles (*pp. 288-298*). Booted Eagle may be taken for a buzzard or kite. Red and Black Kites are larger than harriers, long-winged and long-tailed, with remarkably fluent, graceful flight (but also powerful dives onto prey); Black-winged Kite is unique in Europe, a boldly patterned, short-tailed bird of prey that often hovers. Marsh Harrier is the most 'buzzard-like' or 'kite-like' harrier, with obvious male and female plumages.

Identify by size and shape | flight action | underside pattern | tail colour/pattern

whitish on back; pale patch near wingtip

♀ Ad

BONELLI'S EAGLE
(*p. 279*)

tail pale with black tip

Ad

Juv

dark midwing band may be more complete, or absent

white body/dark underwing

Ad

pale forewing diffuse; 2/3 tail-bands

pale forewing, dark midwing band; dark tail-bands

Juv

SHORT-TOED EAGLE
(*p. 281*)

Juv

Ad
DARK-HOODE

Ad
PALE

rusty head/breast streaks; almost uniform pale underwing

white trailing edges to wings and tail; white neck spot, pale rump

Juv

BOOTED EAGLE (p.280)

Juv
PALE FORM

Imm
DARK FORM

Ad

BLACK-WINGED KITE (p.278)

1W

tapered wings with black tips; white tail

RED KITE (p.282)

Ad

Ad

bold white primary patch

pale covert tips form line

Juv

Juv

Red and Black Kites have pale forewing band above

pale covert tips on Juv

BLACK KITE (p.282)

Ad

dull primary patch

Ad

Imm

Juv

pale covert tips; brighter pale primary patch

no pale forewing band

♂Ad

♂Ad

MARSH HARRIER (p.283)

Juv

♀Ad

LC **Black-winged Kite** *Elanus caeruleus*

LC | **L** 30–37 cm | **W** 77–92 cm

Fairly small (pigeon-sized (*p. 239*)), typically upright bird of prey with large head and short tail. **Ad** | back **pale grey**, '**shoulder**' **black**; head white with **black 'mask'**; underparts white. Wingtip extends beyond tail on ♀; equal on ♂. **Juv / 1W** | back grey-brown with whitish feather edges; nape and breast yellow-buff.

V | Occasional shrill "*chee-ark.*"

FL | **Wings raised** in glides; **hovers**. Broad wings taper to a point. **Ad** above, black 'shoulder', square, pale grey tail; underwing white with black tip. **Juv** like **Ad** but grey mottled with brown.

Ad

Juv

1W
OCT–APR

Often hunts at dusk; hovers like heavy-bodied Kestrel (*p. 310*) or Barn Owl (*p. 251*).

Ad
ALL YEAR

Juv
MAY–N

Scarce and local resident

Wooded river valleys, drier plains

LC **Osprey** *Pandion haliaetus*

LC | **L** 52–60 cm | **W** 150–180 cm

👁 Short-toed Eagle *p. 281*

Very large, long-winged, short-tailed, upright bird of prey. Brown above, white below with blurred breast-band. **Ad** | **head white with black band**. Bill and legs blue; eye yellow. **Juv** | buff feather edges on upperparts. Bill bluish; legs and eye yellow.

V | High, whistling "*weilp weilp weilp*" or "*kew kew kew.*"

FL | Wings **bowed**, gull-like, but tips broad, upswept. **Hovers, dives for fish**, resting briefly on surface. Upperwing dark, tail barred brown and buff; **crown white**. Underside white with **black midwing band** and '**wrist' patch**.

On average, ♀ Ad has wider body, longer tail, broader wings, larger head and darker breast-band than ♂ Ad.

Juv

Ad

Juv
JUN–NOV

Two sspp. recorded: *haliaetus* (widespread); *carolinensis* (vagrant from N America), **Ad** darker above, breast-band spotted, eye orange; **Juv** blackish with whitish fringes.

Scarce summer migrant MAR–OCT; rare and local in winter

Lakes, rivers, shallow estuaries and nearby trees

Ad
ALL YEAR

Bonelli's Eagle *Aquila fasciata*

L 55–67 cm | **W** 143–176 cm

Medium-large, powerful eagle; legs long, slender, fully feathered; head flat, bill deep. **Ad** | upperparts dark grey-brown; underparts largely **white**. **Juv** | upperparts brown; underparts **orange-buff**. **1Y / 2Y** | increasingly like **Ad**.

V | Shrill "*ee-ooo*" in display, otherwise silent.

FL | Head long, slim; flat-backed; square-tailed. Active flight fast and dynamic. Wings **nearly flat** when soaring; bulging rear edge, or square, swept back to a point, or angled at front with straight trailing edge (like a big Honey-buzzard (*p. 275*)). **Ad** whitish patch on greyish back; tail grey with **black tip**. Underparts white, **underwing with broad blackish forewing or midwing band** and black trailing edge to flight feathers. **Juv underside orange-buff**, **blackish midwing band** (sometimes broken or absent), primaries white with black tips. Tail pale, narrowly barred grey.

Booted Eagle *p. 280*

Rare and local resident

Cliffs, peaks, wooded gorges

♀ Ad
ALL YEAR

Underparts white with fine dark streaks; long legs fully feathered.

Contrast between white body and dark underwing striking against sky.

Ad

Juv

♀ Ad

tail pale with black tip

♀ Ad
ALL YEAR

Juv
JUN–NOV

SSP. ***fasciata*** occurs in Europe.

LC

Booted Eagle   *Hieraaetus pennatus*

LC **L** 42–51 cm | **W** 113–138 cm

Bonelli's Eagle *p. 279*
Buzzard *p. 272* | Black Kite
p. 282 | Marsh Harrier *p. 283*

Small, round-headed eagle; upperparts dark brown
and buff with **white patch beside neck**. Buzzard-like but lacks mottles/streaks on
underparts; legs feathered. **Ad** | PALE FORM brown above, white below. DARK FORM
all-brown. Both forms marked with buff on 'shoulder' and wing coverts. Intermediates
occur. **Juv** | like **Ad** but more obvious pale buff patches on back and wing coverts.

FL | Head short, rounded; tail square; **wings narrow, held flat or drooped**. Wings and
tail have translucent trailing edge; **white spot each side of neck**, best seen from front
as bird circles. **Ad** upperside brown, with kite-like **pale buff band** across innerwing
and whitish 'U' at base of tail; below, **pale patch** behind bend of wing. PALE FORM body
white, underwing **black-and-white**; tail square, grey. DARK FORM body and underwing
warm brown, with dark midwing band. **Juv** pale and dark forms, similar to **Ad**, or with
paler upperwing band, pale rump and pale cinnamon tail more striking (see similar but
larger juvenile Bonelli's Eagle and especially Black Kite).

Locally common
summer migrant
MAR–SEP; rare in winter

Forested slopes, open
areas with scattered
trees

V | Loud, shrill double
whistles, often high up
in flight

Juv
DARK FORM
ALL YEAR

wings rather
narrow, parallel-
sided (broader,
more rounded
on Buzzard)

Juv
PALE
FORM

Ad
INTERMEDIATE

Ad
DARK
FORM

Juv

pale crescent
on rump

Ad

pale upperwing
band usually
eye-catching

white
neck
spot

broad,
rounded
head

Juv
INTERMEDIATE
ALL YEAR

eye
dark

eye
pale

Ad
PALE FORM
ALL YEAR

Short-toed Eagle *Circaetus gallicus*

Osprey *p. 278*
Buzzard *p. 272*

62–69 cm | **W** 165–180 cm

Medium-large eagle (larger than 'buzzards' (*pp. 270–275*)); head large, **round, owl-like**. Close-up, **gleaming yellow eyes** obvious. Legs unfeathered. **Ad** | upperparts brown; underparts silvery white with brown bars. **Juv** | upperparts pale brown, head streaked rufous and white; underparts white with rufous spots. **Imm** | head and underparts whitish by 2–3 years old, ♂ narrowly streaked below, ♀ broadly streaked.

L | Head large; tail square; wings broad, longer than on Buzzard. **Wings flat when gliding**, slightly raised when soaring. **Hovers frequently**, shaking or trembling wingtips, or with deeper beats, body angled, depending on wind; stoops onto prey. **Ad** brown with paler forewing above; body and underwing white with fine brown bars (**no dark 'wrist' patch or black primary tips**, unlike Osprey or buzzards). Tail pale with 3–4 dark bars. **Juv** underwing almost unmarked on palest birds.

V | Mostly silent; occasional musical whistle.

Locally common
summer migrant
APR–OCT; rare in winter

Open heaths, warm
sunny slopes

SSP. *gallicus* occurs in Europe.

Ad

Juv

Juv

Ad

Dark hood
usually
indicates ♀.

Juv
ALL YEAR

Ad
ALL YEAR

After 8–9 years, head or
head and breast dark
brown (uniform dark
hood on some ♀s).

LC Red Kite *Milvus milvus*

LC | **L** 61–72 cm | **W** 175–195 cm

Large, **red-brown** bird of prey with pale head and long wings and tail.
Ad | dark **red-brown** with pale feather edges on wings. Head whitish; eye yellow.
Juv | narrow rufous tips to greater coverts and secondaries fade to white.

V | Wailing, screaming versions of Buzzard-like (*p. 272*) notes.

Scarce, locally common migrant/

Woodland, mixed/ wooded farmland, villages

SSP. *milvus* occurs in Europe.

FL | Long, flat profile; slow, fluent action; long wings **flat or bowed; long tail deeply notched.**
Ad upperwing brown with **diagonal pale buff band** across innerwing. **Tail pale rufous with dark corners**, whitish below. Underside rufous; large **white patch** near black wingtip. **Juv/Imm** like Ad but whitish line around wing coverts above and below; tail buff, with shallow notch.

Ad

five visible primary tips

Ad

Juv
ALL YEAR

Ad
ALL YEAR

LC Black Kite *Milvus migrans*

LC | **L** 48–58 cm | **W** 135–155 cm

Large, **dull brown** bird of prey with small head, heavily feathered thighs, long wings and tail. Often on ground.
Ad | brown, underparts dull rufous. **Juv** | like **Ad** but rustier; pale feather edges on back and wings, worn to small whitish spots by autumn.

V | Tremulous, vibrant "whee-ee-ee."

Common summer migrant FEB–OCT

Woodland edge, farmland, villages; migrates over narrow sea crossings

SSP. *migrans* widespread in Europe

FL | Elongated profile wings bowed; t notched, triangu when spread. Act flight with swoopi turns, twisting/tilti tail (unlike harrie
Ad upperwing brown with **diagonal pa buffish band** acr innerwing. **Tail brown** with dark bars, pa beneath; underwing shows dull pa primary patch. **Juv** | Ad but more obvic pale patch und primar

Ad

SSP. *migrans*

Ad

six visible primary tips

Ad

SSP. *lineatus*

Juv
ALL YEAR

SSP. *lineatus*
('**Black-eared Kite**', sometimes treated as a species, vagrant from Asia). **Ad** | whiter patch under primaries; crown pale above dark brown band through eye.
Juv | streaked; neck blackish; back/wings spotted buff.

A
ALL Y

SSP. *migra*

Marsh Harrier *Circus aeruginosus*

L 43–55 cm | **W** 120–135 cm

Bulky harrier: ♀ heavy-bodied; ♂ smaller, slim. **♂ Ad** | back brown, head buff, wing pale grey with black tip; **tail grey**; underparts rusty-buff. **♀ Ad** | strikingly **dark brown** with **cream cap** and throat, cream patch on forewing and often pale streaks on breast. **Juv** | like **♀ Ad** but with dark eye; hard to age. A few are brown-black. Fades paler by first summer. **Imm** | eye becomes yellow; ♂ acquires pale grey over 2–3 years.

V | Silent except high chatter over nest in spring.

FL | Broader-winged than other harriers (*pp. 284–287*) but typical low, direct or wavering flight, with supple beats between **glides on raised wings**. Soars high, wings raised like Buzzard; in spring, acrobatic tumbling and foot-to-foot 'food passes' between ♂ and ♀. Straighter wings, rounded tail, lack of pale diagonal on upperwing and glides on raised wings distinguish it from rather similar Black Kite. **♂ Ad** wings grey with buff-and-brown forewing and black tip; tail grey. Some birds have brown tail and dark trailing edge to duller wing. **♀ Ad** all-dark brown except pale buff head, forewing and streaks on body; tail brown, speckled rufous. **Juv** like **♀ Ad** but on underwing, primary coverts tipped rufous-buff (plain on **♀ Ad**) and tail unmarked (dark form Booted Eagle has pale upperwing band and rump).

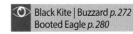

Black Kite | Buzzard *p. 272*
Booted Eagle *p. 280*

Scarce, locally common summer migrant/resident

Reedy marshes, ditches, floods

ssp. *aeruginosus* occurs in Europe.

Juv

Juveniles are dark brown (a minority black-brown), with cream crown and throat, rarely restricted to nape (ABOVE).

♀ Imm
ALL YEAR

♂ Ad

♂ Ad

♀ Ad

♂ Ad

Juv
ALL YEAR

NOTE: Some males breed in immature plumage and never achieve full adult coloration.

♀ Ad
ALL YEAR

♂ more lightly built than ♀

♂ Ad
ALL YEAR

283

Smaller harriers

Hen, Montagu's, Pallid and Northern Harriers can be difficult to identify, having similar plumage patterns and flight actions. Adult males are grey with black wingtips; adult females and juveniles ('ringtails') are brown with a barred brown-and-cream tail. An overall appreciation of shape, wingtip structure and plumage detail is essential for confident identification. With 'ringtails', concentrate on head/neck pattern, colour of underparts and underwing. Females are noticeably larger than males (so a 'small ringtail' might be a male Montagu's or Pallid Harrier, but a juvenile male Hen Harrier must also be ruled out). Note presence/absence in winter months.

LC

Hen Harrier *Circus cyaneus*

NT **L** 45–55 cm | **W** 99–121 cm

Smaller than Buzzard (*p. 272*) but has longer, slimmer wings, tail and legs. ♂**Ad**| grey; **wingtip black**; breast grey, belly plain white. ♂**1Y/2Y**| like ♂**Ad** but back grey-brown. ♀**Ad**| upperparts pale brown; under-parts buff, streaked brown; rump white. **Tail strongly banded brown and cream.** Speckled white crescent from throat beneath broad, dark cheek patch; whitish marks above and below dark eye-patch. **Juv**| like ♀**Ad** but underparts rusty-buff, streaked black.

V| Calls on breeding area, a chattering "*chet-et-et-et-it-it-et*" (♀ deeper than ♂), otherwise silent.

Montagu's Harrier *p. 286*
Pallid Harrier *p. 287*
Northern Harrier *p. 582*

FL| Low, **glides with raised wings** between deep wingbeats. Wingtip rather broad (more so than Montagu's Harrier but slimmer than Marsh Harrier (*p. 283*)); 5 visible primary tips. ♂**Ad** grey above, white below, **rump white**; wingtip black; **dark trailing edge to white underwing.** ♀**Ad** broader-winged than ♂; brown, buff below; **white rump broad**, tail barred brown and cream. 'Wingpit' dark; underwing grey-buff, secondaries pale, barred black. **Juv** like ♀**Ad** but darker brown with buff band across upperwing coverts; underside of secondaries dark, barred blackish; body more rufous-buff.

Scarce resident/ migrant

Moorland, heathland, marshes, grassland

In summer, acrobatic, tumbling display flights, foot-to-foot food-pass between ♂ and ♀.

♂**Ad**

♀**Ad**
white rump wide and obvious

♀**Ad**

Five visible primary tips

Juv

♂**2Y***
ALL YEAR

* brownish tinge on head and back compared with ♂Ad

♂**Ad**
ALL YEAR

♀**Ad**
ALL YEAR

Wings do not extend beyond tail tip.

Smaller harriers in flight

PALLID HARRIER (p. 287)

underwing white, plain

breast white

upperwing plain silver-grey, black 'wedge'

MONTAGU'S HARRIER (p. 286)

black midwing bars

breast grey

black midwing bar

HEN HARRIER

underwing white, dark trailing edge

breast grey

upperwing plain grey, black tip

♂ Ads
♀ Ads

bars thin, broken

axillaries ('wingpit') brown

wings narrow

white rump narrow

bars uniformly broad

white rump narrow

wings rather narrow

axillaries ('wingpit') barred

bars broadest towards wingtip

axillaries ('wingpit') dark, spotted buff

white rump wide

wings broad

Juvs

Juveniles have pale covert tips.

wingtip narrow

white rump narrow

wingtip pointed, pale

underparts orange-buff

PALLID HARRIER (p. 287)

Focus on head/neck pattern to separate Pallid and Montagu's Harriers (see p. 287)

wingtip narrow

white rump narrow

wingtip pointed, dark

underparts orange-buff

MONTAGU'S HARRIER (p. 286)

wingtip narrow

white rump wide

wingtip wide, clearly barred

underparts orange-buff, streaked black

HEN HARRIER

Montagu's Harrier

LC
LC

Circus pygargus

L 39–50 cm | **W** 97–115 cm

Slender harrier; shape, flight actions and basic pattern of ♂ and ♀ like other smaller harriers (a rare dark form occurs in which both sexes are dark brown with subtle hint of 'normal' wing pattern). **♂Ad** | blue-grey, wing crossed by **black bar**; **wingtip black**. Breast grey, belly white with **rufous streaks**; tail side barred rufous. **♀Ad** | brown; underparts buff, streaked brown; rump white; tail strongly banded, **rufous and buff** on side; small dark cheek patch behind **bold white eye-crescents**; eye yellow. **Juv / 1Y** | like ♀ Ad but underparts **unstreaked orange-buff**; wing coverts edged buff; ♂ eye yellow by SEP; ♀ eye dark. **♂1Y** | breast mottled grey. **♂2Y** | like ♂Ad but back brown.

👁 Hen Harrier p. 284 | Pallid Harrier

FL | Slim harrier with light, airy flight; low glides on **raised wings**. **Long wingtip** often swept back; 3–4 visible primary tips.
 ♂Ad grey; **black bar** between **dark forewing/pale hindwing**; extensive black wingtip. White rump small or absent. Belly streaked rufous; underwing white, **barred black and chestnut**. Sides of tail barred.
 ♀Ad brown above, white rump narrow; black bars on hindwing. Below, dark trailing edge continues onto primaries; hindwing has **broad pale band of even width**. 'Wingpit' **barred** black and buff.
 Juv like ♀ Ad but underparts **unmarked orange-buff**. Upperwing has dark trailing edge; underside of secondaries dark.

Scarce summer migrant MAR–NOV

Heaths, grassland, arable land, marshes

V | Calls *"kekekek"* and *"jik-jik-jik"* near nest.

Juv
JUN–OCT

♀Ad

♀Ad

‡ combines Juv patterns with adult-like grey neck and back

♂1Y‡
ALL YEAR
[APR]

Juv
DARK
FORM

♂Ad

♂Ad

white rump narrow

♀1Y*
ALL YEAR

* similar to ♀ Ad but with dark eyes

mixed old, browner and new, grey, feathers

Very long wings (extend beyond tail tip).

♂Ad
ALL YEAR

...ead patterns of juvenile/ ...emale smaller harriers

...venile smaller harriers have white marks ...ove and below the dark eye, and dark ...eek crescents. Adult females have similar ...asic patterns.

...en Harrier: weakest pattern: small white ...arks around eye, **streaked neck** beneath ...arrow pale collar.

...allid Harrier: broad pale edge below ...xtensively dark cheek; **unstreaked** brown ...eck creating dark shawl.

...ontagu's Harrier: bold pattern around ...e, dark cheek with **weak pale edge**; ...nstreaked throat.

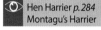

HEN HARRIER (p.284)

PALLID HARRIERS

streaked

STRONGLY MARKED

TYPICAL

MONTAGU'S HARRIER

...allid Harrier *Circus macrourus*

...40–50 cm | **W** 95–120 cm

...ight actions/patterns like Hen Harrier, but ...immer, lighter, more like Montagu's Harrier; ... larger than ♂. **♂Ad** | pale grey above, ...-white below; tail side barred grey. **♀Ad** | ...own above; buff, streaked blackish below; ...mp white; tail banded brown and cream; ...ack-brown cheek patch narrowly edged ...hite; eye yellow. **Juv/1Y** | like ♀Ad but cap ...ark, white crescent under eye, **dark brown ...eek edged white**; brown shawl; underparts ...ufous: ♂ greyish head, eye yellow by SEP; ...eye dark. **♂2Y** | like ♂Ad but back brown.

Hen Harrier p.284
Montagu's Harrier

FL | Slender, ♂ lightweight, with triangular outerwing. Wingtip shows 3–4 visible primary tips. **♂Ad** pale grey, **breast white**; **black 'wedge'** on wingtip. **♂Imm** like ♂Ad but back browner. **♀Ad** upperparts brown with narrow white rump, plain hindwing; underwing has no dark trailing edge to primaries, hindwing blackish with pale band **narrowing inwards**; 'wingpit' brown. **Juv** underparts **orange-buff**; underwing coverts rufous.

Rare and local summer migrant MAR–NOV; rare in winter

Heaths, grassland, arable land, marshes

V | Chattering calls near nest.

♀ Ad

white rump narrow (may be spotted dark)

♀ Ad

Juv
JUL–APR

♂ Ad
ALL YEAR

♀ 1Y*
ALL YEAR

* similar to ♀ Ad but with dark eyes

Closed wingtip reaches or extends beyond tail tip on ♂, falls short on ♀.

♂ 2Y‡
ALL YEAR

‡ darker and browner upperparts than ♂ Ad

NOTE: Hybrids with Hen Harrrier have occurred.

287

Regularly occurring large 'brown' eagles

Six species are regular, four in the genus *Aquila*, two in *Clanga*, all of which have dark brown plumage, a strong, dark bill with yellow base and gape, feathered legs and long, broad wings. These eagles are infrequently seen perched at close range and most likely to be seen in flight (some at great distances over open plains or high peaks). Juvenile and adult plumages are distinct, but juveniles change slowly to adult colours over several years, so intermediates are frequent. Worn/bleached plumage and the effects of moult must be considered, and these large eagles are often difficult to identify. (Also see White-tailed Eagle (*p. 298*), *Tawny Eagle* (*p. 580*), Bonelli's Eagle (*p. 279*), Long-legged Buzzard (*p. 273*) and vultures (*pp. 267–269*).)

Identify by size | set of wings when soaring | wing and tail patterns | wingtip detail, including number of 'fingered' primaries visible when spread

Golden Eagle

Years 1–2
white primary patch; white tail with broad black tip

Years 2–7
white on tail and wings reduces over 6/7 years

Years 5+
no or very little white; greyish tail with brown bars

Imm
ALL YEAR

Black/brown/buff patchwork results from moult and bleaching.

Imm
ALL YEAR

Ad
ALL YEAR

Note different apparent shapes of near and far wingtips. Outermost primary tips more upswept than middle ones, so wing can look broad, pointed or square, depending on angle of view.

PRIMARIES

PRIMARIES

P1 P2 P3 P4 P5 P6 P7 P8 P9 P10

outer primaries (P5-P10) visible in flight; with 'notch' giving indentations

alula ('thumb') (uplifted for control)

MIDWING
greater coverts
median coverts
lesser coverts
FOREWING

SECONDARIES
(HINDWING)

tail

undertail coverts

vent

thigh

Comparison of large 'brown' eagles in flight

		Aquila				Clanga	
		Golden Eagle (p. 292)	**Spanish Imperial Eagle** (p. 294)	**Eastern Imperial Eagle** (p. 295)	**Steppe Eagle** (p. 293)	**Lesser Spotted Eagle** (p. 296)	**Greater Spotted Eagle** (p. 297)
STRUCTURE	**Profile**	HEAD long; TAIL long	HEAD short, broad; TAIL short and square		HEAD short; TAIL short		HEAD round; TAIL short
	Wing shape	very long, TRAILING EDGE 'S'-shaped	long, TRAILING EDGE straight		broad, TRAILING EDGE curved; PRIMARY TIPS 7	less broad; PRIMARY TIPS 6 (7th may project)	very broad; PRIMARY TIPS 7
	Wing in glide	flat, arched	flat		flat, arched	bowed or drooped	bowed
	Wing in soar	obviously raised in 'V'	flat or faintly raised		flat	flat or faintly raised	drooped
PLUMAGE	**Juvenile ABOVE**	blackish-brown; pale crown and nape; **white primary patch**	pale brown; buff line between blackish greater coverts and flight feathers; white trailing edge; inner primaries pale	pale brown; two white lines border black greater coverts; flight feathers blackish, white trailing edge; inner primaries pale	brown; forewing pale, white line between blackish greater coverts and flight feathers; **white streaks on primaries**	brown; **pale nape**; white line between blackish greater coverts and flight feathers; white trailing edge; **inner primaries barred**	dark brown; **dark nape**; 2–3 rows of white spots across blackish coverts; white trailing edge; **inner primaries plain**
		RUMP **brown**; TAIL **white, broad black tip**	RUMP white; TAIL brown	RUMP white; TAIL black	RUMP **buff**; TAIL **blackish with pale tip**	TAIL black-brown; white 'U' at base	TAIL black; white 'U' at base
	BELOW	black-brown; long, broad, **central white wing-patch**	tawny-brown; breast streaked brown, **body unstreaked**; inner primaries pale	tawny-brown; underside **streaked dark**; inner primaries pale	broad white band along length of wing; HINDWING **blackish with white trailing edge**	rusty-brown; HINDWING **darker, with dark bars to tips**; pale crescents at base of primaries	dark brown; HINDWING **paler, with dark bars stopping short of tips**
		TAIL **white with black tip**	TAIL grey-brown		TAIL **black with white tip**	TAIL black-brown	
	Immature	white on tail and wings reduces over 6/7 years	increasingly blotched dark over several years		pale wing bands reduce over several years	like Ad after 2–3 years	
	Adult ABOVE	**golden-buff nape; buff band across coverts**	pale nape; white forewing; white 'braces'	pale nape; white 'braces'	dark brown, nondescript	pale nape; pale patch at base of primaries	dark nape; pale primary shaft streaks *
		TAIL greyish, barred brown	TAIL grey, **broad black tip**		RUMP + TAIL dark brown	**faint whitish 'U'** at base of blackish tail	
	BELOW	flight feathers grey, barred dark grey-brown	black-brown; flight feathers pale greyish	brown; flight feathers greyish; feet striking yellow, vent pale	brown; flight feathers darker, **barred blackish**; **buff-brown patch** at base of primaries	forewing **paler** than hindwing; two pale crescents at base of primaries; vent dark	forewing **darker** than hindwing; single pale patch at base of primaries; vent dark
		tail grey, barred brown, broad blackish tip	tail grey, **thin blackish tip**	tail grey, **broad dark tip**	tail brown, barred dark	tail blackish, white tip	tail blackish, pale tip

* **Greater Spotted Eagle** rare form *fulvescens*
rufous-buff; flight feathers and tail black-brown

Large 'brown' eagles in flight

LESSER SPOTTED EAGLE (*p. 296*)

wing narrow, 6 'free' primary tips (7th may protrude)

Ad

Juv

flight feathers barred

Ad

Juv

GREATER SPOTTED EAGLE (*p. 297*)

wing broad, 7 'free' primary tips

Ad

Juv

flight feathers plain

Ad

Juv

Juv

form *fulvescens*

STEPPE EAGLE (*p. 293*)

flight feathers evenly barred

Juv

broad whi... wing ban...

Imm

290

EASTERN IMPERIAL EAGLE (p. 295)

Ad

SPANISH IMPERIAL EAGLE (p. 294)

Ad

GOLDEN EAGLE (p. 292)

Ad

Juv

body plain

Juv

Imm

white tail base; white patches on underwing

body streaked dark

Ad

white forewing marks

Ad

Ad

white shoulder marks

Juv

Juv

Juv

Imm

white tail base; white patches at base of pimaries

291

LC Golden Eagle
LC *Aquila chrysaetos*

L 80–93 cm | **W** 190–227 cm

Huge, bulky eagle, most likely large
eagle in most of Europe. Bill black with
yellow base. Thighs heavily feathered;
feet yellow, massive. **Ad** | brown; **crown
and nape golden-buff**. Feathers fade to
straw-coloured, giving mottled effect.
♂ smaller, slimmer than ♀, but overlap;
size reliable only with known pairs.
Juv | plain dark brown, nape buff, white
on legs; **tail white at base**. **Imm** | loses
white in wings and tail over 6–7 years
(see *p. 288*), but precise ageing usually
not possible.

V | Yapping, yelping notes.

Two sspp. occur: *chrysaetos* widespread;
homeyeri (Iberia) slightly smaller and
darker.

Ageing difficult
beyond 'juvenile',
'immature' and 'five
years plus'.

White-tailed Eagle *p. 298*
Imperial eagles *pp. 294–295*
Spotted eagles *pp. 296–297*
Steppe Eagle

FL | Wings, tail and head longer
than spotted eagles and buzzards
(*pp. 270–275*); shorter head, longer tail
than White-tailed Eagle; shape most like
the imperial eagles but hindwing more
'S'-shaped. Active flight heavy with deep
beats. Wings arched in glide, flexible;
raised in 'V' when soaring, often to great
height (see Griffon Vulture (*p. 268*)).
Stoops with wings curved back in wide
'teardrop' shape. (See table on *p. 289* for
details of key characteristics.)

Scarce resident, winter
migrant

Mature forest,
mountainsides, coasta
cliffs, crags

Imm
ALL YEAR

Ad

Imm
ALL YEAR

All ssp. *chrysaetos*

Imm
ALL YEAR

Ad
ALL YEAR

Steppe Eagle
Aquila nipalensis

60–81 cm | **W** 165–214 cm

Very large, dark brown eagle (like Imperial and Golden Eagles); long, pale nape (longest **reach back of eye**, unique in large eagles; shortest reach middle of eye, like spotted eagles). Legs heavily feathered, **short**. **Ad** dark brown. **Juv** tawny brown, two pale lines across dark brown wing. **Imm** intermediate ages until maturity after 5–6 years.

| Low, yapping barks.

SSP. *orientalis* occurs in Europe.

Imperial eagles *pp. 294–295*
Golden Eagle
Spotted eagles *pp. 296–297*
Tawny Eagle p. 580

FL | Head/bill quite short; tail short, wide; wings held flat or arched when gliding and soaring; curved trailing edge; wingtip broad, deeply fingered, seven visible primary tips. (See table on *p. 289* for details of key characteristics.)

Rare and local summer migrant FEB–OCT

Open grassy plains; migrates over narrow sea crossings

7 visible primary tips

hindwing barred

Imm
ALL YEAR

Juv

Ad

Ad

Juv
ALL YEAR

Ad
ALL YEAR

Imperial eagles Two species, separated on range. Thighs heavily feathered. In flight, long head, short tail and straight-edged wings give crow-like shape. Juvenile wings narrow at base, so tail looks long. Wings flat in glide; level or faintly raised when soaring. **Ad** | dark brown, crown and nape pale; **white 'shoulder' marks ('braces')**; **tail pale grey with black tip**. **Juv** | paler brown, head and thighs unmarked buff; wing coverts heavily spotted buff, with broad dark brown and buff lines across closed wing.

Golden Eagle *p. 292* | Spotted eagles *pp. 296–297* | Steppe Eagle *p. 293* | Tawny Eagle *p. 580*

VU Spanish Imperial Eagle
VU *Aquila adalberti*

L 74–85 cm | **W** 177–220 cm

See summary box *above*. **Ad** | black-brown, crown and nape buff; **white 'shoulder-stripe' and forewing.** **Juv / 1Y** | bright tawny-brown; breast-band streaked brown, rest of underparts tawny-buff, unstreaked. **Imm** | ageing difficult; variable progression to adult plumage over 5–6 years.

FL | **Ad** gleaming **white leading edge** to wing (visible from great range). (See table on *p. 289* for details of key characteristics.)

Rare and local residen[t]

Open lowland plains, scattered trees, forests

V | Loud barking notes

white forewing band more conspicuous on many individuals

Ad

Juv/1Y
[APR]

Juv
ALL YEAR

Greatly affected by moult/bleaching, but body/wings usually plainer dark brown than Golden Eagle.

Ad
ALL YEAR

Eastern Imperial Eagle

Aquila heliaca

74–85 cm | **W** 177–220 cm

See summary box *opposite*. **Ad** | brown; white 'shoulder-stripe' (but often minute). Wingtips extend beyond tail tip on ♂, equal on ♀. **Juv / 1Y** | tawny-brown, upperparts finely streaked buff, wing **spotted with buff-white**, spots progressively larger across longer coverts and tertials. Underparts **buff** with **thick dark streaks**. **Imm** | ageing difficult; variable progression to adult plumage over 5–6 years.

FL | Ad upperside brown (lacks most pale blotches of Golden Eagle and white leading edge of Spanish Imperial Eagle). Strikingly pale feet and vent. (See table on *p. 289* for details of key characteristics.)

Rare and local summer migrant/resident

Open plains, mountain slopes, forest

V | Loud barking notes.

Juv

Ad

grey base/dark tip to tail fade browner

Ad
ALL YEAR

Juv
ALL YEAR

Imperial eagles *pp. 294–295*
Golden *p. 292* & Steppe Eagles
p. 293 | Tawny Eagle *p. 580*

Spotted eagles
Two brown eagles with subtle structural differences, such as gape length (BELOW); also compare with Steppe Eagle.

LESSER SPOTTED EAGLE
gape slightly shorter than, or equal to, middle of eye

GREATER SPOTTED EAGLE
gape reaches middle of eye

STEPPE EAGLE (*p. 293*)
gape reaches beyond middle of eye

LC
LC
Lesser Spotted Eagle
Clanga pomarina

L 55–67 cm | **W** 146–168 cm

Medium-large eagle; yellow gape slightly shorter than, or equal to, middle of eye. Legs **long**, slim, tightly feathered.
Ad | dark brown, nape slightly paler.
Juv | brown; pale nape; longest wing coverts and flight feathers blacker, tipped white. **Imm** | intermediate stages until maturity after 5–6 years.

V | High bark and yelping or whistling notes in flight.

6 visible
primary tips

Juv

Juv: barring
on hindwing
reaches tips

Ad: hindwing
unbarred

Ad

Scarce summer
migrant MAR–NOV

Plains with forest
or scattered trees;
migrates over narrow
sea crossings

FL | Rather square
winged, short-taile•
slender; relative
light, agile actio•
Wings bowed •
drooped whe•
gliding, flat •
faintly raised whe•
soaring. Wingt•
rather narrow, s•
visible primary tip•
(See table on *p. 28*
for details of ke•
characteristic•

Juv
ALL YEAR

eye pale
brown

Ad
ALL YE

Greater Spotted Eagle
Clanga clanga

59–71 cm | **W** 155–180 cm

Large, heavily built eagle; yellow gape extends back to middle of eye. Legs **long**, slim, tightly feathered. **Ad** | dark brown, without pale nape. Wingtips extend beyond tail on ♂, fall short of tail on ♀. **Juv** | black-brown, **all wing coverts and flight feathers tipped white**. **Imm** | intermediate stages until maturity after 5–6 years.

V | Loud, low bark.

FL | Round-winged, short-tailed; relatively heavy, clumsy action. Wings drooped when gliding and soaring. Wingtip broad, seven visible primary tips, but ♂ smaller, with narrower wings than ♀. (See table on *p. 289* for details of key characteristics.)

Rare summer migrant FEB–NOV; rare and local in winter

Forests, marshes

7 visible primary tips

Juv

Juv
ALL YEAR

Scarce form '*fulvescens*' buff-brown above, with black midwing band, flight feathers and tail; head and underparts rufous-buff.

Juv: barring on hindwing **does not reach** tips

Ad

Ad: hindwing unbarred

Juv
ALL YEAR

eye dark brown

Ad
ALL YEAR

LC **White-tailed Eagle** *Haliaeetus albicilla*

LC **L** 76–92 cm | **W** 200–244 cm

Massive eagle; thighs heavily feathered but legs bare. **Ad** | pale brown, head buff/white; huge bill **all-yellow**. **Tail white**, often stained. Wingtip reaches tail tip on ♂, falls short on ♀. **Juv** | upperparts brown with black, 'teardrop'-shaped spots; breast buff with black lines and 'V's (some individuals are very dark brown with rufous wing). Tail dark, paler streaks show when spread. **Imm** | dark head, pale breast; tail whiter with age.

V | Powerful "*kik-rik-rik*" and "*kee-kee-kee*."

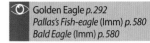
Golden Eagle *p. 292*
Pallas's Fish-eagle (Imm) *p. 580*
Bald Eagle (Imm) *p. 580*

Rare, locally common resident/ migrant

Marshes, lakes inland and coastal cliffs

FL | Very large; less graceful tha Golden Eagle with longer head, short tail. Wings long, very broad, held **fla or drooped in glide**, with long, flexib tips upswept. Deep, powerful bea between glides. Can soar to gre height. **Ad** brown; **white tail** and pa head; ♂ has paler head, more bulgir hindwing than ♀. **Juv** dark; whitis patch under innerwing. **Tail whitis with dark feather edges. Imm** show dark hood, paler belly, whitish 'wingp and lines under wing. Tail become progressively whiter, white with fir dark tips after about 5 year

2Y
ALL YEAR

Imm
ALL YEAR

Ad

Juv
ALL YEAR

Ad
ALL YEAR

Hawks
Four species, from dove- to buzzard-sized; females are larger than males, so size alone can mislead. Wings fall short of the long tail at rest, but are short to quite long and tapered in flight; body broad, narrows to slim tail base on smaller species. Legs longer than falcons', with flexible upper leg joints giving a long reach when capturing prey with feet. Typically secretive, but also soar high up at times; usual flight a series of quick flaps between short glides. Male and female plumages differ slightly; juveniles are browner and more streaked than adults.

Identify by size | head pattern | eye colour | underwing pattern | underparts pattern

SPARROWHAWK ♀
(p. 303)

SPARROWHAWK ♂
(p. 303)

GOSHAWK ♂
(p. 302)

SHIKRA
(p. 305)

GOSHAWK ♀
(p. 302)

LEVANT SPARROWHAWK ♀
(p. 304)

Hawks in flight

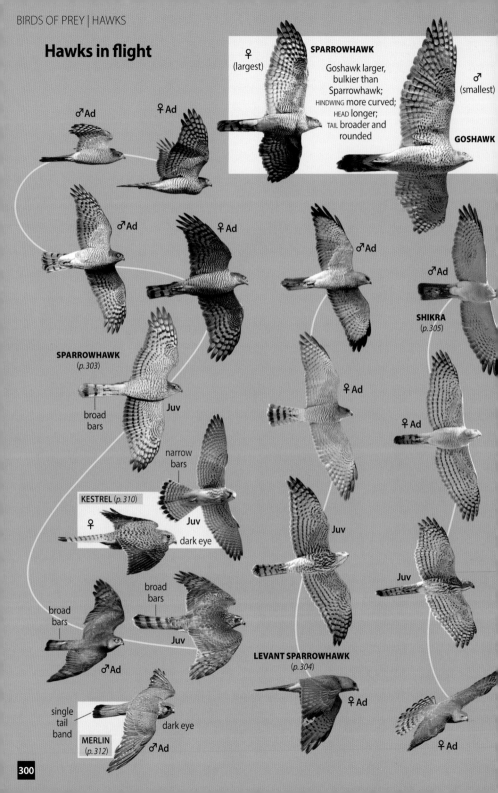

♀ (largest)

SPARROWHAWK

Goshawk larger, bulkier than Sparrowhawk; HINDWING more curved; HEAD longer; TAIL broader and rounded

♂ (smallest)

GOSHAWK

♂ Ad

♀ Ad

♂ Ad

♀ Ad

♂ Ad

♂ Ad

SHIKRA
(p. 305)

SPARROWHAWK
(p. 303)

broad bars

Juv

♀ Ad

♀ Ad

narrow bars

KESTREL (p. 310)

♀

Juv

dark eye

Juv

Juv

broad bars

broad bars

broad bars

Juv

♂ Ad

LEVANT SPARROWHAWK
(p. 304)

single tail band

dark eye

MERLIN
(p. 312)

♂ Ad

♀ Ad

♀ Ad

	Goshawk (p. 302)	Sparrowhawk (p. 303)	Levant Sparrowhawk (p. 304)	Shikra (p. 305)
Active flight	deep beats and short glides	alternates quick beats/ flicks and flat glides	flap-and-glide action	flap-and-glide action
Head, body, tail	HEAD **protrudes**; BODY breast broad and deep; rump broad, TAIL rounded	HEAD **small, broad**; BODY slim, flat-bellied; TAIL long, slim	HEAD **pointed**, BODY + TAIL slim	HEAD slim; BODY **very slim**; TAIL long
Wing shape (soaring)	**long: bulging hindwing** and long, narrow, rounded tip (6 primary tips visible)	**broad-based**, outer half short, rounded; blunt, wide tip (6 primary tips visible, outer one short)	broad-based, parallel-sided, blunt-tipped (5 primary tips visible)	rather long, slender; **hindwing 'S'-shaped**; wingtip narrow (5 primary tips visible

GOSHAWK (p. 302)

Juv

Juv

♂ Ad

♀ Ad

Juv

♂ Ad

♀ Juv

Juv

Note Goshawk's variety of profiles: WINGS swept, flexed or straight out; WINGTIPS flat or upswept; TAIL broad, often rounded; HEAD protruding; CHEST deep

Juv

Juv

Juv

Juv

LC **Goshawk** *Accipiter gentilis*

LC **L** ♂ 49–56 cm | ♀ 58–64 cm **W** ♂ 90–105 cm | ♀ 108–127 cm

Very large, thickset hawk; ♀ approaches size of Buzzard (*p. 272*) but smaller ♂ closer to ♀ Sparrowhawk (can be difficult to judge size). Legs thick. **♂ Ad** | **crow-sized**; upperparts blue-grey; dark cap and band through eye; underparts whitish, barred grey. Eye orange to red. **♀ Ad** | upperparts brownish-grey; underparts dull white, barred grey. Eye yellow or orange. **Juv** | upperparts brown; underparts **buff** with drop-shaped **black streaks**. Eye yellow.

FL | Heavy body with deeply curved breast, protruding head. **Wings long**, with quite narrow, rounded tip (may suggest Honey-buzzard (*p. 275*)). Soars with wings fully spread – shape resembles a soaring falcon (see *p. 307*), tips sweeping gently upwards. Flat-winged, straight-tailed shape when approaching; overhead, wings may curve back like Peregrine Falcon. Displays in early spring with slow flights, deep undulations, vertical stoop into trees. Soars high up; chases prey or stoops like Peregrine Falcon. **Ad** grey with **broad white patch** under tail; hindwing plainer than Sparrowhawk. **Juv** rich brown, **buff beneath**. (See table on *p. 301* for details of key characteristics.)

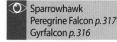

Sparrowhawk
Peregrine Falcon *p. 317*
Gyrfalcon *p. 316*

Generally scarce resident/migrant

Extensive woodland, forest clearings, heath and moor

Five sspp. occur, four breed: ***buteoides*** (N and E Europe) large, pale and lightly barred, with bold white stripe over eye; ***gentilis*** (widespread) smaller, darker, heavily barred (but much overlap); ***arrigonii*** (Corsica and Sardinia) small, dark, head blackish, blackish bars below; ***marginatus*** (Italy and Balkans, E to Caucasus) small, dark; ***atricapillus*** (vagrant from N America) tends to have blacker cap, redder eye, fine streaks through bars on underparts.

V | Call near nest repeated, shouted "*cha-cha-cha-cha-cha*" (recalls Green Woodpecker (*p. 332*)), and high whine.

♂ **Ad**

6 primary tips visible

Juv

♂ **Ad**
ALL YEAR

All ssp. *gentilis*

Juv
ALL YEAR

(Eurasian) **Sparrowhawk**   *Accipiter nisus*

L ♂ 29–34 cm | ♀ 35–41 cm   **W** ♂ 58–65 cm | ♀ 68–77 cm

Small, bird-hunting hawk; elusive but often soars to considerable height. ♂ small; ♀ larger, heavier (size of Kestrel). **Eye yellow** (rules out falcons). **♂ Ad** | upperparts **blue-grey**, cheek orange; underparts whitish to pink-orange, softly barred. **♀ Ad** | upperparts grey (fade browner); nape pale. Pale line above dark eyestripe. Underparts dull white, barred grey. Legs slim (Goshawk's thick). Both sexes often show large white spots on upperparts. **Juv** | upperparts brown with rusty-buff feather edges; underparts buff, barred rufous.

FL | Slim body and small head; tail long, slim. Wings show blunt, wide wingtip when soaring but curved back to short point in fast glide (compare longer wingtip of Merlin, Kestrel). 'Flap-and-glide' action more repetitive than Kestrel's less regular flight. Catches birds after slanting dive, or short, fast chase; also sits and waits in thick cover. Displays (FEB-APR), with fast, steep, bounding undulations and high flights with slow, deep beats (which may prompt thoughts of Goshawk); fast vertical stoop into wood. Never hovers. Underwing pale, uniformly barred. (See table on *p. 301* for details of key characteristics.)

👁 Goshawk | Shikra *p. 305* | Levant Sparrowhawk *p. 304* | Merlin *p. 312* | Kestrel *p. 310* | Cuckoo *p. 322*

Common resident/ summer migrant

Forest, well-wooded parks, gardens, farmland

Three sspp. occur: *nisus* widespread; *wolterstorffi* (Corsica, Sardinia) small, dark; *granti* (Madeira, Canary Is.) heavily barred.

V | Calls chattering *"kewkewkewkewkew"* near nest, otherwise silent.

Juv JUL-NOV

All SSP. *nisus*

6 primary tips visible, outer one short

Juv

♀ Ad

♂ Juv

♀ Ad (large) ALL YEAR

♀ larger than ♂ in any one area, but ♂ of N and E similar in size to ♀ of S and W Europe.

♂ Ad ALL YEAR

LC Levant Sparrowhawk
LC *Accipiter brevipes*

L ♂ 30–35 cm | ♀ 34–37 cm
W ♂ 64–70 cm | ♀ 68–74 cm

Small long-tailed hawk; sexes similar in size. **Head plain**; eye **dark** orange; **dark throat stripe**. ♂**Ad** | upperparts and cheek blue-grey; breast whitish, barred orange. ♀**Ad** | head and upperparts dull grey; underparts white, **barred** rufous. **Juv** | upperparts brown with rufous feather edges; underparts white with brown spots and streaks, flank barred. **1Y** | slowly gains adult colours but retains barred underwing.

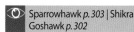 Sparrowhawk *p. 303* | Shikra Goshawk *p. 302*

FL | Slim with small, pointed head, slim tail. Wings straight-edged and blunt-tipped when soaring, but swept back to point in active flight: most falcon-like of the smaller hawks. Displays with high circling, but undemonstrative. Migrants form **flocks**, soar to great height then glide. Rarely hovers. Underwing pale with **thin black tip, dark trailing edge**. ♂**Ad** underwing whitish, secondaries unbarred. ♀**Ad** underwing barred greyish, flight feathers paler with fine dark bars. (See table on *p. 301* for details of key characteristics.)

Locally common summer migrant
APR–SEP

Lowland forest, clearings, wooded plains; migrates over narrow sea crossings

V | Shrill *"kewik kewik."*

Juv
JUN–SEP

♂**1Y**
ALL YEAR

5 primary tips visible, outer one short

♀**Ad**

Juv

♂**Ad**

Random white spots on upperparts, as on this brown juvenile, are often seen on smaller *Accipiter* hawks.

As on many other birds of prey, new feathers are grey but gradually become duller, browner.

♀**Ad**
ALL YEAR

♂**Ad**
ALL YEAR

Shikra *Accipiter badius*

♂ 30–33 cm | ♀ 34–36 cm
W ♂ 64–70 cm | ♀ 68–74 cm

Small, slim, long-tailed hawk. Upperparts pale blue-grey (Levant Sparrowhawk darker). Underparts whitish, breast barred rufous. **Ad** | head plain grey; thin, obscure dark throat stripe: **♂ Ad** | upperparts clear grey, eye orange to orange-red; **♀ Ad** | upperparts slightly browner, eye yellow to orange-yellow. **Juv** | upperparts brown; underparts buff with dark rufous spots and streaks, bars on flank, and dark throat stripe. Eye yellow at first.

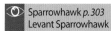

Sparrowhawk *p. 303*
Levant Sparrowhawk

FL | Very slender, with small, narrow head and long, slim tail. Wings have **'S'-shaped trailing edge**. Displays with high circling, stoops and tumbling aerobatics. Does not hover. **♂ Ad** upperside pale grey, wingtips darker; underside whitish, wingtips **dark grey**. **♀ Ad** wingtips less contrasted than **♂ Ad** and **barred** below; underside heavily barred. (See table on *p. 301* for details of key characteristics.)

Very rare and local resident; occasional vagrant elsewhere

Woodland, from parks/ gardens to open forest

ssp. *cenchroides* occurs in Europe.

V | A shrill chatter.

Juv*
JUL–NOV

This individual is growing adult-type grey feathers on the head and barred feathers on the breast; eye is becoming orange.

* **NOTE:** bird shown is African ssp. *sphenurus*; European ssp. *cenchroides* looks similar but is slightly larger and paler.

5 primary tips visible, outer one short

♀ Ad

♂ Ad

Juv

Eye colour ranges from yellow to orange-red, reddest on adult ♂.

♂ Ad
ALL YEAR

Ad
ALL YEAR

Ad
ALL YEAR

305

Falcons

Ten regularly occurring species, most scarce or local but prone to wander. All have a rounded head and bill. Closed wings are longer than those of hawks; eyes are dark. The legs look shorter than those of hawks, but similarly have a long reach to snatch prey. Sexes differ (especially in kestrels); females are larger than males. Juveniles are distinctive or look more like adult females. Moult timings and rate of maturity vary greatly between individuals and geographical areas. Species such as Kestrel and Peregrine Falcon are mature by the end of their second calendar year (in 'second winter', about 18 months old), while even some smaller species, such as Merlin and Hobby, may have another year of immaturity. A typical falcon pattern (not seen on hawks) is a dark hood and 'moustache', with a white or pale cheek/neck patch. Falcons catch their prey (insect, reptile, mammal or bird) with their feet, in the air (small items being transferred to bill) or on the ground.

Identify by size | head pattern | upperwing and tail colour and pattern | leg colour | flight action

MERLIN (p.312)
♂Ad
♀Ad

KESTREL (p.310)
♀Ad
♂Ad

RED-FOOTED FALCON (p.313)
♂Ad
♀Ad

LESSER KESTREL (p.311)
♀Ad
♂Ad

ELEONORA'S FALCON (p.315)
Ad DARK FORM
Ad PALE FORM

HOBBY (p.314)
Ad

GYRFALCON (p.316)
Imm 'PALE'
Juv

PEREGRINE FALCON (p.317)
Ad

LANNER FALCON (p.319)
Ad

SAKER FALCON (p.318)
Imm

Falcons in flight

have a rounded head and stout or tapered body. The tail is narrow when closed (often narrower at the tip) or spread in a broad fan; wings are long, quite broad-tipped when fully spread or curved back to a tapered point. Flight typically has deep, quick wingbeats, with more constant flapping than hawks, but also often prolonged glides; some soar frequently, wings held flat or slightly upswept, and use fast chases or steep diving 'stoops'; others have a less dynamic flight action and three species habitually hover.

Identify by upperpart colour/pattern (brown or grey, uniform, or with darker wingtips, or dark tail-band) | head/neck contrast | underparts barring or streaking | underwing pattern

Larger falcons in flight

Ad
'GREY'

Imm
'PALE'

Ad
'GREY'

GYRFALCON
(p. 316)

Juv

Ad
'GREY'

Ad

Ad

PEREGRINE
FALCON
(p. 317)

Juv

Juv

Imm

SAKER FALCON
(p. 318)

LANNER
FALCON
(p. 319)

Juv

Ad

Ad

Ad

Fading and moult in adults produces mixtures of old, brownish and new, greyer feathers, confusingly like immatures.

Kestrel
(for size comparison)

307

Smaller falcons in flight

Smaller grey-backed falcons may breed at
one year old, when they look like adults
but often show retained brown or barred
juvenile feathers in the wings and/or tail.

Ad
DARK
FORM

Ad
DARK
FORM

ELEONORA'S FALCON
(p. 315)

Juv

Ad
PALE
FORM

Juv

Juv

Ad
PALE
FORM

single
tail band

♂ Ad

Ad

♂ Ad

MERLIN
(p. 312)

Ad

rufous
'thighs'

♀ Ad

♀ Ad

HOBBY
(p. 314)

Juv

tail
barred

Juv

pale
'thighs'

PEREGRINE
(for size comparison)

Juv

♂Ad

♂Ad

♀Ad

♀Ad

♂1S

RED-FOOTED FALCON
(p. 313)

♂1S

♂1S highly
variable

♂1S

Juv

Juv

♀1Y

♂Ad

♂Ad

♀Juv

KESTREL
(p. 310)

♀

♂Ad

♂Ad

♀

LESSER KESTREL
(p. 311)

309

FALCONS IN FLIGHT pp. 307–3

LC (Common) **Kestrel** *Falco tinnunculus*

LC **L** 31–37 cm | **W** 65–82 cm

Small falcon. Sits upright or sloping on wire/post; long, slim tail; **hovers**. Claws black. ♂**Ad** | head grey, dark 'moustache'. Back **orange-rufous**, **spotted black**; tail grey with black tip. Underparts buff to orange-buff with black spots. ♀**Ad** | upperparts and tail **ginger-brown**, thickly **barred black** (tail/rump often greyer than back); wing covert bars straight. Cheek streaked. Underparts buff, spotted black-brown **Juv** | like ♀**Ad**; uppertail coverts barred brown on ♀**Juv**, greyish on ♂**Juv**. ♂**1Y** | may be like ♂**Ad** with barred side to tail, but ageing often difficult.

FL | Wings straight or angled back to point. Tail slender, opens to full fan. Soars on blunt-tipped wings. **Persistent hovering** (sometimes very high, often at dusk). Direct flight has relaxed, irregular beats, but capable of fast, agile aerobatics. Display flight fast, rolling, with flickering beats. **Two-tone upperwing** rufous with **dark flight feathers** (matched only by Lesser Kestrel). ♂**Ad** tail grey with black terminal band. Body streaked; underwing grey-buff with fine grey bars. ♀**Ad**/**Juv** ginger-brown; buff below, underwing buff, barred greyish.

Lesser Kestrel | Hobby *p. 314*
Merlin *p. 312*
Red-footed Falcon *p. 313*

Locally common resident/ summer migran

Farmland, moorland, heaths, marshes, crags and gorge

Three sspp. occur: *tinnunculus* (widespread); *canariensis* (Madeira and W Canary Is.), smaller, darker; *dacotiae* (E Canary Is.) smaller, more spotted on underparts.

V | Sharp, whining "kee-kee-kee-kee

♀

♂1Y
ALL YEAR

back spotted

♀ Ad

♀ Ad

♂ Ad

underparts can be quite orange

♂ Ad (moulting)

Breeding pairs isolated, feeds alone.

All SSP. *tinnunculus*

♀ Ad
ALL YEAR

♂ Ad
ALL YEAR

all ages and sexes have black claws

Lesser Kestrel *Falco naumanni*

L 29–33 cm | **W** 58–73 cm

Small falcon, often around buildings; **hovers**. ♂ distinctive; ♀ very like ♀ Kestrel. **Claws pale** (close-up view or photographs). **♂ Ad** | head blue-grey, dusky around eye ('moustache' weaker than on Kestrel). Back **unspotted pale rufous**, wings crossed by **blue-grey patch**. Tail blue-grey with black tip. Underparts orange-buff with small black spots. **♀ Ad** | upperparts and tail **ginger-brown**, narrowly barred black; smaller wing covert bars 'V'-shaped. Cheek pale, unstreaked; head may be greyish. Underparts buff, spotted brown. **Juv** | like ♀ Ad; bars on upperside browner, edged pale. **♂ 1Y** | back unspotted rufous, wing coverts mottled black; lacks grey in wing.

FL | Wings quite straight; short innerwing gives slightly stiff, quick action; **often hovers. Two-tone upperwing**, like Kestrel. **♂ Ad** tail narrow, often 'wedge-shaped' tip, grey with 'V'-shaped black band. **Blue-grey midwing band** may be conspicuous. Body deep buff, **underwing white. ♀ Ad / Juv** rufous, barred black; underwing buff, barred greyish (no reliable differences from ♀ Ad / Juv Kestrel). **♂ 1Y** tail grey in centre, outer feathers barred brown.

Kestrel | Hobby *p.314*
Merlin *p.312*
Red-footed Falcon *p.313*

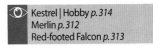

Rare, locally common summer migrant FEB–OCT; very locally resident

Dry plains, scattered trees, towns/ruins

V | Hoarse, grating "*chay-chay-chay.*"

♂ Ad

♀

♂ 1Y
ALL YEAR

back plain

♂ Ad

♀

♂ Ad

♀ Ad
ALL YEAR

Breeds in colonies, feeds socially.

♂ Ad
ALL YEAR

all ages and sexes have pale claws

LC **Merlin** *Falco columbarius*

LC **L** 29–32 cm | **W** 58–73 cm

Smallest breeding falcon: ♂ size of ♂ Sparrowhawk; ♀ close to Kestrel. **♂ Ad** | upperparts **blue-grey**, underparts orange-buff with **dark streaks**; faint 'moustache'. Tail **grey with black tip**. **♀ Ad** | upperparts dull **brown**; brown 'moustache'. Tail brown, **barred cream**. **Juv** | like **♀ Ad** but rufous fringes above; underparts darker buff; tail bands rufous on ♂, whitish bands on ♀.

FL | Fast, **low**, direct; **quick beats**, few glides. Wings broad-based but sharply pointed; body deep at front, tapers to tail. (Kestrel has blunter wingtip; Sparrowhawk wider wing-base, shorter tip). Rarely soars; does not hover. Approaches small birds with a thrush-like action, wingtips flicked in-out like hunting Hobby (*p. 314*), before fast, twisting chase. **♂ Ad** grey above, tail barred grey with **black tip**. **♀ Ad / Juv** brown above, tail **barred brown and cream**.

Peregrine Falcon *p. 317* | kestrels *pp. 310–311* | Sparrowhawk *p. 303*

Scarce migrant/ resident

Open grassland, heathland; winters on marshes, pastures.

Five sspp. recorded: *aesalon* (widespread) and smaller *subaesalon* (Iceland and migrants elsewhere in winter); and vagrants *insignis* and *pallidus* (from Asian steppes), pale and strikingly pale and larger, respectively; and *columbarius* (from N America), darker, ♂ **Ad** tail barred grey and black.

V | Sharp "*ki-ki-ki-ki*" or nasal "*week-week week-week-week*"

♀ **Ads**
ALL YEAR

♀ Ad typically dull brown (less rufous than Kestrel (*p. 310*)), but some have greyer upperparts with rufous feather edges.

♂ **Ad**
ALL YEAR

♀ **Ad**
ALL YEAR

♀ **Juv**
ALL YEAR

SSP. *aesalon*

ed-footed Falcon *Falco vespertinus*

28–34 cm | **W** 65–76 cm

small falcon, between Hobby and Kestrel in shape and character.
Claws pale. **♂Ad** | grey; thighs and belly **rufous. Base of bill, eyering
and legs red. ♀Ad** | upperparts grey, **barred black**; underparts
unmarked rufous. **Cap rufous-buff, fades to white; black 'mask' and
white cheek**; legs orange. **Juv** | like ♀ **Ad** but upperparts barred grey-
brown and buff; underparts buff-white with black streaks. Most have
distinct pale collar (two small pale spots on Hobby). **♂1S** | upperparts
grey; **breast rufous**, rest of underparts grey. **♀1S** | like ♀ **Ad** but wing
and tail mixed grey (new) and brown (older) feathers.

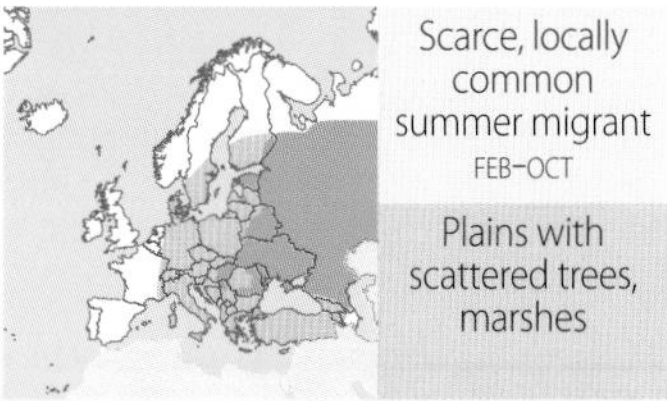

L | Drifts over open space, hovers like Kestrel (migrants infrequently).
Glides, stalls, catches insects with feet. Migrates in flocks. **♂Ad** grey;
windwing silvery-grey, wingtip pale. ♀**Ad** / **Juv** back grey, barred
black; underparts rufous. Underwing whitish with dark spots and
dark trailing edge. **♂1S** like ♂ **Ad** but has more uniform upperwing;
underwing barred/chequered with **Juv** (barred) and newer (grey)
flight feathers in contrasting patches.

Hobby *p. 314* | kestrels *pp. 310–311*
Eleonora's Falcon *p. 315*
Amur Falcon p. 583
♂*Ad - Sooty Falcon p. 583*

Scarce, locally
common
summer migrant
FEB–OCT

Plains with
scattered trees,
marshes

V | High, thin, squeaky *"kweee kweee"* and
wavering *"kwi-kwi-kwi-i-i."*

♀ Ad

♂Ad

♂1S

♀ Ad

♂Ad

♂1S
FEB–OCT

Juv

Most breed
colonially, in old
Rooks' nests.

♂Ad
ALL YEAR

♀Ad
ALL YEAR

Juv
JUL–OCT

FALCONS IN FLIGHT pp. 307–3(

LC

Hobby *Falco subbuteo*

LC **L** 29–35 cm | **W** 68–84 cm

Small, long-winged, aerial falcon, slimmer than Peregrine Falcon and kestrels. **Ad** | upperparts dark grey; **hood and 'moustache' black**, neck **white**; tail plain grey. Underparts white, **thickly streaked** black. Thigh/vent rusty red (bright and unmarked on ♂; dull streaked on ♀). **Juv** | upperparts grey-brown with buff feather edges; head like **Ad** but side of neck buff, small buff spots on hindneck. Underparts **streaked black and buff**, no red. **1S** | like Juv but buff tips wear off, some wing coverts grey.

FL | Delicate, elegant; long wings arc to narrow tip; tail tapered or half-fanned. **Changes in pace** obvious when hawking insects: glides on flat wings, accelerates with deep, whippy beats into upward glide/stall. Flicks wings in long, slanting dive before fast stoop with swept wings onto small birds. Body narrow, especially rump/tail base. Head small, short. **Looks dark** in flight, heavily streaked below: close view/good light needed to see detail, but **white neck patch** shows well.

Peregrine Falcon *p. 317* | kestrels *pp. 310–311* | Merlin *p. 312* Eleonora's Falcon | Red-footed Falcon *p. 313* | Amur Falcon *p. 583*

Scarce, but locally common summer migrant MAR–OCT

Heaths, wooded farmland, marshes, lakes

ssp. ***subbuteo*** occurs in Europe.

V | Rather ringing, bright "*kew-kew-kev kev*

Rump narrow, same shade as back/tail (broad and pale on Peregrine Falcon). ♀

Eats insect prey while in flight.

Ad

Juv

1S
MAR–OCT

Ad

Ad

Juv

Not generally social, but may feed in loose groups.

Juv
AUG–OCT

Ad
ALL YEAR

Eleonora's Falcon *Falco eleonorae*

L 36–42 cm | **W** 84–105 cm

Medium-large, long-winged, aerial falcon. Sexes alike, but eyering and bill-base yellow on ♂ **Ad**, bluish on ♀ **Ad**. Two colour forms.
Ad | PALE FORM upperparts grey-brown; dark hood and 'moustache', white cheek and throat; **underparts rufous-buff**, streaked black, darker under tail. **DARK FORM entirely grey-brown**; legs yellow.
Juv | like **Ad** pale form but pale buff bars on upperparts; dark tail tip; bill base, eyering and legs grey.

FL | Flight quick, agile, acrobatic, hawking insects or chasing small birds. Long-winged, long-tailed, angular silhouette. **Ad** PALE FORM **underwing pale grey with blacker coverts** (Peregrine Falcon (*p. 317*) and Hobby lack contrast). DARK FORM all-dark except paler grey under flight feathers, contrasting with blackish coverts. **Juv** like pale form Ad but browner above, more broadly streaked black below; underwing rufous, closely barred black.
mm tail pale, barred buff.

Peregrine Falcon *p. 317*
Hobby | Red-footed Falcon *p. 313*
DARK FORM - *Sooty Falcon p. 583*

Locally common summer migrant
MAR–NOV

Island cliffs, crags, gorges

V | Grating "*kye-kye-kye*."

Juv
DARK FORM

Juv
PALE FORM

Juv
PALE FORM
JUL–NOV

Ad
PALE FORM

Ad
DARK FORM

Ad
DARK FORM
ALL YEAR

Social; hunts in small groups.

Ad
PALE FORM

Ad
PALE FORM
ALL YEAR

Gyrfalcon *Falco rusticolus*

LC
LC **L** 53–63 cm | **W** 120–134 cm

Large, bulky falcon. **SCANDINAVIAN FORM Ad** | mid-grey or **brownish-grey** with dark hood/'moustache'; upperparts barred white. Underparts whitish, breast spotted, flank barred grey. Legs and eyering yellow.
Juv / Imm | brownish-grey; broad, dark 'moustache'; underparts streaked grey-brown; legs and eyering bluish, yellower by MAR. **ICELANDIC FORM Ad** | pale grey. **Juv / Imm** | browner. **GREENLAND FORM Ad** | white with dark spots.
Juv / Imm | heavily spotted.

FL | Wingspan as Buzzard (*p. 272*)/female Goshawk. Long, broad innerwing results in slower, shallower action than Peregrine. Wingtips blunt; **tail/rump broad**; breast deep. Back/rump/tail uniform in tone (Peregrine has paler rump). **Ad** | underwing coverts **spotted dark, flight feathers pale**. **Juv / Imm** | grey-brown, upperwing with pale barring; underwing coverts dark; **flight feathers and tail paler**. Breast heavily streaked.

Peregrine Falcon | Saker Falcon *p. 31.*
Lanner Falcon *p. 319* | Goshawk *p. 30.*

Rare resident/ winter migrant; Icelandic and Greenland birds occur as vagrants

Tundra, islands and crags, open moorland

V | Harsh, deep cackling (slower tha Peregrine Falcon

Imm
'PALE'

Ad
'GREY'

On 'grey' forms, dark grey hood/ 'moustache' is **less contrasted** than on Peregrine Falcon.

Juv

Ad
'GREY'
(Scandinavia)
ALL YEAR

Imm
'PALE'
(Iceland)
ALL YEAR

Juv
JUN–APR

closed wingtip falls short of tail tip

Beware escaped falcons, including confusing hybrids, that create problems in identifying darker Gyrfalcons outside the normal range (see p. 319).

Peregrine Falcon
Falco peregrinus

♂ 38–45 cm | ♀ 46–51 cm
ᗯ ♂ 87–100 cm | ♀ 104–114 cm

Large falcon, rather heavy, broad-bodied; large feet. **Crown blackish.** Wide, lobe-shaped, **black 'moustache'**; white neck. **Ad** | grey above, white below, belly/flank barred grey. Legs and eyering yellow. **♂ Ad** | upperparts bluish; underparts tinged pink, breast white. **♀ Ad** | dull grey, underparts less pink than ♂. **Juv** | browner, but **head pattern similar** to **Ad**; underparts buff, streaked black; tail tip yellow-buff. Legs and eyering bluish.

ᗯ | Around nest: loud, coarse "*haar-aair-haair*," chattering "*kek-kek-kek-ek*;" various whining sounds.

Five sspp. recorded in Europe: *peregrinus* (widespread); *brookei* (Iberia to Turkey) smaller, more rufous below; *calidus* (N European tundra) large and pale, crown and narrow 'moustache' greyish; *tundrius* (vagrant from N America/Greenland) pale – like *calidus* with white forehead, but blacker crown and 'moustache', **Juv** paler sandy-brown; *pelegrinoides* ('**Barbary Falcon**', sometimes treated as a separate species) (Canary Is.), which is smaller, bluer-grey than *peregrinus*, with some rufous on nape, but often hard to tell apart.

FL | Direct, muscular; **deep, whippy beats**; few or no glides in straight flight, but frequently circles or soars without flapping. Rump broad, pale (narrow, darker on Hobby). Wings wide-based, tapered (blunt-tipped on ♀, more pointed on ♂) or curved back (short, tapered tail creating 'anchor' shape). Soars masterfully (wings faintly upswept) to great height. Chases prey in fast, direct pursuit, or with rolling swoop from beneath, or stoops with closed wings (creating loud 'rush'). Shapes resemble pigeon, Raven (*p. 475*), even Fulmar (*p. 91*), at times.

Gyrfalcon | Eleonora's Falcon *p. 315* Lanner Falcon *p. 319* | Saker Falcon *p. 318* | Hobby *p. 314* | Goshawk *p. 302*

Scarce resident/migrant

Cliffs, crags, lakes and coastal areas, towns and cities

Ad

Ad

ssp. *peregrinus*

Ad

highly variable, ranging from light to dark

Ad

Juv

Ad

'Barbary Falcon' ssp. *pelegrinoides*

Juv
MAY–MAR

Ad
ALL YEAR

Ad
ALL YEAR

'Barbary Falcon' ssp. *pelegrinoides*

closed wingtip reaches tail tip (falls short on Gyrfalcon)

ssp. *peregrinus*

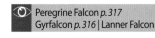

Saker Falcon *Falco cherrug*

L 45–57 cm | **W** 97–126 cm

Very large, bulky falcon (closer in size to Gyrfalcon than Peregrine Falcon); ♂ slimmer than ♀. **Ad** | upperparts **tawny-brown**; crown streaked brown. Bright pale stripe above eye, fine dark stripe through eye and thin 'moustache'; cheek and throat cream. Underparts pale with dark spots, **flank and thigh dark**. Legs, eyering and cere rich yellow. **Juv / Imm** | (ageing difficult) underparts buff, variably streaked dark brown; flank streaked or **solidly dark**; legs and eyering bluish.

FL | Heavy, powerful; wingtips **angled upwards** when soaring. Uppertail **barred or spotted buff, paler than back and wings**. Underparts pale. On ♂**Ad** and **Juv**, blackish underwing coverts form **large dark patch**; flank dark; pale patch at base of primaries contrasts with dark wingtip. ♀**Ad** many have pale underwing coverts.

Peregrine Falcon *p. 317*
Gyrfalcon *p. 316* | Lanner Falcon

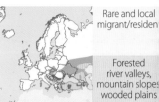

Rare and local migrant/residen

Forested river valleys, mountain slopes wooded plains

Sspp. *cherrug* occurs in Europe.

V | At nest, hoarse, cackling *"kyak-yak-ya ak;"* otherwise siler

Ad

Juv

black underwing patch

Imm

eyering and cere bluish

Juv
JUN–DEC

Imm
ALL YEAR

eyering and cere yellow

Ad
ALL YEAR

closed wingtip falls short of tail tip

Lanner Falcon *Falco biarmicus*

L 39–48 cm | **W** 88–113 cm

Large falcon, slimmer than Gyrfalcon and Saker Falcon, longer tailed than Peregrine Falcon. **Ad** | upperparts grey, barred brown; **rear crown, cheek and hindneck rufous** (but see Peregrine Falcon ssp. *pelegrinoides*). Dark stripe through eye; **thin**, blackish 'moustache'. Underparts white, barred grey; thighs **pale**. Legs and eyering yellow. **Juv** | thighs streaked buff and brown; tail dark. Black 'moustache' joins blackish eye patch. Legs and eyering greyish.

FL | Wings rather **narrow, drooped**, tips smoothly upswept when soaring; direct flight has supple wingbeats, faster and deeper in pursuit of prey. **Upperside greyish** (less brown than Saker Falcon). Underparts dark, streaked black, with extensive pale buff area around legs and undertail; **dark coverts or midwing band** contrast against pale flight feathers; tail dark.

Peregrine Falcon *p. 317*
Gyrfalcon *p. 316* | Saker Falcon

Rare and local resident/winter migrant

Open dry plains, lower mountain slopes

Two similar sspp. recorded: *feldeggii* (S/SE Europe) and *erlangeri* (vagrant from NW Africa) paler blue-grey upperparts.

V | At nest, hoarse cackling, rapid chatter and long-drawn squealing notes.

Ad

Juv

dark midwing band

Ad

NOTE: NE African/Middle Eastern ssp. *tanypterus* shown; European ssp. *feldeggii* looks similar but is slightly smaller.

Juv
JUN–DEC

closed wingtip reaches tail tip

Ad
ALL YEAR

Cross-breeding in captivity produces almost unidentifiable birds, *e.g.* Gyrfalcon × Saker Falcon (ᴛᴏᴘ) and Peregrine Falcon × Lanner Falcon (ʙᴏᴛᴛᴏᴍ), any of which may 'escape'.

319

Cuckoos, kingfishers, bee-eaters, rollers, hoopoes

are a collection of 'near passerines', most with distinctive 'two toes forward, two back' ('zygodactyl') feet.

CUCKOOS 6 species
[3 vagrants] *(pp. 321–323, 584)*

CUCKOO

Slender and long-tailed; long wings often drooped when perched, giving a more bulky or angular profile. All are long-distance migrants. **Flight** Slightly heavy, with quick beats of broad-based wings; small head raised.
Sexing, Ageing and Moult Sexes look alike (differ slightly in some species). No seasonal differences; juveniles are browner than adults. Adults have complete moult after autumn migration; juveniles have partial moult to 1st-year plumage, when like adult with some juvenile wing feathers retained.

Identify by pattern on upperparts (spotted or plain) | underwing pattern | voice

Nearctic cuckoos *(p. 584)*

Two species occur as vagrants from North America but rarely survive long.

YELLOW-BILLED CUCKOO

KINGFISHERS 4 species
[1 vagrant]
(pp. 324–325, 586)

KINGFISHER

Upright, short-tailed, very short-legged; large head and dagger-like bill give a top-heavy appearance when perched. Feet small with two outer toes partly fused together. Not all kingfishers eat fish or dive into water, but the European species do so. Resident (with short movements related to weather), although one is migratory in some regions.
Flight Fast and low: Kingfisher heavy, on short, whirring or flicked wings; larger species longer-winged, more manoeuvrable; all swoop upwards to perch. **Sexing, Ageing and Moult** Sexes look slightly different. Adult shows no seasonal differences. Juvenile duller. Adults have complete moult after breeding, partial in spring, but highly variable and more irregular with age; wing and tail moult even asymmetrical. Juveniles moult after fledging (begin Mar-Oct), some not until Dec.

Identify by overall colour/pattern (all are distinctive)

BEE-EATERS 3 species
[1 vagrant] *(pp. 326, 585)*

BEE-EATER

Rather long and slim with an elongated tail, pointed, slightly downcurved bill and very short legs. The two breeding species are long-distance migrants. **Flight** Long-winged and agile, feeding on flying insects caught in the bill. **Sexing, Ageing and Moult** Sexes look alike. Adults duller after complete moult Jul-Feb, and have partial moult Dec-Mar. Juveniles are duller than adults and moult to 1S by Mar.

Identify by colour of upperparts | head pattern

ROLLERS 2 species
[1 vagrant] *(pp. 327, 585)*

ROLLER

Distinctively coloured, somewhat crow-like *(p. 471)*. **Flight** Strong, direct, when brilliant blues are revealed in the wings; 'tumbling' display-flight. **Sexing, Ageing and Moult** Sexes look alike. Adults have slight seasonal differences, duller after a complete moult Jun-Dec; partial moult Jan-Mar. Juveniles are duller than adults, moult to 1W Sep-Dec and often have a partial moult to 1S Jan-Mar.

Identify by tail shape | colour of primaries

HOOPOE 1 species
(p. 328)

HOOPOE

Unmistakable if seen clearly (but beware Jay *(p. 473)*) – slender-bodied and broad-winged with a large, fan-shaped crest that can be raised or flattened; walks on short legs and probes for invertebrates with its long, slim bill.
Flight Bounding. **Sexing, Ageing and Moult** Sexes look alike. Adult moults from Jul or Sep to Feb, but probably does not have a pre-breeding moult. Juvenile dull, moults Aug-Feb.

Great Spotted Cuckoo *Clamator glandarius*

35–39 cm | **W** 60–65 cm

Large, slim cuckoo; upperparts grey with **white spots**; underparts unmarked buff-white. Perches with long tail closed, wingtips often drooped; often hops on the ground. **Ad** | **cap and short crest pale grey**, nape blackish; upperparts dark grey, covered with **triangular white spots** (browner, with smaller white spots MAR-AUG); eye yellowish to dark brown, eyering grey. **Juv** | **cap black**; upperparts blackish-brown with rounded white spots; flank and belly olive-brown; eye dark brown, eyering orange-red. **1S** | individually variable; cap mixed grey and blackish, wing with some rufous.

♫ | Scratchy, unmusical, vaguely woodpecker-like chatter, a decelerating "*kek-ek-ekekekekekek ek ek ek.*"

Scarce summer migrant FEB–NOV; very local resident

Heathland, pine woods, olive groves

FL | Shape and action recall long-winged Magpie (*p. 479*). **Ad** upperwing grey with long **rows of white spots. Juv** rufous across all primaries. **1S** like dull **Ad** with rufous on outer primaries.

NOTE: All ages moult JUL–FEB; replacement feathers vary with date, so some 1S look like Juv, others more like Ad.

1S
adult-like individual

1S
MAR–OCT

Juv

rufous patch in outerwing

Ad

Juv
MAY–SEP

Ad/1S
ALL YEAR

Juvenile has a black cap and a rufous patch in outerwing that is most obvious in flight.

321

LC (Common) **Cuckoo** *Cuculus canorus*

LC **L** 32–36 cm | **W** 54–60 cm

Large, long, slim cuckoo; upperparts uniform grey, or brown with black bars; **underparts white with black bars. Head small; bill short, downcurved.** Wingtips frequently drooped below long, raised, **white-spotted tail.** ♂| upperparts and neck/breast grey. ♀| some as ♂, but most have buff on neck/breast; rare rufous form also occurs. **Juv**| upperparts greyish or rufous-brown, barred black and white; nape whitish; tail as rufous ♀ but black bars wider than rufous.

V| Soft, far-carrying "*cu-coo.*" ♀ has loud, bubbling, chuckling trill. ♂ also calls low, wheezy "*gek-eh-eh-eh-eh.*"

FL| Wings **broad-based, tapered to swept-back point**; tail wide. Wingbeats quick, below body; **slender head raised; underwing has pale central band.**

Rather scarce summer migrant
MAR–SEP

Heathland, moorland, grassland, woodland edge, reedbed/marsh

Two sspp. occur but intergrade: *canorus* (widespread) and slightly smaller *bangsi* (Iberia, Balearic Is.).

Juveniles call loudly to be fed, with a vibrant "*zssiiiii*" note; this individual's foster parent is a Great Reed Warbler, but Reed Warbler, pipits and Dunnocks are more frequent.

Juv
MAY–SEP

Barred brown or grey-brown juvenile recalls Sparrowhawk but is rounder-headed and shorter-legged.

buff on side of neck on nearly all ♀, very rare on ♂

♀ **Ad** (or possibly ♂ **Ad**)

All ssp. *canorus*

♀ **Ad**
RUFOUS FORM
ALL YEAR

undertail coverts sparsely spotted black

♂ **Ad**
ALL YEAR

♀ has rare rufous form: red-brown with black bars on upperparts and rufous-and-black-barred tail (rufous bars widest).

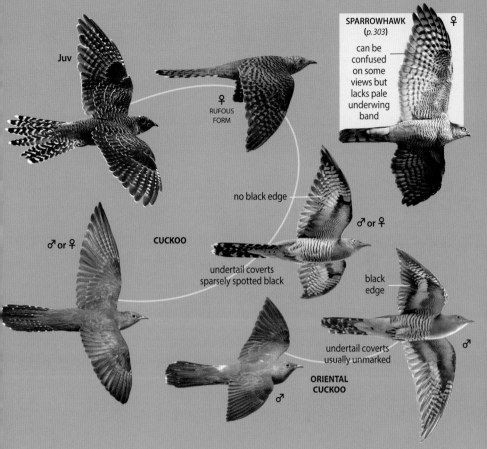

Juv

♀
RUFOUS
FORM

SPARROWHAWK
(*p.303*) ♀

can be
confused
on some
views but
lacks pale
underwing
band

no black edge

♂ or ♀

CUCKOO

♂ or ♀

undertail coverts
sparsely spotted black

black
edge

undertail coverts
usually unmarked

**ORIENTAL
CUCKOO**

♂

♂

Oriental Cuckoo
Cuculus saturatus

30–34 cm | **W** 50–55 cm

Very like Cuckoo, but bill slightly thicker;
undertail coverts buff, usually unmarked.
♂ | neck and breast grey. ♀ | neck barred
black and buff. **Rufous ♀ / Juv** | like
rufous ♀ Cuckoo (some **Juvs** much
greyer), but all have broader black/grey
bars on back and tail, and darker throat.

FL | Shape and action as Cuckoo;
broad white band under wing
edged blackish.

V | Fast sequence of double notes,
equal emphasis, "*pu-pu pu-pu pu-pu*"
(**more like Hoopoe** (*p. 328*) **than
Cuckoo**).

Very locally
common
summer migrant
MAY–SEP

Conifer and birch
forest, orchards

SSP. *optatus* occurs in Europe.

undertail
coverts usually
unmarked

♂
ALL YEAR

323

KINGFISHER ♂

♀

PIED KINGFISHER Ad

WHITE-BREASTED KINGFISHER Ad

LC **VU** (Common) **Kingfisher** *Alcedo atthis*

L 17–19 cm | **W** 25 cm

Distinctive small (smaller than Starling (*p. 379*)), stocky kingfisher with very short tail. Upperparts **blue/green**, **underparts orange**. **Ad** | crown, back and wings **greenish to deep blue**; **rump brilliant blue** (vivid electric blue in bright sunlight); white patch behind orange ear coverts. **Legs orange** (duller in winter). ♂ | bill black, one-third or less of lower mandible orange. ♀ | two-thirds of lower mandible orange. **Juv** | duller than **Ad**, with darker breast-band; dark bill and legs.

V | Often heard first: the sudden 'plop' of a dive, or sharp, high whistle in fly-by, "*chi-k-keee*" or "*ki-kee*," and trilled variants.

Scarce, locally common resident/migran

Freshwater areas; lakes, rivers, marshes in winter, coast and saltmarsh

Two sspp. occur: *ispida* (widespread); *atthis* (S Europe), which differ only slightly in size, and intergrade.

FL | Heavy-bellied, but quick, blurred wings; **streak of electric bl** immediately obviou

Depending on light and situation, white neck and throat patches may be most striking marks (on seemingly 'dark' bird), or bright blue back more obvious.

♀ **ALL YEAR**

♂ **ALL YEAR**

feet bright red

Juv MAY–NOV

Juvenile dull and dark-legged; like adult from NOV although legs patched orange (but some adults' legs similar).

ied Kingfisher *Ceryle rudis*

25–30 cm | **W** 30–33 cm

nmistakable large **black-and-white** ngfisher with short, spiky crest; legs ack. Social where common. ♂| broad ack breast-band above narrower one. | single broken breast-band. **Juv**| like ♀ ith one complete grey-black breast-band, ut some grey feather edges on underparts.

| Noisy: loud, squeaky whistling notes nd trills.

Very local resident
Rivers, lakesides

ssp. ***rudis*** occurs in Europe.

FL| Hovers frequently; wings long, black-and-white with prominent white patch in outerwing.

♀

single breast-band

♀ **ALL YEAR**

♂ **ALL YEAR**

two breast-bands

hite-breasted Kingfisher

alcyon smyrnensis

27–29 cm | **W** 30–33 cm

arge **blue-and-brown** kingfisher with ther upright stance. **Ad**| head brown; ack, wings and tail vivid pale blue; roat/upper breast white; underparts ufous. **Bill and legs red**. **Juv**| duller, -eyer-brown than **Ad**; white throat/upper reast and dull blue back finely scaled arker; bill dark red-brown; legs brownish.

| Song loud, fast, bubbling trill; call a pid, strident *"pi-pi-w-wi-wiwiwiwiwiw."*

Very local resident
Rivers, lakesides

ssp. ***smyrnensis*** occurs in Europe.

FL| Low, quick, rather heavy; wings long, mostly **bright blue with prominent white patch in outerwing.**

Juv
MAY–NOV

Ad
ALL YEAR

Juvenile is darker and browner than adult on head and wing at first, with duller bill and legs, but pattern unmistakable.

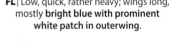

LC (European) **Bee-eater**
LC *Merops apiaster*

L 25–29 cm | **W** 36–40 cm

Slim, brightly coloured aerial feeder with long, downcurved bill and long tail; sits on open perches. **AdBr** | crown and nape **dark rufous**; upperparts **rusty-brown**, **golden-buff** on side; **throat yellow, outlined in black**; underparts dull green-blue. Tail has central spike. Eye usually red. **AdNb/Juv/1Y** | duller, greener, tail spike short or absent. Eye brown on **Juv**.

V | Far-carrying, deep, throaty, soft, rolling whistles, "*prr-up, prr-up.*"

Juv
JUN–FEB

Juvenile like non-breeding adult but duller and with a shorter tail.

Both bee-eaters similar to *Asian Green Bee-eater p.585*

FL | Long, triangular wings; tail with **pointed central spike.** Underwing has **thick black trailing edge on inner half, thinner** towards wingtip. Deep, quick, rowing beats between **flat, straight-winged, circling glides**, with **sudden spurts** to catch flying insects

♂**AdBr**
MAR–OCT

central wing cover bright red-brown on ♂; edged blue-green on ♀

Locally common summer migrant
MAR–OCT

Loses tail spike during moult
JUL–FEB.

Orchards, woodland edge, sandy cliffs and banks

LC **Blue-cheeked Bee-eater**
LC *Merops persicus*

L 28–32 cm | **W** 35–39 cm

Size and shape as Bee-eater but **crown, upperparts and underparts green**; throat yellow with diffuse **red-brown patch** (no black border). **AdBr** | black 'mask' with pale blue/white above and below. Tail has long central spike (longer than Bee-eater). **AdNb/Juv/1Y** | duller; tail spike short or absent.

V | Rolling whistles like Bee-eater but slightly higher and thinner.

Juv/1W
JUN–MAR

Juvenile has pale streak above dull rufous throat.

FL | Shape and actions as Bee-eater. Tail has **long central spike**; black trailing edge to underwing **narrow along full length.**

AdBr
MAR–OCT

Scarce and very local summer migrant
MAR–OCT

Loses tail spike during moult
JUL–FEB.

Open areas, bushy river valleys

ssp. **persicus** occurs in Europe.

1S (#1)*

Ad

Ad

BLUE-CHEEKED
BEE-EATER

BEE-EATER

1W
AUG–MAR

1S
(Ad similar)
MAR–AUG

1S (#2)*
MAR–SEP

* NOTE: 1S may be like
AdNb (#1) or AdBr
(#2); on Ad, primaries
and primary coverts
uniform blue-green.

Ad

Juv

Ad

ROLLER

Ad

(European) **Roller**
Coracias garrulus

29–32 cm | **W** 35–39 cm

Unmistakable crow-like bird: similar to
jackdaw (*p. 476*) in shape but has **large,
broad head**, longer bill, slim tail and very
short legs. Can look dull when perched,
but vivid colours are eye-catching in flight.
Ad | head, wing and underparts dull or
brighter green-blue; **back pale rufous-
brown**. Buff feather fringes in autumn.
Juv / 1W | much duller than **Ad**: upperparts
pale sandy-rufous; underparts pale blue-
green with subtle streaks; forehead and
throat buffish; dark eyestripe.

SSP. *garrulus* occurs in
Europe.

 *Abyssinian Roller p. 585*

V | Short, harsh, crow-like, calls.

FL | Quite long-winged, long-tailed;
action like pigeon (*p. 240*) or lapwing
(*pp. 163–165*). Upperwing **bright
turquoise**, blue and black.

Pale fringes obscure
colours AUG–MAR.

Scarce summer
migrant APR–OCT

Woodland edge,
heathland, scattered
trees, wooded
farmland

Ad
ALL YEAR

Juv
JUN–OCT

Juveniles have buff-
brown feather edges;
less eye-catching than
adults.

327

LC **Hoopoe** *Upupa epops*

LC | **L** 25–29 cm | **W** 44–48 cm

Unmistakable mainly ground-feeding bird with **barred black-and-white wings and tail** and long crest. **Long, low**, flat-backed shape with short legs; long, **faintly downcurved bill**. Crest usually flattened into **narrow 'wedge'**, briefly raised in broad semicircular **fan of bright orange-buff**. **Ad** | upperparts **barred black and white**, blending with shadow and light when feeding unobtrusively on ground. Upper back pale brown; head and breast grey-buff to orange-pink. **Juv** | duller, slightly greyer on nape.

FL | Slightly undulating, with bouncy, rhythmic but uneven in–out wingbeats below body level; wings broad, oval; **black and white bars** striking.

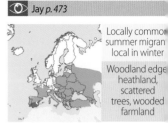

Jay *p. 473*

Locally common summer migrant, local in winter

Woodland edge, heathland, scattered trees, wooded farmland

ssp. **epops** occurs in Europe.

V | Simple, far-carrying, soft, quick repetition of quite low, hollow "*poo-poo-poo*," given with throat inflated, bill angled down and crest lowered.

Ad

Ad

Ad

Ad

Ad
ALL YEAR

Ad
ALL YEAR

Crest may be raised in early stages of courtship, but more often when a bird is nervous, disturbed, or is feeding chicks.

Woodpeckers have strong, dagger-like bills, and 'zygodactyl' feet (two toes forward, two back), giving good grip on tree trunks and branches. Residents or partial migrants. **13 species [2 vagrants].**

WRYNECK [1 species] *(p. 337)* Small, pointed bill; rounded tail; unique brown, grey and buff pattern. **Flight** Direct, undulating. **Sexing, Ageing and Moult** Sexes alike. No seasonal change. Adult has complete moult Jun-Sep, partial moult Feb-Mar. Juvenile very like adult; partial moult after fledging, completed in winter.

OTHER WOODPECKERS Stiff, pointed tail gives support against perch; pointed bill used to extract food from bark, excavate nest hole and to 'drum' on branch, serving as song. Loud contact calls. May feed on the ground but fly to trees if disturbed. **Flight** Strong, direct, with bursts of wingbeats between swooping undulations with closed wings. **Sexing, Ageing and Moult** Sexes almost alike. No seasonal changes. Adult has single complete moult, after nesting to Nov. Juvenile has different head pattern from adult; starts moult before fledging, complete by Nov. This group can usefully be divided into four 'subgroups':

Black Woodpecker [1 species] *(p. 331)* Very large; all-black except red crown/nape and pale bill.

'Spotted' woodpeckers [5 species] *(pp. 334–337)* Black, white and buff, some with red on head and under tail; best identified by size, head/neck pattern, and distribution.

Three-toed Woodpecker [1 species] *(p. 338)* Resembles 'spotted' woodpeckers but yellow on head, no red.

'Green' woodpeckers [3 species] *(pp. 332–333)* Green, paler below, yellower on rump; no black-and-white markings, but patterns of red and black on head.

Identify by size | body colour (brown, black-and-white, green or black) | head pattern | pattern on upperparts

LESSER SPOTTED *(p. 337)*   MIDDLE SPOTTED *(p. 335)*   WHITE-BACKED *(p. 336)*   WRYNECK *(p. 337)*

BLACK *(p. 331)*   SYRIAN *(p. 335)*   GREAT SPOTTED *(p. 334)*   THREE-TOED *(p. 338)*

GREEN *(p. 332)*   IBERIAN GREEN *(p. 333)*   GREY-HEADED *(p. 333)*

Woodpeckers in flight

BLACK WOODPECKER (p. 331) ♀

Juv

GREEN WOODPECKER (p. 332)

GREY-HEADED WOODPECKER (p. 333) ♂

♀

IBERIAN GREEN WOODPECKER (p. 333)

♂

♂

THREE-TOED WOODPECKER (p. 338)

Ad

WRYNECK (p. 337) Ad

♀

LESSER SPOTTED WOODPECKER (p. 337)

Ad

♂

Juv

WHITE-BACKED WOODPECKER (p. 336) ♀

GREAT SPOTTED WOODPECK (p. 334)

♂

Ad

MIDDLE SPOTTED WOODPECKER (p. 335)

Ad

SYRIAN WOODPECKER (p. 335) ♀

Ad

Black Woodpecker
Dryocopus martius

L 45–55 cm| **W** 64–84 cm

Very large woodpecker with typical shape and actions, but **black plumage** unique. Often heard first. On tree, perches upright, but also hops around fallen logs and stumps on ground. Head rounded, or with angular nape; bill whitish, dagger-like. **Ad**| **black, with red on head**; eyes white. ♂| extensive red cap. ♀| red only on nape. **Juv**| very like adult but dull black, crown dull red; eyes darker.

V| Loud, raucous, ringing or jangling "*kwik-kwi-kwi-kwi-kwi-kwi-kwi*." Single penetrating, ringing "*kweeeih*." Drum is hard, loud, machine-gun burst up to 3 seconds long.

FL| Quick, head held up, wings flicked down; not so undulating as other woodpeckers and appears slightly unsteady (often recalls Nutcracker (*p. 478*)); tail pointed.

pointed tail

Ad

ROOK (*p. 475*)

rounded tail

♀
ALL YEAR

♂
ALL YEAR

Scarce resident

Mixed and coniferous forest, particularly with large pines, Beech, oaks

SSP. *martius* occurs in Europe.

'GREEN' WOODPECKERS Long-bodied, dagger-billed woodpeckers with loud, ringing calls; green above but rump strikingly yellow. Black or red-and-black moustache. Mostly ground-feeders, hopping tail-down, using long, sticky tongue to probe for ants.

LC (Eurasian) **Green Woodpecker** *Picus viridis*

LC **L** 31–33 cm | **W** 45–51 cm

Large woodpecker, bigger than a Blackbird (*p. 385*); head up-tail down, short-legged stance on ground. Often clings upright out of sight, behind tree or post. **Ad** | upperparts bright green, **cap glistening red**; rump yellow; underparts very pale greenish. 'Moustache' black on ♀, black with red-centre on ♂. Pale eye set in black patch gives staring impression. **Juv** | cheek streaked; upperparts green with soft, whitish spots; underparts whitish, spotted black.

FL | Rises with burst of quick beats, then bounds away in deep undulations. Rump **bright yellow**, eye-catching.

Golden Oriole [♀/Imm] *p. 376*

Locally common resident

Deciduous and mixed woods, heaths, grassy areas

Two sspp. occur: *viridis* (widespread); *karelini* (Italy, SE Europe), which is duller, with greyer upperparts and whiter underparts.

V | Very distinctive loud, striking, shouted "*kew-kew-kew*" call; song longer, ringing laugh, sudden "*kyu-kyu-kyu!*" and longer "*kyu-yu-yu-yu-yu.*" Rarely drums

SSP. *viridis* ♂

SSP. *karelini*
♀
ALL YEAR

red 'moustache' with black border

SSP. *viridis*

black patch surrounds white eye in both sexes

♂
ALL YEAR

♂ Juv
MAY–OCT

Juveniles are greyer, more spotted, than adults, and have a 'primitive', almost 'reptilian' look.

Iberian Green Woodpecker
Picus sharpei

L 31–33 cm | **W** 45–51 cm

Large woodpecker, very much like Green Woodpecker but underparts more yellowish-green.
Ad | cheek dusky, **dark grey patch around eye small, ill-defined** (black on Green Woodpecker). ♂ | has red 'moustache' without black edge. ♀ | has all-black 'moustache'.
Juv | like ♀ with small dark spots and 'V'-shaped bars below.

V | Low "*kyack*" and explosive "*kyik*" calls, sharper, more tinny, than Green Woodpecker; similar laughing calls, up to 20 "*kiu*" notes. Rarely drums.

FL | Deeply undulating, like Green Woodpecker, revealing yellow rump.

Scarce, local resident
Mixed woodland

LC Grey-headed
LC Woodpecker
Picus canus

L 28–33 cm | **W** 40–50 cm

Large 'green' woodpecker; round-headed, neckless shape; bill smaller and rear body more tapered than Green Woodpecker's; often located by **call**.
Ad | upperparts olive-green; **head grey** with **thin** black 'moustache'. ♂ | has **red forehead**. ♀ | **no red**. **Juv** | head grey, no red; weak moustache; scarcely marked below.

V | Distinctively **slowing and falling in pitch and volume** "*kwee-kwee-kwee-wee-wee-wi wi wi wi*." Long, hollow drum with even pitch and pace.

FL | Undulating, like Green Woodpecker, but more oval shape, thicker neck. Rump **dull** pale yellow.

Scarce, locally common resident
Mixed upland forest, riverside trees, parkland

♂
ALL YEAR

red 'moustache' lacks black border

dark grey patch around eye (mainly in front) in both sexes

♀
ALL YEAR

black triangle in front of red eye

♀
ALL YEAR

♂
ALL YEAR

SSP. *canus* occurs in Europe.

333

'SPOTTED' WOODPECKERS Five species occur in Europe: small-medium-sized woodpeckers; thickset, short-legged, dagger-billed, black-and-white above and buff/white below. Can hang beneath branch but usually on top or side, propped up on tail. Feed with swinging, hammer-like strikes of bill. Flight undulating, swooping, with bursts of wingbeats. Calls are useful for locating birds; most also 'drum' in spring.

Three species (**Great Spotted**, **Syrian** and **Middle Spotted Woodpeckers**) have **long, white shoulder patches**; the other two (large **White-backed** (*p. 336*) and small **Lesser Spotted** (*p. 337*) Woodpeckers) have **white bars** across the back.

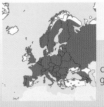 Three-toed Woodpecker *p. 338* | Yellow-bellied Sapsucker *p. 585*

LC Great Spotted Woodpecker *Dendrocopos major*

LC **L** 23–26 cm | **W** 38–44 cm

Medium-sized, noisy and conspicuous woodpecker, often visits feeders. Upperparts black-and-white with **long white shoulder patch**; underparts often stained darker by tree resin; large, **vivid red patch** under tail. White cheek separated from **white triangle on neck** by **black cross-bar**. ♂| red patch on nape. ♀| nape black. **Juv**| red cap (extends behind eye on ♂, smaller on ♀); red under tail paler than on **Ad**. Outer tail feathers white with thin black bars.

V| Loud, sharp, abrupt "*tchik*," squeaky rattle of alarm. Drums in spring: loud, hollow, fast "*brrrrp*" of about half a second (but often faint especially from ♀). Young call loudly from nest hole with scratchy, squeaky cacophony.

FL| Bounding undulations, may be high with smooth, even sweeps; bursts of wingbeats.

Common resident

Deciduous, mixed and coniferous forest, gardens, wooded parkland

Seven sspp. occur, many of which intergrade: those in N larger, heavier-billed with whiter underparts than in S; *hispanus* (Iberia) may have red on breast and belly; *canariensis* (Tenerife) and *thanneri* (Gran Canaria) are olive below, with white flank.

Juv

♂

♂
ALL YEAR

black nape

red nape

♀
ALL YEAR

Both ssp. *major*
(Scandinavia)

ssp. *pinetorum*
(W, C & S Europe)

On Juv, black bar between cheek and neck may be broken, more similar to Syrian Woodpecker, but outer tail feathers **mainly white, barred black**.

♂ Juv
APR–OCT

Middle Spotted Woodpecker

Leiopicus medius

L 20–22 cm | **W** 35–38 cm

Medium-sized, slim woodpecker. **Pale red under tail fades into streaked belly**; crown all-red (no black edge); **face white, without black bar** from base of bill to neck. ♂ has 'fuzzy', flame-red crown that can be raised. ♀ | as ♂ but slightly smaller, bill shorter; less red on crown. **Juv** | duller than **Ad**, less pink under tail; crown red, flecked grey.

V | Fast repetition of weak "*kik*" note. Does not drum; song short, nasal, descending "*wair, wair, aiir*."

Scarce resident

Deciduous woodland

Three sspp. occur but near-identical and intergrade; *medius* (widespread) becomes darker with stronger flank streaks farther S; *anatoliae* (W & S Turkey); *caucasicus* (N Turkey & Caucasus).

FL | Undulating, like Great Spotted Woodpecker but less powerful.

Ad
ALL YEAR

Ad
ALL YEAR

♀ often indistinguishable from ♂; crown may be duller, cheek more buff (individual above probably ♀).

All SSP. *medius*

Juv
APR–OCT

Syrian Woodpecker

Dendrocopos syriacus

L 23 cm | **W** 38 cm

Medium-sized, 'spotted' woodpecker; like Great Spotted Woodpecker, upperparts black with **long white shoulder patch**, but paler **pink-red under tail. White cheek continues into white on neck** with no black cross-bar. ♂ | nape red. ♀ | nape black. **Juv** | crown red; reddish breast-band; often streaked on flank. Outer tail feathers black with thin white bars.

V | Abrupt "*kik*," softer than Great Spotted Woodpecker. Drum slightly longer than Great Spotted Woodpecker's, slightly fades out (but Great Spotted Woodpecker's varies greatly, especially from ♀).

Locally common resident

Open woodland, orchards, riverside trees

FL | Bounding undulations, like other 'spotted' woodpeckers.

Cheek and neck continuous white; lacking the black bar seen on Great Spotted Woodpecker.

♂
ALL YEAR

♀
ALL YEAR

♂**Juv**
APR–OCT

Since some Juv Great Spotted Woodpeckers have similar face pattern; Juv Syrian Woodpecker is best identified by **less white** on outer tail feathers.

335

LC **White-backed**
LC **Woodpecker**

Dendrocopos leucotos

L 23–26 cm | **W** 35–44 cm

Medium-sized, but the largest 'spotted'
woodpecker, black above, dull white
below. Upperparts black, **barred white**
across wing. Forehead and cheek white;
broad black 'Y'-shape on side of neck.
Underparts dull white, streaked grey.
♂ | **diffuse pinkish-red under tail**;
cap red, edged black. ♀ | cap black.
Juv | duller, browner than **Ad**; black areas
less glossy, white areas more grey. Crown
dull red, flecked dark.

V | Low, solid "*tchik*" or "*chuk*." Drum fast,
hollow, fading to weaker, faster finish.

FL | Strong with long, deep undulations.

Rare and local resident

Mixed, old forest with
dead trees

♂

Both ssp. *leucotos*

♀

♂
ALL YEAR

Both ssp. *leucotos*

♀
ALL YEAR

♂
ALL YEAR

ssp. *lilfordi*

Two sspp. occur: *leucotos* (C and
N Europe) [MAIN IMAGES] has a broad,
unmarked white lower back and rump;
lilfordi (Pyrenees, E to Balkans and Turkey,
'Lilford's Woodpecker') [ABOVE] has lower
back and rump barred black-and-white;
wings broader than ssp. *leucotos*.

Lesser Spotted Woodpecker

Dryobates minor

L 14–16·5 cm | **W** 24–29 cm

Very small (**sparrow-sized** (*p. 505*)) woodpecker; unobtrusive, in treetops or spindly thickets; best located by call. **Ad** | Upperparts black with **white bars** merging into square patch on back; underparts white, **no red under tail**. ♂ | crown red. ♀ | crown black. **Juv** | like ♀ **Ad** but black parts browner: ♂ **Juv** forecrown red; ♀ **Juv** little or no red.

Scarce resident

Deciduous forest, thickets, wooded parkland

V | Weak "*tchik*" and nasal "*pee-pee-pee-pee-pee*." Drum is a rattling roll for 1·2 to 1·8 seconds, often twice in quick succession, but Great Spotted Woodpecker's (*p. 334*) can be confusingly faint.

FL | Fluttery in upper branches, weakly undulating over distance. Often with tit flocks.

♀
ALL YEAR

♂
ALL YEAR

Seven sspp. occur, darker/smaller from N to S and larger/paler from W to E; distinguishable only by range.

Wryneck   *Jynx torquilla*

L 16–18 cm | **W** 25–27 cm

Unusual and distinctive small brown woodpecker, which typically perches motionless for long periods in a bush or tree, or hops on the ground feeding unobtrusively. (Vaguely resembles Barred Warbler (*p. 437*).) Grey-brown; large pale head with dark brown band through eye; upperparts pale grey with **dark central stripe** on nape and back; wings spotted rufous. Rump and long tail **pale grey**, tail barred brown. Underparts buff-white with brown bars. Bill stout, sharp, **quite small**. **Ad** | eye red-brown. **Juv** | like **Ad**, but paler; throat deeper orange-buff; eye grey.

Two sspp. occur: *torquilla* (widespread; some winter in Iberia and Balearics) and *tschusii* (Corsica, Sardinia, Italy and E Adriatic coast; some winter in S Italy), which is smaller and more reddish.

V | Migrants generally silent; spring song distinctive quick, whining, nasal "*ti-ti-ti-ti-ti-ti*" or "*kyee-kyee-kyee-kyee-kyee*," rather like Kestrel (*p. 310* or Lesser Spotted Woodpecker (*p. 337*).

FL ● | Shallow undulations and long bounds on closed wings (can be mistaken for Barred Warbler (*p. 437*)).

Scarce, locally common, summer migrant MAR–OCT; resident in far S Europe

Mixed or coniferous forest; migrants on grassland, heath, bushy places

Ad

All ssp. *torquilla*

Ad
ALL YEAR

Wrynecks look unlike anything else but can be hard to see.

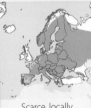

LC Three-toed Woodpecker
LC *Picoides tridactylus*

L 20–22 cm | **W** 35–40 cm

Quite small, dark woodpecker; **no red.** Upperparts black with **long white central stripe.** Head has three **broad black stripes**, separated by white; throat white. ♂| cap **yellow.** ♀| cap whitish, finely streaked grey. ♂**Juv**| like ♂ but yellow crown duller, white on back barred grey. ♀**Juv**| similar to ♂**Juv** but most lack yellow crown.

V| Nasal "*quick-wick-wick-wik*" and soft "*kwuk.*" Drum long, even, or with accelerating downward fade at end.

FL| Quick, deeply undulating.

Ad

SSP. *tridactylus*

♀

Scarce and local resident

Mixed or coniferous forest, wooded mountainsides

♂
ALL YEAR
SSP.
alpinus

♂
ALL YEAR

SSP.
tridactylus

♀
ALL YEAR

Two sspp. occur: *alpinus* (C and E Europe) [ABOVE] appears dark and has small white patch on back spotted black, flank thickly barred grey, breast streaked black; *tridactylus* (N Europe) [MAIN IMAGES] has broad white band down back and almost unmarked white underparts.

erial feeders are a small group of birds that spend much of their time in the air and feed
n airborne insects. Long-distance migrants (one also resident in south); frequently concentrate near or over
vater, or in lee of tall trees, in wet or windy weather, when mixed flocks may number in the thousands.

SWIFTS (pp. 340–343, 588) **10 species [4 vagrants]**
Exclusively aerial except at nest or when roosting: do not perch and cannot stand. Nest in holes and
crevices or construct nest under sheltered overhang. Bill minute but gape very wide; feet tiny but
strong hooked claws grip upright surfaces. Stiff, scythe-shaped wings distinctive in European
species. **Flight** Varies from slow glide to fast, twisting or racing action, singly or in groups, high or
low, often with marked changes in height; breeding groups noisy.
Sexing, Ageing and Moult Sexes look alike. No seasonal change but dark feathers often fade
browner; juveniles have paler feather edges than adults.

Identify by size | colour of underparts/rump | tail shape

SWALLOWS and MARTINS (pp. 344–347, 586–587) **12 species [7 vagrants]**
Less exclusively aerial than swifts, feeding in the air but perching on branches, wires, roofs *etc.*,
especially on migration. Nest in cliff holes or on or inside buildings. Bill small but gape wide; feet
small, feathered in some species. Wings broader, more angled and less scythe-like than swifts'.
Flight Fluent, swooping action or more fluttery effect, with frequent glides, sometimes high up.
Sexing, Ageing and Moult Sexes look alike or differ slightly (swallows). Seasonal changes
insignificant; juveniles are duller than adults, swallows also with shorter tail.

Identify by colour | head/throat pattern | rump colour | tail shape

Upperparts patterned or bluish

Upperparts plain brown

LITTLE SWIFT
(p. 343)

WHITE-RUMPED SWIFT
(p. 343)

ALPINE SWIFT
(p. 342)

SWIFT
(p. 340)

PALLID SWIFT
(p. 341)

PLAIN SWIFT
(p. 342)

HOUSE MARTIN
(p. 346)

SWALLOW
(p. 344)

SAND MARTIN
(p. 346)

CRAG MARTIN
(p. 346)

RED-RUMPED SWALLOW
(p. 345)

Swift, Pallid Swift and Plain Swift (*p. 342*) are difficult to tell apart when seen against bright sky; identification based on single photographs can be misleading (one wing may even suggest one species (*e.g.* Swift), the other wing another species (*e.g.* Pallid Swift), depending on lighting angle and intensity).

LC

(Common) **Swift** *Apus apus*

LC **L** 17–18·5 cm | **W** 40–44 cm

Fairly large swift, bigger and longer-winged than swallows and martins: **all blackish**; **stiff, scythe-like wings.** Exclusively aerial when not at nest (never perches on wire, branch or roof). **Ad** | **blackish-brown**; chin whitish. Underwing shines paler in sun. Fades browner JUN-SEP (see Pallid Swift). **Juv** | white in front of eye, dark patch through eye over cheek; fine whitish feather edgings above and below; underwing coverts blackish, contrasting with paler flight feathers.

V | Screeching whistle "*scrrreeee*," ♀ higher pitched than ♂, often in duet. Fast-flying 'screaming parties' in breeding season.

FL | Often high, fast, but also chases around rooftops; deep flickery beats between soaring glides; also slower, erratic action with wings almost beating singly. Wingtip pointed; deep tail fork.

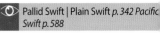

Pallid Swift | Plain Swift *p. 342* Pacific Swift *p. 588*

Locally common summer migrant
MAR–NOV

Aerial: over open spaces, water, towns, cliffs, older buildings

Two sspp. occur, which intergrade: *apus* (widespread) and *pekinensis* (vagrant from Middle East, Asia), which is browner and Juv has wider white fringes to feathers on underparts.

pointed wingtip

NOTE: Some individuals can show white patches (*e.g.* rump) and resemble rarer species.

fades browner, upperwing approaches Pallid Swift

weak 'mask'

underparts plain or subtly mottled, lacking pale 'scales' of Pallid Swift

head short, narrow; forehead steep

Ad
ALL YEAR

pale on throat restricted

SSP. *apus*

Ad
ALL YEAR

SSP. *apus*

Ad
ALL YEAR
[MAY]

Juv
JUN–DEC
[AUG]

Juv moults body feathers only, in winter range; 1S retains juvenile wing/tail but most do not return to Europe until the following year.

SSP. *pekinensis* may be indistinguishable from Pallid Swift.
(NOTE: This image was taken in Kazakhstan, where supposedly only intergrades with SSP. *apus* occur.)

SSP. *apus*

Pallid Swift *Apus pallidus*

16–18 cm | **W** 39–44 cm

Swift | Plain Swift *p. 342*
Pacific Swift *p. 588*

Common large swift of S Europe. Like Swift, with same rapid, chasing flight on **stiff, scythe-like wings**; also exclusively aerial.
Ad | **paler, browner** than Swift, with paler 'face' and more pronounced dark 'mask'; **upperwing dull brown** with **paler area** each side of dark back; underparts browner with **paler feather edges giving scaly' appearance** and paler underwing against darker wingtips.
Juv | like **Ad** but inner primaries unmoulted; large dark eye isolated in dull greyish 'face' and cheek; buff feather edgings on upperside and underside wider than on juv Swift; underwing coverts brown, blending into paler midwing.

♪ | Very like Swift, usually perceptibly lower and slightly disyllabic.

FL | Rapid, flickering wingbeats and glides on stiff wings; like Swift but fractionally rounder wingtip, shallower tail fork.

Locally common summer migrant
FEB–NOV

Aerial: over towns, villages, cliffs

Two sspp. occur: *brehmorum* (widespread) and *illyricus* (Adriatic coast), which is slightly darker; also, paler ssp. *pallidus* (N Africa) possible vagrant.

relatively blunt wingtip

pale area across innerwing

distinctive dark 'mask'

underparts appear 'scaly'

head long, broad; forehead sloping

Ad
ALL YEAR

Ad
ALL YEAR

All ssp. *brehmorum*

Ad
ALL YEAR
[AUG]

Ad
ALL YEAR

Unlike Swift, Ad moults inner primaries and coverts in late summer before migration: note new dark innermost primary growing, others pale and worn.

large pale throat patch

LC **Plain Swift** *Apus unicolor*

LC **L** 14–15 cm | **W** 36–38 cm

Very like Swift (*p. 340*) and Pallid Swift (*p. 341*) but pale throat patch diffuse and lacks pale face/dark 'mask'. Body long; tail closed in spike or spread wide with deep fork. **Ad**| dark brown, underwing coverts blacker; faint black/buff bars on body. **Juv**| like **Ad** but broader pale bars below, JUN–AUG, when edges are least distinct on **Ad**.

V| Calls high-pitched, squealing screams, much like Swift.

Fairly common resident/migrant (Macaronesian Is.): very rare breeder/migrant Iberia.

Aerial: over forests, open space

Swift *p. 340* | Pallid Swift *p. 341*

FL| Quick, dashing, sometime through treetop

Ad
ALL YEAR

Ad
ALL YEAR

Short head/ narrow wing/long rear body create slightly different shape from Swift/ Pallid Swift.

SWIFT (*p. 340*)
THROAT PATCH distinct

PLAIN SWIFT
THROAT PATCH diffuse

PALLID SWIFT (*p. 341*)
THROAT PATCH large;
DARK 'MASK' obvious

LC **Alpine Swift**

LC *Tachymarptis melba*

L 20–23 cm | **W** 57 cm

Very large and powerful swift; typical shape and actions with **stiff, scythe-shaped wings**. Upperparts mid-brown. Underside of wing and rear body dark brown; **belly white** (rear edge square or rounded); white throat and brown breast-band visible at close range.

V| Distinctive, especially from colonies or roosting groups, chorus of fast chittering notes at varying speed and pitch, "*ti-ti-ti-ti ti ti tee tee tee ti ti-ti.*"

Locally common summer migrant MAR–OCT

Aerial: over crags and gorges, upland river valleys, coastal cliffs

FL| Dynamic, covering large are of sky at high speed, diving dow beside cliffs, or to water surface: st beats of scythe-like wings betwee tilting glide

Ad
ALL YEAR

Ad
ALL YEAR

white throat often inconspicuous

SSP. *melba* occurs in Europe.

Little Swift *Apus affinis*

12–13·5 cm | **W** 32–34 cm

SSP. ***galilejensis*** occurs in Europe.

FL | Stiff, fluttering flight with short glides; wings **rather broad and straight**.

Small, dumpy swift with a **short, square tail** and rather broad, straight wings. **Ad** | glossy blackish except for white chin and prominent wide **white rump** (more like House Martin than narrow white curve of White-rumped Swift). **Juv** | like **Ad** but duller, with no gloss.

√ | High-pitched twitter.

Rare and local summer migrant APR–OCT

Aerial: over towns, villages

rump patch wide, wraps around sides

Ad
ALL YEAR

Ad
ALL YEAR

tail broad, square (blunt fan when spread)

Ad
ALL YEAR

White-rumped Swift

Apus caffer

14 cm | **W** 32–33 cm

FL | Flight quick, with fast, deep beats and long, twisting glides.

Small, slender, dark swift with a **deeply forked** tail (often closed in long point) and long, narrow wings that **curve back to long point**. **Ad** | black-brown with sharply defined white chin and **narrow, 'U'-shaped white rump**. From below, innerwing slightly paler, lashes silvery, with thin white trailing edge. **Juv** | very like **Ad** but has pale fringes to coverts on upperwing (soon wear away); white trailing edge often more prominent.

√ | Unmusical, staccato notes that may merge into trill.

Rare and very local summer migrant APR–OCT

Aerial: over towns, villages

Rump patch narrow

Ad
ALL YEAR

long, forked tail (wide, pointed triangle when fully spread)

Ad
ALL YEAR

Ad
ALL YEAR

Ad
ALL YEAR

343

LC (Barn) **Swallow** *Hirundo rustica*

LC **L** 17–21 cm (incl. tail 3·0–6·5 cm);
Juv 14–15 cm | **W** 29–32 cm

Small, slender, fork-tailed aerial feeder, with swooping flight. Legs tiny but often uses prominent perches; flocks on wires. **Throat and breast-band dark**; underparts white to pinkish-buff. **Ad** | upperparts dark, glossy blue; **forehead and throat deep red**. Tail **deeply forked**, with long streamers; long **white spots** show from beneath or when tail spread. ♂ | has longer tail and wider, glossier blue-black breast-band than ♀. **Juv** | similar to **Ad** but forehead and throat pale brownish-red; tail short, fork shallow.

Builds mud nest: an open dish on ledge or beam.

Red-rumped Swallow

FL | Direct flight fast; often swerves, wings swept back, less stiff/flickery than House Martin (*p. 346*) or Red-rumped Swallow. Often low over fields or water; in wind and rain, in lee of hedgerows or trees. When feeding, rises to momentary pause, or makes sudden sideways twist. On sunny days, chirruping groups feed at much greater height.

Common summer migrant MAR–NOV

Farms, towns, villages; lakes, marshes, open space, coastal belt

V | Calls sharp "*vit vi* chirrupy "*shrrip*" or "*trit it*" (similar to Goldfinc (*p. 487*) or White/Pie Wagtail (*p. 366*)); son rapid musical twitte with quick trill or rattl

throat dark

tail has white spots

Usually looks short-bodied, long wings swept back, tail inconspicuous thin spike unless spread or at close range.

Ad

uniform dark blue upperparts

Juv
MAY–DEC

♀
ALL YEAR

♂
ALL YEAR

All ssp. *rustica*

Loses tail streamers during moult in winter quarters
JAN–MAR.

Two sspp. recorded: *rustica* (widespread) and *erythrogaster* (vagrant from N America), which has narrow, often broken, breast-band and rufous underparts.

Red-rumped Swallow
Cecropis daurica

L 14–19 cm (incl. tail 3–5 cm)
W 27–32 cm

Small, sleek, slender, fork-tailed aerial feeder with **pale rump**; structure and behaviour much like Swallow. **Throat pale**; underparts pale buff-white with **sharply contrasting black tail**.
Ad | cap blue; **nape rusty-red, cheek pale rufous-buff**; back glossy blue; **rump pale rusty-red** or orange-buff, rear half often paler. Tail deeply forked with long streamers; **all-dark** (no white spots as on Swallow). **Juv** | like **Ad** but rump duller, no tail streamers; underwing buff.

Builds mud nest with short entrance tunnel under overhang in caves, cliff ledges, buildings.

Swallow | House Martin *p. 346*
Cliff Swallow *p. 587*

FL | **Stiffer, less elegant** action than Swallow; wings held straighter, outstretched in steadier glide, and less often swept back beside tail; thicker tail streamers often in single obvious 'spike'.

Scarce, locally common summer migrant MAR–NOV

Drier open areas with farms, villages, lakes, orchards

V | Call distinctive, hard "*djrrup*" or "*djuit;*" song slower than Swallow, less musical, with sparrow-like, chirruping quality.

Ad

no white spots on tail

throat pale buff

tail all-black

Juv
JUN–OCT

two-tone pale rump

Sexes alike but ♂ has longer tail than ♀.

Ad

All ssp. *rufula*

Usually looks slightly stocky, wings straight; tail thick and obvious, spread wide in sudden twists and turns when feeding.

Ad
ALL YEAR

Ad
ALL YEAR

Vagrant Asian ssp. *daurica* or *japonica* more streaked below than regularly occurring ssp. *rufula*; rufous collar broken by blue nape; rump single tone of orange-buff.

Loses tail streamers during moult in winter quarters
JAN–MAR.

LC (Northern) **House Martin**
LC *Delichon urbicum*

L 13·5–15 cm | **W** 26–29 cm

Small aerial feeder: size between Sand Martin and Swallow (*p. 344*); tail short, forked; wings triangular; legs short, white-feathered. Collects mud for nest from puddles; perches on roofs and wires (less likely on TV aerials or bare branches than Swallow). **Ad** | sexes alike; upperparts blue-black with black-brown wings and tail; **rump white**. Underparts and **throat white**. **Juv** | rump brown-buff, underwing grey; upperparts dull black; tertials tipped white.

Ad
ALL YEAR

Red-rumped Swallow *p. 345*
'White-rumped' swifts *p. 343*
Tree Swallow *p. 586*
Asian House Martin *p. 586*
Juv - Cliff Swallow *p. 587*

Two sspp. occur: *urbicum* (widespread), becomes smaller to S; *meridionale* (S Europe) smaller still.

Builds round mud nest with entrance at top under overhang (*e.g.* eaves).

LC (Eurasian) **Crag Martin**
LC *Ptyonoprogne rupestris*

L 14–15 cm | **W** 27–32 cm

Stocky martin; like Sand Martin but greyer; also larger, more elongated, with longer, broader wings and less forked tail. Perches on cliff ledges, under overhangs. **Ad** | sexes alike; upperparts **pale grey-brown**, becomes browner as grey 'bloom' wears away in spring. Underparts pale grey-buff, throat slightly browner and finely streaked; darker under tail. **Juv** | like **Ad** but feathers on upperparts edged buff.

Purple Martin *p. 586*
Pale Crag Martin *p. 587*
African Plain Martin *p. 587*

Ad
ALL YEAR

Builds open mud nest under cliff ledge or on building.

LC **Sand Martin** *Riparia riparia*
LC
L 12–13 cm | **W** 26–29 cm

Brown-and-white martin, smaller than House and Crag Martins. Perches (especially in autumn) along dead branches/wires over water, sometimes forms dense flocks on leafy bush or tree. **Ad** | sexes alike; upperparts sandy-brown; underparts white with **brown breast-band**. At long range, breast and underwing look dark, contrasting with **white belly** and throat (breast-band harder to see). **Juv** | like **Ad** but has pale feather fringes and edges to rump (uniform on autumn **Ad**).

African Plain Martin *p. 587*

Ad
ALL YEAR

ssp. *riparia* occurs in Europe.

Nests in a deep burrow in earth/sand cliff.

V| Short, dry, chattering "*trrrit, trri-it*" call; twittering song.

Locally common summer migrant
MAR–NOV

Towns and villages; lakes, coastal areas, open space

wide white rump

short, forked tail

throat white

Ad
ALL YEAR

underwing coverts pale

Ad
ALL YEAR

All SSP. *urbicum*

Juv
MAY–DEC

Juv has 'dirty' rump and underparts

FL| Stiffer action than Swallow, **more likely circling above house height** (but swallows and martins often mix high up or over water). Wings outstretched in glide; angled back, quick flutters and flicks in active flight; rear body/tail wide.

V| Hard, fast twittering, short clicking notes, short chirps, mostly insignificant.

Locally common resident/ summer migrant

Cliffs, gorges, peaks, rocky riversides; coasts in winter

underwing coverts dark

Ad
ALL YEAR

white tail spots

Ad
ALL YEAR

FL| Agile and elegant, swooping and gliding more than other martins, often backwards and forwards across face of cliff. Handles strong winds and updraughts with ease. **Dark underwing coverts** create small dark 'wedge' on front of wing from below. Tail wide, triangular when spread, with shallow notch when closed; dark brown with **row of large white spots** near tip, most obvious from below.

V| Dry, light, short twittering, rasping notes; trill or sharp "*chirr*" if alarmed.

Locally common summer migrant
MAR–OCT

Over water, quarries, earth/ sandbanks/cliffs, open areas

Ad
ALL YEAR

Ad
ALL YEAR

brown breast-band

Juv
JUL–OCT

FL| Agile but flickering or fluttery, less graceful than larger swallows; wings triangular, swept back; tail inconspicuous, short, slim, forked. When feeding, makes upward swoops and twists, with quickening rise/stall at intervals and little or no gliding. In poor weather, flocks flutter low over water, head to wind.

Larks, pipits and wagtails

POSSIBLE CONFUSION GROUPS Small, streaky brown birds on the ground include finches and sparrows (*p. 480*), buntings (*p. 508*) and Dunnock (*p. 373*) but these all hop double-footed, or shuffle and perch more freely, often in trees or bushes. Pipits are most similar in plumage to larks, and walk, but most are slimmer, with a finer bill, or are longer-legged. Wagtails are brightly coloured or boldly patterned as adults and in all plumages the back and underparts are unstreaked.

LARKS 20 species [7 vagrants] (*pp. 349–358, 590–591*)

SKYLARK

Small, mostly streaked brown birds that walk on the ground, with slender legs and long toes, some with elongated hind claws. Larks are stockier and shorter-tailed than pipits, with a thicker, more triangular bill. Some have a crest (flattened or raised as an upstanding triangle). Most have a dark tail, paler in the centre, with white edges. Some species have a distinctive head pattern. **Flight** Broad-winged and heavy-bodied, some quite angular, with a short or very short tail; flurries of wingbeats between short glides, with little undulation. Sing in prolonged high song-flights. **Ageing, Sexing and Moult** In most species, the sexes look alike with no seasonal change, but a few have marked differences. Adult has complete moult Jun–Oct; juvenile has complete moult Aug–Nov; after this first moult ageing is not possible as birds have acquired adult plumage.

Identify by head shape/pattern | breast-band | upperwing and underwing colour/pattern | tail pattern | primary projection | leg colour | calls and song

PIPITS 13 species (1 Macaronesian islands only) [3 vagrants] (*pp. 359–365, 525, 589–590*)

MEADOW PIPIT

Small, streaked birds that walk on the ground, with slender legs and long toes, unlike finches (*p. 480*) and buntings (*p. 508*). The dark tail with white sides is similar to many buntings and wagtails. Most are smaller, longer-tailed, thinner-legged and finer-billed than larks. None has a crest. **Flight** Pipits' broad-based wings taper to narrow wingtips and the tail looks slim. Larger species have a strong, bounding action; smaller ones are more hesitant and flitting in short, quick bounds with light, bouncy undulations, although they are long-distance migrants. Most sing in flight, rising steeply before a slow, parachuting descent with raised wings and tail. **Ageing, Sexing and Moult** In all but one species, the sexes look alike, with no seasonal differences. Adult has complete moult Jun–Oct and partial moult Dec–Apr; juvenile has partial moult Jun–Oct and again Dec–Apr – generally becoming inseparable in the field by autumn.

Identify by head pattern | back and underpart streaking | tail pattern | leg colour | calls and song

WAGTAILS 5 species (2 with complex subspecies) [1 vagrant] (*pp. 366–371*)

YELLOW WAGTAIL

Juv

♂

♀

Small, long-tailed birds with slender legs that walk on the ground, like pipits, but with a more constant tail-bobbing action. The slim tail has white sides. Colours and patterns vary between species and also unusually distinct subspecies. **Flight** Over longer distances, long, sweeping undulations; shorter flights are fast, dashing or flitting, settling on ground or perch with 'wagging' tail. **Ageing, Sexing and Moult** Sexes look different and seasonal differences are obvious; juveniles and 1st-winter birds are separable. Adult has complete moult Jun–Oct and partial moult Dec–Apr; juvenile has partial moult Jun–Oct and again Dec–Apr.

Identify by overall colour | head/breast pattern | leg colour | calls

Larks Most are brown, streaked darker; a few uniquely patterned. Two species (Crested Lark and Thekla Lark) have a pointed crest and two (Woodlark and Skylark) a blunter crest that can be raised; short crests on the two 'short-toed' larks are rarely obvious. Several species have a streaked breast-band, others a dark patch at the side of the breast. Together with upperwing, underwing and tail patterns, these create diagnostic combinations.

GREATER SHORT-TOED LARK
(p.350)

CALANDRA LARK
(p.353)

THEKLA LARK
(p.355)

Woodlark *Lullula arborea*

L 13·5–15 cm | **W** 27–30 cm

Small, rounded lark with very short tail and distinctive voice. **Black-and-white patch** on edge of wing; pale legs. Crown rounded, or raised in a blunt triangle. Creeps on ground, crouches. **Ad** | upperparts streaked brown, buff and black; cheek rufous; **whitish stripes over eyes meet on nape**. Underparts white, breast streaked black. **Juv** | upperpart feathers rounded, with wide, pale buff fringes.

Call quiet, or loud "*t'loo-ee*" (emphasis on second syllable, falling at end). Song prolonged, melodic, notes **repeated**: "*loo-o-loo, leeu leeu leeu, toodl-oodl-oodl*," from perch or in very high, circling song flight before steep, silent plunge; often sings at night.

Skylark *p.355*
Greater Short-toed Lark *p.350*
Lesser Short-toed Lark *p.351*
Oriental Skylark *p.590*

FL | Wing broad and rounded, tail very short. Wings show **no white trailing edge** but black-and-white patch on leading edge. Underwing has pale midwing band. Tail has white 'corners'. In groups of usually 2–10. Flushes at close range, bounds away before dropping out of sight; direct flight undulating.

Scarce resident/ migrant

Heathland, woodland edge, clear-felled areas in sandy plantations; winters on downs, farmland

Two sspp. occur: *arborea* (widespread); *pallida* (S & SE Europe) paler, greyer.

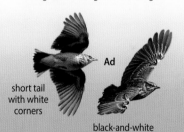

Ad

short tail with white corners

black-and-white patch on edge of wing

streaked crest may be raised briefly

SSP. *arborea*

Ad
ALL YEAR

Ad
ALL YEAR

SSP. *pallida*

Ad
ALL YEAR

'Short-toed' larks

Primary projection beyond the tertials is important for identification, but is **not reliable in juveniles** (until Aug/Sep) nor when adults are moulting tertials/primaries (Aug–Sep). Typical difference shown (*right*).

Greater and Lesser Short-toed Larks are similar. | Skylark *p. 355*
Woodlark *p. 349* | *Black-crowned Sparrow-lark* [♀] *p. 591*

TYPICAL PRIMARY PROJECTION

none/minimal

long

GREATER SHORT-TOED LARK

LESSER SHORT-TOED LARK

LC Greater Short-toed Lark
LC *Calandrella brachydactyla*

① | **L** 14–16 cm | **W** 26–31 cm

Small, pale lark with **unstreaked breast**, very short crest. Tertials **cover closed wingtip** (no obvious primary projection). **Ad** | upperparts streaked buff and dark brown. Head pattern resembles female sparrows (*p. 505*); **cap brown or rufous; whitish band over eye**. Wing crossed by **row of dark spots** and thin pale wingbar. Breast pale with **small** darker patch at side (faint marks sometimes join across centre). **Underparts plain buff-white. Juv** | upperparts barred black and buff.

V | Call **chirruping** "*drit*," "*chrrit*" or "*chirrrip*," recalling House Martin (*p. 346*) or snatch of Linnet (*p. 494*); hard, sparrow-like "*chip chip*." Song fast, chattering notes.

Fl | Short head, round body, finch-like (*p. 480*). Wings angular, tapered; two pale wingbars but **no pale trailing edge**; underwing very pale. Tail dark with pale centre and white sides. Groups of usually 10–50, sometimes 100s. Song flight has bursts of wingbeats in time with song phrases.

NOTE: Images have been selected to show variation within and between sspp.

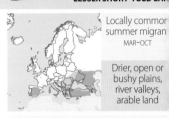

Locally common summer migran
MAR–OCT

Drier, open or bushy plains, river valleys, arable land

Seven sspp. occur, averaging paler, greyer and less streaked in E, more rufous, more streaked above in W (sspp. rarely identifiable in the field): **brachydactyla** (S Europe); **hungarica** (Hungary, N Serbia); **hermonensis** (S Turkey); **woltersi** (S Turkey); **artemisiana** (C Turkey to Transcaucasia); **longipennis** (Ukraine, SW European Russia); **rubiginosa** (Malta).

SSP. **longipennis**

Ad

SSP. **longipennis**

Ad

small dark patches (extreme example: dark patches/streaks usually smaller)

Ad

Crown usually rounded but crest may be raised briefly.

Ad

SSP. **brachydactyla**

Ad

Ad
ALL YEAR

SSP. **rubiginosa**

Ad

wingbars
obvious

wings
plain

GREATER SHORT-TOED LARK

LESSER SHORT-TOED LARK

esser Short-toed Lark
audala rufescens

● | **L** 14 cm | **W** 26–31 cm

mall, pale lark with round head, short
rest, stout bill. Like Greater Short-toed
ark but has **streaked breast-band**
ecalling Skylark) and **short tertials**,
eyond which **primaries project**
n **closed wing** (obvious primary
rojection). **Ad** | upperparts streaked buff
nd dark brown; streaky cap indistinct;
reast buff, finely streaked black.
uv | crown and upperparts barred rufous
nd buff.

| Call distinctive: **dry, buzzed** "*drrrr-p*" or
ttled "*cheer-it*" (not sparrow-like chirrup
f Greater Short-toed Lark, but both vary
nd can be similar). Song fast, musical,
icludes much mimicry.

Fl | Short head, round
body, finch-like (*p. 480*).
Wings angular, plain;
no pale trailing edge.
Tail has pale centre and
white sides. Groups of
usually 10–50, rarely
100+. Song flight drifts:
slow wingbeats between
quick flutters.

Scarce and
localized
resident/
summer migrant
MAR–OCT

Rough, grassy or
dry open spaces,
salt pans

Seven sspp. occur; best identified by range
but slight differences in measurements
and songs (fast, rattling in W, more musical
in E). Sometimes grouped into two
species: '**Mediterranean Short-toed Lark**'
A. rufescens (includes *rufescens* (Tenerife);
polatzeki (E Canary Is.), *apetzii* (Iberia)
and *minor* (S Turkey)); and '**Turkestan
Short-toed Lark**' *A. heinei* (inlcudes
heinei / *pseudobaetica* (Ukraine, Caucasus,
E Turkey) and *aharonii* (C Turkey)).

ssp. *pseudobaetica*

Ad

Crown usually rounded
but short, streaked crest
may be raised briefly.

**Ad
ALL YEAR**

primaries extend beyond
tertials on closed wing
(see *opposite*)

streaked breast, no
dark crescent at side

ssp. *minor*
Ad

ssp. *apetzii*
Ad

LC White-winged Lark *Alauda leucoptera*

LC ❶ | **L** 17–19 cm | **W** 35 cm

Large lark; frequently **hops**. Upperparts brown with **rufous shoulder**. Stripe behind eye, collar and underparts white. ♂**Ad** | forehead, shoulder patch and midwing band bright rufous. ♀**Ad** | crown grey-brown; rufous parts duller than ♂**Ad**. **1W** | less rufous than ♀**Ad**. **Juv** | crown and back streaked grey-brown, buff and black.

👁 Skylark *p. 355* | Snow Bunting *p. 509*

V | Call twittering or more vibrant "*drwi drwit*." Song complex, fast, with dee trills and high, thin, whistled note similar to Skylar

Fl | Forewing pale rufous, broad **whit hindwing patch** and blackish outerwin

Rare resident, winter migrant

Grassland, heathland

white stripe over eye

white hindwing patch

♂

♀
ALL YEAR

rufous crown and shoulder

♂
ALL YEAR

LC Black Lark *Melanocorypha yeltoniensis*

CR ❶ | **L** 18–20 cm | **W** 37 cm

Large, rounded lark; no crest. **Bill thick, whitish**. ♂**Ad** | blackish, fresh feathers edged white. ♀**Ad** | grey-brown, spotted blackish. Head/neck similar to Calandra Lark: crown streaked black, white line over eye, black crescent on side of neck. ♂**1W** | like ♀**Ad** with 'scaly' black marks on head and underparts; wing coverts black, edged white. **Juv** | dull brown; wings blackish with broad buff-white feather edges.

👁 ♀ - Calandra Lark

V | Call vibrant "*djrriw;*" song mix hesitant notes and fast, shrill, bunting-li phras

Fl | Thickset, long-winged; tail broa square or notched. Underwing da coverts blacki

Local resident, winter migrant

Grassland, salt flats

colder grey-brown than Calandra Lark

♀

♂

♂**Ad**
ALL YEAR

♀**Ad**
ALL YEAR

Calandra Lark
Melanocorypha calandra

L 18–20 cm | **W** 28–35 cm

Large, long-winged lark with long, thick bill; crest very short. Upright or crouched down. **Ad** upperparts streaked grey-buff and blackish. Stripe over eye and throat white; **black patch below white crescent on neck** (almost hidden if neck withdrawn). Underparts white. **Juv** paler grey-brown, with more spotted neck patch.

Dry, rolling "trrrreep." Song fast, rich, with far-carrying thinner notes and whistles, like Skylark.

Locally common resident/migrant

Open fields and dry grassland

Three sspp. occur, which differ slightly in colour (individuals rarely identifiable): *calandra* (S Europe); *hebraica* (SC Turkey); *gaza* (SE Turkey eastwards).

FL Wing long, broad and pointed; tail short. Upperwing shows **wide white trailing edge; underwing black** with prominent **white trailing edge**. Tail has **white sides**. Usually solitary or in groups of up to 10, sometimes 500+. High, drifting **song flight** with **slow** beats of outstretched wings.

white trailing edge

Ad

Ad

blackish underwing

Ad

heavy bill

extensive black neck patch

Ad
ALL YEAR

Bimaculated Lark
Melanocorypha bimaculata

L 16–18 cm | **W** 33–36 cm

Large, long-billed lark; crest very short. Upright or crouched low. **Ad** upperparts brown, darker spots across wing coverts. White line above black stripe through eye, **cheek rufous; black neck patch** quite narrow. Underparts white. **Juv** crown and back spotted black with crescentic buff feather edges.

Calls twittering or rolled "trri-er-chrrup." Song varied, quick, forceful; sharp, rippled notes resemble those of Calandra Lark and Skylark but fewer thin, musical whistles.

Scarce summer migrant MAR–OCT

Semi-arid, stony plains and slopes

Fl Wing broad, angular, pointed; tail very short. Head raised, pointed; body deep (Starling-shaped (p. 379)). Wing lacks white trailing edge, underwing grey; tail brown with narrow white tip. Wingbeats quicker than Calandra Lark in song flight, tail more fanned.

Ad

Ad

plain grey underwing

face pattern more 'striped' than Calandra Lark

rather narrow black neck patch

Ad
ALL YEAR

'Crested' larks

Skylark, Crested Lark and Thekla Lark all have a crest, which may be raised or held flat. Skylark is shorter-crested (less pointed) and distinctive, but Crested and Thekla Larks are a very difficult pair.

Identify by breast streaking | back/ rump contrast | tail pattern | underwing colour

Skylark, Crested Lark and Thekla Lark are all similar.
Short-toed larks *pp. 350–351* | Bimaculated Lark *p. 353*
Calandra Lark *p. 353* | Dupont's Lark *p. 357* | *Oriental Skylark p. 590*

THEKLA/
CRESTED
LARK wing plain

CRESTED LARK

SKYLARK wing with whitish trailing edge

lower edge ± convex

lower edge ± straight

THEKLA LARK

CRESTED LARK

SKYLARK

LC **Crested Lark** *Galerida cristata*

LC ❶ | **L** 17–19 cm | **W** 29–38 cm

Large, thickset, pale lark of open ground, very similar to scarcer Thekla Lark. Crest flat, pointed **'spike'**, or raised in **pointed triangular fan**, lightly streaked. Bill quite long with straight lower edge. **Plain wing; short, buff-edged tail. Ad** | upperparts streaked sandy-buff and black-brown. Pale buff fringes in OCT/NOV wear off and dark streaks fade, so more uniform by MAR/APR. Underparts buff-white, breast with **blurred** black streaks; some birds have sharply defined streaks (like Thekla Lark). **Juv** | upperparts broadly barred buff, breast spotted black; identical to **Ad** after OCT.

Locally commo[n]
resident

Arable fields, dr[y]
slopes and rive[r]
valleys, sandy
places

FL | Wings broad, square; **tail very sho**[rt]
Wings **plain**; rump buff-brown, **blen**[ds]
into **dull** uppertail coverts. Tail sho[ws]
buff sides, greyish beneath. **Underwi**[ng]
pink-buff with greyer wingtips (ha[rd]
to see against sky). Direct flight h[as]
irregular undulations. Usually alone or [in]
groups of up to 5, sometimes up to 3[0].

V | Call bright, slurred or clear, even-pitched *"tswit-sew,"* *"tree-loo-peeuw,"* *"tree-pe-loo-pee."* Song intermittent from ground; prolonged in undulating, **wandering song flight**; mixes calls, shorter twittering sounds and **prolonged** strident phrases.

underwing pink-buff, primaries greyish

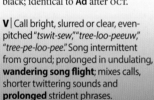

Ad

crest may be lowered

Ad
ALL YEAR

pointed crest

SSP. *pallida*
(Spain)

SSP. *neumanni*
(Italy)

Ad

Ad

rump has no distinct contrast

Ad

Ten sspp. occur in Europe, with minor differences in colour, breast streaking and bill length, but separation often impractical due to overlap and the effects of wear and bleaching.

SSP. *meridionalis*
(Greece)

Ad

Eurasian) **Skylark**
lauda arvensis

| **L** 16–18 cm | **W** 30–36 cm

arge lark, almost the size of Starling
. *379*). Crest flat or raised in **blunt
iangle**. Walks on the ground, perches
nly on low bush or post to sing.
d | upperparts streaked brown, buff
d black, wing coverts/tertials edged
uff. **Breast-band brownish, streaked
ack**, fading whiter by JUN/JUL; belly
hite. **Juv** | upperparts dark, spotted
ack, with rounded buff feather edges.

| Call chirruping "*chrrup*;" winter flocks
ve high, thin whistles. Song usually
rising hover in **long, unbroken
quence**; distinctive rhythm of varied,
st trills between longer notes; deeper
tes are 'lost' at distance, leaving thin,
ratic trills.

_ | Wings broad, angular, trailing edge
raight; tail short. Upperwing shows
hitish trailing edge; underwing pale
ey. Tail has **white sides**. If flushed flies
f fast, low. Migrants (or snow-driven
ocks) high, in straggling lines, revealed
frequent calls. Flocks up to 100s.

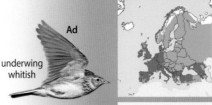

Locally common
resident/migrant

Grassland,
moorland,
heathland, marshes,
downland; winters
in arable fields

Ad

underwing
whitish

SSP. *arvensis*

Five similar sspp. occur and intergrade,
so identification outside breeding ranges
impractical: *arvensis* (widespread); *sierrae*
(Iberia); *cantarella* (S Europe); *armenica* (SE
Turkey); *dulcivox* (SE European Russia) palest.

short crest may
be raised or flat

**Ad
ALL YEAR**

SSP. *armenica*

Ad

SSP. *cantarella*

hekla Lark *Galerida theklae*

| **L** 17–19 cm | **W** 29–38 cm

arge lark of open ground and stony/
ushy slopes, very similar to Crested
rk. Crest flat or **raised in blunt
iangle**, streaked blackish. Bill quite
ort, with slightly convex lower edge.
d | upperparts streaked grey-brown and
uff; well-defined pale fringes in OCT/
ov, but becomes plainer and greyer
ith wear. Whitish below, breast with
ear-cut black streaks. **Juv** | upperparts
ackish, broadly barred buff, breast
otted black; identical to **Ad** after OCT.

| Varied, "*trt-tchu-wee-u*" and strident
reep-treep-tr-weep" (much like Crested
ark). Song in low song flight slightly
ore musical with **short**, trilled phrases.

L | Wing broad, square; **tail very short**.
ings **plain**; rump greyish, **contrast
ith rufous** uppertail coverts. Tail shows
sty-buff sides, blackish beneath.
nderwing grey-buff, weak pinkish area
n primaries (hard to see against sky).
ocks usually fewer than 10.

SSP. *theklae* occurs in
Europe.

Scarce, locally
common resident

Rocky plateaux,
stony slopes with
scattered trees,
bushy river valley
sides, open plains

underwing
grey-buff,
primaries
pinkish

Ad

triangular
crest

rump contrasts
with brighter
uppertail coverts

distinct
streaks

**Ad
ALL YEAR**

355

LC **Shorelark** *Eremophila alpestris*

LC **1** | **L** 16–19 cm | **W** 30–34 cm

Slim, short-legged lark, size of Skylark (*p. 355*). Creeps/walks/shuffles on flat/stony ground. Dark grey-brown in poor light; underparts whitish, **unstreaked** but with dark breast-band. **Legs black.** **♂Br** | head pale **yellow and black** with raised 'horns'; **black breast-band**. **♀Br** | crown and nape streaked, 'horns' short or absent. **AdNb** | head/breast pattern of ♂ less distinct, but some individuals still striking; **blackish 'mask'**. Narrow black breast-band above a brown band, or a broader blackish breast patch. **Juv** | (until AUG–OCT) breast and flank buff, mottled grey; back buff-brown, spotted black and buff.

V | Short, simple, squeaky "*eeh*", "*tseep*" or "*ee-du*." Song recalls Skylark but has shorter, more hesitant, more jingling phrases.

Up to six sspp. occur: ***flava*** (N Europe, winters NW) black cheek separated from breast-band; ***balcanica/penicillata*** (SE Europe) greyer back, **♂Br** | black cheek joins broad black breast-band; ***alpestris/ praticola/hoyti*** (N America) (see *above*).

⬦ *Temminck's Lark p. 591*

Subspecies *alpestris*, *praticola* or *hoyti* ('American Horned Lark') (vagrant from N America) similar to widespread SSP. *flava* but browner above, wing coverts rufous; face less yellow; pinkish on breast and rump; rufous on flank.

Scarce and local migrant/resident

Breeds northern tundra, mountainside and rocky plateaux; in winter, in fields, coastal marshes, sand beaches, muddy tidelines

Fl | Like large pi (*pp. 364–365*)/sm slender thrush (*p. 38* as much as a la tapered wings; qui easy, swerving flig Fairly uniform exce dark tail with p centre and white si

1Y/Ad

streaks on crown

♀ Br
MAR–JUL

♂Br
MAR–JUL

SSP. *penicillata*

♂Br
MAR–JUL

SSP. *flava*

black breast-band

black legs

SSP. *flava*

AdNb/1W
OCT–MAR

SSP. *flava*

♂Br
MAR–JU

Woodlark *p. 349*
Crested Lark *p. 354* | Thekla Lark *p. 355*

Dupont's Lark *Chersophilus duponti*

L 17–18 cm | **W** 26–32 cm

Large, elusive, secretive lark; **runs if approached**, rarely flies. Easier to locate (not necessarily to see) in **high song flight** at dawn and dusk. No crest. Slender, slim and upright when alert, head and bill uptilted. **Bill long and slim**, slightly **downcurved**. **Ad** | upperparts grey-brown, streaked darker; underparts whitish with well-defined black streaks on neck and breast. From OCT, fresh plumage brighter with broad buff feather edges. **Juv** | like **Ad** but obvious buff feather edges above.

| Call vibrant, slightly yodelled whistle, "*hoo-ee.*" Song whistled, slightly Linnet-like (*p. 494*) with nasal, whining, vibrant quality.

SSP. *duponti* occurs in Europe.

Fl | Wings long, rounded; tail slender. Upperwing plain. Tail dark with pale centre and white sides. Very high song flight.

Ad

Ad

pale rufous underwing, darker coverts

very thin pale/ translucent trailing edge

slim, downcurved bill

Ad
ALL YEAR

Scarce, localized resident

Short, tussocky, dry grassland plains

Bar-tailed Lark *p. 591* | Arabian Lark *p. 591*

Desert Lark *Ammomanes deserti*

L 15–16 cm | **W** 25–30 cm

Small, thickset, pale grey-buff lark without crest; tertials/wingtips/tail darker; throat and breast slightly streaked. Head flatter, bill thicker and more yellowish at base, and legs stouter than similar Bar-tailed Lark.

| Call a low ripple. Song, in flight, repeated short, fluty, rapid thrush-like (*p. 383*) rippling phrases.

SSP. *isabellina* occurs in Europe.

Fl | Wings dull or pale rufous; tail **orange-buff** with ill-defined dark triangle at tip.

Ad

Ad
ALL YEAR

unstreaked

Very local resident; vagrant elsewhere

Arid plains, desert

357

Larks in flight

SKYLARK
(p. 355)

THEKLA LARK
(p. 355)

CRESTED LARK
(p. 354)

WOODLARK
(p. 349)

BIMACULATED LARK
(p. 353)

DUPONT'S LARK
(p. 357)

WHITE-WINGED LARK
(p. 352)

♀

CALANDRA LARK
(p. 353)

SHORELARK
(p. 356)

DESERT LARK
(p. 357)

GREATER SHORT-TOED LARK
(p. 350)

♂

BLACK LARK
(p. 352)

♂

LESSER SHORT-TOED LARK
(p. 351)

Pipits

Pipits include species that are common and widespread, some resident, others summer or winter visitors to particular geographical areas. A few are extremely local in Europe, or rare migrants/vagrants. Finding which species are likely in particular areas and times of year is an essential first step in identification. They are elongated but deep-bellied, sometimes almost round-bodied when relaxed, but tend to stand upright when alert. They walk like larks and wagtails, rather than hop, and may perch in trees. Pipits are long-tailed, thin-legged and slender-billed. The majority have pinkish legs, so birds with dark legs reduce the options to a few species. Most are streaked black on the breast and flank, others very lightly marked. They may then be identified by size, precise details of head, rump, wing and tail patterns and calls, but some remain difficult.

Pipits and their flight/alarm calls at a glance

MEADOW PIPIT (*p. 362*)
Thin "*tseep*" or series, e.g. "*seeip-sip-sip-p*" or stronger "*sip sip sip ip-ip.*" Flocks, "*ip*" or "*pipit.*" Sharp "*stip-stip*" in alarm.

TREE PIPIT (*p. 362*)
Buzzy, abrupt "*teess*" or "*spiz.*" Sharp "*sip-sip*" in alarm.

1W/♀ Nb
SEP–FEB

RED-THROATED PIPIT (*p. 362*)
High, long, thin "*p'seeee!,*" with strong start and finely drawn finish, or quiet but explosive "*psee-see-see.*"

ssp. *littoralis*

ROCK PIPIT (*p. 361*)
As **Meadow Pipit** but more slurred, "*feest*" or "*sfeep.*"

OLIVE-BACKED PIPIT (*p. 365*)
Vibrant "*teeess*" or "*tizz*" (weaker than **Tree Pipit**).

PECHORA PIPIT (*p. 364*)
Often silent on migration but occasionally a short, metallic "*dzrep.*"

WATER PIPIT (*p. 360*)
Between **Rock** and **Meadow Pipits**: loud "*tsweeep*" or slightly vibrant "*feest.*"

TAWNY PIPIT (*p. 365*)
Vibrant "*tsreeep*" or "*sfeep,*" sparrow-like "*chwee*" and short "*chup.*"

RICHARD'S PIPIT (*p. 364*)
Throaty, sparrow-like "*shrree*" and "*shrroo,*" with rolled 'r'.

Rock and Water Pipits
are two closely similar, rather large, dark-legged pipits, noticeably stockier than Meadow Pipit (p. 362). Rock Pipits breed on the coast and remain largely coastal but occur in a wider range of habitats in winter. Water Pipits breed at high altitudes on mountain ranges inland, but move down to wetland and coastal areas in winter, when they look more like Rock Pipits in non-breeding plumage.

LC

Water Pipit *Anthus spinoletta*

LC

 L 15·5–17 cm | **W** 23–28 cm

Medium-sized, bold, **dark-legged** mountain/waterside pipit; similar to ssp. *littoralis* of Rock Pipit. Upright, full-breasted, with dark back, pinkish front, surprisingly like Wheatear **on upland meadows APR–AUG**. Strong, dark bill; legs dark red-brown; tail side white. In winter, likely to fly far off if disturbed (Rock Pipit tends to flit along shore). **AdBr** | back plain brown; head **grey** with **white stripe over eye**; throat and breast **pale pink**. Few or no flank streaks. **AdNb** | upperparts brown, head greyish. **Dull white wingbars; whitish stripe over eye**. Underparts **dull white** with few grey-brown streaks; **white bib** outlined with grey-brown. **Juv/1W** | outermost greater covert edged whitish (brown on **Ad**).

Rock Pipit | Buff-bellied Pipit p. 589
Long-billed Pipit p. 589 |
Wheatear p. 404

Locally common; migratory

High altitude pastures; in winter beside lakes, pools, and on saltmarshes

V | Call between Rock Pipit and Meadow Pipit (p. 362): loud "*tsweeep*" or slight vibrant "*feest*," fuller, thicker, more slurred than Meadow Pipit. Song short, separate phrases, each of 5–6 sharp, high notes

FL | White sides to tail. Quite strong for a smaller pipit, bursts of quick, flitting beats, may go quite high. Rising/falling song flight like Rock Pipit

SSP. *coutellii*

Nb
JUL–APR

Subspecies *coutellii* (Caucasus, Turkey) is more orange, less buff/pink on breast in spring than widespread ssp. *spinoletta*; grey on head contrasts with heavily streaked back; rump is pale and lesser coverts pale grey; calls shorter, more buzzing.

dark legs

Br
APR–JUL
[JUN]

All three
ssp. *spinoletta*

Nb
JUL–APR

Br
APR–JUL
[APR]

Br

Br

Nb

Nb

ROCK PIPIT

WATER PIPIT

Rock Pipit *Anthus petrosus*

L 15·5–17 cm | **W** 23–28 cm

Medium-sized, thickset, waterside pipit with a long, strong bill, **grey side to tail** and **slurred call**. **Legs dark** red-brown or blackish. In summer, on **rocks, cliffs, grassy slopes above cliffs**; in winter, often approachable on piers or promenades and in marshes (Water Pipit usually shy); usually in groups of up to 10, not in larger flocks like Meadow Pipit. **Ad** see sspp. box below. **Juv/1W** outer greater coverts slightly worn, inner ones new (all similar on **Ad**).

Three sspp. occur: ssp. *petrosus* (Great Britain, Ireland, W France): upperparts olive-brown, softly streaked dark grey; head greyish-olive, usually weak stripe over eye; white eyering. Underparts dull yellowish to whitish with **broad, blurred streaks**; ssp. *littoralis* (Scandinavia, moves S in winter): usually inseparable from ssp. *petrosus* in winter; stripe over eye and outer tail sometimes whiter. **AdBr** FEB–AUG, crown, nape and back **grey**, rump browner; whitish stripe over eye; **breast pinkish**, variably streaked grey, flank streaked brown; ssp. *kleinschmidti* (Faroes, Scotland): much like ssp. *petrosus* but paler above, yellower below.

Water Pipit | *Buff-bellied Pipit p. 589*

Locally common resident/migrant

Grassy places above rocky coasts, coastal cliffs, adjacent buildings; in winter, saltmarshes

V | Call resembles Meadow Pipit (*p. 362*) but 'thicker', more slurred, "*feest*" or "*sfeep*," not so often tripled. Song, a series of quick trills and song flight resemble Meadow Pipit.

FL | Typical pipit undulations, quite strong but usually low, often keeping low along rocky shore. Rising song flight, 'parachutes' to ground like other pipits.

dark, dull, olive-brown

SSP. *petrosus*

often yellow base to bill

Nb JUL–APR

greyish, becoming paler with wear

brownest type; others greyer on head, breast more pink and less streaked

SSP. *littoralis*

SSP. *petrosus*

Br APR–JUL

Br APR–JUL

dark legs

361

Meadow Pipit
Anthus pratensis **NT**

❸ | **L** 14–15·5 cm | **W** 22–25 cm

Small, streaked, **pale-legged** pipit.
Perches on bushes, not usually inside
canopy. Often crouched, nervous; round-
bodied, neckless. Loose flocks, closer in
flight. Bill slender. **Legs orange-pink;
hind claw long. Ad**| upperparts olive-
brown, some yellowish, streaked grey-
black. Head pattern diffuse; complete
pale eyering. **Rump scarcely streaked.**
Breast yellow-buff, whiter by JUL–SEP,
streaked black; **long, thick streaks on
flank. Juv**| brighter and slightly more
boldly streaked. **1Y**| very like **Ad**, some
with fresh lesser coverts and worn tail.

V| Calls thin, squeaky "*tseep*,"
or short series with varying
rhythm, *e.g.* "*seeip-sip-sip-sip*"
and stronger "*sip sip sip ip-ip*."
From flocks, short "*pip*" or "*pipit*."
Sharp "*stip-stip*" when perched.
Song long sequence of **simple,
rapidly repeated** long notes
and quick trills, from ground or
in song flight.

Tree Pipit
Red-throated Pipit [Nb/Juv]
Pechora Pipit *p. 364*
Buff-bellied Pipit p. 589
Berthelot's Pipit p. 525

Ad (WORN
APR–JUL
[JUN]

Tree Pipit
Anthus trivialis **LC**

❸ | **L** 14–16 cm | **W** 22–25 cm

Small, streaked, **pale-legged** mostly
solitary pipit, often in tree; walks
confidently on branch or ground,
head pushed forward, dipping tail.
Bill strong. **Legs pink; hind claw short.
Ad**| upperparts olive-brown, streaked
blackish. Head pattern quite strong:
buff stripe over eye, pale eyering broken
in front; pale ear-spot. **Rump scarcely
streaked.** Breast yellowish, streaked black;
thin streaks on flank; belly white.
Juv| like Ad but more buff, less olive,
until OCT, when inseparable from **Ad** in
the field.

SSP. ***trivialis*** occurs in Europe.

V| Call buzzy, abrupt, vibrant
"*teeess*" or "*speeze*," or "*spiz*."
Song richer, more accomplished
than Meadow Pipit, in similar
song-flight or **from tree;**
canary-like trills with **long
final notes**, "*see-a, see-a, see-a,
seee-a*" characteristic.

Meadow Pipit
Red-throated Pipit [Nb/Juv]
Olive-backed Pipit *p. 365*
Pechora Pipit *p. 364*

Ad (WORN)*
APR–JUL
[JUN]

Red-throated Pipit
Anthus cervinus **LC**

❸ | **L** 14–15 cm | **W** 25–27 cm

Stout, streaked, **pale-legged** pipit. Adult
distinctive; juvenile difficult to tell from
Meadow Pipit except by **call.** Subtly
stocky, broad-bellied and short-tailed
compared with Meadow Pipit; bobs tail
like wagtail. **Rump streaked.** Bill **black-
and-yellow. Ad**| upperparts streaked
black, buff and cream. **Face and throat
pink-red,** paler on many ♀ s; palest
SEP–FEB (**Nb**). Underparts white, streaked
black. **Juv/1W**| upperparts greyish,
streaked black; **two pale stripes down
back.** Underparts whitish with **bold black
streaks on flank. Rump streaked/spotted
dark.** Develops pinkish face by FEB–MAR.

V| Call **distinctive**: high, long,
thin "*p'seeee!*" with strong start
and finely-drawn finish, or quiet
but explosive "*psee-see-see*."
Alarm call simple "*ship*." Song
combines high, thin, ringing
notes and buzzing trill.

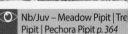

Nb/Juv – Meadow Pipit | Tre
Pipit | Pechora Pipit *p. 364*

pink-red face/throat,
paler SEP–FEB (absent
on some ♀ s)

bill black
and-yello

Ad
ALL YEAR

L | White sides to tail. Rises in **short, springy bounds**, hesitant; disturbed winter flocks (up to 300) circle and disperse. Song flight rises steeply, descends **to ground**, tail and wings raised in 'shuttlecock' shape.

Flight call (see p. 359) **thin, squeaky**.

1Y/ Ad

long hind claw

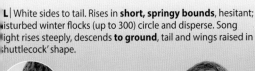

long, thick streaks continue onto flank

faintly streaked rump

1Y/ Ad (FRESH) AUG–APR [OCT]

orange-pink legs

Common migrant/resident

Heathland, moorland, marshes; rough grassland, arable fields

L | White sides to tail. Direct flight strong, quick. Rarely forms flocks. Parachuting song flight usually **starts and finishes on perch** (sapling or high branch).

Flight call (see p. 359) **short, buzzy**.

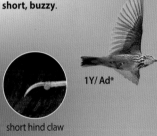

1Y/ Ad*

short hind claw

* From OCT **Ad** and **1Y** birds are indistinguishable in the field.

faintly streaked rump

streaks few and thin on flank

1Y/ Ad (FRESH)* AUG–APR [OCT]

pink legs

Scarce, locally common summer migrant MAR–OCT

Woodland/ heathland/ plantation edge, bushy slopes

L | White sides to tail. Typical small pipit flitting undulations after initial quick rise.

Flight call (see p. 359) **high, long and thin**.

Ad

*AdNb variably pink-buff or pink on throat but some ♀ Nb lack pink and can be difficult to tell from 1W.

black and cream stripes down back

bold black streaks on flank

1W/♀ Nb* SEP–FEB

streaked rump

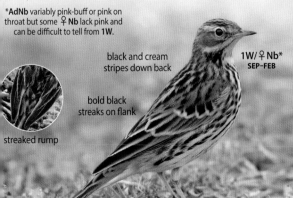

Scarce, locally common summer migrant MAR–OCT

Tundra and open mountainsides; migrants coastal grassland, marshy edges

LC Richard's Pipit *Anthus richardi*

3 | **L** 17–20 cm | **W** 26–30 cm

Large, long-legged pipit, close to Skylark (*p. 355*) in size and colour, but legs and tail longer. Often upright, pear-shaped. Walks steadily through long grass; may bob tail. Dark crescent under eye but **pale between eye and bill with diffuse dark mark.** Crown finely streaked. Bill strong, thrush-like. **Hind claw very long. Ad** | upperparts streaked brown, black and buff; some are more orange-brown. Dark line under eye and beside throat. Underparts buff-white, breast streaked black, flank plain. **Juv** | as Ad but median coverts tipped white (not buff). **1W** | mixed Ad/Juv median coverts.

Regular but rare migrant from Asia, rare in winter

Rough grassland, coastal marshes

Tawny Pipit | *Blyth's Pipit p. 589*

V | Calls variable: loud, rough or grating, with rolled 'r'; sparrow-like "*shrree*" or shorter "*speew*;" softer, flatter or downslurred "*shrroo*." 'Explosive' shouted notes distinctive but quieter notes from undisturbed birds.

FL | Strong, bounding; leaps up if disturbed; may hover before settling. Long tail dark with white sides.

Ad

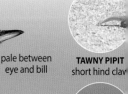

pale between eye and bill

TAWNY PIPIT short hind claw

RICHARD'S PIP long hind claw

1W
AUG–MAR

ssp. *richardi* occurs in Europe.

LC Pechora Pipit *Anthus gustavi*
VU

3 | **L** 14–15 cm | **W** 23–26 cm

Small, boldly streaked. Primaries project beyond tertials, unlike other small pipits. Legs pink; bill pink at base. **Ad** | upperparts brown; two **broad, whitish stripes;** two **broad white wingbars. Rump streaked blackish** (like Red-throated Pipit (*p. 362*)). Stripe over eye short, weak; crown/nape have thin/few streaks; white eyering broken in front of eye (complete on Red-throated Pipit). Breast buff, belly white, **long black streaks** on breast and flank. **Juv** | like Ad but streaks below broader, more blurred; not ageable after SEP/OCT.

Very localized summer migrant MAY–OCT; vagrant elsewhere

Breeds in boggy, bushy tundra

V | Call a short, metallic "*dzrep*," infrequent. Song a series of fast buzzing and slower tinkling trills.

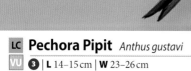

eyering complete

RED-THROATED PIPIT

primaries project beyond tertials

Red-throated Pipit *p. 362* | Tree Pipit *p. 362* | Meadow Pipit *p. 362*

Ad

FL | Relucta to fly; ma shoot up an away b usually on for a sho distanc

eyering broken

Ad
ALL YEAR

ssp. *gustavi* occurs in Europe.

Tawny Pipit *Anthus campestris*

3 | **L** 15·5–18 cm | **W** 25–28 cm

Large, **pale**, elongated pipit, round-bellied like a wagtail; a little smaller than Richard's Pipit, usually less boldly upright or 'chesty' looking; may bob tail. **Blackish line from eye to bill**. Bill fine-tipped. **Hind claw short, arched**. **Ad** | upperparts grey-buff, wing darker with buff feather edges and **black spots across 'shoulder'**. Dark line under eye and beside throat. Underparts unstreaked creamy-white. **Juv** | upperparts brown with buff feather fringes. Less rufous, more 'scaled,' less streaked than Richard's Pipit. Breast streaked black. Moults OCT–JAN to **1W** which has plainer upperparts (some birds migrate in juvenile plumage).

Richard's Pipit | *Blyth's Pipit p. 589*
Long-billed Pipit p. 589
Yellow Wagtail [♀ / Juv] *p. 368*

V | Calls sparrowy "*ch'lee*" or vibrant "*tsreeep*" (some very like Richard's Pipit); short "*shilp*" and "*chup*." Song repeated "*si-rru-ip*" in undulating flight.

FL | Strong, bounding. Long tail dark with white sides.

Scarce summer migrant MAR–OCT

Dry fields, plains, stony/rocky slopes,

dark between eye and bill

Ad
ALL YEAR

row of dark spots

Ad

Juv
JUN–OCT

Olive-backed Pipit

Anthus hodgsoni

3 | **L** 14–15·5 cm | **W** 24–27 cm

Small, delicate pipit, often under trees. Bobs tail like wagtail (*p. 366*). Legs pale pink; bill pale at base. **Ad** | upperparts **greenish-olive**, **softly streaked greyish**. Wide bright **cream stripe** over eye, crossed at rear by black eyestripe, creating **isolated pale spot at back of cheek**. Breast cream to yellowish, **thickly streaked black**. **Juv** | browner above, underpart streaking longer, broader but more blurred, but like **Ad** by SEP/OCT.

V | Call like Tree Pipit's hoarse "*teess*" or "*tizz*." Song mixed rippling trills and longer, sweet notes

Tree Pipit *p. 362*

FL | White sides to tail. Weak, undulating action; often flies up into trees if disturbed.

Ad

head pattern weakly defined

isolated pale ear spot

TREE PIPIT

Ad
ALL YEAR
[SEP]

Ad
ALL YEAR
[JUN]

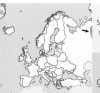

Very localized summer migrant MAY–OCT; vagrant elsewhere

Damp woods, clearings and grassy areas near trees

SSP. *yunnanensis* occurs in Europe.

Wagtails

include species that are common and widespread and both resident and summer visitors; a few occur as rare migrants/vagrants in the west. They are elongated and long-tailed, but rather round-bodied when relaxed. Except for Grey Wagtail, which has rather short, pale legs, they walk freely and quickly on slim, dark legs, with a markedly bobbing head. Males have bold patterns/colours but some species are difficult to identify in other plumages.

LC White/Pied Wagtail *Motacilla alba*

LC | **3** | **L** 16·5–19 cm | **W** 28 cm

Round-bodied but long-tailed wagtail; no bright yellow in any plumage. Tail **black with broad white side**. Legs **black**. Face white and **black bib in summer**; **black breast-band in winter**. **Distinctive calls**. Walks, runs, constantly bobs tail. Characteristic urban/suburban bird, roosts in town centre trees, warehouses, greenhouses, also near water, on ploughed fields, around livestock. Flocks up to 500, rarely 1,000. Age/sex difficult to determine from **1S**, with individual variation in moult and plumage coloration.

V | Cheerful, **musical** "*tsuwee*" or "*churee-wee*," may approach Yellow Wagtail's call; descending "*see-uw*," "*tissip*" or harder "*tissik;*" sharp "*tsip*" or "*tchisspip-tchip*."

Yellow Wagtail [Juv/1W] *p. 368*
Citrine Wagtail [Juv/1W] *p. 370*
Eastern Yellow Wagtail [1W] *p. 369*

Common and widespread resident/migrant

Towns, villages, roadsides/car parks, parks, open grassland, riversides and pastures

FL | Quick, bounding, often low but direct flight with markedly deep undulations.

White Wagtail (ssp. *alba*) widespread in mainland Europe; **Pied Wagtail** (ssp. *yarrelli*) Great Britain, Ireland and adjacent parts of NW Europe. Separation is easier in spring, but problematic in autumn/winter. **Rump colour** is the most consistent difference, but birds of any age (except breeding male Pied Wagtail) can show mixed and/or intermediate features.

pale to dark grey (never all-black)

♂Br

mid-grey (or grey, spotted black) to black

♂Br

WHITE WAGTAIL
ssp. *alba*

♀ like ♂ but rear edge of black crown is more blurred

♂Br
MAR–AUG

♀Br
MAR–AUG

PIED WAGTAIL
ssp. *yarrellii*

♀Br
MAR–AUG

♂Br
MAR–AUG

Juv | greyish, underparts off-white; untidy, narrow, blackish breast-band. NOTE: sspp. are inseparable as juveniles.

rump (all ages)	**WHITE WAGTAIL** (SSP. *alba*)	**PIED WAGTAIL** (SSP. *yarrellii*)
	grey	black/dark grey
♂**Br**	back and flank pale grey	back black; flank blackish
♀**Br**	back dusky grey; flank pale grey	back dark grey; flank extensively dark grey
AdNb	crown olive-grey, little or no black (some ♂'s show more); face often yellowish; rump grey to dark grey	crown and nape black; face white; flank dark grey; rump blackish
♂**1W**	crown grey, front edge black (overlap with Pied Wagtail); cheek greenish-white/olive, pale stripe over eye. Black breast-band narrow. Underparts bright white, flank pale grey. Back pale olive-grey, rump darker grey, uppertail coverts usually black	**crown all-black**, forehead white/yellowish; most have black nape; face white, some faintly yellow. Black breast-band broad. Flank dark grey. Back grey, rump black; uppertail coverts always black
♀**1W**	**nape and crown olive-grey;** narrow whitish forehead	as ♂ but rump blackish-grey

Comparison of White/Pied Wagtail plumages

1W
AUG–MAR

♀**Nb**
AUG–FEB

♂**Nb**
AUG–FEB

PIED WAGTAIL SSP. *yarrellii*

1W
AUG–MAR

♀**Nb**
AUG–FEB

♂**Nb**
AUG–FEB

WHITE WAGTAIL SSP. *alba*

Vagrant subspecies: SSP. *subpersonata* ('Moroccan Wagtail', Africa) ♂**Ad** | cheek mostly black; SSP. *personata* ('Masked Wagtail', Asia) ♂**Ad** | head and breast black with white forehead/'mask', back grey, broad white panel on wing; SSP. *leucopsis* ('Amur Wagtail', Asia) ♂**Ad** | throat, forehead and front of crown white, flank white (or pale grey on ♂1W), broad white panel on wing (with darker central smudges); ♀**Ad** | similar or slightly duller; **1W** | upperparts grey. **V** | Higher-pitched than White Wagtail, closer to Grey Wagtail (*p.371*).

'MOROCCAN WAGTAIL' SSP. *subpersonata*   'MASKED WAGTAIL' SSP. *personata*   'AMUR WAGTAIL' SSP. *leucopsis*

Yellow Wagtail *Motacilla flava*

LC

③ | **L** 15–16 cm | **W** 25 cm

Slender 'yellow' wagtail with **black legs**. Underparts yellow or buff, unstreaked; rump greenish; tail black, side white. **♂Br| upperparts green, underparts bright yellow. ♀Br**| upperparts greyish- or brownish-olive, buff-white wingbars; underparts **yellow-buff**. **Juv**| upperparts grey-brown; underparts buff, yellower under tail and on underwing. Dark crown side, 'moustache' and stripe beside throat; narrow blackish bib (see juvenile White/Pied Wagtail). Two white wingbars and whitish fringes to tertials.

V| Call sweet "*tsee*" or "*schlee*," loud "*sfeesp*" or "*sureee*." Eastern subspecies have harsher notes. Song weak repetition of short, slurred notes.

FL| Swooping, **long, deep undulations** between bursts of wingbeats; twisting drops to the ground. Underwing greyish. Migrant flocks up to 100.

Grey Wagtail *p. 371*
Juv - White/Pied Wagtail *p. 366*
♀ / Juv - Tawny Pipit *p. 365*
Eastern Yellow Wagtail

Often found around livestock.

Scarce but locally common summer migrant MAR–OCT

Arable land, pastures with livestock, grassy areas beside lakes, estuaries, coastal grazing marshes

YELLOW   **EASTERN**

The hind claw of Yellow Wagtail averages shorter than that of Eastern Yellow Wagtail but measurements overlap, so hind claw length is not a diagnostic feature.

♀ SSP. *flava*

♂Br SSP. *flava*

♀ SSP. *flava*

♂Br MAR–JUL

'BLUE-HEADED' SSP. *flava*

'ASHY-HEADED' SSP. *cinereocapilla*

♀Br MAR–JUL

'GREY-HEADED' SSP. *thunbergi*

'BLUE-HEADED' SSP. *flava*

Juv JUN–AUG

1W Yellow Wagtails lacking any olive/buff coloration, can look similar to Eastern Yellow Wagtail. This lack of olive/buff is frequent in eastern sspp. but rare in western sspp.

♀ Nb AUG–MAR

Six sspp. occur: variable, hybridize and intergrade. ♂ **Br** | usually identifiable, ♀ / **Juv** | usually not identifiable.

All ♂ Br
MAR–JUL

'BRITISH'
ssp. *flavissima*
Crown green; yellow over eye, throat yellow.

'BLACK-HEADED'
(so-called *superciliaris*)
As *feldegg* with white stripe over eye.

'BLACK-HEADED'
ssp. *feldegg*
Crown black; chin yellow; back bright green; call harshest, most rasping, "tsee-rr."

'GREY-HEADED'
ssp. *thunbergi*
Crown dark grey, nape paler, cheek blacker; chin yellow; back grey-green, wings browner.

All ♂ Br
MAR–JUL

'CHANNEL WAGTAIL'
hybrid *flavissima × flava*
Crown and cheek pale blue-grey; white over eye; chin white.

'BLUE-HEADED'
ssp. *flava*
Crown grey-blue, cheek darker; white stripe over eye, white spot beneath eye; chin yellow.

'IBERIAN'
ssp. *iberiae*
Crown like 'Blue-headed' or bluer, thinner white stripe over eye; chin white.

'ASHY-HEADED'
ssp. *cinereocapilla*
Crown blue-grey; no white stripe over eye; chin white.

 Yellow Wagtail
1W - White/Pied Wagtail *p. 366*

Eastern Yellow Wagtail
Motacilla tschutschensis

3 | **L** 15–16 cm | **W** 25 cm
Very like Yellow Wagtail. ssp. *plexa* (NE Siberia, most likely in Europe) ♂ | hood black/grey, no white spot below eye. ♀ and **1W** | (most likely to occur, may require DNA and/ or sound recording to confirm identification), typically **cold grey-and-white. Upperparts grey**, wings fringed olive/yellow; broad white wingbars. Dark cheek joins nape; **white over eye.** ♀ underparts white, 1W underparts off-white, may be tinged yellow.

♪ | Rasping "dzeep," lower than Citrine Wagtail, less harsh than 'Black-headed' Yellow Wagtail (ssp. *feldegg*).

Vagrant from Asia

Wet grassland

dark cheek joins nape

♂ Br
MAR–JUL

1W
SEP–MAR

369

♂Br

♀

AdNb/1W

CITRINE WAGTAIL **YELLOW WAGTAIL** **GREY WAGTAIL**

Citrine Wagtail
Motacilla citreola

3 | **L** 16 cm | **W** 25 cm

Slim, black-legged wagtail; tail black-and-white; legs black. **♂Br** | **upperparts grey, hindneck black**; head and underparts yellow. **♀/Juv/1W** | upperparts greyish; stripe around dark cheek, throat and underparts pale yellow on **♀Ad**, whitish on **Juv/1W**. **Broad white wingbars and tertial fringes**; usually **pale** between eye and black bill; **pale band surrounds** 'hollow' dark cheek; **white under tail**.

V | Call **harsh**, loud, grating "*zrrip*" ('Black-headed' Yellow Wagtail similar). Song simple, thin "*slip slip*," repeated, and occasional short, richer warble.

 Yellow Wagtail *p. 368*
Eastern Yellow Wagtail p. 369
Juv/1W - White/Pied Wagtail *p. 366*

Two sspp. occur: *citreola* (N Europe) and *werae* (E & SE Europe), **♂Br** of which has paler grey upperparts and paler underparts.

FL | Quick; long, bounding undulations, like Yellow Wagtail. Underwing white.

Scarce summer migrant MAR–OCT; occasional vagrant elsewhere

Pools, marshes, open forest bogs

♂Br

Some ♀s have blackish mottles on crown, cheek and beside throat.

♀Br
MAR-AUG

♀Br
MAR-AUG

1W
SEP-MAR

♂Br
MAR-AUG

Grey Wagtail *Motacilla cinerea*

3 | **L** 17–20 cm | **W** 25–27 cm

Elongated wagtail with **short, pale legs**, very **long tail**, **yellow rear body**. **Upperparts pale slate-grey**; tail has broad white side. **Rump yellow-green**; **bright yellow under tail**. Lively, active, bobbing and flirting tail, often on rocks beside fast-flowing river, tree-lined streams with rapids, weirs. Does not form flocks. ♂**Br**| chin black, underparts yellow. ♀| throat pale or mixed black/white. **AdNb**| throat pale. **Juv**| like AdNb but pink-buff beneath; wing coverts paler. **1W**| from SEP/OCT wing coverts mixed grey and black.

◀ | Call explosive, metallic "*zi-zi*" or "*tsivit!*" Song rapid, sharp "*tiss-iss- iss*" and "*si-si-si*", penetrating noise of rushing water.

👁 Yellow Wagtail *p. 368*

Four subspecies occur: *patriciae* (Azores) (ABOVE [OCT]) and *schmitzi* (Madeira) have darker upperparts, and *canariensis* (Canary Islands) deeper yellow underparts, than widespread SSP. *cinerea*.

Widespread, locally common, resident/migrant

Flowing, clean freshwater streams, mill races, open or tree-lined; in winter beside lakes, saltmarsh edge, garden ponds, rooftop puddles in towns

FL| Deeply undulating with brief bursts of rapid wingbeats, typically settles with extravagantly **bobbing tail**. Long, slender tail; **white band** along underwing.

AdNb/1W

AdNb/ 1W
SEP–MAR

All SSP. *cinerea*

♀ Br
MAR–AUG

yellow-green rump

♂ Br
MAR–AUG

short pale legs; short claws

1W
SEP–MAR

Wrens

1 species Tiny, rounded bird of woodland, scrub and moorland; barred brown, short tail often raised. **Flight** Fast, whirring. **Sexing, Ageing and Moult** Sexes look alike, no seasonal variation; juvenile and first-year birds hard to separate from adult.

ssp. *indigenus*
(Great Britain and Ireland)

LC Wren *Troglodytes troglodytes*

LC ❸ | **L** 9–10·5 cm | **W** 13–17 cm

Tiny, **rotund**, **brown**, with quick, jerky movements, low in undergrowth, ditches, gardens; more rarely treetops. Often appears at top of bush, calls irritably, dives back down. Little variation with age, sex or season. Warm brown. **Pale stripe over eye.** Flank rufous-buff, faintly barred grey; rump rufous. Tail and wings **barred** with brown and rufous, primaries black and buff. Tail narrow, often (not always!) raised.

V | Short "*chek*," scratchy "*tret-et*," longer, rolling/rasping "*cherrrr*" and irregular scolding rattle. Song **loud** and vibrant: sudden powerful, ringing, rapid warble with low, quick **trill** at or near the end.

 Dunnock

Common, locally abundant resident/migrant

From coastal cliffs to upland tops, islands, moorland, heathland, woods, parks, gardens

Twelve sspp. occur: most differ little from *troglodytes* (widespread); those on isolated island groups are most distinctive, *e.g. islandicus* (Iceland), *zetlandicus*, *fridariensis* and *hirtensis* (N & W Scotland), all slightly larger, darker or greyer and more heavily barred than spp. *troglodytes*, with minor differences in song.

FL ● | Low, whirring, often rising, to perch briefly, bobbing, with tail cocked.

ssp. *hirtensis*
(St Kilda)

ssp. *zetlandicus*
(Shetland)

1Y/Ad
ALL YEAR

ssp. *troglodytes*
(mainland Europe)

ssp. *islandicus*
(Iceland)

Accentors 5 species

Small, shuffling on ground, often flicking wings and tail as they progress, without sparrow-like hops; fine-billed, pale-legged. **Flight** Round-bodied; wings rounded, tail slender. Low, quick, turning sharply into cover. **Sexing, Ageing and Moult** Sexes look alike, seasonal variation slight or absent, and ageing very difficult (juvenile eye colour may help at first, but not always distinct).

Identify by head/throat pattern | underparts colour

Wren
Other accentors *pp. 374–375*
Black-faced Bunting p. 607

Dunnock *Prunella modularis*

2 | **L** 13–14·5 cm | **W** 19–21 cm

Small accentor with dull pattern, rather **dark**, streaky. Bill thin, unlike sparrows (*p. 480*). **Creeps and shuffles**, legs flexed; flicks wings and tail. Sometimes higher up, towards canopy. **Ad** | upperparts **dark brown, heavily streaked blackish**; cheek streaked brown, surrounded by grey band; underparts **grey** with blurred **dark brown streaks** on browner flank. Eye red-brown. Legs orange-pink. **Juv** | like **Ad** but underparts yellowish with dark grey spots and streaks. Darker than juvenile Robin (*p. 389*), back more heavily marked, with pale bar across plain dark wing. Eye dull. Soon becomes almost indistinguishable from **Ad**. **1W** | like **Ad** with larger pale tips/black centres to inner greater coverts, eye dull until DEC.

V | Bright, even whistle, "*peeeh*" and thin, vibrant "*si-i-i-i-i-i-i.*" Song fast, thin, high, slightly 'flat' warble, of even speed and pitch. Shorter, less varied, less rambling than Robin.

Common resident/migrant

Heathland, moorland, bushy and wooded areas, clifftops, parks and gardens

FL | Low, quick dash, often turns sideways into cover with dark wings and tail spread.

Eight sspp. described, perhaps three species: '**Common Dunnock**' *modularis* (widespread) with six sspp. ranging from dark and rufous (e.g. SSPP. *hebridium* and *occidentalis* in W) to grey-brown (e.g. SSP. *modularis* in N/C); '**Iberian Dunnock**' *mabbotti* (Iberia, S France) which has a plainer, browner head; '**Caucasian Dunnock**' *obscura* (N Turkey eastwards), which is dull and pale.

SSP. *hebridium*
(Ireland, Hebrides)

Ad
ALL YEAR

SSP. *modularis*
(N & C Europe)

Ad
ALL YEAR

1W birds have larger pale tips to the greater coverts than adults

SSP. *occidentalis*
(Great Britain, W France)

1W
AUG–MAR

'Iberian Dunnock'
SSP. *mabbotti*
(Iberia, S France)

Ad
ALL YEAR

👁 Radde's, Siberian and Black-throated Accentors are similar. | Dunnock *p. 373*

LC Black-throated Accentor
LC *Prunella atrogularis*

② | **L** 14–15 cm | **W** 19–20 cm

Small accentor with bold head pattern. **AdBr** | cap and throat blackish, creamy-white stripe over eye; back streaked rufous and black. Underparts clear creamy-buff, streaked black on flank. **AdNb** | crown grey with black sides, cheek streaked black and rusty-buff; broad buff stripe over eye. Underparts buff, sparsely streaked grey and black. **Juv** | drab, bunting-like (*p. 508*); cap and cheek grey, stripe over eye buff, streaked grey. Back dull but wings rufous and black. Underparts yellowish-grey, streaked dark grey. **1W** | like **Ad**, pale fringes obscure pattern but gradually wear off.

V | Dunnock-like "*ti-ti-ti*" call. Song from exposed perch short, wistful phrases of Robin-like (*p. 392*) warbling.

FL | Low, fast; flitting action.

Very locally fairly common summer migrant APR–OCT

Forest bogs

black head with white stripe over eye

AdBr
MAR–AUG

black streaks on flank

1W
SEP–MAR

SSP. *atrogularis* occurs in Europe.

LC Radde's Accentor
LC *Prunella ocularis*

② | **L** 14–15 cm | **W** 19–20 cm

Small, greyish accentor with bold head pattern. Flits in and out of cover and flicks wings like Dunnock. **Ad** | upperparts grey-brown, streaked grey-black; broad cap black-brown; **broad black 'mask'** between **whitish stripe** over eye to nape and pale chin curling back onto neck. Breast pale orange-buff, flank greyer, finely streaked blackish. **Juv** | crown and cheek olive-brown, stripe over eye and throat pale yellowish; underparts buff-white, streaked dark grey. **1W** | like **Ad**, pale fringes obscure pattern but gradually wear off.

V | Dunnock-like "*ti-ti-ti*" call. Song bright, clear, thin phrase with high trills.

FL | Low, fast; flitting action.

Scarce and local resident

Alpine meadows, rocky slopes

black mask, white stripe over eye

Ad
ALL YEAR

pale orange-buff breast

Juv
MAY–OCT

SSP. *ocularis* occurs in Europe.

Siberian Accentor
Prunella montanella

2 | **L** 13–14 cm | **W** 19–20 cm

Small, brightly patterned accentor; rather shy. **Ad** | **narrow** black crown; **broad, bright buff band** over eye. **Neck grey,** throat **unmarked orange buff.** Back rusty-brown, streaked black. Underparts softly mottled peachy-buff with greyer flank. **Juv / 1W** cap dark grey, cheek blackish with pale spot in corner, **buff stripe** over eye. Underparts buff, flank greyish, streaked rufous.

V | Dunnock-like *"ti-ti-ti"* call. Song from bush or tree, short, fast but melodious or squeaky warble.

FL | Low, fast; flitting action.

orange-buff over eye and on throat

Scarce and very local summer migrant
APR–OCT

High altitude low thorny thickets, stunted spruce

1W
SEP–MAR

greyish flank finely streaked darker

ssp. *montanella* occurs in Europe.

Alpine Accentor   *Prunella collaris*

2 | **L** 18 cm | **W** 25 cm

Thickset accentor with dull head pattern and brighter-coloured body; distinctive patterns at closer range. **Ad** | **grey with rufous flank** and **blackish band on wing** between lines of **white spots.** Upperparts olive-grey, **streaked black.** Head pale grey, drabber by APR/MAY. Throat spotted dark, with whitish line beneath. Tail has white tips on outer feathers. Breast grey, flank **chestnut-brown** with **black streaks at rear.** Bill **yellow-and-black. Juv** | head paler grey than **Ad** and throat whitish; underparts buff, streaked grey, with no rufous. Prominent white spots create curved wingbar. **1W** | like **Ad** with some browner juvenile wing coverts.

V | Song, by both sexes, a quick series of musical or hard trills and whistles, quite repetitive (compare with Black Redstart (*p. 397*) from high up on rocks in similar places). Calls subdued, trilled *"chrrup-chrup,"* flight call harder, lark-like *"chup-up chrrt."*

Dunock *p. 373*

Scarce, locally common resident/migrant

High altitude stony pastures; in winter, lower down on grassland, rocks

FL | Like small, low, fast thrush (*p. 383*); broad black midwing band, buff and white spots on tail tip.

pale bill can be eye-catching; pale, spotted throat inconspicuous

dark band on wing more obvious than rusty flank streaks

Both ssp. *collaris*

Juv
MAY–OCT

Ad
ALL YEAR

Three sspp. occur: *collaris* (SW Europe) back olive and buff; *subalpina* (SE Europe) paler, grey; *montana* (Caucasus, N/E Turkey) olive-grey, rufous flank extensive.

Orioles **1 species** Thrush-like, elongated, short-legged. Secretive and usually elusive in tree canopy

but presence revealed by song and calls. **Flight** Thrush-like (*p. 383*), long-winged; flies quickly across open spaces. **Sexing, Ageing and Moult** Sexes look different; juvenile/first-year birds differ slightly from adult female. Adult and juvenile have a partial moult Jun–Aug and a complete moult Nov–Feb.
(NOTE: Baltimore Oriole (*p. 609*) is an unrelated N. American icterid.)

Waxwings **2 species [1 vagrant]** (*pp. 377, 609*) Like stocky, large-headed, short-tailed starlings

with very short legs; usually perched but visits pools to drink, barely walking. **Flight** Heavy body, short tail; triangula starling-like wings; head/bill short; fast, swooping, often in flocks. Aerobatic flycatching, especially in breeding season. **Sexing, Ageing and Moult** Sexes look different, no seasonal variation; juvenile differs from adult at first but sex and age become difficult to determine. Social in winter; movements south and west in winter, in response to berry availability, erratic. Adult has a complete moult Aug–Nov (or later); juvenile a partial moult Aug–Nov.

Identify by wing pattern | colour of undertail coverts

LC
LC Golden Oriole *Oriolus oriolus*

4 | **L** 19–22 cm | **W** 44–47 cm

Elongated, thrush-like (*p. 383*) form, with short legs and **long wings**. Male brightly coloured but difficult to see in leafy canopy. Distinctive voice. ♂**Ad** | brilliant **yellow and inky black**; black from bill to eye; bill pinkish-red. ♀**Ad** | pale yellow, back greenish, flank faintly streaked grey; grey from bill to eye; wing greenish-black with pale yellow spot near edge; **tail blackish with yellow corners**; green-yellow rump (recalling Green Woodpecker). Bill dull pink-red. **Juv** | upperparts greenish; underparts white with grey streaks, yellow under tail; wing dark with small whitish spot; rump/tail as ♀**Ad**; bill grey. **1W** | like **Juv** but streaking reduced, darker between bill and eye; bill becomes pink-red. ♂**1S** | like ♀**Ad** but has fine grey streaks on underparts and bolder yellow wing patch.

'Green' woodpeckers *pp. 332–333*

Scarce, locally
common
summer migrant
APR–SEP

Broad-leaved
woodland,
riverside poplars

V | Strained, harsh, gasping "eee-aahk.
Song unmistakable: a short, rich, fluty
yodel or whistle, "ee-dl-oo," or "dl'oo," or
"ee-deeoo-dli-do."

FL | Direct; steady wingbeats, no
undulations

♀Ad/♂1S

♂Ad

♂Ad
ALL YEAR

1W
SEP–MAR

♀Ad/♂1S
ALL YEAR

(Bohemian) **Waxwing** *Bombycilla garrulus*

L 18–21 cm | **W** 32–35 cm

Almost unmistakable, Europe's only regular waxwing, but see vagrant Cedar Waxwing, which is pale, not rufous, under the tail. Stocky, with upright, pointed **crest**, **short bill** and **short legs**. Starling-like size and flight profile, but more sedate when perched, often inactive in treetops for lengthy periods, and rarely on the ground unless drinking. Agile fly-catcher, especially in summer. **Acrobatic** when feeding on berries/shoots. Winter flocks spend much time inactive in treetops, with **distinctive calls**; drop to puddles to drink. **Ad** | **pale pink-grey-brown** (can appear dull and greyish in poor light). **Chin and 'mask' black**, **rump grey**. Tail has **yellow tip**; **rufous under tail**. **Juv** | until SEP/OCT, no black bib, underparts streaked, pale chestnut under tail and short crest. **1W** like ♀ Ad but no pale 'V' on primary tips (see *annotations below*).

Starling (in flight) *p.379*
Cedar Waxwing p.609

Scarce, locally common; migratory

Northern damp coniferous forest; in winter, parks, gardens, urban areas

SSP. *garrulus* occurs in Europe.

V | **Calls** help locate feeding or resting groups: far-carrying, soft, silvery trill, "*sirrrr*." Greenfinch (*p.490*) and Blue Tit (*p.463*) can make remarkably similar sounds in spring but Waxwing calls, especially from flock, distinctive. Song short, simple trill.

FL | Quick, dashing or swooping, with longer body profile/larger head/shorter bill than Starling.

often in large flocks

1W

♀ Ad
ALL YEAR

diffuse edge to black chin patch

well-defined edge to black chin patch

relatively short crest

1W
OCT–MAR

♂ Ad
ALL YEAR

thin white 'tips' on primaries

thick white 'tips' on primaries

no white 'tips' on primaries

Starlings
4 species [1 vagrant] *(pp. 378–380, 592)*   Small, size between sparrows *(p. 480)* and smaller thrushes *(p. 383)*. Pointed bill, strong legs, pointed triangular wings and short, square tail (tail much less evident or mobile than on most thrushes); typically walk or run. Strongly social. **Flight** Heavy body tapered to pointed bill; broad, short tail; wings triangular. Fast, direct or undulating; dense flocks from 10s to millions. **Sexing, Ageing and Moult** Sexes show minor differences; seasonal variation marked. Juvenile differs from adult: juvenile Starling and Spotless Starling moult Jun–Oct, most already like adult by autumn, but striking intermediate stages; juvenile Rose-coloured Starling remains separable from adult until later in the year. Adult has complete moult between Jun and Oct.

Identify by overall colour | extent of pale spotting | juvenile bill colour and wing/rump contrast

Starling and Spotless Starling are similar. | Blackbird *p. 385* | Waxwing (in flight) *p. 377* | Nutcracker *p. 478* | Juv - Rose-coloured Starling *p. 380* | Brown-headed Cowbird *p. 609* | Daurian Starling *p. 592* | Mynas *p. 622*

LC Spotless Starling *Sturnus unicolor*

LC ❶ | **L** 20–22 cm | **W** 35–40 cm

Blackish starling, difficult to separate from Starling in some plumages. **AdBr** | solidly dull black, with weak 'greasy' gloss rather than iridescent sheen. **No pale spots**. Head and breast have very long, loose plumes. **Legs pink**. Bill lemon-yellow; base bluish on ♂, pink-brown on ♀. **AdNb** | dull, greyish; **face unspotted**, without contrasted dark 'mask'. **Wings plain**, lacking bright feather edges. Underparts, and back on ♀/**1W**, have tiny pale spots and weak crescents under tail. **Juv** | plain dark brown, wing feathers thinly edged paler brown; paler face with darker cap and 'wedge' from eye to bill; **throat mottled brown and white**.

V | Rattles, churrs and *"squeer"* calls like Starling; song similar medley but some longer, rising or falling, clearer whistled notes.

FL | Shape and action like Starling. In sunshine, wingtips may look dark red-brown against light.

Locally common resident

Towns and villages, arable fields, marshy areas

♂AdBr
JAN–SEP

♀ AdBr
JAN–SEP

♀ Nb/1W
SEP–MAR

lightly spotted

Juv (moulting)
MAR–OCT

Juv (moulting)

♂Br

♀ Ad

STARLING

Ad

Juv

SPOTLESS
STARLING

Juv

ROSE-COLOURED
STARLING

(Common) **Starling** *Sturnus vulgaris*

❶ | **L** 19–22 cm | **W** 35–40 cm

Slim, small-headed; smaller than Blackbird with **shorter tail** and pointed bill. **Walks/runs on the ground** with tail held clear. Looks blackish at a distance. Gregarious, tight flocks in trees, on the ground, in flight. **AdBr** | black with **purple and green gloss**; buff feather edges on wings and around tail. Bill base blue on ♂, pinkish on ♀. **AdNb/ 1W** | **large white spots** on underparts. Head and throat densely spotted white (soon wearing off) with **dark eyestripe**. Legs **orange-brown**. **Juv** | brown; pointed **blackish bill**; **dark 'wedge'** in front of eye. Moults into black body with white spots, while head/neck fade to buff, creating characteristic **dark body/pale head**.

♪ | Strident whistles, buzzing "*cheer*." Alarm sharp, clicking "*plik*." Frequent staccato chatter and low, nasal squeals. Song (with puffed-out throat, waving half-open wings) prolonged rattling, whistling and warbling, including mimicry of other birds and mechanical sounds; also, on perch or ground, long, rambling subsong.

➤L | **Pointed head, square tail, triangular wings**. Groups twist, swirl, suddenly settle together. Pre-roost gatherings (100s to millions) cross the sky and swirl and dive in coordinated manoeuvres. Often catches insects high in the air. Solitary bird makes long, direct flight to nest with food.

Common, locally abundant resident/migrant

Almost any open area, woodland edge, reedbeds, gardens

Seven sspp. occur, hard to distinguish: *vulgaris* (widespread); *faroensis* (Faroe Is.) **Ad** darker, duller with fewer white spots, **Juv** blackish; *zetlandicus* (Shetland Is.) **Juv** black-brown; *granti* (Azores) smaller; *purpurascens* (E Turkey), *poltaratskyi* (Urals) and *caucasicus* (Caucasus) **Ad** less green, more purple.

Juv
(moulting)
JUL–OCT

♀ AdBr
MAR–AUG

♂ AdBr
MAR–AUG

All sp. *vulgaris*

AdNb/1W
JUL–MAR
heavily
spotted

black
bill

Juv
MAY–AUG

379

LC **Rose-coloured Starling** *Pastor roseus*

LC ❶ | **L** 19–22 cm | **W** 37–42 cm

Typical starling form and behaviour, but **short, blunt bill**; large, rounded head. **AdBr** | unmistakable, **pink-and-black** with **ragged crest**. **AdNb** | pink areas sullied brown. **Juv** | moults later than Starling, unlike **Ad** until OCT/NOV. Pale beige-brown, pale below, **rump pale**; brown wing feathers edged buff. Bill **yellow with darker tip** (blackish on young Starling). Bold dark eye in plain pale face without dark 'wedge'. **1W** | dull version of **AdNb** after patchy transition: grey-brown above, pinkish-buff below.

V | Calls like Starling but less harsh; soft chattering clamour from flock.

FL | Pointed head, broad wings narrow at base, less triangular than other starlings. Note pale rump/dark tail/dark wing contrast on **Juv** (occasional sandy-coloured young Starling more uniform). Large flocks are elongated and twist, turn and swirl in synchrony, like Starling.

Juv - Starling *p. 379*

Scarce, locally fairly common summer migrant APR–NOV

Farmland and grassland with scattered trees

1W
OCT–MAR

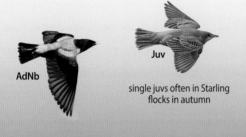

AdNb

Juv

single juvs often in Starling flocks in autumn

AdBr

AdNb
SEP–MAR

♂**AdBr**
MAR–SEP

Juv
MAY–NOV

yellow bill

Dippers
1 species Small, stocky, short-billed but strong legs and toes; always beside water (by coast only in hard weather). **Flight** Heavy-bodied; wings short, rounded. Fast, low. **Sexing, Ageing and Moult** Sexes look alike but male larger, no seasonal variation; juvenile differs until Oct; first-year has some white-edged wing coverts.

Dipper *Cinclus cinclus*
○ | L 17–20 cm | **W** 25–30 cm

Unmistakable **round-bodied, short-tailed waterside bird**, size of Starling (p. 379) but shape like Wren (p. 372). Usually seen standing on rock or bank by running water or stony lakeside, **bobbing** distinctively on flexed legs, or in water, **swimming**/drifting buoyantly; **frequently dives** or walks into water. **Ad** | black-brown, with **white breast**. **Juv** | dull, mottled grey-brown and blackish, white breast blurred by dark feather fringes. **1W** | some wing coverts thinly edged white; eye dark (red-brown after 3–4 years).

♪ | Call hard, thick, deep, rasping "*dzzit*" or "*strit*." Song a bright, prolonged, disjointed warble with whistles and trills, penetrating streamside noise.

FL | Flies off at least disturbance, or dashes past, low, following stream on jerky, **whirring** wings, giving **distinctive call.**

1W

All SSP. *cinclus*

Locally fairly common resident/migrant

Rocky or tree-lined freshwater streams, upland lake sides; in winter, lower rivers, coastal sites

ALL YEAR*

Juvenile has pale fringes above and dark mottles on breast, reducing contrast, but shape and character are unmistakable.

Juv
MAR–AUG

*bird shown is 1W (AUG–MAR) – some wing coverts with thin white edges

At least five sspp. occur, but difficult and complex: *gularis* (Great Britain), dull brown on head; *hibernicus* (W Scotland, Ireland), blackest on head and upperparts; *aquaticus* (C & S Europe east to Greece), paler above; and smaller *caucasicus* (Turkey to Caucasus) all have **red-brown band** under belly. SSP. *cinclus* (NW Europe to N Spain, Corsica) – 'Black-bellied Dipper' – has brown upperparts and **black belly**, but browner individuals occur and black becomes browner with wear. Belly colour varies individually and with age; *cinclus* and *aquaticus*-types live side-by-side in Spain.

Ad SSP. *hibernicus* **(ALL YEAR)**

Ad SSP. *gularis* **(ALL YEAR)**

Ad SSP. *aquaticus* **(ALL YEAR)**

Babblers 1 species

Somewhat like a long-tailed thrush (*p. 383*), or over-large warbler (*p. 412*) with long, rounded tail often raised, but thick, curved bill. Usually found in small, social groups. **Sexing, Ageing and Moult** Sexes look alike, no seasonal variation; juvenile paler, less streaked than adult. Adult has a prolonged complete moult Mar–Nov, depending on breeding activity; juvenile moults May–Dec.

LC **NT** ## Iraq Babbler
Argya altirostris

② | **L** 20–24 cm | **W** 25–26 cm

Slim, thrush-like, with **long, slender, tapered, faintly barred tail** often raised. Tail shape may suggest a large warbler (*p. 412*), but bill short, thick and slightly **downcurved**. Typically in small groups. **Ad** | upperparts pale brown, crown striped dark, back lightly streaked grey. Underparts paler buff, flank brighter orange-buff, throat whiter. **Juv** | paler and more faintly streaked.

V | Soft, trilled calls, "*phee-rree-rreee;*" song similar, descending in pitch.

FL | Low, short, flitting flights between bouncy hops on ground.

Rare and very local resident

Reeds, orchards, thickets

Ad
ALL YEAR

Bulbuls 5 species

[1 vagrant, 2 introduced]
(*pp. 382, 592, 620*) Like small, plain thrushes (*p. 383*) but short-billed, square-tailed, with distinctive head pattern. Feed on fruit and berries; bubbly calls. **Sexing, Ageing and Moult** Sexes look alike, no seasonal variation; juvenile has weaker head pattern. Adult has a complete moult May–Nov; juvenile a partial moult May–Nov.

LC **LC** ## White-spectacled Bulbul
Pycnonotus xanthopygos

① | **L** 20–25 cm | **W** 20–25 cm

Like a small, plain, greyish thrush with a **black hood**, raised into a peaked crown, and narrow white eyering. Bill short, slightly curved, black. **Ad** | bright **yellow** undertail coverts; dark tail. Underparts pale buff-grey. **Juv** | dusty-greyish; dull blackish face and throat, crown and nape dark grey-brown.

V | Short, quick, bubbly phrases, "*ship-er ship-er ship-er,*" "*b'dip-adip-adip-adip-er,*" and harder, grating "*tcherp tcherp.*"

👁 *Common Bulbul p. 592*

FL | Quick, flitting; thrush-like, tail rather short and square.

Very locally fairly common resident

Orchards, plantations, thickets

Juv
MAY–AUG

dark hood

Ad
ALL YEAR

Thrushes, chats, wheatears and Hypocolius

POSSIBLE CONFUSION GROUPS Dunnock (*p. 373*) fine bill, streaked flank. | **Buntings** (*pp. 508–522*) thick bill, most have white tail sides, upright on perch or horizontal on ground. | **Flycatchers** (*pp. 448–451*) upright on very short legs; wide bill.

THRUSHES 21 species [13 vagrants: 7 from America, 6 from Asia (*pp. 596–598, 611*)]

REDWING

Small–medium-sized, larger than chats and starlings (*p. 378*), smaller than doves (*p. 239*). Stocky-bodied, short-billed, strong-legged, with a rather long, broad tail. Typically hop and run on ground, pausing, upright, with head up, looking down or tilted. Some are resident, others long-distance migrants, others include both resident and migrant populations that may mix in winter. Some form flocks outside the breeding season and several species often mix loosely together. Many are fine songsters. **Flight** Strong, direct, often swooping into cover or up onto perch; mostly quite long-winged. **Sexing, Ageing and Moult** The sexes look alike or differ, slightly or markedly. Juvenile differs from adult but looks much more like adult after autumn moult, told by pale tips to wing coverts and faded primary feathers. Adult has a complete moult between May and Oct depending on species, location and date of breeding; juvenile has a partial moult Jul–Oct.

Identify by overall colour | presence/absence of spots | head/breast pattern | rump/tail pattern | underwing colour

American vagrants include two similar species (see *p. 598*), the other five being smaller and rounder with more or less spotted underparts (see *p. 611*).

CHATS 23 species (1 Macaronesian islands only (*p. 525*)) [7 vagrants (*pp. 593–594*)]

REDSTART

Larger chats look much like small thrushes; small chats are rounded, short-tailed and strong-legged. Some are resident, others long-distance migrants. Very varied, but rather stout-bodied with quite short wings and tail, short, strong bill. Strong legs and feet are not well adapted to clinging (so these are not especially acrobatic birds, unlike, for example, tits (*p. 452*)). They feed on or near the ground. **Flight** Compact, with round wings, broad tail; low, quick, rising steeply to perch. **Sexing, Ageing and Moult** (see *p. 389*) Most show marked differences between male and female (others, such as the Robin and nightingales, have sexes virtually alike). There are small seasonal differences in most species and juveniles differ, but many are less distinctive by their first winter. Adult has a complete moult Jul–Oct, and in some species a partial moult Jan–Apr. Juvenile has a partial moult Jun–Sep, in some species another Jan–Apr.

Identify by head and breast colour and pattern | rump and tail pattern

WHEATEARS 14 species [4 vagrants (*p. 595*)]

PIED WHEATEAR

A distinct group of small, terrestrial birds, feeding on bare ground or in short vegetation. Deep-bellied body tapers into head and broad tail; stand rather upright. Most have bold patterns (including black-and-white tail and rump, usually with some form of a distinctive 'T'-shape created by dark central tail feathers and a band across the tip). **Flight** Low, fast, for short distances on quite long, broad wings. Some sing in short song-flights. **Sexing, Ageing and Moult** Sexes look different; juveniles and non-breeding males look much like females and ageing becomes difficult after first autumn. Adult has a complete moult Jun–Sep and a partial moult to breeding plumage Jan–Mar; juvenile has a partial moult to first-winter plumage Jun–Sep, partial again Jan–Apr.

Identify by head pattern | rump and tail pattern

HYPOCOLIUS 1 species [vagrant] (*p. 592*)

Appearance between a shrike (*page 466*) and a slender bulbul (*page 382*): slim, upright, round-headed but long-tailed; crown may be raised. **Flight** Low, quick, on short, rounded wings; long, slender, round-tipped tail. **Sexing, Ageing and Moult** Sexes look alike, no seasonal variation; juvenile sandy-brown, dusky tips to tail. Adult has complete moult May–Nov.

LC **Ring Ouzel** *Turdus torquatus*

LC ❷ | **L** 24–27 cm | **W** 41–45 cm

Large, **dark** thrush; wings and tail long, dark-legged. On ground, sleek, flat-backed; tail often held up but not habitually raised and lowered on landing. ♂**Br** | **black with white breast-band**. Pale feather edges create **silvery-grey panel on wing**. ♂**Nb** | pale lacy pattern on underparts; breast-band dull. ♀**Ad** | browner than ♂**Ad**, **pale feather edges** on wings and underparts, breast-band duller. **1W** | has dull wing panel, pale scaly feather edges, obscure breast-band. ♂**1S** | has some pale tips to wing coverts.

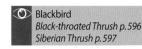

Blackbird
Black-throated Thrush p. 596
Siberian Thrush p. 597

V | Scolding, hard "*tuc tuc tuc*," rolling "*churr*." Song wild, loud, similar to Mistle Thrush (*p.387*), based around a few clear whistles, phrases distinctly separated: "*tuleee tuleee tulee; tiu-lee tiu-lee tiu-lee*."

FL (see *p. 388*) | Fast, dashing, often disappears over skyline; bursts of beats between glides, often glides on half-folded wings. **Pale upperwings** catch the eye more than dull whitish underwing.

Scarce, migratory; loca[l] in winter

Mountain crags, moorland, peat bogs; migrants on hills, heaths

Juv
MAY–SEP

♀**1W**
AUG–MAR

♂**Br**
SSP. *alpestris*

Juv (*left*) lacks a distinct breast-band but has short, whitish bars over dark underparts and short, curved pale streaks on upperparts; ♀**1W** (*right*) least distinctive, with dull pale wing panel, dull pale feather fringes ('scaly' effect) and only obscure breast-band.

Three sspp. occur, varying slightly in extent of pale feather edges: **torquatus** (N Europe, Great Britain, Ireland) dark; **alpestris** (C and S Europe) paler, with paler wing panel and more obvious pale scales below; **amicorum** (Caucasus) white breast-band wider.

All SSP. *torquatus*

♀
ALL YEAR

pale
breast-band

pale wing

♂**Br**
MAR–AUG

Eurasian) **Blackbird**
urdus merula

◐ | **L** 23·5–29 cm | **W** 40–45 cm

arge, **dark** thrush; round-headed, ong-tailed, dark-legged. **Tail raised** fter a short flight, lowered slowly. ♂**Ad** | ntensely **black**; **bill and eyering yellow**. ♂**1W** | blackish, wings brown; bill dark ntil DEC/JAN. ♂**1S** | black, wings dark rown. ♀ | brown, **darker** and darker-egged than Song Thrush (*p. 386*). hroat often whitish; breast dark brown, treaked blackish. Bill dark or **yellow** ▸ith dark tip. **Juv** | **rusty-brown**, nderparts barred and spotted brown nd buff (♂ has black tail); some are eddish below, may have ill-defined paler ▸reast-band. ♂**Juv** | briefly has blackish ▸ody but faded buff-brown head, like noulting juvenile Starling (*p. 379*).

◉ Ring Ouzel | Starling *p. 379* | Blue Rock Thrush *p. 390* | Black-throated Thrush *p. 596* | Siberian Thrush *p. 597* | Tickell's Thrush *p. 598* | American Robin *p. 598* | Red-winged Blackbird *p. 609*

V | Vibrant, "*shrreee;*" soft "*chook;*" loud "*chak;*" repeated loud "*pink pwink pwink*" especially at dusk. In mild alarm a short, rhythmic phrase repeated endlessly; full alarm **clattering, screechy rattle**. Song strongest at dawn/dusk: long, **musical, throaty and flute-like**, falls into rattles and squeaks.

FL (see *p. 388*) | Quick, strong, dashing through low shrubbery; longer flights higher with irregular wingbeats between very short glides on half-folded wings. **Pale outerwing**; long rounded tail.

Common resident/ migrant

Forests, woodland clearings, heathland, gardens, parks, farmland with trees, hedgerows

♂**Juv** MAR–SEP

♂**1W** JUL–MAR

♂**1S** MAR–SEP

Blackbird ♂ ageing sequence: Juv (MAR–SEP) rusty brown and spotty with black tail (♀ has brown tail); **1W** (JUL–MAR) with dark bill until DEC/JAN and brown in wings; **1S** (MAR–SEP) retains brown in wings with yellow bill; thereafter plumage as adult. NOTE: ♀ follows a similar pattern but harder to discern the differences in wing colour.

Five sspp. occur, slightly variable: *merula* (widespread); *azorensis* (Azores) and *cabrerae* (Madeira) ♂ has stronger gloss; *aterrimus* (SE Europe) both sexes smaller and duller; *syriacus* (Turkey) both sexes greyer.

♀ **1W** JUL–MAR

♂**Ad** ALL YEAR

All SSP. *merula*

♀ ALL YEAR

385

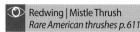

Redwing | Mistle Thrush
Rare American thrushes p. 611

LC

LC Song Thrush *Turdus philomelos*

LC ② | **L** 20–22 cm | **W** 33–36 cm

Small, compact, '**spotted**' thrush, typically in pairs/families, but **not larger flocks**. **Ad** | upperparts **warm pale brown**, wings plain. Underparts creamy-buff with dusky flank and **blackish 'V'-shaped spots**. Subtle dark cap and pale line over eye (less contrast than Redwing). **Juv** | feathers of back and wing coverts each have pale streak. **1W** | as **Ad** with large pale tips to some greater coverts.

V | Thin, sharp "*tik*" or "*sip;*" alarm like weak Blackbird (*p. 385*) rattle. Song strident with rich, fluty whistles, shouted and squeaky notes, in short phrases, each repeated – even-paced repetition rules out Blackbird and more flowing Mistle Thrush. Loud 'slap' when smashing snail on stone characteristic.

Three sspp. occur: *philomelos* (widespread); *clarkei* (Great Britain, Ireland) slightly darker; *hebridensis* (W Isles of Scotland) darkest above, whiter beneath.

FL (see *p. 388*) | Tends to fly low into cover if disturbed. Higher flight slightly zigzagging, with fast, regular wingbeats. Underwing pale orange-buff; tail plain.

ssp. *clarkei*

'V'-shaped spots

Ad ALL YEAR

Common resident/migrant

Mixed and deciduous woodland, parks, gardens, farmland with trees, hedges

1W (AUG–MAR) angular pale tips to some (juv) greater coverts

Song Thrush | *Dusky Thrush p. 597*
Eyebrowed Thrush p. 598

LC Redwing *Turdus iliacus*

NT ② | **L** 19–23 cm | **W** 30–34 cm

Small, dark, spotted/streaked thrush with **strong head pattern**. Mixes with Fieldfares and other thrushes in winter. Resting flocks often in treetops. **Ad** | upperparts dark brown. **Cream stripe over eye** and below **dark cheek**. **Lines of dark streaks** on whitish underparts; flank **brick-red**. **Juv** | brown back streaked pale buff. **1W** | as **Ad** with pale tips to some greater coverts.

V | High, thin "*seeeeh*" (often heard at night); rattling notes. Song short phrase mixing fluty and subdued grating notes. Rambling 'subsong' chorus from resting flocks.

Two sspp. occur: *iliacus* (N & E Europe); *coburni* (breeds Iceland, winters mainly in NW Scotland and Ireland) darker, broad streaks almost coalesce on underparts.

FL (see *p. 388*) | Fast, slightly zigzagging, sometimes fluttery, recalling Skylark (*p. 355*), but sleeker, long-headed. Smaller than Fieldfare. Feeding flocks wary, dash off low. **Underwing pale red-brown**; pale spot beside tail.

Locally common breeder, migratory

Coniferous, birch or mixed woodland; winter on fields, in deciduous forest, parks, gardens

pale stripe over eye

ssp. *coburni*

ssp. *iliacus*

ALL YEAR*

** bird shown is **1W** (AUG–MAR) – some wing coverts with thin buff edges*

Mistle Thrush *Turdus viscivorus*

L 26–29 cm | **W** 43–45 cm

Large, long-tailed, often **upright**, 'spotted' thrush. Hops with strong, springy action. Markedly larger but relatively smaller-headed than Song Thrush. Typically in pairs or groups of 10–20. **Ad** | upperparts pale greyish- or buffish-brown; **dark shoulder spots**, **pale feather edges** on wings; tail has whitish sides and corners. Underparts uniform yellowish-cream, **round black spots** often broader and merging on side of breast. **Juv** | pale, buffish, back marked with **dark-edged, drop-shaped cream spots**; pale wingbars. **1W** | as **Ad** but underparts brighter buff.

| Call dry, rattling "*tchrrr-tchrrr-tchrrr*." Song similar to Blackbird (*p. 385*) but **less varied**; brief, flowing phrases far-carrying, with wild, shouted quality, often from high treetop.

SSP. *viscivorus* occurs in Europe.

FL (*see p. 388*) | Fast, **often high**, a little tail-heavy. Long, shallow undulations, rather slow wingbeats. Small head, long, squared tail, broad wings. Family group or small loose flock, often in line. Prominent **white underwing** (like Fieldfare); tail has **white sides**.

Ad / 1W
ALL YEAR

rounded spots

Common resident/ migrant

Woodland of all kinds, heathland, moorland edge, villages, farmland with old trees

---

Fieldfare *Turdus pilaris*

L 24–28 cm | **W** 40–42 cm

Large, contrastingly patterned thrush. In winter, often with Redwings in flocks of tens/hundreds; also feeds on berries in bushes. Head-on, looks 'orange-buff'; tail-on, brown/grey/black. **Ad** | **head grey**, back red-brown, **rump grey**, **tail black**. Black around eye and yellow on bill give bold expression. Breast pale to deep **orange**, **streaked black** (blackish bank in spring). Wide black tail, white belly/vent. ♂ | streaked blackish on bluish crown, tail black; ♀ | narrowly streaked grey on dull crown, tail browner. **Juv** | brown back streaked pale buff. **1W** | as **Ad**, usually with pale-tipped greater coverts.

| Low, throaty, **chuckling chatter** "*chak-chak-ak*" or "*chuk-uk-uk-uk*," often in chorus from flock; nasal "*swee-eep*" almost like Lapwing (*p. 163*)). Song weak, chattering, repetitive sequence. Occasional subsong from spring flocks.

FL (*see p. 388*) | Strong, rather direct, with long, shallow undulations and rather slow wingbeats. Flocks often trail in ragged lines; **white underwing** (Mistle Thrush similar but more elongated, with pale tail).

Locally common breeder, migratory

Woodland, copses, parks; winters on heathland, farmland

grey rump

Ad / 1W
ALL YEAR

Thrushes in flight

FIELDFARE
(p. 387)

MISTLE THRUSH
(p. 387)

SONG THRUSH
(p. 386)

RING OUZEL
(p. 384)

♂

♂

REDWING
(p. 386)

BLACKBIRD
(p. 385)

♂

♀

Chat ageing/sexing

In most small chats/wheatears the sexes look different (but not in *e.g.* Nightingale and Robin). Most also have seasonal changes.

Juvenile chats & wheatears

(*shown here*) are distinct, duller and more spotted than adults. 1st-winter and 1st-summer (one-year-old) birds are told from adult birds by having juvenile wings and tail, which fade and/or wear paler.

NIGHTINGALE
(*p. 394*)
MAY–AUG

ROBIN
(*p. 392*)
MAY–SEP

BLACK-EARED WHEATEAR
(*p. 406*)
JUN–JUL

REDSTART
(*p. 396*)
JUN–SEP

STONECHAT
(*p. 400*)
MAY–AUG

WHEATEAR
(*p. 404*)
MAY–AUG

BLACK REDSTART
(*p. 397*)
JUN–SEP

BLUETHROAT
(*p. 393*)
MAY–SEP

Chat moult sequence

Sexes alike in juvenile plumage; differ by 1st-winter after moult.

1ST-WINTER keeps juvenile flight feathers, tail, tertials, many wing coverts, all these browner, more worn than new feathers; difficult to separate from adult by next summer, when heavily worn.

ADULT ♂
SEP–FEB (FRESH)
FEB–AUG (WORN)

ADULT ♀
SEP–FEB (FRESH)
FEB–AUG (WORN)

1ST-WINTER ♂
JUL–MAR

→ **Post-juvenile moult**
JUVENILE → 1ST-WINTER
JUL–SEP: head, body, some wing coverts, from 4–6 weeks, completed at 2–3 months old.

→ **Adult moult**
ADULT: single complete moult (takes 50 days) JUL/AUG – SEP/OCT; fresh feathers have pale tips, lost by spring.

1ST-WINTER ♀
JUL–MAR

389

LC Blue Rock Thrush *Monticola solitarius*

LC **②** | **L** 21–23 cm | **W** 37–40 cm

Large, dark, thrush-like chat with long wings, broad, dark tail and **long bill**. ♂**Br** | slaty-blue, wings and tail blacker; looks dark but **rich blue** at close range. ♂**Nb** | blue partly obscured by paler fringes. ♀ | dull, dark brown, **wings and tail darker**; underparts with dark-edged buff spots. **Juv** | like ♀**Ad** but greyer above, yellowish below with dark bars on flank. ♂**1Y** | like ♂**Ad** but duller, paler, often finely barred, with some browner wing coverts and tertials contrasting with adult-type blue scapulars.

V | Bright "*peep-eep*" and "*chuk*." Song loud, wild, melodic phrases like simple Mistle Thrush (*p. 387*).

FL ● | Dashes across gorge with strong, rapid wingbeats. Looks dark, plain, long-winged, long-tailed. Drops steeply from ledge or flicks along skyline before diving behind rock/building.

Scarce and loca resident, migran

Upland crags, cliffs, gorges, coastal rocky areas, buildings

Two similar sspp. occur: *solitarius* (SW and CS Europe); *longirostris* (Greece eastwards), slightly smaller and paler, ♀ less spotted.

♂**Nb**
AUG–MAR

Pale bars and fringes wear away by spring to reveal blue coloration.

♂**Br**

All SSP. *solitarius*

♂**Br**
FEB–JUL

♀
ALL YEAR

dark brown, w drop-shaped dark-edged buff spots o underparts

(Rufous-tailed) **Rock Thrush** *Monticola saxatilis*

L 18 cm | **W** 32–35 cm

Medium-large, thrush-like chat with long wings and short, **rufous tail**. Perches on boulders, wires. ♂**Br**| **head blue**, **wing dark brown**. **White patch on lower back**. **Underparts orange**. ♂**Nb**| colours partially obscured by buff feather tips. ♀| sandy-rufous; upperparts dark, with cream feather edges wearing off in summer. Fine blackish bars on orange-buff flank. **Rufous tail**. **Juv/1W**| paler, greyer; broad whitish feather edges above, white tips to primaries; **underparts pale orange-buff**. ♂**1S**| often inseparable from ♀.

| Hard "*tshak*," "*tchak-tchak*" and fluty whistle. Song, often in fast, fluttery, wheatear-like (*p.403*) song flight, a fast, flowing warble with mimicry.

| Quick, on long, dark, slightly rounded wings (less triangular than starlings). Short **rufous tail**; **rufous underwing**.

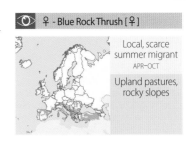

♀ - Blue Rock Thrush [♀]

Local, scarce summer migrant
APR–OCT

Upland pastures, rocky slopes

♂**Nb**
AUG–FEB

Pale feather edges wear away by spring to reveal distinctive colours.

♂**Br**

♂**Nb**

sandy-rufous, with pale bars on upperparts; rufous uppertail coverts

♀
ALL YEAR

♂**Br**
FEB–AUG

LC (Eurasian) **Robin** *Erithacus rubecula*

LC **2** | **L** 12·5–14 cm | **W** 22–25 cm

Small chat of mid-level canopy and the ground beneath, often around buildings. May be upright and slim, or squat and rounded, but actions and silhouette remain distinctive. Curtseys and bows, flicks wings and tail. Hop-and-stop bouncy action, or deft drop to ground and quickly back up to perch. **Ad** | upperparts mid-brown; **face and breast red-orange**. Late summer adults (JUL–SEP) are very faded; fresh and bright by SEP–OCT. Red not vivid but can be conspicuous, even in dark recesses, but provides good camouflage in bright autumn leaves. Underparts olive-buff, often a white fleck near bend of wing.
Juv (*p. 389*) | no red; pale spots above, dark crescents below; yellowish wingbar, dull tail; pale legs. (juvenile Redstart has black legs) Gradually develops patchy red on breast JUN–SEP, and then like **Ad**.
1Y | as **Ad** but may have contrast within greater coverts, some fringed yellow-brown with pale tips (**Juv**) others new, olive, usually without pale tips (**Ad**).

V | Sharp "*tik;*" thin, high, elusive "*see.*" Song **long**, fluent, melodic, **more or less melancholy** (in spring, stronger passages); **frequent changes in speed**; long-drawn notes characteristic. Often **sings at night** near street lights.

FL ● | Short, quick dashes, twisting between branches; longer flights slow, nervous, with irregular bursts of wingbeats. Round-winged, narrow-tailed. No upperparts/tail contrast.

Bluethroat | Red-flanked Bluetail
Juv - Redstart [Juv] *p. 389*
Juv - nightingales [Juv] *p. 389*

Very common resident/migrant

Coasts to high ground, forest, scrub, gardens parks, suburban areas

ssp. *superbus*
Ad
ALL YEAR

ssp. *melophilus*
Ad
ALL YEAR

1Y / Ad

1Y
SEP–JUL

ssp. *rubecula*

Four sspp. occur: *rubecula* (widespread) pale, olive, bluish neck patch, wary; *melophilus* (Great Britain, Ireland) browner, approachable, familiar garden bird. Sspp. *marionae* (Gran Canaria) and *superbus* (Tenerife) more contrasted, with white eyering, bright red breast.

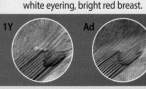

1Y   **Ad**

Pale tips and contrast between greater coverts indicates 1Y (often difficult to judge), but some 1Y birds replace all coverts so uniform coverts may indicate Ad or 1Y; both fade paler during spring/summer, until autumn moult.

Bluethroat *Luscinia svecica*

L 13–14 cm | **W** 23–25 cm

Small chat, resembles dark Robin; runs/hops, raises and dips **slender tail** with exaggerated action. **♂Br** | upperparts dark brown; **white stripe over eye**; **electric-blue breast** above bands of black, white and rufous. Throat blue, with red or white spot depending on subspecies. **♂Nb** | blue, black, white and chestnut bands on breast (sspp. not safely distinguishable). **♀** | very variable (sspp. usually inseparable): dark crown and cheek, white over eye; wide white bib with dark stripe beside throat. Typically lacks blue, but a few can be almost as blue as **♂**. **Juv** (p.389) | (MAY–JUL/SEP) streaked blackish and buff. **1W** | like **♀Ad** but some greater coverts pale-tipped; **♂** throat and breast may have at least some blue and chestnut; **♀** always whitish on throat and breast.

| Call a loud, arresting "*shlak*." Song strong, clear whistle with fast, variable flourish, including mimicry.

L ● | Low dash to cover, longer flights fast, direct. Wing broad, rounded; tail broad with **red sides** and **blackish tip**.

Robin | Redstart [♀] p.396
Siberian Rubythroat [♀] p.594

Scarce, locally fairly common summer migrant MAR–OCT; scarce in winter

Willow thickets, riverside growth, reedbeds

Six sspp. occur: red-spotted group *svecica* (N Europe), *volgae* (E Europe) and *namnetum* (SW France); white-spotted (rarely all-blue) *cyanecula* (S & C Europe); and all-blue-throated *azuricollis* (Iberia) and *luristanica* (E Turkey, Caucasus).

red sides to tail
♂Br SSP. *azuricollis*

♂Br MAR–OCT SSP. *azuricollis*

♂1W AUG–MAR

♂Nb OCT–MAR SSP. *cyanecula*

♂Br MAR–OCT SSP. *cyanecula*

white stripe over eye

♀1W AUG–MAR

♂Br MAR–OCT SSP. *svecica*

♀ ALL YEAR

Nightingale and **Thrush Nightingale** are two closely similar, elusive chats found close to the ground in dense thickets. They usually sing from dense cover and are typically heard first, then glimpsed on a song-post or on the ground under low foliage. Tail often raised and conspicuous above long undertail coverts, or pointing down when perched. Rufous or brown with paler underparts; head plain with large, dark eye and pale eyering.

FL ● | Low, slow, with short bursts of wingbeats between glides. Slim, rather long-winged and long-tailed.
Nightingale: No contrast, pale back **blends into rustier tail** (Redstart (*p. 396*) has dark centre to redder tail);
Thrush Nightingale: Dull back **contrasts with rusty tail**.

LC (Common) Nightingale
LC *Luscinia megarhynchos*

❷ | **L** 15–16·5 cm | **W** 26–28 cm

Short first primary extends beyond primary coverts. Closed wingtip shows **seven** feather tips. **Ad** | upperparts rusty-brown, **rump brighter**; neck greyer. Throat white; breast plain grey-brown, underparts and under tail plain buff-white. **Juv** (*p. 389*) | upperparts spotted buff; faint darker mottling on buff breast. **1Y** | tips of tertials and greater coverts buff (ssp. *golzii* **1Y** inner greater coverts paler than outermost).

V | Low, **grating** "*kerrrr*;" clear, whistled "*wheep*." Song has marked **variation in pace**, pitch and quality: **long, thin sounds** change **abruptly** to **short, deep notes** and long crescendo "*sseee, ssseee, ssseee seeeee*" and 'collapse' into deep, fast phrase.

Three sspp. occur: ***megarhynchos*** (widespread); *africana* (Caucasus, Turkey) paler; *golzii* (vagrant from Asia) palest with stronger face pattern, pale stripe over eye, pale feather edges on longer wings and tail.

ssp. *golzii*

1Y
ALL YEAR

Scarce, locally common summer migrant APR–SEP
Dense, often damp, thickets, woods, woodland edge

Ad
ALL YEAR

ssp. *megarhynchos*

LC Thrush Nightingale
LC *Luscinia luscinia*

❷ | **L** 16 cm | **W** 27–28 cm

Close views/photographs may confirm large yellow gape and **absence** of visible first primary (usually hidden beneath primary coverts). Closed wingtip shows **eight** feather tips. **Ad** | upperparts grey-brown. Tail **contrastingly brighter rufous**. Throat white with faint dark outline; breast-band **softly mottled olive-grey**. Faint grey bars under tail. **Juv** | upperparts spotted pale buff; breast greyish, mottled darker.

V | Song loud and far-carrying, many deep, full-throated, rippling notes, but more fast rattles/clicking sounds than Nightingale, and lacks 'crescendo' sequence.

Scarce summer migrant APR–SEP
Deep, damp thickets

Ad
ALL YEAR

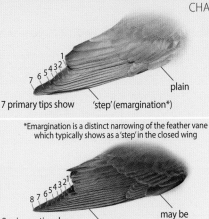

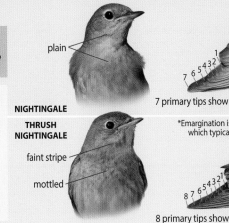

Rufous Bush Robin
Redstart [♀] *p. 396*
Juv - Robin [Juv] *p. 389*
Veery p. 611

Nightingale and **Thrush Nightingale** are difficult to see and identify. With good views, focus on details of the throat and upper breast, and in particular the structure of the wingtip (number of visible primary tips) and colour of the alula.

NIGHTINGALE

plain

plain

7 6 5 4 3 2 1

7 primary tips show   'step' (emargination*)

THRUST NIGHTINGALE

faint stripe

mottled

*Emargination is a distinct narrowing of the feather vane which typically shows as a 'step' in the closed wing

8 7 6 5 4 3 2 1

8 primary tips show   no 'step'   may be two-tone

Rufous Bush Robin *Cercotrichas galactotes*
Rufous-tailed Bush-robin, Rufous Bush Chat)

2 | **L** 15–16 cm | **W** 26–28 cm

lim, **long-tailed**, upright, pale brown or greyish chat, usually on or near the ground; moves with bouncy hops on strong legs, **tail often raised**, fanned and slowly lowered again. Bill long; pale stripe over eye, paler streak under eye, dark line below cheek, whitish throat.
Ad | Upperparts and wings rather uniform. **Juv** | paler, more buff, with paler edges to wing feathers. **1Y** | has paler tips to some greater coverts.

V | Call a high whistle or low, grating buzz. Sings with vibrating throat and dipping tail; disjointed, thin song has short quick phrases, pauses ike weak Song Thrush (*p. 386*).

FL ● | Low, dashing; longer flights rather slow, with bursts of quite low, even wingbeats. Pointed, triangular wings; long tail. Tail all-rufous in western birds except **black-and-white spots** at tip, striking only when spread, from below and in flight. In eastern birds, tail has darker centre and more extensive black markings.

Nightingales

Scarce and local summer migrant
APR–SEP

Open, bushy slopes, orchards, cactus thickets

SSP. *syriaca*

1Y/Ad

SSP. *familiaris*

1Y/Ad

Three sspp. occur: *galactotes* (Iberia) bright, pale, plain rufous-buff above with rusty tail; *syriaca* (Balkans to W & S Turkey) and *familiaris* (SE Turkey) duller, browner, greyer on back and crown, more isolated rufous rump and tail side.

SSP. *familiaris*

1Y/Ad

SSP. *galactotes*

1Y/Ad
ALL YEAR

LC (Common) **Redstart** *Phoenicurus phoenicurus*

LC ❷ | **L** 13–14·5 cm | **W** 25 cm

Slender chat, like slim Robin, constantly **quivering orange-red tail**. Perches high in trees or lower in bushes. **♂Br** | **forehead white**; **face and throat black**, **back grey**. Breast rufous. Rump and tail **orange**. **♂Nb** | white forehead/black face partly obscured by buff feather edges. Wing dark, often with pale panel. Breeding plumage revealed by wear during winter/spring. **♂1W** | browner, head pattern even more obscured. **♂1S** | duller than **Ad**, wings browner. **♀/♀1W** | upperparts brown, underparts **orange-buff**. Plain face with bold black eye and pale eyering. **Rusty tail**. **Juv** (*p. 389*) | (JUN–AUG/SEP) spotted, with **rusty tail**. Black legs (juvenile Robin has pale legs).

V | Call a sweet, strong "*sweep*" (like Chaffinch (*p. 500*) or Chiffchaff (*p. 432*)); "*wheet-tik tik*" or fast ticking (like Hawfinch (*p. 485*)) in alarm. Song, often from high perch, seems unfinished: low, indrawn, vibrant "*srree srree srree*" followed by quick, musical warble.

Black Redstart | *Daurian Redstart* p. 593 | White-winged Redstart p. 39
♀ - Bluethroat [♀] p. 393
♀ - Red-flanked Bluetail [♀] p. 398
♀ - White-throated Robin [♀] p. 39
♀ - nightingales p. 394
Juv - Robin [Juv] p. 389
♀ - Moussier's Redstart [♀] p. 593
♀ - Eversmann's Redstart [♀] p. 593

Locally commo
summer migra
MAR–OCT

Mixed/
deciduous
forest, heath/
woodland/
moorland edge

♀1W
AUG–MAR

(BRIGHT)

♂1W
AUG–MAR

(DULL)

♀s difficult to age

SSP. *samamiscus*

♂Br
MAR–AUG

FL | Short, flitting, low over ground; floats on wide wings in strong wind. Longer flights thrush-like (*p. 383*); rather long body and tail, and broad wings.

♂Br

All SSP. *phoenicurus*

Two sspp. occur: *phoenicurus* (widespread); *samamisicus* ('Ehrenberg's Redstart') (Turkey and Caucasus), **♂Br** shows bright white edges to tertials secondaries and primaries. **♂1W** shows buffish-white panel (similar on some **♂Nb/♂1W** SSP. *phoenicurus*).

pale, brownish; underparts orange-buff

♀
ALL YEAR

♂Br
MAR–AUG

Black Redstart *Phoenicurus ochruros*

L 13–14·5 cm | **W** 25 cm

Small, rounded, grey-black chat; behaviour like Wheatear (*p. 404*) on ground, rocks, buildings. **♂Br** | smoky-grey, **blacker on face and breast**, white wing panel. Uppertail coverts and side of tail rusty-orange. **♂Nb/♂1Y** | (often breeds in this plumage) greyer; wing browner. **♀/1W** | **brownish-grey** (greyest on ♂); head plain grey except for pale eyering; wing panel weak. Uppertail coverts and tail side rusty-red (rufous extends to rump on Redstart). **Juv** (*p. 389*) | throat, belly and vent grey-buff; breast has weak darker scales, not spotted. Black legs (juvenile Robin (*p. 389*) has pale legs).

♪ | Call a sharp "*weet*" or "*weet-t'k t'k*." Song far-carrying but not loud: a trill followed by curious dry crackle and musical flourish.

Redstart
Plumbeous Water-redstart p. 593

Locally common migrant/resident

Cliffs, gorges, towns, villages; locally urban/ industrial areas; winters coasts, urban sites

FL | Short, flitting, low over ground; floats on wide wings in strong wind. Longer flights thrush-like (*p. 383*); rather long body and tail, and broad wings.

ssp. *ochruros/ semirufus*

ssp. *phoenicuroides/ rufiventris*

♂Br
JAN–SEP

♂Br
JAN–SEP

♂Br

♀/1W

Up to six sspp. recorded in Europe: *gibraltariensis* (widespread) described above; *ochruros* (C Turkey eastwards) and smaller *semirufus* (SE Turkey) variably dull rufous on belly with weak pale wing panel. These grade into sspp. *phoenicuroides/xerophilus/rufiventris* ('**Eastern Black Redstart**') (vagrants from Central Asia): **♂Br** | forehead often white. Breast black; lower breast, flank and belly orange-red; wing all-black. **♀Ad** | grey-brown, belly whitish. **♂1W** | forehead/back grey; breast blackish, more extensive than on ♂ Redstart; underparts reddish. **♀1W** | inseparable from ssp. *gibraltariensis*.

All ssp. *gibraltariensis*

♀/♀1W
ALL YEAR

♂1Y
ALL YEAR

rather uniform brownish-grey

♂Br
JAN–SEP

397

LC LC White-winged Redstart
Phoenicurus erythrogastrus

Redstart *p. 396* | Daurian Redstart *p. 593*
♀ - Eversmann's Redstart [♀] *p. 593*

2 | **L** 15–16 cm | **W** 30 cm

Small chat, but larger than Redstart, with **plain rufous rump and tail**. ♂ | white crown, black back and bib; **extensive white patch on wing. Underparts deep rufous.** ♀ | plain sandy-brown, paler below with faint orange-buff mottles, or grey bib and orange-buff underparts more defined; rump and tail rufous. **Juv** | grey, weakly spotted buff; rump and tail duller; wing dull brown. **1W** | grey bib mottled darker; underparts orange-buff; dull white wing panel on ♂.

♂
ALL YEAR

LC LC White-throated Robin
Irania gutturalis

♀ - Redstart [♀] *p. 396*
♀ - Red-flanked Bluetail [♀]

2 | **L** 15–17 cm | **W** 25–27 cm

Large chat; forages on the ground. Resembles a small, slender, slim-tailed thrush (*p. 383*). ♂**Br** | upperparts pale grey, **underparts orange**. White stripe over eye, **black band across cheek**, narrow **white throat**. White under tail. Tail dull black. ♀ | pale greyish, face grey, cheek browner; **white eyering**. Breast-band pale orange, more or less mottled grey; flank and underwing dull or brighter **orange**. White beneath blackish tail. **Juv** | like ♀ but upperparts spotted buff, wing coverts tipped buff; breast-band grey with buff spots. **1W** | like respective **Ad**s but wings browner, pale tips to wing coverts, wearing off by **1S**.

♂**Br**
FEB–AUG

LC LC Red-flanked Bluetail
Tarsiger cyanurus

Robin *p. 392* | ♀ - Redstart [♀] *p. 396*
♀ - White-throated Robin [♀]
♀ - Siberian Blue Robin [1W] *p. 594*

2 | **L** 14 cm | **W** 25–26 cm

Small, Robin-like chat with **bluish tail**. Flicks wings, dips tail. Rather shy and elusive. Often skulks low down. ♂**Br** | upperparts blue, with white line over eye. **White bib**, greyish breast, **orange flank** edged white. **Vivid blue tail.** ♀ | upperparts pale greyish olive-brown. Distinct **white throat** and **white eyering**. Side of neck merges into paler brownish breast; **flank pale orange. Tail grey-blue.** Legs black. **Juv** | olive-brown with head and back spotted cream; whitish throat and eyering. **1W** | like ♀ but pale tips to wing coverts.

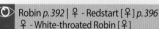

♂**Br**
APR–AUG

V | Call weak *"tsee,"* harder *"tek"* or *"tak-tak-ak;"* loud *"tseee-tek-tek"* in alarm. Separated, short phrases of rich, melodious but slightly metallic warbling.

FL | Low, direct, on long, broad but pointed wings; **long white band along wing on ♂.**

extent of grey bib individually variable

♀
ALL YEAR

♀
ALL YEAR

Rare, local resident

Alpine slopes, rocky plateaux

SSP. *erythrogastrus* occurs in Europe.

V | Call squeaky *"tsip"* and hard trill in alarm. Song a repeated, rapid, hard or rolling, warbled phrase.

FL ● | Direct, agile. Wings long, rounded; tail long, rather broad. Grey, with blackish tail.

♀
ALL YEAR

Local and scarce summer migrant
MAR–SEP

High, rocky, bushy slopes

V | Calls a hard *"tak"* and sharp, thin, whistled *"szip szip."* Song like Redstart, a short, deep, clear phrase.

FL ● | Low, flitting; longer flights slow, agile with bursts of wingbeats between glides. Wings broad and rounded. Tail narrow, blue or slaty.

♀/1W
ALL YEAR

Rare, local summer migrant APR–OCT

Coniferous forest; migrants in deciduous copses, especially Sycamore

LC (Common) **Stonechat**
LC *Saxicola torquatus*

2 | **L** 11·5–13 cm | **W** 21–23 cm

Small, dark, pot-bellied chat; perches on bush-top or upright stem, occasionally in tree. ♂**Br** | upperparts **black-brown. Hood, including throat, black** with contrasting **white neck patch.** Rump white, finely streaked black. **Breast rufous,** flank orange, belly white. White wing patches spread in display. ♂**Nb** | dark areas suffused paler brown; underparts dull buff-brown. ♀/**1W** | upperparts brown, streaked black. Hood dark brown; neck patch dull whitish; dark throat, often pale on lower edge. Rump brown, thickly streaked black. **Juv** *(p. 389)* | pale stripe over eye, whitish chin (more like Whinchat but stripe over eye shorter, throat streaked with whitish lower edge, tail all-dark).

V | Sharp whistle "*whee*" or "*whee-tak*." Song fast, chattering, squeaky warble, sometimes in flight.

Two sspp. across most of Europe: *hibernans* (Great Britain, Ireland, W France, Portugal); *rubicola* (widespread), in S Europe, may look like eastern/Siberian subspecies (see *opposite*), with unstreaked white rump and white collar reaching nape, but ♂ | flank orange, ♀ | rump more streaked.

Stonechat and Whinchat are similar. *Fuerteventura Stonechat p. 525*

FL ● | Low, whirring; settles with flurry of quick wing flicks. Small head; short, round wings. White mark each side of back. **Short, broad tail black.**

Locally common resident/migran

Heathland, moorland, open rough grassland around walls and fence-lines

primaries brownish

PC

SC

UNDERWING: primary coverts (PC) **darker** than secondary coverts (SC)

rump streaked

♂

♂**Nb**
AUG–MAR

♀
ALL YEAR

ssp. *rubicola*

♂**Br**
FEB–SEP

rump streaked

streaked rump

LC **Whinchat** *Saxicola rubetra*
LC **3** | **L** 12–14 cm | **W** 22–24 cm

Small, upright chat with **pale stripe over eye. White panel on each side of tail at the base.** ♂ | upperparts streaked black and straw-buff. **Long white stripes** above and below black 'mask'; apricot throat and breast. White patch on outerwing. Fades to more black-and-white effect by JUL/AUG. ♀ | pale, buffish; back bright buff with long dark streaks; long buff line over eye, pale throat curls up behind dark cheek. Underparts buff. **Juv/1W** | both sexes more buff above, scalloped; stripe over eye less striking; throat/cheek contrast reduced, approaching some Stonechats, but white side to tail.

V | Sweet "*siu*" and "*siu-tek tek*." Song variable, sometimes like Robin (*p. 392*) with added rattles and clicks, often dry, ticking sequence before more musical, fast flourish.

Typically perches on bush-top, isolated tall stem, wire or post. May perch high on a tree but usually low down.

♂**Br**
APR–AUG

'Eastern'/'Siberian Stonechat' subspecies *maurus/stejnegeri/hemprichii/variegatus* (sometimes treated as separate species; local residents/migrants or vagrants from Asia). <u>**DNA analysis recommended for certain identification**</u>. **Rump unstreaked rufous-buff (whiter in winter)**. On ♂'s underwing coverts **black, with primary coverts paler** (on sspp. *hibernans* and *rubicola* underwing coverts **grey, with primary coverts darker**); greyish on all ♀s. ♂**Br** | like ♂ *rubicola* Stonechat but white neck patch extends to nape; smaller orange breast patch; belly whiter. ♀**Br** | throat pale. **AdNb / 1W** | **pale stripe over eye**, pale throat; cheek and nape buff, streaked brown. Back greyish/buff, streaked darker. Sspp. *maurus* and *stejnegeri* often inseparable but most *stejnegeri* darker, warmer buff-brown; pale neck and rump patches smaller; bill slightly wider (4·7–5·7 mm; *maurus* 4·2–4·9 mm). 'Caspian' sspp. *hemprichii/variegatus* ♂ | much white in base of tail, white on wing and collar more extensive; ♀ buff base to outer tail feathers.

primaries silvery
ssp. *maurus*
rump unstreaked
ssp. *hemprichii*
white sides to base of tail
♂**Br**
♂**Br** FEB–SEP
PC
SC
UNDERWING: primary coverts (PC) **paler** than secondary coverts (SC)
ssp. *stejnegeri*
♂**Nb** AUG–MAR
ssp. *maurus*
♂**Br** FEB–SEP
ssp. *maurus/stejnegeri*
rump unstreaked
1W AUG–APR

FL ● | Low, slow, uneven flitting through vegetation. Short wings and tail. **White on each side of tail at the base**; ♂ has white shoulder-patch.
white in tail
♂**Br**
pale stripe over eye
♀ ALL YEAR
Less squat/round-bellied than Stonechat.
1W AUG–APR
Scarce, locally fairly common summer migrant APR–OCT
Rough grassy heaths, moorland, bracken slopes, young conifer plantations

Wheatears – males in breeding plumage

Rump/tail patterns are consistent for all ten regularly occurring wheatears in all plumages. Breeding males also have distinctive upperpart colours and crown/'mask'/throat patterns; whether the black on the face joins the wing or back is a useful feature.

BLACK WHEATEAR (p. 403)

KURDISH WHEATEAR (p. 410)

WHEATEAR (p. 404)

ISABELLINE WHEATEAR (p. 405)

RED-TAILED WHEATEAR (p. 410)

BLACK-EARED WHEATEAR (p. 406)
The extent of black on tail is variable in all subspecies and forms.

PIED WHEATEAR (p. 408)

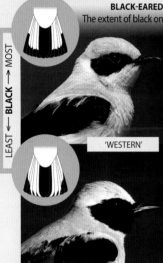

'WESTERN'

'EASTERN'

LEAST ← **BLACK** → MOST

DESERT WHEATEAR (p. 410)

FINSCH'S WHEATEAR (p. 408)

CYPRUS WHEATEAR (p. 408)

Wheatears in flight

KURDISH WHEATEAR (p. 410) ♂

ISABELLINE WHEATEAR (p. 405) ♂

RED-TAILED WHEATEAR (p. 410) ♂

WHEATEAR (p. 404) ♂

DESERT WHEATEAR (p. 410) ♂

CYPRUS WHEATEAR (p. 408) ♂

PIED WHEATEAR (p. 408) ♀

FINSCH'S WHEATEAR (p. 408) ♂

BLACK-EARED WHEATEAR (p. 406) ♂

BLACK WHEATEAR

White-crowned Black Wheatear p. 595
Pied Bushchat p. 594

Black Wheatear

Oenanthe leucura

3 | **L** 18 cm | **W** 30 cm

Large, dark wheatear of rocky slopes. **Black with conspicuous white rear end**, dark plumage becoming browner with wear. Rump, vent and under tail white. **Tail white with black 'T'**, broad black band at tip of **even width** (tail white with black tip from below). **♂ Ad** | dull black. **♀ Ad** | black-brown. **Juv** | duller, greyish.

NOTE: Unique in range but vagrant White-crowned Black Wheatear may lack white crown; white tail has black centre but only **dark spots** across tip.)

♫ | Call a thin "*pee-pee-pee*" or hard, clicking "*chik*." Song seems 'distant', subdued, fast chattering, often in undulating song flight.

SSP. *leucura* occurs in Europe.

FL | Fast, low, on long wings. Looks all-dark with bold white rump/tail with black 'T'.

Locally fairly common resident

Rocky slopes, crags

♀
ALL YEAR

white from legs to tail

♂
ALL YEAR

LC (Northern) **Wheatear**
LC *Oenanthe oenanthe*

3 | **L** 14–16·5 cm | **W** 27–28 cm

Medium-sized wheatear. Strong-legged, short-tailed. Extensive **white rump** and white tail with **black centre and tip** ('T' shape). ♂**Br**| upperparts blue-grey; **black 'mask'**, blackish wings; underparts pinkish to yellowish-buff, white by JUL (♂**1S** as ♂**Br** but wings brown.). ♀**Br**| upperparts grey-brown; pale stripe over **slightly darker ear coverts**, dark brown wings. Underparts buff. Fades to brown above, whiter below by JUL, wings creating dark diagonal band. ♂**Nb**| from AUG onwards: like ♀ but blackish between eye and bill; wing darker brown with greyish feather edges. ♀**Nb**/♂**1W**| wing brown, feathers **edged bright buff**; blackish or brown between eye and bill. ♀**1W**| brown between eye and bill (some **1W** birds indeterminate). **Juv** (*p. 389*)| pale spots on back until JUL/SEP.

V| Whistled "*wheet*" and hard "*chak*." Song, often in short **fluttery song flight**, or from low perch, a quick-fire phrase of chattering and ticking notes with musical chirps.

Isabelline Wheatear
Black-eared Wheatear *p. 406*
[♀/Imm] Pied Wheatear *p. 408*
[♀/Imm] Desert Wheatear *p. 410*

Locally common summer migrant
MAR–NOV

Upland pastures, stony slopes, coastal grassland; migrants on ploughed fields, short turf, shingle beaches

FL ●| Repeatedly flies ahead if disturbed. Wings long and broad but pointed, giving more graceful action than other wheatears; tail broad and short. **Prominent white rump**; black 'T' on tail; underwing dull grey.

underwing coverts dull grey, flecked blackish

♂**Br**

♂**Br**

♂**Nb**
SEP–FEB

pale stripe over eye whitest and broadest **behind** eye

1W
AUG–MAR

All ssp. *oenanthe*

blue-grey back

dark wing coverts

♂**Br**
FEB–SEP

♀
ALL YEAR

Wheatear subspecies Four sspp. occur. ssp. *leucorhoa* ('Greenland Wheatear') (migrant through NW Europe in MAY, smaller numbers SEP–OCT, when most fly non-stop to Spain/N Africa) larger than ssp. *oenanthe* (widespread), ♂**Br**| browner back and orange-buff underparts, but some *oenanthe* (including ♂**1S**) also dark in spring. In autumn, inseparable without measurements, but 7 or 8 primary tips visible on closed wing (ssp. *oenanthe* 6 or 7). ssp. *libanotica* (Spain, Greece) ♂**Br**| paler above, ♀| blacker 'mask' and greyer back than ssp. *oenanthe*. ssp. *seebohmi* (vagrant from Africa) ♂**Br**| has black throat.

♂**Nb**
AUG–FEB

'GREENLAND WHEATEAR' ssp. *leucorhoa*

♂**1S**
FEB–SEP

Ad has
black wings

ssp. *libanotica*

♂**Br**
FEB–SEP

'SEEBOHM'S WHEATEAR' ssp. *seebohmi*

Isabelline Wheatear *Oenanthe isabellina*

3 | **L** 15–16·5 cm | **W** 26–28 cm

Large, upright, strikingly pale wheatear, **buff-brown**. Quite plain wings (paler edges from AUG), except **blackish alula**. White line over eye narrows above dark cheek. Bill thick ♂**Br**| black between eye and bill. ♀**Br**| brown between eye and bill. **Juv**/**1W**| broad buff edges on closed wing, pale stripe over eye whitest and broadest in front (reverse on Wheatear).

V| Call bright, low "*chiu*" and "*chak*." Song, often in flight, includes chattery notes, fast, crackling/spluttering warbles and longer, fluty "*whi-oww*" whistles.

Wheatear
Desert Wheatear [♀] *p. 410*
Black-eared Wheatear [♀] *p. 406*
Pied Wheatear [♀] *p. 403*

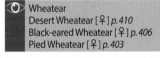

Locally common summer migrant
APR–OCT

Short grass, stony arable and semi-desert

FL ●| Wings long and broad, tail short. **Broad black tail-band but short 'T'-stem. Underwing silvery-grey/whitish** but hard to see.

underwing coverts silvery-grey/whitish

♂

♂
ALL YEAR

black between eye and bill

pale stripe over eye whitest and broadest **in front of** eye

pale wing coverts

brown between eye and bill

♀
ALL YEAR

Black-eared Wheatear
LC
LC *Oenanthe hispanica*

❸ | **L** 13·5–15·5 cm | **W** 25–26 cm

Small, slim wheatear. Two subspecies (sometimes treated as separate species, '**Western**' and '**Eastern**'), both with dark- and pale-throated males. ♂**Br** (both sspp.) | pale; **wing/shoulder band blacker**, broader than on Wheatear, does not meet throat on dark-throated form, unlike Pied Wheatear. **Juv** (see p. 389).

TAIL PATTERN VARIATION

Pied Wheatear p. 408
Wheatear p. 404
Finsch's Wheatear p. 408
Desert Wheatear p. 410
[♀/Imm] Isabelline Wheatear p. 405

Locally common summer migrant
APR–OCT

Dry bushy and stony areas, higher rocky plateaux

V | Harsh, low, grating "*chek chek*" c "*churk*" calls. Song a fast, rattling, churrin phrase, often in diving song flight, wit tail spreac

FL ● | Low, quick, direct. Broad wings, sho tail. White rump; **black tail-band variabl – narrow** or broken by white, **curls up onto sides. Underwing blackish** (greye on ♀

Comparison of Black-eared Wheatear subspecies

	'WESTERN' ssp. *hispanica*	'EASTERN' ssp. *melanoleuca*
♂Br	UPPERPARTS: **orange-buff**, whiter by JUN/JUL	UPPERPARTS: **dull whitish**, white by MAR/APR
	BLACK ABOVE BASE OF BILL: **none**	BLACK ABOVE BASE OF BILL: **thin band**
	narrow black 'mask' or black face/throat **not extending** onto breast	**broad** black 'mask' or black face/throat **extending** onto upper breast
♂Nb	like ♂**Br** with pale fringes on wing	**greyer**, darker; fewer pale fringes on head and wing coverts than ssp. *hispanica*
♀	wing darker than upperparts	
	upperparts brown or **rusty-brown**; dark brown/blackish through eye; some have pale chin/dark throat, most have all-pale underparts with **little contrast**	upperparts brown (generally **less rusty-brown on back** than ssp. *hispanica*); dark brown line through eye; some have dark throat; orange breast usually contrasts with paler belly
Juv/1W	brown, spotted bright buff; wings black with broad, bright ginger fringes; ♂1W brighter than ♀ 1W – see *opposite*	
1S (♂+♀)	similar to **Ad** but crown and back darker. Some have faint pale fringes on back (like Pied Wheatear, from which may be inseparable)	

1W

♂Br

(shows underside)

'WESTERN' BLACK-EARED WHEATEAR ssp. *hispanica*

♂Br
JAN–AUG

♀
ALL YEAR

WING: thin pale fringes

1W (probably ♂)
AUG–MAR

♀1W
AUG–MAR

'WESTERN'
BLACK-EARED WHEATEAR
SSP. *hispanica*

Non-breeding and 1st-winter birds particularly difficult to tell apart and separate from Pied Wheatear: '**Western**' back orange-buff, underparts pale; '**Eastern**' back brown, breast darker than belly (♂1W of both sspp. brighter than ♀, some black wing coverts after AUG); **Pied** back cold grey-brown with pale fringes; breast/flank browner than belly, vent/undertail clear white.

'EASTERN'
BLACK-EARED WHEATEAR
SSP. *melanoleuca*

♂1W
AUG–MAR

PIED WHEATEAR

♀1W
AUG–MAR

WING: broad pale fringes

'EASTERN' BLACK-EARED WHEATEAR
SSP. *melanoleuca*

♂Br
JAN–AUG

generally less rusty-brown on back than SSP. *hispanica*

♀
ALL YEAR

white-throated form
'*vittata*'

♂**Br**

♀

tail-band
usually
narrow

♂**Br**
JAN–JUL

closed wing
long

Three similar species – see also
Black-eared Wheatear *p. 406*
♀ – Wheatear [♀] *p. 404*
♀/Imm – Isabelline Wheatear *p. 405*
♀/Imm – Desert Wheatear [♀] *p. 410*
Hooded + Mourning Wheatears *p. 595*

LC Pied Wheatear
LC *Oenanthe pleschanka*

❸ | **L** 14–16·5 cm | **W** 25–26 cm

Small wheatear; breeding male
distinctive, other plumages extremely like
Black-eared Wheatear (**some inseparable**).
♂**Br**| **black-and-white; unbroken black from
throat to wingtip**. Most have black throat;
minority white throat/black 'mask'. Crown and
hindneck mottled greyish-white. Underparts
white, tinged buff. ♂**Nb**| pale greyish feather
edges obscure black. ♀**Br**| upperparts **grey-
brown**. Underparts buff. Throat usually **dark**;
extensive greyish bib above diffuse buff-brown
breast-band. ♀**Nb**| as ♀**Br** but upperparts
cold grey-brown; curved **pale feather edges**.
Juv/1W| upperparts brown, spotted buff; wings
black with broad ginger/buff feather edges;
♂ has obscure dark throat and bib; ♀ throat
greyish or whitish above diffuse breast-band.

LC Cyprus Wheatear
LC *Oenanthe cypriaca*

❸ | **L** 13.5 cm | **W** 25 cm

Like Pied Wheatear, but smaller.
♂**Br**| **black-and-white**; crown and nape grey
with white border, all-white by MAY. Upperparts
glossy black. Underparts **orange-buff**, fading to
white by MAY. ♀**Br**| like dull, browner ♂; dark
grey cap outlined with white; black-and-white
like ♂**Br** by JUL. ♂**Nb**/♀**Nb**| crown and back
dark grey; underparts deep rusty-buff. **Juv/1W**|
back and breast greyish, spotted buff; thin
orange-buff wingbar.

♂**Br**

♂**Br**
JAN–JUL
WORN [APR]

tail-band
usually
broad

closed wing
short

LC Finsch's Wheatear
LC *Oenanthe finschii*

❸ | **L** 15–16 cm | **W** 25–26 cm

Medium-sized wheatear. ♂**Br**|
black-and-white; crown pinkish-white, with
greyer centre when worn; **white continuous**
from nape, down back to rump (but closed
wings usually cover rump). Extensive **black
throat joins black wing**. ♂**Nb**| white parts
tinged buffish. ♀| back and shoulder pale
grey; pale edges on primary coverts outline
dark midwing band; black alula. Throat and
cheek mixed grey/black, or pale grey-buff with
browner cheek. **Juv**| softly spotted buff-white.

ssp. *finschii*

♂**Br**

♂**Br**
FEB–AUG

♂1W
AUG–MAR

♀/1W
ALL YEAR

♀
ALL YEAR

FL ● | Direct, low, on pointed wings. White rump; a few have broad black 'T' on tail, most have **narrower tip, widening on corners**. Underwing coverts blackish.

V | Dry, churring and "*tack*" notes; song whistling, chattering, strangled trills, often in song flight.

(dark-throated 'Eastern' Black-eared Wheatear has smaller dark throat patch above well-defined orange breast-band)

Scarce, local summer migrant APR–OCT

High rocky slopes, barren stony grassland

FL ● | Low, direct; broad wings, short tail. **Tail white with black 'T' broad across tip. Underwing all-blackish.**

♂Br
JAN–JUL
FRESH [MAR]

♀
ALL YEAR

V | Song sustained repetitive buzzing or sawing "*bizz bizz bizz*" usually from high perch.

Locally common summer migrant APR–OCT

Rocky slopes

FL ● | Low, quick, direct; raises and lowers tail rhythmically on landing. On ♂ **white back joins crown and rump**. Wings blackish, outer half paler. Underwing silvery with black coverts. Tail white with black 'T', **tip of uniform width**.

SSP. *barnesi*

♀
ALL YEAR

V | Short "*tsit*" and hard tacking note. Song (in flight) slow, bright whistling phrases.

Scarce, local summer migrant MAR–OCT

Rocky slopes and hilltops

Two sspp. occur: *finschii* (CS & SE Turkey); *barnesi* (E Turkey, S & E Caucasus), which is longer-billed and longer-winged.

409

LC Kurdish Wheatear

LC *Oenanthe xanthoprymna*

3 | **L** 14–15 cm | **W** 25 cm

Small, dark **grey-brown** wheatear with **rufous rump; tail white with black tip**. ♂ | black throat joins blackish band along closed wing; white stripe over eye. Underparts creamy-buff, deeper rufous under tail. ♀ | ♂**1W** | greyer, dark cheek and throat less contrasted; rufous under tail. **Juv** | spotted buff on head and back.

♂**Br**

♂**Br**
FEB–AUG

⊙ Red-tailed Wheatear and Kurdish Wheatear are similar.
Buff-rumped Wheatear p. 595

LC Red-tailed Wheatear
EN

Oenanthe chrysopygia

3 | **L** 14–16 cm | **W** 27–28 cm

Small, pale greyish wheatear with weak head pattern, **pale throat**, grey nape and hindneck, browner back, pale rufous flank. Rump and tail pale buff-orange, closed tail black. Individual variation makes sexing difficult, but ♂**Br** | bluish-grey over eye, around nape and side of neck, surrounding dark cheek; blackish between eye and bill. ♀**Br** | like ♂ but often has plainer, browner head/neck. **AdNb/1W** | pale and grey, wing and tail feathers tipped orange-buff (individuals with greyest head presumed ♂). **Juv** | like ♀**Ad** with rufous wingbar and edges to flight feathers; tail side paler.

AdBr
JAN–AUG

AdNb
(probably ♂)
AUG–FEB
[NOV]

⊙ Black-eared Wheatear *p. 406*
Wheatear *p. 404* | Finsch's Wheatear *p. 585*
♀ - Isabelline Wheatear *p. 405*

LC Desert Wheatear
NT

Oenanthe deserti

3 | **L** 14·5–15·5 cm | **W** 25–26 cm

Small, **pale buff** wheatear with **black tail**. ♂**Br** | buff; **black face/throat joined to black wing**. ♀**Br** | upperparts yellow-buff, tinged grey; underparts whiter; pale shoulder, darker midwing, black wingtip. ♂**Nb/♂1W** | blackish face obscured by pale tips to feathers, which wear off by APR. ♀**Nb/♀1W** | like ♀**Br** with pale fringes on wing; **Juv** | grey-brown; faint pale spots on head and back, whitish feather edges on blackish wing; pale throat, grey-buff breast with pale spots.

♀ **Br**

♂**Br**
FEB–AUG

square white rump
and black tail

L ●| Rump rufous; tail **white** with thick black 'T'; outerwing dark. **1W** tail rufous with black 'T'. Underwing silver-grey, coverts blackish.

V| Whistle and hard "*tchak*" calls. Song prolonged, rambling, musical warble.

♀
ALL YEAR

♀
ALL YEAR

Scarce, local summer migrant MAR–OCT

Rocky slopes and hilltops

L ●| Rump and **tail pale buff-orange with black 'T'**; outerwing (above) and underwing coverts paler than on Kurdish Wheatear. Underside of tail plain rufous.

V| Calls quick, low, nasal "*tcher-tcher-tcher*." Song short, musical, warbling phrases.

Ad/1W
ALL YEAR
[NOV]

Ad/1W
ALL YEAR
[OCT]

Scarce, very local summer migrant MAR–OCT

Barren, rocky upland slopes

FL ●| Low, quick, direct. **All-black tail**, square white rump. Dark underwing coverts.

V| Dry, trilling call. Song short, descending whistle, slowly repeated.

♂Nb
AUG–FEB

♂1W
AUG–MAR

♀
ALL YEAR

ssp. *deserti*

ssp. *homochroa*

Two sspp. occur: *deserti* (breeds SE Europe); *homochroa* (vagrant from Africa), smaller, ♂ pinker.

Scarce and very local summer migrant MAR–OCT; vagrant elsewhere

Arid areas

Warblers, crests, cisticolas and prinias

OLD WORLD WARBLERS 67 species (1 restricted to the Canary Islands) [16 (+1 possible) vagrants] *(pp. 416–447, 599–602, 527)*

All have a thin 'insect-eater' bill and tend to be slender-legged and tapered, unlike the stubby-billed, bulky-bodied tits *(p. 452)*. Some are dull, some bright, some uniform, others patterned, but they can be divided into six broad groups. These are the best starting point for identification and each is illustrated in this introduction.

Flight Wings short, broad, rounded, tail slim. Rarely seen above treetop height (some have bouncy song-flights); quick, slightly jerky or hesitant.

Sexing, Ageing and Moult Sexes look alike in most species but differ in others (especially *Sylvia* species). Juvenile differs slightly from adult (*e.g.* pale fringes to feathers or richer colours); plumage is quickly replaced (giving 1st-winter). Spring migrants less than a year old (1st-summer) are like adult but have old juvenile wing feathers.

Identify by general structure and coloration | tail shape | behaviour

broad tail

***Cettia* – 1 species** *(p. 418)*: Small, secretive, in dense water-side vegetation. **STRUCTURE**: thick-set; **broad tail**. **PLUMAGE**: sexes alike; dark red-brown and pale grey-buff. **CALLS**: short *"plit"*. **SONGS**: loud outburst, distinct structure.

graduated tail

curved edge to wing

UTCs long

***Locustella* – 6 species** [2 vagrants] *(pp. 416–417, 599)*:
Look like *Acrocephalus* warblers, exceedingly skulking in grasses/wetlands. **STRUCTURE**: slim bill, flattish head; short wings with markedly **curved outer edge**. Tail graduated; mottled **undertail coverts (UTCs) as long as outer tail feathers**. **PLUMAGE**: sexes and ages look alike; olive-brown to rusty-brown, plain or streaked. **SONGS**: distinctive insect-like 'reeling', often at dusk or at night.

Identify by subtle plumage differences, especially underpart and tail patterns

slightly rounded tail

UTCs long

***Acrocephalus* – 9 species** [1 vagrant] *(pp. 418–423, 599)* and ***Arundinax* –1 species** [vagrant] *(p. 599)*:
Found in reeds/waterside/fen vegetation. **STRUCTURE**: most species have rather long bill and flattish head. Wings short, **tail quite long**; plain **undertail coverts (UTCs) long** (but fall short of outer tail feathers). **PLUMAGE**: sexes and ages look alike; plain or streaked brown above, unstreaked buff below. **SONGS**: mostly fast and rhythmic (some given in flight).

Identify by wing detail | subtle structure and plumage differences, especially head patterns and rump colour

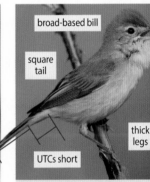

broad-based bill

square tail

thick legs

UTCs short

***Hippolais* – 4 species** *(pp. 424–425)* and ***Iduna* – 4 species** *(pp. 426–428)*:
STRUCTURE: mostly a little larger, bulkier than *Phylloscopus* warblers, with broad-based bill, **square-ended tail** and **short undertail coverts (UTCs)**. **PLUMAGE**: sexes look alike; juvenile bright fringes to wing feathers. Unstreaked greenish/brownish; some have pale edges to wing and tail feathers. **CALLS**: mostly hard notes. **SONGS**: fast, erratic or with repetitive pattern.

Identify by wing detail | subtle plumage and behavioural differences

Sylvia – **20 species [3 vagrants]**
(*pp. 436–447, 602*)

Small to medium-sized warblers, in bushes, scrub, woodland. STRUCTURE: quite **thick bill**, **thick legs**; crown may be raised. Wings short, tail short and square to long and tapered. PLUMAGE: sexes differ in most species but are alike in some; juvenile like adult female or with incomplete male pattern. No consistent colour/patterns, but sub-groups of closely similar species. CALLS: mostly short and hard, "*tak*" or churring notes. SONGS: (some in flight) rapid chattering, or rich, musical warbles. NOTE: *Sylvia* warblers are sometimes separated as 'Sylviid Babblers'.

Identify by head pattern | back colour | call and song

Phylloscopus – **22 species (1 restricted to Canary Islands) [9 (+1possible) vagrants]** (*pp. 429–435, 527, 600–601*)

Very small/small warblers, in foliage; active, not often on ground. STRUCTURE: slim bill; **thin legs**; **tail square/notched, undertail coverts short**. PLUMAGE: sexes look alike; juvenile yellower than adult in some species but like adult after autumn moult; mostly unstreaked, greenish, with combinations of stripes over and through eye, crown stripe, pale eyering, and pale wingbars. CALLS: most soft, whistled, disyllabic ("*hoo-eet*"), but some have harder notes closer to *Sylvia* warblers. SONGS: musical cadence, or repeated, staccato notes, or metallic trill; no harsh notes.

Identify by leg colour | wingbars | head pattern | call and song

CRESTS 4 species (1 restricted to Madeira) [1 vagrant (kinglet) from America] (*pp. 414, 526, 615*)

Acrobatic feeders in foliage, from ground level to treetops. STRUCTURE: tiny, rounded, with short tail, short wings. PLUMAGE: sexes differ slightly. Greenish; crown has yellow/orange/red centre, usually inconspicuous but fanned in display; underparts pale, unstreaked; wings have white bar and black patch. CALLS: high, thin notes. SONGS: simple, rhythmic phrase or trill. **Sexing, Ageing and Moult**. Juvenile lacks adult's distinctive head stripe at first. Adult has a single complete moult Jun–Oct; juvenile has a partial moult Jul–Nov.

Identify by head pattern

short, rounded tail

long, slender tail

CISTICOLAS
1 species (*p. 415*):

Very small, in tall grasses. STRUCTURE: tail **short, rounded**. PLUMAGE: sexes alike; pale buff-brown, streaked ; **black-and-white spots under tip of tail**. SONGS: repeated sharp, high note.

PRINIAS
1 species (*p. 415*):

Very small, in low bushes. STRUCTURE: tail **very long, slender**. PLUMAGE: sexes alike; pale brown, streaked. SONGS: repeated metallic notes.

AMERICAN WARBLERS
28 species [all vagrants]
(*pp. 612–615*).

Bear a structural resemblance to Old World Warblers. Occur mainly in autumn in first-winter plumages, many species with quite striking patterns that are generally noticeably different from the regular species in Europe.

Crests are tiny, rounded, warbler-like; olive-green; white bar and black patch on wing. Often high in canopy, can be low down, occasionally hovering; song best clue. **FL** | Quick, bouncy flits.

ALL YEAR ♂

LC LC (Common) **Firecrest**
Regulus ignicapilla

❷ | **L** 9–10 cm | **W** 14–15 cm

Head boldly patterned. **1Y/Ad** | upperparts bright green with **bronzy-yellow shoulder**. White 'wedge' over black eyestripe, black 'moustache'. Crown black with yellow/orange central stripe. Underparts white. **Juv** | no crown stripe; head pattern subdued until AUG–OCT.

♂ has orange central crown, spread in display; mostly yellow on ♀.

All SSP. *ignicapilla*

Locally common resident/migrant

All kinds of woodland, thickets, large gardens

Four sspp. occur: *ignicapilla* (widespread); *caucasicus* (W Caucasus) and *tauricus* (Crimea) poorly defined; *balearicus* (Balearic Is.) paler, greyer.

👁 Goldcrest
Pallas's Leaf-warbler p. 601
Yellow-browed Warbler p. 434
Madeira Firecrest p. 526

V | Call single or 2–3 note first longer: "*zee-zi-zi*" (ma be very like Goldcrest). Sor accelerating trill, witho repetitive rhythm or flourish Goldcrest: "*zi-zi-zi-zizizizizi*

Juv
MAY–AUG

white stripe over eye

1Y/Ad
ALL YEAR

LC LC **Goldcrest** *Regulus regulus*

❷ | **L** 8·5–9·5 cm | **W** 14–15 cm

Face rather 'plain'. **1Y/Ad** | upperparts pale olive-green. Pale area around eye; weak black 'moustache'. Crown black with yellow central stripe (vivid orange on ♂ when spread). Underparts whitish. **Juv** | lacks crown stripe until AUG–OCT.

ALL YEAR ♂

♂ has orange central crown (hidden unless spread); all-yellow on ♀.

Common resident/migrant

Mixed or coniferous woodland, thickets, gardens, parks; migrants in coastal scrub

Seven sspp. occur: *regulus* (widespread); *buturlini* (Crimea) slightly greyer, less yellowish; five on Macaronesian islands (see p. 526).

👁 Firecrest | Blue Tit p. 463
Yellow-browed Warbler p. 434
Ruby-crowned Kinglet p. 615

V | Call 3–4 notes: "*zree-zre zree*" (more emphatic tha Long-tailed Tit (p. 460)), single, stronger note; feedi flocks call sharp "*sit*." Sor high-pitched, rhythmic w **slight terminal flourish,** " *sissi si-sissi si-sissi sissi-siswee–*

All SSP. *regulus*   no white stripe over eye

Juv
MAY–AUG

1Y/Ad
(probably ♀)
ALL YEAR

Sedge Warbler *p.423*
Aquatic Warbler *p.422*

Zitting Cisticola
Cisticola juncidis

L 10–11 cm | **W** 12–15 cm

Tiny, pale brownish, warbler-like. Tail slender, square, rounded when fanned. Perches upright low down in grass/bush, with slight nervous wing-flicking. **Ad** upperparts streaked black and buff-brown, becoming darker, more uniform with wear. Throat white, underparts buff. Tail striped black and buff with **white spots on tip**, largest on underside. Eye pale brown. Inside of mouth black on **↗Br**, pink on ♀. **Juv** more rufous than Ad, with dull brown streaks and darker eye. **1W** as Ad (minority show contrast between old and new flight feathers).

V Rapid "*tsip-tsip-tsip-tsip…*" calls. Song in **high, bounding** flight, repeated, rasping, metallic "*dzip, dzip…*."

Three sspp. occur: *cisticola* (W France, Iberia, Balearic Is.); *juncidis* (S France to W Turkey) upperparts more buff, less brown; *neuroticus* (CS Turkey, Cyprus) rump less rufous.

FL Short, broad wings; short, broad brown tail blackish towards tip above, **bold black and white spots** below.

1Y/Ad

SSP. *cisticola*

Ad **ALL YEAR** [MAR]

Ad **ALL YEAR** [SEP]

Ad **ALL YEAR** [JAN]

SSP. *juncidis*

spots under tail

SSP. *cisticola*

Locally common resident

Marshes, open drier grassland, crops

Graceful Prinia
Prinia gracilis

L 10–11 cm | **W** 12 cm

Tiny, short-winged, brownish, warbler-like. Perches on low vegetation, raising and swaying **long, thin tail**. Upperparts grey-brown, finely streaked grey. Underparts white. **♂Br** bill black; black inside mouth obvious when singing. **↗Nb**/♀/**Juv** bill pale.

V Call a metallic, ringing trill "*prrr-rr-rr-rr.*" Song a shrill "*shrr-rr-rr-rr*" or more rhythmic "*shi-jip shi-jip shi-jip shi-jip.*"

SSP. *akyildizi* occurs in Europe. NOTE: Graceful Prinia is split into two species by some taxonomic authorities, with *akyildizi* a ssp. of **'Delicate Prinia'** *Prinia lepida*.

FL Fast, low, whirring; wings very short, tail long and narrow.

SSP. *akyildizi*

♂Br **MAR–AUG**

♂Nb/♀ **ALL YEAR**

(NOTE: Middle Eastern SSP. *carpenteri*)

Locally common resident

Dense undergrowth, grassy areas

LC LC (Common) **Grasshopper Warbler** *Locustella naevia*

4 | **L** 12·5–13·5 cm | **W** 16–18 cm

Small, secretive, rather elongated, **softly streaked** warbler; **creeps** in low, dense vegetation. **Long, dark-streaked undertail coverts** extend well down tail. Tertials dark with **diffuse** pale fringes. **Ad** | upperparts olive- to yellowish-brown, streaked greyish; underparts buff, some with diffuse flank streaks. **Juv / 1W** | often more yellowish; some finely streaked on throat.

V | Sharp "*tik*" or "*psit*." **Song** a **prolonged, reeling trill**, may last several minutes; fast, mechanical, loud ticking, thinner at distance. (Savi's Warbler has faster "*buzz*.")

FL ● | May flush at close range, flits ahead on rounded wings, twists back down, **round tail** fanned; looks **pale, dull yellowish**; rump barely contrasted.

> Three sspp. occur: *naevia* (widespread) and slightly more olive *obscurior* (E Turkey, Caucasus) both larger and darker than *straminea* (E European Russia), which has more contrasted streaks.

> 👁 Grasshopper Warbler and Lanceolated Warbler are very similar.
> Sedge Warbler *p. 423*
> Aquatic Warbler *p. 422*
> Pallas's Grasshopper Warbler *p. 599*

Ad
ALL YEAR

Scarce summer migrant APR–SE

Marshes and drier areas with long grass and bushy growth

Juv/1W

TERTIALS: broad pale fringes

All ssp. *naevia*

considerable individual variation; ageing difficult as post-juvenile moult late, from OCT–FEB

Juv/1W
JUN–MAR

LC LC **Lanceolated Warbler**
Locustella lanceolata

4 | **L** 12 cm | **W** 16–18 cm

Small, extremely skulking, short-tailed, **distinctly streaked** warbler. **Long undertail coverts** extend well down tail. **Tertials blackish** with **well-defined** narrow pale fringes. **Ad** | upperparts grey-brown, streaked blackish; wing slightly rufous; underparts whitish, flank buff, both finely streaked blackish. **Juv** | underparts yellowish, with diffuse blackish streaking (more extensive than on juvenile Grasshopper Warbler).

V | Call a sharp click. **Song** prolonged, high-pitched, soft reeling trill (Grasshopper Warbler's more metallic, ticking trill).

FL ● | Short, low dash on rounded wings.

ssp. *lanceolata* occurs in Europe.

Ad
ALL YEAR

Scarce, local summer migrant APR–OCT

Swamps, marshes, wet scrub

TERTIALS: narrow pale fringes

Juv

considerable individual variation in plumage

Juv
AUG–OCT

wo similar *Locustella* warblers with
plain upperparts. **FL ●** | Low, quite
low, on short, triangular wings; head
pointed; tail often fanned into oval-
shape; head and tail often raised slightly.
No plumage contrasts.

River Warbler
ocustella fluviatilis

● | **L** 14·5–16 cm | **W** 16–18 cm

airly small, slim, grey-brown warbler.
lain wing has noticeably pale, long,
urved outer edge. Resembles Savi's
Warbler but **throat and breast subtly
streaked dark**, long undertail coverts
ark with **pale crescentic tips**, and has
distinctive song. Ad | upperparts grey-
rown. Faint pale stripe over eye, cheek
mottled brown. Underparts dull white,
reast buff with subtle wavy brown
treaks, flank slightly browner. **Juv / 1W** |
end to be more yellowish on underparts
han **Ad**, but much individual variation
n both; like **Ad** after FEB.

◐ Savi's Warbler and River Warbler are
similar. | *Reed Warbler p. 419*
Marsh Warbler p. 420
Blyth's Reed Warbler p. 420
Gray's Grasshopper Warbler p. 599

Savi's Warbler
ocustella luscinioides

● | **L** 13·5–15 cm | **W** 16–18 cm

airly small but rather heavy-bodied,
rownish warbler; bill slim, head flattish,
ery long, **brown undertail coverts** and
road tail. Obvious curve to edge of
lunt-tipped closed wing. Plain plumage
esembles Reed Warbler. Usually located
y **distinctive song, from dense reeds**.
d | upperparts **uniform** brownish;
nderparts pale buff, **darker** beneath
ail (similar Reed Warbler has shorter,
limmer, whiter undertail coverts).
uv / 1W | underparts duller than on **Ad**.

Three sspp. occur: *luscinioides*
(widespread) and *sarmatica* (far E Europe)
very similar but the latter faintly more
olive-brown; *fusca* (Turkey eastwards)
greyer.

V | Call a sharp "*zic zic*." **Song** a prolonged,
unbroken, sharp, metallic, shaking trill,
fast, rhythmic or mechanical: "*schili-schili-
schili-schili-schili….*"

Scarce summer
migrant APR–SEP

Wet thickets, dense
waterside forest

Ad
ALL YEAR

V | Call a sharp, metallic "*pvit*." **Prolonged
song**, often at night, like Grasshopper
Warbler but **lower and faster**, more
purring or buzzing than ticking/reeling.

Scarce summer
migrant APR–SEP

Reedbeds

SSP. *luscinioides*

Ad
ALL YEAR

LC # Cetti's Warbler *Cettia cetti*

LC **3** | **L** 13–14 cm | **W** 18–20 cm

Medium-sized, dark, dumpy warbler; easy to hear, but skulks, sings, moves unseen to sing again nearby. (Wren often in same watery habitat, forages and crosses open spaces in similar manner.) Sexes and ages look alike: upperparts dark **rufous-brown**, tail rufous, wearing to dull black at tip. **Pale stripe over eye**. Throat whitish, **cheek and breast grey**; flank rufous. Undertail coverts **brown with pale tips**.

V | Short, hard, sharp "*quilp!*" or "*plit*" calls: loud and distinct or quiet. Song (both sexes) a sudden, loud outburst: short notes, momentary pause, then fast series of ringing notes, "*chwee; chwee: chuwee-wee-wee-wee-wee chwit-it!*"

FL ● | Low, quick on rounded wings; half flies, half leaps between clumps. Tail long, **square, dark rufous**.

Reed Warbler | Wren *p. 372*
Moustached Warbler *p. 422*

Two similar sspp. occur and intergrade: *cetti* (widespread); *orientalis* (Turkey E, Cyprus) grey on back, rump/tail more contrasted rufous.

1Y/Ad*
ALL YEAR

*1Y may have some paler greater coverts (uniform on Ad)

Often tilts forward, tail raised.

SSP. *cetti*

Locally common resident/ summer migrant

Marshes, riverside thickets, overgrown ditches

Plain brown *Acrocephalus* warblers – key features	Reed Warbler is the 'standard' plain *Acrocephalus* warbler in reedbeds in summer, but locally other species may be as frequent. Important to note calls/song, precise head pattern, wingtip length, the number of visible primary tips and contrasting paler feather fringes.			
General appearance		Head pattern	Tertials	Wingtip
Marsh Warbler (*p. 420*)	Olive; barely brighter rump	Weak stripe over eye; bolder eyering	Strongly contrasted pale fringes; just longer than secondaries	PRIMARY PROJECTION long; PALE TIPS TO PRIMARIES 8 visible (wear off in summer) — sharp contrast
Reed Warbler (*p. 419*)	Warm brown; rustier rump/tail	Weak stripe over eye; white throat	Weakly contrasted paler fringes; same length as secondaries	PRIMARY PROJECTION long; PALE TIPS TO PRIMARIES 7 visible (dull) — diffuse contrast
Blyth's Reed Warbler (*p. 420*)	Olive; very uniform	Stripe over eye bulbous in front	Very plain	PRIMARY PROJECTION short; PALE TIPS TO PRIMARIES 6 visible 1ST-WINTER has bronzy panel on secondaries — plain
Paddyfield Warbler (*p. 421*)	Bright; sandy/rusty. Long tail	Stripe over eye edged dark above and below	Obvious paler fringes	PRIMARY PROJECTION short; PALE TIPS TO PRIMARIES 5–7 visible — pale fringes

(Common) **Reed Warbler** *Acrocephalus scirpaceus*

⬤ | **L** 12·5–14 cm | **W** 18–20 cm

mall, slim, **unstreaked** brown warbler. Sidles up vertical stem,
ives back down or dashes across open space. Breeding birds forage
n trees, migrants in bushes. Breeding birds best told by **song** but
nigrants difficult to tell from Marsh and Blyth's Reed Warblers. Bill
im, pointed; nape rounded, crown often raised. Tail slim, square.
ale stripe over eye stronger than faint eyering. **Tertial fringes and
rimary tips are scarcely paler**, alula scarcely darker. Legs grey-brown.
Ad | upperparts mid-brown, **rump and tail brighter rufous-brown**.
hroat white, puffed out when singing; underparts pale **orange-buff**.
uv / 1W | like **Ad** but upperparts uniformly rufous-brown.

⬤ | Low, slurred "*tcharr,*" softer "*kresh,*" grating "*krrrr*" calls. Song, from
pright stem (not in flight) rhythmic, repetitive, each phrase repeated
–4 times, lower, more even than Sedge Warbler (*p. 423*), without high
rills, "*chara-chara, krrik-krrik-krrik, charee charee charee….*"

Three sspp. occur: *scirpaceus* (widespread), *ambiguus** (Iberia, S France)
fractionally more buff, less migratory; *fuscus* (Cyprus, Turkey, vagrant in W)
paler, greyer, rump sandy-grey, supercilium and underparts whiter. *NOTE:
ssp. *ambiguus* is sometimes treated as a ssp. of another species, **African
Reed Warbler** *Acrocephalus baeticatus ambiguus*.

Marsh Warbler *p. 420*
Blyth's Reed Warbler *p. 420*
Savi's Warbler *p. 417*
Paddyfield Warbler *p. 421*
Great Reed Warbler *p. 421*
Booted/Sykes's Warblers *p. 427*
Olivaceous warblers *p. 426*

Locally common
summer migrant
APR–OCT

Reedbeds, mixed
fen, waterside
willows

FL ⬤ | Low, quick; often a rustle/twitch
of reeds before a short flight. Wings
triangular; head pointed; tail quite long.
Back and rump lack contrast.

Ad
ALL YEAR
ssp. *ambiguus*

Ad
ALL YEAR
ssp. *scirpaceus*

1W
JUL–MAR
ssp. *scirpaceus*

Plain *Acrocephalus* warblers are unstreaked, olive- to rufous-brown wetland birds that often perch upright on a tall stem. Undertail coverts are longer than those of *Iduna* warblers (*pp. 426– 428*); shorter than those of *Locustella* warblers (*pp. 416– 417*). Breeding birds best told by song; migrants difficult to tell apart (and very like Booted and Sykes's Warblers). **Compare all with Reed Warbler.**

👁 Reed Warbler (see *p. 418–419*) | Savi's Warbler *p. 417* | Booted and Sykes's Warblers *p. 427*

LC **Marsh Warbler**
LC *Acrocephalus palustris*

4 | **L** 13–15 cm | **W** 18–20 cm

Olive-brown. Bill fractionally shorter and thicker than on Reed Warbler; nape angular. Eyering bolder than short pale stripe over eye. **Tertial fringes and primary tips contrastingly pale** (worn off on **Ad** AUG–DEC); **alula dark**. Legs dusky pinkish. **Ad**| upperparts sandy-olive, rump brighter but **not rufous**. Underparts **lemon-buff**. **Juv/1W**| like Ad but rump warm brown; primaries tipped whitish.

V | Dry, rattling "*terrrr*" or soft "*chek*" calls. Song lively, flowing; great variety of accurate mimicry. Most vocal at dawn/dusk; may be quieter, Reed Warbler-like, during day. Includes distinctive nasal "*tzay-beeee*," but many grating notes.

FL ● | Low, quick, on triangular wings; tail quite long, head pointed. Back dull, tail slightly brighter.

Scarce, locally fairly common summer migrant MAY–SEP

Dense waterside vegetation, marshy thickets

LC **Blyth's Reed Warbler**
LC *Acrocephalus dumetorum*

2 | **L** 12·5–14 cm | **W** 16–18 cm

Dull olive-brown. Bill long, slender, pale, with ill-defined dark tip; forehead low. Tail rounded; **wing short and uniform. Broad, pale patch in front of eye**; eyering weak. Legs dark grey-brown. May perch with head and tail raised (characteristic 'banana'-shaped pose). **Ad**| upperparts greyish olive, underparts buff. **Juv/1W**| like Ad but rump warm brown; bronzy panel on closed wing.

V | Hard "*tek*" call. Song slow, repetitive, lacks Reed Warbler's churring rhythm; includes mimicry, descending whistling 'scales', churrs and bright whistles.

FL ● | Low, quick, on triangular wings; tail quite long, head pointed. Uniform olive-brown.

Locally fairly common summer migrant APR–OCT

Wet forest edges, riverside marshs

1ST-WINTER has bronzy panel on secondaries

bill relatively short and thick

head pattern weak

tertial fringes pale

wingtip long

Ad
ALL YEAR

bill long, slim, pale, with ill-defined dark tip, merges into low forehead

Ad
ALL YEAR

tertials plain

wingtip short

Paddyfield Warbler

Acrocephalus agricola

2 | **L** 12–13·5 cm | **W** 15–17 cm

Bright rufous-brown. Bill short, rather thick, yellowish with sharply defined black tip. Tail long; wing short with dark centres to tertials. Legs pale brown. Duller or paler individuals are very like Booted and Sykes's Warblers. **Ad** | upperparts rusty-brown, underparts bright buff. Strong **pale stripe over dark eyestripe**; crown brown with **darker side**. Rump/uppertail often **bright rufous-brown**. **Juv / 1W** | wing feathers edged buff, but inseparable from some **Ad**s that moult wings before migration.

V | Grating "*tsairrk*" call.
Song fast, churring phrases, grating twitters/chatters and bright, Robin-like (*p. 392*) whistles.

FL ● | Low, quick, on short, rather oval-shaped wings; tail narrow. Rump and tail brighter rufous than back.

Locally fairly common
summer migrant
APR–OCT

Reedbeds

SSP. *septimus* occurs in
Europe.

Reed Warbler *p. 419* | Olive-tree Warbler *p. 424*
Basra Reed Warbler, Thick-billed Warbler p. 599

Great Reed Warbler

LC
LC

Acrocephalus arundinaceus

3 **4** | **L** 16–20 cm | **W** 25–30 cm

Large and bulky warbler, plain rufous-brown with well-marked head pattern. Bill large, heavy, **pale with dark tip**. **Crashing movements** in tall reeds. **Ad** | upperparts rufous. Bold **pale stripe over eye** fades out behind, above **thick, dark eyestripe**. Underparts whitish, flank buff. **Juv / 1W** | like **Ad** but underparts bright buff.

V | Call a hard "*crek*." **Song loud, coarse, repetitive**; **deeper** notes than Reed Warbler; also high squeaks, sometimes hesitant, but unique in full flow: "*krr-krr kreek kreek kreek krrr krr grik grik chwee chwee chwee kerra kerra kerra….*"

FL ● | Low, short flights, twisting and diving into reeds; wings long, pointed, tail long, broad, often slightly raised. Large, long head protrudes, often slightly raised.

Locally fairly common
summer migrant
APR–SEP

Reedbeds

Ad
ALL YEAR
SSP. *arundinaceus*

Two sspp. occur:
arundinaceus
(widespread.); *zarudnyi*
(SE European Russia)
paler and greyer.

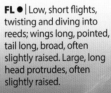

bill short, yellowish
with sharply defined
black tip

head pattern
strong

Ad
ALL YEAR

tertial fringes
pale

wingtip
short

421

Sedge Warbler
Cetti's Warbler *p. 418*

LC
LC

Moustached Warbler
Acrocephalus melanopogon

 | **L** 12–13 cm | **W** 15–17 cm

Dark, rufous; closed wingtip **short**. Flicks or raises tail; tilts forward before dropping into cover. **Ad** | upperparts rufous, softly streaked dark grey, becoming plainer, less rufous with wear; wings marked blackish; pale buff fringes to blackish tertials. **Cap blackish** (faintly streaked); **broad white stripe** over eye widens to rear; cheek grey, fine **dark 'moustache'**. White throat **contrasts with rufous flank** and buff breast; belly white. **Legs dark**; bill blackish. **Juv / 1W** | like **Ad** but underparts faintly streaked blackish.

V | Low, hard "*trrk*" call. Song slightly faster, more even chatter than Reed Warbler (*p. 419*); repetition of quick, piping notes like Nightingale (*p. 394*).

FL ● | Low, quick. Wings rounded; tail fairly long, slim. Dark rufous rump shows little contrast.

Three sspp. occur: *melanopogon* (S Europe to W Turkey); *albiventris* (far E Europe) and *mimicus* (E Turkey eastwards) both larger, less rufous, with browner crown, paler flank (more like Sedge Warbler).

Locally frequent resident/migrant

Dense riverside/marshy vegetation

ssp. *mimicus*

blackish crown

Ad
ALL YEAR

Ad / 1W
ALL YEAR

ssp. *melanopogon*

 Sedge Warbler
Zitting Cisticola *p. 415*
Grasshopper Warbler *p. 416*

VU
VU

Aquatic Warbler
Acrocephalus paludicola

 | **L** 11·5–13 cm | **W** 16–18 cm

Yellow-buff with long, black streaks; wingtip quite short and rounded; uppertail coverts **pointed**. **Ad** | Back boldly marked with **cream stripes** and blackish streaks; rump orange-brown, streaked black. **Crown blackish with unstreaked pale cream central stripe**; broad buff stripe over eye. Dark eyestripe falls **short of bill**. Breast and flank greyish-buff with **fine black streaks**. Legs pale pink. **Juv** | similar to **Ad** but crown stripe streaked (although pattern still strongly contrasted); underparts plain yellowish.

V | Ticking "*chak*," "*ch'k*," or deep "*tuk*" calls. Song like slow Sedge Warbler with frequent hard, dry, rasped "*trrrrt*" between bright whistles.

FL ● | Low, quick. Wings rather narrow; tail fairly long, slim. Streaked rump shows little contrast.

Rare and local summer migrant
APR–SEP

Low, wet fen vegetation

pale crown stripe

Ad
ALL YEAR

streaked rump and uppertail coverts

Juv
JUL–DEC

Streaked *Acrocephalus* warblers are small, stocky, short-tailed wetland birds, with soft or bolder streaking on the back and wings, and strong head patterns. Rump streaked or plain. Compared with *Locustella* warblers (*pp. 416– 417*), shorter undertail coverts and a squarer tail; more often visible on low but exposed perches.

Juv

Ad

SEDGE WARBLER

AQUATIC WARBLER

Can be confusing, especially in autumn when well-marked juvenile Sedge Warblers can show a distinct pale crown stripe.

Sedge Warbler

Acrocephalus schoenobaenus

L 11·5–13 cm | **W** 18–20 cm

Pale, rufous-buff with diffuse **greyish streaks**; wingtip quite long and pointed; uppertail coverts **rounded**. **Ad** | back buff-brown, **softly streaked** darker grey-brown; rump plain **pale sandy-buff** framed by dark brown tertials with pale fringes. By AUG, darker and more uniform, except streaky wings. Cap dark grey-brown; **white stripe over eye** widens to rear; dark eyestripe reaches bill. **Throat white**; underparts buff, brighter on flank. **Legs pale** brownish; bill pale at base. **Juv / 1W** | like Ad but more yellowish or gingery; central crown has pale stripe; dark eyestripe reaches bill. Breast has faint dark streaks.

Aquatic Warbler | Moustached Warbler
Zitting Cisticola p. 415 | Grasshopper Warbler p. 416

Song-flight is a simple smooth rise and fall, with quick, deep, stiff-winged beats.

Common summer migrant APR-OCT

Mixed marsh and riverside vegetation, bramble patches, thickets

V | Hard "*tuk*," short, flat "*trrrr*." Song **energetic, scratchy** or musical, lacks rhythm of Reed Warbler (*p. 419*). Sings upright, exposed or hidden in bush, or in **song flight**.

FL ● | Low, quick, short flights between bushes or reeds; wings rounded, narrow; tail slim. **Plain rump contrastingly pale**.

grey-brown crown

Ad
ALL YEAR

plain rump and uppertail coverts

Juv
JUL–SEP

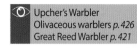 Upcher's Warbler
Olivaceous warblers *p. 426*
Great Reed Warbler *p. 421*

FL ● | Direct, fluent, on long, slightly pointed wings; tail square. Head elongated.

Ad
ALL YEAR

LC **Olive-tree Warbler**
LC *Hippolais olivetorum*

❹ | **L** 16–18 cm | **W** 22–24 cm

Large, bold, greyish warbler; size as Barred Warbler (*p. 437*) or Great Reed Warbler but hard to judge on isolated individual. Moves heavily through foliage, **tail waved** like a shrike (*p. 466*) and sometimes dipped like Eastern Olivaceous Warbler. **Wingtip projection long**, almost length of tertials; **tail long, bill long, heavy**, pointed. **Ad** | greyish, more olive in spring, duller, browner or darker bluish-grey by JUL/AUG. Short pale stripe from bill to above eye, edged dark above; pale eyering. Closed wing has **whitish fringes**, worn off by AUG/SEP. Tail blackish with white sides/corners. Bill pale orange-yellow with dark ridge; legs blue-grey. **Juv** | dull; eyering dull, tail sides greyish.

V | Call deep "*tuc*," chattering alarm and nasal, Jay-like (*p. 473*) screech. Song slowish, repetitive sequence of raucous phrases, coarse and unmusical: "*chak-chi-chak-chu chu-chak-crik crik chak.*"

Scarce, local summer migrant APR–SEP

Oak woodland, olive groves, almond orchards

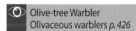 Olive-tree Warbler
Olivaceous warblers *p. 426*

FL ● | Direct, fluent; slightly pointed wings; tail square.

LC **Upcher's Warbler**
LC *Hippolais languida*

❹ | **L** 14–15 cm | **W** 21–25 cm

Medium-sized warbler with dark tail; resembles slightly larger Olive-tree Warbler and slightly smaller Eastern Olivaceous Warbler. Noticeably **long bill**, legs and tail give angular look. **Waves tail**. Wingtip projection medium to long, almost three-quarters length of tertials. **Ad** | grey-brown head and back, browner wing, blacker tail with whitish side; faint pale wing panel. Underparts buff-white. Faint darker side to crown, above whitish stripe from bill to top of eye and white eyering; dark eyestripe. Bill orange-yellow. **Juv / 1W** | like **Ad** but bright pale edges to wing feathers (worn on **Ad** until moult from DEC).

V | Hard "*zak*" and churring notes. Song fast, varied, nasal warble, slightly cyclical pattern.

Ad
ALL YEAR

Scarce, local summer migrant APR–SEP

Scrub, orchards, farmland

Both **Hippolais warblers** have plain upperparts. **FL ●** | Direct but slightly fluttering; wing rounded, tail rather long. Head elongated.

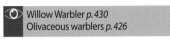

Willow Warbler *p. 430*
Olivaceous warblers *p. 426*

cterine Warbler *Hippolais icterina*

4 | **L** 11·5–13 cm | **W** 22 cm

Medium-sized, green-and-yellow warbler with teep forehead, angular crown, long body; lively, onspicuous. Slightly larger and bulkier than Willow Warbler, with stronger bill and legs. Pale between eye and bill. **Wing structure** mportant: wingtip projection **equals length** of ongest tertial, giving **long wingtip**. **Pale wing panel** worn off on a few adults, weaker on juveniles). **Ad** | upperparts pale grey-green; underparts yellow brightest in spring, whiter by AUG/SEP, when paler han Melodious Warbler). **Juv / 1W** | underparts /hite; throat and upper breast pale yellow.

V | Infrequent hard "*tek*" call. Song **disjointed**, includes harp, scratchy "*chip chip*" and sparrowy churr, and quick, nasal, twanging or buzzing notes.

WINGTIP PROJECTION = longest tertial (**long-winged effect**); usually prominent pale wing panel.

Locally common summer migrant
MAR–OCT

Dense woodland, wooded parkland

LC Melodious Warbler *Hippolais polyglotta*

LC **4** | **L** 12–13 cm | **W** 20–21 cm

Medium-sized, green-and-yellow warbler with rounded head (crown raised in alarm/song), body rounded or pear-shaped; skulking and subdued. Typically has **plain wing**. **Wing structure** crucial: wingtip projection **half length** of longest tertial, giving **short wingtip**. **Ad** | upperparts olive-green; underparts yellow (greener above and more uniformly yellowish below than Icterine Warbler, even in autumn when both have worn, faded plumage). **Juv / 1W** | fresh wing feathers have pale fringes, but rarely shows an obvious pale panel like Icterine Warbler.

V | Call a subdued sparrow-like chattering, and short "*tchret-tret*." Song fast, a relatively even, rambling or sparrow-like chatter.

WINGTIP PROJECTION ½ length of longest tertial (**short-winged**); usually no pale wing panel.

Locally common summer migrant
MAR–OCT

Woodland, bushy places, scattered trees

Ad
ALL YEAR

Ad
ALL YEAR

Juv / 1W
JUL–MAR

Juv / 1W
JUL–MAR

425

Western Olivaceous
LC
LC ## Warbler *Iduna opaca*

4 | **L** 13–14 cm | **W** 18–21 cm

Tail plain (no whitish edges) and **not frequently dipped**. **Ad** | upperparts grey-brown. No strong head pattern except thick, **complete whitish eyering**. Wing dull brown with no pale panel. Bill long, broad, orange-yellow. Underparts whitish, with small grey-buff patch on flank. Legs grey-brown. **Juv / 1W** | well-defined pale feather edges (on **Ad**, feathers worn until moults, from OCT or NOV).

V | Call short, hard, sparrow-like "*chup chup*." Song rambling, like Reed Warbler but less repetitive; lacks cyclical pattern of Eastern Olivaceous Warbler.

Both **olivaceous warblers** are medium-sized, plain and pale 'brown', separated on range when breeding but difficult otherwise.
FL ● | Low, direct; wings and tail broad, head elongated. No contrasts.

Other *Iduna* warblers | Reed Warbler *p. 419* | Olive-tree Warbler *p. 42*
Within ranges: WESTERN – Melodious Warbler *p. 425* |
EASTERN – Upcher's Warbler *p. 424* | Icterine Warbler *p. 425*

eyering complete

pale
between
eye and
bill

Ad
ALL YEAR

tail plain

Scarce and local
summer migrant
MAR–OCT

Bushy heathland,
woodland edge,
scattered trees

Eastern Olivaceous
LC
LC ## Warbler *Iduna pallida*

4 | **L** 12–13·5 cm | **W** 18–21 cm

Tail has whitish edges and tips to outer feathers and is **frequently dipped**. **Ad** | upperparts pale brownish-grey. Side of forehead darker; **slight dark line from bill to eye**, below short, weak pale stripe. **Thin, broken, whitish eyering**. Slight pale panel on closed wing. Long tail has whitish edges and tips to outer feathers. Bill long, broad, orange-yellow. Underparts all buff-white. Legs grey-brown. **Juv / 1W** | well-defined pale feather edges (on **Ad**, feathers worn until moult from OCT).

V | Call soft "*tchat tchat*;" fast, sparrow-like chatter. Song unmusical, quick, scratchy chatter with rhythmic **cyclical repetition**.

ssp. *elaeica* occurs in
Europe.

1W
AUG–MAR

Frequently dips tail downwards.

eyering broken

dark
between
eye and
bill

Ad
ALL YEAR

tail edged
white

Locally fairly
common
summer migrant
MAR–OCT

Woods, orchards,
scattered trees

⊙ Other *Iduna* warblers | Reed *p. 419* | Marsh *p. 420* | Blyth's Reed Warblers *p. 420* | Siberian Chiffchaff *p. 433*

Booted Warbler
Iduna caligata

🄳 | **L** 11–12·5 cm | **W** 18–21 cm

Small, pale buff- to grey-brown warbler; large head, sharply pointed bill. Very like Sykes's Warbler but shorter body, deep belly stops abruptly against **short undertail coverts** (like a *Phylloscopus* warbler), but forages low (like an *Acrocephalus* warbler), with frequent wing/tail flicks. **Ad** | short, pale rusty-**buff stripe over eye** well defined; **weak, dark eyestripe reaches bill**; side of crown may look dark. **Bill short, fine, usually dark at tip. Tertials dark-centred, tips evenly spaced**; wingtip short. Tail **square**, with very thin pale edges, shafts darker. Legs pinkish-brown. **Juv / 1W** | like **Ad** but wing feathers pale-edged (worn on **Ad** until moults, from DEC).

🔊 | Call a short, dry "*chrek.*" Song a quick, repetitive churr, like Reed Warbler but less rhythmic; a richer, throatier warbling than Sykes's Warbler.

FL ● | Low, quick, on short, rounded wings; head rounded; tail square-tipped.

Scarce and local summer migrant
MAR–OCT

Low scrub, bushy grassland

pale stripe over eye well defined at rear

undertail coverts short

tail tip square

Ad
ALL YEAR

TERTIALS dark/pale contrast; tips evenly spaced

Sykes's Warbler
Iduna rama

🄳 | **L** 11·5–13 cm | **W** 18–21 cm

Small, pale, plain warbler, very like Booted Warbler but **longer body** tapers into longer undertail coverts like an *Acrocephalus* warbler (*p. 412*), but forages higher, more like a *Phylloscopus* warbler, with frequent wing/tail flicks. Also similar to Eastern Olivaceous and Blyth's Reed Warblers. **Ad** | whitish stripe over eye **poorly defined**; usually pale between eye and bill; dark side to crown. **Bill long, all-pale. Tertials plain, tips unevenly spaced**; wingtip short. Tail **graduated**, thin pale edges visible in **frequent flicks**; shafts not darker. Legs pinkish-brown to grey. **Juv / 1W** | like **Ad** but wing feathers pale-edged (worn on **Ad** until moults, from DEC).

🔊 | Call a short, dry "*chuk.*" Song quick, varied, chattering and chirruping, mixed with thin, hard notes; less rich or musical than Booted Warbler.

NOTE: Plumage features/measurements of vagrant Booted/Sykes's Warblers may sometimes seem to be contradictory.

FL ● | Low, quick, on short, rounded wings; head rounded; tail round-tipped, with pale sides.

Locally frequent summer migrant
MAR–OCT

Scrub

pale stripe over eye diffuse at rear

TERTIALS plainer; tips unevenly spaced

Ad
ALL YEAR

undertail coverts quite long

tail tip rounded

Iduna warblers

Reed p. 419 | Marsh p. 420 | Blyth's Reed p. 420 | Paddyfield Warblers p. 421

The four *Iduna* species are similar to one another, with overlapping subtle and variable features. **Booted** and **Sykes's Warblers** are extremely similar, and **Sykes's Warbler** is also very much like **Eastern** and **Western Olivaceous Warblers**, which themselves can be difficult to tell apart except by range. They can also look very similar to *Acrocephalus* warblers, although *Iduna* **warblers have shorter undertail coverts**. Differences between the species are summarized below. (Upcher's Warbler (*Hippolais* – p. 424) is long-billed and dark-tailed.)

	Booted Warbler (p. 427)	Sykes's Warbler (p. 427)	Eastern Olivaceous Warbler (p. 426)	Western Olivaceous Warbler (p. 426)
Jizz	*Phylloscopus* warbler-like	longer body shape than Booted Warbler; *Acrocephalus* warbler-like	long body shape; *Acrocephalus* warbler-like	
	slight wing/tail twitches	**frequent upward/ sideways tail twitches**	**tail-dips repeatedly**	**does not dip tail**
Behaviour	forages low (like an *Acrocephalus* warbler)	forages higher (like a *Phylloscopus* warbler); 'nervous', quick actions	forages at all levels; relaxed, less 'nervous' actions	forages at all levels
Call	**sharp, clicking "chek"**		short, low "tch't"	short, hard "chup"
Head	PALE STRIPE OVER EYE **distinct** (whitish to rusty-buff), **extends behind eye**; CROWN **dark on side**; LORES **slight dark spot**; eye large.	PALE STRIPE OVER EYE **diffuse** (variable but never rusty-buff), **very short behind eye**; CROWN **scarcely darker** on side; LORES pale.	thick-necked, large-headed effect PALE STRIPE OVER EYE weak, short (buff); EYERING broken; LORES **slight dark line** from bill to eye.	PALE STRIPE FROM BILL TO EYE short, below faint dark side to forecrown; EYERING complete; LORES **pale brown**.
Bill	typically **shortish** to medium-long, lower mandible with diffuse darker tip (may be faint or absent)	**long, thin**, straight; pale tip (may be faint dark smudge)	long, broad-based, orange-yellow; slight downcurve, curved cutting edge	distinctly long and broad (more so than Eastern Olivaceous Warbler); orange with dark ridge and tip
Upperparts	**pale tawny- to sandy-brown**	plain greyish-brown	pale brownish-grey, tinged olive	pale brown, no olive tinge
Underparts	whitish below, **flank brighter** buff/ochre	whitish below without brighter flank	bright, pale and 'clean'; flank tinged grey-brown	throat whitish; flank pale grey-buff
Legs	pinkish-brown	pale greyish-pink	greyish	grey-brown
Wing	WINGTIP short; tips < half tertial length · contrasting paler edges	plain	WINGTIP longer; tips ± half tertial length · slight pale panel on some	no pale panel
	TERTIALS (+ GREATER COVERTS) dark with **contrasting paler edges**; TERTIAL TIPS **evenly** spaced	TERTIALS **plain**; TERTIAL TIPS **unevenly** spaced	TERTIALS plain; TERTIAL TIPS **evenly** spaced SECONDARIES may show **slight pale panel**	SECONDARIES no pale panel
Tail	moderate length, diffuse/ very little white on outer two pairs, does not extend onto inner web	clearly long, diffuse white on tip of outer two pairs may extend onto inner web	long; **whitish edges and tips** to outer feathers	wide, rounded; plain; white tip on outer feather very narrow or absent

Phylloscopus warblers

Small, mostly greenish warblers with white/yellowish underparts. Note the presence/absence/precise details of head stripes (centre of crown and over and through eye, and whether these meet above or fall short of the bill); wingbars; pale tertial fringes/tips; and pale rump. Leg colour may also be useful. Calls and songs often provide vital identification clues. Rare vagrants (*pp. 600–601*) share/combine similar features.

CHIFFCHAFF

Flight usually short, low, rather hesitant.

Without wingbars
pp. 429–433, 600

With wingbars
pp. 434–435, 601

Typical calls of the region's breeding *Phylloscopus* warblers		
Chiffchaff	*p. 432*	almost monosyllabic "*hweet*"
Willow Warbler	*p. 430*	"*hoo-eet*", more firmly **disyllabic** than Chiffchaff
Iberian Chiffchaff	*p. 433*	**descending** "*swee-oo*"
Wood Warbler	*p. 429*	high, sweet, sad "*siuuh*"
Siberian Chiffchaff	*p. 433*	flat, monosyllabic "*eep*" or "*speep*" (like Dunnock (*p. 373*))
Mountain Chiffchaff	*p. 433*	simple "*peu*" (like Siberian Chiffchaff)
Western Bonelli's	*p. 431*	a long "*tu-eee*"
Eastern Bonelli's	*p. 431*	**distinctive short** "*chip*"
Yellow-browed	*p. 434*	sharp, **high, loud, rising** "*tchu-wee!*," "*tssooee*" or "*tsweest*"
Arctic Warbler	*p. 434*	hard "*dzit*"
Greenish Warbler	*p. 435*	bright, disyllabic "*tsi-li*" or "*chilip*"
Green Warbler	*p. 435*	high "*shri-wee*" or three-syllable "*chi-su-wee*" call (like White/Pied Wagtail (*p. 366*))

 Willow Warbler *p. 430*
Bonelli's warblers *p. 431*

Wood Warbler
Phylloscopus sibilatrix

4 | **L** 11–12·5 cm | **W** 16–22 cm

Small, bright 'green' warbler of woodland canopy above open leaf-litter, often **located by song** (Bonelli's warblers sound similar). Wide-bellied; long wings often droop beside **short, broad tail**; undertail coverts long, white. **Ad** | upperparts rich green; **long, yellow stripe over eye** and broad, dark eyestripe. Lower face and upper breast pale lemon-yellow contrasting with white underparts (some barely yellow except on face). Wings **dark with yellow-green feather edges**, tertials with blackish centres. **Juv / 1W** (see *p. 431*) | like **Ad** but duller; tertials fringed white, primaries with minute white tip.

FL ● | Rather long wings and short tail; easy, light action with deep wingbeats.

V | Call a high, sweet, sad "*siuuh*." Song mixes a rhythmic repetition of call note, and more frequent metallic ticking, strengthening into short, fast trill.

Ad
ALL YEAR

Sings from tree canopy but also from open perches in the space beneath.

Scarce, locally fairly common, summer migrant APR–SEP

Deciduous or larch woodland without dense understorey

Ad
ALL YEAR

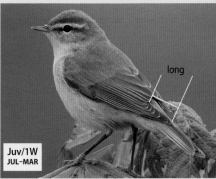

CHIFFCHAFF (*p. 432*) Bill small, mostly dark; round head; white crescent under eye; short wings/tail; dark legs.

WILLOW WARBLER Bill mostly pale; sloping forehead; long stripe over eye; long wings/tail; pale feet.

1Y/Ad **ALL YEAR** ssp. *collybita*

Juv/1W **JUL-MAR**

short

long

Willow Warbler and **Chiffchaff** are by far the most common *Phylloscopus* warblers in the region. Some individuals can be confusing as leg and plumage colours can vary. They can most reliably be told from one another at all ages by the length of the primaries, as shown above.

Wood Warbler | Bonelli's warblers
Chiffchaffs *pp. 432–433*
Greenish Warbler *p. 435*
Green Warbler *p. 435*
Sulphur-bellied Warbler *p. 600*

FL ● | Short, rounded wings; light, often rather jerky, zigzagging action.

Common summer migrant APR-OCT

Woodland, moorland and lowland heath with scattered trees, thickets

LC Willow Warbler
LC *Phylloscopus trochilus*

❹* | **L** 11–12·5 cm | **W** 15–21 cm

Ad **ALL YEAR**

ssp. *trochilus*

legs usually pale

Ad **ALL YEAR**

ssp. *acredula*

Small, pale, 'green' warbler. Like Chiffchaff but subtly brighter, slightly longer. Head flat, bill stronger than Chiffchaff's, **wingtip long**, legs **pale**. Flicks wings, twitches tail but no constantly repeated 'dip' (unlike Chiffchaff). **Ad** | upperparts pale greenish; underparts yellow-cream, belly and vent white. Quite **strong yellowish line over eye**; eyering weak; cheek pale, bill orange-based. **Legs orange-brown** (some dark with pale feet). Wings plain. **Juv / 1W** (see *above*) | yellow stripe over eye, underparts solidly **yellow** including under tail.

V | Call "hoo-eet", more firmly **disyllabic** than Chiffchaff. **Song** distinctive, a sweet, whistling, descending cadence with slight flourish, irregularly repeated.

Two sspp. occur: *trochilus* (widespread); *acredula* (Scandinavia to E Europe) greyer above, whiter below, but the two are highly variable and individuals cannot always be assigned to subspecies.

　* adult has two complete moults per year

Juv/1W
MAY–MAR

Juv/1W
MAY–MAR

WESTERN BONELLI'S
WARBLER

WOOD WARBLER (*p. 429*) Green, yellow and clean white; strong head pattern.

BONELLI'S WARBLERS Both species very similar: dull olive-grey, yellowish and white; very weak head pattern.

The two **Bonelli's warblers** are closely similar, very small, slender, pale warblers, greyer than Willow and Wood Warblers, with contrasting greener wing, rump and tail. Check edges of tertials and tail feathers. Often located by song; call vital for out-of-range vagrant.

FL ● │ Short, rounded wings, rather short tail. Light, often somewhat jerky, zigzagging action.

Willow Warbler | Wood Warbler *p. 429*
WESTERN (RANGE) – Iberian Chiffchaff *p. 433*

	Western Bonelli's Warbler	Eastern Bonelli's Warbler
Call	a long "*tu-eee*"	a **distinctive short** "*chip*"
Song	short, bubbling or 'shaking' trill on one note, "*prr-r-r-r-r-r-r-r-r-r*" (less metallic than Wood Warbler, without opening 'ticking' notes)	very like Western Bonelli's Warbler but a fraction shorter, firmer or flatter

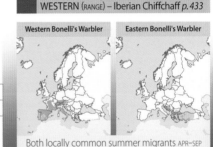

Western Bonelli's Warbler | Eastern Bonelli's Warbler

Both locally common summer migrants APR–SEP

| All woodland types; edges and clearings | Woodland, often oak or pine |

Western Bonelli's Warbler
Phylloscopus bonelli

④ │ **L** 10·5–11·5 cm │ **W** 18–20 cm

Ad│ upperparts brownish-green; **rump brighter yellowish-green**. Wing and tail feathers **edged pale green**. **Head rather plain**, with weak grey line behind eye; short pale stripe over eye. Underparts **silky white**; underwing bright yellow. Bill sturdy, with pale base, dark tip; legs mid- or dark brown. **Juv**/**1W** (see *above*)│ like **Ad** but browner, upperparts more uniform.

Ad
ALL YEAR

Eastern Bonelli's Warbler
Phylloscopus orientalis

④ │ **L** 11–12 cm │ **W** 18–20 cm

Ad│ upperparts greyish; **rump brighter green**. Tertials and tail feathers **edged white**. Rather **plain-faced**. Underparts white; underwing whitish. Bill sturdy, with pale base, dark tip; legs dark brown. **Juv**/**1W** (see *above*) │ like **Ad** but browner, upperparts more uniform.

Ad
ALL YEAR

431

Chiffchaffs – very small, delicate, active, dull greenish/brownish warblers with only a hint of a wingbar at most; pale eyering and stripe over eye. In foliage from ground to treetop height. Flick wings and **regularly and rhythmically dip tail**. Legs thin, very dark. All have calls that are a variation on the *Phylloscopus* "hoo-eet" or "swee-oo," but songs are distinctive. **FL ●** | Short, rounded wings, medium-length tail. Light, often rather jerky, zigzagging action.

Chiffchaffs compared				
	(Common) **Chiffchaff**	**Iberian Chiffchaff**	**Siberian Chiffchaff**	**Mountain Chiffchaff**
Adult General colour	dusky olive-green/ brownish; WINGS dark, with green fringes; UNDERPARTS dull	UPPERPARTS pale green; WINGS yellowish fringes; UNDERPARTS white	grey-brown and buff; no green on head or back; WINGS/TAIL green fringes until MAR; UNDERPARTS whitish, flank buff	grey-brown, tinged olive; WINGS edged whitish or olive (no green); throat whitish, UNDERPARTS dull whitish, breast yellower
Head	pale stripe above dark eyestripe; strong white crescent under eye; cheek dull	long pale stripe over eye yellowest at front; weak pale crescent below eye; cheek pale	long, broad, buff stripe over eye; thick dark eyestripe; cheek buff-brown/rufous	short white stripe over eye fades out behind
Under tail	whitish	yellow	whitish	buff
Bill	dark	lower half pale	black, paler base	dark
Legs	brown-black	pale/brown	black	blackish
Wingtip	short	medium (short in S Iberia)	short	very short
Juv/1Y as adult but	sometimes contrast between old and new wing coverts, but not always reliable			
	tend to be yellower on underparts		tend to be browner	

⊙ Willow Warbler *p. 430* | Bonelli's warblers *p. 431* | Booted/Sykes's Warblers *p. 427* | Arctic Warbler *p. 434*
Greenish Warbler *p. 435* | Dusky Warbler *p. 600* | Radde's Warbler *p. 600*
Where ranges overlap *Plain Leaf-warbler p. 600* | Canary Islands Chiffchaff *p. 527*

LC (Common) **Chiffchaff**
LC *Phylloscopus collybita*

❸ | **L** 10–12 cm | **W** 15–21 cm

Like Willow Warbler, but head rounder, bill finer, **wing short, legs dark**.

V | Almost monosyllabic "*hweet*" call (Willow Warbler's more disyllabic). In JUL/ AUG, slurred "*shrilip*" or "*shlip*." Short "*hoot*" from migrants, SEP–OCT. Song even-paced notes in random sequence, "*chip-chap-chi-chap-chap-chi- chee,*" interspersed with low "*grrt-grrt*."

Common migrant/resident

Woodland, parks, large gardens, riverside and lakeside trees and thickets

Four sspp. occur: *collybita* (widespread) 'olive-and-yellow'; *abietinus* (Scandinavia, E Europe to Urals) greyer above, whiter below (these two highly variable); *brevirostris* (N Turkey) very like *collybita*; *caucasicus* (Caucasus eastwards) whiter below, legs blacker.

SSP. *collybita*

Yellow may fade paler but underparts remain more uniform than on Willow Warbler.

1Y/Ad
ALL YEAR

legs dark

SSP. *abietinus*

1Y/Ad
ALL YEAR

regularly dips tail

Mountain Chiffchaff
Phylloscopus sindianus

3 | **L** 10–11 cm | **W** 12–18 cm

Very like Chiffchaff (darker and browner, lacking most green and yellow) and Siberian Chiffchaff. Wings edged brown, olive or buff, not yellow or green.

SSP. *lorenzii* occurs in Europe.

V | Simple "*peu*" call, like Siberian Chiffchaff. Song like Chiffchaff but more irregular.

Locally fairly common summer migrant
MAR–OCT

Mixed montane woodland

grey-brown overall

wing-feathers edged whitish (no green)

1Y / Ad
ALL YEAR

Iberian Chiffchaff
Phylloscopus ibericus

3 | **L** 11–12 cm | **W** 15–21 cm

Very like Chiffchaff (some impossible to distinguish on plumage), but head pattern more like Willow Warbler. Wingtip slightly longer, legs and bill paler.

NOTE: Southern Iberian populations have a shorter primary projection, like Chiffchaff.

V | Call a **descending** "*swee-oo.*" **Song** typically three sections beginning like Chiffchaff, "*djup djup djup wheep wheep chittichittichittichitta*" or "*chop chop wheep wheep chuckachuckachucka.*"

Locally common summer migrant
APR–OCT

Mixed or deciduous woodland

yellowish base to bill

yellow stripe over eye

yellow throat

1Y / Ad
ALL YEAR

white belly

yellow vent

Siberian Chiffchaff
Phylloscopus tristis

3 | **L** 10–12 cm | **W** 15–21 cm

Very like Chiffchaff. Looks 'cold' grey, buff-brown in bright light. Green fringes on wing recall Bonelli's warblers but wear off by MAR, when more like Booted/Sykes's Warblers. No yellow but yellow underwing may show.

Often treated as a subspecies of Chiffchaff.

V | Flat, monosyllabic "*eep*" or "*speep*", like Dunnock (*p. 373*). Song "*chivvi-tee, chooee, chivvi-tee, chooee-tee, chivvy*" (unlike Chiffchaff).

Locally common summer migrant
APR–OCT; rare in winter

Mixed or deciduous woodland

buff-brown cheek

distinct eyestripe

brown-and-buff overall

1Y / Ad
ALL YEAR

wing-feathers edged green

Arctic Warbler

LC **LC**

Phylloscopus borealis

4 | **L** 11·5–13 cm | **W** 17–19 cm

Small, stocky but long-necked, stout-billed warbler. Very like Greenish Warbler but tail shorter, legs thicker. Call distinctive. **Ad** | upperparts dull, darkish olive-green. Eyestripe long, **broad**, **dark green**, **reaches bill**. Cheek mottled green and yellow. Stripe over eye to nape long, **yellow-cream, falls short of bill**. **Pale wingbar** and thin, short upper wingbar; wear off by JUN/JUL. Underparts greyish-white, may show faint darker streaks. Bill strong with **dark mark** on bottom edge near tip. Legs pale, feet yellower. **Juv** / **1W** | like **Ad** but fresh, bright greenish and white; wingbar more obvious than on worn **Ad**.

V | **Call** a hard "*dzit.*" Song a loose trill, lower than Wood Warbler (*p. 429*); slightly disyllabic "*chuchu-chuchu-chuchu-chuchu-chuchu…*"

FL ● | Short, rounded wing; slightly larger, heavier than Chiffchaff (*p. 432*); often rather jerky, zigzagging action.

Greenish Warbler | Green Warbler
Two-barred Warbler *p. 601*
Eastern Crowned Warbler *p. 601*
Pale-legged Warbler *p. 601*
Tennessee Warbler *p. 614*

Locally fairly common summer migrant
APR–SEP

Birch or mixed forest, bushy areas

Ad
ALL YEAR

wingbar thin

Yellow-browed Warbler

LC **LC**

Phylloscopus inornatus

3 | **L** 9–10·5 cm | **W** 15–16 cm

Tiny, active but inconspicuous warbler; **often calls**. Wings/tail constantly twitched. **Ad** | upperparts greyish- or olive-green, with **long, cream/yellow stripe over eye**, eyestripe dark; crown has diffuse pale centre. Prominent **broad yellow-cream midwing bar**. Tertials tipped white. Underparts silky-white, faintly streaked greyish. **Juv** / **1Y** | almost indistinguishable from **Ad**; some are fractionally browner.

V | Sharp, **high, loud, rising** "*tchu-wee!*", "*tssooee*" or "*tsweest;*" weaker, whispy, at distance; sometimes rapidly repeated for a minute or more. Song short, high, thin, slightly Robin-like (*p. 392*) phrase, "*tsu, tsuwe-si-seeee.*"

FL ● | Short wings and tail, recalling Goldcrest; light, often jerky action.

Firecrest *p. 414* | Goldcrest *p. 414*
Pallas's Leaf-warbler *p. 601*
Hume's Warbler *p. 601*

Very locally fairly common summer migrant APR–SEP, scarce passage migrant (OCT) rare in winter

Woodland

crown subtly paler, no distinct stripe

pale stripe over eye long, wide, tapered

wingbar broad

1Y / Ad
ALL YEAR

Greenish Warbler

Phylloscopus trochiloides

4 | **L** 9·5–10·5 cm | **W** 16–18 cm

Very small, 'green' warbler; flicks wings and tail. Very like Arctic Warbler but legs thinner, tail longer. Call distinctive. **Ad** | upperparts pale green with greyish tinge. Head pattern and bill colour individually variable but usually dark eyestripe **does not quite touch bill**; **cream stripe over eye** extends in thin line over bill. **Thin, pale wingbar** diffuse, narrows inwards. Underparts unmarked whitish. Bill small, lower half usually **all-pale**. Legs dark grey-brown. **Juv / 1W** | like **Ad** but wingbar bright (thin, dull or worn off on **Ad** by JUN/JUL).

V | **Calls** bright, disyllabic "*tsi-li*" or "*chilip*." Song slightly jerky sequence of high-pitched notes, with a flourish at end.

FL ● | Short, rounded wings, medium-length tail. Light, often rather jerky, zigzagging action.

SSP. *viridanus* occurs in Europe.

Arctic Warbler | Green Warbler
Willow Warbler *p. 430*
Two-barred Warbler p. 601
Eastern Crowned Warbler p. 601
Pale-legged Warbler p. 601

Locally fairly common summer migrant
APR–SEP

Mixed or deciduous woodland, wooded parks

wingbar thin

Ad
ALL YEAR

Shape of stripe over eye similar on Greenish and Arctic Warblers, but stripes meet above bill on Greenish Warbler and usually fall short on Arctic, Green (and *Two-barred*) Warblers

Green Warbler

Phylloscopus nitidus

4 | **L** 10–11 cm | **W** 15–17 cm

Very small, 'bright green-and-yellow' warbler; favours trees, flicks wings and tail. **Ad** | upperparts bright greenish; underparts **yellow** (brighter than on Greenish and Yellow-browed Warblers), with long, pale yellow stripe over eye; throat and cheek **yellowish**. **Two yellow wingbars** (worn thinner, upper one broken but still visible by SEP/OCT). Legs dark grey-brown. **Juv / 1W** | bright green, with pale yellow wingbars.

V | High "*shri-wee*" or three-syllable "*chi-su-wee*" call (like White Wagtail (*p. 366*)), sometimes monosyllabic notes. Song lisping, slightly deliberate, jingling phrase, "*swi swi, swi-pi-tu, swish-too.*"

FL ● | Short, rounded wings, medium-length tail. Light, often rather jerky, zigzagging action.

Greenish Warbler | Arctic Warbler
Willow Warbler *p. 430*
Two-barred Warbler p. 601

Locally fairly common summer migrant
MAY–SEP

Mixed forest on mountain slopes

stripe over eye long, narrow

wingbar narrow

Ad
ALL YEAR

underparts distinctly yellow

435

Sylvia warblers

While sharing certain features, notably a short, thick bill, often peaked head/puffy throat, short wings and slim tail, this is a very varied group, but with closely similar pairs/trios. Some have a long, slender tail, which may be raised. Colours and patterns vary from almost plain brown (Garden Warbler) or grey (Marmora's Warbler) to boldly patterned (*e.g.* Rüppell's Warbler) or 'colourful' (*e.g.* Whitethroat). Sexes differ in almost all species. Calls are short and hard, unlike the softer *Phylloscopus* warbler (*p. 429*) notes; songs may be extremely musical (*e.g.* Blackcap) or rapid, scratchy, chattering phrases.

BLACKCAP

♂

Flight direct; heavier, less flitting than *Phylloscopus* warblers.

👁 Garden Warbler | ♂ - Marsh/Willow Tits *p. 464* | Sardinian Warbler *p. 446* | Orphean warblers *p. 444*

LC
LC

Blackcap *Sylvia atricapilla*

❷ | **L** 13·5–15 cm | **W** 20–23 cm

Small, stocky, slightly sluggish; wintering birds visit bird tables. Marsh and Willow Tits superficially similar, but have stockier shape and black bib. **♂** | plain grey-brown, paler below; round black cap falls short of gape; pale grey collar. **♀/Juv** | pale grey-brown, buffish below, pale undertail may show as streak; rufous cap. **♀ 1W** | has brown cap; **♂ 1W** | brown cap mixed with black.

V | Hard "*tek*" or "*tak*" calls; quick, anxious series if alarmed. Song is a fast, **fluty warble**, **vigorous and musical**; increases in speed and volume, becoming more strident, more forceful than Garden Warbler (which it may mimic). Faster, less varied and shorter than Nightingale (*p. 394*). Sings from bush to tall tree-top height; sometimes two or three together in brief skirmish, with prolonged songs.

Common and widespread migrant/resident

Woodland, thickets, large gardens

Five similar sspp. occur: *atricapilla* (widespread); *gularis* (Azores) long-billed; *heineken* (Iberia, Madeira, Canary Is.) small, dark; *pauluccii* (E Spain to S Italy, Mediterranean Is.) greyish; *dammholzi* (E Turkey) paler, greyish.

FL ● | Quite fast, direct, on rather narrow rounded wings. Slightly lighter than Garden Warbler

Marsh and Willow Tits (*p. 464*) are superficially similar to ♂ but are stockier and have a **black bib**.

MARSH TIT

Juv
MAY–OCT

♂ 1W
JUL–MAR

♀ cap brighter rufous than on Juv

♂
ALL YEAR

♀
ALL YEAR

Barred Warbler *Sylvia nisoria*

3 | **L** 15·5–17 cm | **W** 22–25 cm

SSP. *nisoria* occurs in Europe.

Large, long, heavy-bodied, square-tailed warbler; bill thick, thrush-like (*p. 383*). Moves slowly or remains still for long spells in thick scrub. ♂| upperparts steely-grey; **two white wingbars**, **white tertial tips**; **grey bars** on white underparts. Eye yellow, in dark face. ♀| like ♂ but bars on underparts more broken; eye generally duller, but often inseparable. **Juv / 1W** | **grey-buff**, paler below. Eyering pale; short pale line over **dark eye**. Rounded pale tips to coverts create two **thin wingbars**; tertial tips pale. Pale bars on rump; tail long, **dark with white side**. Underparts pale greyish; scaly bars on rear flank, particularly under tail.

V | Call a long, loud, fading rattle "*trr-rr-rr-t-t-t*." Song a rapid, rich, even warble, sometimes in rising, fluttering song flight.

FL ● | Heavy, on long, triangular wings; tail long, narrow at base. Direct, low, with full, even wingbeats (vaguely resembles Wryneck (*p. 337*)).

Juv / 1W
MAY–MAR

♀
ALL YEAR

♂
ALL YEAR

Locally fairly common summer migrant
APR–OCT

Heathland with tall bushes, scattered trees

Garden Warbler *Sylvia borin*

4 | **L** 13–14·5 cm | **W** 20–22 cm

Medium-sized, pale, plain brown warbler with blue-grey, slightly **thick and stubby bill** (for a warbler) and grey legs. Favours woodland, skulking in foliage. **Ad** | sexes alike. Upperparts pale brown. **Head plain** with thin whitish eyering and faint pale stripe over eye; diffuse greyish neck patch. **Juv / 1W** | like **Ad** with well-defined, pale feather edges on wing and tail.

FL ● | Quite fast, direct, on rounded wings; slightly heavier than Blackcap.

Locally common summer migrant
APR–SEP

Woodland, bushy clearings, thickets

Blackcap [♀] | Spotted Flycatcher *p. 449*

Two similar sspp. occur: *borin* (W, C & N Europe); *woodwardi* (E & SE Europe), which is slightly paler, greyer

NOTE: Ad (**ALL YEAR**) very similar but wings rather more uniform.

V | Call "*chek*" or "*tsak*," duller/more wooden than Blackcap's; alarm softer, 'chuffing' "*cha cha cha*." Song may be like Blackcap's but generally longer, simpler, more even with **fast, flowing/bubbling tempo**, less forceful finish. Sings from low bramble to tall tree height.

SSP. *borin*

1W
JUL–MAR

LC (Common) **Whitethroat**
LC *Sylvia communis*

3 | **L** 13–15 cm | **W** 18–22 cm

Medium-sized bright, pale, lively warbler with **rufous** on wing, **white throat** and long tail. Alert, perky; frequently raises and swings tail, dives into dense vegetation. Agitated male raises crown, puffs out throat. Broad **rufous feather edges** on wing (tertials have **broad, rounded** dark centres). Tail long, slim, **white-sided**. Legs **pale yellow-orange**. ♂ | head **grey** (browner AUG/SEP), with broken white eyering; eye pale; **throat white**. Back brown. ♀ | head grey-brown, cheek gingery; some nearly as grey as ♂ (may be almost indistinguishable in autumn). **Rufous wing patch**, back and rump dull olive. **Juv / 1W** | neat, bright; dark eye; wing covert pattern diffuse, tail side dull.

Three sspp. occur: *communis* (widespread); *icterops* (Turkey) slightly darker; *volgensis* (European Russia) larger, paler, upperparts greyer, underparts whiter.

V | Varied calls including nasal, slightly buzzy "*aid-aid-aid;*" longer, buzzing "*churr;*" rhythmic "*wichety-wichety.*" Song (in **bouncy, wing-waving song flight**, from exposed perch, or from cover) fast, **churring, scratchy warble** with fast rise-fall rhythm.

Locally common and widespread summer migrant APR–SEP

Heathland, hedges, overgrown ditches and nettle beds, bramble thickets

FL ● | Quick, jerky, lon tail twitched, showin white sides; direc flight light, agile, o short, round wing

♂

tertials edged rufous with **rounded** dark centres

long

♂ ALL YEAR

♀ ALL YEAR

Immature 'rufous' *Sylvia* warblers

Juvenile/first-winter Whitethroat, Spectacled Warbler and Subalpine/Moltoni's Warblers all have a brown or grey-brown head with a white eyering and contrasted white throat; grey-brown to rufous upperparts; broad or narrow rufous fringes on wing; long tail with white sides; pinkish or buff underparts. Focus on overall size; greater coverts/tertials pattern; primary projection beyond the tertials; eyering; detailed tail pattern and calls.

WHITETHROAT Large, long, bright; wingtip quite long; dark-centred greater coverts.

dark centres

Juv/1W
JUN–MAR

Whitethroat and Spectacled Warbler are similar. | ♀/Juv/1W – Subalpine and Moltoni's Warblers [♀/Juv/1W]
pp. 440–441 | Menetries's Warbler *p. 446* | *Tristram's Warbler p. 602* | Lesser Whitethroat *p. 445* | *Desert warblers p. 602*

Spectacled Warbler
Sylvia conspicillata

3 | **L** 12–13 cm | **W** 18–20 cm

Small, active warbler with **rufous** on wing and **white throat**; resembles Whitethroat, but smaller, with smaller bill, shorter wingtip, longer tail. Broad **rufous feather edges** on wing (tertials have **thin, pointed** dark centres). Legs bright yellow-orange. ♂| **blue-grey hood** with **blackish 'mask'** and white eyering. White throat with **grey centre** merging into darker breast. Greyer rump and rear flank. ♀| head buffish-brown, strong white mark above and below eye; **bright rufous wing panel. Juv / 1W**| like ♀ **Ad** but head duller, browner.

Two sspp. occur: *conspicillata* (mainland Europe); *orbitalis* (resident Madeira and Canary Is.) slightly darker.

V| Quiet, dry, **rasping call**: short "*drrrt*" or longer, quick rattle "*drrrr-rr-rr-rr-rr-rrr.*" Song high, quick warble, with whistling notes intermixed, often in quick, fluttery song flight.

FL ●| Direct, slightly whirring, on rounded wings; narrow tail dipped and waved.

Scarce, locally common, summer migrant MAR–SEP, locally winters (Macaronesian subspecies resident)

Low heathland, bushy stony slopes, saltflats

tertials edged rufous with **pointed** dark centres

short

♂ **ALL YEAR**

Both SSP. *orbitalis*

♀ **ALL YEAR**

SPECTACLED WARBLER Small, short, bright; wingtip short; plain rufous greater coverts.

plain

Juv/1W
JUN–MAR

SUBALPINE and MOLTONI'S WARBLERS (*p. 440–441*)
Long, greyish; wingtip short; back and wing dull.

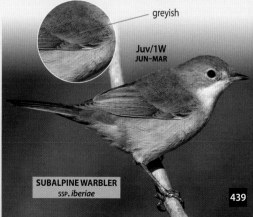

greyish

Juv/1W
JUN–MAR

SUBALPINE WARBLER
SSP. *iberiae*

439

Subalpine and **Moltoni's Warblers** are very similar and identification is not straightforward. The subalpine warbler complex in Europe includes three subspecies, sometimes treated as two species: **'Western Subalpine Warbler'** ssp. *iberiae* (Iberia, S France, NW Italy) and **'Eastern Subalpine Warbler'** sspp. *cantillans* (C & S Italy, Sicily) and *albistriata* (NE Italy, Balkans to W Turkey). Despite its similarity, **Moltoni's Warbler** is considered to be a separate species. ♂s| apart from tail pattern and call, differences are subtle and colours can look different, depending on light conditions. ♀s / **Juv**s| are all very similar; tail pattern and call essential for identification. (See table *opposite*.) **FL** ●| Low, quick, on short, round wings; rather long tail shows white sides.

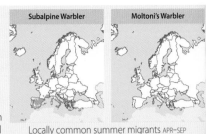

| Subalpine Warbler | Moltoni's Warbler |

Locally common summer migrants APR–SEP

Low bushy places, orchards, thickets, heathland

◉ Menetries's Warbler *p. 446* | Juv/1W - Whitethroat *p. 438* | Spectacled Warbler *p. 439* | Sardinian Warbler *p. 446*
Dartford Warbler *p. 442* | Tristram's Warbler *p. 602* [Juv/1W]

LC
LC

Subalpine Warbler   *Sylvia cantillans*

❸ | **L** 12–13 cm | **W** 17–21 cm

Small, secretive warbler with short bill, short wings, slim tail. Male raises crown and throat feathers to give large-headed effect. Very similar to Moltoni's Warbler (see table *opposite*) for summary of key features). ♂| upperparts **bluish-grey**; underparts pale brownish to **brick-red** or **pink** (obscured by white feather tips in autumn); **white 'moustache'**. Eye and eyering red. ♀ / **Juv** / **1W**| paler, browner than ♂ (old ♀s may look like dullest ♂s); underparts whitish or cream; slight white 'moustache'. **Red around eye** inside **whitish eyering**.

V| **Calls** important for identification (see table *opposite*). Song (all subspecies) **rapid**, a churring, stuttering warble with sudden variations in pitch and quality.

'WESTERN'
ssp. *iberiae*
♀
ALL YEAR

Females are identifiable to subspecies only by a clear view of the tail and a definitive call.

'WESTERN'
ssp. *iberiae*

'EASTERN'
ssp. *cantillans*

'EASTERN'
ssp. *albistriata*
♂
ALL YEAR

♂
ALL YEAR

'WESTERN'
ssp. *iberiae*

'EASTERN'
ssp. *cantillans*

♂
ALL YEAR

Identification of Subalpine and Moltoni's Warblers – summary of key features

	ID Criteria	Call	Tail pattern		Male
Eastern 'Subalpine' ssp. *albistriata*	FROM 'WESTERN SUBALPINE' WARBLER and MOLTONI'S WARBLER: tail pattern	**Dry, rolling "trret"**	White on 2nd outermost feather (T5) **extends up shaft** on inner web forming large white 'wedge'; **much white** on 3rd outermost feather (T4)	T4 T5	UPPERPARTS: pale grey; UNDERPARTS: pale brownish or buffish-pink extending to belly; WHITE 'MOUSTACHE': broader
Eastern 'Subalpine' ssp. *cantillans*	DNA often required to confirm subspecies	similar to 'Western Subalpine'			
'Western Subalpine' ssp. *iberiae*	FROM 'EASTERN SUBALPINE' WARBLER: tail pattern FROM MOLTONI'S WARBLER: call	Hard, clicking "tek" or "tek-tek-tek"	Small white tip on 2nd outermost feather (T5) **does not extend up shaft; little white** on 3rd outermost feather (T4)	T4 T5	UPPERPARTS: blue-grey, dusky or purplish; wings browner grey; UNDERPARTS: brick-red to deep pink breast and flank; paler belly; WHITE 'MOUSTACHE': thinner
Moltoni's Warbler	FROM 'EASTERN SUBALPINE' WARBLER: tail pattern FROM 'WESTERN SUBALPINE' WARBLER: call	**Dry, rolling, "trrrr,"** like Wren (*p. 372*), fading at end			UPPERPARTS: pale grey; UNDERPARTS: pale brownish or buffish-pink extending to belly; WHITE 'MOUSTACHE': intermediate

Moltoni's Warbler *Sylvia subalpina*

L 11·5–13 cm | **W** 18–21 cm

mall, secretive warbler. Very similar to Subalpine
Varbler (see description of that species (*opposite*) and
able (*above*) for summary of key features).

| **Call diagnostic: rolling, dry** "*trrrr*," like Wren (*p. 372*),
ding at end. Song a fast, chattering or twittering warble
n even pitch.

1W
JUL–MAR

♀ / **Juv** / **1W** | 'Western Subalpine' and Moltoni's
Warblers inseparable without **call**; 'Eastern Subalpine'
separable from Moltoni's Warbler only by **tail pattern**.

♂
ALL YEAR

♂
ALL YEAR

♀
ALL YEAR

Usually skulking, but will perch in the open presenting a distinctive profile.

SSP. *dartfordiensis*

NT
NT

Dartford Warbler *Sylvia undata*

2 | **L** 13–14 cm | **W** 16–18 cm

Small, short-winged, pot-bellied warbler, but can look slender, **long, slim tail** exaggerating size. Tail often but not always raised. Located by call or song, usually hard to see well. ♂ | upperparts **dark blue-grey**, browner on back when worn. Throat and breast **brownish-red**. ♀ | dull brownish grey, throat paler. Underparts pale orange-buff, belly white. **Juv** / **1W** | greyish, underparts paler; wings brown.

V | Call distinctive (but Whitethroat's (*p. 438*) can be similar) soft, buzzing churr: low, nasal "*chairrrr.*" Song fast sequence of whistles and buzzy notes in jumbled warble, usually from half- or fully hidden perch in gorse.

FL ● | Low, slow, direct, with **whirring** wingbeats; tail obviously **long and slim**, dipped or flicked.

Marmora's Warbler | Balearic Warbler
♀ /1W - Subalpine and Moltoni's
Warblers [♀ /1W] *pp. 440–441*
Tristram's Warbler p. 602

Very localized, scarce to common resident

Low, dense heathland, gorse scrub

Two similar sspp. occur: *dartfordiensis* (S England, W Europe); *undata* (S Europe) darker grey.

1W
AUG–MAR

SSP. *dartfordiensis*

♂

white throat spots quickly wear off

♀
ALL YEAR

SSP. *undata*

♂
ALL YEAR

Marmora's and Balearic Warblers may be near impossible to identify except by voice; separated by range when breeding. Both are small and keep to low, dense shrubs. Size, shape and behaviour much like Dartford Warbler. May look slim or rounded; tail often raised. Both are almost all-grey (females slightly browner on upperparts), with red eye and eyering and pale orange-brown legs. FL| Low, slow, direct, with whirring wingbeats; tail obviously long and slim, dipped or flicked.

👁 Dartford Warbler

Balearic Warbler *Sylvia balearica*

② | **L** 12–13 cm | **W** 15–16 cm

Compared with Marmora's Warbler: body smaller and tail longer. Bill slim, pointed, orange-red merging into black tip. ♂| small dark smudge through eye; throat pale grey/whitish. **Underparts pale grey, flank tinged buffish-brown.** ♀| like ♂ but flank tinged pinkish. **Juv / 1W** | like ♀ but duller overall.

Scarce, very localized resident

Low, bushy and rocky heathland

♥| Calls short, nasal "*churr*," soft "*tset*" or "*tret*." **Song** fast, repetitive, **grating** and mechanical, with rattling effect, quickly changing pitch.

LC Marmora's Warbler *Sylvia sarda*

LC **②** | **L** 12–13 cm | **W** 15–16 cm

Compared with Balearic Warbler: body slightly heavier, tail shorter, broader; **underparts darker grey without buff-brown tinge.** Bill short, broad, pink with black tip. ♂| dull black forehead and 'mask'; throat dusky grey; small white chin spot. ♀| like ♂ but upperparts faintly tinged brown. **Juv / 1W** | drab, flank tinged brown.

Scarce, localized resident

Low, bushy heathland

V| Calls short, harsh "*tchrit*," often running into quick chattering series, or richer "*tchrak*." **Song** short, fast, **liquid** outburst, less grating, more trilling than Balearic Warbler's.

Juv
MAY–AUG

♂
ALL YEAR

Juv/1W
JUL–MAR

♂
ALL YEAR

443

👁 Lesser Whitethroat | Blackcap *p. 436*

Orphean warblers are two very similar, fairly large warblers, separated by range. Adults are grey-brown, with a **dark grey cap, blending into blacker cheek** to create a **dark hood** contrasting with a whitish throat; the bill is quite long and strong, and the legs thick, grey. **♂Ad** | eye contrastingly whitish. Out-of-range vagrants are best identified by subtle details of undertail coverts and outermost tail feather. **FL ●** | Direct, fast, on rather long wings; long tail shows white sides.

Eastern Orphean Warbler showing distinctive white tail pattern and grey on undertail coverts (see *opposite*).

LC Western Orphean Warbler
LC *Sylvia hortensis*

❸ | **L** 15 cm | **W** 25 cm

Undertail coverts **unmarked buff**. Outermost tail feather has long **white streak**, extending over both webs. **♂Ad** | upperparts grey with little hint of brown. Underparts whitish, only faintly pink on breast. **♂1S** | like ♂Ad but eye dark. **♀** | like ♂ but slightly paler, upperparts browner. **Juv / 1W** | upperparts grey-brown; hood grey with darker cheek; eye dark. Throat white, underparts buff.

V | Call a dry, churred "*trr-trr-t*" or Blackcap-like "*tak*." **Song** a simple repetition of short phrases, "*tlui tlui tlui, tsee-ip tsee-ip tsee-ip*."

LC Eastern Orphean Warbler
LC *Sylvia crassirostris*

❸ | **L** 15 cm | **W** 25 cm

Undertail coverts white, with **grey, arrow-shaped spots**. Outermost tail feather has **short, broad white patch and white outer edge**; small white tips to next three. **♂Ad** | upperparts brownish-grey. Underparts pinkish-buff. **♂1S** | like ♂Ad but eye dark. **♀** | like ♂ but slightly paler crown and nape and browner back, buff (less pink) breast. **Juv / 1W** | upperparts grey-brown; hood grey with darker cheek; eye dark. Throat white, underparts buff.

V | Call a hard "*tak*" and harsh rattle. **Song** repeats rich, varied and melodious phrases.

1W
JUL–MAR

ssp. *hortensis* occurs in Europe.

♀
ALL YEAR

♂
ALL YEAR

1W
JUL–MAR

ssp. *crassirostris* occurs in Europe.

♀
ALL YEAR

♂
ALL YEAR

1W
EASTERN ORPHEAN

♂

WESTERN ORPHEAN
UTERMOST TAIL FEATHER
**(T6) long white
streak extends
cross both webs**

T6

plain
under tail

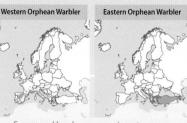

EASTERN ORPHEAN
UTERMOST TAIL FEATHER
**(T6) white streak
long outer web
nd broad white
ip to inner web** T6

grey
chevrons
under tail

Scarce and local summer migrants APR–SEP

Woodland, heathland with scattered trees

Lesser Whitethroat
Sylvia curruca

 L 11·5–13·5 cm | **W** 17–22 cm

airly small, sleek warbler with no bright
olours; resembles a compact, short-
ailed, greyish Whitethroat. Tends to be
ather skulking. Sexes look alike. **Ad** |
pperparts dull grey-brown, **no rufous.**
lead grey, **cheek contrasts with white
hroat. Legs blue-grey**; eye dark. **White
uter tail feathers. Juv / 1W** | neat, pale.
White eyering; dark mark from eye to bill.
light feathers dark brown, edged pale
rey-buff. Ageing difficult in autumn.

👁 Orphean warblers
Whitethroat *p. 438*

V | Clicking, hard "*tet*" or "*tuk*" calls, sharper
than Blackcap's (*p. 436*); also high "*see.*"
Song a low warble before loud, **wooden
rattle**: "*tuk-atuk-atuk-atuk-atuk-atuk-
atuk*" (sometimes rattle before warble, or
one element missing).

FL ● | Low, fast, on rather short round
wings; slender tail shows white sides.

Generally scarce
summer migrant
APR–OCT

Dense thickets, old
hedgerows

Ad
ALL YEAR

Both ssp. *curruca*

1W
JUL–MAR

Three or four sspp. occur: *curruca* (widespread); *blythi* (vagrant from Asia) paler head and whiter line over eye; *minula/
halimodendri* (vagrants from Asia) ('**Central Asian'/'Desert Lesser Whitethroat**') brown nape, buff flank, pale lores, short
wings/long tail, much white in outer tail, tit-like (*p. 460*) call. (ssp. *minula* is sometimes treated as a full species.)

1W
JUL–MAR

ssp. *blythi*

1W
JUL–MAR

ssp. *halimodendri*

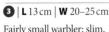 Sardinian, Menetries's, Cyprus and Rüppell's Warblers are similar to one another. | Blackcap *p. 436*
♀/Juv/1W - Subalpine and Moltoni's Warblers [♀/Juv/1W] *pp. 440–441*

LC Menetries's Warbler
LC *Sylvia mystacea*

❸ | **L** 13 cm | **W** 20–25 cm

Fairly small warbler; slim, dark tail often raised to reveal white underside. ♂| upperparts grey; cap and cheek dull, dark grey; **throat contrastingly bright white. Red eyering edged white.** Wing and tail browner. Underparts pinkish-white. ♀/**Juv**| paler than ♂, upperparts brownish-grey; head grey-brown; thick **whitish eyering**; throat dull greyish-white. ♂**1W**| underparts often pinkish-white. ♀**1W**| underparts pale grey.

V| Call fast, harsh "*chrr-rr-t*". Song a scraping warble with rolling churrs and whistles.

FL ●| Low, direct; wings short, rounded; tail slender.

Scarce, local summer migrant APR–OCT

Thornbush on rocky slopes

Two sspp. occur:
rubescens (SE Turkey) ♂ whitish throat;
mystacea (NE Turkey, Caucasus) ♂ pinkish-white throat/breast, white below dark cheek.

LC Sardinian Warbler
LC *Sylvia melanocephala*

❸ | **L** 13–14 cm | **W** 18–22 cm

Medium-sized, greyish warbler. Tail long, slender, blackish with white side. Elusive in low vegetation. ♂| grey with **blackish hood** extending over cheek, throat white; eyering red. ♀| drab, brownish-grey. **Hood grey**, throat pale greyish; eyering pale red. **Juv/1W**| brown, throat white against dark underparts; crown blackish on ♂, browner on ♀.

V| Call loud, hard "*tsek;*" distinctive **hard rattle** "*tuet-et-et-et-et-et-et*," often triple "*trra trra trra*." Song fast, even-pitched churr, often in fluttery song flight.

FL ●| Low, fast, with short wings and long slender tail (shows white 'corners' or **white-spotted rim** in low, fast flight to next bush).

Common resident/migrant

Heath, scrub, bushy/rocky places, gardens

Two sspp. occur:
melanocephala (S Europe) ash-grey;
leucogastra (Canary Is.) darker grey-brown.

♀ 1W
JUL–MAR

♂
ALL YEAR

SSP. *mystacea*

♀
ALL YEAR

♀ 1W
ALL YEAR

All SSP. *melanocephala*

♂
ALL YEAR

Rüppell's Warbler *Sylvia ruppeli*

L 14 cm | **W** 23–25 cm

Medium-sized, greyish warbler; adult male distinctive, other plumages more difficult. ♂ | grey, with **dark hood and black bib**, separated by **diagonal white stripe**. Eyering red. Whitish feather edges on wing; tail dark with white side. ♀ | grey; dark grey hood, white **white 'moustache'**; bib whitish, sometimes with dark spots. Alula blackish. **Juv / 1W** |
much like ♀ **Ad** but throat pale, upperparts browner, less white on second/third outermost tail feathers. Dull, whitish eyering; pale edges to blackish tertials. Pale tips to primaries wear off by AUG/SEP (when still fresh on **Ad**).

V | Hard "*tak*" and 'clock-winding' ticking "*ticticticictic*" calls. Song, often in parachuting song flight, short, dry, chattering phrases mixed with clear whistles.

FL ● | Low, quick, direct but slightly heavy, on short, rounded wings; tail narrow.

Locally fairly common summer migrant
APR–SEP

Dense thornbush, heathland with scattered trees

LC Cyprus Warbler *Sylvia melanothorax*

LC **❸** | **L** 13 cm | **W** 16–18 cm

Fairly small, slim warbler; grey with peaked dark cap and broad white 'moustache'; red eyering. Often cocks tail. ♂ | upperparts grey; **white streak** below black cheek. Underparts densely **spotted grey-black** with white feather edges (often blackest on bib); belly white with **grey 'V'-shapes under tail**. ♀ | brownish-grey; throat and breast greyish, softly spotted black. **Juv / 1W** | upperparts buffish-grey. Wings darker; blackish coverts and tertials with fine white fringes. Underparts pale grey, throat white, breast unmarked, undertail coverts spotted dark grey.

V | Call fast, harsh "*tch'k tch'k*" or "*tst tst tst tst*." Song a short, low, rapid, scratchy chatter.

FL ● | Low, fast, direct, on short, rounded wings; tail slender.

Very localized, scarce to common summer migrant MAR–OCT, some all winter

Bushy heathland

♀
ALL YEAR

♂
ALL YEAR

♀
ALL YEAR

♂
ALL YEAR

Flycatchers   9 species [4 vagrants (excluding American flycatchers) (p. 603)]

Flycatchers are small, slender or rounded, with long wings, slim tail and very short legs. They perch upright and are much less mobile in foliage than warblers, usually sitting still between aerial forays. Catch insects in wide-based bi that looks slightly thicker than on many warblers and fringed with bristles. **Flight** Long-winged, slender-tailed; brie flycatching flights from perch with short, quick, aerobatic chase. **Sexing, Ageing and Moult** Sexes differ in the six *Ficedula* species but are alike in the three *Muscicapa* species; juvenile always separable from adult. In *Muscicapa* species (*e.g.* Spotted Flycatcher), juvenile has a partial moult Jul–Sep and a complete moult in winter; adult has a partial moult Jul–Sep and a complete moult Nov–Mar, so 1st-summer identifiable only by fresher plumage. *Ficedula* species (*e.g.* Pied Flycatcher) juvenile has a partial moult from Jun–Aug and a partial moult in winter; adult has a complete moult from Jun–Sep and a partial moult from Jan–Mar, so first-summer often identifiable by remaining juvenile (faded brown) feathers in wing.

(NOTE: Eight species of American flycatcher have also been recorded; these are not closely related to the Old World flycatchers covered here and are included in this book in the vagrant American passerines section (see *p. 610*).)

Identify by overall colour | wing pattern | tail pattern

LC Red-breasted Flycatcher
LC *Ficedula parva*
3 | **L** 11–12 cm | **W** 18·5–21 cm

Small, short-legged flycatcher. Perches low down on edge of clearing, or moves restlessly higher in trees. Droops wingtips, **raises tail**. Upperparts dark brown; rump/uppertail coverts brown. **Tail black with rectangular white panel each side**, inconspicuous when perched, eye-catching in flight. Underparts buff to white. Bill pale at base. ♂**Br** | head greyish; **throat orange-red**. ♂**Nb** | head brownish, retains red throat. ♂**1S** | throat buff. ♀ | head and back pale olive-brown; distinct white eyering; throat pale. **Juv** | upperparts spotted buff; throat and breast peachy-buff, mottled dark grey. **1W** | like ♀ but dull, thin, rusty-buff wingbar and tertial fringes.

 Taiga Flycatcher p. 603

♂**Br**

White patches on the tail are most conspicuous when the tail is raised. Red extends onto breast on some males.

V | Soft "*tuc*" or "*tic;*" short, hard "*t't*" or longer, dry, "*t-trrt*" calls. Song deliberate, tit-like (p. 452), whistled phrase, "*sit-sit-sit-su-sit-su, sitsu-su-su-su-su.*"

Locally fairly common summer migrant
MAY–OCT

Mixed and deciduous woodland, often nea water

FL ● | Short, qui forays, revealir **white in tail**; mo undulati than warble

♀
ALL YEAR

1W
AUG–MAR

♂**Br**
MAR–AUG

white sides to base of tail

Spotted Flycatcher
Muscicapa striata

L 13·5–15 cm | **W** 23–25·5 cm

Medium-sized flycatcher; upright, short-legged, pale brown, quietly alert, mostly inactive between flycatching flights. Large head with flattened forehead, rounded nape; large, dark eye, quite thick, broad bill. **Long wingtip and tail**. Quick, jerky wing-flick and/or tail dip when perched. Sexes look alike.
Ad | upperparts pale, dull brownish; **crown streaked dark brown**. Wing dark brown with silvery-buff feather edges (Pied Flycatcher has whiter streak/panel). Underparts grey-buff or dull white, streaked grey-brown on breast; white under tail. Legs short, black. **Juv** | back and wings spotted buff; yellow-buff wingbar. **1W** | greyish-brown; loses buff juv spots by SEP.

Pied Flycatcher [♀] *p.451* | Garden Warbler *p.437*
Asian Brown Flycatcher p.603 | *Dark-sided Flycatcher p.603*

Juv
JUN–SEP

Juveniles soon replace spotted head and back feathers with plain ones.

Locally fairly common summer migrant APR–SEP

Woodland and edges of clearings, parks, gardens

V | Calls, from perch or in flight: thin, scratchy, slightly vibrant "*sirrr*" or "*tseeet*." Song variable, a weak repetition of calls, or longer, more musical, thin, squeaky phrases.

FL ● | Sits on open perch and flies out to snatch flying insect, **returning to same perch** or close by. Direct flight regular, with short bursts of wingbeats.

SSP. *striata*

1W
AUG–MAR
narrow pale tips to greater coverts

SSP. *striata*

Ad
ALL YEAR

Ad
ALL YEAR

SSP. *balearica*

Five sspp. occur: *striata* (widespread); *inexpectata* (Crimea) and *neumanni* (Crete to the Caucasus) paler, more grey-and-white. Sspp. *balearica* (Balearic Is.) and *tyrrhenica* (Corsica, Sardinia) are smaller, paler, warmer brown and less streaked, and sometimes treated as a species, **'Mediterranean Flycatcher'** *Muscicapa tyrrhenica*.

'Pied' flycatchers are medium-sized flycatchers. Breeding males are distinctively black-and-white: check head pattern/collar, extent of white in wing and colour of rump. Females and immatures are more difficult to identify: focus on details of the white wing markings (including the patch at the base of the primaries) and the colour/contrast of the rump. **FL ●** | Quick, flitting; long wings; often **drop to ground** to feed, flying up to **new perch**.

Pied, Collared and Semi-collared Flycatchers are very similar. | ♀ - Spotted Flycatcher *p. 449*

'Pied' flycatchers compared

♂ Br	Pied Flycatcher	Semi-collared Flycatcher	Collared Flycatcher
Head/neck	FOREHEAD 1 or 2 spots; WHITE THROAT **curves under cheek**	FOREHEAD white spot; WHITE THROAT **extends as narrow, broken band**	FOREHEAD broad white patch; WHITE THROAT **extends as broad collar**
Wing	WHITE PATCH extensive; WHITE PRIMARY PATCH small; UPPER WINGBAR absent	WHITE PATCH broad; WHITE PRIMARY PATCH **medium-sized**; UPPER WINGBAR **present**	WHITE PATCH very broad; WHITE PRIMARY PATCH wide; UPPER WINGBAR absent
Rump	grey-black	pale grey	**white**
♀ /1W	brown and white; **no collar**	greyish-brown and white; hint of collar (some birds not identifiable)	greyish-brown and white; hint of collar
Wing	WHITE TERTIAL FRINGES narrow; WHITE PRIMARY PATCH narrow, **straight, falls short of edge of wing**; UPPER WINGBAR absent/faint	WHITE TERTIAL FRINGES narrow; WHITE PRIMARY PATCH widens towards edge of wing; UPPER WINGBAR **present**	WHITE TERTIAL FRINGES **wide**; WHITE PRIMARY PATCH widens to broad rounded tip near edge of wing; UPPER WINGBAR absent
Rump	brown	brown	dull whitish
Call	sharp "*pwit*," sweet "*huit*," "*huit-tik*"	simple, flat "*hweep*"	sharp, emphatic "*pseeu*" or "*tsee*"
Song	hesitant, whistled phrase; several variants in irregular sequence	even-pitched sequence like Pied Flycatcher, but quieter, weaker	repeated short phrase of high whistles and full warbles

PIED FLYCATCHER

♂ Br
MAR–AUG

Individually variable: some with two white forehead spots; others with a single narrow patch.

All SSP. *hypoleuca*

Autumn males of all three species resemble female but have bolder white pattern on blacker wing.

♂ Nb
JUL–MAR

♂ Br
MAR–AUG
SSP. *iberiae*

♂ Br
MAR–AUG
SSP. *speculigera*

PIED FLYCATCHER Three sspp. recorded: *hypoleuca* (widespread); *iberiae* (Iberia) ♂ Br | has more extensive white on neck, sometimes almost complete collar, larger forehead patch and broader white patch in wing; *speculigera* (vagrant from Africa), sometimes treated as a species, **'Atlas Pied Flycatcher'** *Ficedula speculigera*, ♂ Br | has a very large white wing patch and extensive white forehead patch.

Pied Flycatcher
Ficedula hypoleuca

3 | **L** 12–13·5 cm | **W** 21·5–24 cm

See table *opposite* for key features. By far the most widespread 'pied' flycatcher, both breeding and migrant. **Juv** like ♀ but upperparts spotted buff, underparts grey-buff, throat edged grey-brown.

Locally common summer migrant APR–OCT

Mainly deciduous woodland; autumn migrants in trees, bushes near coast

no collar

♀ ALL YEAR

♂Br MAR–AUG

primary patch narrow, straight, falls short of wing edge

Semi-collared Flycatcher
Ficedula semitorquata

3 | **L** 12–13·5 cm | **W** 22·5–24·5 cm

See table *opposite* for key features. Intermediate between Pied and Collared Flycatchers; ♀/**Imm** best told by location; migrants difficult. **Juv** like juvenile Pied Flycatcher but short upper wingbar.

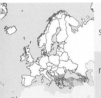

Locally fairly common summer migrant APR–OCT

Deciduous or mixed woodland

♀ ALL YEAR

short white upper wingbar

incomplete collar

primary patch widens close to wing edge

♂Br APR–AUG

Collared Flycatcher
Ficedula albicollis

3 | **L** 12–13·5 cm | **W** 22·5–24·5 cm

See table *opposite* for key features. Range overlaps with Pied Flycatcher, but rare migrant/vagrant in N and W Europe; autumn migrants difficult. **Juv** like juvenile Pied Flycatcher but collar/ wing/rump differences as for ♀/1W.

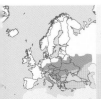

Locally fairly common summer migrant APR–OCT

Deciduous woodland, parks

♀ ALL YEAR

large white forehead patch

complete collar

white rump

♂Br APR–AUG

wide white tertial fringes

primary patch 'club-shaped', close to wing edge

Nuthatches, treecreepers and Wallcreeper

NUTHATCHES 6 species [1 vagrant (*p.615*)] NUTHATCH

Small, with large, wedge-shaped head, neckless shape, flat back and short tail; legs short but feet large; use strong grip to climb more freely than treecreepers and woodpeckers (*p.329*), in any direction, and hammer, stab and probe with pointed bill. Often cling head-down on tree trunk, with head raised at right angles. **Flight** Long head, round wings, very short tail. Strong but undulating, with bursts of wingbeats. **Sexing, Ageing and Moult** Sexes show minor differences, no seasonal variation; juvenile similar to adult. Adult has a complete moult May–Aug; juvenile has a partial moult May–Aug and again Jan–Jul.

Identify by head pattern | tail pattern | range and habitat

TREECREEPERS 2 species (*pp.457–457*) TREECREEPER

Small, slim, with long, spiky tail and fine, decurved bill; upperparts brown, underparts whitish; creep up tree with jerky, hesitant action, using tail for support (occasionally on rocks/walls, rarely on the ground). **Flight** Slim, with narrow head, rounded wings, very narrow tail. Weak, undulating, hesitant, with bursts of wingbeats. **Sexing, Ageing and Moult** Sexes and ages look alike. Adult has a complete moult Jun–Sep; juvenile has a partial moult Jun–Sep and again Jan–Jul.

Identify by calls and song | upperpart/underpart contrast | wing patterning

WALLCREEPER 1 species (*p.456*) WALLCREEPER

Small, uniquely patterned, round-winged, short-tailed, slender-billed; feeds on rocks, both exposed and under overhangs or in wet cavities, from low gorges to high peaks in summer, locally on buildings/bridges. **Flight** Extremely broad, rounded wings, short tail. Bounding, erratic, with fluttery wingbeats between glides. **Sexing, Ageing and Moult** Sexes look slightly different, small seasonal differences; juvenile identifiable. Adult has a complete moult Jun–Sep; juvenile has a partial Jun–Sep and again Jan–Jul.

Tits

14 species (1 Canary Islands only (*p.526*)) BLUE TITS

Small, lively, acrobatic inhabitants of woodlands, gardens, hedgerows and often reedbeds (one, Bearded Tit, is virtually restricted to reedbeds). Most are stocky, thick-necked, short-winged and short-tailed, less slender than most warblers, with very short, bluntly triangular bill (used for hammering seeds, excavating soft wood and probing into bark, as well as picking small insects from foliage and bark). Long-tailed Tit, Bearded Tit and Penduline Tit are not closely related to the others, each belonging to their own individual family; the first two of these are much longer tailed than the rest. Voice is often useful in identification, but in some species is remarkably varied. **Flight** Wings rounded, tail slim; some species have very long tail. Quick: small species weak, jerky, whirring between short undulations; larger species more confident, bounding. **Sexing, Ageing and Moult** The sexes look alike in some species but differ slightly or markedly in others, and juveniles are recognizable. In typical tits (*e.g.* Great Tit), adult has single complete moult May–Sep; juvenile partial moult Jul–Oct, retaining juvenile primary coverts. In Long-tailed and Bearded Tits, both adult and juvenile have a complete moult between May–Dec, after which ageing is impossible. In Penduline Tit, adult has complete moult Jul–Sep and partial moult Oct–Dec; juvenile partial moults Jul–Sep and Oct–Dec.

Identify by voice | head pattern | tail length

NUTHATCH

WESTERN ROCK NUTHATCH (p. 454)

EASTERN ROCK NUTHATCH (p. 454)

EYESTRIPE tapers

EYESTRIPE tapers

EYESTRIPE broad

TAIL black-and-white corners

TAIL plain

TAIL grey with darker corners

Rock nuthatches p. 454 | Krüper's Nuthatch p. 455
Red-breasted Nuthatch p. 615

(Eurasian) **Nuthatch** *Sitta europaea*

L 12–14·5 cm | **W** 22·5–27 cm

Medium-sized nuthatch, alert, bouncy, agile. Climbs up and down tree trunks and branches, searching and probing methodically, often hanging upside down; sometimes on walls and also hops on the ground. **Ad** | upperparts **blue-grey**, **black eyestripe**. Underparts buff/white, flank rufous. Rufous and buff mottling under tail. **Tail short, square** with **black-and-white corners**. ♂ | deeper chestnut flank and undertail than ♀ and **Juv**.

Distinctive: loud, clear, ringing or shouted whistles, often fast series, "ch'wit;" "hwit hwit hwit;" tit-like (p. 452) "sit" calls. Song clear "wheee wheee wheee."

L | Flitting/bounding, straight, quite high but no agility; heavy body/very short tail.

Common
resident

Mixed and
deciduous
woodland, parks,
gardens

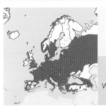

Ad
ALL YEAR

SSP. *asiatica*

SSP. *europaea*

♂
ALL YEAR

Eight sspp. occur sharing head and tail patterns but differ in size, underpart colour and size of bill. Much overlap, but on average: *caesia* (widespread) bill thick, underparts buff, flank darker; *europaea* (Scandinavia) large; bill blunt, underparts white, rear flank rufous on ♂, legs buff; *asiatica* (erratic migrant W from Russia) small and pale; bill pointed, underparts white, no rufous on flank, white line over thin eyestripe, legs blackish; *hispaniensis* (Iberia) small; bill pointed, underparts pale with orange-buff flank; *cisalpina* (Switzerland, Croatia, Italy and Sicily) small; underparts bright; *levantina* (S Turkey) underparts more pink, less buff; *persica* (SE Turkey) small; bill pointed; *caucasica* (NE Turkey, Caucasus) upperparts darker, whitish line over short, thick bill, underparts deep orange-buff.

both SSP. *caesia*

♀
ALL YEAR

♂
ALL YEAR

453

LC **Eastern Rock Nuthatch**
LC *Sitta tephronota*

2 | **L** 15–16 cm | **W** 25–30 cm

Large, pale nuthatch with **long, heavy bill**. Clambers over rocks, often clinging and probing under overhangs. Sexes and ages look alike. Upperparts pale grey; long, **broad black stripe** through eye **continues down beside nape**. Underparts white, becoming buff-brown on belly and under tail. Tail **grey with darker corners**.

V | Powerful whistles, "*tyew-tyew-tyew*" and nasal, Starling-like (*p. 379*) trills, "*tsrr-airp, tsrairp*." Song Thrush-like (*p.386*) "*tchow, chow-chow-chow chup chup*."

Locally fairly common resident

High rocky slopes, ravines

 Eastern and Western Rock Nuthatches are very similar. Nuthatch p.453

Two similar sspp. occur: *dresseri* (SE Turkey); *obscura* (NE Turkey) smaller, darker.

FL | Quick, bounding direct, on rounde wings; tail very shor

SSP. *dresseri*

Ad
ALL YEAR

LC **Western Rock Nuthatch**
LC *Sitta neumayer*

2 | **L** 13·5–14·5 cm | **W** 23–25 cm

Medium-sized nuthatch with **long bill** (longer than on Nuthatch). Often on cliffs, boulders, ruins. Sexes and ages look alike. Upperparts pale grey; black eyestripe **tapers** back from eye. Underparts pale buff; **no dark marks on flank or undertail** (can resemble Nuthatch sspp. in SE Europe, which are paler than those in W Europe). **Tail plain grey**.

V | Loud, liquid "*whit-wit-wit-wit*," sharper "*pliy pliy plit*" and grating, nasal buzz "*tcher*". Song a **loud series of repeated whistles** of varying pitch and speed.

Locally fairly common resident

Rocks, crags, ruins

Four similar sspp. occur: *neumeyeri* (S Balkans) large; *zarudnyi* (Lesbos, W Turkey) small, pale; *rupicola* (N Turkey to Caucasus) darker, fine-billed; *syriaca* (SE Turkey) pale, short-billed.

FL | Quick, slight jerky, on rounde wings; tail very shor

SSP. *syriaca*

Ad
ALL YEAR

Nuthatch *p.453*
Red-breasted Nuthatch *p.615*

Krüper's Nuthatch
itta krueperi

L 12·5 cm | **W** 21–23 cm

mall, fine-billed nuthatch of pine forest.
Jpperparts and most of underparts grey;
hestnut breast patch and vent. Tail
rey, with black sides and paler corners.
↗| **forecrown black** (well-defined **cap**),
white stripe over eye, black eyestripe,
white cheek. ♀| head pattern like ♂ but
lack on forecrown less well defined;
nderparts paler, with buff tinge. **Juv**|
ke ♀ but duller, with small breast patch.

▼| Very vocal: loud, nasal "*pyaa-ya-ya-ya-
a*" call. Song a short, 'shaking' "*shak-a-
hak-a-shak*" or faster, bouncy trill.

FL| Quick, direct, undulating, on rounded
wings; tail very short.

♂
ALL YEAR

Scarce and local
resident

Mostly
coniferous forest

Red-breasted Nuthatch *p.615*

Corsican Nuthatch
itta whiteheadi

L 12 cm | **W** 21–22 cm

mall nuthatch with rather short, slim,
agger-like bill; identify by **range**. Form
nd actions as Nuthatch; clings to bark
t all angles but usually in thinner outer
wigs, tit-like (*p. 452*). Upperparts grey,
nderparts buff; **head boldly patterned**.
↗| **black crown** and eyestripe, **broad
white stripe over eye**. ♀/**Juv**| head
attern like ♂ but eyestripe and crown
rey.

| Calls nasal, yelping "*tchew-tchew-
hew-chew-tu*" and harsh "*tscher-tscher*."
ong bright, fast, clear trill.

FL| Quick, slightly jerky, on rounded
wings; tail very short.

♀
ALL YEAR

♂
ALL YEAR

Rare, localized
resident

High altitude
pine woodland

455

| **LC** | **Wallcreeper** *Tichodroma muraria* |

LC ❷ | **L** 16 cm | **W** 27–32 cm

Unmistakable small, grey, short-tailed, short-legged 'creeper' with red in wings. Flutters/climbs around cliffs/rock faces with springy, bouncy action, probing for food with fine bill; perches with wings tightly closed, with frequent rhythmic in-out flicks of outerwing. Upperparts grey; wing black and **intense red** with **large white spots when opened**. ♂**Br** | black bib. ♀**Br** | black throat edged white. **AdNb** | white throat. **Juv** | brownish throat.

V | Call twittery "*whit-it-it.*" Song slow, piping whistles with little form.

FL | Bounding, fluttery, laborious with slow wingbeats. Floats on upcurrents on **broad, rounded wings**. Thin head/bill; short tail. **Crimson on upperwing**; outerwing black with rows of **white spots**. White spots and black underwing more obvious than red at long range.

Scarce resident/winter migrant

High peaks, rocky gorges; lower in winter, sometimes on buildings, bridges

Treecreepers are small, slim, brown-backed 'creepers' with a spiky brown tail and white underparts; sexes and ages look alike. Usually seen **creeping upwards** on tree trunk or large branch, with jerky movements, **using tail as support**. Occasionally on rocks/walls, rarely on the ground. Very difficult to identify, although **call and song are diagnostic**. Structural and plumage differences between the two species are subtle and summarized in the table below: **focus on the shape of the broad buff bar across the closed wing, and contrast on underparts. FL** | Weak, undulating, hesitant; obvious broad **pale band along length of wing** both above and below.

Short-toed Treecreeper

Common resident

Woodland, parks gardens

Four sspp. occur, most rufous in W: *megarhynchos* (W Europe); *brachydactyla* (S, C and SE Europe); *rossocaucasica* (Caucasus); *dorotheae* (S Greece, Crete and Cyprus), which is greyest, with whitest underparts and has slower song.

Treecreeper

Common resident

Mixed or coniferous woodland

Six sspp. occur, palest in N & E, darkest in S & W Europe: *familiaris* (Fennoscandia & E Europe to NW Turkey) underparts whitest; *britannica* (Great Britain and Ireland) darkest. Sspp. *macrodactyla* (W, C and S Europe), *caucasica* (N Turkey through Caucasus) and *persica* (SE Azerbaijan) are intermediate. ssp. *corsa* (Corsica) underparts buff.

♂**Br**
FEB–SEP

Nb

Nb
SEP–FEB

♀**Br**
FEB–SEP

SSP. *muraria* occurs in Europe.

Short-toed Treecreeper
Certhia brachydactyla

2 | **L** 13 cm | **W** 17·5–21 cm

(Eurasian) Treecreeper
LC
LC
Certhia familiaris

2 | **L** 12·5–14 cm | **W** 17·5–21 cm

hind claw shorter on
Short-toed Treecreeper (*left*)

SSP. *megarhynchos*

ALL YEAR

SSP. *macrodactyla*

ALL YEAR

SSP. *familiaris*

ALL YEAR

	Short-toed Treecreeper	(Eurasian) Treecreeper
Stripe over eye	Dull, indistinct in front, **does not reach** forehead	Long, broad, whitish/white, **reaches** forehead
Forehead	Plain brown	Streaked white
Throat	White; **contrasts** with underparts	White; **no contrast** with underparts
Underparts	Grey/buff; FLANK more rufous	Silky-white; FLANK grey/buff
PRIMARIES:	WHITE TIPS **large** REAR EDGE OF BUFF BAR **sharp points or 'sawtooth' against black-brown**	WHITE TIPS **small** REAR EDGE OF BUFF BAR **evenly stepped against black-brown**
Call	Strong, penetrating "***tsoot***"	Thin, long, faintly vibrant "***srreeee***"
Song	**Distinct separate notes**, without terminal flourish, "*tseet tseet, tseet-it eeroit-it*" (some mimic Treecreeper!)	Thin, high, quiet but far-carrying, sweet, **free-flowing** phrase with a flourish at end

457

Tits – compared

Most tits are readily identified by their head pattern.

CRESTED TIT (p. 460)

BLUE TIT (p. 463)

AZURE TIT (p. 463)

Dark-capped 'brown' tits
Five very similar species. (pp. 464–465)

SIBERIAN TIT

COAL TIT (p. 460)

GREAT TIT (p. 462)

LONG-TAILED TIT (p. 460)

Bearded Tit

LC

Penduline Tit

LC *Remiz pendulinus*

3 | **L** 10–11·5 cm | **W** 16–17·5 cm

Small, acrobatic, tit-like (unrelated to other tits), with very thin, pointed bill, black legs. **Ad**| back **rusty-brown**, dark purple-brown band across wing; underparts buff; head pale grey. ♂| rufous band above **broad black 'mask'**. ♀| narrower rufous band, narrow 'mask' often broken under eye. **Juv**| face plain buff, eye black; wing chestnut. Legs black.

Four sspp. occur: *pendulinus* (widespread) and *menzbieri* (S & E Turkey, Armenia) very similar; *caspius* (SW Russia) often has chestnut hood, black 'mask' and reddish-buff breast, but frequent hybrids/ intergrades occur; *jaxarticus* (winters S Turkey) small, pale; bill very fine.

V| Call distinctive (but beware thin, high Reed Bunting (p. 512) notes): a long, downward "*tseee*." Song descending "*tseee-e-ow-ow*" or chirruping notes.

FL| Tiny, rounded, wings short and round. Slow, hesitant, rather warbler-like, with short undulations, slightly zigzagging.

Generally scarce, locally common, resident/migrant

Riverside willows, poplars; in winter, marshes, reedbeds

Juv
MAY–NOV

♀
ALL YEAR

SSP. *pendulinus*

♂
ALL YEAR
SSP. *caspius*

♂
ALL YEAR

Bearded Tit (Reedling) *Panurus biarmicus*

L 14–15·5 cm | **W** 16–18 cm

Small, **long-tailed**, tit-like (unrelated to other tits); secretive and generally confined to reedbeds and dense, low vegetation. Acrobatic among reed stems; feeds on the ground/in reed litter beneath. **Bright orange-tawny** with **black and cream wing streaks**. Bill short, triangular, golden-orange. Eye yellow. ♂ **Ad** | head narrow-crowned, **blue-grey** with long, pointed **black 'moustache'**. Black under tail. ♀ **Ad** | head plain. White beneath long, brown, white-sided tail. **Juv** | back and tail streaked blackish: ♂ **Juv** | black between yellow bill and eye; ♀ **Juv** | dusky between dark bill and dark eye.

♪ | **Calls distinctive**: quite loud, metallic, pinging "*ching*" or "*p-chink;*" scolding alarm. Song a little-heard, soft "*tchin-tchick-tchray.*"

Penduline Tit

Scarce, locally common resident/irruptive migrant

Reedbeds; in winter, other wet fen vegetation

Three similar sspp. occur, minor differences in plumage: *biarmicus* (widespread); *russicus* (EC & E Europe to C Turkey) slightly paler; *kosswigi* (S Turkey) slightly darker.

FL | Short, low flights over reeds; wings short, tail long, waved; may fly up high and fast on irregular long-distance flights.

♂ Ad

♀ Ad

All ssp. *biarmicus*

yellow bill, dark eye patch

♂ Juv
MAY–AUG

dark bill, faint eye patch

♀ Juv
MAY–AUG

♂ Ad
ALL YEAR

♀ Ad
ALL YEAR

'EUROPAEUS GROUP'

Juv
APR–AUG

SSP. *rosaceus*

SSP. *europaeus*

Ad
ALL YEAR

LC **Long-tailed Tit**

LC *Aegithalos caudatus*

❶ | **L** 13–15 cm | **W** 16-19 cm

Small, acrobatic, tit-like (unrelated to other tits), with **long, slim tail** and **tiny bill**. Sexes look alike. **Ad** | black, pink and dull white; tail black, edged white. **Juv** | dull grey-black and whitish; face brown. Acquires **Ad** plumage after moult (from MAY–JUL, depending on hatching date).

V | High, thin *"see-see-see"* or *"si-si-si;"* abrupt *"brr-p"* mixed with dry, trilled *"ts-rreet"* and metallic *"pit."*

FL | Erratic, weak, bounding/flitting, on short, rounded wings; long slim tail.

LC **Coal Tit** *Periparus ater*

LC **❷** | **L** 10–11·5 cm | **W** 17–21 cm

Small, large-headed tit; **no bright yellow, blue or green**. Quick, acrobatic, often in mixed flocks. Sexes look alike; ageing difficult after AUG. **1Y/Ad** | upperparts olive-grey; **two white bars** across wing. **Underparts buff.** Head black, with **white rectangle on nape; cheek white; throat black. Juv** (see also *p. 462*) | similar to **Ad** but head and back tinged greenish, cheek and underparts yellowish.

V | Sharp *"tsooo"* or *"tsee"* calls and melancholy variations; short, sharp, hard 'spitting' *"split."* Song has emphatic two-note rhythm, *"see-too, see-too"* (resembles Great Tit but less strident).

FL | Fast, dashing, slightly undulating, on short, round wings.

SSP. *britannicus*

Juv
APR–AUG

Diagnostic white nape patch (may be hidden when viewed from side

SSP. *ater*

1Y/Ad*
ALL YEAR

👁 Coal and Crested Tits similar. | Great Tit *p. 462* | Marsh/Willow Tits *p. 46*

LC **Crested Tit**

LC *Lophophanes cristatus*

❷ | **L** 10·5–12 cm | **W** 17–20 cm

Small, buff-brown tit; **distinctive head pattern** and **pointed crest**. Sexes look alike. **1Y/Ad** | underparts buff; black eyestripe extends around cheek; **black throat and collar.** Eye red-brown. **Juv** | slightly browner on head than **Ad**; crest blunt; eye grey/brown, gradually becoming brighter.

V | Thin, trilling, rolling or purring note with distinct rhythm, *"p'trrr-up"* or *"burrur-ur-eet;"* also high, thin *"seeet"* notes. Song weak, thin *"si-si-si si-r-rrup."*

FL | Fast, dashing, slightly undulating, on short, round wings.

SSP. *weigoldi*

1Y/Ad*
ALL YEAR

'CAUDATUS GROUP'
ssp. *caudatus*

'ALPINUS GROUP'

Ad
ALL YEAR

ssp. *italiae*

Ad
ALL YEAR

Common resident

All kinds of woodland, bushy places, hedgerows, gardens

Fourteen sspp. occur, in three groups: '*caudatus* group' (N Europe) **white head**; '*europaeus* group' (S & W Europe) **black bands on head**, variably **pink** on upperparts; '*alpinus* group' (Mediterranean Europe) **greyer or browner** head and back, with or without pink. Intergrades make subspecific identification difficult outside normal ranges.

May show small crest.

* Subtle differences in wing coverts difficult to discern and ageing individuals is often not possible.

ssp. *cypriotes*

ssp. *ater*

1Y/Ad*
ALL YEAR

1Y/Ad*
ALL YEAR

Common resident/ migrant

Mixed and particularly coniferous woodland, thickets

Ten sspp. occur, with minor but noticeable differences in greyness of back, yellowish tinge on cheek and presence of tiny pointed crest on nape, but intergrades confusing: *ater* (widespread); *britannicus* (Great Britain); *hibernicus* (Ireland); *vieirae* (Iberia); *sardus* (Corsica, Sardinia); *cypriotes* (Cyprus); *moltchanovi* (S Crimea); *michalowskii* (Caucasus); *derjugini* (NE Turkey); *phaeonotus* (SE Azerbaijan).

* Subtle differences in wing coverts difficult to discern and ageing individuals is often not possible.

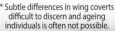

ssp. *cristatus*

1Y/Ad*
ALL YEAR

Locally common resident

Woodland, mostly coniferous

Seven sspp. occur, with minor differences: *cristatus* (N & E Europe) greyest, side of head white, black throat small; *scoticus* (Scotland) and *weigoldi* (Iberia) back grey-brown, flank bright buff; *abadiei* (W France) and *mitratus* (SC Europe) back rufous-brown, flank rufous-buff, side of head grey-buff, black bib extensive; *baschkirikus* (Urals) and *bureschi* (Balkans) paler and greyer.

461

Juvenile tits can be seen APR–SEP and are duller, typically yellowish, versions of the respective adults.

GREAT TIT

BLUE TIT

COAL TIT (p. 460)

LC **Great Tit** *Parus major*

LC ❷ | **L** 13·5–15 cm | **W** 18–20 cm

Large, boldly patterned tit; acrobatic feeder, also creeps through low vegetation and feeds on the ground. **Ad** | head blue-black with bold **white cheek**. Back green; wings blue-grey with white bar; **tail edged white**. Underparts pale yellow; **black throat extending to central stripe** (widens on ♂, tapers on ♀). **Juv** | dull green, grey, yellow-buff; cap greenish, cheek greenish-yellow. **1Y** | like **Ad** but retains dull **Juv** primary coverts until MAY/JUN.

V | Strident calls, "*pink*" or "*chink*," "*pink-a-tchee tchee*," "*tsweet*," "*tsi-uti-uti*." Song loud, see-sawing two- or three-note whistle: "*tsee-tsoo tsee-tsoo tsee-tsoo*" or "*tchee-tchu*" or "*tchi-too-tcha*."

FL | Strong, undulating, quite fast with short bursts of rapid wingbeats. Wings broad and rounded, tail quite long.

👁 Blue Tit | Coal Tit *p. 460*

Common resident

All kinds of woodland, parks, hedgerows, gardens

Eight sspp. occur, with minor differences (*e.g.* in bill size) not noticeable in the field: *major* (widespread); *newtoni* (Great Britain and Ireland); *corsus* (Iberia); *mallorcae* (Balearic Is.); *ecki* (Sardinia); *aphrodite* (S Italy, Greece, Cyprus); *niethammeri* (Crete); *karelini* (SE Azerbaijan).

1Y/Ad
ALL YEAR

SSP. *major*

SSP. *aphrodite*

♀
ALL YEAR

♀
ALL YEAR

Both SSP. *major*

♂
ALL YEAR

Blue Tit

Azure Tit *Cyanistes cyanus*

2 | **L** 13–14 cm | **W** 16–18 cm

Medium-sized, long-tailed, **blue-and-white** tit; active, acrobatic in foliage; like Blue Tit but tail longer, with rounded tip. Sexes look alike. **Ad** | **cap white**; tail blue with **white side and tip**. Blue-black line through eye, extending around nape; cheek and underparts white; broad white band across dark blue wing. **Juv** | cap and back pale greyish. **1Y** | like **Ad** but retains dull **Juv** primary coverts until MAY/JUN.

V | Calls a quick, sharp whistle and nasal buzz. Song "*tsi-tsi-tshurr-tsi-tsi-tshurr*" (similar to Blue Tit).

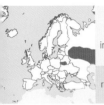

Scarce, local resident, occasional irruptive migrant

Woodland, riverside willows

 Great Tit | Azure Tit
African Blue Tit p.526

(Eurasian) **Blue Tit**
Cyanistes caeruleus

2 | **L** 10·5–12 cm | **W** 17–18 cm

Small, boldly patterned tit; acrobatic feeder. Appears 'green' or 'yellow', with **white cheek**; blackish chin, eyestripe and collar. **Ad** | **cap blue, surrounded by white band**. **Wing and tail pale blue**, white wingbar. Underparts yellow with **thin** dark blue streak. Sexes look similar but ♂**Br** | wings and tail vivid blue MAR–JUN. **Juv** | cap greenish; cheek pale yellow. **1Y** | like **Ad** but retains green **Juv** primary coverts until MAY/JUN.

V | High, sharp "*si-si-si*," frequent rhythmic "*sisi-du*" and "*tzisi-di-di-di*" calls. Song a slurred, trilled "*see-see-si-surrrrr*."

Common resident

All kinds of woodland, bushy places, hedgerows, gardens, reedbeds

---

Two sspp. occur: ***cyanus*** (E Europe) intergrades with ***hyperriphaeus*** (SW Urals), which is paler, greyer, less blue.

FL | Quite slow, undulating with short bursts of rapid wingbeats. Wings short and rounded; tail quite long.

Seven sspp. occur, with minor differences in size and intensity of colour, becoming paler eastwards: ***caeruleus*** (widespread); ***obscurus*** (Great Britain and Ireland), ***balearicus*** (Mallorca); ***ogliastrae*** (Iberia); ***calamensis*** (Greece); ***orientalis*** (SE European Russia); ***satunini*** (Caucasus).

FL | Quite slow, direct, with short bursts of rapid wingbeats; seemingly 'stops dead' on perch. Wings short and rounded.

1Y/Ad
ALL YEAR

1Y/Ad
ALL YEAR

1Y/Ad
ALL YEAR

Azure Tit × Blue Tit hybrids (and subsequent generations) range from like Azure Tit with less white in tail and hint of yellow on breast, to like Blue Tit with whitish underparts.

1Y/Ad
ALL YEAR

ssp. *caeruleus*

Dark-capped, 'brown' tits lack green, blue or yellow. Sexes look alike, juveniles duller (1Y may have duller primary coverts but often not visible in the field). **Marsh Tit** and **Willow Tit**, widespread; black-capped; identification requires several features, **plus call**. **Siberian Tit**, **Sombre Tit** and **Caspian Tit** have large grey/grey-brown cap; **identify by range. FL** | Quite slow, undulating with bursts of rapid wingbeats. Wings short, rounded.

👁 Willow and Marsh Tits, and Siberian, Sombre & Caspian Tits are similar. | Coal Tit *p. 460* | Blackcap [♂] *p. 436*

LC

Willow Tit   *Poecile montanus*

LC   ② | **L** 12–13 cm | **W** 17–20 cm

Medium-sized, black-capped tit.
1Y/Ad | long, **diffuse-edged** white cheek and distinct **pale wing panel**.

Scarce resident

Woodland, thickets, old hedgerows, often damp areas

V | Deep, buzzy "*tsi-tsi chair chair chair*;" single, buzzing "*chairr*" note (longer, more deeply nasal than Marsh Tit); short, sharp "*tsi tsi*." Song "*tsew-tsew-tsew*" or, rarely, a brief, melodic, warble.

Six sspp. occur: **borealis** (N Europe) and **uralensis** (SE European Russia) **grey upperparts**, **white underparts** and **wing panel**; *kleinschmidti* (Great Britain) brown upperparts, **rusty-buff** flank; *rhenanus* (NW France to N Italy), *salicarius* (NC Europe) and *montanus* (E Europe) brown upperparts, buff flank.

1Y/Ad
ALL YEAR

SSP. *borealis*

SSP. *montanus*

1Y/Ad
ALL YEAR

Marsh and Willow Tits compared | NOTE: orange features = overlap between species		
	Willow Tit	**Marsh Tit**
Distinctive calls	deep, nasal buzz	bright "**pit-chew**"
Bill	typically all-dark (a few with a pale patch)	most with a pale patch on edge of upper mandible
Black cap	usually dull	usually glossy
Chin/ throat patch	typically small, wide, inverted 'V'-shape	typically small, narrow, squarish
Cheek	long, white, diffuse-edged	white, well-defined
Pale wing panel	**distinct**	weak or none
Flank	white/rusty	dull buff
Flocking	often in mixed flocks	not often in mixed flocks

V | Bright, **whistled** "*pit-chew!*" Thin "*si-si*" notes; quick "*tsi-tsi-di-di-di*" and nasal "*tsi-nair-nair-nair*" (less harsh than Willow Tit). Song even rattle, "*chi-ip-ip-ip-ip*" or more ringing "*witawitawitawita.*"

1Y/Ad
ALL YEAR

SSP. *palustris*

LC

Marsh Tit   *Poecile palustris*

LC   ② | **L** 11·5–13 cm | **W** 18–19·5 cm

Medium-sized, black-capped tit. **1Y/Ad** | **well-defined** white cheek and **plain** wing with at most a weak pale wing panel.

Scarce resident

Woodland, parks, often damp areas

Five sspp. occur, slightly larger and paler in E: *palustris* (widespread); *dresseri* (Great Britain, W France), *italicus* (French Alps, Italy, Sicily), *stagnatilis* (E & SE Europe); *kabardensis* (Caucasus & NE Turkey).

SSP. *italicus*

1Y/Ad
ALL YEAR

Siberian Tit *Poecile cinctus*

2 | **L** 13·5–14 cm | **W** 17–18 cm

Large, brown, large-headed tit.
1Y/Ad| upperparts **brown**; underparts
buff-white with extensive rusty-buff
flank. Cap **brown** with pale grey sheen;
cheek white, broad; bib black, long
and wide (most extensive in breeding
season). Wing greyish with pale streak
on secondaries.

Locally fairly
common
resident

Old conifer and
birch forest,
bushy slopes

Two poorly defined sspp. occur, which intergrade: *lapponicus*
(Scandinavia to N European Russia); *cinctus* (NE European Russia).

V| Call "*pitzi-chay chay chay*" (like Willow
Tit). Song a buzzing/bleating "*chi-urr
chi-urr chi-urr.*"

1Y/Ad
ALL YEAR

Sombre Tit *Poecile lugubris*

2 | **L** 14–15 cm | **W** 18–20 cm

Large, greyish tit (resembles Willow Tit);
active in trees, bushes, around rocks
and walls. **1Y/Ad**| upperparts **greyish**,
underparts pale grey with little hint of
buff. Cap large, **blackish-brown**; cheek
long, triangular white 'wedge'; bib black,
wide.

Locally common
resident

Mountain forest,
thickets on lower
slopes

Three poorly defined sspp. occur, with only minor differences in size and
coloration: *lugubris* (Balkans); *lugens* (Greece); *anatoliae* (Turkey).

V| Churrs, fast trills, chirps: "*sip-ch-rrr-rrr.*"
Song a simple repetition of sharp, harsh,
grating/rolling note.

ssp. *anatoliae*

1Y/Ad
ALL YEAR

Caspian Tit *Poecile hyrcanus*

2 | **L** 14–15 cm |**W** 18–20 cm

Large, **brown-capped** tit; active,
acrobatic in trees. **1Y/Ad**| upperparts
grey with pale panel on secondaries;
cap dark grey-brown, tinged chestnut;
blackish bib merges into pale neck and
underparts; underparts grey-buff with
pinkish flank.

Very localized
resident

Upland
woodland

V| Calls thin "*zsit*" and nasal "*chev chev.*"
Song melancholy, rhythmic "*siuw-siuw-
siuw-su.*"

1Y/Ad
ALL YEAR

Shrikes 12 species [6 vagrants (pp. 604–605)]

Thrush-sized (p. 383), predatory birds of woodland edge, scrub, heathland and moorland, shrikes can be obvious, perched on treetops or wires, but spend long periods low down or inside bushes, when they can be elusive. All have strong feet with sharp, hooked claws (with which they grasp and carry prey) and slightly hooked bill. **Flight** Most species are short-winged and long-tailed and fly with bursts of wingbeats creating deeply undulating action. **Sexing, Ageing and Moult** Male and female differ in some species, but show little seasonal change; juveniles/first-winters tend to be browner and more barred. Most are long-distance migrants and have a partial moult Jul–Sep and a complete moult Nov–Apr (except Brown Shrike, with both moults complete). Juv has partial moult Aug–Sep, complete Nov–Apr. Ageing after the winter moult is impossible, except in some first-summer Woodchat Shrikes that retain older wing feathers. In resident Iberian Grey Shrike, adult has complete moult Jun–Oct, partial moult Feb–Apr; juvenile has partial moult Jul–Nov and again partial Feb–Apr.

Identify by overall colour | head pattern | head/back/rump contrasts | tail colour and pattern | relative proportions of wing/tail, and length of wingtip (primary) projection on closed wing

---

LC Red-backed Shrike *Lanius collurio*

LC **4** | **L** 16–18 cm | **W** 24–27 cm

Small shrike, upright, thrush-like (p. 383); perches on exposed twigs or inconspicuously on side of bush/hedge; easily overlooked. Broad, rounded head; thick, hook-tipped bill. **Long, slim tail** (often spread, flaunted with sideways twist). Male unmistakable; other plumages have hint of dark 'mask' and fine, crescentic bars on underparts (juvenile/1st-winter vagrant 'brown' shrikes similar, see comparison on p. 605). ♂**Ad** | crown and hindneck blue-grey; black 'mask', white throat; back red-brown; breast pale pink. **Tail black with white side**, rump grey. ♀**Ad** | upperpart/underpart contrast strong. Back rufous; **dark 'mask' from bill to cheek**; greyish crown, nape and rump; underparts white with fine brown crescentic bars. **Juv/1W** | upperparts rufous-brown, barred dark brown. Pale patch between bill and large, dark eye; **dark cheek** contrasts with pale throat. Crown, nape and rump **grey-brown**. Underparts whitish with crescentic dark brown bars on breast and flank. Tail dull to rufous-brown, underside **greyish**.

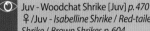

Juv - Woodchat Shrike [Juv] *p. 470*
♀/Juv - *Isabelline Shrike / Red-tailed Shrike / Brown Shrikes p. 604*

Scarce summer migrant APR–OCT

Bushy heathland, moorland edge, thorny thickets

V | Short, harsh notes. Song combine sharp whistles, warbles and faste chattered phrases

FL ● | Low, fast, undulating, on rathe long, narrow wings, with short glides; ta long, square

♀ Ad
ALL YEAR

Juv/1W
JUN–MAR

♂ Ad
ALL YEAR

GREAT
GREY
SHRIKE
(p. 468)
SSP. *excubitor*
Ad

LESSER
GREY
SHRIKE
(p. 469)
Ad

♂Ad
RED-BACKED
SHRIKE
♀

IBERIAN
GREY
SHRIKE
(p. 469)
1S/Ad

WOODCHAT
SHRIKE
(p. 470)
SSP. *niloticus*
1S

♀Ad
MASKED SHRIKE

Masked Shrike *Lanius nubicus*

3 | **L** 17–18·5 cm | **W** 25–26 cm

Small, slender shrike with rounded head, long, slender tail and small, hook-tipped bill. **♂Ad**| **black-and-white. Upperparts black, forehead, side of neck and shoulder patch white**. Throat white, underparts whitish, flank **pale orange**. **♀Ad**| similar to ♂ but upperparts dark grey. **Juv / 1W**| upperparts grey-brown, barred grey-buff; rump and tail dull black. Shoulder and wing coverts barred, white with black crescents, may create white patch after JUL–AUG moult. Underparts pale grey-buff, flank finely barred pale brown.

V| Calls a harsh "*chairk*" and dry rattles. Song a simple repetition of harsh, scratchy, rattling phrases.

FL ●| Relatively weak, scarcely undulating; wings short and round, tail long and slim.

Juv - Woodchat Shrike [Juv] *p.470*

Scarce, local
summer migrant
MAR–OCT

Bushy areas,
orchards

Although Masked Shrike is a
'slender' bird, individuals , like all
shrikes, may strike a 'rounded' pose.

Juv
JUN–NOV

♀
ALL YEAR

♂Ad
ALL YEAR

467

LC

Great Grey Shrike *Lanius excubitor*

LC ❸ | **L** 21–26 cm | **W** 30–34 cm

Large, thrush-sized (*p. 383*) shrike, **pale**, grey, white and black. Can appear as an obvious 'white spot' on distant bush-top, tree or wire, but often unobtrusive. Head rather large, bill thick. Wings short, tail long, slim (spread, tilted or twisted for balance). **Ad** | very pale, upperparts grey, underparts white. **Black 'mask'** with thin white line above; **wings and tail black-and-white**. ♀ slightly duller than ♂, underparts greyer with very faint dark barring. **Juv** | underparts faintly barred. **1W/1Y** | like **Ad** but wing coverts browner.

V | Short, harsh calls. Grating, chattering song; low, rambling subsong.

Five sspp. recorded: *excubitor* (widespread); *homeyeri* (SE Europe); *pallidirostris* ('**Steppe Grey Shrike**', sometimes treated as a full species) (vagrant from Asia), which is very pale, with a paler bill, weaker 'mask', larger white primary patch, longer wingtip and shorter tail; *koenigi* (Canary Islands – see *p. 525*) upperparts dark, underparts greyish, black 'mask' extends narrowly over bill; *algeriensis* (vagrant from Africa) mid-grey-and-white with bold black 'mask' and very short white line over eye.

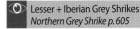 Lesser + Iberian Grey Shrikes
Northern Grey Shrike p. 605

Scarce migrant/ resident

Heathland, moorland, forest edge and clearings

FL | Bounding, sweeping up to perch; if repeatedly disturbed will move far away in long, high, swooping flight, sometimes gliding with wings half-closed. Hovers for up to 40 seconds or more. Long white band across outerwing, sometimes extending inwards; white sides to tail.

SSP. *pallidirostris*

1W

Ad

SSP. *koenigi*

1W
AUG–MAR

SSP. *excubitor*

SSP. *excubitor*

Ad
ALL YEAR

both
SSP. *pallidirostris*

1Y/Ad
ALL YEAR

1W
AUG–MAR

Lesser Grey Shrike
Lanius minor

4 | **L** 19–21 cm | **W** 28–30 cm

Medium-sized grey, black and white shrike. Compared with other 'grey' shrikes, slightly stockier, more bull-necked, often more bolt-upright; closed wing **slightly longer, more pointed, tip reaching beyond tail base**; bill thicker, blunter. ♂**Ad** | upperparts grey, underparts **pink**, throat white. Black 'mask' extends as **broad band across forehead**. ♀**Ad** | like ♂ but 'mask' brownish-black; underparts dull whitish. **Juv/1W** | pale edges to blackish wing feathers. Crown and back pale grey with faint bars; underparts plain; no forehead band but weak, blackish 'mask'.

V | Chacking call note, or series in alarm: "*tzek-tzek-tzek-tzek*". Variable, hesitant song has bubbling warbles mixed with screeching and sparrow-like (*p. 504*) notes.

FL ● | Scarcely undulating, unlike other 'grey' shrikes; wings rarely closed. White wing patches broader than on other grey shrikes; broad white tail sides.

♀
ALL YEAR

1W
AUG–MAR

♂**Ad**
ALL YEAR

Scarce and fairly local summer migrant MAR–OCT

Open arable land with scattered trees, orchards, heathland

Iberian Grey Shrike
Lanius meridionalis

3 | **L** 24–25 cm | **W** 30–33 cm

Large, grey, black, white and pinkish shrike, closely resembles Great Grey Shrike but **darker**. **Ad** | upperparts **slaty-grey**. White throat contrasts with **pink-grey** underparts. Grey crown contrasts with short, curved white line over black 'mask'. Can appear almost **as grey beneath as above**. ♂ | underparts pinkish. ♀ | underparts pinkish-grey or buffish-grey. **Juv/1W** | wing coverts fringed buff; underparts dull brownish-grey. **1S** | like **Ad** but may have browner primaries.

V | Call slightly trilling "*trreep*," nasal, buzzing "*nairr*" and longer whining notes. Song weak, irregular repetition of short warbling notes.

FL | Long undulations and short glides with wings half-closed. Hovers. White wing patch restricted to primaries.

Scarce, locally common resident

Heathland, bushy arable and drier stony land with scattered trees

Juv
JUN–AUG

Ad
ALL YEAR

LC **Woodchat Shrike** *Lanius senator*

LC ❹ | **L** 24–25 cm | **W** 25–27 cm

Smallish, stocky, relatively short-tailed shrike; often perches on wire, bush top. **Ad** | back dark with **white oval patch each side**; broad white wing patch (except on ssp. *badius*). Underparts white. ♂ | **black 'mask'**; cap and nape **rufous**; back blackish, rump paler. ♀ | back 'mask' interrupted by whitish marks, cap pale rufous; back and rump brownish-grey. **Juv / 1W** | upperparts 'cold' **greyish, rump whitish** with grey barring. Line of **whitish feathers**, each with black crescent, along shoulder. Underparts whitish with grey barring ('scaly' effect). **1S** | like Ad but with some browner wing coverts and flight feathers.

V | Quick, harsh, chattering calls. Song fast, rambling, chattering and grating notes.

FL ● | Fast, direct, undulating. Sometimes hovers. White patches beside dark back; white band on outerwing (absent in ssp. *badius*).

Juv - Masked Shrike [Juv] *p. 467*
Juv - Red-backed Shrike [Juv] *p. 466*

Scarce and fairly local summer migrant MAR–OCT

Bushy arable land, heathland, orchards

Four sspp. occur: *senator* (widespread) broad white primary patch, little white on central tail feathers; *rutilans* (Iberia) white in primaries reduced; *badius* (W Mediterranean islands) thicker bill, less black on forehead, white primary patch absent; *niloticus* (Cyprus, S Turkey eastwards) extensive white across base of central tail feathers.

♂1S
ALL YEAR

well defined black 'mask'

blacker back than ♀

no white primary patch

ssp. *badius*

brownish back

ssp. *senator*

♀1S
MAR–AUG

♂Ad
ALL YEAR

ssp. *rutilans*

Juv
JUN–AUG

ssp. *rutilans*

ssp. *senator*

greyer back than ♂

♀Ad
ALL YEAR

Corvids (jays, crows, magpies and nutcrackers)

16 species [3 vagrants and 2 introduced species (*p. 608*)], including 1 distinct ssp. often treated as a species. Large, strongly built birds with a short, arched bill and strong feet. Small prey may be killed with the bill, and food is broken up with the bill, but with little or no use of the feet. Typical crows are black or black and grey, with a colourful sheen. Jays (2 species), magpies (2 species) and Nutcracker are boldly patterned or more brightly coloured. Most species are social, at least when feeding, and Rooks are colonial nesters. Some species (*e.g.* the choughs, jays and Nutcracker) rely on specific habitats and foods, while others are adaptable and opportunistic. Hooded/Carrion Crows, for example, can be found in almost any dry habitat from towns to high peaks and, while they are solitary nesters, flock to feed on fields spread with manure and on sandy beaches exposed at low tide. Vocalizations are mostly simple and short, but may develop into longer, more complex, but subdued, performances. **Flight** Combines deep wingbeats and short glides, but differs greatly between species. Raven, Rook, choughs and others soar well and glide frequently; jays, Nutcracker and magpies have weaker, more laboured action. Crows are usually obvious and easy to see; jays much more secretive. **Sexing, Ageing and Moult** The sexes look alike in all species and there are no seasonal variations; juveniles are duller than adults but otherwise not very distinct. Moult differs between species but in most typical crows adult has a complete moult May–Oct (Raven Mar–Oct), juvenile has partial moults Jun–Sep and Jan–Mar. Jay and Magpie adult moults Jun–Oct, juvenile partial moults Jun–Oct; Nutcracker adult moults Apr–Aug, juvenile has partial moult May–Aug.

Identify by size and shape | head/neck/body contrasts | tail shape and colour | voice

BLACK CORVIDS COMPARED

JACKDAW (*p. 476*)

ROOK (*p. 475*)

Juv

CHOUGH (*p. 477*)

CARRION CROW (*p. 474*)

HOODED CROW (*p. 474*)

ALPINE CHOUGH (*p. 477*)

RAVEN (*p. 475*)

Corvids in flight

RAVEN
(p. 475)

CARRION CROW
(p. 474)

Juv

HOODED
CROW (p. 474)

ROOK
(p. 475)

CHOUGH
(p. 477)

JACKDAW
(p. 476)

ALPINE
CHOUGH
(p. 477)

MAGPIE
(p. 479)

IBERIAN AZURE-WINGED
MAGPIE (p. 479)

SIBERIAN JAY
(p.478)

JAY
(p.473)

NUTCRACKER
(p.478)

(Eurasian) **Jay**
Garrulus glandarius

2 | **L** 32–35 cm | **W** 50 cm

Medium-sized, wide-winged, broad-tailed, strongly contrasted corvid. Dusky pink overall, back greyer; wings **black-and-white**, **rump white**, tail black. Crown white, streaked black, **black 'moustache'**. Patch of **electric blue** on wing visible at close range. **Ad** | blue on wing closely barred dark. **Juv** | blue on wing with irregular dark bars.

Fifteen sspp. occur, varying slightly in size, but much overlap in shades of grey, rufous or pink, and some with black on crown (*): *glandarius* (N Europe to Urals); *hibernicus* (Ireland); *rufitergum* (Great Britain, France); *fasciatus* (Iberia); *corsicanus* (Corsica); *ichnusae* (Sardinia); *albipectus* (Italy; Balkans); *graecus* (W Balkans); *cretorum* (Crete); *glaszneri* (Cyprus); *samios* (Samos); *anatoliae** (Turkey); *iphigenia** (S Crimea); *krynicki** (NE Turkey, Caucasus); *hyrcanus** (SE Azerbaijan).

Hoopoe p.328 | Siberian Jay p.478

V | Subdued or loud 'mewing'; more frequent distinctive **harsh screech** of alarm or irritation – a hoarse, tearing "*shraairk!*"

FL | Wing broad, rounded; wingtips spread and pressed well forward in springy, elastic beats; head raised, tail lower. **Large white rump**. Quick and elusive in dense trees but flies higher between patches of woodland and during regular autumn movements.

Common resident/ migrant

All kinds of woodland, thickets, parks and large gardens

ssp. *rufitergum*
Ad

Ad
ssp. *krynicki*

Ad
ALL YEAR

ssp. *glandarius*

Ad
ssp. *anatoliae*

CARRION CROW

CARRION CROW

RAVEN

ROOK

HOODED CROW

Some Carrion and Hooded Crows (and a few Rooks and Ravens) have a prominent symmetrical white pattern on the wings and, on a few, across tail. This partial leucism is due to a genetic abnormality.

 Rook | Raven | Jackdaw *p. 476*
Choughs *p. 477* | House Crow *p. 621*
Leucistic - Pied Crow *p. 608*
Daurian Jackdaw *p. 608*

LC **Carrion/Hooded Crow**
LC *Corvus corone*

 | **L** 44–51 cm | **W** 85–90 cm

Large crow: **all-black** (ssp. *corone*, Carrion Crow) or **grey with black head, wings and tail** (ssp. *cornix*, Hooded Crow, which is sometimes treated as a separate species). **Crown broad, low; bill short, arched. Face black.** Mixes with Rooks when feeding, but not at colony; flocks usually less numerous than Rook's, but can be in the hundreds.

Carrion Crow: Ad | glossy black. Like juvenile Rook but plumage neater; bill shorter, black; basal bristles smoother. **Juv / 1W** | like **Ad** but duller, brownish. **1S** | like **Ad** with some worn/brown feathers in wing.

Hooded Crow: Ad | pale grey with black head, wings and tail. **Juv / 1W** | like **Ad** but duller. **1S** | like **Ad** with some worn/brown feathers in wing.

V | Calls varied, not so 'musical' as Rook: hard, rough "*kraang-kraang-kraang*" or "*kraaa*," and harder, faster "*dairr dairr*" or soft "*krr-krr-krr*."

FL | Short head/neck/bill; short, **square tail**. Wings oblong, broad at tip, held rather straight. Soars less than Rook; direct flight more even and direct.

In addition to all-black **Carrion Crow**, ssp. *corone* (widespread), three similar 'Hooded' sspp. occur: *cornix* (widespread); *sharpii* (far E/SE Europe, Balkans, Crete, S Italy, Sicily, Sardinia) paler; *pallescens* (S Turkey, Cyprus) smaller, palest.

1Y/Ad
ALL YEAR

In narrow zone of overlap, Hooded and Carrion Crows interbreed and intergrades are frequent. These have 'shadow' of Hooded Crow pattern, but grey areas darker or streaked black; hybrid patterns may persist for generations.

NOTE: Mixture of old, worn, brown feathers and new blacker ones in wing and tail.

Common resident/ migrant

Cliffs from coast to high peaks, moorland, heathland, forested areas, pastureland

HOODED CROW
ssp. *cornix*

1S
MAY–JUL

CARRION CROW
ssp. *corone*

Ad
ALL YEAR

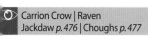

Carrion Crow | Raven
Jackdaw *p.476* | Choughs *p.477*

Rook *Corvus frugilegus*

L 41–49 cm | **W** 80–90 cm

arge, black crow. **Crown peaked; bill ong, tapered, wide-based.** Often **loose lank/belly feathers. Social,** flocks up o 1,000s, often with Jackdaws. Nests n **treetop colonies. Ad** black, glossed urple; **face grey-buff,** bill grey. **Juv** face lack.

Deep caws/croaks, "*craa-craa-craa;*" oud, high "*crroo-crroo-crroo;*" choked rumpeting notes, musical squeals; nechanical rattle in flight.

Common resident/migrant

Farmland, moorland edge, woods, copses, low coastal cliffs with grassy tops, suburbs

FL Head/bill long; tail **long, rounded** (see Raven); wings tapered, often swept back. Aerobatic; **often soars** very high. May use slow, deep beats, or glide with wings raised in 'V'.

CARRION CROW — smooth, evenly curved bill

Juv APR–JAN — bulging nasal bristles; slim-tipped bill

Ad ALL YEAR

SSP. *frugilegus* occurs in Europe.

Carrion Crow | Rook
Brown-necked Raven *p.608*
Fan-tailed Raven *p.608*

Five very similar sspp. occur: *corax* (widespread) purplish; *varius* (Iceland, Faroe Islands) duller; *hispanus* (Iberia, Mediterranean islands) bluer; *laurencei* (E Greece, Turkey, Cyprus) neck browner; *canariensis* (Canary Islands) smallest, short-billed, black-brown.

(Common) Raven *Corvus corax*

L 54–67 cm | **W** 125–135 cm

ery large, black crow (size can be hard o judge in isolation). Crown rounded, eaked or flat; spiky 'beard' may be uffed out; **bill long, deeply arched. oice distinctive.** Flocks (10s–100+ here common). **Ad** all-black. **Juv / 1Y** ke Ad but duller, more brownish.

Loud, abrupt, hollow "*prruk-prruk-rruk;*" ringing "*tonk!*" and many other calls ncluding "*quak quak*" in synchrony from airs; quiet whistles, rattles, clicks.

L Long, tapered wings often **swept ack** or **angled down.** Tail long, ounded or **diamond-shaped** when pread. **Soars expertly.** Diagnostic nomentary roll onto back.

Common resident/migrant

Farmland, mountain and moorland areas, woodland edge, lowland pasture, beaches, cliffs

deep-based, arched bill

close up, darker feather edges give 'scaly' effect

NOTE: 1st-year birds have mixed glossy black and dark brown (juvenile) wing coverts and tertials.

SSP. *corax*

1Y/Ad ALL YEAR

475

JACKDAW
ssp. *monedula*

CHOUGH
ssp. *barbarus*

ALPINE CHOUGH
ssp. *graculus*

Alpine Chough, Chough and Jackdaw are similar. | Carrion Crow *p. 474* | Rook *p. 475*

Carrion Crow *p. 474* | Rook *p. 475*

 LC
LC # (Eurasian) **Jackdaw**
Corvus monedula

❷ | **L** 30–34 cm | **W** 70–75 cm

Three sspp. occur: *spermologus* (W, C & S Europe); *monedula* ('Nordic Jackdaw') (Scandinavia) greyer, side of neck **pale grey to whitish**; *soemmerringii* (E/SE Europe) strong whitish collar.

Small, grey-black crow; shape resembles a Feral Pigeon (*p. 241*) but stouter, longer-legged and more upright; head rounded but broad; **bill short and stout.** Flocks up to 100s. **Ad** | grey-black; **face and cap black** against **pale grey shawl.** Eye whitish. **Juv** | duller than Ad; dark cap ill-defined. **1Y** | glossy wing coverts, browner flight feathers and tail.

V | Metallic "*jak*," "*chak*," "*kya*," but very varied: single bird can create prolonged, rapid, bouncy cacophony, with short, sharp, barked, shouted or squeaky notes. Noisy, quick-fire, staccato chorus from flocks going to roost.

FL | Wings slightly rounded, often slightly curled back with **bulging** front edge; smoother, rounder shapes than Rook or choughs. Quick, with **flickery beats**; frequently soars, groups swirling out from trees or cliff, turning in synchrony. Mixes with Rooks, crows and pigeons.

Common resident/migrant

Arable and pasture land, woodland, parks, coastal cliffs, quarries, suburban areas

Juv
MAY–SEP

ssp. *soemmerringii*

1Y/Ad
ALL YEAR

Ad
ALL YEAR

ssp. *spermologus*

Ad
ALL YEAR

ssp. *monedula*

Alpine (Yellow-billed) Chough *Pyrrhocorax graculus*

L 37–39 cm | **W** 75–85 cm

Medium-sized, all-black, social crow, like Chough but **rounder profile**, smaller, rounder head and **longer tail** extending beyond closed wingtip (tail does not extend beyond wingtip on Chough). **Ad** glossy black. **Bill bright pale yellow**, legs red. **Juv** dull, with dark legs and bill-tip.

Sharp squealing notes resemble Chough, but frequent swizzling, **shrill, high whistling calls**, "*tsree,*" "*shriiiii,*" "*shirrish.*"

FL Wings **rounded** (less square-ended than Chough's), and tail long, **rounded**. **Wing coverts blacker than flight feathers**. Often large flocks (100s), swirling in the air or foraging widely over upland grassland. Flies with bounding action and easy, buoyant glides, like Chough but larger flocks may be tighter, spiralling, with distinctive calls.

Two very similar sspp. occur: *graculus* (widespread); *digitatus* (Turkey) stronger bill and feet.

Ad
ALL YEAR

SSP. *graculus*

Locally common resident

Alpine pastures, lower cliffs and gorges

(Red-billed) **Chough** *Pyrrhocorax pyrrhocorax*

L 37–41 cm | **W** 75–90 cm

Medium-sized, **glossy black** crow with long body and long, slim, **downcurved bill**. Moves with bouncy hops and walk, **long wingtips** dipped and raised, head often bowed. Tail falls short of closed wingtip on ♂; equal on ♀ (tail extends beyond wingtip on Alpine Chough). Flocks typically 10–100. **Ad** black, with green or blue gloss; **bill and legs red**. **Juv** compared with **Ad**, bill shorter, orange; legs duller. **1W** like **Ad** but wings browner.

Ringing, piercing, shouted "*chee-aah,*" "*chaaa,*" "*chrri*" (similar to Jackdaw but more emphatic).

FL Wings broad, **square-ended**, deeply fingered, two-tone **black with greyer flight feathers beneath**; head quite long and narrow; tail short and square. Dives with half-closed wings, often followed by steep, bounding rise.

Four sspp. occur: *erythroramphos* (widespread) large, greenish gloss; *pyrrhocorax* (Great Britain and Ireland) smallest, blue gloss; *barbarus* (Canary Islands) long-winged, greenish gloss; *docilis* (SE Europe) small-billed, dull greenish gloss.

♂ Ad
ALL YEAR

SSP. *erythroramphos*

Scarce, locally common resident

Coastal and inland cliffs, deep shafts and quarries, adjacent grassy areas and high peaks

👁 Starling *p.379*

LC **Nutcracker**
LC *Nucifraga caryocatactes*

2 | **L** 32–34 cm | **W** 40-50 cm

Medium-sized, large-headed, upright, corvid; stocky but short-tailed, often on high, open perch. **Ad** | brown with **blacker cap**, large **white patch under tail**. **White spots** all over face, neck and body, but wings dark, plain, glossy. Tail has broad white tip. **Juv** | like **Ad** but has broad white bar on duller wing. **1Y** | black wing coverts include some **Juv** feathers with a thin white line across tip (minute triangle on **Ad**).

V | Calls low, rasping "*tchairr;*" higher, louder "*trair trair trair;*" thin, squeaky mew.

FL | Heavy-bodied; wing broad and rounded, tail short and broad. Quick, floppy, deep wingbeats and short glides. May drop from high perch to ground with closed wings.

Two sspp. occur: ***caryocatactes*** (Europe) has a slightly shorter and thicker bill than 'slender-billed' ***macrorhynchos*** (Urals eastwards), which sometimes spreads westwards in winter if pine cone crop fails.

Locally common resident, occasional irruptive migrant

High altitude pine forests, tree-lined meadows, thickets

'slender-billed'
ssp. *macrorhynchos*

1Y
ALL YEAR

'thick-billed'
ssp. *caryocatactes*

Ad

Ad
ALL YEAR

👁 Jay *p.473*

LC **Siberian Jay**
LC *Perisoreus infaustus*

2 | **L** 25–31 cm | **W** 40-48 cm

Small, round-headed, very short-billed and rather long-tailed corvid. Often clings beneath branches when feeding. **Ad** | brownish-grey with **rufous patches on wing and side and base of tail**. Dusky cap above large black eye; small white spot above base of bill. **Juv** | plumage slightly duller and looser than **Ad**.

V | Short mewing "*myayk*" and whistled "*kui*" call. Song is a chattering twitter.

Two similar sspp. occur: *infaustus* (Scandinavia eastwards), rufous; *rogosowi* (NE European Russia), greyer.

FL | Short, round wing and fairly long ta Olive-grey with brig orange-rusty are in outerwing and c rump and sides of ta Lightweight glide often circles down perc

Ad

Ad
ALL YEAR

ssp. *infaustus*

Scarce, fairly local resident

Old and often dense coniferous forest

Pied Crow p.608

Eurasian) **Magpie** *Pica pica*

L 40–51 cm (incl. tail 20–30 cm) |
W 56–61 cm

Unmistakable large, **long-tailed, black-and-white** corvid; usually solitary or in pairs, sometimes up to 40. **Ad** head and breast dull black; wings glossed blue; **white shoulder patch and belly**. Long tail black, glossed green, blue and purple. **uv** has shorter tail than **Ad** but still unmistakable.

♪ Loud, chattering, staccato "*cha-cha-cha*" calls, and variations.

Common resident

Farmland, villages, gardens, parks, woodland edge, heathland

Three sspp. occur: *pica* (widespread) rump grey, mixed with white and black; *fennorum* (N Scandinavia eastwards) slightly larger, with a little more white on rump and wing; *melanotos* (Iberia) rump black; sometimes bluish patch behind eye.

FL Wing short, rounded; tail very long. **White wingtips**; white shoulders, black back. Steady, quick wingbeats and steep dives to perch characteristic.

Ad

Both ssp. *pica*

Ad
ALL YEAR

berian Azure-winged Magpie *Cyanopica cooki*

L 34–36 cm | **W** 45-50 cm

airly large, slender, long-tailed, social orvid. **Ad** body pink-beige with contrasting **glossy black cap** and **white throat**. Wing and long, slender tail **pale late-blue** (clearer blue in good light). **uv** browner than **Ad**, cap speckled with white. **1W** like **Ad** but with mixture of d (dull) and new (bright) wing and tail athers.

♪ Loud, rattling alarm and long, rising, asal notes.

Locally fairly common resident

Woodland edge, orchards, heathland with scattered trees, especially pines

FL Wing broad and rounded, tail long, narrow, with wedge-shaped tip. Small, lively groups move quickly through trees or bounce briefly on ground; fly from tree to tree with quick, flappy, undulating action, sweeping up to perches.

Ad

Ad
ALL YEAR

Finches and sparrows are small birds

characterized by short, triangular bill, short legs, broad, rounded or flat-topped head, broad wings and short, usually notched, tail. All hop two-footed or shuffle (like buntings (*p. 508*), but unlike larks and pipits (*p. 348*)).

Flight Whirring wingbeats, often in bursts between bounds with closed wings, giving undulating effect. Flocks may be loose (*e.g.* Chaffinch, sparrows) or tightly synchronized (*e.g.* Siskin).

FINCHES 33 species (4 restricted to Macaronesian islands) [3 vagrants] (*pp. 492–484, 527–529, 606, 616*)

Resident or migratory; some semi-colonial breeders are social all year round, others form flocks (often of mixed species) outside the breeding season. Insect-eaters in summer, but bills adapted to cope with seeds at other times, from soft seeds (Goldfinch, Serin) and buds (Bullfinch) to hard fruit stones (Hawfinch) and seeds within large, hard, cones (crossbills). Some are accomplished singers (often in distinctive display flight).

Identify by bill shape/colour | overall colour and pattern | head pattern | wing and tail pattern | colour of rump | calls and song

SPARROWS 8 species (*pp. 504–507*)

Mostly resident but some (*e.g.* Spanish Sparrow, Dead Sea Sparrow) are migratory in some areas. Some species are social, forming large, dense flocks (*e.g.* House Sparrow), and some are colonial breeders (*e.g.* Spanish Sparrow). Essentially finch-like; some have striking breeding patterns in male, but rock sparrows are less distinct. Songs are less developed than those of finches.

Identify by head pattern | tail pattern

upper mandible generally smaller than lower; backward point at gape

REED BUNTING

BRAMBLING (FINCH)

backward point at base

HOUSE SPARROW

square at base

Sexing, Ageing and Moult

FINCHES Sexes usually look different; seasonal changes may be marked. Juvenile differs from adult until partial (body) moult in Jul–Sep, in some species still identifiable during first half of the following year (in many by minor differences in feather pattern and structure). Adult has a complete moult within the period Jul–Oct, but breeding colours are revealed through loss of pale feather tips in late winter–spring.

SPARROWS Sexes differ in some, not so in rock sparrows; seasonal changes slight. Juvenile looks like female, moult Jun–Sep. Adult moults Jun–Sep or Oct, when pale feather fringes obscure patterns. Breeding colours show when pale fringes fall away in spring. Timing varies according to breeding season and success, and individually, so different stages may be seen at any one time.

Adults and juveniles have a single moult each year.	Post-juvenile moult →	Adult moult
	Flight feathers and some coverts retained for a full year, becoming very abraded.	Complete moult after breeding (body moult may rarely continue into spring); breeding plumage assumed by abrasion/disintegration of dull feather tips.

Juv
APR–SEP

♂

♀

Ad
SEP–JAN (fresh)
JAN–AUG (worn)

♂

SISKIN

1W
AUG–JUN

The types of finches

Finches fall into several groups and can, with experience, be told apart by their frequent flight calls or by their songs.

REDPOLL

GREENFINCH

GOLDFINCH

Greenfinch, **Linnet** and **Twite** all have pale (yellow or white) streaks on the outer edges of their wing and tail feathers. Greenfinch is uniquely largely plain, unstreaked green in most plumages. **Siskin** (*opposite*) is green but strongly streaked, with boldly barred wings. **Goldfinch** and **Siskin**, and the streaky brown **Redpoll**, cling to tall stems and seedheads to feed, while **Linnet** and **Twite** stand on the ground and reach up to seedheads with their bill, or pull them down under one foot. **Siskin**, **Redpoll** and **Goldfinch** also feed in treetops.

CHAFFINCH

HAWFINCH

BULLFINCH

COMMON CROSSBILL

Chaffinch and **Brambling** are remarkably similar in shape, structure and pattern but differ in colour details. They tend to feed on the ground, or take caterpillars from foliage in summer.

Hawfinch is large-billed, able to deal with tough foods like cherry stones, but also feeds a good deal on beech mast under trees. **Bullfinch** is a more secretive feeder on soft buds, shoots and berries.

Crossbills are treetop feeders, prising open scales of cones with crossed bill tips. When they fly off, they can be extremely vocal.

GREAT ROSEFINCH

TRUMPETER FINCH

WHITE-THROATED SPARROW

Trumpeter Finch (and rock sparrows) inhabit cliffs and boulder-strewn slopes in warm regions, perching on the ground and drawing attention by frequent calls. **Rosefinches** include birds of harsher mountain conditions in the east of Europe, such as **Great Rosefinch**.

AMERICAN FINCHES & 'SPARROWS'
Vagrants from North America (see *pp. 616–617*). American 'sparrows' are related to Old World buntings.

Selected finches and sparrows in flight

GOLDFINCH
(p. 487)

Ad

♀

♂

CHAFFINCH
(p. 500)

SISKIN
(p. 488)

♂

♂

BRAMBLING
(p. 500)

♂

CITRIL FINCH
(p. 491)

♂

Ad

SERIN
(p. 489)

♀

GREENFINCH
(p. 490)

♂

♀

♂

♀

COMMON
ROSEFINCH
(p. 496)

TWO-BARRED
CROSSBILL
(p. 500)

♂Imm

COMMON
CROSSBILL
(p. 498)

♂

♀

PARROT
CROSSBILL
(p. 499)

♂

♂Common
Crossbill similar
but head/bill
smaller

♀

♂

Juv

PINE GROSBEAK
(p. 496)

♂

BULLFINCH
(p. 486)

♂

♀

TWITE
(p. 495)

Nb

Nb

Nb

Nb

REDPOLL
(p. 492)

♂ Br

Nb

HAWFINCH
(p. 485)

Nb

Nb

LINNET
(p. 494)

Nb

Ad

Ad

ROCK SPARROW
(p. 507)

Ad

TREE SPARROW
(p. 505)

♂ Br

ITALIAN SPARROW
(p. 504)

♂ Nb

HOUSE SPARROW
(p. 505)

♂ Br

♀

Ad

SPANISH SPARROW
(p. 504)

♂ Br

♂ Nb

**WHITE-WINGED
SNOWFINCH**
(p. 484)

483

LC **White-winged Snowfinch** *Montifringilla nivalis*

LC ❶ | **L** 17–18 cm | **W** 30–34 cm

Stocky, sparrow-like (*p. 504*) finch, usually on the ground, often around ski resorts. **Black-and-white wings** rule out all but Snow Bunting (ranges do not overlap). **Greyish head**, dull **brown back** and **white underparts**. ♂**Br** | (MAR–AUG) head blue-grey, throat black; bill black; rump black. ♂**Nb** | head brownish, black on throat partly obscured, bill orange. ♀ | head brownish-grey, black throat small, obscured by white tips AUG–MAR. Rump brown. **Juv** | (until AUG–OCT) head brown, throat grey; after moult to **1W** like **Ad**.

> Three sspp. occur: *nivalis* (S Europe) head grey, upperparts brown; *leucura* (S & E Turkey) grey-brown head hardly contrasts with grey-brown back; *alpicola* (Caucasus) crown brown, nape greyish, back dark brown.

👁 Snow Bunting p. 509

Scarce and local resident/winter migrant

High altitude peaks, rocky plateaux and snowfields

V | Chattering notes, trills and chirps; sparrow-like song.

FL | Long, broad, tapered wings white with black tip; tail long, white on sides. Fast, direct, undulating action.

♂**Br**
MAR–SEP

SSP. *leucura*

SSP. *nivalis*

Ad
ALL YEAR

SSP. *nivalis*

Nb
SEP–MAR

♀
ALL YEAR

SSP. *nivalis*

long white band
along closed wing

grey head

white
underparts

♂**Br**
MAR–SEP

SSP. *nivalis*

Hawfinch
Coccothraustes coccothraustes

② | **L** 16·5–18 cm | **W** 29–33 cm

Large, striking, colourful but shy and elusive finch with **large, pale bill**. May sit upright on treetop, bulky and thick-necked (recalls Common Crossbill (*p. 498*)). Often feeds on the ground. **Ad** | back brown, chin black. **White wing band**. Underparts buff. Bill blue-and-black (yellowish SEP–MAR). **♂** | forehead and cheek **bright orange-buff**, hindneck grey; black between eye and bill. Secondaries steely-blue. **♀** | head dull brownish; grey-brown between eye and bill; secondaries grey, forming pale patch. **Juv** | pale buff-brown, underparts barred or spotted blackish. Broad **white wing panel** and **tail tip**. **1W** | like ♀ but head plainer and wing greyer.

👁 *Evening Grosbeak p. 616*

V | Call hard, dry, clicking or ticking "*tik!*" or "*tziit*." Sharp, quietly explosive "*tix*" or "*chip*" (very like Robin (*p. 392*)); "*tik-ik-ik*" or Redstart-like (*p. 396*) tick. Song quiet, variable, like repeated calls.

FL | Wing long, broad, with bulging hindwing; short tail. **White tail tip** eye-catching especially in shade under trees; overhead, **long, angular white panel** on underwing. Fast, direct, very slightly undulating; flocks up to 50.

Scarce resident/migrant

Deciduous woods, well-wooded parkland

Two similar sspp. occur: *coccothraustes* (widespread) and *nigricans* (Crimea, C & S Caucasus, NE Turkey), which has darker back (but intergrades).

Juv
MAY–SEP

Juv has same basic pattern as Ad but dull, pale, with dark mottles and bars on underparts.

♀ Nb/1W
SEP–MAR

head and bill duller in winter

♂ Br
FEB–AUG

All ssp. *coccothraustes*

whitish shoulder patch and pale band on wing

♀ Br
FEB–AUG

white tail tip

485

LC

(Eurasian) **Bullfinch** *Pyrrhula pyrrhula*

LC ❷ | **L** 15·5–17 cm | **W** 22–29 cm

Large, thickset, broad-headed, short-billed finch. Broad **white rump and vent**, blue-black wings and broad **whitish wingbar** in all plumages. Quiet, reclusive but not necessarily shy. Parrot-like actions when feeding; sometimes hovers. Call distinctive. ♂ | **cap, chin and bill black**, back pure grey, **breast red-pink**. ♀ | cap/chin black, back grey-brown, underparts **unstreaked pinkish** grey-buff. **Juv** | like ♀ but head plain, no black cap or chin.

V | Call a low, hollow whistle, "*peooo*" or "*heeew*," particularly penetrating in spring. Song quiet, vibrant, reedy, creaky sounds. 'Trumpet' call sometimes given is diagnostic of ssp. *pyrrhula*.

FL | Plump, short-necked, broad-winged. White rump and vent (broader than Brambling's (*p. 500*)). Overhead, pale underwing; white vent and square, dark tail distinctive. Rarely forms flocks.

👁 Pine Grosbeak *p. 496*

Locally fairly common resident/migrant

Deciduous woodland, orchards, thickets, parks, large gardens

Six sspp. occur, differences mostly insignificant but N/E European ssp. *pyrrhula* larger than southern sspp., ♂ underparts **deep red**, white rump **extends high up** onto blue-grey back; *europaea* (N/W Europe) is dull; *pileata* (Great Britain, Ireland) small; *iberiae* (SW Europe) ♂ bright pink, ♀ pale and grey; *rossikowi* (N Turkey, Caucasus) ♂ bright red, ♀ dark grey-brown; *caspica* (Azerbaijan) intergrades with *rossikowi*, small but with large bill.

♀

♂

head plain

Juv
MAY–OCT

♂
ALL YEAR
ssp. *pyrrhula*

♀
ALL YEAR

ssp. *pileata*

♂
ALL YEAR

white rump

ssp. *europaea*

Goldfinch *Carduelis carduelis*

L 12–13·5 cm | **W** 20–25 cm

Unmistakable small, slim finch, with **wide yellow band on black wing**; tail deeply notched. Often 5–10, flocks to 100s. **Ad** | pale crown and buff; dark buff breast side. **Face red; white cheek edged black**. **Juv** | head greyish-buff; buff feather tips on wing and tail. **1W** | may retain brown juv wing coverts among new black ones.

Common and widespread resident/ migrant

Heath, moorland edge, woodland edge, bushy thickets, gardens

V | Call like Swallow (*p. 344*), slurred "*swip*" or "*swilip*;" harsh, churring rasp. Song fast, tinkling trills, chattery notes and prolonged chirruping subsongs.

FL | Wings long and broad. Broad pale band across black wing; white rump; pale body/dark hindwing from below. Light, erratic, as if bounced by gust of wind. Flocks only loosely coordinated.

Nine sspp. occur, often indistinguishable: *carduelis* (widespread); *britannica* (Great Britain, Ireland, NW France to W Netherlands) darker on back; *parva* (SW Europe, Balearic Is., Madeira, Canary Is.) small, greyish; *tschusii* (Corsica, Sardinia, Sicily), *balcanica* (Balkans to Greece, Crete, NW Turkey), *brevirostris* (E Turkey), *colchica* (Crimea, N Caucasus) and *niediecki* (Rhodes, W, SC & NE Turkey, S Caucasus, Cyprus) all greyish; *volgensis* (S Ukraine, SE European Russia) larger.

Juv
MAY–OCT

head plain greyish-buff

unique red/white/black head

Sexes look alike, but on ♂ red face tends to extend farther over eye; blacker between eye and bill.

Ad
ALL YEAR

ssp. *britannica*

Linnet *p. 494* | Twite *p. 495*

LC Red-fronted Serin *Serinus pusillus*

LC **2** | **L** 11·5–12 cm | **W** 18–20 cm

Small, dumpy, dark finch with tiny blackish bill. Rump and side of tail **orange-yellow**. **Ad** | head blackish, **forecrown red**. Upperparts brown, streaked black; shoulder rufous; wing black-and-yellow, two white wingbars. Underparts yellow-buff, streaked black. **Juv** | head and back rusty-brown, streaked black. **Broad rufous** wingbars. Underparts buff, streaked grey-brown. **1W** | like **Ad**, red on forehead from OCT–DEC.

Scarce and local resident/winter migrant

Upland forest, meadows, ravines

V | Bright, twittery trill. Song long, fast, high trilling.

FL | Wings broad, rounded. Undulating, jerky, erratic; flocks tightly coordinated.

1W
AUG–DEC

Juv
MAY–SEP

broad rufous wingbar

forehead red

Ad
ALL YEAR

Juvenile small, streaky finches

Streaked juvenile finches can be difficult in isolation from adults (and suspected out-of-range vagrants may need to be separated from escapes, *e.g.* Canary (*p. 527*) of various forms). Check general colour; pattern around eye and cheek; colour of wing and wingbars/tertial fringes; presence/absence of streaks/patches on side of tail; bill shape and size; leg colour; calls.

REDPOLL (*p. 492*)

APR–SEP

Brown, streaked dark; small, plain head; **buff** wingbar; **black** legs.

TWITE (*p. 495*)

APR–SEP

Buffy-brown, lightly streaked; **buff throat**; **buff** wingbar; **white fringes** on wing and tail; legs pinkish, **dark** by AUG.

LINNET (*p. 494*)

APR–SEP

Rusty-buff, breast streaked brown; **pale crescents** above and below eye; **rufous-buff** wingbar, **white fringes** on wing and tail; **pale** legs.

LC ## Siskin *Spinus spinus*

LC **3** | **L** 11–12·5 cm | **W** 18–22 cm

Small, slender, greenish finch with deeply notched tail. Acrobatic feeder, with other finches or tit flocks. Flocks up to 100+. Broad **black and yellow** bands across wing; white belly; yellow side to tail. ♂| **cap and chin black**. Upperparts green, rump yellow; breast yellow, belly white. ♀| upperparts greyish. Underparts white with long black streaks. **Juv** | like ♀ but back more streaked, wingbars narrow. **1W/1S** | like **Ad** but some wing coverts contrastingly browner.

Serin | Greenfinch *p. 490* | Citril Finch *p. 491* | Corsican Finch *p. 491* Canary (including escapees) *p. 527*

V | Call ringing, squeaky "*tluee*" or "*tzsy-ee.*" Hard, harsh churr; fast medley from flocks. Song fast, twittery, squeaky with trills and light, buzzy, wheezy notes.

FL | Short, broad wings; short, notched tail. Long yellow stripe along blackish wing. Light, bounding; large flocks **tightly coordinated**.

Locally common resident/migrant

Mostly coniferous woods; winters in alder, birch thickets, gardens

♀ 1W
AUG–JUN

yellow-green bar across blackish wing

lacks black cap

♂ 1W
AUG–JUN

black cap, yellow behind eye

♂ Ad
ALL YEAR

underparts whitish, flank streaked black

♀ Ad
ALL YEAR

yellow side to tail

SISKIN
MAY–OCT

Greenish; **yellow** on head; two **yellowish** bars on brown wing; **pale** legs.

RED-FRONTED SERIN
(p. 487)
MAY–SEP

Rufous; rusty-brown on head; **broad dark rufous** bars and tertial fringes on blackish wing; **pale** legs.

CITRIL FINCH *(p. 491)*
APR–OCT

Greyish; two **buff-white** bars on blackish wing; **pale** legs.

SERIN
JUN–SEP

Rufous/buff; thin **rufous-buff** bars on grey-brown wing; **pale** legs.

(European) Serin *Serinus serinus*

2 | **L** 11–12 cm | **W** 18–22 cm

Small, **small-billed**, **streaked** finch, adults with **yellow rump**. Upright, inconspicuous in treetops; crouches/hops on ground. ♂ | **forehead clear yellow.** Upperparts olive, streaked black. Throat and breast yellow; flank streaked black. ♀ | less yellow than ♂, crown streaked brown. **Juv** | buff-brown, streaked black; wingbar buff. Rump buff. **1W/1S** | like **Ad** but some juvenile wing coverts with browner centre.

Siskin | Citril Finch *p. 491*
Corsican Finch *p. 491* | Greenfinch *p. 490* | [Juv] Linnet *p. 494*
Canary (including escapees) *p. 527*

V | Call jingling trill; upswept "*tu-wee*."
Song fast jingle, often in song flight.

FL | Broad wings but slender, forked tail.
Yellow rump. Light, fast, bouncy or jerky.

Common resident/ migrant

Warm bushy places with scattered trees, orchards, villages

♀ 1W
AUG–MAR

pale lower cheek

1W
(probably ♂)
AUG–MAR

pale crescent under eye

♂
ALL YEAR

dark 'moustache'

buff wingbar

♀ 1S/Ad
ALL YEAR

black streaks on flank

yellow rump

LC **Greenfinch** *Chloris chloris*

LC **2** | **L** 14–16 cm | **W** 24–27 cm

Large, **thick-billed** finch with **yellow streak along edge of wing**. Perches upright, horizontal on ground; feeds in fields, under trees. ♂ | **apple green**; grey on wing. **Pale bill**, dark 'frown'; **broad yellow streak** along wing and side of tail. In winter (SEP–MAR) dull feather fringes. ♀ | brownish-green, softly streaked darker above; narrow yellow streak along wing. **Juv** | like ♀ but but paler and diffusely streaked brown; thin yellow streak along wing still characteristic. **1W** | may show contrast between **Juv** and new **Ad**-type wing and tail feathers but often difficult to age.

V | Call short "*jup*;" erratic trill "*jup-jup-up-up*" (heavier, louder than Linnet (*p. 494*), less metallic than Redpoll (*p. 492*)). **Juv** | loud "*chup*," like Common Crossbill. Song, perched or in **song flight**, includes loud, nasal "*dweeez*;" ringing, musical trills of varying speed and rhythm.

FL | Heavy-bodied; wings long, tapered, tail short and notched. Yellow streaks on wing, but **yellow on tail** more obvious in rear view. Wingbeats more emphatic than Chaffinch (*p. 500*): long undulations. Bat-like, **stretched-winged song flight**. Flocks more coordinated than Chaffinch, up to 300.

Common resident/ summer migrant

Woods, thickets, farmland, gardens

Eight similar sspp. occur, those in S & E Europe brightest green: *chloris* (widespread); *harrisoni* (Great Britain, Ireland); *muehlei* (SE Europe); *aurantiiventris* (Spain to W/S Greece, Madeira, Canary Is.); *madaraszi* (Corsica, Sardinia); *vanmarli* (NW Spain, Portugal); *chlorotica* (CS Turkey eastwards); *bilkevitchi* (Crimea, Caucasus, NE Turkey).

♂1W
AUG–MAR

Judging age/sex can be difficult; 1W has narrower streak on wing then Ad; ♂'s broader than ♀'s of the same age.

Juv
APR–SEP

faint dark streaks on breast

black eye in plain head

thick, pale bill

♂Ad
ALL YEAR

yellow streak on wing

yellow sides to tail

♀
ALL YEAR

👁 Citril and Corsican Finches are similar. | Greenfinch | Siskin *p. 488*
Serin *p. 489* | [Juv] Linnet *p. 494* | Canary (escapees) *p. 527*

Citril Finch *Carduelis citrinella*

2 | **L** 11·5–13 cm | **W** 20–22 cm

Small, social finch; often in small groups, rarely 200+. Green, yellow and grey. Size/structure resemble Siskin but tail longer and adults **not streaked**. Wing blackish, with **two broad pale wingbars**. ♂| upperparts green, face yellowish, nape and side of neck grey. **Two broad greenish-yellow wingbars**. Underparts yellow-green. ♀| side of head, nape and back dull grey, tinged brown. Throat and breast greenish-grey or grey. **Juv**| pale buff-brown. Head greyish; throat and underparts buff-brown, streaked brown. Two broad, whitish wingbars.

Locally common resident/winter migrant; vagrant elsewhere

Mountain forests with clearings or adjacent alpine meadows

V| Calls loud, simple, squeaky chirrups and nasal cheeps. Song combines hard, rapid rattles, low buzz and sweet trills, sometimes in flight.

FL| Wing broad, pointed, tail slim. Slightly undulating, flocks uncoordinated.

Juv
APR–OCT

* 1Y birds similar to **Ad** but lower wingbar with some whie fringes – see *p. 10*

♀ 1S*

grey collar

♂
ALL YEAR

♀
ALL YEAR

Corsican Finch *Carduelis corsicana*

2 | **L** 11 cm | **W** 20 cm

Small finch with small bill, round head, **yellow underparts** and **two broad, pale wingbars**. ♂| forehead, cheek and throat yellow, nape and side of neck pale grey; much like Citril Finch (identify by location) but back **warm brown, streaked grey**. Underparts bright yellow. ♀| crown brownish, face greenish-yellow, back streaked grey-brown; underparts greenish-yellow with fine grey streaks. **Juv**| head pale, buffish with yellower throat, upperparts brown, streaked dark brown, wing dark with two narrow buff wingbars; tail slim, edged whitish (similar to ♀/Juv Linnet).

Scarce and local resident

Heath and scrub

V| Calls high, thin "*tseet*" and short chirrups. Song fast trills (less varied than Citril Finch).

FL| Wing broad, pointed, tail slim. Typical slightly bouncy finch action.

♀
ALL YEAR

♂
ALL YEAR

LC # Redpoll *Acanthis flammea*

LC **2** | **L** 11–14 cm | **W** 16–26 cm

Small, slim, lightweight, streaky 'brown' finch with short bill. **Red cap**; small, inconspicuous **black chin**. **Buff-white wingbar**. ♂**Br** | (JAN–JUL) **breast pink-red**, rump pink. ♂**Nb** | pink obscured by buff fringes. ♀ | small red cap, black around bill and eye. Underparts white, flank buff with **black streaks**. **Juv** | lacks red cap, sometimes through **1W**, which has mixed dull/bright greater coverts.

V | Hard chattering calls: fast, metallic "*chuch-uch-uch-uch-uch*;" twangy "*tsooeee*" (more forceful than Linnet, more metallic than Greenfinch (*p. 490*)). Song (bouncy song flight) mixes calls with jingly trill "*trrrreeee*."

FL | Broad wing, narrow tail; bouncy undulations; flocks move in tight groups. Flocks may exceed 100.

Locally common resident/migrant

Birch and mixed woodland, heath, moorland edge; winters in areas with birches, poplars, willows

Five subspecies occur, sometimes treated as three species:

'Lesser Redpoll' SSP. *cabaret* (S Sweden south to Alps, Great Britain, Ireland) smallest, darkest; rump buff, streaked brown; broad **buff wingbar**, fades whiter by MAR/APR.

'Common (or Mealy) Redpoll' sspp. *flammea* (N Europe) large, quite pale, especially on head; whitish lines on back, **rump white/greyish** with short, dark streaks; **whitish wingbar and fringes on blackish wing feathers**; *rostrata* (Greenland, vagrant), large, dark, heavily streaked.

'Arctic Redpoll' sspp. *hornemanni* (NE Canada & Greenland) and *exilipes* (N Eurasia) large, large head, **very short bill**, **narrow grey streak** (occasionally 1–3 on *hornemanni*) **or all-white under tail** (dark streaks on other sspp.). Head **bright buff** from AUG/SEP (almost white by JAN on *exilipes*; deeper orange-buff, often until MAR/APR, on *hornemanni*); white flank lightly marked or unstreaked (but 3–5 lines on some *hornemanni*). ♂ | *exilipes* can be strikingly white, but other plumages are less distinctive. **Ad** | broad white wingbar, **extensive white rump**. ♂ breast pale pink; rump pink MAR–MAY. **Juv** | unmarked white band on rump, streaked upper edge, or fine streaks overall, more like 'Common Redpoll'.

Twite *p. 495* | Linnet *p. 494*
Common Rosefinch *p. 496*

'LESSER REDPOLL'
SSP. *cabaret*

♂**Br**
JAN–JUL

'COMMON REDPOLL'
SSP. *flammea*

♂**Br**
FEB–JUL
[MAR]

'ARCTIC REDPOLL'
SSP. *exilipes*

♂**Br**
JAN–JUL
[MAY]

'LESSER REDPOLL' ssp. *cabaret*
Smallest, darkest; darkest wingbar (fades); rump brown/pink; buff edges on wings; streaks under tail.

1W
SEP–JUN

'LESSER REDPOLL'
distinctly streaked under tail

'COMMON REDPOLL'
ssp. *flammea*
streaks under tail

'ARCTIC REDPOLL'
unstreaked white under tail
(rarely 1–3 lines)

'COMMON REDPOLL'
Large, pale; white wingbar; rump grey-white/dark streaks; white edges on blackish wings; streaks under tail.

AdNb
ssp. *flammea*

♀ Ad
ALL YEAR

AdNb / 1W
SEP–MAR

ssp. *flammea*

ssp. *rostrata*

'ARCTIC REDPOLL'
Arctic Redpoll has a large, round head and tiny bill seemingly 'pushed in' to face. White rump or white upper band. Adult males may be obvious, females and juveniles much less so.

ssp. *hornemanni*

AdNb
ssp. *hornemanni*

1W
SEP–MAR

ssp. *exilipes*

AdNb
SEP–MAR

493

LC

Linnet *Linaria cannabina*

LC

2 | **L** 12·5–14 cm | **W** 20–24 cm

Small, short-billed, short-legged 'brown' finch with twittering calls. Distinct face patterns; grey bill. Stands to feed, not clinging onto stems. Flocks up to 500. **♂Br** | **back plain pale red-brown; head grey**, forehead red. **White streaks along wing and tail side**. Underparts buff, **breast red**. **♂Nb** | buff tips obscure grey and all or most of red. **♀/♀1W** | no red; head greyish, back lightly streaked. Breast finely streaked, belly white. In poor light looks dark, greyish with whitish throat, cheek marks, eyering. **Juv** | buff-brown, breast and flank heavily spotted brown. **♂1W** | usually has red on face/breast, obscured by buff fringes.

Twite | Redpoll *p. 492*
Serin [Juv] *p. 489*
Red-fronted Serin *p. 487*
Citril Finch [Juv] *p. 491*
Corsican Finch [Juv] *p. 491*

V | Call a twittering, dry "*chet-et-et*" (less forceful than Greenfinch (*p. 490*), less forceful than Redpoll.) Also a twangy "*tsooee.*" Song musical sweet warbling.

FL | Tapered wing and notched tail show **white edges** to outer feathers. Bursts of wingbeats; long undulations with closed wings. Flocks coordinated, drop into low vegetation rather than trees.

Locally common
resident/migrant

Bushy heathland and moorland, arable land, coastal areas; winters in fields, around estuaries

SSP. *cannabina*

grey bill

♂Nb
AUG–MAY

pale cheek spot in all plumages

SSP. *mediterranea*

Juv
APR–SEP

pale crescents above and below eye

white wing streak

SSP. *canne*

♀Ad/1W
ALL YEAR

white tail sides

SSP. *cannabina*

♂Br
MAR–AUG

Seven similar sspp. occur: *cannabina* (widespread); *autochthona* (Scotland) darker, more streaked; *mediterranea* (Iberia, Mediterranean islands, Italy, Greece) bill thin; *bella* (Crimea, WC Turkey eastwards, Caucasus, Cyprus) paler, red parts pinker, bill thick; *guentheri* (Madeira), *meadewaldoi* (W & C Canary Is.) and *harterti* (E Canary Is.) all small.

SSP. *mediterranea*

♂Br
MAR–AUG

SSP. *bella*

♂Br
MAR–AUG

Twite *Linaria flavirostris*

2 | **L** 12·5–14 cm | **W** 22–24 cm

Small, social 'brown' finch, much like Linnet. Combines **buff-brown** body and buff wingbar of Redpoll with **white wing/tail streaks** of Linnet; **throat tawny-buff**. Flocks (may exceed 100) feed low down in herbs, often circling saltmarsh before dropping down. **♂ Br** | pale brown, boldly streaked black-brown; throat patch buff; **rump deep pink**. Bill greyish. **♀ Br** | like ♂ but lacks pink. **Nb** | throat tawny-buff, **bill yellow** (grey on Linnet), wingbar buff. Long white streak on closed wing and side of tail. **Juv / 1W** | like ♀ Ad but upperparts more rufous, paler buff throat thinly streaked brown: **♂ 1W** | rump pinkish, few streaks; **♀ 1W** | rump brown, streaked dark. **1S** | like **1W** but wing coverts more worn.

👁 Linnet | Redpoll *p. 492*
Serin [Juv] *p. 489*
Red-fronted Serin *p. 487*

V | Flight notes "*chet-chet-chet*" (more metallic than Linnet) and distinctive twangy, nasal, buzzing "*twaa-it.*" Song fast, twittering, mixing twangy call and rattling trills.

FL | Broad, tapered wing and narrow, notched tail show **white edges** to outer feathers. Quick, bouncy action; winter flocks often in tight, synchronized groups.

Scarce, locally common resident/migrant

Rough grazing, weedy fields; winters around estuaries, saltmarsh

Three sspp. occur: *pipilans* (N Ireland, N Great Britain) dark, streaked; *flavirostris* (N Scandinavia and N European Russia) paler; *brevirostris* (Turkey, Caucasus) – see *inset*.

1W/Nb

1W/Nb
SEP–MAR

yellow bill (both sexes)

1S/AdBr
MAR–AUG

SSP. *brevirostris*

SSP. *brevirostris* (E Turkey/Caucasus) has dark tawny-brown back (greyer when worn) and white wingbar; underparts buff, heavily streaked black.

All SSP. *flavirostris*

♀ Br
MAR–OCT

tawny throat

pink rump

♂ Br
MAR–OCT

brown rump

Common Rosefinch
LC *Carpodacus erythrinus*

2 | **L** 13·5–15 cm | **W** 24–25 cm

Fairly large finch, with bulbous bill. **Bold dark eye** in **plain face**; plain tail rules out most buntings. ♂ | **head, breast and rump bright deep red** (most intense MAR–JUN); belly and tertial tips pinkish-white. ♀ | upperparts olive-buff, subtly streaked brown; **two pale buff wingbars**; underparts white, breast subtly streaked brown. **Juv** / **1W** | like Ad ♀ but wingbars broader (thin by JAN).

V | Call soft, upswept "*tiu-eek*." Song rhythmic, whistling phrases, "*weedy-weedy-weedy-wu*."

FL ● | Broad wings, notched tail; direct, with short, regular undulations; often flies high (above tree-tops).

All SSP. *erythrinus*

♂**Br**
MAR–AUG

Great Rosefinch
LC *Carpodacus rubicilla*

2 | **L** 19–20 cm | **W** 25–30 cm

Large, long-tailed, largely terrestrial rosefinch with stout bill. ♂ | crown, throat and underparts mostly **deep red** with **pale spots**. Rump pink-red. ♀ | pale brown, **head finely streaked**; underparts buff, densely streaked grey-brown. **Juv** / **1W** | like ♀ but more buffy, with thinner streaks on underparts.

V | Bright, chirrupy "*so-ee*" or "*swee-su-suee;*" shorter "*sup*" in flight. Song hesitant, sparrow-like "*tswee-see chi-chu-chu*."

FL | Long wings and tail dark, contrasting with pale rump.

♂**Ad**
ALL YEAR

pale spots on underparts.

Pine Grosbeak
LC *Pinicola enucleator*

2 | **L** 18–20 cm | **W** 30–35 cm

Large, bulky (in cold weather) or rather slender, slim-tailed finch with **bulbous bill** and **white wingbars**. ♂ | **pale red and grey**, wings blackish. ♀ | bronzy-yellow and grey (yellow extensive or confined to head and neck); primaries edged yellow-green. **Juv** / **1Y** | like Ad ♀ but primaries edged white; ♂ may have some orange-red, recalling young male crossbill.

V | Call a bright, squeaky "*ply-zee*." Song bright, full, Robin-like (*p. 392*) phrases.

FL | Bulky, broad-winged and long-tailed; direct, thrush-like (*p. 383*). Flocks up to 20, rarely 100s.

two white wingbars

♂**1Y**
MAR–SEP

♂**Ad**
ALL YEAR

dark eye in plain face

♀ **Ad**
ALL YEAR

Juv/1W
JUN–MAR

two thin, pale wingbars

breast subtly streaked

Redpoll *p. 492* | Trumpeter Finch *p. 502* | Great Rosefinch | *Pallas's & Long-tailed Rosefinches p. 606* *Indigo Bunting p. 616*

Locally common summer migrant
APR–SEP

Woodland, wet thickets, parks

Two sspp. occur: *erythrinus* (widespread); *kubanensis* (N&E Turkey, Caucasus) male paler pink-red, less hooded.

stout bill

♀ **Ad**
ALL YEAR

no obvious wingbars

underparts densely streaked

Common Rosefinch

Scarce and local resident

High altitude rocky slopes/ meadows

SSP. *rubicilla* occurs in Europe.

bulbous bill

Juv
JUN–AUG

Crossbills *pp. 498–500*
Bullfinch *p. 486*

Scarce resident/ winter migrant; occasional vagrant

Extensive old coniferous forest; sometimes in parks, gardens

SSP. *enucleator* occurs in Europe.

♀ **Ad**
ALL YEAR

Common, **Scottish** and **Parrot Crossbills** share similar plumages and general character; not easily identifiable: concentrate on size of head and bill, and calls. Even Parrot and Common Crossbills can be very difficult, while Scottish Crossbill is intermediate, often impossible to identify without analysis of sound recordings. Look in conifers, listen for falling cones; feed very quietly but may create a sudden outburst of loud calls, often before flying away. Frequently drink from pools.

👁 Two-barred Crossbill p. 500
[♀] Greenfinch p. 490
Pine Grosbeak p. 496

	Bill and cheek		Voice
Common Crossbill*	SMALLEST — TIP OFTEN LONG, CURVED		Calls deep, purring notes, build to ringing "*jip-jip-jip*" as bird flies off. In flight, hard, forceful "*djeep-djeep-djeep*" (generally higher pitched than Parrot Crossbill but variable). Song buzzing, trilling, whistled sounds.
Scottish Crossbill	DEEP — CHEEK 'BULGING'		*Between Common Crossbill and Parrot Crossbill: analysis of sound recordings required for confirmation.*
Parrot Crossbill	DEEPEST, ROUNDEST — TIPS BARELY CROSS — CHEEK 'FLAT'		Calls typically deep "*tup*," "*tup-tup-tup...*" (generally deeper with harder quality than Common Crossbill). Song hesitant, varied strident trills and chirruping notes, "*tsip-tsip-tsip, see-tru see-tru, stip-rri-rrip.*"

*Common Crossbill populations from different regions may be separable by analyzing recordings of calls: flocks in same area in successive years may be different 'types' (which may eventually be treated as subspecies).

LC
LC

Common Crossbill
Loxia curvirostra

❷ | **L** 15–17 cm | **W** 27–30 cm

Large, round-headed finch with **cross-tipped, arched bill**. Often upright on treetop (recalls Hawfinch (p. 485)). Agile when feeding. **♂Ad** | dull red, **rump bright red**. **♂Imm** | greenish, patched orange-red. **♀** | greenish, **rump yellow**; **wings plain** (unlike Greenfinch). **Juv** | dull, streaked dark brown; may have thin white wingbars and tertial fringes (like Two-barred Crossbill but tertial tips never white).

FL | Round-body, large-head; wings narrow, tapered; tail short, notched. Fast, bounding over treetops, often over long distances. Flocks noisy, coordinated, dense or elongated, often 10–20, rarely 100+.

Locally common resident; irruptive migrant

Coniferous forest and plantations

Five similar sspp. occur, which differ subtly in bill size, intensity of red and voice: *curvirostra* (widespread); *balearica* (C&S Spain, Balearic Is.); *corsicana* (Corsica); *poliogyna* (S Italy); *guillemardi* (E Balkans, Turkey, Caucasus & S Ukraine).

Juv
JAN–OCT

All ssp. *curvirostra*

♂Imm
JAN–OCT

♀
ALL YEAR

♂
ALL YEAR

FL | All crossbills fly with a direct, bounding action and look large-headed. Call frequently. Parrot Crossbill is especially thick-necked but otherwise the species look similar. Stout body narrows abruptly to deeply forked tail. Wing broad-based, angular, with tapered tip.

COMMON
CROSSBILL

PARROT
CROSSBILL

Juv

♂

Scottish Crossbill
Loxia scotica

2 | **L** 16–18 cm | **W** 27–30 cm

Intermediate between Common Crossbill and Parrot Crossbill and **only reliably identified by analysis of sound recordings**. All three species are found in the same forests in N Scotland. Bill deep, heavy; head rather 'fat-cheeked'.

FL | Bounding action; indistinguishable from Common Crossbill.

Scarce and very local resident

Pine forest and plantations

♂
ALL YEAR

fat, 'bulging' cheek

♀
ALL YEAR

Parrot Crossbill
Loxia pytyopsittacus

2 | **L** 17–18 cm | **W** 30–33 cm

Largest crossbill but often difficult to identify. **Bill deep, bulging** (like ball pressed into face), slightly 'hanging'; tip hooked, barely crossed. Feeds from large pine cones. **♂Ad** | dull red, **rump bright red**. **♂Imm** | grey-green, patched orange-red. **♀/1W** | grey-green; bill smaller than on ♂ but on average Parrot Crossbill has a larger, **deeper, blunter bill**, wider head (thicker neck, often showing as a 'ruff' when hunched) and smaller eye than Common Crossbill.

FL | Heavy head and body, tapered wings, but shape and actions indistinguishable from Common Crossbill; flocks usually under 20, rarely up to 50.

Locally common resident; irruptive

Pine forest

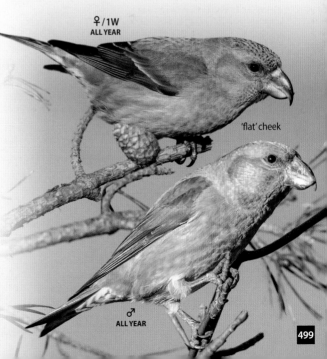

♀/1W
ALL YEAR

'flat' cheek

♂
ALL YEAR

499

LC **Two-barred Crossbill**
LC *Loxia leucoptera*

2 | **L** 14–16 cm | **W** 25–29 cm

Small crossbill with **slender bill, broad white wingbars** and **white tips to tertials**. ♂ | **raspberry-red**. ♀ | pale grey-green. **Juv** | olive-grey, streaked darker; white wingbars and tertial tips thin (some Common Crossbills have thin white wingbars but not white tertial tips).

Two sspp. recorded: *bifasciata* (regular); *leucoptera* (vagrant from N America), which is fractionally smaller-billed.

♂Ad
ALL YEAR

head/body deeper red, more streaked, and wings much blacker than other crossbills

All ssp. *bifasciata*

LC (Common) **Chaffinch**
LC *Fringilla coelebs*

2 | **L** 14–16 cm | **W** 24–28 cm

Fairly large, long-bodied finch with **bold white wingbar, shoulder and tail side**; dips tail. Rump **olive-green**. ♂**Br** | cheek and breast orange-pink; cap, nape and bill bluish. ♂**Nb** | buff feather edges (wear away by MAR); bill pinkish. ♀ / **Juv** | dull olive-grey; dark side to nape. Underparts **unstreaked olive-buff**. **1W** | like **Ad** but some duller wing coverts.

Seven similar sspp. in mainland Europe: *coelebs* (widespread); *gengleri* (Great Britain, Ireland); *solomkoi* (Balkans, Crimea, W Caucasus); *transcaspia* (S Caucasus); *sarda* (Sardinia); *syriaca* (Cyprus, SE Turkey eastwards); *alexandrovi* (winters E Turkey). Another five sspp., with distinctive ♂s, occur on Atlantic islands (see p. 528).

♂Nb
AUG–MAR

♂Br
FEB–AUG

white shoulder (can be hidden)

LC **Brambling**
LC *Fringilla montifringilla*

2 | **L** 14–16 cm | **W** 25–26 cm

Fairly large, long-bodied finch with **orange shoulder** and **white rump**; contrasted **white belly, flank spotted** black. ♂**Br** | hood, bill and back black; **shoulder and breast orange, belly white**. ♂**Nb** | bill bright yellow. Pale fringes on head/back wear away by FEB/MAR. Breast **orange** against **white belly**. ♀ / **Juv** | **pale nape** between dark bands, **pale grey collar**; breast dull orange; buff shoulder and wingbar. **1W** | like **Ad** but greater coverts and/or primary coverts browner and tail feathers pointed (round-tipped on **Ad**).

pale feather edges wear away to reveal solid black in spring

♂1W
SEP–APR

♂Br
FEB–AUG

Juv
FEB–JUL

thin white wingbars, white on tertials

♀
ALL YEAR

broad white wingbars, large white tertial spots

👁 Common Crossbill p. 498
Chaffinch

Scarce and local resident; irruptive

Larch woods

V | Call high, sharp *"chip-chip-chip;"* piping *"feet"* distinctive. Song fast trills, rising and falling, *"chrr-twi-twi-twi-chrr'p-chrr'p, swi-swi-swi…."*

FL | Slim, with narrow wings and notched tail. Fast, direct, slightly undulating.

bill never yellow

♀
ALL YEAR

All ssp. *coelebs*

dull belly, plain flank

👁 Brambling | Two-barred Crossbill

Common resident/migrant

Woods, thickets, parks, villages, gardens, fields with hedgerows; some urban areas

V | Call ringing *"pink;"* in flight, soft *"chup."* Spring/ summer, monotonous *"huit."* Song bright, rattling *"chip-chip-chip cherry-erry-erry,"* accelerating into final flourish.

FL | Broad wings, long, notched tail. Striking white on wings and tail; dark rump. Flocks loose, uncoordinated, up to 300.

yellow on bill

orange shoulder

♀ 1W
SEP–APR

white belly, dark flank spots

tail feathers pointed (rounded on Ad)

👁 Chaffinch

Locally common migrant

Breeds in upland birch woods; winters in woods, parks, arable land

V | Call twangy *"tswairk;"* in flight, hard *"chup."* Song includes deep buzzing note.

FL | Broad wings, long, notched tail. Narrow **white rump**. Slightly jerky/ hesitant; flocks quite loose, up to 300 (roosts occasionally huge numbers).

501

LC **Trumpeter Finch** *Bucanetes githagineus*

LC | ❷ | **L** 12·5–15 cm | **W** 21–25 cm

Small, social, round-headed, sparrow-like finch, with **short, deep bill**. **Unstreaked** buff-grey and pink. **Pink in wing**. ♂**Br** | face pink-red; black eye and white eyering; crown and cheek greyer. Broad **grey and pink edges on black-tipped wing** and tail. Underparts pink, rump and vent darker pink. **Bill orange or red**. ♀**Br** | sandy-buff; thin pink edges on wing (minority show pink on face). Bill orange-yellow. ♂**Nb**/♀**Nb/1W** | like ♀ **Br** but greyer, bill yellow. **Juv** | buff-brown, vent pink; bill yellow.

V | Call short, abrupt, off-key note. Song nasal, buzzing or hooting 'toy trumpet' sound.

FL | Quick, whirring wingbeats, short undulations. Underwing dark grey with broad, pale band across flight feathers.

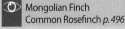

👁 Mongolian Finch
Common Rosefinch *p. 496*

Local resident; vagrant elsewhere

Rocky semi-desert

♀**Nb/1W**
AUG–FEB

seasonal changes quite marked

♂**Br**
FEB–JUL

SSP. *crassirostris*

♂**Br**
FEB–JUL

♀**Br**
FEB–JUL

SSP. *zedlitzi*

Three similar sspp. occur: *zedlitzi* (SE Spain) dullest; *amantum* (C & E Canary Is.); *crassirostris* (S & E Turkey eastwards) palest, large-billed.

LC **Mongolian Finch** *Bucanetes mongolicus*

LC | ❷ | **L** 12–13 cm | **W** 18–20 cm

Small, pale brown finch with short yellowish bill, white belly. **Ad** | head plain brown; upperparts pale brown, back streaked dark grey, rump unstreaked. Wing streaked pink and black with **two bands of pinkish-white**. Tail shows **white side**. ♂ | bright pink-brown; rump pink. ♀ | pink areas paler than on ♂, more restricted to throat and flank. **Juv** | lacks pink; buff-brown, like Trumpeter Finch but bill smaller, two buff wingbars and pale tertial tips; paler buff patch on closed secondaries.

FL | Quick, whirring, dumpy, round-winged. **Ad** pale wingbar and **white hindwing patch**; Juv plainer, browner.

👁 Trumpeter Finch

Scarce and very local resident

High altitude rocky areas

V | Call a rising "ch-veet." Song a short musical phrase

No seasonal change, but pink becomes brighter with feather wear, MAY–JUL.

♀
ALL YEAR

♂
ALL YEAR

Desert Finch

Eurasian Crimson-winged Finch *Rhodopechys sanguineus*

2 | **L** 13–15 cm | **W** 21–25 cm

Stocky, large-headed finch with **short, deep bill**. Brown, spotted black on cheek, back and breast; belly white. **Pink in wing**. **♂Br** | **crown black**. Upperparts rufous-brown. Broad **pink-red band** on black-tipped wing. **Rump and tail side pink**. Bill yellow. **♀Br** | dull brown; cap grey, rump brown. Pink wing band narrow. Bill yellow. **♂Nb/♀Nb/1W** | like **♀Br** but bill grey. **Juv** | bill yellow; head plain sandy-brown.

FL | Broad wings, bounding action and voice resemble Woodlark (*p. 349*). Pale rump contrasts with dark wings and blackish tail with thin pale sides.

Scarce and local resident/migrant

High altitude bare rocky areas, ravines; lower in winter

V | Low, full calls, "*chivli*," "*chu-vu-vu-vu*." Song a musical phrase repeated from rock or in song flight.

Seasonal change as dull feather tips wear off, revealing brighter colours, FEB–JUL.

♀ Br
FEB–JUL

♂ Br
FEB–JUL

Desert Finch
Rhodospiza obsoleta

2 | **L** 13–14 cm | **W** 20 cm

Small, pale, sparrow-like (*pp. 504–507*), social finch. Head and body grey-buff; **wingtip black and white**; tail **white with black centre**. **Ad** | wings streaked pink and black. **AdBr** | bill black. **AdNb** | bill yellowish. **♂** | black patch between eye and bill; tertials black, edged white. **♀** | brown or blackish between eye and bill; tertials grey, edged whitish. **Juv** | lacks pink in wings; bill pale pink-grey.

FL | Thickset, short-tailed. Wings and tail closely streaked **black, pink and white**. Broad **pale band** on grey underwing.

Juv
MAY–AUG

 Eurasian Crimson-winged Finch

Scarce and local resident

Open country, semi-arid farmed land

V | Call a whistled "*pink pink*." Song a musical sequence of varied trills.

No seasonal change except bill yellowish AUG–FEB and plumage worn paler by JUL–AUG.

♂ Br
FEB–JUL

♀ Br
FEB–JUL

Common Sparrows are similar looking. **House**, **Italian** and **Spanish Sparrows** are social and noisy; flocks can be in the hundreds; **Tree Sparrow** much more secretive. **FL**| Rounded body, large head; wings broad, rounded, rather tail-down. Dull brownish, grey-buff rump. Flocks of the three social species form **tight, whirring groups**.

LC

LC ① Spanish Sparrow *Passer hispaniolensis*

①|**L** 15–16 cm|**W** 18–25 cm

Underparts **thickly streaked** on ♂. **♂Br**| red-brown **crown** and black throat contrast with **white cheek, collar and broken stripe over eye.** Upperparts rufous-and-black. Underparts streaked black (some only on breast side MAR–APR). **♂Nb**| crown grey-brown, sparse streaks on breast. **♀/Juv**| like ♀ House Sparrow; underparts often subtly streaked grey; ♀ **Ad** may show faint dark bib, pale cheek.

V| Fast, repetitive, squeaky chirps, prolonged "*chi-li ch-li chi-li chi-li.*"

Locally common resident/migrant; occasional vagrant

Damp willows, thickets, trees near stork nests; around buildings

Two sspp. occur: *hispaniolensis* (widespread); *transcapicus* (Cyprus, E Turkey) paler.

VU Italian Sparrow *Passer italiae*

①|**L** 15–16 cm|**W** 18–25 cm

Upperparts brown, streaked buff and black, **underparts unstreaked.** Plumages like House Sparrow but ♂**Ad** head pattern resembles Spanish Sparrow. **♂Br**| crown and hindneck rich **red-brown**. Face white, bib black, but **underparts unstreaked.** (NOTE: In S Italy, breast streaked on ♂, closer to Spanish Sparrow.) **♂Nb**| bib small, crown with greyish fringes to feathers. **♀/Juv**| indistinguishable from House Sparrow.

V| Calls like House Sparrow. Loud, rambling, chirruping chorus at roost.

Locally common resident

Farmland, villages, towns and cities

♀ **ALL YEAR**

often subtle grey streaks on underparts

All SSP. *hispaniolensis*

♂ **Nb** AUG–MAR

♂ **Br** FEB–AUG

black streaks on underparts

♀ **ALL YEAR**

♂ **Br** MAR–SEP

♂ **Nb** SEP–MAR

plain underparts

NOTE: In S Italy, appears more like Spanish Sparrow.

All four species are similar. | Dead Sea Sparrow [♀] *p. 506* | ♀ - rock sparrows *p. 507* | *American sparrows p. 617*

House Sparrow *Passer domesticus*

❶ | **L** 14–16 cm | **W** 18–25 cm

Upperparts streaked, **underparts unstreaked**. **♂Br** | **crown-stripe grey**, hindneck red-brown. Cheek pale grey; **throat and bib black**. Upperparts red-brown, streaked buff and black; rump greyish. Broad white wingbar. Underparts pale grey. Bill black. **♂Nb** | **small black chin patch**; grey crown obscured by buff tips. Bill yellowish. **♀/Juv** | upperparts **pale brown, streaked buff**; **broad buff stripe behind eye**. Underparts grey-buff. Bill yellowish.

Common resident

Farms, villages, town parks, arable land, coastal areas

V | Loud chirrups and cheeps, "*cheep*," "*shreep*;" rapid, buzzing chatter "*st-t-cht-cht-cht-cht-chrr.*" Song includes calls in long, loud, chirruping sequence.

Four similar sspp. occur: *domesticus* (widespread); *balearoibericus* (S Europe) and *biblicus* (Cyprus, SE Turkey) paler; *hyrcanus* (SE Azerbaijan) small.

♀
ALL YEAR

All ssp. *domesticus*

grey crown and cheek

♂ Nb
SEP–MAR

♂ Br
MAR–SEP

plain underparts

LC (Eurasian) **Tree Sparrow**
LC *Passer montanus*

❶ | **L** 12–14 cm | **W** 18–22 cm

Small, thick-billed, rather quiet sparrow. Upperparts streaked, underparts plain. **Sexes look alike**. Hops with tail uptilted; round-headed, small-billed appearance. **Ad** | **crown and nape all-brown**; cheek white with square **black spot**. Black bib **small** and neat. Almost complete white collar. Upperparts streaked buff, brown and black, rump buff-brown. Underparts unmarked grey-buff. Bill buffish-grey AUG–FEB, black FEB–AUG. **Juv** | centre of crown diffusely pale/grey; as **Ad** by AUG–OCT.

Locally common resident/migrant; disperses in winter

Farmland, parkland with old trees, wet thickets and waterside places, old town/village walls

V | Distinctive hard "*tek*" or "*tet-et-et*" calls in flight, and cheerful "*tsuwit.*" Song high-pitched chattering.

Two sspp. occur: *montanus* (widespread); *transcaucasicus* (E Turkey eastwards, Caucasus) upperparts greyer, underparts whiter.

All ssp. *montanus*

Juv
APR–AUG

black cheek spot

AdNb
AUG–FEB

AdBr
FEB–AUG

♀ - House Sparrow [♀] *p.505*
♀ - Spanish Sparrow [♀] *p.504*
♀ - rock sparrows

LC VU Dead Sea Sparrow
Passer moabiticus

❶ | **L** 12 cm | **W** 15–18 cm

Small, social sparrow. Back streaked black and brown, underparts plain. **♂| bright rufous midwing panel. ♂Br|** head pattern distinctive: crown grey, yellow-buff stripe over eye, white stripe from bill extends into **yellow band below grey cheek**. Bill, line to eye and **throat black. ♂Nb|** head browner, black throat patch smaller; **yellow-buff crescent below cheek. ♀/Juv|** upperparts streaked grey-brown and buff, like small, pale female House Sparrow; pale stripe over eye long and tapered, pale throat extends into yellowish point beneath cheek. Wide **buff patch on base of primaries**.

Scarce and local summer migrant

Waterside shrubs, tamarisk scrub in semi-arid regions

FL| Wings short, rounded; tail short. Fast, whirring action; ♂ shows rufous patch on innerwing and grey rump.

V| Call a high-pitched "*trrirp*". Song strong, rhythmic, chirruping chorus (more musical than House Sparrow)

♀
ALL YEAR

buff patch

♂ Br
FEB–AUG

head pattern distinctive

rufous wing panel

SSP. *moabiticus* occurs in Europe.

♀ - rock sparrows

LC LC Chestnut-shouldered Bush-sparrow
Gymnoris xanthocollis

❶ | **L** 13–14 cm | **W** 18–20 cm

Slender, pale sparrow with a **long, pointed bill**. Upperparts greyish-brown, underparts buff-white. Two white wingbars: upper broad, lower narrow. **♂| chestnut shoulder. ♂Br|** bill black; chin white, throat yellow. **♂Nb|** bill pale. **♀/Juv|** head grey-buff with diffuse whitish band over eye. White upper wingbar on brown wing.

Scarce and local summer migrant
MAR–SEP

Open forest, scrub, gardens, cultivation

FL| Wings rather long and tapered; fast, whirring action.

V| Call a liquid "*chirrup*" or "*chilp*". Song a mixture of rapid chirrups and cheeps (faster than House Sparrow (*p.505*))

♀
ALL YEAR

long, pointed bill

broad white upper wingbar

♂ Br
FEB–AUG

chestnut shoulder

SSP. *transfuga* occurs in Europe.

Rock and Pale Rock Sparrows are similar. | House, Italian + Spanish Sparrows [♀] *p. 504–505*
Dead Sea Sparrow [♀] | Chestnut-shouldered Bush-sparrow [♀]

Rock Sparrow
Petronia petronia

❶ | **L** 14–15 cm | **W** 20–22 cm

Small, pale sparrow, inconspicuous against pale rocks or earth; often detected by calls. Small groups. Sexes look alike: resembles ♀ *Passer* sparrow. Upperparts **pale grey-brown with dark brown streaks**; underparts paler buffish with broad, **grey-brown flank streaks**. **Head broadly striped: pale buff stripe down centre of dark crown** and **over eye** (head pattern strong, colours subdued). Two white wingbars and pale tertial tips, which wear off APR–JUL. **Bill large**, pale orange at base. **Ad** | pale yellow breast spot. **Juv** | lacks yellow.

Three sspp. occur: *petronia* (S Europe to W Turkey, Madeira, Canary Is.) rather dark; *puteicola* (S Turkey) distinctly paler and very large-billed; *exigua* (C Turkey to Caucasus) pale with browner streaks.

FL | Rounded body, large head; long wings and obviously short tail. Fast, whirring action. Pale tips to tail feathers show as row of **whitish spots**.

V | Calls nasal, slightly twangy, deliberate double notes, "woo-siee" or "puyyi." Song simple repetition of "sle-vit," "pswi-iyp" and variations.

Locally common resident

Cliffs, gorges, boulders, earth banks, road cuttings, buildings

striped head

Ad
ALL YEAR

Ad
ALL YEAR

ssp. *puteicola*

Ad
ALL YEAR

ssp. *petronia*

whitish spots on tip of tail

Pale Rock Sparrow
(Pale Rockfinch)
Carpospiza brachydactyla

❶ | **L** 14–15 cm | **W** 20–22 cm

Slender, elongated, unstreaked, pale brown sparrow. Sexes look alike: resembles washed-out ♀ House Sparrow. Upperparts **plain** grey-brown; underparts whitish-buff. **Bill thick, slightly arched**. **Ad** | head grey-brown with diffuse pale stripe over eye and whiter throat. Two pale wingbars (may wear off by MAY); wingtip blackish, edged white. **Juv** | paler, more buffish than **Ad** with whiter underparts and plain head.

FL | Wings broad, rounded. Tail has **small whitish spots** across tip, most obvious beneath.

V | Call a soft "pluip" in flight. Song wheezing, buzzing trill.

Scarce and local summer migrant
MAR–SEP

Semi-arid or bushy hillsides

slightly arched, thick bill

Ad
ALL YEAR

pale wingbars wear thinner by MAY

Ad
ALL YEAR

whitish spots on tip of tail

BUNTINGS COMPARED *pp.510–51*

Buntings

NOTE: The vagrant American sparrows are most closely related to buntings (see *pp.616–617*).

24 species [**6 vagrants** (*pp.606–607*)] Small seed-eating and insectivorous birds with similarities to finches (see *page 480*). They occupy many habitats, from arid deserts to Arctic tundra. Many are migrants and become social in winter, sometimes joining finches and other species in mixed flocks. In spring they are territorial; males sing mostly simple, repetitive songs from regular perches. They have a short, thick bill (often with a smaller upper mandible and a broad, deeper lower mandible with a bulging upper edge, but on some the bill forms a small, neat triangle). Many (but not all) have a dark tail with white sides (excluding many finches). Most (again, not all) are streaked above and below. **Flight** Quite quick, slightly jerky, with bursts of wingbeats and shallow undulations. Some species frequently form flocks.

Identify by head, wing, rump and tail patterns | streaking | leg colour | calls and song

Sexing, Ageing and Moult

Males and females look different in most species; males have distinct breeding plumage. Juveniles/1W may be separable. **Adults and juveniles have a single moult each year.**

♀
1ST-WINTER
SEP–MAR
♂
♀
ADULT (WORN)
APR–AUG
♂
♀
ADULT (FRESH)
SEP–MAR
♂

REED BUNTING

Post-juvenile moult →

JUL–SEP: usually retaining most secondaries, primaries and tail feathers and some coverts. Unmoulted juvenile primary coverts dark brown, edged rufous, worn and frayed. Iris dark grey-brown, slowly becoming chestnut.

Adult moult

JUL–SEP: complete moult after breeding. Fresh primary coverts have firm grey tips. Iris dark chestnut. Fresh plumage has pale feather tips obscuring the pattern beneath. Tips break away (or become worn) in spring to reveal bolder pattern in the breeding season.

Buntings can be particularly difficult to identify. Throughout this book, simple language has been used to describe the parts of a bird. Learning a few technical terms helps to improve precision when looking for the key identification features of some species, including the rarer buntings. The feather tracts marked on this Little Bunting are applicable to other birds throughout the book (see also the annotated birds on *p.7*).

LITTLE BUNTING

stripe over eye
crown
eyestripe
side of crown
nape (hindneck)
eyering
pale cheek spot
cheek
throat
back
dark line by throat
lesser coverts ('shoulder')
median coverts (upper wingbar)
'moustache'
greater coverts (lower wingbar)
tertials
breast
rump [obscured]
wingtip
vent
flank
outer tail feather

White-winged Snowfinch *p. 484* |
White-winged Lark *p. 352*

Snow Bunting
Plectrophenax nivalis

2 | **L** 15·5–18 cm | **W** 32–38 cm

Large, short-legged, terrestrial bunting, often approachable but inconspicuous on ground. **Underparts unstreaked.** Wings reveal **white patches in flight. Legs short, black.** Flocks may number hundreds, only rarely with other species. Breeding plumage revealed by wear. Sex at all ages told by white smaller wing coverts and broad, black centre of scapulars on ♂; dark-centred coverts, pointed, brown centre of scapulars on ♀. **♂Br** | mostly white; upperparts, wingtips and tail black. Bill black. **♀Br** | head and upperparts buff, streaked black. Underparts dull white. **AdNb** | crown, cheek and breast side bright **tawny-brown.** Bill yellow. Tawny feather tips wear off by APR. **1W** | like **Ad**, ageing difficult but **1W** tends to show worn, faded tertials, pointed tail feathers (**Ad** tertials also faded by MAR–APR) and mixed old/new feathers giving contrast in coverts (all similar on **Ad** except during moult AUG–SEP). On ssp. *insulae*, greyish head distinctive. **Juv** | head and upperparts grey; underparts pale grey, softly streaked dark grey.

V | Characteristic rippling, rhythmic *"til-lil-il-it!"* or bright, whistled *"pseu,"* often combined. Song short, disjointed phrases mix full, vibrant or strident whistles and thin, wistful notes.

FL | Long, broad wings; wide, notched tail. Fast, direct; flocks undulate, white wing patches giving 'flickering' effect. **♂ white wings** with black tip; **♀** shorter white band on wing; **1W** less white in wing than **Ad**.

Scarce, locally common migrant/resident

Mountain peaks and plateaux, open rocky slopes, tundra; winters on beaches, uplands, grassland

Three sspp. occur. ssp. *nivalis* (N Europe) ♂ rump rusty-buff, wearing to all-white. ♀/**1W** mid-back frosty grey-buff contrasts with darker, browner scapulars; rump pale, breast-band rufous-buff. ssp. *insulae* (Iceland) ♂ rump white with broad dark streaks. ♀/**1W** back and scapulars show little contrast, all darker rufous or brown; rump and breast-band dark rufous. ssp. *vlasowae* (NE European Russia) large, pale, with very extensive white rump.

♂ Nb

♀ Nb/1W

♂ Br

SSP. *nivalis*

SSP. *nivalis*

♀ 1W
AUG–MAR
SSP. *insulae*

SSP. *nivalis*

♂ Nb/1W
AUG–MAR

SSP. *nivalis*

♀ 1W
AUG–MAR

SSP. *insulae*

SSP. *nivalis*

SSP. *insulae*: black tips to rump feathers.

SSP. *nivalis*

♂ Br
MAR–AUG

♀ Br
MAR–AUG

Buntings compared

Most **male buntings** in breeding plumage are best separated by their head patterns; they fall into several groups of similar species. Check bill colour; crown and cheek patterns; colour of stripes between cheek and throat.

PALLAS'S REED (p.513)

REED (p.512)

♂ Br
♂ Nb

YELLOW-BREASTED (p.518)

LAPLAND (p.510)

RUSTIC (p.514)

YELLOWHAMMER (p.520)

CIRL (p.522)

PINE (p.521)

ROCK (p.514)

RED-HEADED (p.518)

BLACK-HEADED (p.518)

PINE BUNTING × YELLOWHAMMER (p.521)

SNOW (p.509)

ORTOLAN (p.516)

CRETZSCHMAR'S (p.516)

GREY-NECKED (p.516)

CINEREOUS (p.514)

LC LC Lapland Bunting
Calcarius lapponicus

② | **L** 15–16 cm | **W** 24–27 cm

Large, short-legged, terrestrial bunting. **Rufous wing panel bordered each side by thin white bar**. Legs blackish. Flocks up to 100. **♂Br** | cap black; black face and bib outlined by **white band**; bill yellow. Nape rufous. Upperparts streaked rufous and black. Underparts white; side of breast/flank mottled black. **♂Nb** | broad buff stripe over eye; **cheek edged black**; hindneck rufous. Bib mottled blackish; **flank thickly streaked black**. **♀Br** | head like dull ♂**Br** but throat and cheek pale. **♀Nb/1W** | **pale central crown stripe**; black 'corners' to cheek. Hindneck greyish to rufous. Upperparts striped brown, black and cream. Underparts white, flank streaked black. **Juv** | head brownish, streaked.

V | Calls dry, hard, low rattling trill "*trrr-r-r-r-t*" or "*trr-r-r-t'k*" (lighter "*ticky-ticky-tik*" at distance); soft, or longer, loud "*teu*." Song combines long, thin and rich, warbling notes in repeated musical phrase.

FL | Wings long, tail quit short (shape more like Snow Bunting (p.509) than Ree Bunting); direct, level; bes told by ca

♂ Br
MAR-JUL

♂ Nb
JUL-MAR

streaks on side of breast extend onto flank

Female and 1st-winter buntings are mostly similar; some pairs/groups are difficult. Check crown pattern (*e.g.* central stripe); stripe over eye; eyering; cheek pattern, including extent of dark surround and pale 'spot' at rear; colour of stripes between cheek and throat; calls.

PALLAS'S REED (p. 513)   REED (p. 512)   LITTLE (p. 513)

YELLOW-BREASTED (p. 518)   LAPLAND (p. 510)   RUSTIC (p. 514)

YELLOWHAMMER (p. 520)   CIRL (p. 522)   PINE (p. 521)   ROCK (p. 514)

RED-HEADED (p. 518)   BLACK-HEADED (p. 518)   CORN (p. 522)   SNOW (p. 509)

ORTOLAN (p. 516)   CRETZSCHMAR'S (p. 516)   GREY-NECKED (p. 516)   CINEREOUS (p. 514)

♂ Br

chestnut greater coverts bordered by white

Nb

Rustic Bunting p. 514 |
Reed Bunting p. 512 |
American sparrows p. 617

Scarce migrant

Upland willow thickets, tundra, mountain plateaux and open moorland; winters coasts, open grasslands

♀ Nb/1W
JUL–MAR

crown with pale centre and dark sides

dusky rufous nape

♀ Br
MAR–JUL

dark corners to cheek

SSP. *lapponicus* occurs in Europe.

Pallas's Reed Bunting | Lapland Bunting *p. 510* | Rustic Bunting *p. 514*
| Yellowhammer [Juv/♀] *p. 520* | Pine Bunting *p. 521*
♀/Juv - Black-faced Bunting *p. 607* | American sparrows *p. 617*

Locally common
resident/migrant

Wet moorland,
boggy
heathland,
marshes and
riversides

LC
(Common) **Reed Bunting** *Emberiza schoeniclus*

LC ❸ | **L** 14–16 cm | **W** 21–28 cm

Large, slim, streaked, bunting; **tail blackish with white side.** Lesser
coverts reddish. Bill slightly arched. Legs **grey.** Flocks 10–20,
occasionally up to 50–100. ♂**Br** | **head black** with broad **white collar.**
Upperparts streaked black, rufous and cream. Underparts white,
streaked grey. ♂**Nb** | pale tips obscure black head until MAR. Rump
greyish. ♀**Br** | back streaked black, brown and cream; rump brown.
Pale band over eye; cheek dark with **blacker surround;** Underparts
white, streaked grey. ♀**Nb/Juv/1W** | buff band over eye, cheek pale.
Thin pale eyering; dark stripes on face reach bill. Rump grey-brown.

V | **Call** a simple "*tseup*" or high, thin "*tseee*" (no metallic 'tik' note). Song,
monotonously repeated from low perch, disjointed, short, slow "*sup-
jip-chilee-up*." Flocks 10–20, occasionally up to 50–100.

FL | Wings short and blunt; tail quite long. Low, quick dashes, erratic;
long black-and-white tail obvious.

Ten sspp. occur; minor plumage
variations, but bill size and song differ.
THIN-BILLED GROUP: *schoeniclus* (N & W
Europe), *lusitanica* (Iberia) darker. MEDIUM-
BILLED GROUP: *stresemanni* (SE Europe) dark;
ukrainae (Ukraine, SW European Russia)
paler; *incognita* (SE European Russia) very
pale, rump grey-white. THICK-BILLED GROUP:
witherbyi (Iberia, S France, Mediterranean
islands) dark; *intermedia* (Italy, Balkans)
flank striped rufous; *tschusii* (R Danube
in Bulgaria & Romania) pale; *caspia* (E
Turkey to Caucasus) and *reiseri* (S Balkans
to C Turkey) large and dark. Some do
not interbreed where ranges overlap;
taxonomic status under review.

'THIN-BILLED GROUP'

♂ **Br**
MAR–AUG

ssp. *schoeniclus*

'THICK-BILLED GROUP'

♂ **Nb**
AUG–FEB

ssp. *intermedia*

Appearance changes with loss of dull
feather tips on head/breast/rump in
spring, to reveal full breeding colours,
then darkening as feather edges on
back wear away in summer.

♀ **Br**
FEB–JUL

Black cheek marks
almost reach bill.

ssp. *schoeniclus*

♀ **Nb/1W**
AUG–MAR

Little Bunting *Emberiza pusilla*

L 12–13·5 cm | **W** 18–20 cm

Small bunting; resembles female/1W Reed Bunting, but bill small, **straight-edged**. **White eyering** in plain face; **cheek rufous**; face pale/rufous. Dark eyestripe and edge of cheek **do not reach bill**. Lesser coverts dull; legs **pale pink**. **♂Br** | crown black with rufous central stripe. Upperparts streaked grey, black, brown. Underparts white, streaked black. **♀Br** | duller than ♂, face browner. **AdNb / Juv / 1W** | upperparts dull brown; cheek rufous, crown rufous with dark sides.

Scarce and local summer migrant APR–OCT; occasionally winters

Mixed or coniferous forest

👁 Reed Bunting [1W/♀] | Rustic Bunting *p. 514*
Yellow-browed Bunting p. 607 | Chestnut-eared Bunting p. 607

FL ● | Broad, rounded wings, narrow tail. Direct, finch-like (*p. 480*), slightly undulating.

V | **Call** draws attention, a sharp, clicking "*zik*" or "*tik*." Song loud, musical phrase, repeated "*wiss-wiss-wiss sweee siwee*," rattling start resembling Chaffinch (*p. 500*) or thinner, like Yellowhammer (*p. 520*).

Black cheek marks fall short of bill.

♂ Br
MAR–AUG

Nb/1W
AUG–FEB

Pallas's Reed Bunting

Emberiza pallasi

L 13–13·5 cm | **W** 20–25 cm

Small, streaked bunting with small, straight-edged bill, long tail. Upperparts grey-buff, streaked black; rump buff or whitish. **Lesser coverts dull grey**. **♂Br** | head black, broad white collar; upperparts pale buff-brown, streaked black; underparts white. **♂Nb / ♀ / 1W** | cap pale brown without dark side, no dark eyestripe; **pale cheek** with **black spot** in corner. Lesser coverts and rump brown; **two whitish wingbars**. Underparts almost **unmarked**. Bill pink-based. **Juv** | breast streaked blackish (vagrants may be in this plumage).

V | **Call** sparrow-like (*p. 504*) "*chee-ulp*." Simple song, like Reed Bunting.

L | Wings broad, tail narrow; slightly undulating.

Rare and very local summer migrant APR–SEP

Open grassy or marshy areas

ssp. *polaris* occurs in Europe.

👁 Reed Bunting
♀/Nb/1W - Rustic Bunting *p. 514*

1W
AUG–FEB

Buff fringes wear off, looks dark-backed.

♂ Br
FEB–JUL

♀ Br
FEB–JUL

Rustic Bunting

Emberiza rustica

3 | **L** 13–14·5 cm | **W** 20–24 cm

Small bunting with peaked crown, **rufous breast and flank stripes** and white wingbars. Rump unstreaked **red-brown**. Bill pink with dark tip. ♂**Br** | **head black** with **stripe over eye**, nape, cheek spot and throat **white**. Upperparts rufous, streaked black. Underparts white with **rufous breast-band**. ♂**Nb** / ♀**Br** | like ♂**Br** but head pattern blurred; breast-band streaked red-brown. **Juv / 1W** | central crown pale, **side streaked black**; buff stripe behind eye; black eyestripe and edge of cheek, white cheek spot.

FL ● | Wings short and broad, tail long with white sides. Direct but slightly undulating.

♂ Br
MAR–SEP

1W/Nb

white underparts

Rock Bunting   *Emberiza cia*

2 | **L** 16 cm | **W** 20–27 cm

Large, long-tailed bunting. Rarely forms flocks. Upperparts brown, streaked black. Underparts rufous. Weak **white wingbars**; tail black with white side. ♂**Br** | head and bib grey; black lines beside crown, through eye and **on edge of cheek** give **striped** effect. Bill black-and-grey. ♀**Br** | individually variable: some resemble ♂**Br** but with dark streaking on flank and less distinct crown stripe; others with much duller stripes on head. **AdNb** | head pattern obscured by dull feather tips. **Juv** | head finely streaked, lacks black stripes. ♂**1W** | head grey, blackish head stripes distinct from OCT; breast plain. ♀**1W** | head brownish, stripes ill-defined; breast streaked.

FL | Wings short and broad, tail long and narrow. Direct, slightly undulating. White tail sides.

All ssp. *cia*

♂ Br
FEB–SEP

♀ Br
FEB–SEP

Cinereous Bunting

Emberiza cineracea

3 | **L** 16–17 cm | **W** 22–25 cm

Large, long-tailed, **greyish**, terrestrial bunting; head yellowish; large white tips on outer tail feathers. Bill **grey**. ♂ | upperparts pale grey-brown, finely streaked darker grey; head tinged yellow-green; yellow streak beneath cheek; **throat yellow**; white eyering. Underparts unstreaked. ♀ | upperparts brown, streaked grey; two thin white wingbars. Pale eyering; throat yellowish-buff. **Juv / 1W** | grey-brown; crown and cheek finely streaked brown. Underparts buff, streaked brown, belly and undertail white. **Bill grey**.

FL | Wings broad, rounded. Direct, slightly undulating.

ssp. *cinerace*

♂ Br
MAR–SEP

♂ Br
MAR–SEP

ssp. *semenowi*

Call a sharp "*zit*." Song rich, fluty, thrush-like p.383)) warbling phrase, egularly repeated.

♀ Br
MAR–SEP

rufous flank markings

1W
JUL–MAR

brick-red rump

👁 Lapland Bunting p.510 | Reed Bunting p.512 | Little Bunting p.513 | Pine Bunting p.521 Yellowhammer p.520 *Yellow-browed Bunting p.607* *American sparrows p.617*

Scarce and local summer migrant APR–SEP

Wet mixed or coniferous forest, thickets

Persistent call a simple, high, sharp, thin "*si*" (elusive, like Cirl Bunting p.522)). Song short, starting slowly and with a quick, jingling ending.

♀ Nb/ ♀ 1W
AUG–MAR

♂ 1W
AUG–MAR

👁 *House Bunting p.606* *Striolated Bunting p.606*

Locally common resident/winter migrant

Boulders, rocky slopes, cliffs and gorges

Two sspp. occur, gradually intergrade: *cia* (C & S Europe to Balkans and N Turkey); *par* (Crimea, Caucasus, E Turkey eastwards) slightly darker.

Call a sharp "*tchrip*." Song short, rolled or slightly rasping "*shrreet, shree-we-wo, shreevit*."

SSP. *semenowi*

1W
AUG–MAR

♀ Br
MAR–SEP

👁 Ortolan, Cretzschmar's and Grey-necked Buntings p.516 Cirl Bunting p.522

Scarce and local summer migrant MAR–SEP

Stony slopes, dry heathland

Two sspp. occur: *cineracea* (E Greek islands, W Turkey) ♂ **Ad** underparts plain grey with white belly; *semenowi* (SE Turkey) ♂ **Ad** underparts yellow, grey-green on breast.

Ortolan, Cretzschmar's and Grey-necked Buntings are large, slender buntings with similar patterns; males have a green, blue-grey or grey head and a pale eyering and throat. Females and juveniles/1st-winter are more subtle and harder to separate. **FL** | Wings broad, tapered; tail quite long, white-sided. Direct, slightly undulating.

Ortolan Bunting

LC
LC

Emberiza hortulana

❸ | **L** 15–16·5 cm | **W** 21–27 cm

Pale bunting. **White or yellow eyering** in plain face. Bill **pinkish**; legs pink. **♂Br** | head and breast-band green; throat and **stripe below cheek yellow.** Upperparts brown, streaked black (darker by JUL); **rump buff**. Underparts **orange**. **♂Nb** | pale buff feather edges (wear off by MAR). **♀** | crown and breast pale greygreen, finely streaked blackish; underparts orange-buff, breast streaked black. **Juv / 1W** | head brown with **white eyering**. Back and **rump brown**, tertial edges buff. Underparts buff, breast streaked black.

green head and yellow throat

♂ Br
FEB–SEP

♀ Br
FEB–SEP

Cretzschmar's Bunting

LC
LC

Emberiza caesia

❸ | **L** 14–15·5 cm | **W** 23–26 cm

Rufous bunting. **White eyering** in plain face. Bill thick, **orange-pink with grey ridge**; legs pink. **♂Br** | head and breast-band blue-grey; throat and stripe below cheek **orange**. Upperparts **rufous**, streaked black; **rump rufous**. Underparts **rufous**. **♂Nb** | pale buff feather edges, dark streaks and white flecks on head (all wear off by MAR). **♀** | crown and breast buff-brown; white eyering; **orange-buff** stripe below cheek. Underparts rufousbuff, brightest under tail. **Juv / 1W** | head dull brown with white eyering; back, **rump and tertial edges rufous**. Underparts buff, streaked black.

♀ Br
FEB–SEP

bill pink with grey ridge

blue-grey head and orange throat

throat and stripe below cheek orange-buff

♂ Br
FEB–SEP

Grey-necked Bunting

LC
LC

Emberiza buchanani

❸ | **L** 14–15·5 cm | **W** 23–26 cm

Pale, rufous-brown bunting. **White eyering** in plain face. Bill **slim, all orange-pink**; legs pink. **♂Br** | head grey with **bold white eyering**; throat and stripe below cheek **very pale** yellow. Upperparts **pale rufous**, streaked brown; **rump greyish**. Underparts **mottled** orange-red and buff. **♂Nb** | pale buff feather edges (wear off by MAR). **♀** | like ♂ but underparts paler buffish. **Juv / 1W** | head grey-brown with white eyering; back pale **grey-brown**, tertial edges and rump pale rusty-pink. Underparts buff, scarcely streaked.

bill all-pink

blue-grey head; pale yellow throat mottled grey

♂ Br
MAR–SEP

♀ Br
FEB–SEP

Ortolan, Cretzschmar's, and Grey-necked Buntings are similar. Rock Bunting *p.514*

V | Metallic "*chip*" or "*sli*" calls alternating with fuller "*plit.*" Song short, fluty phrase, 3–5 rhythmic notes before longer, lower ending – "*sliu sliu sliu slu-slu wrrrrr,*" repeated, sometimes at a different pitch.

1W
AUG–MAR

Locally fairly common summer migrant
MAR–OCT

Dry, bushy slopes, farmland with hedgerows, trees

tertial edges/ rump buff

V | Like Ortolan Bunting, but sharper, rasping call. Song also similar, with two or three short notes and a longer one, but less clear and ringing.

1W
AUG–MAR

Locally fairly common summer migrant
MAR–OCT

Dry, bushy, stony slopes, rocky mountainsides

tertial edges/ rump rufous

V | Call short, sharp "*tchupe.*" Song low, quick, with longer, higher note before final flourish, "*tsee-tsee-tsee soo-siseep.*"

1W
AUG–MAR

Locally fairly common summer migrant
MAR–OCT

Bare mountainsides

SSP. *cerrutii* occurs in Europe.

tertial edges/rump pale rusty pink

517

Red-headed and Black-headed Buntings are large, slim buntings; males are distinctive but females and juveniles/1st-winter are difficult or impossible to separate without DNA sampling. **FL**| Elongated; wings broad but pointed, tail long with **no white**. Direct, slightly undulating.

LC Red-headed Bunting
LC *Emberiza bruniceps*

❸ | **L** 15–16.5 cm | **W** 20–21 cm

Large, slim bunting, with long, **plain brown tail**. **♂Br**| head and breast red-brown; back streaked yellow and black. **Underparts, neck and rump yellow**. **♂Nb**| pattern obscured by pale feather tips; wing feathers broadly edged rufous. **♀/Juv/1W**| upperparts dull brown, underparts buff. **Rump pale, usually tinged pale yellow/green**; crown **unstreaked**.

♂ Br

♂ Br
MAR–OCT

LC Black-headed Bunting
LC *Emberiza melanocephala*

❸ | **L** 15·5–17.5 cm | **W** 20–23 cm

Large, slim bunting with long, **plain greyish tail**. Occasional flocks of 10–50. **♂Br**| **black hood**; back red-brown, rump rufous or golden-yellow. Throat, neck and **underparts yellow**. **♂Nb**| pattern obscured by white feather tips; wing feathers broadly edged white. **♀**| upperparts dull buff-brown, faintly streaked grey; greyish hood. Throat and underparts **pale yellow**. **Rump brown or slightly rusty-brown. Juv/1W**| like ♀ but duller, underparts greyish-buff, yellow under tail. Rump usually **rusty-brown**; crown **finely streaked** blackish.

♂ Br
MAR–OCT

♂ Br

♂ Nb
SEP–MAR

CR Yellow-breasted Bunting
CR *Emberiza aureola*

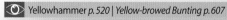

👁 Yellowhammer *p.520* | Yellow-browed Bunting *p.607*

❸ | **L** 15 cm | **W** 20–22 cm

Fairly large, slender bunting with yellowish underparts and **pinkish bill**. **♂Br**| back and rump chestnut; shoulder white; **face black; underparts yellow** with **brown breast-band**. **♂Nb**| pattern obscured by pale feather tips. **♀**| back dull brown, streaked grey. Underparts **pale yellow** streaked black. **Dark stripe** beside **pale crown**. **Juv/1W**| upperparts streaked yellowish-brown, black and buff. **Pale central crown stripe**; cheek greyish, edged black, with yellow spot; throat pale yellow. **Two white wingbars**. Rump grey-brown, streaked black; side of tail white.

♂ Br
MAR–SEP

♂ Nb

♂ 1S
MAR–SEP

V | Calls sharp, sparrowy "*schlip*." Sings with head raised, rump puffed out, wings drooped, or in song flight: song simple, accelerating, ticking "*sip*" notes merging into higher, trilled warble with thin, low flourish.

rump pale, tinged yellow/green

♀
ALL YEAR

Juv / 1W
JUN–MAR

NOTE: Field identification of Juv/1W Black-headed and Red-headed Buntings may not be possible without DNA samples.

Very locally fairly common summer migrant APR–SEP

Steppe grassland with bushy patches, semi-desert

V | Call a fine high "*psip*." Song, simple metallic notes accelerating into bright, warbling phrase; repeated.

rump rusty-brown

♀
ALL YEAR

Locally fairly common summer migrant APR–AUG

Open, bushy farmland, orchards, scattered trees

FL | Wings short, pointed; tail short, black with white sides. Slightly undulating.

♂ Nb
SEP–MAR

♀
ALL YEAR

♀ / 1W

pale crown stripe

V | Call a high, sharp, metallic "*tsip*." Song chattery, hesitant notes mixed with repeated, short, bright, fluty warbling phrases.

Rare and local, rapidly declining summer migrant MAY–AUG

Deciduous woodland, riverside thickets

SSP. *aureola* occurs in Europe.

Juv / 1W
JUN–MAR

519

LC

Yellowhammer *Emberiza citrinella*

LC ❷ | **L** 16–17 cm | **W** 23–29 cm

Large, slim bunting. Head and underparts **yellow** or yellowish; back brown, streaked black. **Rump rufous-orange, tail blackish with white side**. Flocks may exceed 100, often with other buntings/finches. ♂**Br** | head and breast **bright yellow**, crown and cheek edged black; greenish breast-band; flank streaked orange-brown. ♂**Nb** / ♀ | crown yellowish with dark side; cheek dark with pale spot. Crown feathers mostly yellow, with fine or no dark streak (♂) or less yellow but clear black streak (♀). Underparts **yellowish**, ♀ with black streaks, broadest on flank, little or no green on breast. **Juv** | streaked on chin and throat; ageing after moult to **1W** unreliable.

V | Calls clicking "*tswik*" and rasping "*tzu.*" Song even-pitched, high, metallic "*sip-ip-ip-ip-ip-ip- seee-u*" or ending with longer "*-seeee.*" Also faster, trilling version (more like Cirl Bunting).

FL | Broad-based wings; long, narrow tail. Rises quickly into fast, jerky flight, with long undulations; **rufous rump** and white tail sides.

Cirl Bunting *p. 522* | Pine Bunting
Reed Bunting *p. 512*
Rustic Bunting *p. 514*
Yellow-breasted Bunting *p. 518*
Chestnut Bunting p. 607

Locally common
resident/migrant

Bushy heathland,
grassland,
pastures/
arable land with
hedgerows

♂ Nb

♂ Nb
SEP–MAR

♂ Br
FEB–SEP

rufous rump

All ssp. *citrinella*

♀
ALL YEAR

1W
SEP–MAR

Juv
JUN–SEP

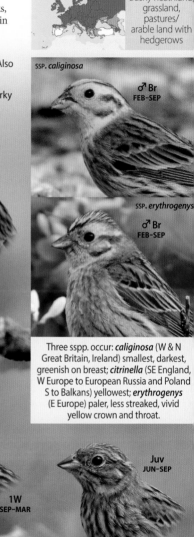

ssp. *caliginosa*

♂ Br
FEB–SEP

ssp. *erythrogenys*

♂ Br
FEB–SEP

Three sspp. occur: *caliginosa* (W & N
Great Britain, Ireland) smallest, darkest,
greenish on breast; *citrinella* (SE England,
W Europe to European Russia and Poland
S to Balkans) yellowest; *erythrogenys*
(E Europe) paler, less streaked, vivid
yellow crown and throat.

Pine Bunting *Emberiza leucocephalos*

3 | **L** 16–17·5 cm | **W** 25–30 cm

Large, slim bunting; shape and size as Yellowhammer, but **no yellow**.
♂**Br** | **crown, cheek and breast-band white**; chestnut patch over eye
edged black, **throat chestnut**; **underparts white, streaked rufous**.
♂**Nb** | head pattern obscured by pale feather edges, SEP–MAR.
♀ | streaked light brown, like pale Yellowhammer, **lacking yellow**;
primaries and secondaries edged white. **Juv / 1W** | like ♀; head more
contrasted in ♂ than ♀.

V | Sharp "*tswik*" call, like Yellowhammer. Song a vibrant,
trilled phrase, "*tititi-ti-tip-tip-tip-tip tsssee*" (pattern like
Yellowhammer but slightly more strident).

Yellowhammer | Reed Bunting *p. 512*
Rustic Bunting *p. 514*

Scarce, local
summer
migrant MAR–SEP;
occasionally
winters

Forest clearings,
shrubby
grassland

FL | Broad-based wing, long, narrow tail;
long undulations. Bright **rufous rump**
and white tail sides.

SSP. *leucocephalos*
occurs in Europe.

♂ **Nb**
AUG–MAR

♀
ALL YEAR

♂**1W**
SEP–MAR

♀**1W**
SEP–MAR

wing feathers
narrowly
edged white
(never yellow)

♂ **Br**
FEB–SEP

Infrequent hybrids/intergrades with Yellowhammer occur: many are clearly
intermediate; those closest to Pine Bunting show yellow edges on primaries.

♀ **1W**
SEP–MAR

♂ **Br**

Yellow edges to primaries
indicate the presence of
Yellowhammer genes.

♂ **Br**
FEB–SEP

♂ **Br**

Some individuals
may recall Rock
Bunting (*p. 514*).

♀   ♀

Yellowhammer
Yellow-breasted Bunting p. 518
Cinereous Bunting p. 514

LC

Cirl Bunting *Emberiza cirlus*

LC

❸ | **L** 16–16·5 cm | **W** 22–25 cm

Large, slim bunting with reddish
upperparts and yellowish underparts.
Like Yellowhammer but rump **dull olive**.
♂**Br** | breast-band green, **face black-
and-yellow**, **throat black**. ♂**Nb** | black
areas obscured by buff tips. ♀/**Juv**/**1W** |
crown dark, plain; dark line behind eye;
cheek with dark edge and prominent
whitish spot; pale eyering. Upperparts
brown, red-brown on shoulders, streaked
black. **Rump dull olive-grey**. Underparts
yellow-buff, finely streaked black, mostly
around upper breast; flank streaks thin.

V | **Call** distinct but elusive: high, thin,
quiet "*si*" or "*zit*." Song (may resemble
Yellowhammer's), a short trill on **one
note**; fast, thin and metallic "*ts-r-r- r-r-r-r-r-
r-r*;" or slightly slower, more distinct "*tsi-tsi-
tsi-tsi-tsi- tsi-tsi-tsi*." Less wooden, hollow or
rattling than Lesser Whitethroat (*p. 445*).

FL | Broad-based wing, long, narrow tail;
long undulations. **Dull olive rump** and
white tail sides.

Cirl Bunting (*left*) has an olive-grey rump;
Yellowhammer (*right*) a rufous rump.

Scarce, locally
common resident

Old pasture, arable
fields with hedgerows
and scattered trees,
bushy slopes

♂ **Br**
FEB–SEP

♂ **Nb**
SEP–MAR

♀/**1W**
ALL YEAR

LC

Corn Bunting

LC

Emberiza calandra

❶ | **L** 16–19 cm | **W** 26–32 cm

Large, brown, streaked, **plain-tailed**
bunting. Small flocks, mixes with
other buntings and finches. Head and
upperparts **pale buff-brown**, streaked
blackish. Breast whitish with dark streaks
merging into central dark patch. **Bill
thick, arched; tail plain brown**. **Ad** | sexes
alike; seasonal differences minimal. **Juv** |
paler, yellower than **Ad**, cheek more boldly
outlined dark; like **Ad** from AUG/OCT.

V | Call a loud, full "*quik*," "*pik*" or "*plip*"
(like a snapped stick). Song highly
characteristic: short, monotonous,
crunching glass/shaking keys quality –
short notes followed by rising, straining
trill "*tuc-tuc-tuc-tss-rr- rreeeee*."

FL | Wing broad, tail long. If disturbed,
groups fly up hurriedly to bush,
hedgerow or wires. **No white** on tail.

Three similar sspp. occur: *calandra*
(wiespread); *clanceyi* (Hebrides) darker;
buturlini (SE Turkey) paler, greyer.

Ad
plain tail

Scarce,
locally
common
resident

Arable
land, grassy
downland

streaks on breast merge
to form dark patch

Ad
ALL YEAR

ssp. *calandra*

Ad
ALL YEAR

ssp. *buturlini*

Endemic landbirds of the Atlantic islands

Three island groups of the eastern Atlantic – the Azores, Madeira and the Canary Islands – are covered in this book. (Together with the Cape Verde islands, these archipelagos are jointly referred to as Macaronesia.) The geographically dispersed nature of Macaronesia is reflected in the wildlife of the Azores being closer to that of Europe, whereas that of the other island groups is more African in nature. Some birds are endemic to Macaronesia (i.e. breed nowhere else in the world) but occur on one or more of the island groups, although a number of species are restricted to individual islands within them. Endemic landbirds, as well as African Blue Tit, that, within Europe, are entirely restricted to Macaronesia and have not been recorded as vagrants elsewhere, are included in this section (endemic species are indicated by **E** in the status box). Other species, notably the seabirds (see pp. 96–97), Plain Swift (p. 342) and African Houbara (p. 238) (which, in Europe, breeds only in Macaronesia) have (or may have) occurred as migrants or vagrants and are therefore included within the main body of the book.

The following table summarizes the distribution of the landbirds that are considered to be Macaronesian specialities. This includes Goldcrest (p. 414), the subspecies of which, in the Canary Islands at least, are separated as a species by some taxonomic authorities. Many other species that occur in Macaronesia are represented by endemic subspecies, most of which are only subtly different from their mainland European counterparts and these are covered in the relevant part of the book. However, the Macaronesian subspecies of Chaffinch (p. 500) are especially distinctive and are included in this section (p. 528).

Species		Page	Azores	Madeira	El Hierro	La Palma	La Gomera	Tenerife	Gran Canaria	Fuerteventura	Lanzarote	Notes
					Canary Islands							
Madeira Laurel-pigeon		524		●								
Dark-tailed Laurel-pigeon		524			●	●	●	●				
White-tailed Laurel-pigeon		524				●	●	●				
Plain Swift		342		●	●	●	●	●	●	●	●	Also Iberia (very rare)
Berthelot's Pipit		525		●	●	●	●	●	●	●	●	
Fuerteventura Stonechat		525								●		
Canary Islands Chiffchaff		527			●	●	●	●	●			
Madeira Firecrest		526		●								
Goldcrest	ssp. *ellenthalerae*				●	●						Sometimes treated as a species, 'Tenerife Kinglet'
	ssp. *teneriffae*						●	●				
	ssp. *inermis*	526	●									W and C Azores
	ssp. *sanctaemariae*		●									Santa Maria, SE Azores
	ssp. *azoricus*		●									São Miguel, E Azores
African Blue Tit	ssp. *teneriffae*						●	●				In Europe, occurs only on the Canary Islands. Sometimes treated as one or more separate species, and referred to as, e.g., 'Canary Blue Tit' (ssp. *teneriffae*) and 'Palma Blue Tit' (ssp. *palmensis*)
	ssp. *degener*									●	●	
	ssp. *hedwigii*	526							●			
	ssp. *palmensis*					●						
	ssp. *ombriosus*				●							
Azores Bullfinch		528	●									
Canary		527	●	●	●	●	●	●	●	●	●	
Tenerife Blue Chaffinch		529						●				
Gran Canaria Blue Chaffinch		529							●			

Macaronesian 'laurel' pigeons Three species of pigeon are restricted to the upland laurel and tree-heath forests of Madeira and the Canary Islands. They are secretive and most often seen flying low over the forest canopy or across clearings, but may venture into more open areas to feed. Woodpigeon p. 243

LC Madeira Laurel-pigeon

LC *Columba trocaz*

L 40–45 cm | **W** 70–75 cm

Large, dark grey pigeon. **Ad** | silvery patch on side of neck. **Juv** | browner, without neck patch.

V | Song a hoarse, weak coo "*uh-uh-hooh-hooh-ho-ho*."

FL | Wide **pale grey band on tail**. Underwing dark.

E Madeira Scarce resident	Laurel/tree heath forest, rocky slopes, adjacent arable fields

Ad

Ad
ALL YEAR

LC Dark-tailed Laurel-pigeon

LC *Columba bollii*

L 35–37 cm | **W** 65–68 cm

Large, deep-chested, broad-winged pigeon. **Ad** | dark greyish, breast purple-pink; shiny green patch on side of neck. **Juv** | upperparts dark brown above, underparts rufous-brown.

V | Song a deep, quiet, four-syllable coo.

FL | Dark, with paler midwing band. Tail dark with **grey central band** on both upperside and underside. Underwing dark (Rock Doves/Feral Pigeons (*p. 241*) in same areas show white rump and underwing).

E W Canary Is. Scarce resident	Laurel/juniper/tree heath forest

Ad

Ad
ALL YEAR

NT White-tailed Laurel-pigeon

NT *Columba junoniae*

L 37–38 cm | **W** 65–70 cm

Large, bronze-brown and grey pigeon. **Ad** | head glossed green, lower neck purple; back and rump blue-grey; underparts pinkish-brown. **Juv** | dull brown with pale feather edges.

V | Song a hoarse, bouncy coo.

FL | Dark brownish; **rump pale grey**, fading to **whitish tail tip**. Underside of tail dark with striking **broad white tip**; tail often fanned.

E W Canary Is. Scarce resident	Laurel/juniper/tree heath forest and adjacent open areas

Ad
ALL YEAR

Ad

Ad

524

Barbary Dove
Streptopelia roseogrisea

Canary Is. | Escape/ introduced resident

Gardens, farmland

L 29–30 cm | **W** 48–50 cm
Like pale Collared Dove with **less contrasted wingtip.**

V | Soft "*coo, crrroo.*"

COLLARED DOVE

Ad/1W ALL YEAR

👁 Collared Dove p. 245

Great Grey Shrike: ssp. *koenigi* (Canary Islands) is an endemic and rather distinctive subspecies of Great Grey Shrike (*p. 468*): dark above, greyish below; black mask extends narrowly over bill.

Ad

Ad ALL YEAR

E | Macaronesia | Common — Stony slopes, fields, heath

Berthelot's Pipit *Anthus berthelotii*

L 15–18 cm | **W** 24–26 cm

Pale, greyish pipit with bright buff fringes on wing; row of blackish shoulder spots; pale stripe over eye. Underparts cold buff-white, dark streaks on breast.

V | Short "*tswee*" call. Song frequent, dry, repeated "*schli, schli, schli….*"

Two similar sspp. occur: *berthelotii* (Canary Is.); *madeirensis* (Madeira) breast densely streaked.

👁 Meadow Pipit p. 362

NOTE: Sexes and ages look alike; no seasonal changes.

1Y/Ad ALL YEAR

ssp. *berthelotii*

Fuerteventura Stonechat
Saxicola dacotiae

L 11–12 cm | **W** 20–25 cm

Small, upright chat. ♂| head black-brown, **white stripe over eye, white throat.** Back brown, white shoulder patch. Underparts buff/white. Moults MAY–JUL, fresh plumage pale, collar dull; brown feather edges wear off by DEC to reveal blackish head and back, underparts whiter with orange breast patch; **collar broad and white.** ♀ / **Juv** | browner; stripe over eye thin. ♂**1W** | wing coverts brown.

V | Pebble-tapping "*tack-tsak-tsak*" like Stonechat; song short, thin, musical phrases.

👁 Stonechat | Whinchat p. 400

E | Fuerteventura | Scarce resident — Semi-arid areas and scrub

♀ **ALL YEAR**

♂ **ALL YEAR [OCT]**

♂**1W AUG–APR [DEC]**

525

LC NE African Blue Tit *Cyanistes teneriffae*

L 11–12 cm | **W** 20–25 cm

Subtly different island subspecies (regarded as up to five separate species by some). Actions and pattern as Blue Tit, but stronger contrasts. **Ad** | back grey-blue, **cap blackish-blue**; broad, black collar; wing blue-grey; underparts bright yellow. **Juv** | yellowish on head.

V | Calls include *"chi-cher-cher-er-er-errr;"* song musical *"chichi-chirichi-chirichi."*

Canary Is.	Woodland, gardens, dry
Fairly common	scrub

African Blue Tit – Canary Islands subspecies plumage detail:

palmensis	La Palma	BELLY white; WINGBAR thin; BACK greenish-blue
ombriosus	El Hierro	BELLY yellow; WINGBAR thin; BACK greenish
teneriffae	La Gomera and Tenerife	BELLY yellow; WINGBAR none; BACK slate-grey
hedwigii	Gran Canaria	as SSP. *teneriffae* but different call
degener	Lanzarote and Fuerteventura	BELLY yellow; WINGBAR obvious; BACK blue-grey

👁 Blue Tit *p. 463*

SSP. *teneriffae*

SSP. *degener*

Ad
ALL YEAR

Ad
ALL YEAR

E Madeira	Tree heath, broom, laurel
Fairly common	forest

LC LC Madeira Firecrest *Regulus madeirensis*

L 8–9 cm | **W** 15–20 cm

Like fine-billed, long-legged Firecrest. **Ad** | grey nape and neck isolate crown and face pattern within subtle grey hood; larger black patch on wing. **Juv** | grey head, broken white eyering, no crown stripe.

V | Calls resemble Firecrest, also fuller *"wheez."* Song thin, high *"see, si-si-si-si, see sisip"* with little rhythm, lacking acceleration of Firecrest.

MACARONESIAN GOLDCRESTS

Two sspp. of **Goldcrest** (*p. 414*) are endemic to the Canary Islands: *teneriffae* (Tenerife and La Gomera), dull with black forehead band, lower-pitched calls; SSP. *ellenthalerae* (La Palma and El Hierro), identifiable by range. These are sometimes separated as a full species, but are visually similar to Goldcrest in mainland Europe. Also, three sspp. occur on the Azores: *azoricus* (São Miguel, E Azores), *sanctaemariae* (Santa Maria, SE Azores) and *inermis* (W and C Azores), which look like mainland European sspp. but have erratic, less rhythmic songs.

Ad
ALL YEAR

SSP. *teneriffae*

Ad
ALL YEAR

👁 Firecrest *p. 414*

Chiffchaff *p. 432*

Canary Islands Chiffchaff
Phylloscopus canariensis

L 12–14 cm | **W** 18–22 cm

Small, dark-legged warbler; like Chiffchaff (spring/autumn migrant to the Canary Islands) but is darker, looks longer-tailed (due to having shorter wings) and does not 'dip' tail. Often clings to upright stem while probing large flower. Greyish-olive to brighter greenish above; whiter throat with dusky breast side, or cleaner yellow below; long, thin pale stripe over eye.

V | Calls flat, low *"schlip," "shweeu"* or *"tsooi"* and twittering, finch-like *"titip."* Song has fast, bouncy rhythm, *"chipchapcheff-cheff-cheff-chipchap…."*

E Canary Is. | Common | Woodland, gardens, parks

Two similar sspp. described: *canariensis* (W Canary Is.); *exsul* (Lanzarote [probably extinct]) paler, dark-legged.

Ad
ALL YEAR

SSP. *canariensis*

Serin *p. 489* | Siskin *p. 488* | Greenfinch *p. 490*

Canary *Serinus canaria*

L 12–13 cm | **W** 20–30 cm

Small, greenish finch; shorter wings, longer tail, longer bill than smaller Serin. ♂**Ad** | band around cheek and whole of underparts dull yellow (Serin is more contrasted yellow-and-white); rump greenish-yellow. Wings blackish with two yellow wingbars. ♀**Ad** | duller, more streaked, grey on crown, side of neck and upper breast. **Juv** | browner, streaked, like young Serin; size and structure important for identification.

V | Calls squeaky *"soee,"* quick *"whi-ti-tip"* and falling *"siu."* Song (less rich than domestic birds) varied trills, rolling phrases and sweet notes.

E **Macaronesia**
Common; occasional escape | Farmland, dry scrub, gardens

Juv   Juv

SERIN   CANARY

Juv
MAR–NOV

♂
ALL YEAR

♀
ALL YEAR

Juv
JUN–OCT

Ad
ALL YEAR

E São Miguel, Azores | Rare | Forest

VU
VU

Azores Bullfinch
Pyrrhula murina

L 16–17 cm | **W** 25–29 cm

Both sexes like female Bullfinch with buff wingbar, duller rump; some ♂| faintly pinker below. **Juv**| lacks black cap.

V| Short, fluty whistle.

Bullfinch [♀] *p. 486*

MACARONESIAN CHAFFINCHES

Five local subspecies of **Chaffinch** (*p. 500*) occur on Macaronesian islands: all have same characteristic white shoulder, wingbar and tail sides but ♂ Ads show distinctive colours:

Maderia: ssp. *maderensis*: cap dark bluish, upper back green.
Canary Islands: sspp. *ombriosa* (El Hierro), *palmae* (La Palma), *canariensis* (La Gomera, Tenerife, Gran Canaria), upperparts slaty-bluish, throat/breast pinkish, flank grey.
Azores: ssp. *moreletti*: similar to *canariensis* but back bright green.

V| (All sspp.) song full-throated but may lack final flourish of mainland European sspp.; some calls very different, *e.g.* long, single or duet, bubbly "*chu-chuit-chuit.*"

SSP. *canariensis*
♂
ALL YEAR

SSP. *maderensis*
♂
ALL YEAR

SSP. *moreletti*
♀
ALL YEAR

SSP. *moreletti*
♂
ALL YEAR

Tenerife Blue Chaffinch
Fringilla teydea

E Tenerife, Canary Is. | Scarce   Pine forest

L 16–18 cm | **W** 26–29 cm

Shape and actions as Chaffinch, but ♂**Ad**| grey-blue with greyish wingbars. ♀**Ad**| quite dark greyish, with browner upperparts; **no white in tail**; bill blue-grey.

V| Calls high *"chi-chip,"* rippled *"chi-chew-a,"* lower *"chi-chruwa;"* song short, weak, Chaffinch-like *"chi-chi-chi-chup che-dairr."*

♂1W
AUG–MAR

♀
ALL YEAR

♂
ALL YEAR

Gran Canaria Blue Chaffinch
Fringilla polatzeki

L 16–17 cm | **W** 26–29 cm

Resembles Tenerife Blue Chaffinch but ♂**Ad**| has bolder blackish patch above base of bill; duller, paler below, with **marked whitish wingbars**. ♀**Ad**| very like ♀ Chaffinch, with prominent wingbars, but **tail plain bluish**; bill large, blue-grey.

Both Tenerife and Gran Canaria Blue Chaffinches are similar, but occur on separate islands.
♀s of both blue chaffinch species are similar to ♀ Chaffinch *p. 500* and *opposite*.

E Gran Canaria, Canary Is. | Rare   Pine forest

V| Call *"chrooit."* Song like Tenerife Blue Chaffinch but stronger, more variation in pitch.

♀
ALL YEAR

♂
ALL YEAR

Vagrant birds in Europe

Europe is a vast region, with extensive land borders to the east, an enormous coastline and abundant islands and archipelagos from Iceland to the Canary Islands and from the Balearics to Cyprus. It is ideally situated to receive birds from other parts of the world that become disorientated or displaced during their migrations. Seabirds travel the world's oceans and can appear almost anywhere at sea or offshore. Small passerines that should migrate from northern to south-east Asia in the autumn are prone to head west, in increasing numbers, frequently being found on western European coasts. Islands and headlands dotted all around the European coast are famed for their frequent vagrants and scarce migrants, especially during the spring and autumn. Weather systems crossing the Atlantic in September/October bring a remarkable number and variety of rare birds from North America.

All those vagrants that have reliably been recorded in Europe are illustrated in this book, most on the following pages but a few with similar species in the earlier accounts. Some species were still to be formally accepted at the time of publication but are included for completeness. Judging the origin of individual birds is a problem with some species. While an albatross in the North Atlantic, an American sandpiper on the western European coast, or an unusual Asian swallow can only be a genuinely wild vagrant, a species such as Pied Crow might be a vagrant or an escaped cagebird, or may have arrived on board a ship. While most small Asian passerines are overwhelmingly likely to be vagrants, a few, such as Mugimaki Flycatcher, have led to uncertainty because they are known to have been imported as cagebirds. Unusual bulbuls in south-east Turkey might be wild, but they are kept in captivity there, too, and sometimes even in truckers' cabs, and could escape. For some species there are accepted records of genuinely wild birds, as well as others that are considered to relate to escapes from captivity. Any unusual bird that is encountered should therefore be viewed with an open mind.

In total, an astonishing 331 species have been recorded in Europe only as vagrants: more than a third of the European total. This does not include those species that are regular in some parts of Europe but occur elsewhere as vagrants, but this section does include a handful of 'escapes' that may be confused with other regular or vagrant species, or are becoming established in some parts of Europe, or whose status is debated. A few other species could have been included here but, for comparison purposes, are included in the main body of the book.

Vagrants are like any other species in terms of their identification. Some are practically unmistakable, others require the most careful scrutiny of a range of characteristics to be accepted as proven. Passing seabirds may never be seen again, while some individuals – whether an albatross in a Gannet colony, a wintering gull in an estuary, or a rare thrush in a suburban park – may remain for months. Ecologically, or in conservation terms, they may or may not be of significance, but they add excitement to a day's birdwatching through their unpredictability and can give a fascinating glimpse of the birdlife of another continent.

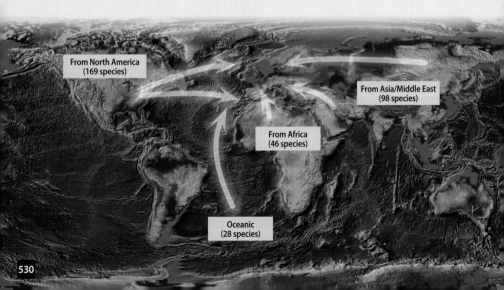

From North America
(169 species)

From Asia/Middle East
(98 species)

From Africa
(46 species)

Oceanic
(28 species)

A summary of vagrant birds in Europe

This table shows the number of species of each 'type' of bird that have been recorded only as vagrants, with an indication of their origin (NOTE: some species may be a vagrant from two regions, indicated by *).

TYPE OF BIRD	North America	Africa	Middle East/Asia	Oceanic	Total	Pages
Wildfowl	21*	1*	3	—	24	*32, 57, 68–71, 532–537*
Grebes	1	—	—	—	1	*538*
Divers	1	—	—	—	1	*538*
Cormorants	1	—	—	—	1	*538*
Seabirds (tubenoses, gannets, tropicbirds, frigatebirds)	—	—	—	24	24	*95, 96, 539–544*
Auks	5	—	—	—	5	*545*
Gulls	7	2	3	—	12	*546–551*
Terns	5*	2*	—	3	9	*552–554*
Skuas	—	—	—	1	1	*555*
Waders	23	2	14	—	39	*157, 169, 555–568*
Large waterside birds (flamingos, spoonbills, storks, cranes, pelicans, herons/egrets, ibises)	9*	10	4*	—	22	*569–575*
Crakes and rails	3	4	—	—	7	*576–577*
Pigeons and doves	1	—	2	—	3	*578*
Sandgrouse	—	1*	2*	—	2	*579*
Nightjars	1	1*	1*	—	2	*579*
Owls	—	1	—	—	1	*584*
Birds of prey	4	5	4	—	13	*580–583*
Near-passerines (cuckoos, bee-eaters, rollers, kingfishers, woodpeckers)	5	2	1	—	8	*584–586*
Aerial feeders (swallows/martins, swifts)	4	3	4	—	11	*586–588*
Passerines — Larks	—	4***	6***	—	7	*590–591*
Passerines — Pipits and wagtails	1*	—	4*	—	4	*369, 589*
Passerines — Hypocolius, starlings, waxwings, bulbuls	1	—	3	—	4	*592, 609*
Passerines — Chats and wheatears	—	3*	9*	—	11	*593–595*
Passerines — Thrushes	7	—	6	—	13	*596–598, 611*
Passerines — Warblers	—	2	14	—	16	*599–602*
Passerines — Flycatchers	—	—	4	—	4	*603*
Passerines — Shrikes and bushshrikes	1	1	4	—	6	*604–605*
Passerines — Finches	1	—	2	—	3	*606, 616*
Passerines — Buntings	—	1	5	—	6	*606–607*
Passerines — Corvids	—	1	3	—	4	*608*
Passerines — Icterids	6	—	—	—	6	*609*
Passerines — American flycatchers	8	—	—	—	8	*610*
Passerines — Mimids	3	—	—	—	3	*611*
Passerines — American warblers, crests and vireos	33	—	—	—	33	*612–615*
Passerines — Nuthatches	1	—	—	—	1	*615*
Passerines — Tanagers and American grosbeaks	6	—	—	—	6	*616–617*
Passerines — American sparrows	10	—	—	—	10	*616–617*

FL| Axillaries ('wingpit') entirely white.
♀ whitish upperwing bar (usually broader than Wigeon).

WIGEON

white

♀

greyish

♀

♀

usually warmer brown head, little hint of 'eyepatch'

♀

ALL YEAR

♂ Br

♂ Nb
APR–OCT

♂ Br
NOV–A...

♀

♂ Br

♀
ALL YEAR

♂ Br
OCT–MA...

MALLARD
♀

white stripes

no white stripes

FL| Dark body,
white underwing

♂

♂
ALL YEAR

LC American Wigeon
Mareca americana

L 48–56 cm | **W** 76–89 cm

Distinctive 'wigeon' form and pattern. **♂ Br**| told from Wigeon by **white forehead and crown** above **dark head band**, grey face; pale purplish/pinkish body. **♀/Imm/♂ Nb**| difficult to pick out and identify. Generally, slightly greater contrast between greyer head and more orange body than ♀ Wigeon, and hint (or more) of male's dark head band/pale forehead (but some Wigeon very similar).

 Wigeon *p. 39*
Hybrids with Wigeon *p. 67*

Annual vagrant from N America
Lakes, marshes

NT Falcated Duck
Mareca falcata

L 46–53 cm | **W** 70–75 cm

Medium-sized dabbling duck. **♂ Br**| soft grey; **head dark, glossed green**, with bulky, drooping nape, white chin; **domed/drooping tertials** above buff-and-black rear end. **♀**| like brown Wigeon with longer grey bill; long, dark tertials.

♀ - Wigeon *p. 39*
♂ - Shoveler × Gadwall *p. 67*

Vagrant from Asia
Lakes, marshes

LC American Black Duck
Anas rubripes

L 53–61 cm | **W** 85–96 cm

♂/♀| Like ♀ Mallard but darker (beware of a variety of farmyard types) with contrasting paler head/neck, yellowish bill (yellowest on male), orange legs. **Dark purple-blue hindwing without white stripes. Juv**| upperwing as adult, but streaked; like dark ♀ Mallard but head/neck contrastingly paler, dark eyestripe. Bill dark olive, blacker in middle.

Mallard [♀] *p. 40*

Vagrant from N America
Lakes, marshes, estuaries

RARE TEAL IDENTIFICATION: MALES straightforward; FEMALES / JUVENILES are similar to Teal (*p. 44*) and Garganey (*p. 45*). Wing and head patterns are important features for identification.

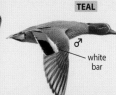

forewing blue

grey patch; whitish midwing and edge bars ♀ — **BLUE-WINGED TEAL**

dark patch; dark midwing bar and white edge bar ♀ — **GARGANEY**

green patch; wide midwing bar and narrow edge bar white ♀ — **BAIKAL TEAL**

♀ — **TEAL**

TEAL ♂ white bar

Green-winged Teal
Anas carolinensis

Sometimes treated as SSP. of Teal

L 34–38 cm | **W** 53–59 cm

Small dabbling duck, very similar to Teal. **♂ Br | vertical white band beside chest;** lacks pale buff edge to green head band and lacks white line along body. **♀/Imm/♂ Nb** like Teal (may have stronger facial stripes and pale spot by bill) and very similar to other, even rarer, species.

 Teal *p. 44* | ♀ - Garganey *p. 45*

Annual vagrant from N America
Lakes, marshes, estuaries

Fl | Usually buff bar above green hindwing patch.

♂ buff bar

♀ ALL YEAR

♂ may show pointed tuft on nape.

♂ **Br** OCT–APR

TEAL

Blue-winged Teal
Spatula discors

L 37–41 cm | **W** 58 cm

Small dabbling duck. **♂ Br | white face crescent;** black bill; dark-spotted tawny flank with white patch at rear. **♀/Imm/♂ Nb** like Garganey and Cinnamon Teal: look for **broken pale line over eye,** white eyering, **white spot against bill** in front of **plain cheek,** white chin, relatively heavy blackish bill and **yellowish legs.**

 ♀ - Garganey *p. 45*
♀ - Cinnamon Teal *p. 71*

Annual vagrant from N America
Lakes

Fl | Blue forewing.

♂

♀ ALL YEAR

♂ **Br** OCT–APR

NOTE: Some 1W and 'eclipse' ♂ Shovelers (*p. 41*) show a face crescent reminiscent of breeding ♂ Blue-winged Teal.

SHOVELER

Baikal Teal
Sibirionetta formosa

L 39–43 cm | **W** 55–60 cm

Small dabbling duck. **♂ Br |** unmistakable: **black/white/buff/green patterned** head. **♀/Imm/♂ Nb** like Teal and Garganey, but plain cheek, **dark-bordered whitish face spot,** slight pale streak beside tail.

 ♀ - Teal *p. 44* | Garganey *p. 45*

Vagrant from Asia
Lakes

cheek plain; white spot in dark patch

♀ ALL YEAR

♂ **Br** OCT–APR

GARGANEY
cheek band; pale spot

TEAL
cheek plain; pale spot absent or weak at best

BLUE-WINGED TEAL
cheek plain; white spot; **heavy bill**

533

LC Ring-necked Duck
Aythya collaris

L 37–46 cm | **W** 65–70 cm

Medium-sized diving duck.
♂ **Br** | (Oct–Apr) like Tufted Duck
with high-peaked head (no
tuft) and grey (not white) flank
(outlined in white and with **white
point at front**); white ring on bill.
♂ **Nb** / ♀ / **1W** | like Tufted Duck
but whitish around bill extends to
chin/throat; eyering and 'spectacle'
line; banded bill like male (see ♀ /
juvenile Pochard, Redhead).

FL | Broad, **grey wing stripe** extends
to end of wing.

 Tufted Duck *p. 48*
Hybrids *p. 67*
♀ - Pochard [♀ / juv] *p. 51*
♀ - *Redhead* [♀ / juv]

Annual vagrant from N America
Lakes

TUFTED DUCK

wingbar
grey

wingbar
white
♀

♂
no pale band

subtly distinctive
head pattern

both sexes have
a pale band
on the bill.

♀
ALL YEAR

♂ B
SEP–J

grey flank with
white 'point' at front

LC Lesser Scaup *Aythya affinis*

L 38–45 cm | **W** 60–65 cm

Small 'scaup'. ♂ | like Scaup with
coarsely barred grey back, white
flank and **small 'bump' on back of
head**. ♀ / **Imm** | like dark Scaup with
slight 'bump' on head; greyer back
and less black on bill tip than Tufted
Duck. *Beware of hybrids.*

FL | Wingbar white on inner half,
outer half grey.

 Scaup *p. 49*
♀ - Tufted Duck *p. 48*
Hybrids *p. 67*

Annual vagrant from N America
Lakes

Identification of ♀ Lesser Scaup
Lesser Scaup: HEAD **peaked at back of crown**; BILL small black tip
Scaup: HEAD **rounded, higher on forehead**; BILL small black tip
Tufted Duck: HEAD **distinct tuft on nape**; BILL wide, dark tip NB white patch on face typically small or obscure

SCAUP

outer part of
wingbar whitish
♀

TUFTED DUCK

♀

**LESSER SCAUP
IDENTIFICATION:**
♂ from **Scaup** by
head shape;
♀ from
Scaup and
Tufted Duck
by head shape
and bill pattern.

outer part of
wingbar greyish
♂

♀

SCAUP

face patch can
be white or
mottled white

both sexes
have head
'peaked' at
rear

♀
ALL YEAR

♂
SEP–

Bufflehead *Bucephala albeola*

L 32–39 cm | **W** 55–60 cm

Small diving duck. ♂ | white with black back; head dark, iridescent, with **broad white band** behind eye and around nape. ♀ | small white panel behind eye, browner body.

Vagrant from N America
Freshwater lakes, estuaries

Hooded Merganser
Lophodytes cucullatus

L 42–50 cm | **W** 75–80 cm

Medium-sized diving duck (sawbill). ♂ | unmistakable: black head with **fan-like**, black-edged, white crest; white on breast, tawny flank; **black bill**. ♀/**Imm** | grey-brown with dusky face blending into wide, fanned, tawny crest; pale bill.

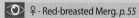 ♀ - Red-breasted Merg. *p. 55*

Vagrant from N America/escape
Lakes, rivers

Redhead *Aythya americana*

L 44–51 cm | **W** 65–70 cm

Like large, dark Pochard with rounder head and steep forehead/**bulging forecrown** when resting (sometimes cocks tail). ♂ | has **golden eye** and pale grey bill with broad black tip beyond diffuse pale band. ♀ | has dark cap, plain, pale face and more uniformly coloured body than Pochard, but whitish under tail.

Pochard *p. 51*

Vagrant from N America
Lakes

Canvasback *Aythya valisineria*

L 49–56 cm | **W** 70–80 cm

Like large, long Pochard with **long, all-black bill** sloping up towards high crown. ♂ | **very pale** grey with dark face. ♀ | greyer than Pochard.

Pochard *p. 51*

Vagrant from N America
Freshwater lakes

like Goldeneye (*p. 52*) with white cheek

♀ **ALL YEAR**

large white nape

♂ **Br** **SEP–JUN**

'fuzzy' crest, dark face

♀/**Imm** **ALL YEAR**

♂ **Br** **SEP–JUN**

dark cap

♀ **ALL YEAR**

both sexes have a 'steep' forecrown

golden eye

♂ **Br** **SEP–JUN**

POCHARD both sexes have pale areas on the bill

♀

♂

♀ **ALL YEAR**

both sexes have a long, sweeping black bill

black foreparts angled against grey

♂ **Br** **SEP–JUN**

535

'Black' sea ducks: **dark wings**

LC **Surf Scoter** *Melanitta perspicillata*

L 45–56 cm | **W** 75–85 cm

Bulky, deep-billed scoter; dives with open wings. ♂ | large-headed; **black** with **white nape patch** and forehead triangle. Bill heavy, boldly patched black, white and orange. ♀ | like Velvet Scoter with double facial spots, sometimes white nape patch; bill more **deeply triangular** with hint of darker basal patch. **Wings all-dark.**

Annual vagrant from N America
At sea (very rarely inland)

NT **Black Scoter** *Melanitta americana*

L 44–54 cm | **W** 70–85 cm

Very similar to Common Scoter. ♂ | has big, wide, **domed yellow patch** at base of bill. ♀ | has **'bump' on bill base** with some yellow streaks.

Vagrant from N America
At sea (usually with Common Scoter)

'Black' sea ducks: **white wing panels**.

LC **White-winged Scoter**
Melanitta deglandi

L 50–57 cm | **W** 78–95 cm

Large scoter. ♂ | **angular 'step'** on **pinkish-red bill** and **yellowish ridge**; white eye patch sweeps upwards. Forehead sweeps up to peaked crown. ♀ | bill **bulges** slightly (like Surf Scoter but has white wing panel).

Vagrant from N America
At sea (usually with Velvet Scoter)

LC **Siberian Scoter**
Melanitta stejnegeri

L 50–57 cm | **W** 78–95 cm

Large scoter. ♂ | has **low, smooth crown** but **angled bill knob**, bill pink-red with yellow streak; short white eye patch hooks upwards. ♀ | like White-winged Scoter but flatter forehead may be visible.

Vagrant from E Asia
At sea

♀ - Velvet Scoter *p. 63*
White-winged Scoter

Some ♀ s have pale nape patch.

♀
ALL YEAR

♂ 1W
AUG–MAY

♂ Br
OCT–JUN

Common Scoter *p. 62*

'Squarer' head than Common Scoter

dark vertical mark on cheek less obvious than on Common Scoter

Bill often slightly swollen at base, with arched nail; some have yellow markings.

♀
ALL YEAR

♂ Br
OCT–JUN

White-winged and *Siberian Scoter* are very similar to each other and to Velvet Scoter *p. 63*

♀ / Juv
ALL YEAR

♂ Br
OCT–JUN

White wing patch may be hidden.

♀
ALL YEAR

White head patches can wear off on all ♀ /Juv scoters.

♂ Br
OCT–JUN

SCOTER IDENTIFICATION: can be difficult, especially at distance. Establish whether white- or dark-winged, then focus on head features – MALES: bill pattern and shape; FEMALES: head pattern and bill shape.

MALES		FEMALES	
'WHITE-WINGED'	'DARK-WINGED'	'WHITE-WINGED'	'DARK-WINGED'

VELVET — slight bulge, yellow

SURF 1ST-WINTER — 'swollen'

VELVET — forehead rounded, concave

SURF — forehead peaked, slight bulge

WHITE-WINGED — bulge, pink

COMMON — black, grey-black

WHITE-WINGED — forehead peaked, concave

COMMON — forehead low, flat, grey-black

SIBERIAN — 'knob'

BLACK — yellow, yellow

SIBERIAN — forehead low, straight

BLACK — forehead bulges, 'bump', some yellow

Spectacled Eider
Somateria fischeri

L 50–58 cm | **W** 90–100 cm

Large, bulky sea duck; typical eider.
♂ **Br** | white above, black below;
head green; white 'disk' around
eye and band over orange bill.
♂ **Nb** / ♀ / **Imm** | barred rufous brown
and black, with pale buffish 'disk'
around eye; short grey bill.

Vagrant from NE Siberia
At sea

EIDER ♀ — No facial 'disk' — long 'lobe' onto forehead — ♀ ALL YEAR

👁 ♀ - Eider [♀] p.75 — forehead fully feathered

♂ **Br** SEP–MAY

537

LC Pied-billed Grebe
Podilymbus podiceps

L 31–38 cm | **W** 45–62 cm

Medium-small grebe. Large, 'reptilian' head, with almost triangular, arched bill. Dark brown, with darker crown; whitish rear end. **AdBr** has black chin and white bill with **vertical black band**; white eyering. **AdNb/Imm** have paler throat and dull grey bill without black band.

👁 Little Grebe *p. 75*

Annual vagrant from N America

Lakes

neck long, slender and erect when alarmed

black band on bill

AdBr
MAR–SEP

spiky tail

AdNb
SEP–MAR

LC Pacific Diver *Gavia pacifica*

L 60–63 cm | **W** 109–122 cm

All plumages as Black-throated Diver but head more rounded (varies with posture) and **bill smaller**. **AdNb** **no white rear flank patch**; slight dark '**chinstrap**' and dark vent band in winter. **Juv** like **AdNb** but has pale scaly bars above.

👁 Black-throated Diver *p. 81*

Annual vagrant from N America

Coasts

AdBr
MAR–SEP

dark 'chinstrap'
AdNb
SEP–MAY

no white on rear flank

AdNb

no 'chinstrap'

BLACK-THROATED DIVE
white flank patch

LC Double-crested Cormorant
Phalacrocorax auritus

L 76–90 cm | **W** 135 cm

Difficult to distinguish from Cormorant; 12 tail feathers, not 14. **Ad** pale stripe above eye separated from bare facial skin by **dark line** between eye and bill; facial skin yellow (often similar on Cormorant) to **deep orange**; very little or no white between face and surrounding dark feathers. Thin, curly feathers above eye in spring. **Imm** has breast paler than belly (usually the opposite on Cormorant, but both variable).

👁 Cormorant *p. 84* | Shag *p. 85*

Vagrant from N America

Coasts

SHAG

CORMOR

Imm

Imm

has wispy crest earlier in spring

edge of throat feathering against bare face straight (no central point)

Imm

Ad

Sooty Shearwater *p. 91*

Short-tailed Shearwater
Ardenna tenuirostris

L 42 cm | **W** 85–95 cm

Heavy-bodied shearwater; like Sooty Shearwater but steeper forehead and rather short, dark bill; throat and underparts paler and greyer. Underwing coverts dull whitish, pale grey or brownish. **FL** | Quick, deep, whippy beats of rather straight, narrow wings, between glides. Feet project just beyond tail tip.

Vagrant from Pacific Oceans

Flesh-footed Shearwater

Ardenna carneipes

L 40–48 cm | **W** 99–116 cm

Large, dark brown shearwater; resembles Sooty Shearwater but broader-winged and **underwing dark** except paler sheen on primaries. **Bill strikingly pale** grey-pink with dark tip. **FL** | Wings long, slightly bowed; tail square.

Vagrant from Indian/Pacific Oceans

White-chinned Petrel
Procellaria aequinoctialis

L 51–58 cm | **W** 134–147 cm

Large petrel; resembles Sooty Shearwater but larger and blacker. **Underwing black**, faintly paler on primaries. **Bill thick, yellowish/white**; tiny white patch on chin (absent in some individuals). **FL** | Slow, elegant beats of long, arched, tapered wings, between low glides.

Vagrant from Southern Ocean

Great-winged Petrel
Pterodroma macroptera

L 42–45 cm | **W** 95 cm

Large petrel; dark brown except variable paler face patch. **Underwing dark** except paler crescent at base of primaries. Bill rather short, black. **FL** | Long, tapered wings, deep breast/belly; tail wedge-shaped. Rises quite high in long, curving glides, between few powerful wingbeats.

Vagrant from S Atlantic/ Southern Oceans

steeper forehead

shorter bill

SOOTY SHEARWATER

SHORT-TAILED SHEARWATER

FLESH-FOOTED SHEARWATER

WHITE-CHINNED PETREL

GREAT-WINGED PETREL

NOTE: Underwing patterns of petrels and shearwaters can be hard to judge due to changing light and shade.

Zino's, Desertas and *Fea's* Petrels
p. 96 | Fulmar *p. 91*

Bermuda Petrel
Pterodroma cahow

L 35–38 cm | **W** 85–92 cm
Stocky, thick-billed, long-winged
petrel; dark above, white below.
Blurred blackish mask, white forehead
and throat; **white crescent above
dark tail**. Underwing **white** with thin
black trailing edge and broader **black
leading edge tapering inwards**
towards wingpit.

Vagrant from W Atlantic

Soft-plumaged Petrel
Pterodroma mollis

L 35 cm | **W** 70 cm
Medium-sized petrel. Dark mask,
white spot over eye. Dark grey crown,
nape and **almost-complete breast-
band**. Throat and underparts white.
Upperparts grey, with **brownish 'W'**
across wings/rump; pale midwing
band. Underwing **dark** (as Zino's Petrel
(*p. 96*)); coverts/hindwing blackish,
midwing/primaries pale grey.
Underside of tail dark, vent white.

Vagrant from S Atlantic

Black-capped Petrel
Pterodroma hasitata

L 40 cm | **W** 98–105 cm
Large, long-winged petrel with
white forehead and **black cap/nape**
above full **white collar; white rump**.
Underwing white with **broad black
trailing edge** and **black diagonal
bar tapering inwards** towards
wingpit.

Vagrant from W Atlantic

Trindade Petrel
Pterodroma arminjoniana

L 35–40 cm| **W** 90–102 cm
Medium-large, agile, long-winged
petrel. Dark **brown** head, upperside
and throat. PALE FORM underside white,
throat brown; DARK FORM mottled grey-
brown. Underwing dark with mottled
grey/white band, **blackish coverts
and wingtip** create long 'W'; **black
vent/tail**.

Vagrant from S & W Atlantic

May show whitish
upperwing band
when moulting.

SOFT-PLUMAGED
PETREL

BERMUDA
PETREL

almost-complete
breast-band

DESERTAS
PETREL

Zino's/
Desertas/Fea's
Petrels (*p. 96*)
are very similar
but do not have
a breast-band.

BLACK-CAPPED
PETREL

Pale
form

TRINDADE
PETREL

NOTE: Separation from Herald Petrel *P. heraldica* and Henderson Petrel
P. atrata, both from the Pacific Ocean, probably impossible at sea;
several indeterminate records in NE Atlantic.

Cape Petrel *Daption capense*

L 39 cm | **W** 85 cm

Like stocky, black-and-white shearwater; dark hood, white below; mottled back, **broad white patches on innerwing and inner primaries**; white tail with broad black band.

Vagrant from S Atlantic

Southern Giant-petrel
Macronectes giganteus

L 86–99 cm | **W** 185–205 cm

May be indistinguishable from **Northern Giant-petrel** *M. halli* [NOT RECORDED / ILLUSTRATED]. Huge, dark brown, hump-backed, deep-bodied, albatross-like seabird. **Ad** | dark brown, pale face/foreneck; large, thick, yellowish bill; pale eyes. **Juv** | sooty-brown, dark eyes, pale pinkish or yellowish bill.

Vagrant from S Atlantic

Swinhoe's Storm-petrel
Hydrobates monorhis

L 18–21 cm | **W** 45–48 cm

Dark brown storm-petrel; size and shape as Leach's Storm-petrel, smaller than Bulwer's Petrel, with **forked tail** and dark rump; **short pale shaft streaks on outer primaries**. Most trapped ashore, identified by biometrics/DNA testing. At sea, hard to separate from rare dark-rumped Leach's Storm-petrel.

Vagrant from Indian Ocean; occasional returning individuals in summer

Black-bellied Storm-petrel
Fregetta tropica

L 20 cm | **W** 46 cm

Fast-moving storm-petrel with dashing, shearing flight. **White rump joins white underside and underwing**. Usually has black or smudgy stripe along belly; if not, could be white-bellied form, or closely similar **White-bellied Storm-petrel** *Fregetta grallaria* [NOT CONFIRMED IN EUROPE, SOME RECORDS INDETERMINATE; NOT ILLUSTRATED]. Black-bellied has larger hood than White-bellied Storm-petrel.

Vagrant from S Atlantic

Ad

CAPE PETREL

SOUTHERN GIANT-PETREL

Adult has yellowish bill with a greenish tip, juvenile a pinkish bill (adult Northern Giant-petrel has pinkish bill with reddish tip, juvenile's bill browner).

Leach's Storm-petrel *p. 99*
Bulwer's Petrel *p. 97*

long, straight wings with prominent joint

pale primary shafts at close range

no pale primary shafts

dark rump

pale rump (usually)

SWINHOE'S STORM-PETREL

LEACH'S STORM-PETREL

EUROPEAN STORM-PETREL

narrow white band

broad white band joins white underside

BLACK-BELLIED STORM-PETREL

European Storm-petrel *p. 98*

541

Gannet *p. 90*

LC Masked Booby
Sula dactylatra

L 75–90 cm | **W** 140–165 cm
Like Gannet. **Ad** | white with more black on wings and tail, **dark mask**, broad-based yellow bill. **Juv** | brown with dark head, blackish face, **pale collar** and mottled rump; dark breast clear-cut above **white** underside; **facial skin and bill pale grey or yellowish** (dark on Gannet).

Vagrant from Caribbean / S Atlantic

LC Brown Booby
Sula leucogaster

L 67–74 cm | **W** 132–150 cm
Like small Gannet in form and actions. **Ad** | rich **dark brown** with **pale bill** and yellowish facial skin; **white belly** and underwing stripe; yellow legs. **Juv** | dark overall: face and bill yellowish-grey; dark breast well defined against mottled pale belly (Masked Booby juvenile blacker around eye, dark breast/white belly).

Vagrant from Cape Verde

LC Red-footed Booby *Sula sula*

L 70 cm | **W** 100 cm
Shape and actions like Gannet; several plumage types. **Ad** | bluish bill, pinkish facial skin, red legs. White form has black flight feathers, some also black tail. Brown form all dark brown, or whiter rump, tail and belly. **Juv** | brown, paler on head and underparts; bill dark, becoming greyish or pink with dark tip; face bluish; feet pink.

Vagrant from tropical Atlantic

EN Cape Gannet *Morus capensis*

L 85–90 cm | **W** 165–175 cm
Very like Gannet: **Ad** | white with **black hindwing band** (except innermost feathers), **black tail** and buff head. **Long black throat (gular) stripe** extends **below bend** in foreneck, ruling out near-adult Gannet (which has dark spots on underwing and uneven hindwing band). **Imm** | normally impossible to identify unless gular stripe seen well.

Vagrant from S Atlantic

542

MASKED BOOBY — Ad — Juv

BROWN BOOBY — Ad — Juv

RED-FOOTED BOOBY — Juv — Ad White form — Imm Intermedia

CAPE GANNET — gular stripe — Ad — Ad — blac tai

Imm (3Y) GANNET — white in hindwing — white in tail

Black-browed Albatross
Thalassarche melanophris

L 80–95 cm | **W** 200–235 cm

Most likely flying over sea, rarely ashore. Bigger than Gannet (*p. 90*); stout-billed, round-headed, **square-tailed**; very long, slender wings. **Ad** | white with black back/upperwings and **dusky tail** (check immature Gannet and adult Great Black-backed Gull (*p. 123*)). Underwing crucial: **broad white band, narrow black trailing edge, broader black leading edge**. Bill yellow/orange. Black eyebrow. **Imm** | similar to adult but darker bill tip, greyish collar and dusky underwing masking pattern.

Annual vagrant from S Atlantic; occasional long-stayer visiting Gannet colonies.

Atlantic Yellow-nosed Albatross
Thalassarche chlororhynchos

L 90 cm | **W** 200–210 cm

Obvious albatross shape/actions. **Ad** | bill black (may glisten paler grey) **with a yellow stripe on ridge** and **narrow black margins to the white underwing**. Head white with soft grey wash on neck. **Imm** | has white head, black bill.

Vagrant from S Atlantic

Tristan Albatross
Diomedea dabbenena

L 110 cm | **W** 275–305 cm

Huge, very long-winged albatross. **Ad** | white with black upperwing, black wingtip on white underwing and long, pale bill. Individuals develop white plumage at differing rates over 20 or more years. Near-identical to Wandering Albatross *Diomedea exulans* (NR) [NOT ILLUSTRATED], which has a slightly longer bill; not usually possible to distinguish the two species at sea.

Vagrant from S Atlantic

Ad

Imm

BLACK-BROWED
ALBATROSS

Ad

ATLANTIC
YELLOW-NOSED
ALBATROSS

Ad

Ad

Ad

TRISTAN
ALBATROSS

Frigatebirds

FL | Fly with **angled wings**; able to soar to great height over sea or adjacent land, or chase other birds/flying fish over waves.

LC Magnificent Frigatebird
Fregata magnificens

L 90–114 cm | **W** 215–245 cm

Huge, long-winged seabird with **long, forked tail** (may close to form a single thick spike); long, hooked bill. ♂ | **black**, glossed purple, with **red throat sac.** ♀ | all-dark except **white breast. Juv** | white head and white patch on belly (which does not extend onto underwing as on juvenile Ascension Frigatebird).

Vagrant from the Caribbean
At sea; rarely storm-blown inland

VU Ascension Frigatebird
Fregata aquila

L 85–105 cm | **W** 205–230 cm

Very similar to Magnificent Frigatebird and practically indistinguishable at sea. ♂ | **black**, glossed green, with **red throat sac.** ♀ | typically all-dark except paler brown breast, but some have white breast patch. **Juv** | white head; **white on belly just extending onto inner part of underwing** (white restricted to belly on Magnificent Frigatebird). Extent of white on underwing increases with age.

Vagrant from S Atlantic
At sea/stranded ashore

LC White-tailed Tropicbird
Phaethon lepturus

L 71–80 cm | **W** 89–95 cm

White seabird with slender wings and long tail; **black band across innerwing** and black-streaked wingtips; long white or yellowish tail streamer; black mask. Bill yellow to orange.

👁 Red-billed Tropicbird *p. 97*

Vagrant from the Caribbean
At sea

♀
black head; white breast/wingpit

MAGNIFICENT
FRIGATEBIRD

♂

white head; white breast/belly; black wingpit

Juv

white head; white belly/wingpit

Juv

ASCENSION
FRIGATEBIRD

Juv

looks all-white at distance (black diagonal bands not always obvious)

white tail streamer very long and straight in direct flight

Ad

WHITE-TAILED
TROPICBIRD

Long-billed Murrelet
Brachyramphus perdix

L 25 cm | **W** 45 cm
Like tiny Guillemot (*p. 103*) with whitish shoulder patches, slim bill, white cheek/throat.

 Little Auk *p. 101*

Vagrant from Pacific
Sea/coasts

1W
OCT–FEB

Ancient Murrelet
Synthliboramphus antiquus

L 27 cm | **W** 45–48 cm
Tiny, pale **grey** auk with black cap, face and bib; **white streak** behind eye; **white neck**; small, pale bill.

 Little Auk *p. 101* | Puffin *p. 101*

Vagrant from N America
At sea, cliffs

AdBr
FEB–AUG

Parakeet Auklet
Aethia psittacula

L 23 cm | **W** 44–48 cm
Tiny auk with black head/upperparts, white below; small red bill, white stripe behind white eye.

Vagrant from Pacific
Sea/coasts

AdBr
FEB–AUG

Crested Auklet
Aethia cristatella

L 18–20 cm | **W** 40–50 cm
Small auk. **AdBr** | blackish overall with red bill, thin white line behind eye, upstanding, forward-curving crest. **AdNb / 1W** | bill dull, crest reduced.

Vagrant from Pacific
At sea

AdBr
FEB–AUG

Tufted Puffin
Fratercula cirrhata

L 36–41 cm | **W** 60–63 cm
Stocky auk; like Puffin but black, with red bill, white face, yellowish crest.

 Puffin *p. 101*

Vagrant from Pacific
At sea

AdBr

AdBr
FEB–AUG

545

LC **Ross's Gull** *Rhodostethia rosea*

👁 1W, AdNb - Little Gull *p.122* | 1W - Kittiwake *p.114*

② **L** 29–32 cm | **W** 73–80 cm

Small, dove-like, round-headed gull with **pointed tail, short dark bill** and short, red legs. **AdBr** grey-and-pink with **black neck ring. AdNb** as AdBr but nape grey. **1W** has black band along wing; wingtip black; legs pink; black neck ring develops by **1S**.

V In winter, harsh, 'chuckling' "*chag-ak*."

FL **Ad** upperwing pale with **broad white trailing edge** stopping short of **grey wingtip; underwing grey. 1W** dark 'W' across upperwings, like Little Gull and larger Kittiwake, but long white 'wedge' into black outer primaries; underwing shows translucent white band against the light. Black patch on tip of tail.

AdNb

1W

AdBr
MAR–AUG

AdNb

AdNb
AUG–APR

1W
SEP–MAR

wingtip grey (white rim on Little Gull)

Rare migrant/vagrant
Breeds in Arctic; winters at sea, coasts

NT **Ivory Gull** *Pagophila eburnea*

LC **②** **L** 41–47 cm | **W** 100–113 cm

Medium-sized, pigeon-like, **white** gull with long wings and short **blackish** legs. **Ad** all-white; bill blue- or greenish-grey **with yellow tip** (tip brighter orange-red in spring). **Juv** white with **scattered blackish spots** and **grey face**.

V Squealing notes, tern-like chattering and short, squeaky "*chee-o*."

Uniquely among gulls, Ad has single moult, between APR and AUG; Juv moults directly into adult plumage between APR and AUG.

👁 Iceland Gull *p.131*
beware aberrant, 'white' individuals of commoner gull species

FL Elegant, but slightly heavy-bodied; wings smoothly tapered. Heavy flier, sometimes with legs lowered. **1W** lines of dark spots on coverts and on tips of flight and tail feathers.

Rare migrant/vagrant
Breeds in Arctic; winters at sea, coasts

Ad

Juv

some birds more heavily spotted on wings

Juv
JUL–APR

Ad

Ring-billed Gull
Larus delawarensis

(3) **L** 41–49 cm | **W** 112–124 cm

Like Common Gull but slightly larger, **paler on back**; **less white** on tertials. **AdBr** | **eye yellow** with dark ring; **bill thick, yellow** with **black band** and paler tip (looks dark-tipped at distance); head white. **AdNb** | as AdBr but head streaked, nape spotted grey-brown. **1W** | back pale; bill thick, pink (yellow by MAR) with black tip. **2W** | as AdNb but smaller white wingtip spots; dark marks on tertials on some.
V | High, nasal squeals run into repeated short "*kyow*" notes.

FL | **Ad** like *pale* Common Gull but wings broader, with more black and smaller 'mirrors'. **1W** like Common Gull but wingtip and trailing edge **blacker**, midwing and inner primaries **very pale**, tail-band **less clear-cut**. **2W** as **Ad** but more black on wingtip, one small white 'mirror'; blackish marks on hindwing/tail (rare on Common Gull).

　Common Gull p. 116
　Herring Gull p. 128

Annual vagrant from N America
Coasts, lakes

'Thayer's Gull'
Larus glaucoides thayeri

(4) **L** 55–60 cm | **W** 125–140 cm

As Iceland Gull (*p. 131*) (of which it is a rather distinct SSP.), but **slightly darker**. **AdBr / AdNb** | plumages like Herring Gull but **duller bill, darker eye**, deeper pink legs. **Juv** | wingtip mid-brown; tertials brown with pale tips; rump/undertail broadly barred brown; bill dark, slender; fades paler during **1W**. **2W** | wingtip dark brown with broad, pale feather tips. **3W** | like **Ad** with variable darker markings on upperwing, more black on wingtip.
FL | **Ad** long white streaks or spots inside **blackish wingtip** (darkest Iceland Gull SSP. *kumlieni* may be similar, but most have smaller, greyer marks); white line along inner edge of outer primary joins white tip.

　Herring Gull p. 128
　kumlieni Iceland Gull p. 131

Vagrant from N America
Coasts, tips

1–2 small 'mirrors'

COMMON GULL

dark trailing edge; pale midwing panel

AdNb

1W

Common Gull bill may have black band, but thinner; sub-adult Herring Gull bill often has black band, but is a much larger bird with a heavier bill.

dark midwing panel

AdNb

AdNb
AUG–MAR

COMMON GULL

1W

AdBr
FEB–JUL

bulkier than Common Gull; back more rounded

very little white between grey and black

2W
JUL–MAR

1W
AUG–MAR

legs long

HERRING GULL

AdBr

ICELAND GULL
SSP. *kumlieni*

PALE

DARK

HERRING GULL

Juv

Juv / 1W

AdNb

AdNb
ICELAND GULL
SSP. *kumlieni*

AdNb
AUG–MAR

Juv

Juv
JUN–APR

547

LC # American Herring Gull
Larus smithsonianus

④ **L** 53–67 cm | **W** 120–155 cm

Two subspecies. ssp. *smithsonianus* (N America) like large, dark Herring Gull (many inseparable).

AdNb | broad, dark streaks on white head and breast. **1W** | **belly dark**.

ssp. *vegae* (NE Asia, often treated as species, **Vega Gull**). **Ad** | like Herring Gull but darker back; wide white tertial crescent; legs dull pinkish (rarely yellowish); bill slim, greenish-yellow with red spot (which may be small); eyering purple-red.

AdNb | head and neck heavily streaked. Still moulting outer primaries in JAN/FEB (Herring Gull complete by DEC/JAN).

FL | ssp. *smithsonianus* **Ad** black on outer 6 primaries extends inwards in black points between long grey 'fingers'. **1W** rump whitish, densely barred dark brown; tail blackish; dark band across greater coverts; underwing dark with paler flight feathers. ssp. *vegae* **Ad** as *smithsonianus* but 'fingers' on primaries whitish. **1W** like 1W Herring Gull, but pale inner primaries have more obvious black streak near tip.

👁 Herring Gull *p. 128*

LC # Kelp Gull *Larus dominicanus*

④ **L** 55–65 cm | **W** 125–160 cm

Large, 'black-backed' gull; bill heavy, **bulbous** at tip; legs long. **Ad** | **black** back; head and breast white; **broad white trailing edge** to wing obvious even when closed; **legs greenish-yellow**. Eye **dark** with yellowish ring. **1W** | dark grey-brown with whitish fringes above; bill black (individually variable). **2W** | whiter head and body. **3W** | like dull Ad with dark band on bill.

FL | **Ad** upperwing dark with wide white trailing edge and single small 'mirror'. **1W** upperwing like Lesser Black-backed Gull; tail more solidly black. **2W** head white; back black; tail white with black markings; upperwing brown. **3W** as Ad but a few dark blotches on underwing/tail.

👁 Great Black-backed Gull *p. 123*
Lesser Black-backed Gull *p. 124*

Vagrant from N America, Asia
Coasts

ssp. *smithsonianus*

SSP. *vegae*

SSP. *smithsonianu*

AdBr
HERRING GULL

AdNb

1W

1W

AdBr →AdNb

HERRING GULL

Ad

AdNb
JUN–MAR

1W
JUL–MAR

SSP. *vegae*

SSP. *smithsonianus*

AdNb
JUN–MAR

Vagrant from S Atlantic
(ssp. *vetula*, S Africa)
Sea, coasts

NOTE: Kelp Gull is a S Hemisphere gull, so seasonal moult sequence is reverse of N Hemisphere species (but long-staying vagrants may adopt northern timings).

GREAT BLACK-BACKED GULL
Slightly larger, has pale pink/whitish legs and pale eye.

Ad

Ad

1W
MAR–OCT

Ad

Glaucous-winged Gull
Larus glaucescens

(4) **L** 48–56 cm | **W** 117–134 cm

Large, heavy gull, like Glaucous Gull with **darker wingtip. Ad** | grey-and-white; **wingtip darker grey with large white spots**. Eye dark (pale on Glaucous Gull). **AdNb** | head white, mottled buff-brown. **Juv** | pale buff, mottled grey-brown above, plain below; **bill black**. **1W** | quite uniform grey-buff; primaries pale with whitish fringes; bill blackish. **2W** | pale grey above; white, blotched brownish, below; bill pink with black band. **3W** | like **Ad** but buff on wing coverts; dark band on bill (individually variable).

FL | **Ad wingtip grey with white tips and large white 'mirror'. 1W** upperwing uniform pale **grey-brown including wingtip**; flight feathers contrastingly pale below. **2W** wingtip **dusky-brown** with paler fringes; tail plain beige-grey. **3W** like **Ad** but greyish tail-band and less white on wingtip.

Glaucous Gull *p. 130*

Vagrant from
N America
Lakes, coasts
GLAUCOUS
GULL
Juv/1W
AdNb
1W
3W
AUG–MAR
1W
AUG–MAR
AdNb
AUG–MAR

Slaty-backed Gull
Larus schistisagus

(4) **L** 61–66 cm | **W** 145–150 cm

Large, **'dark-backed'** gull. Two forms: **AdBr** | dark grey above (colour of Lesser Black-backed Gull SSP. *graellsii*) or paler (colour of Yellow-legged Gull); head white. **Broad white tertial crescent. Legs pink. AdNb** | as AdBr but head streaked. **1W** | sandy-brown, underparts plain; primaries dark brown with pale fringes; tail dark brown; eye dark. **2W** | paler than **1W**, a little grey on back; eye pale. **3W** | grey-backed, like **AdNb**, but brown patches on wing.

FL | **Ad broad white trailing edge** to wing and tertials; **row of white spots** between grey and black on primaries 4–6. **1W** pale brown; hindwing band and tips of outer primaries dark brown; rump buff, barred brown; tail solidly brown with thin buff tip. **2W** like **1W** but grey marks on back; wings brown; rump whitish; thick black-brown tail-band. **3W** like Ad but wing mostly brown.

Lesser Black-backed Gull *p. 124*
Yellow-legged Gull *p. 126*

Vagrant from Asia
Coasts, tips
LESSER
BLACK-
BACKED
GULL
2W
SEP–MAR
AdNb
1W
SEP–MAR
3W
SEP–MAR
AdNb
SEP–MAR

Black-headed Gull *p.119*
Mediterranean Gull *p.120*

All: vagrants from N America

LC Bonaparte's Gull
Larus philadelphia

② **L** 31–34 cm | **W** 79–84 cm

Like a **small**, dainty Black-headed Gull with small head and **black bill**. **AdBr** | **hood black**; thin white eye-crescents. **AdNb/1W** | head white with black ear-spot; nape grey; **legs pink**.

FL | **Ad underwing white** with black trailing edge. **1W** like Black-headed Gull, but inner primary coverts pale, outer ones dark; hindwing band and diagonal band on innerwing blacker. Underwing white; fine black trailing edge. **1S** as 1W but black hood.

Coasts, lakes

LC Franklin's Gull *Larus pipixcan*

② **L** 32–36 cm | **W** 81–93 cm

Small gull with slate-grey upperparts. **AdBr** | **hood black**; thick white eye-crescents meet behind eye. **AdNb/1W/1S** | **dark half-hood**; white face and eye-crescents.

FL | **Ad** white trailing edge curves forward to outline **black-and-white wingtip**; underwing white with black tip; **grey centre to tail. 1W** hindwing, outerwing and tail-band blackish. **2W** more black on wingtip than **Ad**.

Lakes, marshes

LC Laughing Gull *Larus atricilla*

② **L** 36–41 cm | **W** 98–110 cm

Small-medium-sized gull with **slaty-grey upperparts**. **AdBr** | **hood black**; white eye-crescents do not meet behind eye; **bill and legs red. AdNb** | head white with grey cheek and nape. **1W** | back grey; wing grey, blotched brown; **breast-band and flank grey**; bill blackish; legs dark grey. **2Y** | as Ad but flank/wingtip browner.

FL | **Ad** white trailing edge; **large black triangle on wingtip**; primary tips white (wear off by AUG). **1W** back grey; innerwing brown with grey midwing band, outerwing blackish; black tail-band and grey sides accentuate white rump.

Coasts, lakes

BLACK-HEADED GULL

1W
SEP–MAR

1W

AdNb

AdNb

AdNb
AUG–MAR

AdBr
MAR–S

underwing and body whiter than on Laughing Gull

1W

AdNb
AUG–MAR

1W
SEP–APR

AdBr
MAR–SEP

NOTE: Complete moults in both spring and autumn give unusual plumage sequence.

1S
MAR–SEP

1W

AdNb

AdB
FEB–

1W
AUG–MAR

AdNb
JUL–MAR

Grey-headed Gull
Larus cirrocephalus

 L 39–42 cm | **W** 100–115 cm

Medium-sized grey and white gull.
AdBr | hood **grey** with darker border;
eye pale; legs and bill dark red.
AdNb | legs and bill brighter red;
head like Black-headed Gull but eye
pale. **1W** | like Black-headed Gull with
darker wing coverts, larger bill.
2W | like Ad with brown on wing.

FL | **Ad** upperwing has prominent
white patch next to black wingtip;
white 'mirrors'; underwing grey.
1W innerwing grey/brown with broad
black hindwing band; streaked **white
patch** inside **black outerwing**. **2W**
like **Ad** but brown on upperwing.

Black-headed Gull *p.119*
AdBr - Med. Gull [2S] *p.120*

Vagrant from Africa
Lakes, coasts

Relict Gull *Larus relictus*

 L 42–46 cm | **W** 85–100 cm

Medium-sized, pale gull; bill short,
thick, blackish. **AdBr** | hood black
with white eye-crescents; legs dark
red. **AdNb** | grey smudges on white
head. **1W** | **head pale**; neck **spotted**;
legs blackish.

FL | **Ad** wingtip **streaked black**
(like 2Y Mediterranean Gull);
underwing white. **1W** upperwing like
Mediterranean Gull but hindwing
band weak; white spot on outer
primary; tail-band incomplete.

AdNb - Common Gull *p.116*
Mediterranean Gull *p.120*

Vagrant from Asia (ring recoveries only)
Lakes, marshes

White-eyed Gull
Larus leucophthalmus

 L 39–43 cm | **W** 100–110 cm

Medium-sized, dark grey and white
gull with **white collar, long red bill**
and yellow legs. **AdBr** | **hood** and
throat black; white eye-crescents.
AdNb | dusky, streaked hood extends
onto upper breast.

FL | Wings long, with black wingtip
and broad white trailing edge.

Vagrant from Indian Ocean
Coasts

Bridled and Sooty Terns

Large, slim, angular 'sea' terns that are dark above and white below; bill and legs black. Of the two, Sooty Tern is slightly larger and darker with a more contrasting underwing.

LC Sooty Tern
Onychoprion fuscatus

L 42–45 cm | **W** 72–80 cm

Ad | back blackish, fades browner/greyer, but little contrast with **black cap. White forehead extends back to eye** in broad, blunt patch. **Juv** | dark brown, with pale bars above; breast dark, belly pale; bill and legs black.

FL | Blackish above, white below; tail long, forked, blackish, with broad **white** sides. Underwing white with **broad blackish** trailing edge/wingtip.

Vagrant from tropical seas; has bred (Macaronesian islands)

Coasts / at sea

LC Bridled Tern
Onychoprion anaethetus

L 37–42 cm | **W** 65–72 cm

Ad | back grey-brown, contrasts with black cap; white forehead extends behind eye in side view, a striking 'V'-shape from in front.

FL | Dark brown above, white below; tail long, forked, dark brown with narrow white sides. Underwing white with **narrow dark-grey** trailing edge.

Vagrant from tropical seas

At sea, rarely inland

VU Aleutian Tern
Onychoprion aleuticus

L 32–34 cm | **W** 75–80 cm

Small, pale grey tern with black cap; **darker** than Arctic Tern. **Ad** | grey with black cap; **white forehead extends back just over eye; underparts pale grey. Bill and legs black**.

FL | Mid-grey; underwing whitish, with **broad dark trailing edge** to secondaries and outer primaries (broken on inner primaries). Rump and long, forked tail white.

Common Tern *p. 142*
Arctic Tern *p. 143*

Vagrant from N Pacific

Coasts

Darker than Bridled Tern; white forehead stops at eye

Juv
ALL YEAR

Ad

Ad

Ad

Ad
ALL YEAR

Worn birds have dark trailing edge on paler upperwing.

In strong light over sea, underparts can look surprisingly dark.

Ad

Ad

White forehead extends behind eye.

Ad
ALL YEAR

Ad

Ad

Ad

Ad
ALL YEAR

Least Tern *Sternula antillarum*

L 21–25 cm | **W** 41–47 cm

Very small, grey-and-white tern with black cap; rump and tail greyer than very similar Little Tern. Best separated by recordings of distinctive **squeaky double-note** call (Little Tern has a rasping call).

Little Tern *p. 139*

Vagrant from N America

Coasts

Ad

LITTLE TERN

rump and tail white

rump and tail grey

Ad

Ad
ALL YEAR

Forster's Tern *Sterna forsteri*

L 33–36 cm | **W** 64–70 cm

Small, pale tern, very like Common Tern but **upperwing paler. AdBr** | bill red, tipped black; legs red; tail **grey, edged white** (white, edged grey on Common Tern). **Underparts white. AdNb** | bill black; broad **black 'mask'**. Upperwing silvery, outer primaries tipped black, contrasting with pale inner primaries by JAN/FEB. **1Y** | primaries grey, wearing to black; coverts pale.

Common Tern *p. 142*
Arctic Tern *p. 143*
Roseate Tern *p. 144*
Nb - Gull-billed Tern *p. 140*

Vagrant from N America

Coasts

COMMON TERN

tail white with grey edge

tail grey with white edge

outer primary tips wear darker

AdNb
AUG–MAR

1Y
ALL YEAR

AdBr
MAR–AUG

Brown Noddy *Anous stolidus*

L 38–45 cm | **W** 75–86 cm

Medium-large, **dark brown** seabird with **diffuse whitish cap**, black bill and legs. **Tail rounded** or wedge-shaped.

Vagrant from tropical seas

At sea

Ad

Ad
ALL YEAR

'Orange-billed' terns are similar and difficult to identify. Important to assess size and structure (ideally against *e.g.* Caspian/Sandwich Terns) and focus on bill size, shape and colour, and shape of crest.

LC Royal Tern *Thalasseus maximus*

L 42–49 cm | **W** 86–92 cm

Large, pale grey and white tern (larger than Sandwich Tern). Bill long, stout; yellow-orange to bright red (Caspian Tern's is **heavier**). **AdBr** | crown and short, squared crest black. **AdNb** | **black eye surrounded by white** (Caspian Tern has darker forehead). **FL** | Powerful; long-winged. **Ad** rump and tail **white**.

Vagrant from N America, Africa
Coasts

LC Lesser Crested Tern
Thalasseus bengalensis

L 33–40 cm | **W** 76–82 cm

Medium-large, grey and white tern (size as Sandwich Tern). Bill long, rather slim, **bright orange** or orange with paler tip. **AdBr** | cap and short, slightly pointed crest black. **AdNb** | forehead white, **black around eye**. **FL** | Wings rather broad (Sandwich and Elegant Terns have narrower, more angular wings). **Rump and tail pale grey**.

Vagrant from Africa; has bred
Coasts

NT Elegant Tern
Thalasseus elegans

L 39–43 cm | **W** 76–81 cm

Medium-large, grey and white tern (size/shape as Sandwich Tern). **Bill long, slender, droop-tipped**; orange with red base and yellowish tip. **AdBr** | cap and long, drooped crest black. **AdNb** | forehead white, **broad black patch around eye**. **FL** | Long, angular wings (narrower than Lesser Crested Tern). Rump and tail white.

Vagrant from N America, has bred
Coasts

Caspian Tern p. 145

African ssp. *albididorsa* (sometimes treated as a species, '**West Africa Royal Tern**') has slimmer, more yellow-orange b than American ssp. *maxima*.

AdBr

ssp. *albididorsalis*

ssp. *maxima*

AdNb
AUG–APR

upperwing pale, outer primaries dark; underwing white with black trailing edge to outer primaries (as Common Tern (p. 142))

ssp. *albididorsalis*

AdNb
AUG–APR

AdBr
MAR–SEP

ssp. *maxima*

Sandwich Tern p. 141

wing pattern as Royal Tern

AdBr

AdNb
AUG–APR

AdBr
MAR–SEP

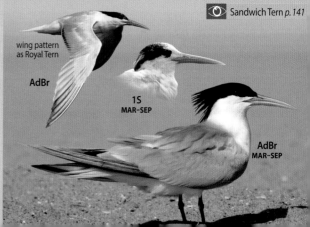

Sandwich Tern p. 141

wing pattern as Royal Tern

AdBr

1S
MAR–SEP

AdBr
MAR–SEP

South Polar Skua
Catharacta maccormicki

L 50–55 cm | **W** 120–130 cm

Large brown skua, very like Great Skua: dark birds in autumn and bleached, paler birds in summer can be almost inseparable. Paler collar, uniform cold greyish-brown underparts, very dark underwing and narrower white crescent at base of primaries all suggest South Polar Skua, but both species individually variable.

 Great Skua *p.150*

Vagrant from S Atlantic
At sea

GREAT SKUA

broader white crescent

paler underwing

Ad
ALL YEAR

Ad
ALL YEAR

Wilson's Phalarope
Phalaropus tricolor

L 22–24 cm | **W** 40–42 cm

Largest phalarope with **long, thin, black bill**. ♀ **Br** | crown and hindneck grey; black eyestripe blends into **rufous neck-stripe**; legs black. ♂ **Br** | back grey, blotched dark; eyestripe grey; neck pale orange-buff. **AdNb** | pale grey and white; legs dark grey-green. **Juv/1W** | very pale, like AdNb; dark mark through eye but no prominent black eye-patch; **legs yellow**.
FL | Wings plain; rump white.
V | Flight call "*chu.*"

 Other phalaropes *pp.196–197*
Juv - Marsh Sandpiper *p.176*
Juv - Spotted Redshank *p.179*
Juv - Ruff *p.192*

Annual vagrant from N America
Freshwater pools, coastal lagoons

Juv
JUL–SEP

Juv → 1W
AUG–OCT

AdNb
JUL–MAR

♀ Br

Intensity of orange on neck varies between individuals in ♂.

♀ Br
MAR–AUG

♂ Br
MAR–AUG

Grey-headed Lapwing
Vanellus cinereus

L 34–37 cm | **W** 75 cm

Medium-sized, long-legged lapwing, upperparts pale brown, underparts white; **grey head** and neck; resembles White-tailed Lapwing with **broad white band on wing** and **yellow legs**, but **yellow bill base**, narrow black breast-band and **black band on tail**.

 White-tailed Lapwing *p. 164*

Vagrant from Asia
Marshes

Ad

Ad
ALL YEAR

Egyptian Plover
Pluvianus aegyptius

L 19–21 cm | **W** 47–51 cm

Unmistakable small, sleek wader with short bill and flat head. Narrow black stripe down back; wing blue-grey; underparts **orange-buff**. Bill small, black; broad black cheek extends onto back and into narrow black breast-band, all edged with white.

Vagrant from Africa
Watersides

FL | Largely **white wings** crossed by **black diagonal** band.

Ad

Ad
ALL YEAR

Crab-plover
Dromas ardeola

L 38–41 cm | **W** 66–78 cm

Large, plover-like wader. **Ad** | white; back and lower edge of closed wing black. Bill black, thick, dagger-like. **1W** | like Ad but back mottled grey; crown and wings pale grey-brown.

 Avocet *p. 158*

Vagrant from Indian Ocean
Coasts

FL | Elongated, long legs trailed. Wing black with white forewing patch; rump/tail white.

Ad

1W
AUG–APR

Ad
ALL YEAR

Semipalmated Plover
Charadrius semipalmatus

L 16–17·5 cm | **W** 31–32 cm

N American equivalent of very similar Ringed Plover: small size and **call** may draw attention. Small webs between toes (one tiny web on Ringed Plover); head rounded; bill short and stubby (Ringed Plover has flatter head, longer bill). **AdBr/1S** faint whitish stripe below cap (bold on Ringed Plover), breast-band thinner. **Juv/1W** dull; white throat extends as point above gape (dark on Ringed Plover).

V Rising "*chewee*," vaguely like Spotted Redshank (*p. 179*).

| Vagrant from N America |
| Coasts |

Ringed Plover p. 170

Juv

RINGED PLOVER

dark

♂Br

wide white stripe

breast-band broad

faint whitish stripe

Juv
JUN–OCT

white point

breast-band narrow

1S
MAR–JUL

Kittlitz's Plover
Charadrius pecuarius

L 12–14 cm | **W** 40–44 cm

Small, long-legged, 'ringed' plover, resembles Kentish Plover.
Ad upperparts **brown with buff fringes**; underparts bright buff; white forehead extends as band under cap; extensive white throat; **black frontal band extends as diagonal line through eye** and below **white nape. Bill and legs blackish. Juv/1W** lacks black-and-white head pattern of Ad; no dark breast-band.

| Vagrant from Africa |
| Grassland, watersides |

Kentish Plover p. 170
Lesser Sandplover p. 558

Juv/1W lack obvious pattern but show buff collar; side of breast bright buff without dark patch.

1W
SEP–APR

AdBr
FEB–JUL

Killdeer
Charadrius vociferus

L 23·5–26·0 cm | **W** 59–63 cm

Like large, long-tailed 'ringed' plover (see *p. 170*); brown above, white below. **AdBr** **double breast-band**. **AdNb/1W** has cinnamon feather fringes on head and back; lower breast-band mottled white.

V Call long, rising "*klu-ee*."

FL Blackish wings with long, wide white stripe; **bright rufous rump** blending into long, dark tail.

| Annual vagrant from N America |
| Coasts, marshes |

AdNb
AUG–MAR

1W
AUG–MAR

double breast-band

AdBr
APR–OCT

557

Sandplovers look like large 'ringed' plovers; the two species have distinctive black, white and rufous breeding plumages but identical non-breeding and immature plumages, when size and structure are vital. Subspecies of both vary in size, bill size and breeding patterns, creating identification problems.

LC VU Greater Sandplover
Charadrius leschenaultii

L 22–25 cm | **W** 53–60 cm

Large 'ringed'-type plover, bulky with deep belly, heavy towards tail; **head large; eye large; bill long, tapered; legs long,** grey-green or olive-green. Subspecies *columbinus* (breeds) has smallest bill, most like Lesser Sandplover, but not so blunt; sspp. *scythicus* and *leschenaultii* (vagrants from Asia) have a **longer** bill. ♂**Br** black 'mask', rufous forecrown/nape; white forehead and throat; breast-band rufous. ♀**Br** 'mask' brown or greyish; breast-band light orange-buff. **AdNb / 1W** breast-side dark brown; remnants of orange indicate Ad. **Juv** like AdNb / 1W but back scaled buff; breast buff.

V | Call a trilled "*trrrr*;" song a rhythmically repeated "*pip-ru-irr*."

FL | Blackish wing with broad white wingbar; rump and tail dark with white sides; darker near tip of tail; toes project beyond tail.

GREATER SANDPLOVER bill 'heavy' but pointed: 'nail' more than half total length

LESSER SANDPLOVER bill blunt: 'nail' less than half total length

SSP. *columbinus*

♀ Br FEB–AUG

♂ Br FEB–AUG

1W AUG–MAR

Rare and local summer migrant

Dry grasslands; shorelines, mudflats

NOTE: In Europe, AdBr in FEB/MAR (or Juv in JUN/JUL) points to Greater Sandplover SSP. *columbinus*; AdBr after MID-AUG points to Lesser Sandplover.

LC Lesser Sandplover
Charadrius mongolus

L 19–21 cm | **W** 55–61 cm

Slightly smaller than Greater Sandplover; head rounder; eye small; **bill shorter, stout, blunt**; rear-body short, slim; legs shorter, dark grey. ♂**Br** | black 'mask'; rufous nape and breast-band; forehead black (SSP. *atrifrons* early in breeding season) or white (sspp. *stegmanni, pamirensis*). ♀**Br** | like ♂**Br** but black reduced. **AdNb / Juv / 1W** | plumages as Greater Sandplover.

V | Sharp "*chitik*" and trilled "*trrrr*" (overlap with Greater Sandplover).

FL | White wingbar; white sides to rump, tail often uniform; toes often do not project beyond tail.

SSP. *atrifrons* (type)

SSP. *pamirensis*

SSP. *pamirensis*

♂ Br APR–SEP

♀ Br APR–SEP

♂ Br APR–SEP

♂ Br APR–SEP

SSP. *stegmanni*

AdNb / 1W SEP–APR

Vagrant from Asia
Shorelines, mudflats

AdNb/1W

♂Br

**GREATER
SANDPLOVER**

. leschenaultii

AdNb/1W

♂Br

p. pamirensis
LESSER SANDPLOVER

CASPIAN PLOVER

♂Br

Juv
JUL–AUG

♂Br

**ORIENTAL
PLOVER**

LC **Caspian Plover**
RE *Charadrius asiaticus*

L 18–20 cm | **W** 55–61 cm

Medium-small, slender, fine-billed, long-legged plover. Pale brown above, white below. Bill black; legs grey-green.
♂Br | cap dark, white over eye, forehead and throat white; broad **rufous breast-band** with thin black lower border.
♀/♂Nb | breast-band grey-brown; stripe over eye, and face and throat yellowish-buff. **Juv/1W** | like ♀/♂Nb but pale feather edges on upperparts.

V | Call "*tyup*;" song, in flight, repeated, ringing trisyllabic notes "*ty-ur-lee*."

Rare passage migrant
APR–OCT; formerly bred

Dry plains, saltpans,
near water

FL | Innerwing pale, outerwing dark, with short, white wingbar. Underwing pale **brown and white**. Toes project beyond tail.

♂Br
MAR–AUG

♀
ALL YEAR

Oriental Plover
Charadrius veredus

L 22–25 cm | **W** 46–53 cm

Similar to Caspian Plover but **♂Br** | has largely **white head**, breast-band rufous, edged black below. **♀Br** | similar to ♂ but head and breast-band buffish-brown. **AdNb/Juv/1W** | grey-brown, white below; white line above dusky cheek; bill rather heavy, black; legs orange-yellow.

V | Calls a whistled "*chip-chip-chip*" and "*hweet*."

FL | Plain brown above, only faint paler wingbar; dark rump. Underwing **plain brown**.

Vagrant from Asia
Wetlands

♂Br
MAR–AUG

AdNb
AUG–MAR

Rare snipes are similar to each other and to Snipe *p. 194*

LC **Pintail Snipe** *Gallinago stenura*

LC **L** 25–27 cm | **W** 44–47 cm

Secretive, dark brown, long-billed snipe; brown above, paler below. Very like Snipe but with slightly shorter bill and tail. Pale buff lines on back are narrower, less continuous.

V | Very quiet call. In high display flight, **squeaky** "*chz-chz-chz-chz-chz,*" then whining noise in dive, followed by nasal hissing notes.

more barred than Snipe

FL | Slower than Snipe. Wings **lack pale trailing edge**. Upperwing dull brown; underwing more uniformly densely barred than Snipe.

Rare and very local summer migrant
APR–OCT

Marshes

ALL YEAR

LC **Swinhoe's Snipe**
Gallinago megala

L 27–29 cm | **W** 40–50 cm

Indistinguishable from Pintail Snipe in the field unless displaying (recorded in Europe), when different calls are diagnostic.

V | Usually silent if flushed. In display flight repeated **harsh** "*kxr-kxr-kxr-kxr-kxr*" with **marked "r" sound**, whining dive then final harsh "*kxr*" notes.

Vagrant from Asia

Marshes

LC **Wilson's Snipe**
Gallinago delicata

L 23–28 cm | **W** 41–44 cm

Very like Snipe; separated by details of underwing and tail. Wilson's Snipe, has thicker dark bars on the axillaries ('wingpits') and a darker, more extensively barred underwing with a slightly narrower white trailing edge. Outer tail feathers have 4 or more dark bars (Snipe 2–4).

Vagrant from N America

Marshes

ALL YEAR

SNIPE

mostly white

quite broad

WILSON'S 'wingpit'
dark ≥ white

SNIPE 'wingpit'
dark < white

WILSON'S SNIPE
extensive black barring

ALL YEAR

rather narrow

Photographs of underwing and tail ideally needed to assess details.

Buff-breasted Sandpiper
Calidris subruficollis

L 18–20 cm | **W** 43–47 cm

Small, grassland wader, with small round head and **yellow legs**. **Ad** | upperparts brown with pale feather edges; underparts buff, white under tail. **Juv** | like **Ad** but paler fringes above give more scaly look.
V | Usually silent.

Annual vagrant from N America

Grassland, marshes

Ad
ALL YEAR

FL | Wing plain; rump dark without white sides.

Juv
JUN–OCT

Ruff *p. 192*

Upland Sandpiper
Bartramia longicauda

L 28–32 cm | **W** 50–55 cm

Small, pale, elongated grassland wader; long tail extends beyond closed wingtip. Bill straight, fine; **legs yellow**. **Two dark stripes** on crown; cream feather edges on upperparts, pale 'notches' on tertials.
V | Usually silent.

Vagrant from N America

Grassland

Juv

FL | Wing and rump dark.

Juv
JUN–OCT

Little Curlew
Numenius minutus

L 29–32 cm | **W** 57–63 cm

Small buff-brown curlew with short bill, **dark rump**. **Ad** | crown brown with buff central stripe; black streak behind eye beneath **buff stripe**. **Juv** | greyer than **Ad** with whitish spots above; crown blackish.
V | Flight call higher, thinner than Whimbrel, a rising "*quip quip quip*."

Vagrant from Asia

Wet grassland, watersides

Ad

FL | Wing and rump dark.

Ad
ALL YEAR

Whimbrel *p. 182*

Slender-billed Curlew
Numenius tenuirostris

L 36–41 cm | **W** 80–92 cm

Small curlew with fine, blackish bill; legs **blackish** with white 'thighs' (beware runt/juvenile Curlew). **Ad** | underparts white with **round/ ace-of-spades-shaped blackish spots**. **Juv** | as **Ad** but flank streaked.
V | High "*cur-lee*" and quick "*kew-ee*."

Very rare passage migrant (extinct?)

Marshes

Ad

FL | Upperwing has dark outer 'wedge'; underwing largely white.

Ad
ALL YEAR

NOTE: Slender-billed Curlew possibly extinct; **Eskimo Curlew** *Numenius borealis* (historical vagrant from N America) also now likely to be extinct.

Curlew *p. 183*
Whimbrel *p. 182*

LC **Greater Yellowlegs**
Tringa melanoleuca

L 29–33 cm | **W** 65–67 cm

LC **Lesser Yellowlegs** *
Tringa flavipes

L 23–25 cm | **W** 65–67 cm

Vagrants from N America [*annual]
Coasts, marshes

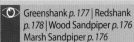

Greenshank p. 177 | Redshank
p. 178 | Wood Sandpiper p. 176
Marsh Sandpiper p. 176

These two grey-brown and white waders with **yellow legs** are hard to tell apart when size cannot be assessed. Best distinguished by size, bill shape, calls and behaviour, but specific differences are summarized in the table and annotations below. **Greater Yellowlegs** is near the size of Greenshank; **Lesser Yellowlegs** like a small, slender, long-legged Redshank. Plumages paler than Redshank, whiter on breast; head pattern stronger with bold white stripe over blackish line from bill to eye. **AdBr** | dark spots on back and breast. **AdNb / 1W** | plainer and greyer than **AdBr**, whiter on breast. **Juv** | back spangled with fine buff spots.

FL | Rump white, square; wing dark (Redshank, Greenshank and Marsh Sandpiper all have long white 'wedge' on back).

AdNb / 1W
AUG–MAR
[DEC]

Greater Yellowlegs (LEFT) 'heavier', less likely to look obviously long-necked, than **Lesser Yellowlegs** (RIGHT); size hard to assess in isolation.

Identification of yellowlegs – summary of key features		
	Greater Yellowlegs	**Lesser Yellowlegs**
Bill	**long** (**longer** than head and ≥ **length of tarsus**); **slightly upturned**; base pale grey	**short** (just longer than head and < **length of tarsus**); **fine, straight**; base dark/yellowish
Closed wingtip	extends **just** beyond tail	extends **well** beyond tail
AdBr	flank	**barred**	**unmarked**
Juv	breast	distinctly streaked	faintly streaked
FL	hindwing	finely spotted pale	unmarked
Voice	3–4 piercing, rhythmic notes "peu-peu-pew" (Greenshank a louder, even "teuw-teuw-teuw")	1–4 weak, hesitant "tew" notes (Redshank a ringing, fading "tyew-yewyew")

REDSHANK

LESSER YELLOWLEGS | Juv

GREATER YELLOWLEGS | Juv

GREENSHANK

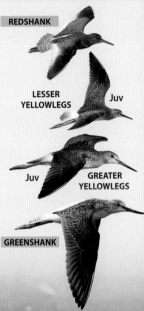

GREATER YELLOWLEGS

AdBr
FEB–AUG

barred

Wide flank with dark bars emphasizes the round-bodied shape.

LESSER YELLOWLEGS

AdBr
FEB–AUG

unmarked

Narrow, pure-white flank and slender shape.

GREATER YELLOWLEGS

Juv
JUN–OCT

Often wades belly-deep, with head frequently under water.

LESSER YELLOWLEGS

Juv
JUN–OCT

Rarely wades in deep water and always feeds from the surface.

Long-billed Dowitcher*
Limnodromus scolopaceus

L 27–30 cm | **W** 48–50 cm

LC Short-billed Dowitcher
Limnodromus griseus

L 25–29 cm | **W** 48–50 cm

Vagrants from N America [*annual]
Coasts, marshes

Stilt Sandpiper p. 565

Dowitchers are hard to separate, particularly AdNb / 1W. Bill length varies and overlaps between the two species. Best distinguished by call, but differences as summarized in the table below. Like oversized Knot (*p. 191*) with long, snipe-like (*p. 194*) bill and long, green legs; 'sewing-machine' feeding action. Prominent dark cap above wide white stripe (pale 'V' from in front) and dark line from eye to bill. **AdBr** | reddish-brown or cinnamon overall, with blackish markings. **AdNb / 1W** | greyish; pale below with grey bars/spots on flank. **Juv** | back brown with rufous feather edges; breast buff, underparts white with grey bars/spots on flank.

FL | Wing dark with broad white trailing edge; **white triangle** on back merges into white rump and tail, which has dark bars.

SHORT-BILLED DOWITCHER
Juv

LONG-BILLED DOWITCHER
AdNb

Identification of dowitchers – comparison summary of key features		
	Long-billed Dowitcher	**Short-billed Dowitcher**
Bill	very slightly curved; typically 2× head length	slightly curved, thick at tip; typically 1·5× head length
Body	rather pot-bellied, with round-backed profile	rather slim-bellied, with flat-backed profile
Tail bars	bars equal width, or **black bars wider than white**	bars equal width, or **black bars narrower than white**
Voice	short, sharp "**kip**" or "**keek**," sometimes (confusingly) two or three quick notes	fast, double or triple, slightly rattling "**tudu**" or "**tududu**"

LONG-BILLED DOWITCHER

white tips

bars

AdBr
MAR–AUG

Breast-side rufous with **dark bars**
(MAR–JUN; **worn away by** JUL)

SHORT-BILLED DOWITCHER

white/buff fringes

spots

AdBr
MAR–AUG

Breast-side rufous with **dark spots**
(MAR–JUN; **worn away by** JUL)

LONG-BILLED DOWITCHER

1W
AUG–APR

In this plumage, tail and call are most useful but other, secondary, 'relative' features are summarized below.

Juv
JUN–OCT

SHORT-BILLED DOWITCHER

SCAPULARS: **irregular markings**; TERTIALS: **dark with rufous bars/ blotches; fringes rufous/buff**

AdNb/1W
AUG–APR

WHITE LOWER EYE-CRESCENT: less obvious; CHEEK: paler; UPPER BREAST: often paler, variably spotted; FLANK: grey 'V'-shapes

Juv
JUN–OCT

LONG-BILLED DOWITCHER

AdNb/1W
AUG–APR

SCAPULARS: well-defined rusty fringes/'notches'; TERTIALS: plain, dark with simple **narrow** pale, rusty fringes; no internal marks

WHITE LOWER EYE-CRESCENT: more obvious; CHEEK: darker; UPPER BREAST: often with 'sooty' wash; FLANK: grey bars

563

LC Hudsonian Godwit

Limosa haemastica

L 37–42 cm | **W** 67–79 cm

Like Black-tailed Godwit but slightly smaller; bill thinner. ♂**Br** | uniform red below. ♀**Br** | barred grey, white and red below; larger and longer-billed than ♂. **AdNb** | grey-brown, streaked blackish above, plain buff below.

V | Descending *"tow-wit."*

FL | Underwing blackish; narrow white wingbar.

 Black-tailed Godwit *p. 181*

Vagrant from N America
Coasts, marshes

narrow white wingbar

♂**Br**
BLACK-TAILED GODWIT
broad white wingbar
underwing white

underwing blackish

♂**Br**
MAR–SEP

♀**Br**
MAR–SEP

LC Spotted Sandpiper

Actitis macularius

L 18–20 cm | **W** 37–40 cm

Very like Common Sandpiper, but **tail shorter**. **AdBr** | back barred, underparts white with **bold black spots**, bill pink. **AdNb** | eyestripe bolder, bill paler, breast side greyer and plainer and legs yellower than Common Sandpiper. **Juv** | tertials plainer than Common Sandpiper.

V | Sharp *"teep-teep"* call.

FL | Wingbar shorter than on Common Sandpiper, broadest in middle; tail has less white at sides.

 Common Sandpiper *p. 174*

Annual vagrant from N America
Waterside, coasts

long white wingbar

AdBr

wingbar narrows on innerwing

AdBr
MAR–AUG

Black spotting below in breeding plumage is diagnostic.

COMMON SANDPIPER

AdBr

tail long

Juv

Juv
JUL–OCT

tail quite short

LC Solitary Sandpiper

Tringa solitaria

L 18–21 cm | **W** 50 cm

Like small, delicate Green Sandpiper but tends to show bolder white eyering, more tapered hind end.

V | High-pitched *"peet-weet-weet."*

FL | **Rump dark** (not white as on Green Sandpiper).

 Green Sandpiper *p. 175*

Vagrant from N America
Coasts, watersides

rump dark

rump white

less distinct eyering

Juv

AdNb
Juv

GREEN SANDPIPER

bold white eyering

Juv
JUL–OCT

Stilt Sandpiper
Calidris himantopus

L 18–23 cm | **W** 38–47 cm

Medium-sized, tall, slim, wader; like large Curlew Sandpiper or small dowitcher but legs **longer**, greenish-yellow; bill angled down, slightly **drooped at tip. AdBr** | underparts **barred**; rufous cheek patch. **AdNb/1W** | grey-and-white; dark cap; grey flank streaks. **Juv** | like AdNb but pale edges on upperparts.

V | Low, single, "*whu*" call.

FL | Rump white.

 Curlew Sandpiper *p. 189*
Dowitcher spp. *p. 563*

Vagrant from N America
Coasts, pools

1W
OCT–APR

Juv
JUL–OCT

bill droop-tipped

legs greenish-yellow

AdBr
APR–SEP

Barred below, cheek rufous in breeding plumage.

Pectoral Sandpiper
Calidris melanotos

L 19–23 cm | **W** 43–47 cm

Larger than Dunlin (*p. 188*), smaller than Ruff. Creeps/crouches in wet vegetation, mud, reedbeds. **Breast-band streaked; belly white; legs pale**; bill faintly downcurved, pale at base. **Ad** | back dull brown. **Juv** | back brown with **cream fringes** and **pale 'V'; breast-band** finely streaked. Legs **yellow-ochre**/greenish-yellow.

V | Call trilled "*krrrt*."

FL | Rump dark-centred; resembles Dunlin but wingbar faint, white.

 Ruff *p. 192* | *Sharp-tailed Sandpiper*

Annual vagrant from N America
Watersides, marshes

DUNLIN
prominent white wingbar

faint wingbar

Juv

AdBr
APR–SEP

Juv
JUL–OCT

pale 'V' on back

bill slightly downcurved with yellowish base

legs yellowish

belly white; well-defined breast-band

Sharp-tailed Sandpiper
Calidris acuminata

L 17–21 cm | **W** 36–43 cm

Like Pectoral Sandpiper, but **AdBr** | has **rufous cap**, **spotted breast** and **'V'-shaped** bars on flank. **Juv** | cap rufous; breast orange-buff, streaked on side/throat (**no breast-band**).

V | High, short notes repeated, "*shilip-sheep-sheep-ip*."

FL | As Pectoral Sandpiper.

 Ruff *p. 192* | *Pectoral Sandpiper*

Vagrant from Asia
Marshes, lakes

AdBr
APR–SEP

breast spotted

cap bright rufous

Juv
JUL–OCT

belly white; breast orange-buff, diffusely streaked

legs yellowish

RARE 'PEEPS' The seven small sandpipers on these pages, plus Little and Temminck's Stints (*pp. 184-185*) are often referred to as 'peeps'. Identification is difficult: look for leg colour (blackish or pale), bill shape, presence or absence of a pale 'V' on the back, upperpart pattern (especially on juveniles), and rump pattern in flight.

Species on this page are similar to Little Stint; in flight, white wingbar and dark-centred white rump. **Calls differ.**

Annual vagrant from N America	Vagrant from N America	Vagrant from Asia
Coasts and pools	Coasts and pools	Coasts and pools
TOES: **small webs between front toes**		TOES: **unwebbed** [as Little Stint]

NT **Semipalmated Sandpiper**
Calidris pusilla

L 13–15 cm | **W** 27–29 cm
Like Little Stint; **bill thicker, blunt-tipped. AdBr** | breast ochre-brown; flank streaked grey. **AdNb** | brownish-grey, white below. **Juv** | (see *table*).

V | Call a **rolled "tchrrrp."**

LC **Western Sandpiper**
Calidris mauri

L 14–17 cm | **W** 27–29 cm
Like Semipalmated Sandpiper; bill **longer and thinner. AdBr** | back rufous, dark **'V'-shapes** on flank. **AdNb** | as Semipalmated Sandpiper. **Juv** | (see *table*).

V | Call a **thin "jeet."**

NT **Red-necked Stint**
Calidris ruficollis

L 13–16 cm | **W** 28–30 cm
Like Little Stint but bill short, thick; legs shorter; body longer. **AdBr** | cheek/neck **orange-red. AdNb** | back greyish, scapulars with dark central streak. **Juv** | (see *table*).

V | Call **"kreet."**

Identification of juvenile dark-legged 'peeps'			
	LITTLE STINT	RED-NECKED STINT	WESTERN SANDPIPER	SEMIPALMATED SANDPIPER
Cap	pale at side	evenly streaked		
Line over eye	forked	scarcely forked	unforked	unforked
Cheek	diffuse	wholly greyish	rufous 'smudge'	greyish 'smudge'
Scapulars DARK CENTRE:	ALL: round	UPPER: round; LOWER: 'anchors'	ALL: pointed 'anchors'	ALL: blunt 'anchors'
EDGES:	buff/rufous/whitish	buff	bright rufous	whitish
Tertials CENTRE:	blackish	grey	grey-brown	grey
EDGES:	rufous	off-white	whitish/buff	buff
Back 'V'	strong	obscure/absent	obscure	obscure/absent

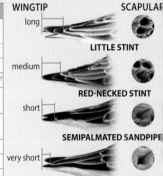

WINGTIP — SCAPULAR

long

LITTLE STINT

medium

RED-NECKED STINT

short

SEMIPALMATED SANDPIPER

very short

WESTERN SANDPIPER

SEMIPALMATED SANDPIPER
NOTE: Has both greyish and more rufous 'types'. Feeds more slowly than Little Stint; picks from surface.

small webs

Juv

wingbar white

LITTLE STINT
V | Call **"stit-tit."**

Juv

WESTERN SANDPIPER
Feeds by probing with long bill.

bill blunt-tipped

unwebbed

bill tapers to a point

Juvs JUL–OCT

RED-NECKED STINT

bill thick-based, slightly downcurved

AdBr

FEB–JUL

Small size; red neck

Baird's Sandpiper
Calidris bairdii

L 14–17 cm | **W** 40–43 cm

Like short-legged stint or White-rumped Sandpiper; **longer wing** extends farther beyond tail. Legs dark. **AdBr** | back and breast rufous, buff and black; broad pale feather fringes. **AdNb** | dull brown; underparts white. **Juv** | **head and breast buff**; upperparts grey-brown with black spots and **neat, white fringes giving scaly effect**; bill all-dark.

V | Call a purring "*prreet*."

FL | Dark-centred rump (unlike White-rumped Sandpiper).

White-rumped Sandpiper
Calidris fuscicollis

L 16–18 cm | **W** 38–40 cm

Like stint or Dunlin; wing extends beyond tail. Legs short, dark. **AdBr** | back bright brown with black spots. **AdNb** | greyish; **grey breast**, dark flank streaks. **Juv** | like juv Little Stint with white 'V' on back, but breast streaked grey; **bill dark, pale-based.**

V | Call a sharp, thin "*tjeet*."

FL | White crescent at tail base (unlike other 'peeps' (see Curlew Sandpiper)).

Least Sandpiper
Calidris minutilla

L 13–14·5 cm | **W** 27–28 cm

Very small; legs **yellow**. **AdBr** | back mottled brown and black. **AdNb** | back greyish, finely streaked blackish. **Juv** | back black and rufous with **pale 'V'**; cap rufous, evenly streaked black; buff line over eye unforked; **thick** dark line from bill to eye; breast-band buff, sides streaked brown.

V | Call a sharp "*kreeet*" or "*kit-kit-eet*."

FL | Thin white wingbar; tail side **grey**.

Long-toed Stint
Calidris subminuta

L 14–15·5 cm | **W** 27–29 cm

Very small; **legs yellow; toes long**. **AdBr** | back brown, rufous and cream. **AdNb** | back greyish, finely streaked blackish. **Juv** | back rufous with **pale 'V'**; cap rufous, streaked black, split by cream stripe; buff line over eye thickest/whitest in front; **narrow** dark line from bill to eye.

V | Call a rippled "*chrrup*."

FL | Thin white wingbar; tail side **grey**.

dark-centred, pale-edged feathers create 'scaly' effect

Juv

bill all-dark

wing very long

legs dark

Juv
JUL–OCT

Annual vagrant from N America

Coasts, freshwater margins

Juv

DUNLIN

Juv

CURLEW SANDPIPER

AdNb
SEP–MAR

rounded, pale-edged feathers

pale base

Juv
JUL–OCT

wing long

legs dark

Curlew Sandpiper *p.189*

Annual vagrant from N America

Coasts, lagoons

usually looks rather squat

Juv

cheek patch reaches eye

Juv
JUL–OCT

bill all-dark, fine-tipped

thick

tertials thinly edged rufous

Vagrant from N America

Watersides

BOTH: pale legs, as Temminck's Stint; pale 'V' on back and grey tail, as Little Stint (*p.184*).

Temminck's Stint *p.185* – legs pale ochre/greenish (Least Sandpiper – orange to greenish-yellow; Long-toed Stint – yellow-ochre)

AdNb
SEP–MAR

often looks long-necked

isolated cheek spot

Juv
JUL–OCT

tertials broadly edged rufous

bill pale at base

legs pale yellow-ochre

narrow

EN Great Knot *Calidris tenuirostris*

L 24–27 cm | **W** 58 cm

Like Knot but bill **longer, thicker**;
wing longer; head relatively small.
AdBr | back spotted rufous, breast
spotted black. **AdNb / 1W** | grey;
breast whitish, **subtly spotted grey**.
V | Generally silent.
FL | Dark 'wrist' patch; rump greyish.

 Knot *p. 191*
Purple Sandpiper *p. 186*

Vagrant from Asia

Coasts

AdNb / 1W
AUG–APR

AdNb
SEP–MAR

AdNb / 1W

AdBr

AdBr
FEB–AUG

breast heavily
spotted black

broad white
wingbar,
widens
across black
wingtip

bill thick,
grey

AdNb / 1W

legs greyish
or greenish

LC Willet *Tringa semipalmata*

L 33–41 cm | **W** 55–66 cm

Like thickset, grey Redshank; bill
thick, grey; legs greyish or greenish.
AdBr | grey, paler below, breast/flank
barred. **AdNb / Juv / 1W** | underparts
dull white, breast side grey.
V | Call nasal "*wey-wup*" and clipped
"*plip-plip-plip*" alarm.
FL | Striking **broad white wingbar**;
underwing **black-and-white**.

 Redshank *p. 178* | Knot *p. 191*

Vagrant from N America

Coasts

Head pattern recalls Spotted
Redshank (*p. 179*), with
broad white stripe over black
line between eye and bill.

AdNb
AUG–APR

Juv
JUL–OCT

bill long;
grey-green
with dark tip

legs yellow

NT Grey-tailed Tattler
Tringa brevipes

L 23–27 cm | **W** 51 cm

Medium-sized, grey wader, like
Redshank but colour of non-breeding
Knot; **legs yellow**.
V | Piping, melancholy "*tweet-weet*."
FL | Wings plain; rump and tail grey.

 Redshank *p. 178* | Knot *p. 191*

Vagrant from Asia

Coasts

LC American Woodcock
Scolopax minor

L 25–31 cm | **W** 40–51 cm

Typical woodcock form; back brown
and pale grey; dark face stripe and
bars across nape; underparts **orange**.

 Woodcock *p. 193*

Vagrant from N America

Woodland, clearings

ALL YEAR

underparts orange

Lesser Flamingo
Phoeniconaias minor

L 90–105 cm | **W** 90–105 cm

American Flamingo
Phoenicopterus ruber

L 120–145 cm | **W** 120–130 cm

Chilean Flamingo
Phoenicopterus chilensis

L 110–130 cm | **W** 120–130 cm

Greater Flamingo *p. 202*

GREATER

IDENTIFICATION OF FLAMINGOS				
	Greater	Lesser	American	Chilean
Bill	pale pink and black	dark red and black	pale grey, pink and black	pale pink and black
Eye	yellow	red	yellow	yellow
Legs	pink	red	grey-pink	grey; red joints

much darker pink than Greater Flamingo

AMERICAN FLAMINGO

CHILEAN FLAMINGO

LESSER FLAMINGO

Ad ALL YEAR

Ad ALL YEAR

Ad ALL YEAR

Vagrant from Africa — Lakes

Escape — Pools

Escape — Lakes

African Spoonbill
Platalea alba

L 90–95 cm | **W** 125–135 cm

Like Spoonbill but **face red**, bill grey and **legs pink** (not black).

Spoonbill *p. 208*

Ad ALL YEAR

Possible vagrant from Africa, occasional escape
Shallow lakes

LC **Yellow-billed Stork**
Mycteria ibis

L 90–105 cm | **W** 150–165 cm

Like White Stork but **face red**; bill bright **yellow, downcurved**; wing coverts barred pink, flight feathers black; legs pink.

White Stork *p. 206*

Ad ALL YEAR

Vagrant from Africa
Marshes

LC **Marabou Stork**
Leptoptilos crumenifer

L 120–130 cm | **W** 300–350 cm

Huge **grey-and-white stork**; bill massive, **dagger-like**, pale grey; head **pink**; legs grey. Plain grey upperwing in flight.

Ad ALL YEAR

Vagrant from Africa
Open ground, tips

569

CR Siberian Crane
Leucogeranus leucogeranus

L 140 cm | **W** 210–230 cm

Very large, **white** crane with black primaries (often hidden); **face red**, bill blackish; legs dark pink.
FL | All-white with black wingtips.

Ad

Ad
ALL YEAR

Passage migrant from Arctic Russia (only 1 remaining individual)
Wetlands

LC Sandhill Crane
Antigone canadensis

L 90–120 cm | **W** 160–230 cm

Large, pale grey crane (often stained browner).
Ad | forehead and crown red; eye yellow; cheek has white streak at top; neck pale grey. Tertials bushy, grey. **1Y** | browner than **Ad**; head red-brown, throat white.

Ad

FL | Underwing pale grey with darker tip and trailing edge.

Ad
ALL YEAR

1W
NOV–MAY

New feathers pale grey, become stained and 'bloom' wears off to reveal darker brown.

👁 Crane *p. 204*

Vagrant from N America
Open ground

LC Pink-backed Pelican
Pelecanus rufescens

L 125–132 cm | **W** 215–290 cm

Relatively small pelican, **brownish-white. Eye black with bulging white 'eyelids'. Ad** | bill yellowish to pinkish or grey, legs grey to yellowish, reddish in spring. **Juv / Imm** | pale brownish; head, neck and bill pale grey, gaining adult coloration over several years.

FL | Upperwing dull, lower back and rump **pale pink**; underwing pale with dull dark flight feathers and **whitish midwing line.**

Ad

Tinged pinkish when breeding (individually variable), otherwise dull white overall.

👁 Other pelicans *pp. 200–201*

Vagrant from Africa
Shallow lakes, coastal marshes

Ad
ALL YEAR

Great Blue Heron
Ardea herodias

L 95–135 cm | **W** 165–200 cm
Like Grey Heron, but slightly larger and **darker slaty grey**; crown boldly white above black stripe, neck brownish-grey. **Ad** | flank stripes, forewing marks and thigh **red-brown, legs blackish**. **Imm** | duller than **Ad**; back and wing feathers edged rusty-buff; crown dull.

Imm
ALL YEAR

FL | Underwing dark grey, more uniform than Grey Heron, lacking thin white leading edge.

AdNb
ALL YEAR

GREY HERON

Grey Heron *p. 212*

Vagrant from N America
Wetlands

LC Black-headed Heron
Ardea melanocephala

L 92–96 cm | **W** 150 cm
Large, slender, blue-grey heron. **Ad** | **crown and hindneck black**; face and throat white; legs dark grey. **Imm** | duller than **Ad**; crown and hindneck greyer; like Grey Heron, dull until following autumn moult. Legs **dark grey** (yellowish on Grey Heron).

Ad

FL | **Underwing black-and-white**.

Imm
ALL YEAR

Ad
ALL YEAR

Grey Heron *p. 212*

Vagrant from Africa
Grassland

Yellow-crowned Night Heron
Nyctanassa violacea

L 55–75 cm | **W** 100–112 cm
Medium-sized, dumpy, thick-billed heron. **Ad** | greyish; **head and bill blackish with pale crown and cheek**. **Juv / 1W** | brown; like Night Heron with white streaks on throat and foreneck, and thinner pale feather edges on wing. **Bill black, stout**.

Ad
ALL YEAR

1W
OCT–MAY

Juv - Night Heron
[Juv] *p. 214*

Vagrant from N America
Pools, marshes

LC African Sacred Ibis
Threskiornis aethiopicus

Ad

L 68 cm | **W** 112–124 cm
Unmistakable large white wading/waterside bird with **curved black bill**, bare **black head** and wispy plumes above black tail.

FL | Black tips to white flight feathers; red band under wing.

Ad
ALL YEAR

Very local but increasing naturalized escape

Marshes, open space, coasts

White herons/egrets similar to each other and to Cattle Egret *p. 209* | Little Egret *p. 210* | Great White Egret *p. 211*

LC Yellow-billed Egret
Ardea brachyrhyncha

L 56–72 cm | **W** 105–115 cm

Medium–large egret (between Little and Great White Egrets in size); head domed, bill relatively **short, yellow**, often with small black-tip; legs and feet all-dark. **Line of gape** reaches only **to rear of eye** (on Great White Egret, extends back behind eye).

Vagrant from Africa

Marshes

GREAT WHITE EGRET

YELLOW-BILLED EGRET

Line of gape (black line) extends behind eye (red line) on Great White Egret; stops beneath eye on Yellow-billed Egret.

Ad
ALL YEAR

LC Little Blue Heron
Egretta caerulea

L 60–76 cm | **W** 95–105 cm

Medium–small heron.
Ad | **entirely blue-grey** with blue face; **bill blue with black tip**; legs dark grey to yellow-green. **Juv/1W** | white with dark wingtip, bill pale with black tip, legs green.
FL | Pale upperwing with **blackish trailing edge and tip**.

Vagrant from N America

Pools

Ad
ALL YEAR

1W
AUG–APR

LC Tricolored Heron
Egretta tricolor

L 50–76 cm | **W** 90–95 cm

Small, slender, dark heron; dark grey with **white foreneck and thighs**. **Face yellow**; bill long, slim, pale with black ridge and tip; legs yellow-green. **Ad** | chin white, throat bright buff, side of neck purplish-brown. **Juv/1W** | upperparts dark slate-grey with chestnut feather edges.

Vagrant from N America

Watersides

Juv→1W
AUG–MAR

Ad
ALL YEAR

Snowy Egret
Egretta thula

L 47–68 cm | **W** 84–91 cm

Medium-sized egret, like Little Egret but **Ad** | feet brighter **golden-yellow**, continuing as stripe **up rear of leg**; **larger patch on face and eye bright yellow**. **AdBr** | also has bushy white crest and long and strongly **upcurved** back plumes. **Juv** | feet and back of leg greenish.

Vagrant from N America

Wetlands

AdNb
JUL–MAR

AdNb

AdNb

LITTLE EGRET

AdNb

AdBr
APR–JUN

AdBr

Little Egret can have a yellowish face but it is never so extensive, bright and sharply defined as on Snowy Egret; also has thin head plumes, never a bushy crest.

Western Reef-egret
Egretta gularis

L 55–65 cm | **W** 86–104 cm

Medium-sized egret, like Little Egret but **bill thicker**, tinged **yellowish**; legs thicker, with yellow blurring up to joint. Two forms: DARK FORM **slaty-grey; throat white;** WHITE FORM all-white. Little Egret is very rarely mottled grey or dark grey overall, but always looks much less blackish than dark-form Western Reef-egret.

Vagrant from Africa

Rocky coasts

Ad
DARK FORM
ALL YEAR

Ad
WHITE FORM
ALL YEAR

Black Heron
Egretta ardesiaca

L 42–66 cm | **W** 105–110 cm

Small, **slaty-grey** heron (blackish at distance). Bill long, grey; legs grey with dull **yellow feet**. Neck thick; long, drooping, pointed feathers from nape, long plumes on breast. Little Egret very rarely mottled grey or dark grey overall, but always looks much less black than Black Heron.

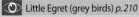 Little Egret (grey birds) *p.210*

Vagrant from Africa

Watersides

Ad
ALL YEAR

Pond-herons similar to each otherandtoSquaccoHeron*p. 209*

LC Chinese Pond-heron
Ardeola bacchus

L 42–52 cm | **W** 79–90 cm
Small heron; bill yellow-and-black, legs yellow-green. **AdBr** | **head and neck purplish-brown**, back **blue-grey**, wings and underparts white. **AdNb / 1W** | like Squacco Heron but often broader dark streaks on dull buff-white neck and breast (narrow streaks on brighter buff on Squacco Heron).

Vagrant from Asia

Pools

LC Indian Pond-heron
Ardeola grayii

L 39–46 cm | **W** 75–90 cm
Like Chinese Pond-heron but **AdBr** | head/neck more buff-brown; back dark red-brown; wing coverts buff, rest of wing white.
AdNb / 1W | may be inseparable from Chinese Pond-heron and Squacco Heron; some show darker stripe between eye and bill; broad breast streaks on dull buff-white.

Occasional escape

Pools

LC American Bittern
Botaurus lentiginosus

L 58–85 cm | **W** 105–125 cm
Large heron: like Bittern in size, shape and actions, but streaked brown with striped face and broad **dark rufous stripes** on foreneck.
FL | Wing coverts pale, flight feathers **unbarred dark grey-brown**.

 Bittern *p. 215*

Vagrant from N America

Reedbeds

AdBr
MAR–AUG

AdNb/1W
SEP–MAR

AdNb
SEP–MAR

Squacco Heron typically has narrow neck stripes, but there is considerable variation.

AdNb

SQUACCO HERON

Brown cap; broader, browner neck streaks

ALL YEAR

ALL YEAR

Black cap; thinner, darker neck streaks

ALL YEAR

BITTERN

Green-backed Heron
Butorides striata

L 35–48 cm | **W** 62–70 cm
Small, **very dark** heron. ssp. *virescens* ('Green Heron'): **Ad** | **slate-green** above; **neck chestnut-red**, striped white; legs orange/yellow. **Juv** / **1W** | brownish-grey (**Juv** neck rufous); cap dull black; face/neck **broadly striped brown and white**; bill and legs yellow-green. ssp. *brevipes* ('Striated Heron'): as *virescens* but neck greyer.

Vagrant from N America (ssp. *virescens*) and Middle East (ssp. *brevipes*)

Watersides

Ad.
ALL YEAR

Ad.
ALL YEAR
ssp. *brevipes*

ssp. *virescens*

1W
MAR–SEP

immature plumages variable in appearance

Schrenck's Bittern
Ixobrychus eurhythmus

L 33–42 cm | **W** 48–59 cm
Small, dark bittern. ♂ (NR) [not illustrated] cap dark; cheek, hindneck and back dark purple-chestnut; large buff patch on wing coverts; underparts buff. ♀/**Juv**/**1W** | chestnut with white spots above, white with dark streaks below; ♂**1W** (NR) wing plain.

◉ Little Bittern p.215

Vagrant from Asia

Pools

Least Bittern *Ixobrychus exilis*

L 23–25 cm | **W** 40–45 cm
Tiny bittern, like Little Bittern but ♂ | face, neck and wing patches **darker rusty-buff**; **white stripe along each side of back**. ♀/**Juv**/**1W** | cap browner than on ♂, neck broadly streaked.

◉ Little Bittern p.215

Vagrant from N America

Marshes

♀
ALL YEAR

♂ 1W
SEP–MAR

♀
hindneck pale; back lacks stripes
LITTLE BITTERN

♂
ALL YEAR

♀
ALL YEAR

Dwarf Bittern
Ixobrychus sturmii

L 25–30 cm | **W** 45–50 cm
Tiny bittern. **Ad** | head, neck and back slate-grey; foreneck and underparts buff with black stripes. **Juv**/**1W** | [not illustrated] buff feather edges on upperparts; underparts orange-buff with dark stripes.

Vagrant from Africa

Wetlands

Ad
ALL YEAR

LC Lesser Moorhen
Paragallinula angulata

L 22–23 cm | **W** 40–50 cm

Like small Moorhen, **facial shield pointed. Ad** has more triangular yellow bill and red facial shield; **legs green or pinkish**. ♂ plumage as Moorhen; ♀ pale grey on face and underparts. **Juv / 1W** dark brown, paler and greyer below; white flank streak diffuse; bill yellowish-brown.

◉ Moorhen *p. 218*

Vagrant from Africa

Swamps, pools

facial shield rounded

Ad

MOORHEN

♀ **ALL YEAR**

♂ **ALL YEAR**

LC Allen's Gallinule
Porphyrio alleni

L 22–25 cm | **W** 48–52 cm

Ad like small, green-backed, violet-breasted Moorhen with red legs and bluish facial shield.
Juv / 1W greenish-brown with buff feather edges (wear off); undertail buff; bill and legs reddish-brown.

◉ Moorhen *p. 218*

Vagrant from Africa

Swamps

Juv MAY–OCT

Ad ALL YEAR

buff under tail

LC (American) Purple Gallinule
Porphyrio martinicus

L 29–33 cm | **W** 50–55 cm

Ad like green-backed, blue-bodied Moorhen with blue facial shield, red-and-yellow bill and yellow legs.
Juv bright buff, back greenish.
1W bright purple-blue breast, bill and facial shield dull blue, legs yellowish. Undertail plain white (lacks central dark band of Moorhen).

◉ Moorhen *p. 218*

Vagrant from N America

Lakes, marshes

1W AUG–APR

plain white under tail

Striped Crake
Amaurornis marginalis

L 18–21 cm | **W** 28–30 cm

Small, dull, dark grey-brown crake, streaked buff above; eye red; bill and legs green; **cinnamon rear flank and undertail.**

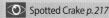 Spotted Crake *p. 217*

Vagrant from Africa

Marshes

African Crake *Crex egregia*

L 20–23 cm | **W** 40–42 cm

Like Water Rail with mottled brown back, well-defined dark cap, greyer face but browner breast, more **sharply barred black-and-white flank,** red around eye and **short, thick, reddish bill** with green tip.

 Water Rail *p. 221*

Vagrant from Africa

Swamps

Sora *Porzana carolina*

L 18–21 cm | **W** 35–40 cm

Similar to Spotted Crake. **Ad** | yellow **bill (no red)**; sharply defined **black face/throat** extends onto breast. **Juv / 1W** | has **plain brown breast,** brown crown with thin central dark stripe. At all ages, tertials **brown with dark centres** (on Spotted Crake, broad buff upper edge and wavy white lines across tertials).

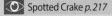 Spotted Crake *p. 217*

Vagrant from N America

Watersides

American Coot
Fulica americana

L 34–43 cm | **W** 58–71 cm

Dark, like Coot but **white under tail**; bill has **dark band** near tip; smooth rounded black face against bill, lacking sharp black point where small facial shield joins bill; top of shield dark red.

 Other coots *p. 219*

Vagrant from N America

Lakes

Ad
ALL YEAR

Ad
ALL YEAR

Ad
ALL YEAR

Ad

tertials barred

SPOTTED CRAKE

1W
SEP–MAR

black point between bill and shield

COOT   Ad

rounded border between bill and shield

white under tail

dark band on bill

Ad
ALL YEAR

577

LC Oriental Turtle Dove
Streptopelia orientalis

L 30–35 cm | **W** 55–60 cm

Small dove, like heavy, dark Turtle Dove; two subspecies. Wings have diffuse whitish bars. Closed wingtip (shows 5 feather tips) equals length of tail projection; longer, narrower (6–7 tips) on Turtle Dove. Eyering **thin**, pinkish (wide, bare 'diamond' on Turtle Dove). Neck patch dull grey.

Subspecies *orientalis* pigeon-like; narrow rufous fringes to wing coverts. Rump grey; tail tip grey-white; belly dark, undertail greyish.

Subspecies *meena* slender; wing coverts have broad, pale rufous fringes. Rump grey; tail tip white; belly pale; vent/undertail cream.

(**Turtle Dove** rump brown; tail tip white; breast/flank pink, belly/vent/undertail white.)

👁 Turtle Dove *p. 244*

Vagrant from Asia

Open spaces, gardens

TURTLE DOVE | **ORIENTAL TURTLE DOVE**
SSP. *meena* | SSP. *orientalis*

rump brown; tip white — rump grey; tip white — rump grey; tip pale grey

grey — bare 'diamond' around eye

3–4 broad black bars on white

grey

Ad — **Ad**

TURTLE DOVE — **Juv**

short tail — 6–7 tips

from 1st-winter, 5–6 thin black bars on grey

Juv

5 tips

long tail

pinkish-brown

SSP. *meena*

1W
AUG–MAY

LC Mourning Dove
Zenaida macroura

L 28–33 cm | **W** 37–45 cm

Small, slim dove with long, **tapered tail**. **Ad / 1W** | back pale olive-brown; head and chest pinkish; wing coverts have scattered dark spots. **Juv** | wing coverts black with pale fringes.

👁 Collared Dove *p. 245*
   Laughing Dove *p. 245*

Vagrant from N America

Open areas

1W

1W
AUG–MAY

long, tapered tail

LC Namaqua Dove   *Oena capensis*

L 22–28 cm | **W** 28–33 cm

Tiny, sandy brown dove with dark spots on wing; 2 black bars on lower back; tail **long, wedge-shaped**. ♂ | head grey, **face and breast black**, bill red-and-yellow. ♀ | head plain.

V | Soft, mournful "*ku-hooo*."

FL | Rises with long tail fanned; flight dashing. Wings mostly **rufous**.

Vagrant from the Middle East

Open areas

rufous wings — ♂
♀

long, pointed tail

black face and breast

♂
ALL YEAR

♀
ALL YEAR

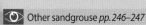

Other sandgrouse *pp. 246–247*

Spotted Sandgrouse
Pterocles senegallus

L 30–35 cm | **W** 53–65 cm

Pale sandy-buff sandgrouse with 'pin' tail. ♂ | neck and upper breast grey; small red-brown patch on crown; face pale yellow-orange; wing coverts dark brown with rows of pale spots. ♀ | crown, neck and breast-band buff, spotted black; wing coverts buff, spotted black-brown.

Vagrant from Africa/Middle East
Grassy plains

FL | Outerwing pale with dark trailing edge. **Underparts pale** with narrow dark brown centre.

♀ ALL YEAR

♀ ALL YEAR

♂

♂ ALL YEAR

Chestnut-bellied Sandgrouse
Pterocles exustus

L 31–33 cm | **W** 48–51 cm

Pale sandgrouse with 'pin' tail; face and neck orange; back brown with buff spots and black bars across wing. ♂ | breast pink-buff with thin black band. ♀ | breast spotted, with faint dark band.

Vagrant from Asia
Grassy plains

FL | Underwing coverts **deep red-brown**; on ♂ no contrast with dark belly.

♀ ALL YEAR

♂ ALL YEAR

Common Nighthawk
Chordeiles minor

L 22–25 cm | **W** 51–61 cm

Small, greyish nightjar, with buoyant, erratic flight. White 'V' on throat; underparts whitish, barred dark.
FL | Underwing barred, outer half black; upperwing has broad pale band; **broad white band near wingtip**. Tail dark (with thin white band on ♂ Ad); **tip notched**.

Vagrant from N America
Open spaces, towns, suburbs

♂ ALL YEAR

♀ ALL YEAR

Juv marbled paler grey than Ad and has whitish primary tips.

Juv
JUN–OCT

Egyptian Nightjar
Caprimulgus aegyptius

L 24–26 cm | **W** 50–60 cm

Pale greyish nightjar with **sandy-buff** spots, few dark marks; underparts finely barred brown on buff.
FL | Pale sandy; flight feathers dark, barred buff; tail weakly barred. ♂ has tiny white spots near wingtip.

Vagrant from Africa/Middle East
Semi-arid grassland, dunes

Ad

Ad
ALL YEAR

Steppe Eagle *p. 293* | large 'brown' eagles *pp. 288–298*

Vagrant from Africa
Open plains

VU ## Tawny Eagle *Aquila rapax*

L 60–75 cm | **W** 160–183 cm

Large, rather dumpy, **pale**, short-winged eagle. **Ad** | buff to dark brown. **Juv** | sandy-brown.
FL | Wings flat/bowed. **Three inner primaries short and pale** in all plumages. **Ad** pale 'U' across uppertail coverts; underparts buff, tail dark, unbarred; underwing narrowly barred. **Juv** white-edged dark bands on upperwing; rump white. Below, forewing buff, wingtips black, hindwing grey.

 Imm - White-tailed *p. 298* & Golden Eagles [imm] *p. 292*

Vagrant from Asia
Wetlands

EN ## Pallas's Fish-eagle *Haliaeetus leucoryphus*

L 72–84 cm | **W** 180–215 cm

Very large; like White-tailed Eagle but tail longer.
FL | Wings long, straight-edged; tail longish. **Ad** dark above with pale head and neck; **tail white with black tip** above and below; underwing dark, paler towards tip. **Juv** grey-brown; dark 'mask'; underwing black on leading edge, hindwing and tip, with whitish diagonal band and inner primaries; tail base pale.

 Imm - White-tailed Eagle [imm] *p. 298*

Vagrant from N America
Waterside

LC ## Bald Eagle *Haliaeetus leucocephalus*

L 70–100 cm | **W** 180–230 cm

Very large; like White-tailed Eagle but tail slightly longer.
FL | Wings flat or bowed. **Ad** (NR) blackish; **head and tail white**, bill yellow. **Imm** very like same-age White-tailed Eagle but more slightly built, head less protruding; underwing whitish with black hindwing and tip like Pallas's Fish-eagle but tail shorter, wedge-shaped, white with dark feather edges; underparts of body dark.

lacks Steppe Eagle's white band under wing

Ad

Ad

Juv

Juv
ALL YEAR

Juv

inner primaries short and pale

Pale Tawny Eagle like Juv Spanish Imperial Eagle; Juv Eastern Imperial Eagle has noticeably streaked body.

Ad
ALL YEAR

Ad
ALL YEAR

Juv
ALL YEAR

Juv
ALL YEAR

Juv
ALL YEAR

Juv
ALL YEAR

Vagrant vultures from Africa   Three very large 'griffon-like' vultures with very long, broad wings and short tail.

👁 Vultures are similar to each other – see also Black Vulture *p. 268* | Griffon Vulture *p. 268*

| Open plains | Open plains, cliffs | Open plains |

White-backed Vulture
Gyps africanus

L 95 cm | **W** 218 cm

Ad | head and neck pale grey-brown; bill **blackish-grey**; body dull brownish. **Juv / Imm** | head whitish, ruff slate-grey, underparts streaked buff.

FL | Wings raised when soaring. **Ad** white lower back obvious on take-off, **underwing coverts pale**. **Juv** single thin white line along underwing coverts, like Rüppell's Vulture.

CR Rüppell's Vulture
Gyps rueppelli

L 100 cm | **W** 230–280 cm

Ad | brown, **broadly scalloped buff**; head and neck grey; **bill pale**. **Juv / Imm** | upperparts plain grey-brown; underparts streaked (like White-backed Vulture but bill paler).

FL | Wings bowed when soaring, trailing edge 'S'-shaped. **Ad / Imm** underwing has **white line** near front and rows of small white spots on coverts. **Juv** has single white line; rest of underwing coverts plain (like Juv White-backed Vulture).

EN Lappet-faced Vulture
Torgos tracheliotos

L 115 cm | **W** 270–280 cm

Head bare, pinkish; body dark brown; bill massive, deep. **Ad** | bill blue at base; head and nape **pink-red**. **Imm** | head greyish; underparts all-brown.

FL | Soars on wide, square-tipped, **flat/drooped wings**. Dark above; underside dark with long white line under wing; white thighs.

Ad

Ad   Ad

Ad

Ad
ALL YEAR

Ad
ALL YEAR

Ad
ALL YEAR

581

Honey-buzzard *p.275*   Hen Harrier *p.284*

LC Swallow-tailed Kite
Elanoides forficatus

L 52–66 cm | **W** 119–136 cm
Ad | unmistakable, slim, long-winged kite with long, forked tail; head and underparts white, back, wings and tail black. Underwing white with black flight feathers. **Juv** | duller; tail less deeply forked than **Ad**.

Ad   Ad

Ad
ALL YEAR

Vagrant from
N America
Open areas

EN Bateleur
Terathopius ecaudatus

L 55–70 cm | **W** 168–190 cm
Unique eagle; long, broad wings **taper to narrow point**. Tail **extremely short**. Flies with 'teetering' action, **wings raised**. **Ad** | **black** with red face, rufous back, black wings with pale 'shoulder'. Underwing white, ♂ with **black rear third**; ♀ with black trailing edge. **Juv** | brown with grey-green face; gains adult plumage over 7–8 years.

♂ Ad

♀ Ad

♀ Ad
ALL YEAR

Vagrant from
Africa
Open plains

LC Oriental Honey-buzzard
Pernis ptilorhynchus

L 52–68 cm | **W** 115–155 cm
Like broad-winged Honey-buzzard, plumages individually variable. **Ad** | grey, buff or barred dark brown below; underwing pale or heavily barred dark grey; tail black with **broad white band**. ♂**Ad** | head pale grey; ♀ **Ad** | head brown. **Juv** | buffish; narrow buff/grey bands on tail similar to Honey-buzzard.

short
6th
primary

HONEY-BUZZARD

Juv
PALE FORM
ALL YEAR

long
6th
primary

Honey-buzzard shows five visible primaries; **Oriental Honey-buzzard** shows six.

Juv
ALL YEAR

wings flat when soaring, more slender on Juv

♂ Ad

♂ Ad

♂ and ♀
both vary greatly

NOTE: Hybrids with Honey-buzzard occur.

♂ Ad
ALL YEAR

Vagrant from Asia
Over migration watchpoints

LC Northern Harrier
Circus hudsonius

L 41–50 cm | **W** 97–122 cm
Very like Hen Harrier, but ♂**Ad** | subtly barred brownish-grey above; underparts and underwing white, spotted rufous and black; tail has dark tip above, narrow dark bars below. ♀ **Ad** | inseparable from ♀ **Ad** Hen Harrier. **Juv** | dark cheek, narrow pale collar, rusty neck. Rufous below, streaked brown on throat/upper breast; 5–6 bars on outer primaries (4–5 on Hen Harrier).

Juv
ALL YEAR

outer primaries with 5–6 **dark bars**

♂ Juv
ALL YEAR

outer primaries with 4–5 **dark bars**

HEN HARRIER

breast and underwing white (no rufous)

♂ Ad

♂ Ad

rufous spots on breast and underwing

♂ Ad
ALL YEAR

Vagrant from N America
Marshes, moorland, grassland

Eleonora's *p. 315* & Red-footed Falcons [♂ Ad] *p. 313*

Red-footed Falcon *p. 313* | Hobby *p. 314*

Sooty Falcon
Falco concolor

L 32–36 cm | **W** 75–88 cm

Medium-sized falcon. **Ad** | like dark-form Eleonora's Falcon but paler grey; eyering, base of bill and legs yellow.

FL | **Ad upperwing pale grey with darker outer half**; underwing plain pale grey (Eleonora's Falcon has darker coverts). **Juv** | like **Juv** Eleonora's Falcon but upperside plainer, without bars or tail-band; underwing coverts barely darker than flight feathers; heavy black spots on dull brown-buff breast (no rufous). Dark 'moustache' less obvious than on juvenile Hobby (*p. 314*)

LC Amur Falcon
Falco amurensis

L 28–30 cm | **W** 63–71 cm

Like Red-footed Falcon but **♂ Ad** | has **white underwing coverts**. **♂ 1S** | like **♂ Ad** but grey-barred underwing coverts increasingly mixed with white. **♀ Ad / ♀ 1S** | upperparts 'cold' grey, **crown grey**; inconspicuous dark 'mask'. Underparts white with dark grey 'V'-shaped bars.

LC American Kestrel
Falco sparverius

L 21–31 cm | **W** 51–61 cm

Small, round-bodied, sharp-winged, 'colourful' falcon. **♂ Ad** | upperparts rufous; **wings grey** with white spots on primaries; **tail rufous** with black band; head pale with vertical **black band** each side of cheek and **black nape spot**. **♀ Ad/1W** | like **♂ Ad** but streaked rufous below; wings rufous, barred dark; head pattern less contrasted.

barred underwing with white feathers

♂ 1S

Ad

Juv

RED-FOOTED FALCON

buff

♀ Ad

♂ Ad

white underwing

♂ Ad

Juv
ALL YEAR

Ad
ALL YEAR

♂ Ad
ALL YEAR

grey

♀ 1S
JAN–OCT

♂ Ad

♀ Ad
ALL YEAR

♀ Ad

♂ Ad
ALL YEAR

♀ 1W
AUG–MAR

Vagrant from Middle East / Africa
Open areas

Vagrant from Middle East / Asia
Cliffs, riverside marshlands

Vagrant from N America
Open areas

LC **Yellow-billed Cuckoo**
Coccyzus americanus

L 29–32 cm | **W** 38–43 cm

Fairly large, grey-brown and white cuckoo; **rufous patch** on wing. Long tail with brown centre and **large white tips** to blackish outer feathers (strikingly bold **black-and-white from below**); white edge to outermost tail feather from above. Underparts white from throat to tail. **Bill yellow-and-black.**

LC **Black-billed Cuckoo**
Coccyzus erythrophthalmus

L 28–31 cm | **W** 40–44 cm

Fairly large cuckoo; similar to Yellow-billed Cuckoo but duller, wings less bright. Long, grey-brown tail with **small white tips** to outer feathers (appearing dull from below). White breast but throat and **undertail buff. Bill grey.**

Juv/1W
JUL–APR

Juv/1W
JUL–APR

Juv/1W

Yellow-billed Cuckoo (ABOVE) has bright wing patch and bold tail pattern (both are duller on Black-billed Cuckoo).

LC **Diederik Cuckoo**
Chrysococcyx caprius

Vagrant from Africa
Bushy areas

L 18–20 cm | **W** 35–40 cm

Small cuckoo with white underparts and shoulder spots. White stripe behind eye in dark hood; short, dark bars on white flank; white spots in tail.
♂| (NR) upperparts glossy green, underparts white.
♀| upperparts greenish coppery-brown, underparts tinged buff.

LC **Marsh Owl**
Asio capensis

Vagrant from Africa
Grassland, marshes

L 31–38 cm | **W** 82–99 cm

Like Short-eared Owl (*p. 257*) but **plain grey-brown** above; dark grey-brown surrounding pale grey-buff face, dark patches around **dark eyes.**

FL| Few broad dark bands on tail; broad **pale trailing edge** to dark upperwing, with barred orange-buff primaries.

♂
ALL YEAR

♀
ALL YEAR

Ad

Ad
ALL YEAR

Short-eared Owl p.257

| Vagrant from Asia | Semi-arid bush, woodland edge |

Asian Green Bee-eater *Merops orientalis*

L 26–28 cm | **W** 30–35 cm

Small, slender, long-tailed, **green** bee-eater with bronze nape, black band through eye, and turquoise-green throat above black band.

V | Nasal "*tree tree tree.*"

Ad
ALL YEAR

Ad

| Vagrant from Asia | Semi-arid bush, woodland edge |

LC ## Abyssinian Roller *Coracias abyssinicus*

L 28–30 cm (+ 12 cm tail streamers) | **W** 35–36 cm

Like Roller. **Ad** | has two **long, straight tail streamers**, **purple** uppertail coverts, **blue** primaries. **Juv** | paler, duller than **Ad** and lacks tail streamers; not safely distinguishable from Roller.

Ad

Ad
ALL YEAR

Yellow-bellied Sapsucker
Sphyrapicus varius

| Vagrant from N America |
| Woodland |

L 18–22 cm | **W** 34–40 cm

Small, unobtrusive woodpecker. Black-and-white with broad **white band along** barred wing. Bold head pattern: black eyestripe, **white band across cheek**, white on nape. **Ad** | forehead red: ♂ throat red; ♀ throat white. **Juv** | like **Ad** but duller, no red. **1W** | like **Juv** but blotchy red on forehead once migration starts AUG-OCT: ♂ throat red; ♀ throat white.

FL | Jerky, bounding undulations.

V | Nasal mewing calls.

♀
ALL YEAR

♂ 1W
SEP–APR

Juv
JUN–SEP

LC ## Yellow-shafted Flicker
Colaptes auratus

| Vagrant from N America |
| Woodland; vagrants in open spaces, on walls *etc.* |

L 28–36 cm | **W** 42–54 cm

Large, brown woodpecker. Black bill, black eye in plain face, **grey crown** and **red nape**. Back barred black. Underparts whitish, spotted black. Underwing yellow. ♂ has black moustache. ♀/**Juv**/**1W** | face plain pink-buff.

FL | Swooping undulations.

V | Long, loud "*kyeer.*"

♂
ALL YEAR

585

Belted Kingfisher *Megaceryle alcyon*

Vagrant from N America | Rivers, lakes

L 28–33 cm | **W** 48–58 cm
Very large; large head, with 'double' crest; black, dagger-like bill. **Blue-grey** above; **white collar; white below.** ♂| broad grey breast-band. ♀| narrower grey upper and rufous lower breast-bands, rufous flank.
V| Fast, hard rattle.
FL| Often high, fast; wings long, wide, with **large white patch** near tip.

♂

Often hovers briefly when hunting.

♀1W
SEP–MAR

rufous spots in breast-bands

♂
ALL YEAR

Purple Martin *Progne subis*

Vagrant from N America | Open areas

L 20 cm | **W** 39–41 cm
Large, swallow-like martin.
♂| (NR) all iridescent purple-blue. ♀ (NR)/ **Juv/1Y**| dark brown above, **bluish on crown and shoulders; pale collar**, dark cheek; whitish below with dark streaks, subtle dark breast-band. **Tail all-dark** (see Crag Martin).

pale collar

Juv/1Y
ALL YEAR

Juv/1Y
ALL YEAR

1Y/♀
ALL YEAR

Crag Martin *p. 346*

Tree Swallow *Tachycineta bicolor*

Vagrant from N America | Clearings, open areas

House Martin *p. 346* | Sand Martin *p. 346*

L 15 cm | **W** 30–32 cm
Ad| Like House Martin but **rump dark**: glossy greenish-blue above; white below.
Juv/1W| Like Sand Martin; plain slaty-brown above; pure white below with pale-greyish breast-band and dark forehead.

Ad
ALL YEAR

dark rump

1W
SEP–APR

1W

breast-band pale, greyish

Juv
MAY–SEP

Asian House Martin *Delichon dasypus*

Vagrant from Asia | Open areas

House Martin *p. 346*

L 12 cm | **W** 28 cm
Like dull, broad-bodied House Martin. Rump white, **streaked grey; underparts greyish**, contrasting with white throat. Underwing coverts **dark**.

Ad/1W

Ad/1W
ALL YEAR

white throat contrasts with grey underparts

white rump with grey streaks (House Martin unstreaked white)

Cliff and *Streak-throated Swallows* are quite similar. | House Martin [juv] *p. 346* | Red-rumped Swallow *p. 345*

House Martin [juv] *p. 346* | Red-rumped Swallow *p. 345*

Vagrant from N America	Open areas

Cliff Swallow *Petrochelidon pyrrhonota*

L 13 cm | **W** 28–30 cm

Small, thickset martin; dark above, except **pale rufous rump**; buff-white below; tail square-ended. **Ad** | **head rufous**, forehead buff; **pale buff collar**. **Juv / 1W** | like **Ad** with pale feather fringes, upper breast mottled grey and buff; throat pale or dark.

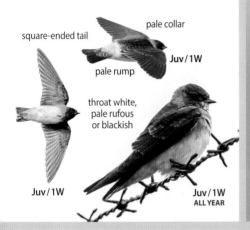

pale collar

square-ended tail

Juv / 1W

pale rump

throat white, pale rufous or blackish

Juv / 1W

Juv / 1W
ALL YEAR

Vagrant from Asia	Open areas

LC ## Streak-throated Swallow
Petrochelidon fluvicola

L 12 cm | **W** 30 cm

Small, short-tailed swallow with pale brown rump and **streaked underparts**. **Ad** | head and neck pale **brown, streaked dark brown**; deep blue above with whitish streaks; pale brown rump; buff below; finely **streaked black** on throat and breast side; tail short, **notched**. **Juv** | like **Ad** but browner; upperside barred buff.

Ad

Ad
ALL YEAR

Vagrant from Africa	Open areas

 Sand Martin *p. 346* | Crag Martin *p. 346*
Pale Crag Martin

African Plain Martin *Riparia paludicola*

L 10–11 cm | **W** 20–25 cm

Like small Sand Martin with short, broad wings; upperside pale greyish sandy-brown; **chin and throat grey-buff**, fading to white; **no breast-band**. Underwing paler than larger Crag Martin; tail lacks pale spots.

NOTE: This bird is in wing moult.

Ad / 1W
ALL YEAR

Ad

no breast-band

Ad
ALL YEAR

Vagrant from Africa	Cliffs, gorges

 Sand Martin *p. 346* | Crag Martin *p. 346*
African Plain Martin

LC ## Pale Crag Martin *Ptyonoprogne obsoleta*

L 11–13 cm | **W** 28 cm

Like Crag Martin but upperparts **paler brown**, throat whiter. Pale spots across tail, **underwing coverts pale**.

Ad / 1W

Ad / 1W

dark underwing coverts

Ad / 1W
ALL YEAR

CRAG MARTIN

LC Pacific Swift *Apus pacificus*

L 17–18 cm | **W** 40–44 cm

Medium-large, slender swift with long rear body and forked tail held in sharp point; throat white; **rectangular white rump band** (less crescentic than on smaller White-rumped Swift); wings plain; white scales on underparts (widest on **Juv**).

FL | Fast, flickering; short glides.

 Swift *p. 340* | Pallid Swift *p. 341*

Vagrant from Asia

Entirely aerial

LC Horus Swift *Apus horus*

L 13–15 cm | **W** 30 cm

Small, blackish swift, like Little Swift but tail **notched**. Head broad, chin whitish. **White rump** intermediate between Little and White-rumped Swifts.

FL | Fast, fluttering.

 Little Swift *p. 343*
White-rumped Swift *p. 343*

Vagrant from Africa

Entirely aerial

LC White-throated Needletail
Hirundapus caudacutus

L 19–21 cm | **W** 50–54 cm

Large, stocky, sabre-winged swift; very dark except for pale back, **white throat** and white 'U'-shape under **very short tail**.

FL | Quick, stiff-winged beats; wings quite straight, between banking glides, dramatic changes of height.

Vagrant from Asia

Entirely aerial

VU Chimney Swift
Chaetura pelagica

L 12–13 cm | **W** 27–30 cm

Small, chunky swift; outerwing broad, base narrow; **tail short and square with minute spiky feather tips.** Dusky grey-brown, paler throat.

FL | Fast, stiff-winged action; wings seem to beat alternately at times.

Vagrant from N America

Entirely aerial

Ad
Ad
ALL YEAR

LITTLE
square tail

notched tail

Ad

WHITE-RUMPED
forked tail

Ad
ALL YEAR

Ad

1Y*/Ad
ALL YEAR

*bird shown is **1Y**
– white forehead patch small;
undertail coverts tipped brown

Ad
ALL YEAR

Ad

Blyth's Pipit *Anthus godlewskii*

L 15·5–17 cm | **W** 23–28 cm

Large, buff or rufous pipit; like Richard's Pipit but more creeping, legs slightly shorter, hind claw shorter. **Bill shorter and finer**; tail slightly shorter; underparts more uniform, orange-buff. **Pale buff** between eye and bill. Crown strongly **striped**.
1W (most migrants) median coverts edged white, some newly moulted ones have **blunt** blackish centre and distinct buff fringe (1W Richard's Pipit's moulted median coverts have **pointed** dark centre and diffuse buff fringe). Outer tail feather/outer web of 2nd white in both species; inner web of 2nd has white patch on Blyth's Pipit, long streak on Richard's Pipit.
V Call slightly higher than Richard's Pipit, less grating "*shreeu*" or "*spiew*." **Diagnostic squeaked** "*chup*" or "*chip*."

 Richard's Pipit *p. 364*

1W
AUG–MAR

Vagrant from Asia
Grassland

Blyth's Pipit and Richard's Pipit
median and greater coverts : Pattern difficult to assess in the field; median coverts shown here:

 JUVENILES: clear-cut, pointed dark centre, buff sides, white tip

1ST-WINTER (NEW)

 RICHARD'S: pointed blackish centre blends into brown fringe

BLYTH'S: blunter, more distinct black centre

'Large' pipit hind claws

RICHARD'S **very long**

BLYTH'S **medium-short, fine**

TAWNY **medium, arched**

Buff-bellied Pipit
Anthus rubescens

L 15–16 cm | **W** c22–25 cm

Large, **dark-legged** pipit.
ssp. *rubescens* (N America): **Nb** like large Meadow Pipit but upperparts faintly streaked. **Pale** between eye and bill. **Underparts buff**, finely streaked grey. **Legs dark**.
ssp. *japonicus* (Asia): **AdNb/1W** upperparts grey-brown. Underparts **whitish**, **black streaks** from **dark neck patch**. Legs brownish-pink.
V Call squeaky "*pseep*," closer to Meadow Pipit than Water Pipit.
FL Tail sides white. Bounding.

 Water Pipit *p. 360*
Meadow Pipit *p. 362*

Vagrant from America/Asia
Lake sides, wet grassland

AdNb/1W
AUG–MAR

AdNb/1W
AUG–MAR

ssp. *japonicus*

ssp. *rubescens*

Long-billed Pipit
Anthus similis

L 16–17 cm | **W** 25–26 cm

Large, long-tailed, long-billed pipit. Upperparts greyish; underparts very pale with **bright buff flank** and **grey streaking** on breast (more extensive than on Tawny Pipit). **Very long** buff stripe over eye.
V Downslurred "*shrwee*," "*shwoo*."
FL Tail sides buffish. Strong, direct.

 Tawny Pipit *p. 365*

Vagrant from Middle East
Dry, rocky slopes, cliffs

Ad/1W
ALL YEAR

LC Oriental Skylark
Alauda gulgula

L 16 cm | **W** 25 cm

Large lark; warm brown, streaked black and buff; black-streaked breast-band merges into buff underparts. Like a small, squat Skylark, longer bill and legs. Crest very **small**, pointed. Long whitish stripe over eye but face pattern otherwise weaker than Skylark. Wing feathers edged **rufous**.

V | Soft buzz or staccato *"baz baz."*

FL | **Short tail and broad wings** (like Woodlark (*p. 349*)); trailing edge of wing and sides of tail rusty-buff.

Open grasslands
Vagrant from Asia

crest short, raised or flat

Ad

Ad

Ad
ALL YEAR

SKYLARK

Ad

Ad

wing feathers edged buff

👁 Skylark *p. 355*

LC Thick-billed Lark
Ramphocoris clotbey

L 17–18 cm | **W** 36 cm

Large, bulky lark; **large, arched pale grey bill**; upperparts brown; tail blackish, side buff; underparts white, heavily spotted black. ♂**Ad** | **face/ cheek black** with white crescent under eye and **white cheek spot**. ♀**Ad** | head pattern less distinct.

V | Call soft, whistled *"h'wee."*

FL | Hindwing black, **white trailing edge**; tail **white** with black bar at tip.

Vagrant from Africa
Desert, arid scrub

♂
ALL YEAR

♀
ALL YEAR

LC Greater Hoopoe-lark
Alaemon alaudipes

L 19–22 cm | **W** 35 cm

Large, slender, long-tailed lark. Upperparts greyish sandy-brown. Head greyish, with white line above black eyestripe and white cheek with black edge. Underparts white, breast softly streaked with black. **Bill long, slim, downcurved**. Legs long, pale grey.

V | Calls short *"chip"* and longer, vibrant *"psseei."*

FL | Eye-catching **black wings with broad white stripes**.

Vagrant from the Middle East/Africa
Semi-arid plains

Ad

Ad
ALL YEAR

Vagrant from Middle East/Africa   Open areas

 Shorelark *p. 356*

Temminck's Lark *Eremophila bilopha*

L 14–15 cm | **W** 25–30 cm

Like a **bright, sandy** Shorelark. **Ad** | face **black-and-white** (no yellow); minute raised 'horns' on crown. **Juv** | upperparts pale sandy-brown, underparts whiter with unstreaked breast. Dark eye in plain face.

V | Simple "*tseep.*"

FL | Low, quick, direct.

♂Br
MAR–JUL

SHORELARK
ssp. *flava*

♂Br
FEB–JUL

Vagrant from Middle East   Semi-desert, bushy areas

 Bar-tailed Lark | Desert Lark *p. 357*

LC Arabian Lark *Eremalauda eremodites*

L 15–19 cm | **W** 30 cm

Large, stocky, pale sandy-brown lark with arched, **pinkish** bill; upperparts softly streaked, more uniform with wear; underparts buff.

V | Call whistled "*daa-dee,*" abrupt "*di-uw;*" in flight, "*swee.*"

FL | Wings plain; tail rusty, with **black sides** when spread, **black** below.

slight dark 'moustache' and stripe behind eye

Ad
ALL YEAR

Vagrant from Middle East   Dry grassland

 Greater Short-toed Lark *p. 350*

Black-crowned Sparrow-lark
Eremopterix nigriceps

L 12–13 cm | **W** 20–25 cm

Small, finch-like lark. **Bill thick, pointed**, pale grey. **♂ Ad** | upperparts brown; **head and underparts black**; **bold white cheek** and **white forehead**. **♀ Ad** | (NR) pale brown with whitish neck patch, dark-centred wing coverts and white belly.

V | Call low, buzzing "*dzzup dzzup.*"

Fl | Tail edged white; **underwing blackish** on both sexes.

♀
ALL YEAR

♂
ALL YEAR

Vagrant from Middle East /Africa   Semi-arid plains

Arabian Lark | Desert Lark *p. 357*

LC Bar-tailed Lark *Ammomanes cinctura*

L 13–14 cm | **W** 25 cm

Small, rather slim, buff lark without a crest; tertials pale, wingtip dark; throat and breast unstreaked. Head more domed, bill smaller and more pinkish, and legs thinner than similar Desert Lark.

V | Rising whistle, "*who-o-eep.*"

Fl | Wings rufous; tail orange-buff with **narrow black bar** across tip.

Ad
ALL YEAR

591

LC Daurian Starling
Agropsar sturninus

Vagrant from Asia/escape

Woodland

L 17 cm | **W** 35 cm

Like small, short-billed Starling in shape. **1W** | pale grey with dark grey back and dark greenish-black wings and tail; **white wing patch**; broad **white rump**. Dark, sharply pointed bill; dark grey legs. ♂ has glossy sheen to wing feathers; ♀ duller.

V | Squeaky chatter, "*slee-slee-slee-slee-slee*" and churring, trilling notes.

♂ 1W
SEP–MAR

Starlings *pp. 378–380*

LC Hypocolius
Hypocolius ampelinus

Vagrant from Middle East

Woodland, riverside trees

L 23 cm | **W** 25 cm

Slender, long-tailed, short-billed. Pale buff-grey, tip of tail black. ♂ | **black 'mask'** onto nape. ♀ | (NR) hint of 'mask' above pinkish throat.

V | Softly bubbling, mewing "*tree-uh*" and soft trills.

FL | ♂ outerwing, black, tipped white; ♀ wing plain grey.

♂
ALL YEAR

♀
ALL YEAR

NOTE: 1W (APR–SEP) has dark wingtip.

Very local resident

Woodland, scrub, urban

LC Common Bulbul *Pycnonotus barbatus*

L 18 cm | **W** 20–25 cm

Slim, thrush-like (*p. 383*) bulbul with peaked nape, curved black bill and long, square tail. Dull brown with darker hood (like dull juvenile White-spectacled Bulbul but brown hood even less contrasted), **no eyering**.

V | Calls rich, bubbling or fluty. Song similar thrush-like phrases.

FL | Fast, flitting; broad tail contrastingly blackish.

SSP. *barbatus* occurs in Europe.

NOTE: breeding in S Spain since 2013

Ad
ALL YEAR

LC White-eared Bulbul *Pycnonotus leucotis*

Vagrant from Middle East

Woodland and scrub

L 18 cm | **W** 20–25 cm

Distinctive bulbul with black head and collar and **broad white cheek**; upperparts grey; underparts buff, **vent yellow**. Tail black, with white tip below.

V | Bubbling calls.

FL | Fast, flitting; upperparts grey-brown, tail black with narrow white corners and tip.

Ad
ALL YEAR

White-spectacled Bulbul *p. 382*

Daurian Redstart
Phoenicurus auroreus

Vagrant from Asia
Woodland, gardens

L 14–15 cm | **W** 22 cm

Medium-sized redstart. ♂| cap pale grey; face, throat, back black; rump, underparts and tail **rufous. Broad white wing patch.** Colours obscured by buff fringes AUG–FEB. ♀/**1W**| (NR) olive-brown; small white wing patch, orange rump and tail.

V| High "*tseep*" and harsh "*tak.*"

FL| ♂ rufous rump and tail, white wing patch.

♀/1W
ALL YEAR

♂
ALL YEAR

Redstart p. 396 | Eversmann's Redstart
White-winged Redstart p. 398

LC ## Eversmann's Redstart
Phoenicurus erythronotus

Vagrant from Asia
Montane forest; open, arid areas (winter)

L 15 cm | **W** 25–27 cm

Large redstart. **Rump and tail side rufous.** ♂**Br**| **crown grey, black 'mask'; throat and back rufous. White shoulder stripe.** ♂**Nb**| colours obscured by whitish feather edges. ♀| grey-brown; wing dark with pale wingbar and primary patch.

V| Call a low, hard, grating "*krrk-rrk.*"

FL| Rufous back, rump merge and tail sides; **white on inner wing.**

♀
ALL YEAR

♂Br
FEB–AUG

Redstart p. 396 | Daurian Redstart
♀ - White-winged Redstart [♀] p. 398

Vagrant from Asia
Riversides

♂ - Black Redstart p. 397

Plumbeous Water-redstart
Phoenicurus fuliginosus

L 14 cm | **W** 20 cm

Medium-sized, rounded redstart. ♂| **slaty-blue;** rump, vent and tail **bright rufous.** ♀/♂**1Y**| grey, underparts mottled white; **rump and vent white;** tail black, **side white.**

V| Call high, thin "*seeet't't.*"

FL| Low, flitting; ♂ dark with rufous tail, ♀/♂**1Y** dark with white rump and white sides to tail.

♂
ALL YEAR

♀/♂1Y
ALL YEAR

Vagrant from Africa
Arid areas

Redstart p. 396

LC ## Moussier's Redstart *Phoenicurus moussieri*

L 12 cm | **W** 20–22 cm

Small, short-tailed chat. ♂| black above with **long white stripe over eye** and **white patch on wing;** orange beneath. ♀/**1W**| grey-brown above, **pale rufous on belly, rump and side of tail;** whitish eyering.

V| Call a short whistle and grating buzz, "*siu-dzzzzz.*"

FL| ♂ long dark tail, sides rufous; **broad white midwing band.** ♀ brown; rump rufous, tail darker.

♀
ALL YEAR

♂
ALL YEAR

LC **Pied Bushchat** *Saxicola caprata*

L 13–14 cm | **W** 20–25 cm

Shape of Stonechat. ♂ | black with white wingbar, vent, rump. ♂**1W** | lacks wingbar. ♀ | grey with rusty rump, short dark grey tail.

V | Call a liquid, descending *"siew."*

⬤ Stonechat *p. 400*
Black Wheatear *p. 403*

Low bushes, grassland

LC **Siberian Rubythroat**
Calliope calliope

L 15 cm | **W** 26–27 cm

Robust, long-legged, rounded but upright, pale brown chat; hops; often cocks tail. **White line over blackish eyestripe**; black and white stripes below cheek. ♂ | all ages throat **vivid red**. ♀ | all ages throat whitish.

V | Call long, descending *"psee-oop."*

FL | Low, flitting; can be fast, direct.

⬤ Bluethroat [♀] *p. 393*

Woodland and scrub

LC **Rufous-tailed Robin**
Larvivora sibilans

L 14 cm | **W** 21–22 cm

Small, rounded chat with long, pale pink legs; hops. Grey-brown with **broad buff eyering**; breast pale with **olive-brown scaling**, flank brown; rump and short tail **rufous-brown**.

V | Call a high *"tsu-ee."*

FL | Underwing plain (dark with pale band on similar American thrushes).

⬤ Veery | Hermit Thrush *p. 611*

Woodland and scrub

LC **Siberian Blue Robin**
Larvivora cyane

L 12 cm | **W** 20–22 cm

Small, short-tailed chat; long, pale pinkish legs; hops. May quiver tail rapidly. ♂ | unmistakable: **dark blue above, white below**. ♂**1W** | bluish. ♀ / ♀ **1W** | brown above; breast buff, mottled dark; white belly; bluish tail.

V | Call high, vibrant, metallic *"shreet."*

⬤ Red-flanked Bluetail *p. 398*

Woodland and scrub

Vagrant from Asia

♂**1W**
AUG–MAR

♀
ALL YEAR

Rare summer migrant to extreme E Europe
MAR–OCT; vagrant

Ad has greyer wing

♀**1W**
AUG–MAR

♂**1W**
AUG–MAR

Vagrant from Asia

1W
AUG–MAR

Vagrant from Asia

♂**1W**
AUG–MAR

♂
ALL YEAR

♀**1W**
AUG–MAR

All inhabit deserts/arid, rocky areas

White-crowned Black Wheatear *Oenanthe leucopyga*

L 18–19 cm | **W** 26–29 cm

Large, **black** wheatear with white rump, white vent; **tail lacks full black tip**. **Ad**| glossy black, crown **usually white**. **Juv / 1W**| dull; crown black.

V| Call a low, chacking "*chik-chik*."

FL| Tail white with short central black line; **dark spots across tip (no bar)**.

Vagrant from Middle East/Africa

Hooded Wheatear
Oenanthe monacha

L 15–17 cm | **W** 26–27 cm

Medium-sized, **long-billed** wheatear. ♂| **black-and-white**; cap and underparts white; face/throat, upperparts and wing black. ♀| brown-and-buff, wings brown; cheek pale rufous, underparts buff.

V| Call a whistled "*vit*."

FL| Rump white. ♂ tail white, centre black; upperwing all-dark; ♀ tail rufous, centre black.

Vagrant from Middle East

Mourning Wheatear
Oenanthe lugens

L 16 cm | **W** 26–27 cm

Medium-sized, short-billed, short-tailed wheatear. Sexes look alike. Cap grey-white; throat, cheek, back and wings black, primary coverts tipped white when fresh; underparts white, **vent buff**.

V| Call a hard "*tak*."

FL| Rump/tail white, short black 'T'; flight feathers pale.

Vagrant from Middle East

Buff-rumped Wheatear
Oenanthe moesta

L 16 cm | **W** 25–29 cm

Medium-sized wheatear with **rufous rump; mostly black** tail. ♂| crown and nape pale grey, face/throat black; back dark grey, wings fringed browner; underparts pale grey, vent buff. ♀| head and rear flank rufous.

V| Call a hard "*tak*."

FL| Rump rufous; tail black. Heavy.

Vagrant from Africa

1W
AUG–MAR

Ad
ALL YEAR

👁 Black Wheatear *p. 403*
Basalt Wheatear

outer tail feathers may have small black markings

♂
ALL YEAR

♀
ALL YEAR

👁 Hooded and Mourning Wheatears are similar.
Pied Wheatear *p. 408* | Finsch's Wheatear *p. 408*

Ad
ALL YEAR

Ad
ALL YEAR

SSP. *warriae*, sometimes treated as a separate species '**Basalt Wheatear**' (vagrant from Middle East, has bred) black; small white rump, broad black tail tip, vent white.

👁 Black Wheatear *p. 403* |
White-crowned Black Wheatear

👁 Red-tailed Wheatear *p. 410* | Kurdish Wheatear *p. 410*

♂
ALL YEAR

♀
ALL YEAR

LC White's Thrush
LC *Zoothera aurea*

L 27–31 cm | **W** 35–40 cm

Large thrush; makes short runs between pauses when feeding. **Ad** | back rich buff with **crescentic black bars** (juv. Mistle Thrush dark-edged pale spots). Black band across primary coverts. Underparts creamy-white with **black crescents**, dusky on side of breast. **Juv** | underparts spotted. **1W** | wing and tail feathers worn (fresh on **Ad** after JUL/AUG).

V | Call short, strong "*wheuuw*." Song a slow sequence of long, high, piping notes of varying pitch.

 Mistle Thrush *p. 387*

FL | Strong, fast, low, undulating; pale bands across upperwing, **black and white bands on underwing.**

1W
OCT–MAR

Rare summer migrant to extreme E Europe MAR–OCT; vagrant

Woodland, thickets

LC Black-throated Thrush
LC *Turdus atrogularis*

L 23–25·5 cm | **W** 40–45 cm

Fairly large, greyish thrush with paler underparts; bill **yellow with black tip**. ♂ | **face/breast black**, cheek grey. ♀ | dull, **dark tail** (no rufous); dark mark from eye to bill; **grey mottles or streaks on breast, grey streaks on flank**. **Juv** | back brown with pale streaks; throat white; breast buff with black spots; flank rufous. **1W** | rufous tips to coverts create pale wingbar; streaks on throat and flank coalesce into blacker breast-band on ♂.

V | Call quick, nasal "*wheep-eep-eep*" and deep chatter. Song a series of slow, rich, throaty phrases.

Blackbird *p. 385*
Ring Ouzel *p. 384*
Red-throated Thrush

♂
ALL YEAR
[DEC]

Pale fringes wear off DEC– MAR to reveal black breast of ♂Br (MAR–AUG); individually variable.

♀1W
SEP–MAR

♂
ALL YEAR
[JAN]

Rare summer migrant to extreme E Europe MAR–OCT; vagrant; occasionally winters

Woodland, pastures, berried bushes

BLACK-THROATED THRUSH

♂Nb

FL (Black-throated and Red-throated Thrushes) | Fast, direct; underwing **rusty-red**.

LC Red-throated Thrush
Turdus ruficollis

L 23–25·5 cm | **W** 35–39 cm

Fairly large thrush, grey-brown above, whiter below; **side of tail rusty-/red-brown**. ♂ | **brick-red** breast and face, in winter more mottled. ♀ | upperparts pale grey; underparts paler grey with weak rusty-buff marks on throat and neck, grey streaks on belly. **1W** | like ♀ but wing coverts edged paler grey; underparts with more extensive dark streaks; rufous breast on ♂.

V | Call quick, nasal "*wheep-eep-eep*" and deep chatter.

 Black-throated Thrush

♂1W
SEP–MAR

Vagrant from Asia
Woodland

Siberian Thrush
Geokichla sibirica

L 20–21 cm | **W** 35 cm

Small, dark thrush with **white stripe over eye**. ♂**Ad** | **slate grey**. ♀**Ad** | brown; whitish below with **dark crescents**. ♂**1Y** | like ♂**Ad** but duller, browner. ♀**1Y** | like ♀**Ad** with buff-tipped wing coverts.

V | Call quiet, very high, thin "*stit*."

FL | Direct; **black and white bands on underwing**, ♂ white on tail tip.

 Blackbird *p. 385*
Ring Ouzel *p. 384*

♂ white tips to outer tail feathers

♀
ALL YEAR

♂1Ys individually variable, becoming greyer with maturity.

♂1Y
ALL YEAR
[MAY]

♂1Y
ALL YEAR
[OCT]

Dusky Thrush   *Turdus eunomus*

L 21–24 cm | **W** 34–38 cm

Small, rufous thrush with white underparts; dark cap, eyestripe and cheek; **bold buff-white bands** above eye and below cheek. **Blackish spots** on breast and 'V'-shaped marks on flank; rufous rump. ♂**Ad** | broad **rufous wing panel**. ♂**1Y** | most rufous on shoulder; pale edges break up dull wing panel; head/throat more speckled. ♀**1Y** | lacks rufous, shoulder and wing panel buff-brown.

V | Call nasal "*wheet-wheet-wheet;*" abrupt flight note, "*chup-chup*."

FL | Fast, direct; upperwing dark with rufous coverts, underwing rusty-red.

 Redwing *p. 386*
Naumann's Thrush

♂

♀1Y
ALL YEAR
[MAY]

♂1Y
ALL YEAR
[JAN]

Naumann's Thrush
Turdus naumanni

L 21–24 cm | **W** 35–40 cm

Small, rufous-brown thrush. **Ad** | back olive; orange-buff wing panel; underparts extensively spotted **orange-rufous**. Rump and tail rusty-brown. Sexes similar, ♀ slightly duller than ♂. **1Y** | like **Ad** but browner, rump dull; greater covert tips pale.

V | Call nasal "*wheet-wheet-wheet;*" abrupt flight note, "*chup-chup*."

FL | Fast, direct; tail orange-brown; underwing greyish.

 Dusky Thrush

1Y
ALL YEAR
[OCT]

1Y
ALL YEAR
[APR]

Vagrant from Asia | Woodland

👁 Redwing *p. 386*

LC **Eyebrowed Thrush** *Turdus obscurus*

L 20·5–23 cm | **W** 37–40 cm

Small, pale thrush. **Ad**| head and upper breast grey;
white stripes over and below eye; flank orange;
1W| browner; head grey-brown, **white stripe over
eye**, dark eyestripe; **flank pale orange**; belly and
vent white.
V| Alarm call sharp, "*chip-chip-chip*," flight call thin,
sharp "*tsip*."
FL| Fast, direct; underwing pale greyish.

1W
SEP–MAR

Vagrant (historical) from Asia | Woodland

👁 Blackbird *p. 385*

LC **Tickell's Thrush** *Turdus unicolor*

L 20–25 cm | **W** 30–40 cm

Small, greyish thrush. ♂| **ashy-grey**, whiter on
belly; **bill and eyering yellow**; legs yellow-brown.
♀| brown, paler below; **bill and legs yellow. Dark
line** below cheek, throat spotted; upper breast
slightly mottled grey, underparts pale grey-buff.
1W| crown, cheek and wings streaked cream, dark
crescents on upper breast.
V| Sharp, abrupt "*twik*" and deep chattering "*trrt-rr-rrt*."
FL| Direct; underwing **grey with rufous coverts**.

♂Ad
ALL YEAR

Vagrant from N America | Woodland

LC **Varied Thrush** *Ixoreus naevius*

L 24 cm | **W** 35–40 cm

Large, grey-and-orange thrush, **orange-buff over
eye** and on wingbars; **dark cheek and breast-band**.
(Rare grey-and-white aberration has been recorded
in Europe.)
V| Low "*chet chet*" and short, hard trill.
FL| Tail black with white tips to outer feathers;
underwing dark with broad pale band.

Ad Nb / 1W
AUG–MAR

Vagrant from N America | Woodland, pastures

LC **American Robin** *Turdus migratorius*

L 22–25 cm | **W** 38–40 cm

Size, shape and actions like Blackbird. **Ad**| slaty-grey
above, paler fringes to wing feathers. Blackish hood,
bold **white marks around eye**; throat paler, streaked.
Underparts pale **brick-red/orange**, darker on ♂.
White with black streaks under tail. **1W**| paler, with
buff feather edges on underparts.
V| Blackbird-like "*cuk*" and strident "*peek*."
FL| Tail black with white tips to outer feathers.

👁 Blackbird *p. 385*

♀ 1W
SEP–MAR

Great Reed Warbler *p. 421*

Vagrant from Middle East | Reedbeds

Basra Reed Warbler *Acrocephalus griseldis*

L 17–18 cm | **W** 25–26 cm

Like **large**, dark, greyish Reed Warbler (*p. 419*) with long bill, long wings and long, thick, legs. Dark crown often raised; may raise and flick tail. Pale stripe above thick dark line between eye and bill; **prominent broken white eyering**.

V | Short, harsh rasping "*skairk*" call.

FL | Low, quick; size and shape intermediate between Reed and Great Reed Warblers.

Ad/1W

Vagrant from Asia | Bushes, thickets

Great Reed Warbler *p. 421*

LC Thick-billed Warbler *Arundinax aedon*

L 16–17 cm | **W** 24–28 cm

Like a pale Great Reed Warbler with a **stout, slightly arched, pale-based bill**, orange gape extends almost to eye. Head plain but **cap slightly darker**. **Pale** between eye and bill; white throat above rusty-buff breast. Closed wingtip short.

V | Emphatic "*tsak*" or "*tsick-tsick*" call notes.

FL | Short wings; **long, rounded, bright rufous-brown tail**.

Ad
ALL YEAR

Vagrant from Asia | Marshes, reedbeds

Grasshopper Warbler *p. 416*

Pallas's Grasshopper Warbler
Locustella certhiola

L 13–14 cm | **W** 16–18 cm

Small, skulking warbler, like contrasty Grasshopper Warbler but cap greyish, streaked dark grey; **whitish stripe over eye**. **Wing coverts and tertials blackish** with **white tips; rump rufous, streaked**. Tail dark, subtly barred, **darker towards whitish tips**.

V | Short click and longer "*trrrrt*" call.

FL | Low, fast; tail becomes blacker before fine whitish tips.

Juv
JUL–OCT

Vagrant from Asia | Meadows, thickets

Savi's Warbler *p. 417* | River Warbler *p. 417*

LC Gray's Grasshopper Warbler
Locustella fasciolata

L 16–18 cm | **W** 18–25 cm

Large, sandy-brown warbler, almost unstreaked; long, **stout, dark bill**; long tail. Head greyish with browner cap and long, pale stripe over eye. Throat whitish, breast softly streaked grey; rump and **vent orange-buff**.

V | Call hard, 'thick' "*tsuk-tuk-tuk*."

Ad
ALL YEAR

All vagrants from Asia [*annual]

LC Plain Leaf-warbler
Phylloscopus neglectus

L 9–10 cm | **W** 15 cm

Tiny, rather drab warbler. Upperparts brownish-grey; wing plain. Indistinct pale stripe over eye; small whitish crescent below eye. Underparts pale greyish. Legs dark brown.
V | Sparrow-like (*p. 504*) "*chleep*."

LC Sulphur-bellied Warbler
Phylloscopus griseolus

L 10–11 cm | **W** 15–20 cm

Very small warbler, often on rocks. Head dark, side of crown dark grey, above long **bright yellow stripe over eye**; dark eyestripe; small white crescent below eye. **Ad** | upperparts grey, olive-brown by Apr/May; underparts greenish-yellow, faintly streaked grey. **1W** | upperparts greyish; underparts buff, less yellow.
V | Call short, abrupt "*tschup*."

LC Dusky Warbler∗
Phylloscopus fuscatus

L 10·5–12 cm | **W** 16–19 cm

Small, skulking warbler, like a **grey-brown** Chiffchaff. Similar to Radde's Warbler (some distinct, others barely separable) but slimmer, browner. **Long, pale stripe over eye** thin in front, wide and **buff behind**. **Cream or buff under tail. Bill fine, pointed**. Legs brown with yellow toes, occasionally all yellow or pinkish.
V | **Call hard** "*tek*," sometimes repeated (like Wren (*p. 372*)), or softer, sucked, "*ch'k*" or "*tsuc*."

LC Radde's Warbler∗
Phylloscopus schwarzi

L 11·5–12·5 cm | **W** 17–19 cm

Small, secretive, stocky, thick-legged warbler. Similar to Dusky Warbler (some very difficult) but more olive. **Long pale stripe over eye** blurred buff in front, well-defined white at rear; broad dark eyestripe. **Orange-buff under tail. Bill thick**, orange/pink; legs orange-yellow.
V | Rather soft "*chuc*," subdued or louder, often in long series; "*chrep*."

Chiffchaffs *pp. 432–433* — Woodland, dry scrub

1Y/Ad
ALL YEAR

Willow Warbler *p. 430* — Woodland, scrub

Ad
ALL YEAR

Wet bushy areas, woodland floor

1Y/Ad
ALL YEAR

Dusky and Radde's Warblers are very similar. | Chiffchaff *p. 432* — Woodland, scrub

1Y/Ad
ALL YEAR

Yellow-browedWarbler*p.434   Yellow-browed Warbler p.434   Greenish Warbler p.435
                                                          | Firecrest p.414   Green Warbler p.435

Hume's Warbler*
Phylloscopus humei

L 9–10·5 cm | **W** 15–16 cm

Tiny, active; rapid wing/tail flicks. Some inseparable from Yellow-browed Warbler without **call** but upperparts slightly greyer or browner; stripe over eye **tinged buff**; wingbars more **buff on grey** (less yellow on green); tertial tips duller. Legs darker.

V | **Call** a dull, flat "*ds-weet*" or longish, slightly falling "*dsee-o.*"

LC Pallas's Leaf-warbler*
Phylloscopus proregulus

L 9–9·5 cm | **W** 14–16 cm

Tiny, **bright green** warbler with **pale yellow rump**; underparts whitish. **Very long yellow stripe over black eyestripe**; narrow **pale central stripe** on green-black crown. **Broad yellow midwing bar**; tertial edges pale.

V | Call soft, rising "*chueee,*" generally rather infrequent.

LC Two-barred Warbler
Phylloscopus plumbeitarsus

L 10–11 cm | **W** 15–20 cm

Very small, dull green warbler. Pale stripe over eye may fall short of bill; cheek mottled green and yellow. Well-defined **long, broad, even-width lower wingbar**; **upper wingbar** usually present; tertials plain. Lower mandible yellow-pink. Legs red-brown.

V | Disyllabic "*chew-wee*" and monosyllabic notes.

Ad/1W
ALL YEAR

Ad/1W
ALL YEAR

1W
SEP–MAR

 Arctic Warbler p.434 | Greenish Warbler p.435

Eastern Crowned Warbler
Phylloscopus coronatus

L 11–12 cm | **W** 18–20 cm

Small; like Arctic Warbler but brighter green on wing and tail; **two narrow whitish wingbars**. Diffuse **pale central stripe** on **dark** olive/blackish crown; stripe over eye greenish-yellow in front, cream behind; white crescent under eye.

V | Loud, downslurred "*schleuw.*"

LC Pale-legged Leaf-warbler
Phylloscopus tenellipes

L 10–11 cm | **W** 15–21 cm

Very small, brownish-green warbler; resembles Arctic Warbler. **Crown and eyestripe dark grey-olive; long** cream stripe over eye falls short of forehead; creamy-white below eye, above dark 'moustache' and mottled cheek; two narrow whitish wingbars (upper obscure); underparts creamy-white; legs pale pink.

V | High, thin, short "*tseep.*"

Pale-legged and **Sakhalin Leaf-warbler** *Phylloscopus borealoides* inseparable without examination in the hand or song (occurrence of the former in Europe confirmed by DNA sample; one other record could not be specifically identified).

Ad
ALL YEAR

SAKHALIN
LEAF-WARBLER

1W
AUG–MAR

Ad/1W
ALL YEAR

LC RE Asian Desert Warbler
Sylvia nana

L 11·5–12·5 cm | **W** 18–20 cm

Small, pale, round-headed warbler; recalls Whitethroat but face bland and **eye yellow**. Upperparts pale **grey-brown**, crown **greyish**. **Rump and tail rufous**, tail feathers and tertials **dark with wide pale rufous edges**.

V | Call a fast, nasal, tit-like (*p. 452*) "*tr-r-r-chair-chair*". Song a rich, fluty warble.

Whitethroat *p. 438*
African Desert Warbler

Vagrant from Asia
(formerly bred very locally)

Semi-arid areas

Ad/1W
ALL YEAR

LC African Desert Warbler
Sylvia deserti

L 11·5–12·5 cm | **W** 18–20 cm

Like Asian Desert Warbler but paler, **brighter sandy-buff** and less rufous on tail; crown orange-buff; tertials and central tail feathers **plain**, without dark centres (no contrast).

V | Call tit-like (*p. 452*), much like Asian Desert Warbler.

Whitethroat *p. 438*
Asian Desert Warbler

Vagrant from Africa

Semi-arid areas

Ad
ALL YEAR

NT Tristram's Warbler
Sylvia deserticola

L 12 cm | **W** 18 cm

Small; very like Dartford Warbler; rounded, short-winged and long-tailed, but ♂ | plainer grey above, except dull **rufous wing-panel**, white eyering and weak pale 'moustache' above white-spotted throat; pale base to bill. ♀ | paler, back olive-brown. **1W/1S** | underparts paler.

V | Call a short, soft "*tchrut*."

Dartford Warbler *p. 442*
Subalpine Warbler *p. 440*
Moltoni's Warbler *p. 441*

Vagrant from N Africa

Dry, bushy heathland

dull brown wings ♂

DARTFORD WARBLER

rufous wing panel

♂Ad
ALL YEAR

1S
MAR–SEP

Any woodland

Asian Brown Flycatcher
Muscicapa dauurica

L 12–13 cm | **W** 19·5–21·5 cm

Like small, plain, greyish, wide-billed Spotted Flycatcher. **Ad** | greyish-brown above, buff-white below; head and breast **unstreaked**; **large eye** with thin **white eyering**; bill clearly **broad and pale at base. Juv** | buff spots. **1W** | pale fringes on wing.

V | High, insignificant "*tsi*" call.

Ad / 1W
ALL YEAR

bill broad-based, with extensive pale base

eyering white

bill relatively narrow, with restricted pale base

eyering buff

SPOTTED FLYCATCHER

Spotted Flycatcher p. 449

Dark-sided Flycatcher
Muscicapa sibirica

L 13–14 cm | **W** 20–21 cm

Like Spotted Flycatcher. **Wingtip longer** than Asian Brown Flycatcher. **Ad** | (NR) flank streaked, dark stripe beside pale throat, pale eyering. **Juv/1W** | back brown (spotted buff until SEP–OCT), wing coverts and tertials fringed rusty-buff; underparts streaked grey-brown, especially on flank and undertail coverts.

V | Call a thin, sharp "*tsi*."

Juv / 1W
JUL–MAR
[OCT]

Ad
ALL YEAR

Mugimaki Flycatcher
Ficedula mugimaki

L 12–13 cm | **W** 18–20 cm

Small flycatcher with long wingtips and short tail. ♂ | **back slaty-grey; white behind eye**, **white shoulder; underparts orange**; tail blackish with thin white edges at base. ♀ | pale grey with faint pale patch behind eye; narrow white wingbar; throat/upper breast pale orange, belly white. Tail plain dark grey. ♂**1W** | like ♀ but browner above and brighter and more orange on throat and breast.

V | Rattling call notes.

♂
ALL YEAR

♀
ALL YEAR

long wingtip often drooped

Taiga Flycatcher
Ficedula albicilla

L 11–12·5 cm | **W** 18·5–21 cm

Like Red-breasted Flycatcher but **uppertail coverts blackish**; bill mostly black. ♂**Br** | **small** orange bib; **grey cheek and breast-band**. ♂**Nb** / ♀ / **Juv/1W** | upperparts brown, breast greyish; wingbar and tertial fringes white.

V | Call dry, creaking chatter. Song rich warble, including fast trill.

Red-breasted Flycatcher p. 448

RED-BREASTED FLYCATCHER
rump + UTC uniformly pale

1W
SEP–MAR

♂
ALL YEAR

uppertail coverts (UTC) contrastingly blackish

'BROWN' SHRIKES Three species occur as vagrants from Asia, favouring open, bushy areas. They are similar in all plumages to female or juvenile/first-winter **Red-backed Shrike** (p. 466). They can be difficult to identify with certainty and often require examination of subtle structural and plumage features, including overall colour and contrasts, tail colour and details of the closed wingtip.

LC Isabelline Shrike
Lanius isabellinus

L 16·5–18 cm | **W** 26–28 cm
Resembles Red-backed Shrike (p. 466). **Tail rufous above and beneath.** Small white primary patch (can be absent on ♀, rarely present on Red-backed Shrike); 6–7 primary-tips show on closed wingtip (typically 8 on Red-backed Shrike). ♂**Ad** | nape greyish, forehead brighter buff, buff line over eye, black 'mask'. **Greyish above, buff below.** ♀**Ad** | faintly barred below; **buff stripe** over eye weak. **Juv / 1W** | sandy-buff above and below; nape as back; no strong 'mask'. **Rump and tail rusty**, including underside. Underparts buff with pale ginger bars.

LC Red-tailed Shrike
Lanius phoenicuroides

L 16·5–18 cm | **W** 26–28 cm
Similar to Isabelline Shrike, but all plumages darker above/whiter below; **crown, nape and rump more rufous** than back; 6–7 primary-tips show on closed wingtip. ♂**Ad** | white stripe over eye, black 'mask'; dull **brown above**, **whitish below**. ♀**Ad** | underparts faintly barred; **white stripe** over eye well defined. **Juv / 1W** | like Isabelline Shrike, but typically whitish feather edges on wings, darker above than below; blackish 'mask'.

LC Brown Shrike
Lanius cristatus

L 18–20 cm | **W** 25–28 cm
Resembles female Red-backed (p. 466), Isabelline and Red-tailed Shrikes but head bigger, **bill thicker** and tail longer, **dark rufous-brown**. Short wingtip shows **5–6 primary tips**. ♂ | brown above, rufous crown and rump; black 'mask' below white stripe; buff underparts. ♀ / **Juv / 1W** | brown from crown to rump, darker above than below; rump brighter. Strong **blackish 'mask'**. Underparts barred like Red-backed Shrike but deeper buff. Bill dark, grey-pink at base.

buffish stripe above eye obscure over bill

♀ Ad

♀ Ad
ALL YEAR

Ad
(presumed ♂)
ALL YEAR

clear white stripe above eye continues over bill

♀ Ad
ALL YEAR

♂ Ad
ALL YEAR

♂ Ad
ALL YEAR

RED-BACKED SHRIKE

All vagrants from Asia

Open bushy areas

 Red-backed Shrike p. 466

ISABELLINE SHRIKE

RED-TAILED SHRIKE

BROWN SHRIKE

1W
SEP–MAR

1W
SEP–MAR

1W
SEP–MAR

7–8 primary tips show (7 on this bird)

6–7 primary tips show

6–7 primary tips show

5–6 primary tips show

1W
SEP–MAR

Vagrant from Asia

Open spaces

Long-tailed Shrike
Lanius schach

L 22–27 cm | **W** 25–26 cm

Large shrike: combines grey crown/back, black 'mask' and white throat with **brown rump**, **deep buff underparts** and **long tail**, often swayed up and down.

V | Call nasal "*tchairk tchairk*."

1W
SEP–MAR

Vagrant from N America

Open spaces and forest edge

LC Northern Grey Shrike
Lanius borealis

L 21–26 cm | **W** 30–34 cm

Extremely like Great Grey Shrike but upperparts faintly ochre-brownish; underparts slightly darker grey with **fine dark bars** (scaly effect).

FL | Undulating, showing bold black-and-white wings and tail.

1W
SEP–MAR

 Great Grey Shrike p. 468

Vagrant from Africa

Dry scrub

LC Black-crowned Tchagra
Tchagra senegalus

L 21–24 cm | **W** 30–32 cm

A bushshrike: recalls a shrike, with a large, hook-tipped, black bill. Greyish, with a black-and-white-striped head and rufous wing.

V | Call a long, loud, rasping "*skrairrrrr*."

FL | Long, graduated tail with white corners.

Ad
ALL YEAR

Long-tailed Rosefinch
Carpodacus sibiricus

L 18 cm | **W** 25 cm

Rounded finch with very short bill and **long**, slim tail. **White shoulder**, wingbar and tertial fringes. ♂| upperparts streaked **dark grey and pink. Dark red eyestripe and collar**. Underparts pink. ♀/**Imm**| head and upperparts brown, underparts buff/white, streaked brown.

V| Call high "*tsee, tsi-si-see.*"

Pallas's Rosefinch
Carpodacus roseus

L 16–17 cm | **W** 25 cm

Large, stout-billed finch with reddish rump, pale wingbars and tertial edges. ♂| **deep pink, streaked black above; forehead whitish; throat spotted white.** ♀/**Imm**| pale brownish, **crown and throat pink**. Rump pink-red, tail edged pink. Underparts **pinkish-buff**, streaked brown.

V| Call very thin, high "*zi-si-si.*"

House Bunting
Emberiza sahari

L 13–14 cm| **W** 22–23 cm

Small, plain bunting; **wings plain, tail edged buff. Upperparts unstreaked**. ♂**Br**| head grey, less striped than Rock Bunting and Striolated Bunting, with pale streak below cheek. Streaked grey bib. Underparts bright orange-buff. ♀/**Juv**/**1W**| head brownish-grey.

V| Call a short "*chup*" or "*dueet.*"

 House and *Striolated Buntings* are similar.| Rock Bunting *p.514*

Striolated Bunting
Emberiza striolata

L 13–14 cm | **W** 20 cm

Small bunting, like dull Rock Bunting or **streaked** House Bunting. ♂| **head and bib streaked**; no white wingbar; underparts dull buff. ♀/**Juv**/**1W**| like ♂ but head greyer.

V| Calls a loud, sparrow-like (*p.504*) "*chep*" or "*chairp.*"

Vagrant from Asia

Bushy areas

♀ ALL YEAR

♂ ALL YEAR

Vagrant from Asia

Bushy areas

♀ ALL YEAR

♂ ALL YEAR

Vagrant from Africa

Dry, rocky areas

♀ ALL YEAR

♂ ALL YEAR

Vagrant from Middle East

Rocky, semi-arid areas

♀ ALL YEAR

♂ ALL YEAR

Chestnut Bunting
Emberiza rutila

L 14–15 cm | **W** 20–21 cm

Small bunting. **Rump rufous**; tail brown, **no white**. ♂**Br** | (NR) head and upperparts plain rufous. ♀/**1W** | upperparts brown, streaked black; wing rufous, two buff wingbars. Pale grey stripe over eye; throat whitish. Underparts yellowish, streaked black.

V | Call a sharp "*zik*."

Lesser coverts show rufous base on ♂1W; brown on ♀1W.

♂1W
SEP–MAR

Chestnut and Chestnut-eared Buntings are similar. | Little Bunting p. 513

Chestnut-eared Bunting
Emberiza fucata

L 15–16 cm | **W** 20–22 cm

Large, long-tailed bunting. ♂**Br** | (NR) head grey, **cheek dark rufous**; throat white with black stripes. ♂**Nb** | (NR) breast yellowish, streaked black, above chestnut band. ♀/**1W** | **cheek chestnut**, lower edge black, with buff spot; white eyering. Shoulder rufous; two buff wingbars. Rump chestnut. Flank buff, sparsely streaked black.

V | Call an explosive "*tzic*."

1W
SEP–MAR

Black-faced Bunting
Emberiza spodocephala

L 14–15·5 cm | **W** 20–23 cm

Small, slim bunting; white tail side. Streaked brown, grey and black. ♂**Ad**/**1W** | head grey (black face from DEC). ♀**Ad**/**1W** | like dull Reed Bunting with greyer neck and rump. Underparts dull greyish or yellowish.

V | Call quiet, thin, metallic "*tip*."

Dunnock p. 373
Reed Bunting p. 512

♀Ad/1W
ALL YEAR

♀Ad
ALL YEAR

♂Ad
ALL YEAR

Yellow-browed Bunting
Emberiza chrysophrys

L 13–14 cm | 20–25 cm

Small bunting. ♂**Br** | (NR) cheek/crown black, white crown stripe, broad yellow stripe over eye. ♂**Nb**/♀/**1W** | crown black, central stripe buff, **white line on nape**; stripe over eye rufous in front, **yellow, fading to white** behind; cheek chestnut, edged black, with white spot. Underparts white, streaked black.

V | Call a thin, high "*sip*."

Little Bunting p. 513
Rustic Bunting p. 514

Nb/1W
ALL YEAR
[OCT]

LC **Fan-tailed Raven**
Corvus rhipidurus

L 45–52 cm | **W** 100–110 cm
Large, thickset black crow, with short, **deep, arched bill**; wingtip extends well beyond short tail when perched. **Ad** | black, **Juv / 1W** | browner.
FL | Two-tone underwing; **very short, broad tail**; broad innerwing.

 Raven *p. 475*

LC **Brown-necked Raven**
Corvus ruficollis

L 52–56 cm | **W** 90–95 cm
Large, black crow with slender wings and tail. **Neck and underparts brownish** (often hard to see). Bill long (but slimmer than Raven's).
FL | Head protrudes; wings long, narrow at tip; tail rounded or wedge-shaped (shape between Raven and Rook); underwing coverts black against paler flight feathers.

Raven *p. 475* | Rook *p. 475*

LC **Daurian Jackdaw**
Corvus dauuricus

L 34–36 cm | **W** 75 cm
Small, black-and-white crow: black with white hindneck and underparts. Short, stubby bill.
FL | From below, head, underwing, vent and tail black and belly white; from above, black with white collar.

Jackdaw *p. 476*
Hooded Crow *p. 474*

LC **Pied Crow**
Corvus albus

L 46–52 cm | **W** 85–90 cm
Large, thick-billed crow; black with **white upper back and underparts**.
FL | Head protrudes; wings long and narrow; tail short but slightly wedge-shaped (shape between Raven (*p. 475*) and Carrion Crow).

Hooded / Carrion Crow (leucistic) *p. 474* | Magpie *p. 479*

Vagrant from the Middle East
Cliffs, arid areas

Ad
ALL YEAR

1W
AUG–MAR

RAVEN

Ad

Vagrant from the Middle East
Cliffs, arid areas

Ad/1W

Ad/1W
ALL YEAR

Vagrant from Asia
Open areas

Ad

JACKDAW

Ad

Ad
ALL YEAR

HOODED CROW

Ad

Vagrant from Africa/escape
Urban areas, farmland

Ad

Ad
ALL YEAR

Ad

Vagrant passerines from North America

80 species [all vagrants] (6 species covered on *pp. 586–587, 598, 605*)
Astonishingly, 80 species of North American passerines have been recorded in Europe, all bar six of which are covered in this section. A further 86 species of non-passerines, near-passerines and a swift have occurred as vagrants from North America (not including distinct American subspecies). Most of these are included in the previous part of this section, the exception being various wildfowl that are most likely to be confused with regular escapees (see *pp. 32, 68–71*).

Each year, a remarkable variety of North American landbirds reaches Europe. In autumn, insectivorous species arrive unaided, carried by the jet stream and often associated with Atlantic storms. In spring, most arrivals are seed-eating birds, often crossing on board ships. Most of these vagrants appear on western coasts and islands.

Only plumages that have been recorded in Europe are shown here, using photographs of the actual birds seen as far as possible.

ICTERIDS Elongated but heavy-bodied, with pointed, triangular bill; mostly colourful or largely black; in bushes, trees or grassland.

LC Bobolink
Dolichonyx oryzivorus

L 16–18 cm | **W** 19–26 cm
Bunting-like (*p. 508*), with pointed bill, pointed tail feathers.
1W | yellowish; dark crown with **buff central line; two cream stripes down back**.

1W

LC Yellow-headed Blackbird
Xanthocephalus xanthocephalus

L 21–26 cm | **W** 42–44 cm
♂ | black; head and breast yellow; white wing patch. ♀ (NR) | brown; stripe over eye, cheek and throat yellow. **Juv / 1W** (NR) | buff-brown; wings and tail black.

♂

LC Brown-headed Cowbird
Molothrus ater

L 16–22 cm | **W** 34–36 cm
Sleek, stocky mainly terrestrial; thick, triangular bill. ♂ | glossy black, **head brown**. ♀/**1W** | grey-brown, head paler. Slim tail often raised.

♀

♂

LC Baltimore Oriole
Icterus galbula

L 17–22 cm | **W** 23–30 cm
Shape and size of a Starling (*p. 379*). **Ad** | orange-yellow; dark wings; two white wingbars. Long, pointed, triangular, grey bill. ♂**Ad** | black head. ♂**1W** | pale orange rump.

♂1W

WAXWINGS Stocky, crested; short legs. Trees, berried bushes.

LC Cedar Waxwing
Bombycilla cedrorum

L 15–19 cm | **W** 30 cm
Like Waxwing but **plain** wing, **white** under tail. **Ad** | flank yellow. **1W** | browner; short crest; buff below.

Ad

1W

⟳ Waxwing *p. 377*

LC Red-winged Blackbird
Agelaius phoeniceus

L 22–23 cm | **W** 37–40 cm
Thrush-like (*p. 383*) but **pointed, triangular bill**. ♀/**1W** | **closely streaked** brown and buff; broad pale stripe over eye, pale cheek and throat. Blackish under-wing.

1W

NT Common Grackle
Quiscalus quiscula

L 26–27 cm | **W** 36–40 cm
Thrush-like (*p. 383*) but forehead flat; bill triangular; tail long, rounded with broad tip. **Ad** | bronze-black, head purple-blue; eye white. **Juv** (NR) | brown with darker tail; dark eye.

Ad

609

AMERICAN FLYCATCHERS Despite their name, tyrant-flycatchers have no close equivalent in Europe; they include various upright, large-headed, large-billed, fly-catching birds. Smaller flycatchers in autumn may pose extremely difficult identification problems, as they are best separated in North America by their songs and calls in spring. Vagrants are usually found in trees or bushes.

LC Least Flycatcher
Empidonax minimus

Ad/1S

L 13–14 cm | **W** 19–22 cm
Small; round-headed; secretive. **Flicks wings** and tail. **Small bill, short tail; closed wingtip short.**
1W | head greyish; back greenish or grey; **buff-white** wingbars and tertial fringes.
V | Call loud "*che-bek*."

LC Acadian Flycatcher
Empidonax virescens

Ad/1W

L 12–13 cm | **W** 17–20 cm
Small; **closed wingtip long.**
1W | thin eyering; **head and upperparts olive-green.** Wings grey with two **white** wingbars, pale tertial fringes. Underparts yellowish. Bill long, pink at base; legs grey.
V | **Call** explosive "*peet-sah*."

LC Alder Flycatcher
Empidonax alnorum

1W

L 13–14 cm | **W** 18–22 cm
Small; round, **dark** head; **closed wingtip short.**
1W | back greyish; two **white** wingbars; white throat; pale tertial fringes.
V | **Call** "*pip*". (NOTE: Willow Flycatcher *E. traillii* (NR) looks very similar, but call "*whit*.")

LC Yellow-bellied Flycatcher
Empidonax flaviventris

1W

L 13–15 cm | **W** 18–20 cm
Small; domed head; small bill; short tail. **1W** | upperparts rich **greenish**; bold yellow-white eyering. Two **yellowish-white** wingbars. Breast olive, tinged yellow.
V | Call "*psiee*" or "*tsu-ee*."

LC Eastern Wood-pewee
Contopus virens

L 13–14 cm | **W** 19–22 cm
Small, active; perches high on open perches. **Peaked crown. Does not flick** long, notched tail; **closed wingtip long. 1W** | two long, buff wingbars.
1W
V | Frequent **calls**, "*peewee*" and "*chip*."

LC Eastern Phoebe
Sayornis phoebe

L 13–14 cm | **W** 18–22 cm
Small; long-tailed. **Ad** | upperparts grey-brown; **dark 'hood', no pale eyering**; bill all-dark. Two **dull buff wingbars**. Throat white; breast grey, underparts buff-white.
1W
V | Call sharp "*chip*."

LC Eastern Kingbird
Tyrannus tyrannus

L 19–23 cm | **W** 33–38 cm
Large, upright; peaked head; long, wide bill. **1W** | large **dark head**. Tail **long, black with white tip**; upperparts grey, wing feathers edged white; underparts white.
1W
V | Call harsh "*kit*" or "*kitter*."

LC Western Kingbird
Tyrannus verticalis

Ad

L 20–24 cm | **W** 38–41 cm
Large; large, rounded head. **Head grey**; throat and breast pale grey. Back grey-brown; tail square, dark with **white side**. Underparts **pale yellow**.
V | Call fast, squeaky twittering, bright "*kwip*."

MIMIDS Thrush-like (*p. 383*) but no close equivalent in Europe; typically found in thickets near the coast.

LC Northern Mockingbird
Mimus polyglottos

L 21–28 cm | **W** 31–38 cm
Pale, slender; **long white-sided tail**. Upperparts **grey**, underparts whitish; two white wingbars and white patch on spread wing. **Ad** | eye dull yellow. **1W** | eye dark.

Ad/1W

LC Brown Thrasher
Toxostoma rufum

L 23–30 cm | **W** 29–33 cm
Ad | Rufous, slender; **long-tailed** with long bill; **two white wingbars**, rufous tail. Underparts white, streaked black.

Ad

LC Grey Catbird
Dumetella carolinensis

L 20–24 cm | **W** 22–30 cm
Dark grey with **long tail, often raised**. Grey, with **dark rufous under tail**; **black cap**, pale cheek.

Ad/1Y

AMERICAN THRUSHES
Elusive, skulking; look like small **Song Thrush** (*p. 386*) and some Asian robins (*p. 594*). **American Robin** and **Varied Thrush** are Larger (covered with the rare Eurasian thrushes (*p. 598*)).

FL | *Catharus* thrushes have dark underwings with a white central band.

SWAINSON'S THRUSH

 Rufous-tailed Robin p. 594 (has pale underwing)

LC Grey-cheeked Thrush
Catharus minimus

L 15–17 cm | **W** 25–30 cm
Upperparts uniformly dull olive-brown; **weak pale eyering, greyish cheek**. Breast buff with diffuse spots; flank greyish, belly white. **1W** | has thin pale wingbar.

1W

LC Swainson's Thrush
Catharus ustulatus

L 16–18 cm | **W** 22–25 cm
Upperparts uniformly sandy-brown; wide, **bright, pale eyering**, pale line eye to bill. Upper breast whitish with diffuse dark spots; underparts whitish, flank lightly mottled grey.

1W

LC Wood Thrush
Hylocichla mustelina

L 17–18 cm | **W** 25–30 cm
Rounded, short-tailed; upperparts **bright brown** with **rusty nape** (overall looks **rufous towards front**). bold **pale eyering**, dark-flecked cheek. Underparts white, with **large, rounded black spots** all over.

Ad/1W

LC Veery
Catharus fuscescens

L 16–18 cm | **W** 22–27 cm
Thick neck, broad tail; upperparts **uniformly warm brown**; greyish cheek, brighter cap. Throat buff with few diffuse grey spots; underparts white, flank plain greyish.

1W

LC Hermit Thrush
Catharus guttatus

L 16–17 cm | **W** 20–25 cm
Upperparts plain brown; wing patch, uppertail coverts and base of tail **rufous** (overall, looks **rufous towards rear**). Weak or bold pale eyering. Underparts buff with black spots over breast, blurred streaks on browner flank.

1W

AMERICAN WARBLERS

Although superficially similar to Old World warblers (*p. 412*), American warblers are not closely related. They usually arrive in Europe after strong winds from the west. Breeding-plumage adults (very rare in Europe) are brightly coloured, but autumn (first-winter) birds are more difficult to identify. All are most likely to be found in wooded, scrubby or marshy areas. Learning their calls is an art: most have a similar very short, high, thin "*tsit*" note that may draw attention.

NT Blackpoll Warbler
Setophaga striata

L 13–15 cm | **W** 20–25 cm
Two **long, curved white wingbars**. **White undertail**; white-edged tail. Legs orange. ♂**Br** | **black cap**, white cheek. **1W** | **soft grey streaks** on olive-green back and yellow breast; flank whiter.

LC Bay-breasted Warbler
Setophaga castanea

L 13–15 cm | **W** 20–23 cm
1W | like Blackpoll Warbler with two long, **curved white wingbars**, but **buff undertail** and larger bill. Grey streaks on back, but **underparts unstreaked**; breast yellowish, flank buff.

LC Yellow-rumped Warbler
Setophaga coronata

L 12–15 cm | **W** 19–24 cm
Rump yellow; yellow patch on breast side; legs black. ♂**Br** | grey with white throat. **1W** | head and back brown, white crescent above and below eye. Two long white wingbars. Underparts whitish; dark streaks on flank.

LC Blackburnian Warbler
Setophaga fusca

L 11–13 cm | **W** 20–22 cm
1W | upperparts green; **pale yellow** stripe over eye; dark, triangular cheek patch; two wide, white wingbars. **Throat orange-yellow**; underparts pale yellow, flank whiter with long grey streaks.

LC Cape May Warbler
Setophaga tigrina

L 12–14 cm | **W** 19–22 cm
♂**Br** | green-and-yellow; dark cap, **rufous cheek**. **1W** | greyish; white crescent above and below eye; pale yellowish side of neck. **Diffuse** pale wingbars. Underparts **grey/white with soft grey streaks**.

LC Magnolia Warbler
Setophaga magnolia

L 11–13 cm | **W** 16–20 cm
1W | back greenish, scarcely streaked; crown greyer; white eyering; **narrow** white wingbars. Underparts **yellow**, flank softly streaked grey. **White band across spread tail**.

LC Yellow-throated Warbler
Setophaga dominica

L 14 cm | **W** 17–20 cm
Grey, black and white; head black-and-white, throat bright **yellow, edged by long black stripe below eye**, white neck spot. Wings black, two **broad white wingbars**. Flank white, streaked black.

LC Prairie Warbler
Setophaga discolor

L 12 cm | **W** 16–17 cm
1W | bright **yellow and green**. White eyering, dark eyestripe, **curved dark band under cheek**. Wingbars dull. **Flank yellow** with **black streaks**. Flicks/bobs tail, showing **white sides**. ♂**1W** | shows chestnut on back.

LC Chestnut-sided Warbler
Setophaga pensylvanica

L 10–14 cm | **W** 16–21 cm
Sleek but pot-bellied shape; green and grey. **1W** crown and upperparts **lime-green**; white eyering; cheek and underparts **pale grey**. At least a hint of **chestnut** on crown, back and flank.

♀ Ad/1W

NT Cerulean Warbler
Setophaga cerulea

L 12 cm | **W** 16–18 cm
1W greenish, **tinged pale blue**; **two white wingbars**. Underparts pale yellow, flank streaked grey; dark spots on undertail coverts. **AdNb** (NR) whiter below, flank streaks well defined.

♀ Ad

LC American Redstart
Setophaga ruticilla

L 13 cm | **W** 16–23 cm
1W head grey with white eyering; back grey-brown; **yellow band** (may be absent) on dark wing. **Tail black** with **yellow side panel**. Underparts white, flank orange (♂) or yellow (♀).

♂ 1W

LC Hooded Warbler
Setophaga citrina

L 13 cm | **W** 18–20 cm
1W **face and cheek yellow**, **contrasted** with green crown and upperparts (some with trace of blackish edge). Wing plain. **Long white spots under tail** visible from below. Underparts yellow. Legs pale pink.

♀ 1W

LC Wilson's Warbler
Cardellina pusilla

L 10–12 cm | **W** 16–20 cm
1W green-and-yellow. Face yellow, cheek greener; **yellow stripe** over eye beneath **dark crown** (blackish cap in ♂). Long tail without white marks. Legs pale pink/brown with yellow soles to feet.

♂ 1W   ♀

LC Common Yellowthroat
Geothlypis trichas

L 14 cm | **W** 20–22 cm
Olive-brown and yellow.
♂ Ad black 'mask', yellow throat.
♀ Ad cheek greyer, **throat yellow**.
1W head plain; weak eyering; throat **yellow-buff**. Flank pale olive.
♂ 1W cheek blackish.

♀ 1W   ♂

LC Yellow Warbler
Setophaga petechia

L 12–13 cm | **W** 16–20 cm
Olive-green and yellow; head plain, weak yellow eyering. Back may have **chestnut** streaks. Tertials edged white. Tail **edged yellow** but no white. **Underparts yellow**, may have faint chestnut streaks. **♂ 1W** gains bright yellow underparts with chestnut streaks.

♂ 1W

LC Black-throated Green Warbler
Setophaga nigrescens

L 12–13 cm | **W** 17–18 cm
Active, large-headed; green, yellow and white. **Crown green, face yellow**; two broad white wingbars. Flank white, boldly **striped dark grey**.

Ad/1W

LC Black-throated Blue Warbler
Setophaga caerulescens

L 13 cm | **W** 17–18 cm
Sluggish, thickset. **♂ Br** blue; white wing patch; **black face and flank**.
♀ / 1W dull green; white line over eye; dark cheek; **white crescent** under eye. **White patch** on primaries (may be small); tail plain.

♀ 1W   ♂ Br

LC Northern Parula
Setophaga americana

L 11–12 cm | **W** 16–18 cm

Small, delicate. Grey, green and yellow. **Head grey, white crescent** above and below eye. **Back green-yellow**, wings grey with **two white bars**. Throat pale yellow, breast white. ♂**1W** | wings grey, feather edges green. ♀**1W** | wings greener.

♂1W

LC Black-and-white Warbler
Mniotilta varia

L 11–13 cm | **W** 20–22 cm

Unmistakable small warbler, **striped black-and-white**. Behaves like Nuthatch (*p. 452*)/Treecreeper (*p. 457*). Pale crown stripe rules out adult Blackpoll Warbler (*p. 612*). ♀/**1W** | often more grey-and-buff than ♂ **1W**.

FL | Looks blue-grey in flight or quick glimpse.

♂1W

LC Tennessee Warbler
Leiothlypis peregrina

L 11·5 cm | **W** 18–20 cm

Small, greenish, like Arctic Warbler but **yellower**. **1W** | **bill fine, grey-based**. Greenish head with weak pale stripe over eye. Faint wingbar. Underparts pale **yellowish**, **white undertail**.

Arctic Warbler *p. 434*

Ad/1W

LC Connecticut Warbler
Oporornis agilis

L 13–15 cm | **W** 22–23 cm

Skulking, elusive; bulky and long-legged. Brownish, green and yellow. **1W** | drab yellowish; **complete white eyering**. Wings and tail plain. Breast slightly darker olive than yellowish underparts.

1W

LC Canada Warbler
Cardellina canadensis

L 13 cm | **W** 19–21 cm

1W | greenish and yellow. **Plain head** with white eyering. Wings and long tail **plain grey**. Legs pale pink-orange. ♂**1W** | hint of grey-black breast-band. ♀**1W** | breast plain.

♀1W

LC Prothonotary Warbler
Protonotaria citrea

L 13 cm | **W** 22 cm

Large, heavy, thick-billed. ♀/**1W** | back greenish, **wings and tail grey**; **underparts yellow**; bill and legs dark grey. ♂**1W** | head orange-yellow. ♀**1W** | head yellow-green. ♂**Ad** (NR) | brilliant yellow head and breast.

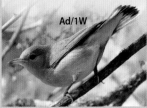

Ad/1W

LC Palm Warbler
Setophaga palmarum

L 14 cm | **W** 17–20 cm

Brownish, pipit-like (*p. 359*), **feeds the on ground** and **bobs tail**. **1W** | upperparts dull brown; long pale stripe over eye. Underparts buff, lightly streaked brown; **yellow patch** under tail. Long, dark legs. **V** | Call a frequent, hard "*chek.*"

1W

LC Northern Waterthrush
Parkesia noveboracensis

L 12–15 cm | **W** 21–24 cm

Small, pipit-like (*p. 359*), **walks on the ground**, **bobbing tail** like a wagtail (*p. 366*). **1W** | upperparts brown, **long pale stripe over eye tapers to nape**. Underparts buff-white with long **dark brown streaks**. **V** | loud, sharp "*chink.*"

1W

LC Ovenbird
Seiurus aurocapilla

L 11–14 cm | **W** 19–26 cm

Small, rounded, **walks on the ground** with deliberate steps; bobs tail, tosses leaves aside. **1W** | upperparts olive-green; **white eyering** and **rusty crown stripe**, edged black. **Underparts white, streaked black.**

Ad/1W

LC Blue-winged Warbler
Vermivora cyanoptera

L 11·5 cm | **W** 18–20 cm
Green, yellow and grey. **Head yellow** with **dark stripe from bill to eye**. Wings bluish-grey, two thin whitish wingbars. Underparts yellow, white under tail. Age/sex difficult Sep/Oct, but extreme ♂**Ad** has **black** eyestripe, **broad white** wingbars.

♂1W

'Brewster's' Warbler
Vermivora chrysoptera × cyanoptera

L 11·5 cm | **W** 15–16 cm
Hybrid Golden-winged × Blue-winged Warbler. Like Blue-winged Warbler but wingbars broad, yellow; underparts paler. Subsequent hybridization gives plumages closer to one parent.

Ad/1W

NT Golden-winged Warbler
Vermivora chrysoptera

L 11·5 cm | **W** 18–20 cm
♂**Ad** | grey, black and yellow. **Forehead yellow; broad black mask and throat**, white 'moustache'. **Broad yellow shoulder**. Underparts pale grey. ♀**Ad / 1W** (NR) | cheek and throat dark grey.

♂Ad

VIREOS Like heavy, sluggish warblers. Woodland/scrub.

LC Red-eyed Vireo
Vireo olivaceus

L 13–14 cm | **W** 22–24 cm
Dull, round-headed. **Dark greyish forehead**/crown, dark eyestripe; diffuse **whitish 'spectacle'**. Broad, diffuse wingbar. Underparts lemon-yellow, brightest on throat and vent.

1W

LC Yellow-throated Vireo
Vireo flavifrons

L 14 cm | **W** 20–24 cm
Large head, thick bill. Sexes and ages look alike except **Ad** | eye pale, **1W** | eye dark. Bright, green, yellow, grey and white. **Pale yellow 'spectacle'**, **yellow throat**. Wings grey with **two white wingbars**; underparts white.

1W

CRESTS (KINGLETS) Tiny, warbler-like. Woodland/scrub.

LC Ruby-crowned Kinglet
Regulus calendula

L 9–11 cm | **W** 16–18 cm
Tiny, like greyish Goldcrest with **dull greyish head**; white eyering but **no crown stripes** or moustache. Black-and-white wingbars. ♂**Ad** | (NR) small red nape (usually hidden).

Ad/1W

⊙ Goldcrest *p. 414*

LC Philadelphia Vireo
Vireo philadelphicus

L 13 cm | **W** 20–23 cm
Dull, round-headed. **Dark greyish forehead**/crown, dark eyestripe; diffuse **whitish 'spectacle'**. Broad, diffuse wingbar. Underparts lemon-yellow, brightest on throat and vent.

Ad/1W

LC White-eyed Vireo
Vireo griseus

L 11–13 cm | **W** 17–20 cm
Small, elusive. Grey-green. **Grey crown, yellow stripe from bill to eye**, narrow eyering. Back greenish; **two white wingbars** and white tertial edges. Flank yellow. **1W** | eye dark. **Ad** (NR) | eye pale.

Ad

NUTHATCHES Small; very short-legged; cling to trees.

LC Red-breasted Nuthatch
Sitta canadensis

L 11 cm | **W** 19–21 cm
Small grey nuthatch with **bright buff** underparts; **dark cap** and eye-stripe; **bold white stripe over eye**. **V** | Loud, excitable "*yank yank*," like a tiny toy horn.

Ad

⊙ Nuthatches *pp. 453–455*

TANAGERS and AMERICAN GROSBEAKS, FINCHES AND SPARROWS Some species in this group resemble Old World finches (*p. 480*) and especially buntings (*p. 508*). **Tanagers** are slender, finch-like, thick-billed, fruit-eating species; **grosbeaks** are heavy-billed and thickset; the **American sparrows** are difficult, more like European buntings and many require careful, detailed observation for certain identification.

LC Scarlet Tanager
Piranga olivacea

L 16–19 cm | **W** 25–30 cm
Stocky, broad-tailed, with arched, conical bill; elusive, skulks in foliage. **1W** green, dull black and yellowish. **Wings dark grey-green** (♀) or **black** (♂); underwing white. Underparts **pale yellow**.

♂ **1W**

LC Summer Tanager
Piranga rubra

L 17 cm | **W** 25–27 cm
Stocky, with rather long, conical bill; feeds high up in foliage, flies out to catch flies. **1W** head and upperparts greenish-brown or orange-brown, rump brighter. Wings plain olive; underwing yellow. Underparts dull orange-yellow.

1W

LC Rose-breasted Grosbeak
Pheucticus ludovicianus

L 18–22 cm | **W** 29–33 cm
Large; **deep, triangular, pale bill.** **1W** upperparts brown; **pale crown stripe**, broad pale **stripe over eye** and pale collar. **Two white wingbars.** Underparts buff, streaked brown. ♂ **Ad** black-and-white with red on breast.

♂ **Ad**
1W

VU Evening Grosbeak
Hesperiphona vespertina

L 20 cm | **W** 30–33 cm
Large finch; large, pale bill; wings black with **large white patch**. ♂ **Ad** head dark grey, forehead yellow; underparts olive-yellow. ♀/**1W** pale greyish, nape greenish-yellow; **wing patch** mottled grey. Underparts pale buff.

♂ **Ad**

⟳ Hawfinch *p. 485*

LC Blue Grosbeak
Passerina caerulea

L 17–19 cm | **W** 25–28 cm
Thickset, upright, with **thick bill**. ♀/**1W** upperparts rufous-brown; **two broad buff wingbars** on dark brown wing; underparts buff. (♂ **Ad** (NR) blue with rufous wingbar.)

1W

LC Dark-eyed Junco
Junco hyemalis

L 13–17 cm | **W** 18–25 cm
Small, shape and behaviour like Chaffinch (*p. 500*); forages on the ground or low in bushes. **Grey-and-white** with very **pale bill**. Side of tail and belly white. ♂ **Ad** slate grey. ♀/**1W** browner, belly less clearly contrasted. ♂ **1S** like ♂ **Ad** but wing browner.

♂ **1S**

LC Eastern Towhee
Pipilo erythrophthalmus

L 17–23 cm | **W** 20–28 cm
Heavily built, slim-tailed; forages in leaf-litter. ♂ **Ad** (NR) black, white and rufous; eye red. ♀/**1W** head, breast, upperparts and tail dark brown; white patches in wing. **Flank dark orange**, **belly white**. Tail shows white side. Eye dark.

♀ **Ad**

LC Indigo Bunting
Passerina cyanea

L 11–15 cm | **W** 18–23 cm
Slim, round-headed with conical bill. **1W** nondescript; black eye in plain head; two weak buff wingbars. Underparts buff, faintly mottled brown. ♂ **Ad** **blue**. ♀ **Ad** brown, **scattered hints of blue**.

♂ **1Y**
♂ **Ad**
1W

LC Lark Sparrow
Chondestes grammacus

L 15–17 cm | **W** 28 cm

Slim, terrestrial; brown-and-grey. **Ad** | **head boldly striped black, chestnut and grey**; white cheek spot. Underparts grey with dark breast spot. **1W** (NR) | head pattern similar, black and white, but cheek grey-brown with white spot.

Ad

LC American Tree Sparrow
Passerella arborea

L 13–14 cm | **W** 18–22 cm

Small, bunting-like (*p. 508*), **rufous-and-grey. Crown and stripe through eye rufous**; broad grey band over eye, pale grey cheek and neck. Wing rufous with two **white wingbars** on. Underparts pale grey with dark central spot. Bill dark above, yellow below.

Ad

LC Savannah Sparrow
Passerculus sandwichensis

L 11–17 cm | **W** 18–25 cm

Small, chunky, 'neckless', heavily streaked; tail short, slim. **Ad** | upperparts brown, streaked black; pale band over eye, **yellow at front; pale central crown stripe**. Underparts whitish, boldly streaked black and rufous-brown. **1W** | as **Ad** but duller overall.

1W

LC Red Fox-sparrow
Passerella iliaca

L 15–19 cm | **W** 26–28 cm

Rounded, streaked; small bill. Upperparts streaked grey and rufous; broad grey band over eye, rufous cheek. Underparts white, heavily streaked rusty-brown.

Ad/1Y

LC Lincoln's Sparrow
Melospiza lincolnii

L 12–14 cm | **W** 18–22 cm

Small, slim, secretive, terrestrial, bunting-like (*p. 508*). Brown, streaked blackish. Brown side to peaked crown; **grey over eye, grey nape**; white eyering; dark 'moustache'. Breast white, streaked **black**, flank buff; tail plain.

1W

LC Song Sparrow
Melospiza melodia

L 11–18 cm | **W** 18–25 cm

Dark, rufous, streaked, with **long, rounded tail. Grey cheek**, **broad grey band over eye**; dark, rusty-brown streaks on back. Underparts **white** with dark rufous streaks and blackish central spot.

Ad

LC White-crowned Sparrow
Zonotrichia leucophrys

L 18 cm | **W** 24–25 cm

Slim. **Ad** | **white crown stripe**, edged black; **white band over eye**; **throat grey. 1W** | crown striped dark **rufous and pale grey**. Throat and underparts grey, virtually unstreaked.

1W   Ad

LC White-throated Sparrow
Zonotrichia albicollis

L 18 cm | **W** 24–25 cm

Head grey-and-black, **band over eye yellow in front, white behind. Throat white**. Upperparts brown, streaked black; two white wingbars. Underparts brownish-grey. **1W** | and 'tan-striped' **Ad** form have buff and brown head stripes.

Ad
Ad/1S
'tan-striped'

LC Dickcissel *Spiza americana*

L 16 cm | **W** 25 cm

♀ / **1W** | like small female House Sparrow (*p. 505*); yellow stripe from bill to eye, yellow 'moustache'; rufous shoulder. ♂ **Ad** | head grey and yellow; black bib in summer.

♂   ♂ 1W

617

Established introductions

Some non-native species, introduced deliberately or having escaped accidentally, have established breeding populations in the wild in Europe, several of which are more likely to be seen than many rare native birds. Almost any species of bird can escape from captivity but most do not breed; only those that have self-sustaining populations have been included in this book. Some of these are covered in earlier sections (*e.g.* Pheasant (*p. 227*)), as are some 'escapes' that may be confused with native species (*i.e.* some introduced or escaped wildfowl (*pp. 69–71*), flamingos (*p. 569*), African Spoonbill (*p. 569*), Indian Pond-heron (*p. 574*), galliforms (*pp. 234–235*), Barbary Dove (*p. 525*) and crows (*p. 608*). The other 30 are featured here.

Escaped birds may be obvious but others can appear on remote islands and headlands, where true vagrants might be expected. These complicate the assessment of vagrants (*e.g.* Mugimaki Flycatcher (*p. 603*), is now included as a vagrant, having been 'upgraded' from 'probable escape' in light of a very recent record).

Laughingthrushes Scrub.

LC Red-billed Leiothrix
Leiothrix lutea

L 14–15 cm | **W** 25 cm

Small; tail notched. Grey-green with whitish cheek, **yellow throat**, rufous upper breast, orange wing patch. **Bill red, legs orange**. Sexes alike.

V | Call a long, shimmering chatter. Song long, complex fluty warble.

Locally fairly common (France, Germany, Italy, Spain) [from Asia]

Parrots and parakeets occur mostly in suburban areas with wooded parks and gardens, sometimes in noisy flocks. The species shown here are recently estabilshed but some have since declined.

LC Rose-ringed Parakeet
Alexandrinus krameri

L 37–43 cm | **W** 42–48 cm

Large **green** parakeet with a **long, pointed tail. Bill and eye red.** ♂ | black chin and collar, becoming pink on nape. ♀ / Juv | head plain green, no collar.

V | Loud, frenzied squeals and screeching notes.

FL | Fast, direct; narrow, blade-like, wings and spike-like tail. Often flocks 10–20 or more.

Locally common, some urban roosts exceed 5,000 [from Asia]

NT Alexandrine Parakeet
Palaeornis eupatria

L 56–62 cm | **W** 50 cm

Very large green parakeet with **long, pointed tail** and **purplish shoulder patch. Bill red, eye white.** ♂ | black chin and collar, back of neck pink; grey on neck and breast . ♀ / Juv | head green, faint yellowish collar.

V | Ringing "*trrrieuw*," loud "*kree-aar*," deep "*klak-klak-klak-klak*."

FL | Fast, direct; narrow wings and spike-like tail; usually 5–10.

Scarce, local (Germany, Greece) [from Asia]

LC Monk Parakeet
Myiopsitta monachus

L 29 cm | **W** 48 cm

Small green parakeet; sexes and ages alike. Forehead, cheek, throat and breast pale grey. Flank and vent lime-green. Primaries dark blue-grey. Bill small, orange-pink.

V | Calls screeching and loud "*quak quaki quak-wi quarr*."

FL | Fast, direct; wings narrow, tail slim and pointed. Outerwing dark blue-grey.

Widespread and locally abundant (Iberia/Mediterranean region, Azores, Madeira) [from S America]

LC Blue-crowned Parakeet
Psittacara acuticaudatus

L 37 cm | **W** 40–45 cm

Large green parakeet with blue forehead; **white eyering**. Bill small, pink. **Rufous** on underside of tail and underwing. Sexes alike.

V | Short, wailing screeches "*chairr chairr chairr.*"

Ad

Scarce and local (Italy) [from S America]

EN Yellow-headed Amazon
Amazona oratrix

L 38–43 cm | **W** 45–50 cm

Large, robust, **short-tailed**, green parrot; sexes alike. **Ad** | forehead and face yellow; red patch on wing. **Imm** | face green.

V | Calls a nasal "*whuup whuup.*"

Ad

Rare, local (Germany) [from S America]

LC Mitred Parakeet
Psittacara mitratus

L 34–38 cm | **W** 40–45 cm

Medium-sized, long-tailed, green parakeet; sexes alike. **Ad** | uniformly bright green, except **red face** and thighs. White eyering; heavy pinkish bill. **Juv** | lacks red.

V | High, ringing "*keer-eet.*"

Ad

Locally fairly common (Spain) [from S America]

LC Yellow-crowned Amazon
Amazona ochrocephala

L 33–38 cm | **W** 40–45 cm

Large, robust, **short-tailed**, vivid green parrot; sexes alike. **Ad** | white eyering; forehead yellow. Red patch on wing and shoulder; wing-tip blue. **Juv** | all-green.

V | A nasal "*whuup whuup.*"

Ad

Rare, local (Germany) [from S America]

NT Red-masked Parakeet
Psittacara erythrogenys

L 33 cm | **W** 40 cm

Medium-sized, long-tailed, green parakeet; sexes alike. **Ad** | **head red**, broad white eyering; large pink bill. Red on shoulder, underwing and thighs. **Juv** | lacks red.

V | Loud screeches and caws.

Ad

Local and scarce (Spain) [from S America]

NT Fischer's Lovebird
Agapornis fischeri

L 14–16 cm | **W** 28–30 cm

Very small parrot with large head, short tail; sexes alike. **Ad** | vivid green with **orange-brown head**, white eyering, small red bill. **Juv** | duller; brown on bill. Various domesticated forms occur.

V | Loud "*tchree-wit.*"

Ad

Locally fairly common (S France) [from Africa]

LC Nanday Parakeet
Aratinga nenday

L 32–37 cm | **W** 40–45 cm

Medium-sized, long-tailed, yellow-green parakeet with **black crown, face and bill**; white eyering. Bluish breast-band; dark blue wingtip and tail; red thighs. Sexes and ages look alike.

V | Sharp, explosive screech.

Ad

Rare, local (Spain, Canary Islands) [from S America]

LC Yellow-collared Lovebird *Agapornis personatus*

L 14–15 cm | **W** 26–28 cm

Shape as Fischer's Lovebird (which hybridizes). **Ad** | vivid green with **blackish hood**, yellow neck and breast, white eyering, red bill. **Juv** | duller overall.

V | "*tchruit*" and fast chatter.

Ad

Locally frequent (S France) [from Africa]

Bulbuls (p. 382) Thrush-like, short-billed, square-tailed; loud, repetitive calls; sexes look alike. Woodlands.

LC Red-whiskered Bulbul
Pycnonotus jocosus

L 18–20 cm | **W** 30–35 cm
Contrasting **black, brown and white; pointed black crest; red cheek spot**. Underparts and tip of undertail **white**; vent **red** (**Ad** only).
V | Bright, musical calls.

Scarce and local (Spain, Canary Islands) [from Asia]

LC Red-vented Bulbul
Pycnonotus cafer

L 18–20 cm | **W** 30–35 cm
Brown, with **blackish head** with **blunt crest. Rump white**. Underparts buff, mottled brown; vent **red**. Tail black with white tip.
V | Loud chattering.

Scarce and local (Spain, Canary Islands) [from Asia]

Parrotbills Small, **long-tailed**, deep-bellied, with very short, deep bill; sexes look alike. Reedbeds.

LC Vinous-throated Parrotbill
Sinosuthora webbiana

L 11–12 cm | **W** 20–25 cm
Pale grey with **bright rufous cap** and **wing** and **pinkish cheek. Eye black**, bill grey.
V | Call a quick "*rit-rit chididi tsseu-tss*."

Scarce, local (Italy, Netherlands) [from Asia]

LC Ashy-throated Parrotbill
Sinosuthora alphonsiana

L 11–12 cm | **W** 20–25 cm
Dark grey, especially cheek, throat and underparts; crown, nape and wing rufous. **Eye and bill white**.
V | Quick chattering call.

Scarce, local (Italy) [from Asia]

Weavers Large, stout; ♂**Br** yellow, ♂**Nb**/♀ like ♀ sparrow (p. 504). Social, nest colonially in waterside trees.

LC Black-headed Weaver
Ploceus melanocephalus

L 14 cm | **W** 30–35 cm
♂**Br** | Back **golden-green**; underparts **yellow-and-rufous; hood and bill black; eye dark**. ♀/♂**Nb**/**Juv** | like ♀ sparrow, **eye whitish**.
V | "*Zit*." Song 'sizzling' trills.

Locally fairly common (Iberia) [from Africa]

LC Village Weaver
Ploceus cucullatus

L 15–17 cm | **W** 35 cm
♂**Br** | Back **black-and-yellow**; underparts **yellow; hood black; bill grey; eye red**. ♀/♂**Nb** | like ♀ sparrow, **eye red. Juv** | eye brown.
V | Song staccato chattering.

Rare (Iberia (may be extinct), Italy) [from Africa]

Bishops Small, finch-like (p. 480); ♂**Br** brightly coloured; ♂**Nb**/♀ drab – ID difficult. Often flocks near water.

LC Yellow-crowned Bishop
Euplectes afer

L 10 cm | **W** 20 cm
Very small, compact, short-tailed. ♂**Br** | **yellow-and-black**. ♀/♂**Nb**/**Juv** | brown/buff, streaked darker; **pale yellow** stripe over eye/cheek.
V | Calls thin, sharp "*szi, sziip*."

Locally fairly common (Iberia) [from Africa]

LC Northern Red Bishop
Euplectes franciscanus

L 13–15 cm | **W** 25 cm
Very small, compact, short-tailed. ♂**Br** | **red-and-black**. ♀/♂**Nb**/**Juv** | dull brown/rich buff, streaked darker; **buff** stripe over eye.
V | Calls high squeaks.

Locally fairly common (Spain, Portugal) [from Africa]

Waxbills, silverbills, munias and relatives (estrildid finches) are very small or small, with a short, conical bill, short wings and long, slender tail (short on munias). Sexes are alike (apart from Red Avadavat).

LC Common Waxbill
Estrilda astrild

L 10–13 cm | **W** 20–25 cm
Ad| grey-brown, **barred** brown; **red stripe through eye**. **Bill red**. Underparts pinkish-brown, belly and **vent black**. **Juv**| bill dark.
V| Twittering; nasal twanging.

Swamps, long grass

Locally fairly common (Iberia, Italy) [from Africa]

LC Black-rumped Waxbill
Estrilda troglodytes

L 10 cm | **W** 20 cm
Ad| pale greyish, **rump black**; **long red band through eye**. **Bill red**. Underparts pale buff-brown, faintly barred; **vent white**. **Juv**| no red on head.
V| Harsh "*chuur*;" nasal "*jeeeu*."

Woodland, thickets

Locally fairly common (Iberia) [from Africa]

LC Orange-cheeked Waxbill
Estrilda melpoda

L 10 cm | **W** 20 cm
Ad| greyish; back and wing pale brown, **rump red**; **cheek orange**. **Bill red**. Underparts pale grey. **Juv**| bill dark.
V| Call a nasal "*jerp jerp*." Song a twittering jingle.

Waterside thickets/trees

Locally fairly common (Iberia) [from Africa]

LC Indian Silverbill
Euodice malabarica

L 11 cm | **W** 22 cm
Slim, brownish; wing and pointed tail dark brown; **rump white**. **Bill blue-grey**. Cheek and throat greyish-white;. ,
V| Call quick, shrill, cheeping notes, "*shrip-ip-reep-ip-shrip*."

Suburban gardens

Locally fairly common (France) [from Asia]

LC Red Avadavat
Amandava amandava

L 9·5 cm | **W** 18 cm
♂| **deep red**, wings brown; **white spots** on wing and flank. **Bill red**. ♀| olive-brown; black band through eye, rump pink-red. **Juv**| brown; bill dark.
V| Call thin "*tsiit*;" twittering.

Waterside thickets/trees

Locally fairly common (Iberia, Italy) [from Asia]

LC Scaly-breasted Munia
Lonchura punctulata

L 11–12 cm | **W** 25 cm
Small, slender, slim-tailed.
Ad| plain dark rufous, rump finely barred white; underparts white with closely spaced, crescentic black bars. **Juv**| paler, underparts plain buff.
V| Calls whistles; "*chip chip*."

Grassland

Locally fairly common (Iberia) [from Asia].

Whydahs Small, ♂**Br** long tail; ♀ like ♀ bishop.

LC Pin-tailed Whydah
Vidua macroura

L 13 cm (♂ 33 cm with tail)
W 25 cm
Tiny, thick-billed. ♂| **black-and-white**; **long black tail**; bill red. ♀/**Juv**| buff-brown, streaked black on back; black bands on head; bill black.
V| Fast, squeaky, calls.

Scrub, grassland

Local (Iberia) [from Africa]

Crows Large, black-and-grey; bold and noisy.

LC House Crow
Corvus splendens

L 37–42 cm | **W** 68–80 cm
Large, thick-billed crow. Dark **grey** with **black crown and throat**; neck/breast sometimes noticeably paler.
FL| Long, slender wings, longish tail.

👁 Carrion Crow *p. 474*
Jackdaw *p. 476*

Urban areas, farmland

Locally introduced/escape [from Asia]

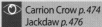

Mynas Starling-like (*p. 379*) but more stocky, with longer, more robust legs; sexes alike.

LC Common Myna
Acridotheres tristis

L 23 cm | **W** 40 cm

Deep **chocolate-brown**, black hood; white vent; patch of bare skin behind eye, bill and legs yellow.

V | Varied chattering, rich "*tchi-ow tchi-ow*," hard trills and churrs.

FL | White wing patches.

Woodland, agricultural areas, urban centres

Local (Portugal) [from Asia]

LC Crested Myna
Acridotheres cristatellus

L 25 cm | **W** 40–42 cm

Ad | **glossy blue-black. Curly tuft** on flat forehead. White patch in wing. Eye and legs yellow. **Juv** | grey-black; no crest, legs grey.

V | Rippling "*chrr-rr-rr-rree*."

FL | White patch on outerwing; tip of tail white.

Suburbs, agricultural areas

Local (Portugal, possibly Spain) [from Asia]

The status and conservation of Europe's birds

BirdLife International

BirdLife International brings together 115 Partner organisations worldwide, including 43 in Europe, striving to conserve birds, their habitats and global biodiversity. Widely recognised as the world leader in bird conservation, BirdLife combines rigorous science with feedback from projects on the ground to implement successful conservation programmes. BirdLife's online Data Zone contains a wealth of information on birds and conservation, including up-to-date global species distribution maps (upon which the maps featured in this book are based). For more information, visit: **http://datazone.birdlife.org/species/search**.

Conservation status

The International Union for Conservation of Nature (IUCN) assesses the global conservation status of animals and plants on a regular basis and maintains a 'Red List'. BirdLife International is the official IUCN Red List authority for birds and updates the categories as new information is provided, undertaking a complete review of all species every four years. In addition, during 2012–2015 BirdLife led a European Commission-funded project, involving a consortium of ornithological organisations, that reviewed the regional threat status of the 533 wild bird species considered to occur naturally and regularly in Europe. The Red List status of each species, both globally (as of 2020) and, if appropriate, for Europe, is included in this book. The categories used are summarized below, the icons being used consistently throughout:

Conservation status codes
(black/red border = included on the European Red List)

RE Regionally Extinct – No reasonable doubt that the last individual in Europe has died.

PE Possibly Extinct – Highly likely that the last individual has died.

CR CR Critically Endangered – Considered to be facing an extremely high risk of extinction in the wild.

EN EN Endangered – Considered to be facing a very high risk of extinction in the wild.

VU VU Vulnerable – Considered to be facing a high risk of extinction in the wild.

NT NT Near Threatened – Close to qualifying for/likely to qualify as CR, EN or VU in the near future.

LC LC Least Concern – Does not qualify as CR, EN, VU or NT.

Not Evaluated

Sources of further information

There is a multitude of sources of information on birds, ranging from books to websites, museums and libraries. To give full details is beyond the scope of this book, but the following have been of particular value in preparing the accounts:

Books

Baker, J. K. 2016. *Identification of European Non-Passerines: a BTO Guide.* British Trust for Ornithology.

Cofta, T. 2021. *Flight Identification of European Passerines and Select Landbirds: An illustrated and photographic guide.* Princeton WILD*Guides.*

Cramp, S. *et al.* 1977–94. *Birds of the Western Palearctic.* Oxford University Press.
(A nine-volume work that remains indispensable.)

Demongin, L. 2016. *Identification Guide to Birds in the Hand.* Laurent Demongin.

del Hoyo, J., Collar, N. *et al.* 2014/2016. *HBW and BirdLife International Illustrated Checklist of the Birds of the World.* Lynx Edicions
(Two volumes that provide invaluable information on the distribution of subspecies.)

Mitchell, D. 2017. *Birds of Europe, North Africa and the Middle East An Annotated Checklist.* Lynx Edicions.

Websites

agami.nl – an unrivalled selection of bird photographs, very many of which are featured in this book.

blascozumeta.com – a detailed online guide to ageing and moult.

bto.org – an invaluable reference with masses of data, and particular reference to the UK.

datazone.birdlife.org – the essential BirdLife International reference upon which much of this book is based.

netfugl.dk – up-to-date information on bird records from across Europe.

oiseaux.net – invaluable reference for identification, distribution and taxonomy.

rspb.org.uk – includes data and maps with particular reference to UK birds.

tarsiger.com – up-to-date information on bird records from across Europe.

xeno-canto.org – a remarkably comprehensive online collection of bird call and song recordings.

Companion volume

Readers wishing for more information about the flight identification of many of the European passerines and related species covered in this book are recommended to refer to *Flight Identification of European Passerines and Select Landbirds: An illustrated and photographic guide.*

● The first field guide to flight identification of European passerines and related landbirds

● Covers 205 European passerines and 32 near-passerines

● Features 850 stunning colour illustrations

● Includes more than 2,400 photos showing typical profiles of each species in flight

● Provides detailed information on flight calls, with a QR link to recordings online

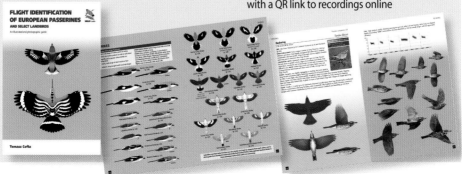

Acknowledgements and photographers

Many people have contributed, directly or indirectly, to the production of this book since its inception five years ago and our sincere thanks go to everyone who has influenced the final product. We would particularly like to acknowledge the efforts of enthusiastic birdwatchers across Europe and beyond who have contributed much of the data on the status and distribution of birds in the region, upon which we have drawn heavily.

In producing the book we have benefitted greatly from the lessons learned from completing two editions of *Britain's Birds*, and especially from the constructive feedback and helpful suggestions from birdwatchers on identification-related matters. Special mention must, however, be made of **Chris Batty** who has painstakingly checked the identification, sex and age of the birds shown in each of more than 20,000 photos that had been shortlisted for possible inclusion. Chris's input has been invaluable in ensuring that the captioning of the images is as accurate as possible, but responsibility for any errors that may have crept in inadvertently remains with us. **Steve Holmes**, **Bob Self**, **Chris Sharpe**, **Anne Donnelly** and **Brian Clews** also made significant contributions with very helpful comments regarding identification tips and ideas for improving the content. Over the years many of Europe's top birders have offered insightful comments on some key identification issues and we particularly acknowledge the input from **Nils van Duivendijk**, **Dick Forsman**, **Dani López Velasco** and **Adam Scott Kennedy**. Thanks are also due to **Joe Hobbs** for his contribution in compiling details of Nearctic passerines in the Western Palearctic, **D. I. M. Wallace** for regular enthusiastic support and encouragement, and to many friends who have provided information along the way.

Thanks, too, go to **Ian Burfield** and **Jim Lawrence** at BirdLife International for their support for the project since the outset, and particularly to **Hannah Wheatley** and **Mark Balman** at BirdLife for preparing distribution maps upon which those that appear in the book are based. **Robert Kirk**, Publisher, Field Guides & Natural History, at Princeton University Press, has encouraged and helped us immeasurably throughout the project. A special mention must also go to **Rachel** and **Anya Still**, **Gill Swash** and **Marcella Hume** for their patience, help and support behind the scenes and the contribution they have made in bring this book to fruition.

Although a substantial number of the images in the book were taken by the authors, the inevitable gaps in our portfolios meant that achieving the aim of showing high quality images of a range of plumages for the 928 species illustrated would not have been possible without considerable help from others. Key to this has been our very close association with the **Agami Photo Agency** in the Netherlands (agami.nl), which represents many of the world's top wildlife photographers. Without access to this resource, and in particular the unwavering help and support of **Marc Guyt**, **Roy de Haas** and **Wil Leurs** in responding to often seemingly obscure requests for details on the origin of particular images, or for additional photos of specific plumages or profiles, it would not have been possible to produce such a richly illustrated and comprehensive book. But even with such a fantastic resource available to us, there were some very specific images that we needed to obtain from elsewhere to complete the coverage. Our great friend **Brian Clews** kindly undertook to help source the majority of these images and took the lead in liaising with very many photographers from around the world.

The quality of the images featured in the book is testament to the skill and dedication of the contributing photographers. In total, an astonishing 4,700 photos are featured, representing the work of 349 photographers. Thanks are due to all for their tremendous support but we would like to make special mention of a few photographers whose work is featured very extensively (*i.e.* 100 or more images): **Daniele Occhiato** (agami.nl), **Markus Varesvuo** (agami.nl), **Ralph Martin** (agami.nl), **Marc Guyt** (agami.nl), **David Tipling** (birdphoto.co.uk) and **Brian E. Small** (agami.nl). We would also like to thank a number of other photographers who generously provided access to their entire portfolio of images: **Martin Bennett**; **Roger and Liz Charlwood** (worldwildlifeimages.com); **Mark Darlaston**; **Greg and Yvonne Dean** (worldwildlifeimages.com); the late **David Kjaer** (davidkjaer. com), who kindly bequeathed to us his extensive collection of wonderful images; **Michael McKee** (michaelmckee.co.uk); and **Denzil Morgan**.

The following is a complete list of all the contributing photographers, with details of their website where requested and the total number of images that are featured in the book. For those wanting more information about any specific image, or to find out which images a particular photographer has taken, a comprehensive and fully searchable schedule of all the images is freely available for download from the Princeton University Press website at **https://press.princeton.edu/books/ paperback/9780691177656/europes-birds**.

In total, 39 images are published under the terms of one of the following Creative Commons licenses: Attribution 2.0 Generic license (CC BY 2.0), Creative Commons Attribution-ShareAlike 2.0 Generic license (CC BY-SA 2.0), Creative Commons Attribution-NoDerivs 2.0 Generic license (CC BY-ND 2.0), Creative Commons Attribution-ShareAlike 3.0 Unported license (CC BY 3.0), Creative Commons Attribution-ShareAlike 3.0 Unported license (CC BY-SA 3.0), Creative Commons Attribution-NoDerivs 3.0 Unported license (CC BY-ND 3.0) or the Creative Commons Attribution-ShareAlike 4.0 International license (CC BY-SA 4.0). In addition, one is in the Public Domain. The relevant license is indicated using the appropriate code after the photographer's name in the list.

A **AbdulRahman Al-Sirhan** (birdsofkuwait.com) [1]; **Georgios Alexandris** (shutterstock.com) [1]; **Duha Alhashimi** [2]; **Andrew M. Allport** [3]; **Jim Almond** (shropshirebirder.co.uk) [1]; **Alpsdake** (CC BY-SA 3.0 via Wikimedia Commons) [1]; **Humoud Alshayji** (flickr.com/photos/showaiji/16327252076) [1]; **Amar-Singh HSS** [2]; **Rafael Armada** (Agami.nl) [12]; **Anand Arya** [1]; **Sigmundur Ásgeirsson** (flickr.com/photos/simmi25) [2]; **Aurélien Audevard** (Agami.nl) [13]; **Kelly Colgan Azar** (flickr.com/ photos/puttefin (CC BY-ND 2.0)) [1];

B **Jem Babbington** [1]; **Zoltan Baczo** [1]; **David Bakewell** [1]; **Danny Bales** (flickr.com/photos/ mudhen) [1]; **Robert Balestra** (flickr.com/183717315@N02) [2]; **Arijit Banerjee** [1]; **Keith Barnes** (tropicalbirding.com) [2]; **Glenn Bartley** (Agami.nl) [48]; **Ferit Başbuğ** [2]; **Bill Baston** (Agami.nl) [6]; **Roy & Marie Battell** (moorhen.me.uk) [1]; **Chris Batty** [1]; **Sam Bayley** [1]; **Tom Beeke** [3]; **Ken Behrens** (tropicalbirding.com) [2]; **Boris Belchev** (borisbelchev.com) [1]; **Darren Bellerby** (flickr.com (CC BY-SA 2.0)) [1]; **Amir Ben Dov** (gull-research.org) [22]; **Martin Bennett** [51]; **Bering Land Bridge National Preserve** (flickr.com/photos/bering_land_ bridge (CC BY-SA 2.0)) [1]; **Alex Berryman** [1]; **Joachim Bertrands** (flickr.com/photos/141891542@ N04) [7]; **Don Bindler** (flickr.com/photos/pheasantwood) [1]; **Anders Blomdahl** [1]; **Carlos Bocos** (bicheandoatope.blogspot.com) [3]; **Richard Bonser** (rothandb.blogspot.co.uk) [4]; **Bas van den Boogaard** (Agami.nl) [12]; **Pasquale Borla** (flickr.com/photos/xrupex) [1]; **Sándor Borza** [1]; **Han Bouwmeester** (Agami.nl) [13]; **John Bowler** [1]; **Colin Bradshaw** [1]; **Dermot Breen** (dermotbreen.blogspot.co.uk) [6]; **Tristram Brelstaff** (CC BY 3.0 via Wikimedia Commons) [1]; **Neil Brimacombe** (flickr.com/photos/neilb0147) [6]; **Christian Brinkman** (Agami.nl) [1]; **Mika Bruun** [1]; **Dave Bryan** [1]; **Simon Buckell** [1]; **Karen Burns** (flickr.com/photos/118130027@N03) [1]; **John Burnside** [1]; **Butterfly Hunter** (shutterstock.com) [1]; **Steve Byland** (shutterstock.com) [2];

C **Martin Cade** (portlandbirdobs.com) [1]; **Mark Carmody** (flickr.com/photos/drcarmo) [2]; **Graham Catley** (grahamcatley.com) [1]; **Marek Cech** (shutterstock.com) [1]; **Richard Chandler** [2]; **Keith Chapman** [1]; **Roger & Liz Charlwood** (worldwildlifeimages.com) [13]; **Ivan Chernatkin** [1]; **Choi Soon-Kyoo** (Aveskorea.com) [1]; **Chun Fai Lo** [1]; **Bruce & Joanne Clayton** (butterflyonmyshoulder.ca) [1]; **Trevor Codlin** [8]; **Pete Coe** [2]; **David Cooper** (eastsussexbirding. blogspot.com) [4]; **Luis Costa** (flickr.com/photos/lcmj) [1]; **Richard Crossley** (crossleybooks.com) [3]; **D. Cuddon** [1]; **Stan Culley** [2];

D **Stephen Daly** (flickr.com/photos/sdaly) [10]; **Mike Danzenbaker** (Agami.nl) [75]; **Mark Darlaston** [36]; **Ian Davies** (Agami.nl) [6]; **Kit Day** (kitday.smugmug.com) [2]; **Greg & Yvonne Dean** (worldwildlifeimages.com) [36]; **Jaap Denee** (Agami.nl) [1]; **Harvey van Diek** (Agami.nl) [17]; **Oscar Díez** (Agami.nl) [14]; **Iosto Doneddu** (iosto.net) [1]; **Dennis W. Donohue** (shutterstock.com) [2]; **Jacob Drucker** (flickr.com/photos/58638795@N08) [1]; **Adrian Drummond-Hill** [1]; **Tony Duckett** [1]; **Menno van Duijn** (Agami.nl) [40]; **Nils van Duivendijk** (Agami.nl) [3];

E Matt Eade [1]; **Dean Eades** (Birdmad.com) [3]; **James Eaton** (Agami.nl) [15]; **Kari Eischer** (Agami.
nl) [13]; **Graham Ekins** (flickr.com/photos/graham_ekins_world_wildlife) [1]; **Ralph Eldridge**
(pbase.com/lightrae) [2]; **Paul Ellis** (flickr.com/photos/the_treerunner) [1]; **Ivan Ellison** (flickr.com/
photos/ivanellison) [2]; **Juan Emilio** (flickr.com/photos/juan_e (CC BY-SA 2.0)) [2]; **Agustin Esmoris**
(shutterstock.com) [1];

F Pekka Fagel (kuwaitbirds.org) [3]; **Frode Falkenberg** (falkefoto.no) [1]; **Efi First** (pbase.com/efifirst)
[11]; **Ian Fisher** [1]; **Charles Fleming** (charlesfleming.smugmug.com) [1]; **Dick Forsman** (Agami.nl)
[39]; **Clement Francis** (Agami.nl) [1]; **Paul French** (nomadbirder.com) [1]; **Richard Frèze** [2];
Ian Fulton (pbase.com/ianfulton) [3];

G Steve Gantlett (Agami.nl) [6]; **Jacob Garvelink** (Agami.nl) [3]; **Saverio Gatto** (Agami.nl) [61];
George Gay [2]; **Hans Gebuis** (Agami.nl) [10]; **Hans Germeraad** (Agami.nl) [6]; **Alain Ghignone**
(Agami.nl) [20]; **Chris Gibbins** (gull-research.org) [2]; **Giedriius** (shutterstock.com) [3];
Doug Gochfeld (flickr.com/photos/29840397@N08) [2]; **Ana Gram** (shutterstock.com) [1];
Danny Green [2]; **Lee Gregory** (flickr.com/photos/lee_gregory) [1]; **António Guerra** (flickr.com/
photos/ajmguerra) [4]; **Antonio Gutiérrez** (gaviotasyanillas.blogspot.com.es) [1]; **Jesús Giraldo**
Gutiérrez del Olmo [1]; **Pablo Gutiérrez Varga** [2]; **Marc Guyt** (Agami.nl) [168];

H Roy de Haas (Agami.nl) [26]; **Marlin Harms** (flickr.com/photos/marlinharms) [2]; **J.J. Harrison** (CC
BY-SA 3.0 via Wikipedia or Wikimedia Commons) [4]; **A.H.J. Harrop** (rutlandbutterflies.wordpress.
com) [2]; **Hugh Harrop** (hughharrop.com) [632]; **Peter E. Hart** (flickr.com/photos/pehart (CC BY-SA
2.0)) [1]; **Harum.Koh** (flickr.com/photos/harumkoh (CC BY-SA 2.0)) [1]; **Stanislav Harvančík** [15];
James Harvey [1]; **Russell Hayes** (birdmanbirds.blogspot.com) [3]; **hedera.baltica** (flickr.com/
photos/hedera_baltica (CC BY-SA 2.0)) [2]; **Tom Heijnen** (flickr.com/photos/theijnen) [1];
Magnus Hellstrom (Agami.nl) [2]; **David Hemmings** (Agami.nl) [5]; **Ron Hindhaugh** [1];
John & Jemi Holmes (johnjemi.hk) [1]; **Richard Howard** [1]; **Steve Howell** [1]; **Paul Huang**
(naturestops.com) [1]; **R.A. Hume** [4];

I John L. Irvine [1]; **Eric Isselee** (shutterstock.com) [1];

J Ayuwat Jearwattanakanok [3]; **Evan Jenkins** (www.flickr.com/photos/evanjenkins) [2];
Tom Johnson [8]; **Gareth Jones** [1]; **Josh Jones** (Agami.nl) [9]; **Arto Juvonen** (Agami.nl) [9];

K Eugenijus Kavaliauskas (dantis.net/x3) [2]; **Joe Kearney** (flickr.com/photos/122825362@N04) [1];
Derek Keats (flickr.com/photos/dkeats (CC BY 2.0)) [5]; **Lior Kislev** [1]; **David Kjaer** (davidkjaer.com)
[37]; **Michal Kocan** (shutterstock.com) [1]; **Steve Kolbe** [1]; **Timothey Kosachev** (shutterstock.
com) [1]; **Maxim Koshkin** [3]; **Hannu Koskinen** [1]; **Robert L. Kothenbeutel** (shutterstock.com) [1];
Aseem Kumar Kothiala [2]; **Prasanna Kumar Mamidala** (Wprasannak (Own work) (CC BY-SA 4.0
via Wikimedia Commons) [1]; **Miroslaw Krol** (flickr.com/photos/mirekkrol) [1]; **Jainy Kuriakose** [1];
Fyn Kynd (flickr.com/photos/79452129@N02 (CC BY 2.0)) [1];

L Laitche (CC BY-SA 4.0 via Wikipedia) [1]; **Mike Lane** (nature-photography.co.uk) [12];
Hugh Lansdown (shutterstock.com) [1]; **Greg Lavaty** [1]; **Jim Lawrence** [1]; **Vincent Legrand**
(Agami.nl) [93]; **Tony Leukering** (flickr.com/photos/tony_leukering) [1]; **Wil Leurs** (Agami.nl) [21];
James Lidster [1]; **David Lindo** (theurbanbirderworld.com) [1]; **Andrew Lipczynski** [2];
Liu Yen Teng [2]; **Martin Lofgren** (wildbirdgallery.com) [2]; **Lonelyshrimp** (flickr.com/photos/
lonelyshrimp (CC BY 2.0)) [1]; **Daniel López-Velasco** (Agami.nl) [6]; **Ann Lowe** [1]; **James Lowen**
(jameslowen.com) [1]; **Thomas Luiten** (Agami.nl) [2];

M Bruce MacQueen (shutterstock.com) [1]; **Bruce Mactavish** (brucemactavish1.blogspot.com) [2];
Benoit Maire [2]; **Ralph Martin** (Agami.nl) [192]; **Jonathan Martinez** (Agami.nl) [1];
Bence Mate (Agami.nl) [12]; **Mateusz Matysiak** (fotomatysiak.smugmug.com) [1]; **Karel Mauer**
(Agami.nl) [21]; **Gerhard Mauracher** (CC BY-SA 3.0 via Wikimedia Commons) [1]; **James McCormick**
[1]; **James McGarry** (flickr.com/photos/41453183@N05) [1]; **Michael McKee** (michaelmckee.co.uk)
[49]; **Arnold Meijer** (Agami.nl) [13]; **Tim Melling** (flickr.com/photos/timmelling) [1]; **Eric Menkveld**
(Agami.nl) [2]; **Ian Merrill** [1]; **Mike's Birds** (flickr.com/photos/pazzani (CC BY-SA 2.0)) [2];
Pegah Mirzaei [1]; **Mjobling** (CC BY-SA 3.0 via Wikimedia Commons) [1]; **David Monticelli** (Agami.
nl) [37]; **Dave Montreuil** (shutterstock.com) [2]; **Andy Morffew** (flickr.com/photos/andymorffew
(CC BY 2.0)) [1]; **Denzil Morgan** (facebook.com/Denzil-Morgan-Photography-786259851389520)
[17]; **Pete Morris** (Agami.nl) [28]; **Tomi Muukkonen** (Agami.nl) [42];

N Jacques van der Neut (Agami.nl) [6]; **Steve Nuttall** [1];

O Jerry O'Brien [1]; **Daniele Occhiato** (Agami.nl) [597]; **János Oláh** (sakertour.com) [4]; **Rob Olivier** (Agami.nl) [3]; **Klaus Malling Olsen** [2]; **Leif Høgh Olsen** [1]; **Maciej Olszewski** (shutterstock.com) [3]; **Arie Ouwerkerk** (Agami.nl) [95]; **Korhan Özkan** (korhanozkan.org) [1];

P Vincent Palomares (oiseaux.net/photos/vincent.palomares) [1]; **Jose M. Pantaleon** [2]; **Jaysukh Parekh "Suman"** [1]; **Tim Parker** (flickr.com/photos/82348328@N05 (CC BY 2.0)) [1]; **Martin D. Parr** (flickr.com/photos/85387952@N00) [4]; **Mital Patel** (shutterstock.com) [1]; **Viral Patel & Pankaj Maheria** [2]; **Tommy Pedersen** (flickr.com/photos/sandmanindubai) [1]; **John Pelechaty** (flickr.com/photos/johnpelechaty) [1]; **Jari Peltomäki** (Agami.nl) [64]; **Joe Pender** (wwwsapphirepelagics.blogspot.co.uk) [3]; **Yoav Perlman** (Agami.nl) [4]; **Lars Petersson** (larsfoto.se) [2]; **Christopher Plummer** (pbase.com/cplummer) [1]; **Jeff Poklen** [1]; **Rene Pop** (Agami.nl) [5]; **Mike Pope** (kuwaitbirds.org/photographers/mike-pope) [6]; **Richard Porter** [1]; **Stephen Powell** (wildaboutspain.com) [1]; **Simon Price** (flickr.com/photos/simons_snapshots) [1]; **Stuart Price** (hakodatebirding.com) [5]; **Rauli Pudas** (flopshots.1g.fi) [1]; **Mathias Putze** (Agami.nl) [2];

R Brian Rafferty (flickr.com/photos/brianrafferty) [1]; **Giorgi Rajebashvili** (Ecotours Georgia: ecotours.ge) [2]; **Markku Rantala** (Agami.nl) [16]; **Steve Ray** (flickr.com/photos/26135972@N05) [1]; **rck_953** (shutterstock.com) [1]; **Mike Read** (mikeread.co.uk) [1]; **Keith Regan** [2]; **George Reszeter** [1]; **Steve Reynaert** (flickr.com/photos/walmerwildlife) [1]; **Chris van Rijswijk** (Agami.nl) [46]; **Ghislain Riou** (oiseaux.net/photos/ghislain.riou/photos.html) [1]; **Simon Rix** (oslobirder.blogspot.com) [1]; **Ricardo Rodriguez** [1]; **Arun Roisri** (shutterstock.com) [1]; **Steve Rooke** [1]; **Kris de Rouck** (Agami.nl) [3]; **Ómar Runólfsson** (flickr.com/photos/omarrun (CC BY-SA 2.0)) [2];

S S1001 (shutterstock.com) [1]; **Juan Sagardia Pradera** [24]; **Pranjal J. Saikia** [3]; **Alan Schmierer** (flickr.com/photos/sloalan (PD)) [1]; **Fabian Schneider** [1]; **Ran Schols** (Agami.nl) [85]; **Reint Jakob Schut** (Agami.nl) [13]; **Ray Scott** [1]; **Will Scott** [1]; **Adam Scott Kennedy** [1]; **Richard Seeley** (shutterstock.com) [2]; **Glyn Sellors** (glynsellorsphotography.com) [6]; **Imran Shah** (flickr.com/photos/gilgit2 (CC BY-SA 2.0)) [2]; **Dubi Shapiro** (Agami.nl) [13]; **Charles Sharp** (flickr.com/photos/93882360@N07) [1]; **Tom Shevlin** (irishbirds.ie) [2]; **Pavel Simeonov** (Agami.nl) [4]; **Dr. Ajay Kumar Singh** (drajaykumarsingh.com) [1]; **Skierx** (shutterstock.com) [1]; **Brian E. Small** (Agami.nl) [101]; **Dave Smallshire** [2]; **Raymond De Smet** (pbase.com/raydes) [20]; **Steve Smith** (birdingpooleharbourandbeyond.blogspot.co.uk) [1]; **Walter Soestbergen** (Agami.nl) [21]; **Song Yingtao** (flickr.com/photos/birdsoong) [1]; **Helge Sørensen** (Agami.nl) [40]; **Mick Southcott** [1]; **Mustafa Sozen** [1]; **Laurens Steijn** (Agami.nl) [14]; **Robert Still** [1, plus 54 illustrations]; **Richard Stonier** (birdsonline.co.uk) [4]; **Colby Stopa** (flickr.com/photos/photographybycolby (CC BY 2.0)) [1]; **Brian Sullivan** [17]; **Andy & Gill Swash** (worldwildlifeimages.com) [316];

T Tom Tams [3]; **Tanoochai** (shutterstock.com) [1]; **Tim Taylor** (wildimaging.co.uk) [2]; **August Thomasson** (augustthomasson.weebly.com) [1]; **Roger Tidman** [9]; **Matt Tillett** (flickr.com/photos/mattyfioner (CC BY 2.0)) [1]; **David Tipling** (davidtipling.com) [113]; **Robert Tizzard** [1]; **Ralph Todd** [2]; **Mark Tomlins** (marktomlins.co.uk) [1]; **Purevsuren Tsolmonjav** (flickr.com/photos/wildlife_of_mongolia) [2];

U Underworld (shutterstock.com) [1]; **Chris Upson** (flickr.com/photos/chris_upson_images_of_nature) [2]; **USFWS Mountain-Prairie** (flickr.com/photos/usfwsmtnprairie (CC BY 2.0)) [1];

V Mitchell Vanbeekum (flickr.com/photos/ozzyhead) [1]; **Markus Varesvuo** (Agami.nl) [489]; **Alex Vargas** (Agami.nl) [5]; **Frank Vassen** (flickr.com/photos/42244964@N03 (CC BY 2.0)) [2]; **Aravind Venkatraman** (flickr.com-photos-arvifotoworld) [9]; **Martijn Verdoes** (Agami.nl) [15]; **Francesco Veronesi** (flickr.com/photos/francesco_veronesi (CC BY-SA 2.0)) [1]; **Fred Visscher** (Agami.nl) [6]; **Renate Visscher** (Agami.nl) [1];

W Wang LiQiang (shutterstock.com) [1]; **Abi Warne** (shutterstock.com) [1]; **Arend Wassink** (Agami.nl) [9]; **Mike Watson** (mikewatsonfoto.com) [13]; **Ulrich Weber**, Switzerland [1]; **Ian N. White** (flickr.com/photos/ian_white) [1]; **Steve Wilce** (breconbeaconsbirder.com) [1]; **Onno Wildschut** (Agami.nl) [2]; **Wim Wilmers** (Agami.nl) [2]; **Peter J. Wilson** [1]; **Edwin Winkel** (Agami.nl) [23]; **Phil Winter** (flickr.com/photos/philwinter) [2]; **Michelle & Peter Wong** [12];

Y Steve Young (birdsonfilm.smugmug.com) [14];

Z Angelo Zimmitti [1]; **RazvanZinica** (shutterstock.com) [1] and **Bildagentur Zoonar GmbH** (shutterstock.com) [4].

Index

This index includes the English and (in *italics*) scientific names of all the birds in the book.

CAPITALIZED text is used for the 'types' of birds; **bold text** highlights main species accounts; regular text is used for subspecies and also species that are not subject to a full account; *italicized numbers* indicate comparative plates.

Alternative English and scientific names that are frequently used by other taxonomic authorities are included in this index, with the actual name used in the book shown (**in darker text in brackets**); this is for the benefit of those who may know a bird by another name.